City Guide
London

D1240717

Roger Woodley

A&C Black • London
WW Norton • New York

Eye Contact

The following images are a selection of the author's most loved and loathed architecture, examples of some of the delights and dismays that London has to offer.

Some delights are ancient. The glorious, and uniquely English, late Gothic lacework of the Henry VII Chapel (begun 1503) at Westminster Abbey should lift the spirit of the most exhausted traveller. (Chapter 14)

While the nearby Houses of Parliament (begun 1835)—creating perhaps the finest view in all London—revived traditional Gothic values for a more democratic age. (Chapter 13)

No one promoted the project for a revitalised but proudly historic city more energetically than the still under-valued Prince Albert. This is his properly magnificent memorial (1863–72) at Kensington. (Chapter 35)

Yet London is not romantic enough to be Gothic at heart. Rational Classicism suits its brisk temperament better, as the perfect ensemble of Somerset House (1776–1806) shows. (Chapter 9)

London's innumerable well-behaved Georgian streets have typically down-to-earth Classical proportions, or equally pleasing disproportions, as at Cornwall Terrace (1826), Regent's Park. (Chapter 25)

So do its churches, whether in the Baroque grandeur of the West Towers of St Paul's Cathedral (1703–5). (Chapter 7)

Or in an imposing but earthier parish church, St Anne Limehouse (1714–25), in the heart of one of London's former dock areas. (Chapter 46)

But not everything in London has to be Classical or Gothic. There have been notable ventures in other visual directions. What about this, the Horniman Museum in Forest Hill (1897–1901)? (Chapter 52)

Or these eye-catching 'French Renaissance' apartments for wealthy Victorians at Whitehall Court (1884) on the Embankment? (Chapter 12)

Although Londoners were always too conservative to welcome Modernism with enthusiasm, a few brave attempts were made, such as the National Theatre (1961–76) and the Royal Festival Hall (1948–51). They work well and look very handsome from the river. (Chapter 32)

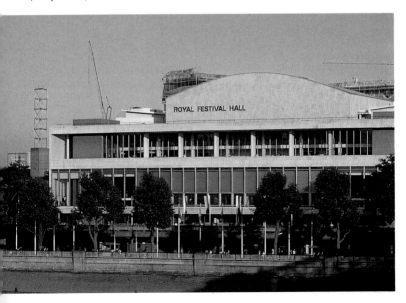

Pre-Modern functionalism was reflected very early in the engineering of London's great 19C stations and elsewhere. This is the Palm House (1848) at Kew Gardens, ravishingly beautiful and still doing the job for which it was built. (Chapter 61)

And in our Post-Modern age, some fine new structures are emerging, such as the City Hall (2002), by Foster & Partners, enriching a hitherto neglected river view near Tower Bridge. (Chapter 30)

However, architecture on the Thames has included some notable absurdities, such as Tower Bridge itself (1886–94): first class engineering made to look silly by its fancy dress. (Chapter 3)

Or first class engineering in completely the wrong place: the London Eye (2000) making a fool of its more dignified neighbours. (Chapter 32)

But the view from the Eye is another matter: the River Thames upstream looks magical (Chapter 75). Travel on the Eye while it turns: it may not be there for ever. But the Thames will.

Contents

Practical information

Background information

The Walks

Maps and plans

Introduction

The 17th edition

This Blue Guide aims to introduce London to you if you do not know it, or to deepen or renew your existing knowledge if it is limited or rusty. If you are coming for a holiday or a fixed period, there is plenty of practical information on getting here, where to stay, and eat, and go, and similar essentials.

This much is familiar material, available in many guidebooks. But the main chapters of this new edition adopt a more novel approach. They comprise a comprehensive series of self-guided walking tours, covering the whole of inner London, including all the main museums, galleries and important buildings, as well as key locations in the suburbs and around the fringe. These walks are arranged spiral-fashion, starting from the City and spreading along the Thames, then rotating clockwise. If you had time to do them all, you would know London as well as a black-cab driver, and in more depth. The style is historical in perspective, architectural and cultural in emphasis, sometimes critical or subjective in tone, but upbeat and enthusiastic in its engagement with the theme. These walks will make you love London more.

In the new century, London is on a roll. Thanks to the millennium and the Heritage Lottery Fund, many museums have had major extensions and improvements; more are planned for 2002 and beyond. Other new and interesting attractions have recently arrived, such as the London Eye. Transport and other aspects of tourist experience are reasonable and improving. Food, drink and shopping are excellent. London's architecture is an irresistible encyclopaedia of the subject itself. There has never been a better time to interact with this great city.

How to use this Guide

The first part of the section called Practical information covers material relevant when **planning your trip**, including sources of tourist information, travel advice and lists of hotels. The rest gives information useful when you are actually in London, such as transport, recommended restaurants and pubs, and lists of museums and other attractions.

The Background information includes a general **survey of London's past** and present, seeking to get to its heart and to fire you up, and a **chronology** of events in the city. This is followed by a list of **further reading**. Throughout the text there are highlighted sections on people of interest and on aspects of London life or history.

The bulk of the *Blue Guide* is divided into **walks**, 73 in all, with two river trips suggested at the end. There is one walk per chapter, dealing with the City and Central London first, then the outer areas (Zones 2–6 in London transport jargon) in clockwise order. London is friendly to walkers—safe, with names at the end of each street and locals who are happy to direct you. The only minus is when it rains. Many of the walks are quite short, so there is plenty of time to pause and take in your surroundings. Follow them all, and you will have visited all the most important and interesting streets and buildings in London.

The approximate **distance** of each walk is shown, together with a guideline for the **time** it takes if you are looking at the environment as you go. In inner London more time needs to be allowed to stand and stare; and always add on time to see interiors, especially museums and galleries. Of course, the walks could be completed much more quickly. Take a Tube train or bus to the starting point of each walk, follow the recommended route, and finish at the designated Tube or bus stop: the nearest Tube **stations** are indicated at the beginning and end of each chapter, and grid references to the **maps** at the back of the book are given along the way (e.g. **Map 9,6**). Buses often pass the door and a bus map is always useful (see Getting around, p 32).

You may want to visit some **museums, galleries or architectural sights** without following a walk. In this case, simply find the relevant pages via the index: the *Blue Guide* suggests self-contained tours of the major museums and galleries, pointing out the main items of interest (although beware, the arrangement or hang may have changed since we went to print). The descriptions of all important museums and galleries, and sometimes those for houses, churches and other places, are accompanied by:
• opening hours
• whether or not there are admission charges
• facilities (cafés, restaurants and shops)
• telephone numbers (☎), to check for up-to-date information, book tickets, etc.
• website address (if available)
• nearest Tube or rail station

If you are in London for only a day or two, look at the list of **unmissable sights** that follows. Then find the page number via the index to find out details.

At the back of the book is a **glossary** of London terms, architectural and other. Finally, there are specially produced maps for use on the walks in the central area; you may wish to supplement these with a street atlas if going further afield.

Getting the most out of the walks
• wear comfortable shoes.
• keep off the kerbs—buses come close!
• stop often to look around, and back, and up: the best Edwardian sculpture, for example, is usually placed at the top of façades.
• use the maps to help with the text. If using another map, transfer the route explained in the text onto your map with a highlighter.
• Monday to Friday are the best days for walking in business areas (Chapters 1, 2, 4–6, 8, 9, 23 and 29), when they are livelier, with more places open, including those for refreshment.
• the middle hours of the day (10.00–15.00) are best for getting into churches, but some walks (e.g. Chapters 10 and 22) are also great at night.
• lightweight binoculars are useful to spot details during some of the walks.

Buildings are demolished from time to time—although those important enough to be mentioned in these walks are likely to be 'listed' and therefore safe—and plenty of interesting new architecture appears. If on your walks you spot important omissions from this *Blue Guide*, or see mistakes in the text, please write to Blue Guides at 37 Soho Square, London, W1D 3QZ or email us at travel@acblack.com. All communications will be gratefully acknowledged.

Highlights—what you must not miss

If you have only **a few hours** in London, take a tour bus (details on p 35), or use the top deck of London buses on a triangular tour defined by routes 11, 38 and 8, or the linear route 15 (details on p 32).

If you have **one day**, take a tour bus and then go back to the favourite place you saw from it to explore further. Or take the 15 bus to the Tower of London, come back on it to St Paul's Cathedral, reboard the bus to go west for a quick visit round Somerset House and the National Gallery, then walk down Whitehall for whatever time is left.

If you have **two or three days**, choose according to taste from the following top places. Sights that have following letters in common can be combined easily.

For history
Tower of London
Westminster Abbey (A)
Houses of Parliament (A)

For art and culture
National Gallery (C)
British Museum

For architecture
St Paul's Cathedral (G)
Somerset House,
  including the Courtauld Gallery (E)

For shopping
Bond Street and Regent Street (D)
Covent Garden (E)
Knightsbridge

For contemporary excitement
London Eye
Docklands

Recent statistics list the top London tourist attractions as (1) British Museum, (2) National Gallery, (3) Westminster Abbey, (4) Madame Tussaud's, (5) Tower of London, (6) Tate Britain (before the spectacularly successful opening of Tate Modern) and (7) St Paul's Cathedral. It is worth noting that of these, three are free to enter: getting the best out of London need not be expensive.

If you have **five to seven days** in London, you could cover all the items above and add according to taste from the following:

For history
Horse Guards (A)
Windsor or Hampton Court
Imperial War Museum, especially
  the Holocaust Exhibition

For art and culture
National Portrait Gallery (C)
Wallace Collection (D)
Tate Modern (G, via Millennium
  Bridge)

Tate Britain
Victoria and Albert Museum

For architecture
Banqueting House (A)
Greenwich
Kenwood House (F)
City churches (G)

For shopping
High Street Kensington
Street markets

For open space
St James's Park (A)
Hampstead Heath (F)
Kew Gardens or Wetland Centre, Barnes

Suppose you can only do five of the walks in this guide: which would provide the richest comparison and variety? We suggest:

Chapter 1 for the City
Chapter 12 for Westminster, adding the Abbey from Chapter 14
Chapter 17 for open space and grandeur
Chapter 36 for smart suburbs
Chapter 46 for the vanishing East End

Blue Plaques

You will find commemorative plaques, and not just blue ones, on a large number of London buildings, referring to famous past residents. They were first erected as long ago as 1867, when the Royal Society of Arts placed one on Lord Byron's home in London; two from 1875, to Dryden and Napoleon III, still remain. The London County Council took over in 1901 and the Greater London Council in 1965. English Heritage became responsible for the scheme in 1986 and now choose about 20 new sites each year from a list of proposed candidates. Individuals are commemorated only once: 100 years from birth, or 20 years from death, must have elapsed before they are considered and the actual building with which they are associated must still stand. There are now about 800 official plaques througout London. Other London bodies also put up plaques to mark historic sites, blue rectangular ones by the City Corporation and green ones by Westminster City Council. To find a particular memorial, check www.blueplaque.com.

PRACTICAL INFORMATION

Planning your trip

When to go

London can be visited all the year round. It is humid on hot summer days and cold and dark in winter, and it often rains, but it is also often bright and fine and the temperature is almost always equable. (Londoners themselves complain about the weather nearly all the time: it is best to ignore them on this point.) British Summer Time starts at the end of March (see p 64.)

There is a season of fashionable events in early summer (see the calendar on p 60), but there are other happenings of one sort or another, in no way inferior, all the year round. Most of the museums, galleries and shops are open seven days a week (except at Christmas). Tourist attractions are much emptier between November and February.

Tourist information

If you live outside the UK, you can obtain information about travel in Britain in general and London in particular from the office of the **British Tourist Authority** (BTA). The BTA's website is www.visitbritain.com (followed by / and the web initials for your country).

The BTA may have an office in your country:

Australia Level 16, Gateway, 1 Macquarie Place, Sydney NSW 2000.
☎ (2) 9377 4400. Fax (2) 9377 4499.

Canada 5915 Airport Rd, Suite 120, Mississauga, Ontario L4V 1T1.
☎ (905) 405 1840. Fax (905) 405 1835.

France Maison-de-la-Grande-Bretagne, 19 Rue des Mathurins, 75009 Paris.
☎ (1) 4451 5620. Fax (1) 4451 5621.

Germany Westendstrasse 16–22, 60325 Frankfurt. ☎ (69) 97 1123.
Fax (69) 97 112 444.

Hong Kong Suite 1401, Natwest Tower, Times Square, Causeway Bay, Hong Kong. ☎ (00 852) 2882 9967. Fax (00 852) 577 1443.

Ireland 18/19 College Green, Dublin 2. ☎ (1) 670 8000. Fax (1) 670 8244.

Italy Corso Magenta 32, 20123 Milano. ☎ (02) 7201 0078.
Fax (02) 7201 0086.

Japan Akasaka Twin Tower 1F, 2-17-22, Minato-Ku, Tokyo. ☎ (3) 5562 2548.
Fax (3) 5562 2551.

Netherlands Aurora Gebouw (5e) Stadhouderskade 2, 1054 ES Amsterdam.
☎ (20) 689 0002. Fax (20) 618 6868.

New Zealand 17th Floor, 151 Queen St, Auckland 1. ☎ (9) 303 1446.
Fax (9) 377 6965.

South Africa Lancaster Gate, Hyde Park Lane, Hyde Park, Johannesburg 2196 or PO Box 41896, Craighall 2024. ☎ (11) 325 0343. Fax (11) 325 0344.

USA 7th Floor, 551 Fifth Avenue, New York, NY 10176-0799.
☎ (212) 986 2200. Toll free 1 800 GO 2 BRITAIN.

For information about London itself, the **London Tourist Board** (LTB) may be contacted at Glen House, Stag Place, Victoria, London SW1 5LT. ☎ 020 7932 2000. Its website is www.londontouristboard.com. It also offers extensive **recorded information**, ☎ 09068 663 344. For a London Line card, which gives even more numbers for information, ☎ 020 7932 2000 or fax 020 7932 0222 during business hours.

The LTB will book **accommodation** for you, ☎ 020 7932 2020, but this line is operative only in business hours.

For particular parts of London, such as many of the areas dealt with in this guide under the term 'villages', there are **local tourist offices** in central locations. Telephone first to obtain their opening hours.

City of London St Paul's Churchyard, EC4. ☎ 020 7332 1456.
Croydon Katharine St, Croydon, CR9 1ET. ☎ 020 8253 1009.
Greenwich Pepys House, 2 Cutty Sark Gardens, Greenwich, SE10 9LW. ☎ 0870 608 2000.
Harrow Civic Centre, Station Rd, Harrow, HA1 2XF. ☎ 020 8424 1103.
Richmond Old Town Hall, Whittaker Avenue, Richmond, TW9 1TP. ☎ 020 8940 9125.
Southwark London Bridge, 6 Tooley St, SE1 2SY. ☎ 020 7403 8299.
Spitalfields 18 Lamb St, E1 ☎ 020 7375 2539.

Passports and formalities

European Union citizens with a current passport can live and work freely in London. Visitors from **other European countries** with a current passport can stay for up to three months: any longer and a visa is required, as is a work permit. For citizens of the **USA, Canada, Australia, New Zealand and South Africa**, a current passport will allow a visit of up to 6 months: a longer stay requires a visa. A work permit is also required. People visiting from elsewhere in the world need a visa.

For **visas**, contact your nearest British Embassy or High Commission. **Work permits** are hard to obtain without the backing of an employer, but persons aged 17–27 may apply for a Working Holiday Entry Certificate which will allow a stay of up to two years during which casual work may be undertaken. Consult your nearest British Embassy or High Commission.

For further details, see the Foreign Office website, www.fco.gov.uk.

Customs

There are restrictions on the amount of tax- or duty-free goods you may bring into Britain, from the European Union and everywhere else. Check the current regulations, ☎ 0845 010 9000 or at your port or airport of departure. If you have nothing to declare, go straight through the green channel at the airport or port of entry.

There are no **exchange controls** in Britain and you can bring in or take out as much UK currency as you wish.

Currency

The currency is still famously the **pound** (£), whose defenders are bracing themselves against the Euro. There are £1 and £2 coins, and £5, £10, £20 and £50 notes. Each £1 is divided into 100 pence or pennies (p). There are silver coins worth 50p, 20p, 10p and 5p, and copper coins worth 2p and 1p.

Credit cards can be used for nearly all forms of payment, unless the amount is under £5—this includes bills in hotels, restaurants and shops, and tickets for theatres and trains. Most public telephones accept cards. You will need **cash** for most station fare machines and when travelling in buses and taxis, shopping in street markets, pubs, coffee shops, newsagents and other small shops, for public telephones (it is easier to use than cards), and for tipping.

There are foreign **exchange facilities** at banks, in shopping streets and at ports and airports: they are often in hotels, too, but at less favourable rates. Banks will exchange **travellers' cheques**. Take your passport or other ID. You cannot use travellers' cheques to pay for goods and services in shops and restaurants.

The big four banks are *Barclays*, *HSBC*, *Lloyds/TSB* and *Natwest*: they and other banks are open 09.30–16.30 Mon–Fri (see also p 59). Most branches have **ATM machines** in the wall outside which accept Visa, Mastercard, and many other cards. Check on any charge that might be made for cash withdrawals with your card company.

Costs London is expensive. An average three-star hotel will charge £100 per night for a double room and £80 for a single: always look around for special packages. The minimum adult fare on the underground is £1.00 (or £1.60 in Zone 1), and on buses 70p (£1 in Zone 1). A coffee or tea will cost from around £1.50, and a basic meal (pizza, pasta, salad, etc) with a drink from £15 upwards. A good dinner out for two with wine will start at £70. Seats in theatres and at concerts begin at around £15, but these are likely to be poorer ones at the back of the upper circle. The good news is, entry to most of the big museums is free.

Health

In case of genuine emergency, you can usually use the accident and emergency service of a **National Health Service** (NHS) hospital in Britain free of charge. For non-emergency treatment you will be charged unless the NHS has a reciprocal agreement with your country. There are such arrangements with EU countries and most other Western European countries, and with Australia and New Zealand. Visitors from the USA, Canada and the Far East would be wise to take out **health insurance** before leaving home.

Travellers with disabilities

While London is still not an easy city for travellers with disabilities, reception arrangements at Heathrow and Gatwick airports are good: for a brochure giving details in advance, ☎ 01233 211 207; and for general travel information and advice, ☎ 020 7688 4601. From the airports taxis offer the best way of getting around, but the *Heathrow Express* is also a good way to get into London (see p 13). A low-floor bus operates the *Stationlink* service between London's main rail stations, ☎ 020 7918 4300.

Much of the underground and national rail system remains inaccessible to wheelchair users, but **buses** are improving and the newer models include a platform that can be lowered for wheelchair access.

Travel advice. *Tube Access Guide*, with a useful map showing problem stations, is available at *London Transport Information Offices* (see p 30) and at many station displays, or ☎ 020 7941 4600. London Transport's general helpline, which also covers the DLR and River Thames boat service, is ☎ 020 7222 1234. Advice can also be obtained from *Transport for London*, general helpline ☎ 020 7941 4600. Textphone 020 7918 3015. www.transportforlondon.gov.uk

Among **hotels**, there have been recommendations for the *Copthorne Tara*, Scarsdale Place, Kensington W8 (☎ 020 7937 7211); *Mount Royal Hotel*, near Marble Arch (☎ 020 7629 8040); *Novotel Hotels* (☎ 020 8237 7474).

More detail about hotels in London and other facilities is obtainable from:
Holiday Care Service 2nd Floor, Imperial Buildings, Victoria Rd, Horley, Surrey RH6 7PZ. ☎ 01293 774 535. www.holidaycare.org.uk
RADAR (Royal Association for Disability and Rehabilitation), 12 City Forum, 250 City Rd, London EC1V 8AF. ☎ 020 7250 3222.

The book *Access in London* is also very well worth obtaining (Quiller Press, ☎ 020 7499 6529).

Getting there

By air

Five airports serve London. Two are large: Heathrow, the busiest in the world, is 15 miles west of London; Gatwick is 28 miles south in Surrey. Two are smaller: Luton lies 33 miles to the northwest, and Stansted, 37 miles northeast, has notable architecture. London City Airport in the former Royal Docks, only 6 miles east of the centre, is mainly for business flights to and from Europe; you need allow only 40 minutes for check-in here.

Heathrow ☎ 0870 000 0123. www.baa.co.uk/main/airports/heathrow
Gatwick ☎ 0870 000 2468. www.baa.co.uk/main/airports/gatwick
Luton ☎ 01582 405 100. www.london-luton.com
Stansted ☎ 0870 000 0303. www.baa.co.uk/main/airports/stansted
London City ☎ 020 7646 0000. www.londoncityairport.com

The following are just some of the airlines that serve London's airports:
From North America and Canada
American Airlines ☎ 800 433 7300 (☎ 0845 778 9789 in the UK)
www.aa.com
Air Canada ☎ 888 247 2262 (☎ 0870 524 7226 in the UK)
www.aircanada.ca
British Airways ☎ 800 247 9297 (☎ 0845 773 3377 in the UK)
www.british-airways.com
Delta ☎ 800 241 4141 (☎ 0800 414 767 in the UK)
www.delta.com
United Airlines ☎ 800 538 2929 (☎ 0845 844 4777 in the UK)
www.ual.com
Virgin Atlantic ☎ 800 862 8621 (☎ 01293 747 747 in the UK)
www.virgin-atlantic.com
From Australia and New Zealand
Qantas ☎ 131313 (☎ 0845 774 7767 in the UK)
www.qantas.com
Air New Zealand ☎ 00 649 366 2400 (☎ 020 8600 7600 in the UK)
www.airnz.com

From Britain and Ireland

Aer Lingus ☎ 01 886 8888 (☎ 0845 973 7747 in the UK)
www.aerlingus.com
Ryanair ☎ 01 609 7800 (☎ 0870 156 9569 in the UK)
www.ryanair.com
British Midland ☎ 0870 607 0555. www.flybmi.com

Security Be careful about packing sharp items, like nail scissors, in hand luggage: they may be deemed a security risk and confiscated. Since 11 September 2001, inevitably waiting times and security checks at airports have become more protracted.

Getting to Central London from the airports

From Heathrow The *Piccadilly Line* on the underground network runs from the two stations serving Terminals 1, 2, 3 and Terminal 4, which are in fare Zone 6. It is slow, taking approximately 50 minutes to Central London, but relatively cheap: a single adult fare costs £3.60 (child fare £1.50). First trains to and from the airport run from around 05.30 and the last around 23.45 (07.00 and 23.30 on Sundays). For enquiries, ☎ 020 7222 1234.

The *Heathrow Express* is a mainline train that runs to Paddington Station. It is fast, taking about 15 minutes (20 minutes to Terminal 4), but relatively expensive: a single fare costs £12. First trains run at 05.10 and the last at 23.40; onwards travel from Paddington will probably be necessary. At present check-in at Paddington itself is limited. For enquiries, ☎ 0845 600 1515.

The *Airbus* or coach, the A2, runs to Russell Square via Paddington and Euston Stations. There are also **National Express** coach services to Victoria Station. These are cheap but not very frequent. For enquiries, ☎ 0870 574 7777 or 0870 575 7747. www.gobycoach.com

Taxis wait in rank at each terminal. Use a black London cab. The fare to Central London is metered and is likely to be above £40 plus a 10 per cent tip; there will be extra charges depending on the number of passengers, pieces of luggage, waiting and time of day. But taxis are comfortable, quick and take you wherever you want to go.

All major car hire companies are represented at the terminals (see p 34). Many others will arrange for a car to be available on arrival.

From Gatwick The *Gatwick Express* is a train running to Victoria Station. It is frequent and reasonably fast, taking 30 minutes. A single fare costs £20. For enquiries, ☎ 0870 530 1530. All trains run to the South Terminal and passengers for the North Terminal need to take a shuttle service.

Thameslink trains go to Blackfriars and King's Cross Stations and beyond. For enquiries, ☎ 0870 000 2468.

Black cabs are not available, although car hire is available as at Heathrow. There are also coach services; for enquiries, ☎ 0870 608 2608. www.baa.co.uk

From Stansted A train, the *Stansted Express*, runs to Liverpool Street Station, calling at Tottenham Hale (connections to the Victoria Line). Single fare £13. For enquiries, ☎ 0870 000 0303. www.baa.co.uk

From Luton A new station, Luton Airport Parkway, with Thameslink trains to King's Cross, Blackfriars and other central London stations. For enquiries, ☎ 01582 405 100. www.london-luton.com

From City Airport A shuttle bus service runs to Liverpool Street Station or Canary Wharf (connections to the Jubilee Line or DLR). There are also many black cabs. For enquiries, ☎ 020 7646 0088. www.londoncityairport.com

By train

Visitors can reach London from Continental Europe by train via the Channel Tunnel. *Eurostar* operates passenger services from Paris (18 trains each day, journey time 3 hours) and Brussels (15 trains each day, 2 hours 45 minutes) via Lille: the current return fare from either city is £79. At present, Eurostar trains terminate at Waterloo Station. For enquiries, ☎ 0870 160 6600. For bookings (not more than three months ahead) ☎ 0870 584 8848. www.raileurope.co.uk Travellers with cars can take the *Eurotunnel* shuttle service from Calais to Folkestone (three trains per hour in the day, one every hour at night, journey time 35 minutes): the current cost is £130–200 per car, passengers free. It is best to book on ☎ 0870 535 3535. www.eurotunnel.com

Visitors coming from other ports of entry arrive in London at Victoria (from Dover), Euston (from Liverpool), Paddington (from Bristol) and Waterloo (from Southampton). For information on domestic train services, see p 32.

By coach

Details of the international coach services run by *National Express* can be obtained on ☎ 0870 580 8080, or from individual ports of entry: the nearest to London are Dover, ☎ 09064 142 103; and Portsmouth, ☎ 09064 142 115. Or try www.gobycoach.com

By car

See details for the Eurotunnel service under 'By train' above.

By sea

It is not difficult to get to London by ferry and then rail, from the Continent or from Ireland. The most frequent services are from Calais to Dover (every 30 mins), and thence to Victoria. There are ferries at only slightly longer intervals for Zeebrugge or the Hook to Harwich (and thence to Liverpool Street). A guide-line single fare from Calais is £25, or £50 from Holland.

For details on travel from France enquire at: *P & O Stena Line*, ☎ 087 0600 0600, www.posl.com or, for Holland, *Stena Line*, ☎ 0875 70 70 70, www.stenaline.co.uk.

From Ireland, the usual route is from Dublin to Holyhead or Liverpool (guide-line single fare £58) and thence to Euston. Enquiries *Irish Ferries*, ☎ 08705 17 17 17, www.irishferries.com or Stena Line above.

 # Where to stay

It is always advisable to book hotel or bed-and-breakfast accommodation in advance, but the **London Tourist Board** (LTB) and other agencies also offer a **booking service** on your arrival in London, which should ensure that no visitor

is without a bed. There is an LTB hotel accommodation service at Heathrow airport, Terminals 1 2, 3 station (see p 13). *Thomas Cook* operates a similar service at Gatwick, and at Victoria, King's Cross and Paddington. Credit-card holders can book by phone, ☎ 020 7932 2020 during business hours.

The range of accommodation in London is huge, from Tent City in Hackney Marshes (£5 per night) to the top Mayfair hotels (well over £500 per night). In between are a number of newer options, including **self-catering apartments** and accommodation in **family homes**, bookable through Home Stay agencies. At the cheaper end of the market are university **halls of residence**, available during vacations.

A good general source of **information** about all these options is *Where to Stay in London*, a low-priced book published annually by the LTB (for contact details, see p 10). This is well worth getting hold of before you travel, if possible. Other good general guides include the AA's *The Hotel Guide* or *The Good Hotel Guide*.

Prices The following list of hotels is classified as shown below. Prices given are per person, per night.

E	quality hotel (£150–£300 or much more)**
D	mid-price hotel (£100–£150)
C	basic hotel (£50–£100)
B	good bed-and-breakfast hotel (£50–£90)*
A	basic bed-and-breakfast hotel (£30–£50)

* The LTB calls these Guest Accommodation.
** This includes hotels normally classified as 4- or 5-star and small townhouse hotels.

This list is intended only to provide examples, not recommendations or otherwise: some areas of London, such as Bloomsbury, Kensington and Bayswater, are more extensively populated with hotels than others, and the greater numbers listed here reflect simply that point. Comments on the accuracy of our listing will be most gratefully received.

Hotel groups

Radisson Edwardian. ☎ 0800 374 411. www.radisson.com
Thistle. ☎ 0800 181 716. www.thistlehotels.com
Best Western. ☎ 08457 737 373. www.bestwestern.co.uk
Holiday Inns Express. ☎ 0800 897 121. www.sixcontinentshotels.com
Marriott. ☎ 0800 221 222. www.marriott.com
Travelodge. ☎ 08700 850 950. www.travelodge.co.uk

City (E1 and EC3)

(E) *Thistle Tower*, St Katherine's Way, E1 9LD. ☎ 020 7481 2575.
Fax 020 7488 4106. Overlooks St Katherine's Dock and Tower Bridge.
(D) *Novotel London Tower Bridge*, 10 Pepys St, EC3N 2NR. ☎ 020 7265 6000.
Fax 020 7265 6060. Very convenient location in the centre of EC3.
(D) *Thistle City*, Central St, EC1V 8DS. ☎ 020 7956 6000. Fax 020 7253 1005.
North of the City (15mins walk) but a rarity in this area.

North Bank (WC2)

(E) *Savoy*, Strand, WC2R 0EU. ☎ 020 7836 4343. Fax. 020 7240 6040.
One of London's most famous, with Art-Deco interiors and river views.

(E) *Waldorf Meridien*, Aldwych, WC2B 4DD. ☎ 020 7836 2400.
Fax 020 7836 7244. Fine Edwardian building next to the Strand.
(E) *Hampshire (Radisson)*, Leicester Square, WC2H 7LH. ☎ 020 7839 9399.
Fax 020 7960 8122. Very convenient but in a noisy location.
(D) *Strand Palace*, Strand, WC2R 0JJ. ☎ 020 7836 8080. Fax 020 7836 2077.
Mid-range, reliable hotel, opposite the Savoy.
(D) *Thistle Royal Trafalgar*, Whitcomb St, WC2H 7HG. ☎ 020 7930 4477.
Fax 020 7925 2149. Adjacent to the National Gallery and Trafalgar Square.
(B) *Royal Adelphi Hotel*, 21 Villiers St, WC2N 6ND. ☎ 020 7930 8764.
Fax 020 7930 8735. Small bed-and-breakfast hotel near Trafalgar Square.

Westminster (SW1)

(E) *Goring*, Beeston Place, Grosvenor Gardens, SW1W 0JW. ☎ 020 7936 9000.
Traditional, comfortable, close to Buckingham Palace.
(E) *Capital*, Basil St, Knightsbridge, SW3 1AT. ☎ 020 7589 5171.
Fax 020 7225 0011. A stone's throw from Harrod's; has outstanding restaurant.
(E) *Berkeley*, Wilton Place, Knightsbridge, SW1X 7RL. ☎ 020 7235 6000.
Fax 020 7235 4330. Top of the range, in the heart of Knightsbridge.
(D) *Quality Hotel Eccleston*, 82–83 Eccleston Square, SW1V 1PS.
☎ 020 7834 8042. Fax 7630 8942. Quiet location, yet close to Victoria.
(C) *Melita House Hotel*, 35 Charlwood St, SW1V 2DU. ☎ 020 7828 0471.
Fax 020 7932 0988. Newly refurbished, family-run hotel near Victoria Station.
(C) *Victoria Inn*, 65–67 Belgrave Place, SW1V 2BG. ☎ 020 7834 6721.
Fax 020 7931 0201. Modern hotel, again close to Victoria
(B) *Collin House*, 104 Ebury St, SW1W 9QD. ☎ and fax 20 7730 8031.
Small, comfortable bed-and-breakfast hotel in a pleasant area
(B) *Victor House Hotel*, 51 Belgrave Rd, SW1V 2BB. ☎ 020 7592 9853.
Fax 020 7592 9854. Small, modern hotel
(A) *Caswell Hotel*, 25 Gloucester St, SW1V 2DB. ☎ 020 7834 6345.
Small family-run bed-and-breakfast hotel
(A) *Huttons Hotel*, 55 Belgrave Rd, SW1V 2BB. ☎ 020 7834 3726.
Fax 020 7834 3389. Convenient bed-and-breakfast hotel near Victoria.

West End (W1 and SW1)

(E) *Dorchester*, Park Lane, W1A 2HJ. ☎ 020 7629 8888. Fax 020 7409 0114.
World-famous hotel, with the prices you would expect.
(E) *Holiday Inn Mayfair*, 3, Berkeley St, W1X 6NE. ☎ 020 7493 8282.
Fax 020 7629 2827. New, close to Piccadilly, and reliable.
(E) *London Marriott*, Grosvenor Square, W1A 4AW. ☎ 020 7493 1232.
Fax 020 7491 3201. Reliable standard and ideal for Mayfair and Oxford St.
(E) *22 Jermyn Street*, SW1Y 6HL. ☎ 020 7734 2353. Fax 020 7734 1750.
Smart townhouse hotel, close to Piccadilly.
(E) *Flemings*, 10 Half Moon St, W1Y 7RA. ☎ 020 7499 2964.
Fax 020 7629 4063. A terrace of Georgian houses: ask for the flexible tariff.
(D) *Regent Palace*, Piccadilly Circus, W1A 4BZ. ☎ 020 7734 7000.
Fax 020 7734 6435. Huge, but reasonable prices and central for everything.
(D) *Sherlock Holmes Hotel*, 108 Baker St, W1M 2LJ. ☎ 020 7486 6161.
Fax 020 7486 0884. Not quite 221B, but closer to the shops!
(C) *Glynne Court Hotel*, 41 Great Cumberland Place, W1H 7LG.
☎ 020 7262 4344. Fax 020 7724 2071.

Small, price-conscious hotel in a convenient location.

(B) *Marble Arch Inn*, 49–50 Upper Berkeley St, W1H 7PN. ☎ 020 7723 7888.
Fax 020 7723 6060. Small, friendly hotel near the western end of Oxford St.

(B) *Hallam Hotel*, 12 Hallam St, Portland Place, W1N 5LF. ☎ 020 7580 1166.
Fax 020 7323 4527. In a quiet location but only 5 minutes from Oxford Circus.

(B) *Bentinck House Hotel*, 20 Bentinck St, W1M 5RL. ☎ 020 7935 9141.
Fax 020 7224 5903. Family-run hotel, perfectly located for the shops.

(A) *Kenwood House Hotel*, 114 Gloucester Place, W1H 3DB. ☎ 020 7935 3473.
Fax 020 7224 0582. Budget bed-and-breakfast hotel on a noisy street.

Bloomsbury and King's Cross (WC1)

(E) *Blooms*, 7 Montague St, WC1B 5BP. ☎ 020 7323 1717. Fax 020 7636 6498.
In a pleasant street, and almost inside the British Museum.

(E) *Hotel Russell*, Russell Square, WC1B 5BE. ☎ 020 7837 6470.
Fax 020 7837 2857. Yet more architecture to enjoy, but not very up-to-date.

(E) *Post House Bloomsbury*, Coram St, WC1N 1HT. ☎ 0870 400 922.
Fax 020 7837 5374. A modern, reliable standard.

(D) *London Ryan Hotel*, Gwynne Place, King's Cross, WC1X 9QN.
☎ 020 7278 2480. Fax 020 7837 3776. A modern hotel convenient for travel.

(D) *Bonnington*, 92 Southampton Row, WC1B 4BH. ☎ 020 7242 2828.
Fax 020 7831 9170. An old faithful in the Bloomsbury area.

(C) *George Hotel*, 58–60 Cartwright St, WC1H 9EL. ☎ 027 387 8777.
Fax 020 7387 8666. See next entry.

(C) *Crescent Hotel*, 49–50 Cartwright St, WC1H 9EL. ☎ 027 387 1515.
Fax 020 7383 2054. Several comfortable hotels in a quiet Georgian crescent.

(A) *Gower House*, 57 Gower St, WC1E 6HJ. ☎ and fax 020 7636 4685.
Small, friendly bed-and-breakfast near the British Museum.

South Bank (SE1)

(E) *London Marriott County Hall*, Westminster Bridge Rd, SE1 7PB.
☎ 020 7928 5200. Fax 020 7928 2233. Beautiful facilities and fine view from
riverside rooms.

(E) *London Bridge Hotel*, 8–18 London Bridge St, SE1 9SG. ☎ 020 7855 2200.
Fax 020 7855 2233. Independent hotel with a good range of facilities.

(D) *Novotel*, 113 Lambeth Rd, SE1 7LS. ☎ 020 7793 1010. Fax 020 7792 0202.
More business than tourist, but useful in area.

(C) *County Hall Travel Inn*, Belvedere Rd, SE1 7PB. ☎ 020 7902 1600.
Fax 020 7902 1619. Of a basic standard but perfect for the London Eye.

(C) *Days Inn*, 54 Kennington Rd, SE1 7BJ. ☎ 020 7922 1331.
Fax 020 7922 1441. New hotel opposite the Imperial War Museum.

Bayswater (W2)

(E) *Thistle Kensington Gardens*, 104 Bayswater Rd, W2 3HL.
☎ 020 7262 4461. Fax 020 7706 4560. Overlooking Kensington Gardens.

(E) *Pembridge Court*, 34 Pembridge Gardens, W2 4DX. ☎ 020 7229 9977.
Fax 020 7247 4982. Victorian house in a trendy area, close to Portobello Rd.

(D) *Central Park Hotel*, 49 Queensborough Terrace, W2 3SS.
☎ 020 7229 2424. Fax 020 7229 2904. Modern hotel close to Queensway.

(D) *Mornington Hotel*, 12 Lancaster Gate, W2 3LG. ☎ 020 7262 7361.
Fax 020 7706 1028. Victorian façade, comfortable interior; opposite Hyde Park.

(C) *Beverley House Hotel*, 142 Sussex Gardens, W2 1UB. ☎ 020 7723 3380.

Fax 020 7262 0324. Refurbished hotel convenient for Paddington Station.
(B) *Barry House Hotel*, 12 Sussex Place, W2 2TP. ☎ 020 7723 7340.
Fax 020 7723 9775. Bed-and-breakfast hotel close to Paddington and Hyde Park.
(A) *Hyde Park Rooms*, 137 Sussex Gardens, W2 2RX. ☎ 020 7723 0225.
Small family-run hotel on the route taken in Chapter 37.
(A) *Caring Hotel*, 24 Craven Hill Gardens, W2 3EA. ☎ 020 7262 8708.
Fax 020 7262 8590. Small bed-and-breakfast hotel close to Paddington.

Kensington (W8) and Earl's Court (SW5)
(E) *Royal Garden*, 2–24 Kensington High St, W8 4PT. ☎ 020 7937 8000.
Fax 020 7361 1991. Luxury appropriate to its location.
(E) *Millennium Gloucester*, 4–18 Harrington Gardens, SW7 4LH.
☎ 020 7373 6030. Fax 020 7373 0409. Large, luxury hotel close to
Knightsbridge.
(E) *Cranley Hotel*, 10–112 Bina Gardens, SW5 0LA. ☎ 020 7373 0123.
Fax 020 7373 9497. Delightful townhouse hotel in a quiet street.
(D) *Harrington Hall*, 5–25 Harrington Gardens, SW7 4JW. ☎ 020 7396 9696.
Fax 020 7396 9090. Close to some remarkable housing and to the museums.
(C) *Swiss House Hotel*, 171 Old Brompton Rd, SW5 0AN. ☎ 020 7373 2769.
Fax 020 7373 4983. Comfortable hotel in a convenient if noisy location.
(C) *Beaver Hotel*, 57–59 Philbeach Gardens, SW5 9ED. ☎ 020 7373 4553.
Fax 020 7373 4555. Quiet Victorian crescent with a breathtaking church,
convenient for South Kensington.
(A) *Ramsees Hotel*, 32–36 Hogarth Rd, SW5 0PU. ☎ 020 7370 1445.
Fax 020 7244 6835. Inexpensive bed-and-breakfast hotel near Earl's Court station.
(A) *Nevern Hotel*, 29–31 Nevern Place, SW5 9NP. ☎ 020 7244 8366.
Fax 020 7370 1541. Small hotel close to Earl's Court and Olympia.

Further afield
Muswell Hill
(D) *Raglan Hall*, 8–12 Queen's Avenue, N10 3NR. ☎ 020 8883 9836.
Fax 020 8883 5002. In tree-lined Edwardian Avenue, on the walk in Chapter 66.
Hampstead
(D) *Comfort Inn*, 5–7 Frognal, NW3 6AL. ☎ 020 7794 0101. Fax 020 7794 0100.
Off Finchley Rd, but not far from the delights of Hampstead.
Blackheath
(C) *Clarendon Hotel*, Montpelier Row, SE3 0RW. ☎ 020 8318 4321.
Fax 020 8318 4378. Large Georgian terrace overlooking the heath.
Greenwich
(D) *Hamilton House*, 14 West Grove, SE10 8QT. ☎ 020 8694 9899.
Fax 020 694 2370. Small Georgian hotel with impressive views.
(C) *Holiday Inn Express*, Bugsby's Way, SE10 0GD. ☎ 020 8269 5000.
Fax 020 8269 5069. Basic but reasonable.
Wimbledon
(E) *Cannizaro House (Thistle)*, West Side, Wimbledon Common, SW19 4UE.
☎ 020 8879 1464. Fax 020 8879 7338. Delightful country house with four-
poster beds, etc; surrounded by parkland.

Bed-and-breakfast agencies
Uptown Reservations, ☎ 020 7351 3445.
London Bed-and-Breakfast Agency, ☎ 020 7586 2768.

Note that many bed-and-breakfast hotels accept cash only. You can find many more on the London Tourist Board website (for contact details, see p 65).

Self-catering apartments These are usually bookable for whole weeks only, although some will offer nightly rates. Prices start from around £300 per week in low season and £350 in high season.

Holiday Serviced Apartments, 273 Old Brompton Rd, SW5, ☎ 020 7373 4477. www.holidayapartments.co.uk. Offers a wide range of locations.

Langorf Hotel and Self-Catering Apartments, 20–22 Frognal, NW3. ☎ 020 7794 4483.

Nell Gwynne House Apartments, Sloane Avenue, SW3. ☎ 020 7584 8317.

Clarendon House Apartments, 48 Ranelagh Rd, W5. ☎ 01424 212954.

Youth hostels London's youth hostels have been cleaned up in the past few years and offer budget bed-and-breakfast accommodation, often in central locations. Seven are run by the **Youth Hostels Association**, which you must join (£12.50 for a year) to stay in their property, which costs from around £20 per person per night. For bookings, ☎ 01629 592 709. www.yha.org.uk

The following are independently run and may be cheaper, depending on your choice of room and the season:

St Christopher's Inn, 48–50 Camden High St, NW1. ☎ 020 7407 1856. www.st-christophers.co.uk. There are five other locations in London.

Ashlee House, 261–65 Gray's Inn Rd, WC1. ☎ 020 7833 9400. www.ashleehouse.co.uk

Hyde Park Youth Hostel, 2–6 Inverness Terrace, W2. ☎ 020 7229 5101. www.astorhostels.com. There are four other locations in London.

The Generator, 37 Tavistock Place, WC1. ☎ 020 7388 7666. www.the-generator.co.uk. Huge, relatively new hostel with 800 beds.

Dover Castle Hostel, 6A Great Dover St, SE1. ☎ 020 7403 7773. www.dovercastlehostel.co.uk

The **YMCA** and **YWCA** also have several hostels in London, many of which offer private rooms rather than dormitory accommodation:

Barbican YMCA, 2 Fann St, EC2. ☎ 020 7628 0697. admin@barbican.ymca.org.uk

London City YMCA, 8 Errol St, EC2. ☎ 020 7628 8832.

Bayswater YWCA, 13 Palace Court, W2. ☎ 020 7727 3009.

University halls of residence Student rooms are often available during vacations, particularly in summer: some have *en suite* facilities, others must share.

Linstead Hall, Prince's Gardens, SW7. ☎ 020 7594 9507. www.ad.ic.ac.uk/conferences/accommodation.htm. Imperial College also has rooms near the Royal Albert Hall and in Notting Hill.

Bankside House, 24 Sumner St, SE1. ☎ 020 7633 9877. www.lse.ac.uk/vacations/bankside-residence.htm. One of four sites run by the London School of Economics.

International Students House, 229 Great Portland St, W1. ☎ 020 7631 8300.

Camping and caravan sites These offer the cheapest accommodation in London (from about £11), although they are far from the centre. You do not need your own tent.

Tent City (June–Sept only), Millfields Rd, Hackney E5. ☎ 020 8985 7656. www.tentcity.co.uk

Lea Valley Campsite (April–Oct only), Sewardstone Rd, E4 7RA. ☎ 020 8529 5689. Fax 020 8559 4070. www.leevalleypark.org.uk
Crystal Palace Camping and Caravanning Site, Crystal Palace Parade, SE19 1UF. ☎ 020 8778 7155. Fax 020 8676 0980.

Further information is available from the LTB (for contact details, see p 10) and from the *Camping and Caravanning Club*, Greenfield House, Westwood Way, Coventry (☎ 01203 694 995) or the *Caravan Club*, East Grinstead House, London Rd, East Grinstead, West Sussex (☎ 01342 326 944).

 # Food and drink

Foods that were once traditionally associated with the capital are not much in evidence in London now: pie and mash, jellied eels, whitebait and beer are still available but in the last few decades have been totally superseded by the full range of international cuisines. Certain areas, including Chinatown and Banglatown, are particularly associated with the food of their new populations. There is a plethora of specialist food shops and an increasing number of successful organic and farmers' markets (see p 55).

Eating out in London has become, for many, one of the highlights of a visit to the capital. The range is vast, in every direction—price, ethnicity, location and style. You can go almost anywhere in the centre of London without giving the matter much thought and obtain reasonable and cheap light meals, coffees and snacks. Outside the centre, for example when walking the higher numbered chapters of this guide, you need to be a little more discriminating, and a pub might be the best bet (but see general remarks on pubs below).

Here we list restaurants in the geographical areas defined by the walks, with some indication of price and style, followed by suggestions for light refreshments and then pubs and wine bars.

Restaurants

Restaurants do not so naturally form part of a walk as pubs or cafés. Lunch, as Kingsley Amis used to allege, may be the finest meal of the day—longer, easier and more digestible than dinner—but experiencing lunch at a good restaurant to the full may find you wrongly placed in terms of both dress and mood for an exploratory walk afterwards. There are exceptions, however, and in many places just outside the central area, and even within it if you look around, lunch (or early evening dinner) can be excellent value.

Moderately priced restaurants include the chains *Bella Pasta*, *Café Pasta*, *Café Rouge*, *Gourmet Pizza Company*, *Pizza Express* and *Pizza Paradiso*. A good lunch in the middle of a day in the National Gallery or the British Museum may surprisingly enhance your appreciation of their contents.

Restaurants of many nationalities now exist in London. **'Modern British'**, the style of cooking emanating from catering courses today, uses traditional ingredients modified by knowledge of foreign cuisines, in smaller and more expensive portions. **'Traditional' British** is another thing altogether—carveries, roast beef and Yorkshire pudding—and is only rarely to be found in high-quality restaurants (such as ***Simpson's in the Strand*** or ***Rules***), but is common enough in pubs, at a lower grade and price. Traditional **fish and chips** are always best in a pub or from a fish and chip shop.

Recommended restaurant guides include *The Good Food Guide* and *Time Out Eating and Drinking*. You should **book a table in advance** for dinner at any of the restaurants listed below, several days ahead in most cases, weeks ahead at a few. Booking for lunch is also advisable. You will be asked for a contact number; if you decide not to go, make sure you phone to cancel the booking. Some top restaurants are open only in the evenings, but most restaurants are also open for lunch. Many are closed on Sunday evenings. In business areas they may open only during the week and in the City only for lunch. Restaurants near theatres offer pre- and post-show meals, which you should still book.

Prices All prices should be displayed outside the entrance. Set lunch or pre-theatre dinner menus offer excellent value, and are becoming increasingly common—they undercut the prices quoted against the relevant restaurants in the lists. Our indication assumes the inclusion of half a bottle of wine per person, as well as VAT and 12.5% service, which is now almost always added to the bill.

£   Moderate (under £25 per head)
££   More expensive (under £40 per head)
£££ Expensive (over £40 per head)
(£) is a sort of halfway statement.

City

£££ *Coq d'Argent*, 1 Poultry. ☎ 020 7395 5000.
Large rooftop restaurant in the Conran stable.
£££ *1 Lombard St*, 1 Lombard St. ☎ 020 7929 6611.
Smart modern food. Could not be more central (Mon–Fri only).
£££ *Prism*, 147 Leadenhall St. ☎ 020 7256 3888.
Harvey Nichols restaurant in a former bank.
££ *Alba*, 107 Whitecross St (near the Barbican). ☎ 020 7588 1798.
Neighbourhood Italian close to the City.
££ *Searcy's*, Barbican Centre. ☎ 020 7588 3008.
Reliable, middle-range food for concert and theatre-goers.
££ *Singapura*, 1–2 Limeburner Lane (near St Paul's). ☎ 020 7329 1133.
Singapore food, plenty of space.
££ *Sweetings*, 39 Queen Victoria St. ☎ 020 7248 3062.
Traditional City oyster bar—a remarkable survival. Lunches only; no bookings.
£ *Moshi Moshi Sushi*, Liverpool St Station. ☎ 020 7247 3227
£ *Moshi Moshi Sushi*, 7–8 Limeburner Lane (near St Paul's). ☎ 020 7248 1808.
Japanese food on colour-coded plates, chosen from a conveyor belt.

North Bank

£££ *City Rhodes*, 1 New St Square, off Fleet St. ☎ 020 7583 1313.
Run by Gary Rhodes, a young(ish) chef famous for his television appearances and books as well as his imaginative, modern British food.
£££ *Bank*, 1 Kingsway. ☎ 020 7234 3344.
Big, noisy, modern, fast (££ at certain times).

£££ *Sheekeys*, 28–32 St Martin's Court, off St Martin's Lane. ☎ 020 7240 2565.
Fish, traditional, high quality (£ set lunches Sat/Sun).

£££ *Simpson's in the Strand*, 100 Strand. ☎ 020 7836 9112.
Traditional in every sense, roasts carved at the table, Sunday lunch a special treat.

££(£) *Admiralty*, Somerset House, Strand. ☎ 020 7845 4646.
Eat good French food between your gallery visits.

££ *Chez Gerard*, The Piazza, Covent Garden. ☎ 020 7379 0666.
A big branch of a reliable quasi-French chain.

££ *National Portrait Gallery Restaurant*. ☎ 020 7312 2490.
New and popular star serving modern British food—book lunch well in advance.

££ *Rules*, 35 Maiden Lane, Covent Garden. ☎ 020 7836 5314.
Oldest restaurant in London (1798), traditional English food. Service can be brisk.

£(£) *Sofra*, 36 Tavistock St, Covent Garden. ☎ 020 7240 3773.
One of a chain of Turkish restaurants. Try the *meze*.

£(£) *Belgo Centraal*, 50 Earlham St, Covent Garden. ☎ 020 7813 2333.
Belgian beers and food, i.e. mussels and *frites*.

£(£) *Bertorelli's*, 44a Floral St, Covent Garden. ☎ 020 7836 3969.
Above average Italian, bistro or restaurant.

£(£) *L'Estaminet*, 14 Garrick St, Covent Garden. ☎ 020 7379 1432.
French, very pleasant (£ pre-theatre, otherwise ££).

£ *Brown's*, St Martin's Lane. ☎ 020 7497 5050.
Basic but high-quality food and obliging service.

£ *Le Café Des Amis*, 11–14 Hanover Place, Covent Garden. ☎ 020 73793444.
Crowded French-style brasserie, ideal for pre-theatre food.

£ *Café Flo*, 51 St Martin's Lane. ☎ 020 7836 8289.
One of a reliable chain, good value.

£ *Tuttons*, 11–12 Russell St, Covent Garden. ☎ 020 7836 4141.
Good value, busy, open all hours.

Westminster (including Belgravia and Knightsbridge)

£££ *Atrium*, 4 Millbank. ☎ 020 7233 0032.
Modern British food in a spectacular setting.

£££ *Halkin Hotel*, Halkin St, Belgravia. ☎ 020 7333 1234.
Milanese cooking in a romantic setting.

£££ *One-O-One*, 101 William St, Knightsbridge. ☎ 020 7290 7101.
Seafood restaurant within the Sheraton Hotel.

£££ *La Tante Claire*, Wilton Place, Knightsbridge. ☎ 020 7823 2003.
Opulent French restaurant, all you could wish.

££(£) *Fifth Floor*, Harvey Nichols, Knightsbridge. ☎ 020 7235 5250.
Within Harvey Nichols department store, but open for dinner. Modern British.

££ *Al Bustan*, 27 Motcomb St, Knightsbridge. ☎ 020 7235 8277.
Comfortable Lebanese.

££ *Justin de Blank*, 50–52 Buckingham Palace Rd, Victoria. ☎ 020 7828 4111
British food, decently cooked and presented.

££ *Simply Nico*, 48A Rochester Row. ☎ 020 7630 8061.
Nico Ladenis's Westminster outpost—very civilised.

££ *Tate Gallery Restaurant*, Tate Britain, Millbank. ☎ 020 7887 8825.
Excellent food and wine, and a Rex Whistler mural to admire. (Lunch only).

£(£) *Olivo*, 21 Eccleston St, Victoria. ☎ 020 7730 2505.
Sardinian food. Crowded but good value.

£ *Ebury Wine Bar*, 139 Ebury St, Victoria. ☎ 020 7730 5447.
More than a wine bar—a full restaurant.

West End

£££ *The Connaught*, 16 Carlos Place, Mayfair. ☎ 020 7499 7070.
Ultra-traditional ultimate French restaurant.

££(£) *Alastair Little*, 49 Frith St, Soho. ☎ 020 7734 5183.
Famous since its 1980s heyday, serious cooking by the eponymous owner.

££(£) *The Criterion*, Piccadilly Circus. ☎ 020 7930 0488.
Startling interior (late 19C), good value lunches, slow service.

££(£) *Mezzo*, 100 Wardour St, Soho. ☎ 020 7314 4000.
Modern European cooking in a giant basement (the Mezzanine is a cheaper option), part of the Terence Conran empire. There is also a café next door.

££(£) *L'Odeon*, 65 Regent St. ☎ 020 7287 1400.
Modern French cooking with views out over Nash's great street.

££ *Bentley's*, 11–15 Swallow St, off Regent St. ☎ 020 7734 4756.
More than an oyster bar, offering seafood from many oceans.

££ *Bleeding Heart*, Bleeding Heart Yard, Hatton Garden. ☎ 020 7242 8238.
French restaurant and bistro.

££ *Gay Hussar*, 2 Greek St, Soho. ☎ 020 7437 0973.
Long-time Hungarian favourite, old-fashioned and elegant.

££ *Greenhouse*, 27A Hays Mews, Mayfair. ☎ 020 7499 3314.
International food in a comfortable setting (good value set lunches).

££ *Langan's Brasserie*, Stratton St, Piccadilly. ☎ 020 7491 8822.
Famous rather than idyllic.

££ *Livebait's Café Fish*, 36–40 Rupert St, Piccadilly Circus. ☎ 020 7287 8989.
First-class seafood. In the Chez Gerard chain.

££ *Mon Plaisir*, 21 Monmouth St, St Giles's. ☎ 020 7836 7243.
Classic French bistro, top of its field for 50 years.

££ *Quo Vadis*, 26–29 Dean St, Soho. ☎ 020 7437 9585.
A Marco Pierre White foundation, modern European, dramatic décor.

£(£) *Rasa W1*, 6 Dering St, nr. Oxford Circus. ☎ 020 7629 1346.
Distinctive vegetarian Keralan cooking from well-regarded small chain.

££ *Red Fort*, 77 Dean St, Soho. ☎ 020 7437 2115.
Relatively expensive but high-quality Indian.

£(£) *Randall & Aubin*, 16 Brewer St, Soho. ☎ 020 7287 4447.
Was a local butcher (see décor inside), now a smart oyster and champagne bar.

£ *Amalfi*, Old Compton St, Soho. ☎ 020 7437 7284.
Basic Italian, cheap and cheerful.

£ *Chuen Cheng Ku*, 17 Wardour St, Soho. ☎ 020 7437 1398.
Chinese old faithful that still pleases.

£ *Poons*, Leicester St, Leicester Square. ☎ 020 7437 1528
and Lisle St, Chinatown. ☎ 020 7437 4549.
Long-established, reliable Chinese.

£ *Soho Soho*, 11–13 Frith St, Soho. ☎ 020 7494 3491.
French standard, part of the Chez Gerard group (£ early and late).

New Road

£££ *John Burton Race at the Landmark*, Marylebone. ☎ 020 7723 7800.
Top chef in top hotel, grand French cooking in grand surroundings.

££ *Birdcage*, 110 Whitfield St, near Warren St. ☎ 020 7323 9655.
Deliberately crazy, world-wide menu, only for the brave.
££ *Nico Central*, 35 Great Portland St. ☎ 020 7436 8846.
The name 'Nico' guarantees high standard, French cuisine (lunch £).
££ *Ozer*, 4–5 Langham Place, nearOxford Circus. ☎ 020 7323 0505.
'Modern Ottoman', by the founder of the Sofra chain (also recommended).
££ *Passione*, 10 Charlotte St, Fitzrovia. ☎ 020 7636 2833.
Easy modern Italian, one among many similar in Charlotte St.
££ *Quality Chop House*, 94 Farringdon Rd. ☎ 020 7837 5093.
Traditional London food, working-class in origin if not in price (consider for lunch in Chapter 29).
££ *St John*, 26 John St, Farringdon. ☎ 020 7251 4090.
Interesting restaurant specialising in British culinary rarities.
££ *Stephen Bull*, 5–7 Blandford St, Marylebone. ☎ 020 7486 9696.
Early Modernism, in décor and cooking; great food.
£(£) *Ibla*, 89 Marylebone High St. ☎ 020 7224 3799.
High-quality Italian, *table d'hôte* controls cost.
£(£) *Tajine*, 7A Dorset St, Marylebone. ☎ 020 7935 1545.
Cheerful welcoming Moroccan restaurant.
£(£) *Villandry*, Great Portland St. ☎ 020 7631 3131.
Excellent for lunches, with bar and foodstore attached.
£ *Asakusa*, 265 Eversholt St, Euston. ☎ 020 7388 8399.
Japanese food, and a great place to learn about it.
£ *Back to Basics*, 21A Foley St, Marylebone. ☎ 020 7436 2181.
Small, crowded, with fish dishes inscribed on a blackboard.
£ *Eagle*, 159 Farringdon Rd. ☎ 020 7837 1353.
A pub essentially, but with restaurant-standard food and a long history.
£ *Wagamama*, 4a Streatham St, Bloomsbury. ☎ 020 7323 9224.
Japanese 'noodle canteen', very popular; branches elsewhere, no bookings.

South Bank

£££ *County Hall Restaurant* (Marriott Hotel). ☎ 020 7902 8000.
Modern British food in a suitably grand London ambience.
££(£) *Livebait*, 43–45 The Cut, Waterloo. ☎ 020 7928 7211.
Ground-breaking fish restaurant, now with branches elsewhere.
££(£) *Oxo Tower*, near Blackfriars Bridge. ☎ 020 7803 3888.
8th-floor restaurant and brasserie, with great river views.
££(£) *Le Pont de la Tour*, Butler's Wharf, Shad Thames. ☎ 020 7403 8403.
Conran enterprise overlooking Tower Bridge.
££(£) *Tentazioni*, 2 Mill St, Shad Thames. ☎ 020 7237 1100.
Expensive Italian, very polished.
££ *Blue Print Café*, Design Museum, 28 Shad Thames. ☎ 020 7378 7031.
Within the museum, interesting menu, river views.
££ *Cantina Vinopolis*, Bankside. ☎ 020 7940 8333.
Attached to the wine museum, with appropriate drinking.
££ *Fish!*, Borough Market, London Bridge. ☎ 020 7234 3333.
First of a reliable chain of fish restarants, now with branches elsewhere.
££ *Neat*, in Oxo Tower (see above). Brasserie ☎ 020 7928 4433, restaurant ☎ 020 7928 5533. On 2nd floor, modern French newcomer.
£(£) *Delfina Studio Café*, 50 Bermondsey St, near London Bridge.

☎ 020 7357 0244. Art gallery and modern restaurant for exciting lunches.
£(£) *Lobster Pot*, 3 Kennington Lane, Elephant and Castle. ☎ 020 7582 5556.
Tiny French fish restaurant, well worth seeking out.
£(£) *RSJ*, 13A Coin St, Waterloo. ☎ 020 7928 4554.
Excellent value, complete reliability.
£ *Tas*, 33 The Cut, Waterloo. ☎ 020 7928 1444.
Excellent value Turkish.

Further afield

Bayswater
££ *Amandier*, 26 Sussex Place. ☎ 020 7262 6063.
Delicious French cooking, with a cheaper option in the Bistro.
£ *Four Seasons*, 84 Queensway. ☎ 020 7229 4320.
Excellent value Chinese, somewhat swisher than Chinatown.

Brixton
£ *Eco*, 4 Market Row, Electric Lane. ☎ 020 7738 3021.
Highly recommended pizzas in the middle of a Caribbean market.

Camden Town
££ *Odette's*, 130 Regent's Park Rd, Primrose Hill. ☎ 020 7586 5486.
Excellent food, amazing value set lunch (£).
£ *Nontas*, 14 Camden High St. ☎ 020 7387 4579.
Excellent value Greek restaurant (there are several more similar in this area).

Chelsea
£££ *Gordon Ramsay*, 68 Royal Hospital Rd. ☎ 020 7352 4441.
Top-of-the-range French cooking from a star chef.
££ *Bluebird*, 350 King's Rd. ☎ 020 7559 1000.
Safe bet European food with a deli attached (£ set lunch).
£ *Soviet Canteen*, 430 King's Rd. ☎ 020 7795 1556.
Amusing compromise between the old days and the new.

Chiswick
£(£) *The Chiswick*, 131 Chiswick High Rd. ☎ 020 8994 6887.
The kind of neighbourhood restaurant that should be in every neighbourhood.
£(£) *Riso*, 76 South Parade, Turnham Green. ☎ 020 8742 2121.
Reasonable value Italian, pizzas included.

Ealing
£(£) *Parade*, 18–19 The Mall. ☎ 020 8810 0202.
Good chef and good value.

Fulham
£££ *Putney Bridge*, Embankment. ☎ 020 8780 1811.
Top-class French cooking, plus river views (££ lunch).
£££ *River Café*, Rainville Rd, Fulham. ☎ 020 7381 8824.
Pricey Italian, run by Rose Grey and Ruth Rogers (wife of Richard Rogers).

Greenwich
££ *Spread Eagle*, 1–2 Stockwell St. ☎ 020 8305 0447.
Pub-type interior but high-class French cuisine (good value *table d'hôte*).

Hackney
£ *Little Georgia*, 2 Broadway Market, London Fields. ☎ 020 7249 9070.
Georgia south of Russia, not USA. Delicious rare cuisine.

Hammersmith
££ *Wilson's*, 236 Blythe Rd. ☎ 020 7603 7267.

Scottish restaurant, ambience to match.

£ *Anglesea Arms*, Wingate Rd. ☎ 020 8749 1291.
Pub food at its outstanding best.

Hampstead

££ *New End*, 102 Heath St. ☎ 020 7431 4423.
Bright and central.

£(£) *Cucina*, 45a South End Rd. ☎ 020 7435 7814.
Good-quality European, with a deli in front.

High St Kensington

££(£) *Belvedere*, in Holland Park (Abbotsbury Rd entrance). ☎ 020 7602 1238.
French restaurant in beautiful surroundings.

££ *Offshore*, 148 Holland Park Avenue. ☎ 020 7221 6090.
Largely high-quality fish, with good value set lunch (£).

Islington

££ *Frederick's*, Camden Passage. ☎ 020 7359 2888.
Seems old-fashioned by Islington standards.

££ *Granita*, 127 Upper St. ☎ 020 7226 3222.
Minimalist in all respects.

££ *Almeida*, Almeida St. ☎ 020 7354 4777.
Conran restaurant serving classic French dishes.

£ *Iznik*, 19 Highbury Park. ☎ 020 7704 8099.
Neighbourhood Turkish, with friendly service.

Kew

££ *The Glasshouse*, 14 Station Parade. ☎ 020 8940 6777.
Delightful place for lunch before exploring Kew Gardens.

Little Venice

££ *Red Pepper*, 8 Formosa St. ☎ 020 7266 2708.
Italian, plenty of character.

£ *Salt House*, 63 Abbey Rd. ☎ 020 7328 6626.
Good value in an up-graded pub.

Notting Hill

££ *First Floor*, 186 Portobello Rd. ☎ 020 7243 0072.
Unconventional environment above a pub, equally distinctive food (£ set lunch).

££ *Kensington Place*, 201 Kensington Church St. ☎ 020 7727 3184.
Noisy and brash, but steady quality in modern British cooking (£ set lunch).

££ *Pharmacy*, 150 Notting Hill Gate. ☎ 020 7221 2442.
Echoing Damien Hirst and Tate Modern; the food's modern, too.

£ *Books for Cooks*, 4 Blenheim Crescent, Ladbroke Grove. ☎ 020 7221 1992.
Primarily a bookshop, where they try out recipes from the books. Lunches only.

£ *Geale's Fish Restaurant*, 2 Farmer St. ☎ 020 7727 7969.
Famous, comparatively stylish, fish and chips.

Richmond

£(£) *Canyon*, Riverside. ☎ 020 8948 2945.
American cooking overlooking the Thames.

£ *Chez Lindsay*, 11 Hill Rise. ☎ 020 8948 7473.
Breton cooking at reasonable prices.

Shoreditch

££ *Real Greek*, Hoxton Market. ☎ 020 7739 8212.
Modern Greek food in a stylish shop conversion.

South Kensington
£££ *Bibendum*, Michelin House, 81 Fulham Rd. ☎ 020 7581 5817.
Converted 1905 French garage in which to eat excellent expensive food.
£(£) *Brasserie St Quentin*, 243 Brompton Rd. ☎ 020 7584 8005.
French all the way, reasonable prices. Part of the Chez Gerard empire.
£(£) *Lundum's*, 119 Old Brompton Rd (near South Kensington tube).
☎ 020 7373 7774. Danish restaurant, unusual in London, high quality.
Wimbledon
£(£) *Utah*, 18 High St. ☎ 020 8944 1909.
American cooking. Good value lunch (£).

Light refreshments

There are many pleasant cafés to be found, in all areas, offering a variety of coffees, sandwiches and cakes. Numbers may be a little less plentiful on Sundays,
and in very touristy spots a minimum charge may be quoted: if you notice this
before ordering, leave and go elsewhere. The five branches of *Patisserie Valerie*
(including Brompton Road, Marylebone High St and Old Compton Street) are
worth a visit, and the following chains should all appeal: *Aroma*, *Caffè Nero*, *Café
Uno*, *Coffee Republic*, *Prêt à Manger*, *Starbucks*. Vegetarians can find sustenance
at *Cranks*, another chain, and at *Neal's Yard* and *Food for Thought*, both in
Covent Garden.

In summer you could buy take-away food and eat in a park, as many office-
workers do daily. **Department stores** often have good eating places (John Lewis,
for example), as do museums. Again, many churches, of all places, contain pleasant cafés: these include St Martin's-in-the-Fields, St Mary-le-Bow, St John's
Smith Square and St Paul's Cathedral.

The English institution of tea-shops is now non-existent in London.
'Afternoon tea' is a very different phenomenon, extremely expensive, and
obtainable only by booking at major hotels, such as the Ritz (see p 229).

Pubs and wine bars

London pubs are quite distinct from the archetypal village inn with roses round
the door. Noisier, plainer, smokier, they are usually still consciously antique,
sometimes confirming it by taking over the premises of old institutions such as
banks. There are far too many with large TV screens and too much loud music,
but the beer should be just as good, and the atmosphere of each characteristic in
its own way.

In central locations, pubs become very crowded at certain times, despite the
relaxation of licensing hours to keep most of them open all day. For reasonable
peace, take **pub lunches** before 13.00, and avoid Friday evenings altogether. Do
not visit pubs that appear to rely on trade from large stations or similarly crowded
places, or are located on busy corners. Go down side streets. (A perfect example
is included on the walk in Chapter 16.) You can not always judge from the outside, so have a look in. Either simply have one drink (a 'half', say) before ordering
any food, to test the service and atmosphere, or walk straight out and try
another. That is the one consolation: London has pubs by the thousand.

Beer In the form of fermented malt and water, flavoured with hops and
pumped from a barrel, beer or ale has been an English staple for centuries. It is still
served in pints and half-pints and is surrounded by ritual. As you start your drink,

you raise your glass and say 'Cheers'. Connoisseurs despise British beer served from a metal keg or a bottle, and go into complicated arguments about preferred temperature, age, colour and bubbliness ('head'). All this is no different to the jargon and elitism surrounding wine. And, just as wine has become more international, traditional English beer is under threat from Continental beers (not ale) or lagers, especially from Belgium and Germany. In response to this, some English brewers have leaned further towards traditional methods of production, but have also introduced new brews to tempt the market. As a result there are some superb draught beers around. London still has two important breweries, Youngs and Fullers, and the products of small country breweries are recommended.

Wine Wine bars are scarcer than pubs, although there are a growing number. Of course you can get wine in a pub, but it will usually be better to stick to beer; the newish chains such as Slug and Lettuce and All Bar One offer a reasonable selection of wines. You can also get beer in a wine bar, but aficionados will say it is not as good (unless it is bottled). Wine bars can be less smoky and sometimes quieter than pubs. Their character is different, more Continental, perhaps not surprisingly, given the nationalistic subtext in English beer. Food is likely to be more expensive.

The following is a list of suggestions of pubs and wine bars, all recommendable at the time of going to press, arranged to match the walks (they can be found either close to the start or finish or half-way round). The chapter number and closest underground or train station (indicated by 'station') are shown in brackets. But find your own favourites for yourself: that is half the fun. For enthusiasts, the *Good Pub Guide* is recommended for more comprehensive research.

City

Balls Bros (wine bar), King's Arms Yard (1; Bank). Several other branches.
The Habit (wine bar), 65 Crutched Friars (2; Tower Hill)
Dirty Dick's, Bishopsgate (4; Liverpool St)
Bishop of Norwich (wine bar), 91–93 Moorgate (5; Moorgate)
Olde London, Ludgate Hill (6 and 7; St Paul's)
Davy's (wine bar), 10 Creed Lane (6 and 7; St Paul's). Several other branches.

North Bank

Black Friar, 174 Queen Victoria St (8; Blackfriars)
Old Bank of England, 194 Fleet St (8; Temple)
Olde Cheshire Cheese, 145 Fleet St (8; Blackfriars)
Seven Stars, Carey St (9; Temple, Chancery Lane)
Lamb and Flag, Rose St, off Garrick St (10; Covent Garden)
Champagne Charlies (wine bar), Villiers St (11; Charing Cross)
Sherlock Holmes, Northumberland Avenue (11; Charing Cross)

Westminster

Lord Moon of the Mall, Whitehall (12; Charing Cross)
Albert, 52 Victoria St (13, 14 and 15; St James's Park)
Nag's Head, Kinnerton St (16; Knightsbridge)
Grenadier, Wilton Row (16; Knightsbridge)

West End

Westminster Arms, Storey's Gate (17; Westminster)
Red Lion, Duke of York St (18; Piccadilly Circus)
Grapes, Shepherd Market (19; Green Park)

Guinea, Bruton Place (19 and 21; Bond St)
Red Lion, Waverton St (19; Green Park)
Argyll Arms, Argyll St (22; Oxford Circus)
Cork and Bottle (wine bar), Cranbourn St (22; Leicester Square)
Dog and Duck, 18 Bateman St (22; Tottenham Court Rd)
Cittie of Yorke, 22 High Holborn (23; Chancery Lane)
Lamb, 92 Lamb's Conduit St (23; Holborn)

New Road

Devonshire Arms, 21a Devonshire St (24; Regent's Park)
Jack Horner, 236 Tottenham Court Rd (26; Goodge St)
Museum Tavern, Museum St (27; Holborn)
Euston Flyer, Euston Rd, opp. British Library (28; Euston)
Head of Steam, Eversholt St, in Euston station forecourt (28; Euston)
Jerusalem Tavern, 55 Britton St (29; Farringdon)
Eagle, 159 Farringdon Rd (29; Farringdon)

South Bank

George, 77 Borough High St (30; London Bridge)
Anchor, Bankside (31; London Bridge)
Market Porter, 9 Stoney St (31; London Bridge)
The Archduke (wine bar), Upper Ground (32; Waterloo)
Fire Station, 150 Waterloo Rd (33; Waterloo)

Further afield

Orange Brewery, 37 Pimlico Rd (34; Sloane Square)
Scarsdale, Edwardes Square, Kensington (36; High St Kensington)
Archery Tavern, 4 Bathurst St, Lancaster Gate (37; Lancaster Gate)
Windsor Castle, 114 Campden Hill Rd, Holland Park (38; Holland Park)
Warrington, Warrington Crescent (39; Maida Vale)
Engineer, 65 Gloucester Avenue (40; Chalk Farm)
Flask, Flask Walk, Hampstead (41; Hampstead)
Holly Bush, Holly Mount, Hampstead (41; Hampstead)
Flask, 77 West Hill, Highgate (42; Highgate)
Compton Arms, 4 Compton Avenue (43; Highbury and Islington)
Prospect of Whitby, 57 Wapping Wall (47; Wapping)
Town of Ramsgate, 62 Wapping High St (47; Wapping)
Trafalgar Tavern, 5 Park Row Greenwich (49; Maze Hill)
Princess of Wales, 1a Montpelier Row, Blackheath (50; Blackheath station)
Mayflower, Rotherhithe St (51; Rotherhithe)
Crown and Greyhound, 73 Dulwich Village (52; North Dulwich station)
Windmill, Clapham Common South Side (54; Clapham South)
Atlas, 16 Seagrave Rd, West Brompton (56; West Brompton)
Bull's Head, 373 Lonsdale Rd, Barnes (58; Barnes Bridge station)
Bull's Head, Strand on the Green (59; Kew Bridge station)
London Apprentice, Church St, Isleworth (59; Isleworth station)
Princes Head, The Green, Richmond (62; Richmond)
White Swan, Riverside, Twickenham (63; Twickenham station)
Castle, West St, Harrow (65; Harrow-on-the-Hill)
Queen's Head, High St, Pinner (65; Pinner)
Fox and Grapes, Camp Rd, Wimbledon (71; Wimbledon)

King's Arms, Hampton Court Rd (72; Hampton Court station)
Highlander, Castle Hill, Windsor (73; Windsor station)

Getting around

London is a civilised city to travel around, most of the time. Of course there are problems with an ageing infrastructure which has for too long been under-capitalised, but for nearly every journey you can devise alternative routes. The way to avoid being late in London is to **allow plenty of time**.

London Transport

This organisation (LT) runs the underground network, usually called the 'Tube', and buses in London, and also co-ordinates riverboat services, trams between Croydon and Wimbledon, and the Docklands Light Railway. For many journeys in South London, some in the east and all (except Amersham) beyond the M25, you need to use national rail services (see below).

London Travel Information Centres are located at Heathrow airport terminals and the following stations: Heathrow Terminals 1, 2, 3, King's Cross, Paddington, Liverpool Street, Oxford Circus, St James's Park (underground) and at Euston, Paddington and Victoria (national rail). They give the best transport advice, free maps and timetables and you can buy travel cards, bus passes and other tickets.

London Travel Information, ☎ 020 7222 1234. www.transportforlondon.gov.uk

> **Travel zones and fares** For the purposes of travel London is divided into six **zones**. Zone 1 covers Central London, an area roughly defined by the Circle Line but also including Waterloo and London Bridge on the South Bank. Zones 2–6 are concentric rings dividing the rest of London into bands, out as far as the M25. The system covers all Tube and DLR services in London; the DLR operates only in Zones 1–3. Buses operate in four zones, Zone 1 being roughly equivalent to that for the Tube, and Zone 4 to Tube Zones 4–6.
>
> On the Tube there is a **standard fare** for travel within a zone, or usually between pairs of zones. The minimum adult single fare is £1.60 in Zone 1 and £1.00 within other zones (child fare 60p and 40p); £1.90 between Zones 1 and 2 or £1.30 between other Zones, 2 and 3, 3 and 4, etc (child fares 80p and 60p). Alternatively, you can buy a batch of ten tickets for single journeys on the Tube within Zone 1 only, called a **'carnet'**, for £11.50 (child fare £5). On the buses, a single journey including Zone 1 costs £1, and 70p in other zones (child fares both 40p).
>
> It is often better to buy a **travelcard**, which gives unlimited travel within a group of zones, or all zones, during a specified time period—a day, a weekend, a week or longer. Travelcards can also be used on buses and trains within the zoned area and most types can be obtained at booking offices in all Tube and rail stations, shops displaying the travel pass logo (such as

newsagents) and at London Travel Information Centres. You will need a photograph for a weekly card: these can usually be obtained from booths in larger stations. Note that one-day travel cards cannot be used until after 09.30 on weekdays (00.01 at weekends), and that fares tend to rise each year in early January, so prices given here are an indication only. **Bus passes** for bus travel only are about half the price of full travelcards and can be obtained at the same outlets, but give you less flexibility.

There are further **discounts** available to children and to family and other groups that are best explained in the *Fares and tickets* booklet published by Transport for London, available from any underground station: it covers the zones, fare structure and ticket options for travel by Tube, bus, DLR and Tramlink. Ask any further questions at a Tube or rail station, not on a bus. If you travel without a correct ticket, you are liable to an on-the-spot fine, or **Penalty Fare**, of £10 on the Tube and some trains, £5 on a bus or the DLR.

On foot

The only deterrent to walking is the weather, and the distances resulting from 'spread' (see p 69). Otherwise, get a good **street map** (the *London A–Z* or Collins' *London Street Atlas*), with the central areas shown in larger scale, and set off. People are polite on the pavements—more so than on the trains or in cars, will get out of your way if you are in a hurry and always help you if you are lost. And as this guide attempts to prove, while walking you will see much more. Remember when crossing the road that traffic drives on the left, and that on the pavement you may encounter cyclists, roller bladers and other mobile hazards.

Instead of using a book to self-guide, you may prefer to join one of the many **guided walks** held in London every day, in many different areas or with specific themes ranging from Shakespeare to Jack the Ripper. Leaflets advertising these are available in hotels, entertainment venues and other sites as well as tourist information offices. Some walks are child-friendly.

Original London Walks, ☎ 020 7624 3978.

Recorded information ☎ 020 7624 9255. www.walks.com

Stepping Out, ☎ 020 8810 6141.

It is possible to arrange tailor-made tours through your hotel or organisations such as *British Tours*, ☎ 020 7734 8734. www.britishtours.com/bt

Tours conducted by **Blue Badge Guides** are to be recommended: these professionally qualified guides are co-ordinated by the London Tourist Board and wear a distinctive badge (they have no connection with the Blue Guides series).

You may also like to follow one of the walks marked on pavements or road-signs, including the **Silver Jubilee Walk** (marked by round metal plaques in the ground); or the more challenging **Thames Path**. There is a good guide to the latter, *National Trail Guide: The Thames Path* by David Sharp (Aurum Press, 1997).

By Tube

'Tube' means the **underground system** run by London Transport. (The original 'tube' was the deep-level tunnels created a century ago by the Northern and Piccadilly Lines, to distinguish their engineering from the 'cut-and-cover' method used earlier for the Circle and District Lines.) There is a **Tube map** at the end of this guide and copies are available on display at nearly all central stations.

Everybody uses the Tube map all the time: created by Harry Beck in 1931, when he was unemployed, it is one of the superlatives of industrial design and is imitated throughout the world.

First trains start running around 05.30 and **last trains** have gone by 01.00 or earlier: check before you travel if you want to return late at night. Try to avoid travelling at rush hour (07.30–09.30 and 16.30–18.30) when carriages can become extremely crowded. Smoking is not permitted on the Tube and it really is a good idea to 'mind the gap' between train and platform at some stations. In busy stations keep a close eye on your personal belongings and do not travel in an empty carriage late at night.

The **Docklands Light Railway** (DLR) is effectively part of the Tube system, although only about 20 years old. It is a 'light rapid transport' system, which means that trains are short, frequent, centrally operated (with no driver), and mostly run at high level, not in tunnels. It is a most enjoyable way to travel round not only the former dock areas (see Chapter 48) but also many other parts of East London, so use it for pleasure as well as convenience.

By bus

Travel by double-decker bus is one of the joys of London. Some of the buses on long-established central west–east routes still have two staff on board, a driver and a conductor who collects the fares and calls out the names of stops (in theory). These **Routemaster** services are more popular with some people because they enable you to 'hop' on and off when the traffic slows, at traffic lights or other dangerous opportunities. But the majority of buses are now 'one-man' operated, less convenient for some but safer and, on a clear road, exhila-ratingly fast. Bus-lanes are facilitating faster bus journeys.

Get a **bus map** from a London Transport Information Centre (see p 30). A map of the central area may be sufficient, but if you intend to tackle some of the sub-urban walks in this guide, ask also for the appropriate area guides, *South-west, North-west, North-east* and *South-east*. Remember that if you are standing at a **request stop** (white on a red background), you must put out your hand to get the driver to halt. Buses should halt at fare stops (red on a white background). Ring the bell to get the bus to stop and let you off.

After about 00.30 day buses stop and **night buses** take over on many routes: the route numbers are prefixed by the letter N. Many go from or through Trafalgar Square. Travelcards are still valid (until about 04.30) and single fares cost the same as on day buses.

By train

Rail services not operated by London Transport are part of the National Rail network, under which individual companies (including SouthWest Trains, Connex and WAGN) run trains on tracks and from stations maintained by Railtrack, whose future at the time of writing is uncertain.

Travel by train is easy, fairly comfortable, relaxing and good for sight-seeing. Of course there are too many disruptions and delays and the fare structure is complex, but ticket office staff are always helpful. Or you can book through the Internet or a travel agent. It is advisable to reserve seats (first or second class) when travelling on main lines in the morning or early evening.

National Rail enquiries, ☎ 08457 48 49 50.
Ticket booking, www.thetrainline.com

There are 11 major **rail termini** in London, located in a ring round the central area—as close as they could get by the mid-19C. Clockwise from the west they are: Paddington (for Oxford, Southwest England and Wales); Marylebone (for Buckinghamshire and Bedford); Euston (for Liverpool, Manchester, Glasgow); St Pancras (for Leicester, Nottingham, Sheffield); King's Cross (for Cambridge, Leeds, York, Edinburgh); Liverpool Street (for East Anglia, including Stansted); Fenchurch Street (for Southend and Tilbury); Cannon Street (for Kent); London Bridge (for Southeast London, Kent and Sussex); Waterloo (for South and Southwest England, and Eurostar to Paris and Brussels); Charing Cross (for Kent and Sussex); and Victoria (for Gatwick, Sussex, Kent). **Thameslink** trains operate a service that runs north–south through the centre of London, via Blackfriars. **Suburban services** such as Silverlink (which curves round north London from North Woolwich to Richmond) run along old tracks that have miraculously survived the 20C, to less visited but no less appealing areas.

By taxi

Black cabs are a London tradition, easily recognised by their standard design, which is carefully regulated by what is still called the Public Carriage Office (PCO) of the Metropolitan Police. The newest cab design is accessible to wheelchairs and should bear a sign indicating as much. Drivers are all examined by a regulator to ensure they have **'the knowledge'** of all remotely possible journeys from one place in London to another, so it is not a good idea to second-guess them on routes. They are almost always helpful. Cabs can be hailed only when they display a lit sign on the cab roof; or hired from a rank at a station or elsewhere, where the convention is to queue; or booked by telephone:
Computacab, ☎ 020 7286 0268.
Radio taxis, ☎ 020 7272 0272.

A taxi is significantly more expensive than the cost of a train or bus, but of course a great deal more comfortable and direct. The **fares** are displayed inside the cab and comprise a standard charge, with additions for the number of passengers, amount of luggage, time of day (possibly), and a metered measurement of distance. For long journeys into the suburbs or beyond (but not to Heathrow), you may need to negotiate a fare in advance. Otherwise, do not bother to argue. If you have a complaint about the fare, take the cab number displayed inside the car and underneath the rear number plate: problems should be referred to the PCO.
Public Carriage Office, ☎ 020 7230 1631.

It is very hard to get a taxi to come to you, but a **minicab** will. There are scores of firms, with their cards all over the place, in your hotel, in Yellow Pages, and elsewhere. Minicabs are private cars insured to carry passengers, but the driver's knowledge of London may be little better than your own. Fares are not metered and should be enquired about, and if necessary negotiated, in advance. Minicabs are not supposed to ply for hire, and should not be commissioned if they do. Women alone should avoid minicabs; the Yellow Pages lists firms with female drivers.

For both black cabs and minicabs, the conventional **tip** is 10 per cent of the bill, or more to round up to whole £s.

By car

Driving is pleasant enough in Britain and London is a more civilised place to drive than many European cities—other drivers are more tolerant, the signage is good and the traffic lights and related systems work. But no one can go very fast because of **congestion**. The roads are often jammed and there are bound to be roadworks all along the route you have chosen as well as bus lanes which cars may not use at certain times. The Mayor of London is doing his best to deter motorists from bringing their cars into town at all, and is planning a congestion charge for all traffic entering a newly defined ring in the centre—somewhat smaller than Zone 1 on the London Transport system (see p 30).

Above all it is very hard to park. Signs by the side of the road or on parking meters indicate whether or not you may park: if in doubt, go and find a separate car park. (A valuable list of **car parks** run by the biggest operator, *National Car Parks*, is obtainable from them, ☎ 020 7499 7050). If you park illegally, you will be fined, or worse may find your car clamped and immovable, or worse still towed away in your absence and only retrievable with great hassle and cost.

The message is, if you are visiting London only, forget the car. The secret is to use the car to get out of London. A self-drive tour of Britain could be one of the most delightful holidays of a lifetime.

If you are determined to drive in London, however, **car hire** is easy. All the big rental companies are represented in London, notably at airports, but also via hotels, or at their own offices. For information and advance reservations try the following:

Avis, ☎ 0870 590 0500. www.avisworld.com
Hertz, ☎ 0870 599 6699. www.hertz.co.uk
National, ☎ 0870 600 6666. www.nationalcar.com
Budget, ☎ 0800 181 181. www.budget.com

You cannot expect to pay less than £150 for a small car for a week, and it may be cheaper to arrange a fly-drive deal before you leave your home country. You will need an International driving licence or a domestic licence with 12 months' driving experience, and must be over 21 years old (25 in some cases).

Drive on the left. In built-up areas the **speed limit** is 30 miles per hour and on motorways 70mph. Wearing a seatbelt is compulsory. Make sure you have adequate insurance cover. Your own driving licence is valid for 12 months in Britain, but you may need an International Driving Permit if your own licence is not in English. For full driving regulations, buy a copy of the *Highway Code* (from bookshops) or see www.dvlc.gov.uk.

Either of the two national motoring organisations, which may also be of help should you break down, can give further advice:

Automobile Association (AA), ☎ 0990 444444. www.theaa.co.uk
Royal Automobile Club (RAC), ☎ 0800 550055. www.rac.co.uk

An alternative is to rent a **chauffeur-driven car**, for London sightseeing or travel further afield. Stretch limousines are very popular for special occasions, but of course there are more humble cars available, sometimes with drivers who have special expertise on London. Get more details from your hotel or via Yellow Pages, or contact the following:

Driver Guides Association, ☎ 020 8874 2745 (official Blue Badge guides).
British Tours, ☎ 020 7734 8734.

By bike

While cyclists still have to cope with poor road surfaces, pollution and the unsympathetic attitude of drivers, London streets are being made progressively more friendly to bicycles, and several boroughs are constructing special routes within the road system for cyclists' exclusive use. A London Cycle Network is now established and publishes a map of suitable routes.

London Cycle Network ☎ 020 7721 7254. www.londoncyclenetwork.org

Remember always to wear a helmet and to secure the bike whenever it is out of your sight. For bike hire, try:

London Bicycle Tour Co., ☎ 020 7928 6838.
Dial-a-Bike, ☎ 020 7828 4040.

By tour bus

This is a good way to get an impression of the layout of the city if you are not familiar with it—especially if you do not have long—and will include a commentary of variable quality. There are three firms offering a hop-on-hop-off service around the centre. All have stops in the obvious places, Trafalgar Square, St Paul's, etc. No advance booking is required.

Original London Sightseeing Tour. www.theoriginaltour.com
London Pride Sightseeing Tours
The Big Bus Company. www.bigbus.com

Some normal bus routes also offer good sightseeing opportunities: try routes 6, 9, 12, 19, 25 and 73 (and see p 32).

By riverboat

The main **piers** operating tourist services on the Thames are at Westminster, Embankment (Charing Cross), the Tower and Greenwich. Boats operate between about 10.00–17.00 in summer, 10.30–16.00 in winter. Several companies run one-way or circular cruises. (See also p 497.)

Thames Passenger Boat Service, ☎ 020 7930 4097. www.westminsterpier.co.uk
Westminster to Greenwich (50 minutes) or the Thames Flood Barrier (1 hour 30 minutes), adult single fare to Greenwich £6.00 (child fare £3.00).

Catamaran Cruisers, ☎ 020 7925 2215. www.catamarancruisers.co.uk
Circular or hop-on-hop-off routes from Waterloo and Embankment (50 mins), adult fare £6.70 (child fare £4.70).

City Cruises, ☎ 020 7740 0400. www.citycruises.com
Westminster to Tower Pier (25 minutes) or Greenwich, adult single fare to Greenwich £6 (child fare £3).

Some of these also run dinner cruises and their tickets give discounts on travel or attractions. **DLR Rail & River Rover tickets** allow a day's travel on the DLR and on City Cruises boats between Westminster, Tower and Greenwich Piers. Adult £7.80. Child £3.90. Family (two adults and up to three children under 16) £20.50. DLR ticket machines sell the single tickets; group tickets can be bought at the piers or from the *DLR Customer Services Department*, ☎ 020 7363 9700.

Westminster Passenger Service Association (Upstream) run a longer trip from Westminster to Hampton Court (April–Oct only) via Kew and Richmond, ☎ 020 7930 2062. www.wpsa.co.uk. The journey takes approximately 3 hours 30 minutes, depending on tides. Adult fare to Hampton Court £10 (child fare £4.00).

Commuter services between the Savoy Pier at Charing Cross Embankment and

Canary Wharf are offered by *CRE*. Linked to early morning and evening travel, services are timetabled between approximately 07.30 and 09.30 and 16.30 and 19.30; ☎ 020 7237 9538. www.thamescat.com

 ## Museums and galleries

London is home to some of the world's great museums and art collections, and you will certainly want to see as many as you have time for. The discovery of less well-known places is always a joy, especially if you come across them unexpectedly. The list below also includes some famous indoor entertainments, such as Madame Tussaud's, which, although not museums in any serious sense, nevertheless provide valid mirrors of popular culture.

Many museums publish their own **guidebooks**, some excellent, some not.

Opening hours Try to find out opening hours in advance to avoid disappointment. Opening times of local history museums in particular vary greatly. The main London museums open 10.00–18.00 all year, except Christmas Day and Boxing Day. **Last admission** is often 30 minutes or 1 hour before closing time.

Recently some of the major institutions have introduced **late-night opening**: Tuesday and Wednesday at the Hayward (until 20.00); Wednesday at the National Gallery (21.00), Barbican Gallery (20.00) and Victoria and Albert Museum (22.00); Thursday and Friday at the National Portrait Gallery (21.00) and British Museum (20.30); Friday at Dulwich Picture Gallery (21.00 during exhibitions) and Tate Modern (22.00); and Saturday at Tate Modern (22.00). The main text gives the latest information available at the time of writing, but around Christmas and Bank Holidays double check before setting out; similarly, if a museum is described as undergoing refurbishment, do not write it off as work may be finished by now.

Admission charges At the time of writing, most of the larger museums are abandoning their admission charges: this has been made possible by the extension of government subsidy but deprives the museums of a source of independent income. This development does not include historic royal palaces like the Tower of London or Hampton Court, which are not public in the same sense. Other museums and galleries still levy for entry, but you should always ask about discounts for senior citizens (60+), children, students and the unwaged.

Membership of certain organisations gives free or discounted entry to a wide variety of museums and stately homes throughout the UK. These include

National Trust, ☎ 020 7222 9251. www.nationaltrust.org.uk
English Heritage, ☎ 020 7973 3000. www.english-heritage.org.uk
National Art Collections Fund ☎ 020 7255 4835. www.art-fund.org

Many individual institutions also have **Friends schemes** which provide additional benefits, especially to regular visitors. Some, like the Royal Academy, also have Friends schemes based abroad.

Tours and lectures Events in museums and galleries, including many especially for children, are advertised in listings magazines and many newspapers. They may need to be booked in advance.

All the institutions listed below are grouped by category, with a page reference to further information; if they are not covered elsewhere in this guide a brief description, address and telephone number is given.

Some other public and historic buildings normally inaccessible are made public on **Open House** days, usually the third weekend in September (see p 61).

Major exhibition centres Events such as the London International Boat Show and London Motor Show take place at *Earl's Court*, Warwick Rd, SW5. ☎ 020 7385 1200. www.eco.co.uk

Other such venues include

Olympia, Hammersmith Rd, W14. ☎ 020 7385 1200.

Alexandra Palace (p 463), Wood Green, N22, ☎ 020 8365 2121.

Royal Horticultural Society Halls (p 107), Vincent Sq, SW1. ☎ 020 7834 4333.

Art exhibitions Within the major national collections, **special exhibitions** may well require payment on entry, as will private exhibitions such as those at the Royal Academy or many smaller galleries. In the dealers' area around Piccadilly, and at art schools, and in a growing number of other venues, exhibitions are free on the basis that the works on show are for sale. Do not hesitate to go in, even if you have no intention of buying—when inside you may be tempted. Similarly, do not hesitate to go into **antique shops**, even if the proprietor's manner is unwelcoming. They warm up remarkably if you buy something.

Painting and sculpture

Bankside Gallery (p 309)
Barbican Art Gallery (p 119)
Camden Arts Centre (p 364)
Courtauld Galleries (p 150)
Dali Collection, County Hall (p 315)
Dulwich Picture Gallery (p 412)
Estorick Collection (p 372)
Guildhall Art Gallery (p 91)
Hayward Gallery (p 313)
Kenwood House (p 359)
Marianne North Gallery (p 446)
National Gallery (p 165)
National Portrait Gallery (p 172)
Old Battersea House (p 421)
Orleans House Gallery (p 454)
Queen's Gallery (p 223)
Royal Academy of Art (p 228)
Saatchi Gallery, in temporary space in Underwood St, N1. ☎ 020 7336 7362.
Serpentine Gallery (p 241)
South London Art Gallery, Peckham Rd, SE5. ☎ 020 7703 6120.

Contemporary art in a 19C Baroque gallery space.
Strang Print Room (p 278)
Tate Britain (p 209)
Tate Modern (p 306)
Wallace Collection (p 262)
Whitechapel Art Gallery (p 379)

Decorative arts, British or international

British Museum (p 279)
Crafts Council Gallery (p 291)
Design Museum (p 298)
Fan Museum (p 403)
Geffrye Museum (p 383)
Gilbert Collection (p 154)
Hermitage Rooms (p 153)
Museum of Domestic Design and Architecture, Middlesex University, Cat Hill, Barnet, Herts. ☎ 020 8411 5244. Open 10.00–17.00 Tues–Sat, 14.00–17.00 Sun.
Percival David Foundation for Chinese Art (p 278)

*Petrie Museum of Egyptian
  Archaeology* (p 278)
Court Dress Collection (p 341)
Victoria and Albert Museum (p 336)
William Morris Gallery (p 467)

Commerce, medicine, nature or technology

*Alexander Fleming Laboratory
  Museum* (p 348)
Bank of England Museum (p 89)
BBC Experience (p 273)
Brunel's Engine House Museum,
  (p 408)
Chelsea Physic Garden (p 326)
Clock Museum at the Guildhall
  (p 90)
Faraday Museum (p 235)
Florence Nightingale Museum (p 317)
*Grant Museum of Zoology and
  Comparative Anatomy*, Gower St, WC1.
  ☎ 020 7679 2647. Old-fashioned
  glass cases of anatomical exhibits.
Kew Bridge Steam Museum (p 434)
London Canal Museum (p 288)
London Fire Brigade Museum (p 302)
London Planetarium (p 265)
London Transport Museum (p 160)
Museum in Docklands (p 392)
Museum of Garden History (p 318)
Natural History Museum (p 330)
North Woolwich Old Station Museum,
  Pier Rd, E16. ☎ 020 7474 7244.
  Child-friendly range of mementoes of
  the railway age.
Old Operating Theatre (p 301)
Old Royal Observatory (p 401)
Royal College of Surgeons (p 148)
Royal Gunpowder Mills, Waltham
  Abbey. ☎ 01992 767 022. Absorbing
  display in a historic setting, with
  Waltham Abbey nearby.
Royal Pharmaceutical Society (p 318)
Science Museum (p 332)
Thames Barrier Visitor Centre (p 403)
Three Mills, Bow. Mill Lane E3.
  ☎ 020 8472 2829. Fascinating
  ancient technology, open summer only.
Veterinary Museum (p 356)

Wellcome Trust Library, Euston Rd,
  NW1. ☎ 020 7611 7211) Small,
  medically themed exhibitions.
Wimbledon Windmill (p 478)

Cultural history and entertainment

Bethnal Green Museum of Childhood
  (p 384)
Fenton House (p 364)
Horniman Museum (p 414).
  ☎ 020 8699 1872 for latest
  information on re-opening of music
  collection.
Madame Tussaud's (p 264)
Museum of the Moving Image, South
  Bank, SE1. Closed until 2003, ☎ 020
  7928 3535 for latest information.
Musical Museum (p 435)
Pollock's Toy Museum (p 276)
Ragged School Museum (p 385)
Rose Theatre (p 305)
Royal Academy of Music (p 265)
Royal College of Music (p 334)
Shakespeare's Globe Exhibition (p 250)
Theatre Museum (p 160)

British history

Bramah Tea and Coffee Museum
  (p 302)
British Library (p 290)
Cabinet War Rooms (p 180)
Churchill's Britain at War Experience
  (p 300)
Clink Museum (p 304)
College of Arms (p 126)
Cutty Sark (p 397)
Firepower! (p 403)
Freemasonry Library and Museum
  (p 259)
Golden Hinde (p 304)
Guards' Museum (p 219)
HMS Belfast (p 299)
Imperial War Museum (p 319)
Jewel Tower (p 193)
London Dungeon (p 299)
National Army Museum (p 325)
National Maritime Museum (p 400)
RAF Museum, Hendon. ☎ 020 8205

2266. Excellent, extensive display of aircraft and related hardware, well worth the journey.
Royal Hospital Chelsea Museum (p 324)
Tower Bridge Experience (p 111)
Tower of London (p 103)
Wellington Arch (p 232)

Royalty, famous people or their houses

Apsley House (Wellington Museum) (p 232)
Banqueting House (p 176)
Boston Manor, Boston Manor Rd, Brentford. ☎ 020 8560 5441. A Jacobean house.
Buckingham Palace (p 221)
Carlyle's House (p 328)
Chiswick House (p 427)
Dickens's House Museum (p 287)
Dr Johnson's House (p 139)
Down House, Downe, near Orpington, Kent. ☎ 01689 859 119. Home of Charles Darwin.
Eastbury Manor House (p 470)
Eltham Palace (p 471)
Freud Museum (p 366)
Ham House (p 451)
Hampton Court Palace (p 479)
Handel House Museum (p 236)
Hatfield House, Hatfield, Herts. ☎ 01707 262823. Great Jacobean house, home of the Earls of Salisbury, an easy journey from King's Cross.
Hever Castle, Edenbridge, Kent. ☎ 01732 865 224. A fascinating medieval castle, the childhood home of Anne Boleyn.
Hogarth's House (p 430)
Keats' House (p 366)
Kensington Palace (p 340)
Knole, Sevenoaks, Kent. ☎ 01732 450 608. Enormous house and park (National Trust), reached via Charing Cross.
Leeds Castle, Maidstone, Kent. ☎ 0870 600 8880). Picturesque lakeside castle with magnificent park and gardens.
Leighton House Museum and Art Gallery (p 345)
Linley Sambourne House (p 344)
Marble Hill House (p 453)
Osterley Park House (p 438)
Pitshanger Manor (p 441)
Prince Henry's Room (p 140)
Ranger's House (p 406)
Royal Mews (p 223)
Sherlock Holmes Museum (p 267)
Sir John Soane's Museum (p 257)
Southside House, Wimbledon (p 477)
Spencer House (p 230)
Strawberry Hill (p 456)
Sutton House (p 377)
Syon House (p 436)
2, Willow Road (p 366)
Wesley's House and Museum (p 118)

Religion

All Hallows by the Tower Crypt (p 100)
Fulham Palace (p 426)
Jewish Museum (p 357 and 465)
Museum of the Order of St John (p 293)
St Bride's Fleet St Crypt (p 138)
St Paul's Cathedral Crypt (p 135)
Southwark Cathedral (p 303)
Westminster Abbey Undercroft Museum (p 202)

Sport

Arsenal Museum. Avenell Rd, N5. ☎ 020 7704 4000. (Fridays only.) A good place to be initiated into the mysteries of football, and of one prestige club in particular.
Lord's Cricket Ground (p 354)
Museum of Rugby (p 455)
Wimbledon Lawn Tennis Museum (p 478)

Local history

Barnet Museum, 31 Wood Street. ☎ 020 8440 8066.
Bromley Museum, The Priory, Church Hill, Orpington. ☎ 01689 873826.

Bruce Castle Museum, Lordship Lane, N17. ☎ 020 8808 8772. Includes a display on the former owner, Rowland Hill, inventor of the Penny Post.

Church Farm House Museum, Greyhound Hill, NW4. ☎ 020 8203 0130. A delightful late 17C property with changing exhibitions.

Croydon Clocktower (p 475)

Crystal Palace Museum, Anerley Hill, SE19. ☎ 020 8676 0700.

Cuming Museum, Walworth Rd, SE17. ☎ 020 7701 1342. Covers the local history of Southwark.

Epping Forest District Museum, Waltham Abbey. ☎ 020 8529 6681. Relates not to the Forest as such but to the surrounding area.

Epping Forest Museum, Chingford. ☎ 020 8529 6681. Fascinating collection covering the history of this ancient hunting-ground of kings.

Grange Museum, Neasden, NW10.

☎ 020 8937 3600. Includes Victorian and Edwardian period rooms.

Gunnersbury Park Museum (p 440)

Hampstead Museum (Burgh House) (p 365)

Harrow Museum and Heritage Centre (p 462)

Kingston Museum (p 459)

Livesey Museum, Old Kent Rd, SE15. ☎ 020 7639 5604. A children's museum with lots of interactive, hands-on exhibits.

Museum of London (p 121)

Museum of Richmond (p 449)

Valence House Museum, Dagenham. ☎ 020 8592 4500. Local history of the Barking area.

Vestry House Museum (p 467)

Wandsworth Museum, The Courthouse, 11 Garrett Lane, SW18. ☎ 020 8871 7074. Housed in the former Surrey County Courthouse.

Wimbledon Museum of Local History (p 477)

Entertainment

Listings

As soon as you arrive in London, or better still before, you are strongly advised to buy **Time Out**, the weekly listings magazine published on Wednesdays (☎ 020 7813 6060 for distribution queries). It describes, with startling brashness but admirable detail, everything going on in the city—theatres, concerts, all other music, clubs, films, guided walks, as well as TV and radio, with all the necessary phone numbers, starting times, and other information. It is better for this purpose than any newspaper.

At the **planning** stage of your visit it may be worthwhile booking tickets for the theatre, concerts, opera or special exhibition in advance. The venue will post you the tickets if there is sufficient time, or keep them for collection when you arrive in London (up to 30 minutes before the performance).

Theatre

The history of the theatre is so closely tied to the history of London that it is worth recording some of the landmarks. London's first theatre was in Shoreditch, established by Richard Burbage in 1576. It was soon followed by several others on the South Bank, of which the **Globe** represents a re-built, living example. These theatres, open to the elements and with audiences who expected to participate, were the birthplaces of the works of Shakespeare, Jonson and Marlowe which have been seminal in the development of English literature.

The Commonwealth government of the mid-17C suppressed all this false and corrupting activity, as they saw it, but the theatre was vigorously revived with the **Restoration** of the monarchy from 1660, in closed buildings with female as well as male actors, and a tendency towards bawdy comedy. More cultivated dramas, and a higher standard of actor (including **David Garrick** and **Sarah Siddons**) and production, gradually appeared in the 18C, but the theatre remained 'downmarket' compared with other literary pursuits, and was subject to continuous government regulation in response to both satire and rowdiness. Drury Lane and Covent Garden were the only licensed theatres, but that did not prevent a huge number of alternative ventures being launched, a tradition which continues in pubs and clubs today.

The golden age of London theatre was probably the early years of the 20C, by which time most of the famous venues were in operation. After the Second World War London saw the establishment of the **National Theatre** (opened 1976) and the arrival from Stratford of the Royal Shakespeare Company (though soon to leave the Barbican) as well as, more dubiously, the predominance of the long-running musical. It is still fair to assert that no visit to London is complete without a theatre experience of some sort.

Buying tickets To find out what is on, buy a copy of *Time Out*, or call in at any theatre and collect a **listing**. The best place to book is at the theatre of your choice: most box offices open from mid-morning up to the time of the evening performance. Performances are usually at 19.30 or 20.00, with matinees on Wed/Thur and Sat. Alternatively you can book by telephone with a credit card and collect your tickets at the theatre shortly before curtain up. Each theatre operates its own policy on **discounts** for students and senior citizens, and they vary greatly in ease of access for the disabled: always check in advance. **Ticket agencies** charge a commission:

Ticketmaster, ☎ 020 8344 4444.
First Call, ☎ 020 7420 0000.

Agencies who set out blackboards in the street also charge commission and are best avoided. In Leicester Square, there is the **Half-Price Ticket Booth**, for that day's performances only, open 10.00–19.00 Mon–Sat.

See the map for the location of West End and South Bank theatres. The list below also indicates long-running successes:

Adelphi, Strand.
☎ Ticketmaster 020 7344 0055.
Albery, St Martin's Lane.
☎ 020 7369 1730.
Almeida, King's Cross (returns to Islington Sept 2002). ☎ 020 7359 4404.
Apollo, Shaftesbury Avenue.
☎ 020 7494 5070.
Apollo, Victoria. ☎ 0870 4000 651

Arts, Great Newport St. ☎ 020 7836 3334.
Barbican Centre ☎ 020 7638 8891 (often Royal Shakespeare Company).
Cambridge, Earlham St.
☎ 020 7494 5080.
Comedy, Panton St. ☎ 020 7369 1731.
Criterion, Piccadilly. ☎ Ticketmaster 020 7344 4444.

Dominion, Tottenham Court Rd.
☎ 0870 607 7460 (often musicals).
Donmar Warehouse, Earlham St.
☎ 020 7369 1732.
Duchess, Catherine St.
☎ 020 7494 5076.
Duke of York's, St Martin's Lane.
☎ 020 7369 1791.
Fortune, Russell St. ☎ 020 7836 2238
(*The Woman in Black*).
Garrick, Charing Cross Rd.
☎ 020 7494 5085.
Gielgud, Shaftesbury Avenue.
☎ 020 7494 5065.
Her Majesty's, Haymarket. ☎ 020
7494 5400 (*Phantom of the Opera*).
King's Head, Upper St, Islington.
☎ 020 7226 1916.
London Palladium, Argyll St,
☎ 020 7494 5020 (*The King and I*).
Lyceum, Wellington St. ☎ 0870 243
9000 (probably a musical).
Lyric, Shaftesbury Avenue.
☎ 020 7494 5045.
National Theatre (Olivier, Lyttelton and
Cottesloe Theatres), South Bank. ☎ 020
7452 3000.
New Ambassadors, West St.
☎ 020 7369 1761.
New London, Drury Lane.
☎ 020 7405 0072 (*Cats*).
Old Vic, Waterloo. ☎ 020 7928 7616.
Open Air Theatre, Regent's Park
(summer only). ☎ 020 7486 2431.
Palace, Shaftesbury Avenue.
☎ 020 7434 0909 (*Les Miserables*).
Phoenix, Charing Cross Rd.
☎ 020 7369 1733.

Piccadilly, Denman St.
☎ 020 7369 1734.
Polka, Wimbledon. ☎ 020 88543 4888
(children's productions).
Prince Edward, Old Compton St.
☎ 020 7447 5400.
Prince of Wales, Coventry St.
☎ 020 7839 5972.
Queen's, Shaftesbury Avenue.
☎ 020 7494 5040.
Richmond, The Green, Richmond.
☎ 020 8940 0088.
Riverside Studios, Hammersmith.
☎ 020 8237 1111.
St Martin's, West St. ☎ 020 7836 1443
(*The Mousetrap*, in its fifth decade).
Sadler's Wells, Rosebery Avenue,
Islington. ☎ 020 7863 8000.
Shaftesbury, Shaftesbury Avenue.
☎ 0870 906 3798.
Shakespeare's Globe, Bankside
(summer only). ☎ 020 7401 9919.
Strand, Aldwych. ☎ 020 7936 8800.
Theatre Royal, Drury Lane.
☎ 020 7494 5000.
Tricycle, Kilburn High Rd.
☎ 020 7328 1000.
Vaudeville, Strand. ☎ 020 7836 9987.
Victoria Palace, Victoria St.
☎ 020 7834 1317.
Westminster, Palace St.
☎ 020 7834 0283.
Whitehall, Whitehall.
☎ 020 7369 1735.
Wyndhams, Charing Cross Rd.
☎ 020 7369 1736.
Young Vic, The Cut. ☎ 020 7928 6363.

Comedy

A sub-division of theatre for which London has developed something of a reputation in the last 20 years is comedy. This can be **stand-up** (scripted) or **improvised**. It has led to the creation of many new stars, whose success is ultimately judged by the viewing figures they can draw on TV, clearly a low common denominator. So by catching them young, in live comedy shows, you are able to sample them at their best. In every venue there is usually a bill of several names, so if you do not like the first one you encounter, just wait. You are advised not to sit in the front rows unless you have a hankering to be drawn into some kind of public performance yourself.

The following is a list of the best-known venues—many are pubs. Further details can be gleaned from *Time Out*:

Banana Cabaret, The Bedford, 77, Bedford Hill, Balham. ☎ 020 8673 8904.
Canal Café Theatre, Delamere Terrace, Little Venice. ☎ 020 7289 6054.
Comedy Store, 1a Oxendon St, Piccadilly Circus. ☎ 020 7344 0234.
Downstairs at the King's Head, The Broadway, Crouch End. ☎ 020 8340 1028.
Jongleurs Battersea, 49 Lavender Gardens, Clapham Junction. ☎ 0870 787 0707.
Jongleurs Bow, 221 Grove Rd, Mile End. ☎ 0870 787 0707.
Jongleurs Camden Lock. ☎ 0870 787 0707.
Laughing Horse, Black Horse, Sheen Rd, Richmond. ☎ 020 8940 0424.
Upstairs at EDT, 1 Lordship Lane, East Dulwich. ☎ 020 8299 4138.

Film

There is plenty in London to satisfy cinema enthusiasts, with the **London Film Festival** every November a special draw. Numerous West End cinemas show new films; some have enormous screens and sound systems to match, and some (like the Curzon chain) are smaller and gentler. Many venues, usually in more off-beat places, specialise in rarities, repertory or recent releases discarded from the West End. Lists are given below. For classics, you can also consult the **National Film Theatre** on the South Bank.

West End

Curzon Mayfair, Curzon St.
☎ 0871 871 0011.
Curzon Soho, Shaftesbury Ave.
☎ 020 7439 4805
Empire, Leicester Square.
☎ 08700 102030
Odeon Marble Arch. ☎ 0870 5050 007.
Odeon Mezzanine, Leicester Square.
☎ as above.
Odeon Panton St. ☎ as above.
Odeon Tottenham Court Road.
☎ as above.
Odeon Leicester Square. ☎ as above.
Odeon Wardour St. ☎ as above.
Plaza, Lower Regent St.
☎ 08700 102 030.
Prince Charles, Leicester Place.
☎ 020 7494 3654.
Screen on Baker St, ☎ 020 7935 2772.
Screen on the Green, Upper St,
Islington Green, ☎ 020 7226 3520.
Screen on the Hill, Haverstock Hill
(Belsize Park Tube), ☎ 020 7435 3366.
UGC Trocadero, Piccadilly Circus.
☎ 0870 907 0716.
Warner Village West End,
Leicester Square. ☎ 020 7437 4343.

Other

Barbican. ☎ 020 7382 7000.
BFI London Imax, Waterloo.
☎ 020 7902 1234.
Coronet. Notting Hill. ☎ 020 7727 6705.
Electric, Portobello Rd.
☎ 020 7727 9958.
Everyman, Holly Bush Vale,
Hampstead.
☎ 020 7431 1771.
Gate, Notting Hill.
☎ 020 7727 4043.
ICA, The Mall. ☎ 020 7930 3647.
Lux, Hoxton Square. ☎ 020 7684
0201.
Metro, Rupert St. ☎ 020 7437 0757.
National Film Theatre, South Bank.
☎ 020 7928 3232.
Renoir, Brunswick Square.
☎ 020 7837 8402.
Riverside, Hammersmith.
☎ 020 8237 1111.
Tricycle, Kilburn High Rd.
☎ 020 7328 1900.

* Often show repertory or classic films.

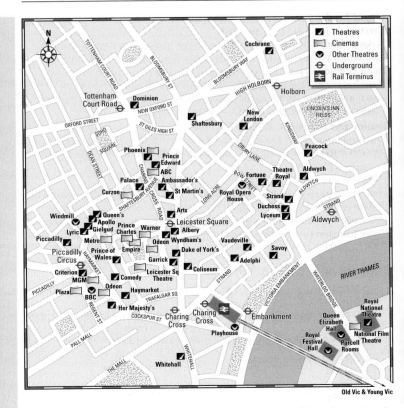

Old Vic & Young Vic

Music

Classical

London can claim several major orchestras of its own, as well as playing host to international names, numerous world-class chamber ensembles and soloists. The three great **concert halls** are the *Royal Albert Hall*, Kensington (☎ 020 7589 8212), the *Royal Festival Hall*, South Bank (☎ 020 7960 4242) and the *Barbican Centre*, home of the London Symphony Orchestra (☎ 020 7638 8891).

The most noted places for **recitals** are the *Wigmore Hall* (☎ 020 7935 2141), *Queen Elizabeth Hall* and *Purcell Room*, South Bank (☎ 020 7960 4242) and *St John's Smith Square* (☎ 020 7222 1061).

There are regular evening concerts at St Martin's-in-the Fields. Out of the centre, good music can be found at *Fairfield Halls*, Croydon. ☎ 020 8688 9291.

In summer, besides the Sir Henry Wood Promenade Concerts at the Albert Hall, better known as the **Proms**, the most democratic of all music festivals, there are also **outdoor concerts** at Kenwood, Marble Hill and elsewhere, ☎ 020 7973 3427. Several smaller **annual festivals** attract distinguished visiting artists. Each has developed a distinctive character of its own:

Spitalfields, June. ☎ 020 7377 1362.
Covent Garden, late May/early June. ☎ 020 7405 7555.

City of London, June/July. ☎ 020 7377 0540.
Greenwich, June. ☎ 020 8317 8687.

Apart from any of the above, simply by wandering around churches at lunchtimes you will find innumerable events, often free, but sometimes with a small charge—organ recitals, song recitals, talks, lectures, debates, or even church services at which, besides worshipping, you can always enjoy the music. There are similar events at the **music colleges**, the Royal College in Prince Consort Road, Kensington and the Royal Academy in Marylebone Road.

Opera and dance

The two famous opera houses in London are the **Royal Opera**, Covent Garden (☎ 020 7304 4000) and the **English National Opera** at the Coliseum in St Martin's Lane (☎ 020 7632 8300). The former is international, serious, self-conscious and on its dignity. It performs works in the language they were written in and is very expensive. The latter (the ENO to its many enthusiastic supporters) is more comfortable and friendly, performs in English and is somewhat cheaper. Opera also appears spasmodically at the Royal Festival Hall (see above), Sadler's Wells, Islington (see the list of theatres above) and the **Holland Park Theatre** (☎ 020 7602 7856), and within the music festivals listed above.

Classical dance in London is not what it was. The Royal Ballet and the English National Ballet appear irregularly at Covent Garden and the Coliseum but the London Festival Ballet and the Ballet Rambert seem to have disappeared from view. Where are they? But there are plenty of wonderful visiting companies to be seen at special seasons at the Royal Opera, the ENO, Sadler's Wells and elsewhere. And contemporary dance is bursting with life. A special pleasure is **Dance Umbrella**, a festival in October at a range of venues, ☎ 020 8741 5881.

Jazz, rock and pop

There are still a series of long-established jazz clubs in London, catering for what has become a specialist clientele and giving them what they want—no experiments. It is best to book a table.

Ronnie Scott's, 47 Frith St. ☎ 020 7439 0747.
100 Club, 100 Oxford St. ☎ 020 7636 0933.
606 Club, 90 Lots Rd, Fulham. ☎ 020 7352 5953.
Jazz Café, 5 Parkway, Camden Town. ☎ 020 7916 6060.
Pizza Express, 10 Dean St. ☎ 020 7437 9595.
Vortex, Stoke Newington Church St (73 bus). ☎ 020 7254 6516.
Bull's Head, Barnes Bridge. ☎ 020 8876 5241.
Pizza on the Park, Knightsbridge. ☎ 020 7235 5273.

Other live music is diverse in the extreme, ranging from giant **pop concerts** at major venues like Earl's Court, Labatt's Apollo at Hammersmith, the London Arena in Docklands and even the Royal Albert Hall, to small smoky clubs in out-of-the-way places. Other clubs, with DJs and bars, make up another huge sector of London's music scene. The following lists should get you started, but for serious detail, *Time Out* is again indispensable.

Major pop concert venues
Earl's Court. ☎ 020 7385 1200.
Labatt's Apollo. ☎ 020 7416 6080.
London Arena. ☎ 020 7538 1212.
Wembley Arena. ☎ 020 8902 0902.

Royal Albert Hall. ☎ 020 7589 8212.

General (mostly former theatres)
Astoria, Charing Cross Rd.
☎ 020 7434 0403.

Brixton Academy. ☎ 020 7924 9999.
Forum, Kentish Town.
☎ 020 7344 0044.
The Grand, Clapham Junction.
☎ 020 7223 6523.
Shepherd's Bush Empire.
☎ 020 8740 7474.

Rock and blues venues
Subterrania, 12 Acklam Rd, Ladbroke
Grove. ☎ 020 8960 4590.
Dover St Wine Bar, 8–9 Dover St,
Green Park. ☎ 020 7629 9813.
Half Moon, 93 Lower Richmond Rd,
Putney. ☎ 020 8780 9383.
Roadhouse, The Piazza, Covent Garden.
☎ 020 7240 6001.
Station Tavern, 41 Bramley Rd,
Latimer Rd. ☎ 020 7727 4053.

12 Bar Club, 22 Denmark Place,
Tottenham Court Rd. ☎ 020 7916
6989.

Clubs
Ministry of Sound, 103 Gaunt St,
Elephant and Castle. ☎ 020 7378
6528.
Salsa!, 96 Charing Cross Rd.
☎ 020 7379 3277.
Fabric, 77a Charterhouse St,
Farringdon. ☎ 020 7336 8898.
Fridge, Town Hall Parade, Brixton.
☎ 020 7326 5100.
Turnmills, 63 Clerkenwell Rd,
Farringdon. ☎ 020 7250 3409.
The Cross, Goods Way Depot, King's
Cross. ☎ 020 7837 0828.

Outdoor London

The walks in the main text take advantage of London's open spaces wherever possible. The boxed text in Chapter 44 says a little about the development of Victorian public parks, but even before this excellent innovation in town and social planning, there were many open spaces in London, thanks not least to the public-spirited attitude of a succession of monarchs. The **royal parks** which extend their green lungs into London from the west were mostly once royal hunting grounds, but, except for Buckingham Palace gardens, are all publicly accessible all day every day, and in some cases (for example, St James's Park), have been for centuries. Many different uses are expected from parks in the suburbs, some of them in conflict with each other: you cannot use the same space for tennis and dog-walking.

There is another kind of outdoor space to enjoy, too: left-over pieces of **countryside**, which by the determined interventions of our predecessors have been saved from developers. These include Hampstead Heath, Wimbledon Common and Clapham Common. Some of these triumphs of the environmentalists over commerce are quite recent, such as the Lea Valley Park and Bow Back Rivers.

Then there are **formal gardens**, some to be found in the royal parks above, and others in the grounds of houses and palaces open to the public, such as Hampton Court and Syon. Or there are gardens open for their own sakes, in particular the world-class botanical gardens at Kew and Chelsea Physic Garden.

A growing number of us get pleasure from walking through **cemeteries**. This was what the Victorians intended, but it did not happen for a long time because of 20C hang-ups about death, a mood from which we are now starting to recover, enabling us to enjoy cemeteries for their quiet peacefulness. A by-product, ironically, is that as a result of being ignored for so long, some burial grounds are rich in undisturbed plants and wildlife.

A special feature of open space in London is the plethora of **residential squares**, a 17C invention which became an essential for all better-class housing developments of the 18C and early 19C. We have inherited some examples of beautiful urban space, often open for us to sit in. Not all are as good as they should be: planting has been terrible and maintenance clearly a low priority. Some you should actively avoid, even if enjoying their surrounding architecture (Bloomsbury and Fitzroy Squares, for example) and many of the finest are firmly locked. But there are a few examples to put the rest to shame. And on Squares Day on the second Sunday in June, a new annual event in the calendar, most of those normally closed are opened up to view.

In addition to all these are specialist open spaces designated for particular activities. These include sports grounds and stadia but the category also covers the London Zoo, the Wetland Centre at Barnes, and other attractions.

The following is a list of the best open spaces in London, grouped under the above categories. The number in brackets indicates the relevant chapter in this guide. If they are not included in a walk, further details are given here.

Formal parks
(for walking, waterfowl, flowers, and perhaps entertainment)
Greenwich Park (49)
Holland Park (36)
Hyde Park (20)
Kensington Gardens (20)
Kenwood (41)
Osterley Park (59)
Regent's Park (25)
St James's Park (17)

Victorian and 20C parks
Battersea Park (55)
Brockwell Park (53)
Dulwich Park (52)
Finsbury Park, intended for the people of Finsbury and Islington, miles away, but still a dignified 19C conception.
Golders Hill, a beautiful space in Golders Green, with a small zoo and The Hill, an early 20C garden, alongside.
Mile End Park (46)
Southwark Park, a fine Victorian park in Bermondsey.
Thames Barrier Park, an exciting, state-of-the-art, French-designed, late 20C park in Beckton, overlooking the Thames and the Barrier.
Victoria Park (44)

Heaths, commons and wildlife reserves
Blackheath (50)
Clapham Common (54)
Epping Forest, extensive remains of the huge forest which covered the area northeast of London, with many beautiful woodland walks at all seasons. It stretches right down to Woodford, but is best explored from Chingford (via Liverpool Street).
Hampstead Heath (41)
Highbury Fields (43)
Lea Valley and Hackney Marshes, a large, partly wild, space following the Lea from Hackney to Hertfordshire, criss-crossed by waterways and football pitches—haunting in winter.
Primrose Hill (40)
Richmond Park (62)
Wetland Centre (58)
Wimbledon Common (71)

Gardens
Capel Manor, Enfield. ☎ 020 8366 4442. Showing garden design from various periods,
Chiswick Park (57)
Embankment Gardens (10)
Hampton Court Palace (72)
Horniman, Forest Hill (52)

Isabella Plantation, Richmond Park (62)
Kew (61)
Queen Mary's Rose Garden,
Regent's Park (25)
Syon Park (59)

Cemeteries and burial grounds
Abney Park, Stoke Newington (44)
Bunhill Fields (4)
Highgate (42)
Kensal Green. ☎ 020 8969 0152. The
first and most ambitious of the cemeteries established under the legislation of
the 1830s. Well worth a special visit.

Old St Pancras (40)
West Brompton (56)
West Norwood. Station: West Norwood
or 68 bus. Like Kensal Green, with fine
views of town.

Squares
Albion Square, Hackney
Finsbury Circus (4)
Hanover Square (19)
St James's Square (18)
Tavistock Square (28)
*Lonsdale Square, Barnsbury Square,
Thornhill Square*, Islington (43)

Water The most obvious stretch of water in London is Father **Thames**, the great brown river that gave birth to the place. Even now he is the largest open space in the metropolis, and the only element of untamed nature left. For so long celebrated for his indispensable contribution to Britain's trade and prosperity, for the defence of London and the primary means of royal transport, the old river god is now pensioned off as a leisure amenity. It is, however, much healthier, having seen the recent return of fish and other wildlife.

The Thames is still inspiring to walk along and contemplate, and one benefit from the loss of the river's true purpose has been the opening up of the **Thames Path**, displacing the old wharves and boatbuilders, but giving us views we could never previously enjoy. There are many opportunities for river trips, as explained in Chapters 74 and 75.

Many of the parks have **boating lakes** where rowing boats can be hired. Regent's Park and the Serpentine in Hyde Park (where you can also swim) are popular examples; also try Greenwich and Battersea Parks. Or—equally delightful, and more distinctively 'London'—you can take a boat trip on the **Regent's Canal**. Details are given in Chapter 39.

Sport

As you will see from any British newspaper, this is a country in which playing games is a serious business, with connotations of national pride and humiliation. And as some of the boxes in the text explain, many of the major world sports were invented in Britain, not least football (sometimes called soccer, but never by the initiated), cricket and tennis. There is plenty of evidence of their popularity in London, although perhaps, in the case of football, less than in a northern city, and plenty of other sport being enjoyed as well.

As of now, huge controversy has surrounded the provision of a major stadium for London. The myth-laden **Wembley Stadium** (for football, rugby, the dogs and pop concerts), is in course of demolition and reconstruction into a state-of-the-art venue for football and rugby, and occasionally athletics. It is being designed by Foster Associates and HOK (who are also redesigning Arsenal—see

Football below) and will have a giant illuminated arch, visible across London. A new cathedral?

Sports Line, ☎ 020 7222 8000 can give information about major sporting fixtures in the Greater London area.

Where to watch sport

Athletics

The main public **athletics meetings** are at *Crystal Palace National Sports Centre* (☎ 020 8778 0131): note that tickets are sold well in advance. For information about future meetings and events, contact the *British Athletics Federation* (☎ 0121 456 5098).

The **Flora London Marathon**, run from Blackheath to the Mall in April, has become a fixture in the British sporting calendar, attracting both world-class athletes and plodders for charity, and large crowds of supporters.

Cricket

The cricket season extends from May to September. In English culture, the game used to rank equally with, if not ahead of, football, but has been in steady decline for years. The big fixtures are the five-day **Test Matches** between England and Commonwealth countries such as Australia, India and the West Indies. It is not easy to get seats for these. A better bet, and perhaps a better introduction to the game if you need one (see Chapter 39), might be a day at a four-day **county game**, or better still a one-day game at one of the following venues:

Lord's, St John's Wood. ☎ 020 7289 1611. www.lords.org.uk. Home ground of the Middlesex county side, and also the home of the MCC.

Oval, Kennington. ☎ 020 7582 6660. www.surreycricket.com. Surrey's home ground and the venue for the final Test in any series.

Local matches are still played on many green spaces and parks throughout the suburbs on Saturday and Sunday afternoons: try Gunnersbury Park, Turnham Green at Chiswick and the Old Deer Park, Richmond. Watching cricket induces powerful feelings of pleasure and lassitude.

Football

The sport is played from August to May, in leagues and for championship cups. There are at the time of writing six London teams in the **Premier League**, out of 20. To get tickets for their home games (mainly played on Saturdays at 15.00) will not be easy, as the great bulk are reserved for supporters, but it is worth a try. You may do better for mid-week evening fixtures. Or watch on TV.

Arsenal. ☎ 020 7413 3366. Tube: Arsenal.

Charlton Athletic. ☎ 020 8333 4000. Station: Charlton (from Charing Cross).

Chelsea. ☎ 020 7386 7799. Tube: Fulham Broadway.

Fulham. ☎ 020 7893 8383. Tube: Putney Bridge.

Tottenham Hotspur. ☎ 020 8365 5050. Station: White Hart Lane (from Liverpool St).

West Ham United. Tube: Upton Park. ☎ 020 8548 2700.

Below the Barclaycard Premier League is the **Nationwide League**. For these games you stand a much better chance of obtaining tickets, which are cheaper, declining in price according to division.

Brentford (Div. 2). ☎ 020 8847 2511. Station: Brentford (from Waterloo).

Crystal Palace (Div. 1). ☎ 020 8771 8841. Station: Selhurst (from Victoria).

Leyton Orient (Div. 3). ☎ 020 8926 1111. Tube: Leyton.

Millwall (Div. 1). ☎ 020 7231 9999. Station: South Bermondsey (from London Bridge).
Queen's Park Rangers (Div. 2). ☎ 020 8740 2575. Tube: White City.
Watford (Div. 1). ☎ 01923 496010. Station: Watford High St (from Euston).
Wimbledon (Div. 1). ☎ 020 8771 8841. Station: Selhurst (from Victoria).

Listings are given in all the daily papers on Saturday mornings, and in *Time Out*, which also lists **women's fixtures**.

Greyhound racing

A night at the dogs, originally confined to London's working class, has become more generally popular in recent years. Betting thrills can be combined with a meal in a restaurant overlooking the track, but phone to book a table.

Catford, Adenmore Rd. ☎ 020 8690 8000. Station: Catford (from Victoria).
Crayford, Stadium Way ☎ 01322 557 836. Station: Crayford (from Charing Cross).
Romford, London Rd. ☎ 01708 762345. Station: Romford (from Liverpool Street).
Walthamstow, Stadium Way. ☎ 020 8531 4255. Tube: Walthamstow.
Wimbledon, Plough Lane. ☎ 020 8946 8000. Tube: Wimbledon Park.

Horse racing and equestrianism

There are five racecourses accessible to Londoners and visitors alike, listed below. The most famous event is the Derby at **Epsom**, still a popular day out, always on the first or second Saturday in June. More appropriate for dressing up is **Ascot** Week (also in mid-June), patronised by royalty and other media stars. The flat season is from April to September and hurdling from August to April. Details are in the daily newspapers.

Ascot. ☎ 01344 622 211. Station: Ascot (from Waterloo).
Epsom. ☎ 01372 726 311. Station: Epsom Downs (from Waterloo).
Kempton Park. ☎ 01932 782 292. Station: Kempton Park (from Waterloo).
Sandown Park. ☎ 01372 463 072. Station: Esher (from Waterloo).
Windsor. ☎ 01753 865 234. See Chapter 73.

The annual **Horse of the Year Show** is held at Wembley Arena in October. ☎ 020 8902 0902 for bookings.

Rowing

The major events are shown in the calendar (p 60–61). For more details, follow up the telephone numbers given there.

Rugby

The top venue is **Twickenham** ('Twickers'), where internationals and the Cup Final are contested (see Chapter 63). To book tickets (though these are virtually unobtainable), ☎ 020 8892 2000. www.rfu.com. It may be better to visit a **club game** at one of the following grounds, where it is not even essential to book in advance. In some cases, the winter afternoon game could be pleasantly combined with a walk: relevant chapter numbers are given below.

Blackheath, Rectory Field, Charlton Rd. ☎ 020 8858 1578. (50)
Station: Blackheath.
Harlequins, Stoop Memorial Ground, Craneford Way. ☎ 020 8892 0822.
Station: Twickenham (from Waterloo).
London Irish, The Avenue, Sunbury on Thames. ☎ 01932 783 034.
Station: Sunbury (from Waterloo).
London Scottish, Athletic Ground, Kew Foot Rd, Richmond. ☎ 020 8332 2473. (62)
London Welsh, Old Deer Park, Kew Road, Richmond. ☎ 020 8940 2368.

Wasps, same as Queen's Park Rangers football club. ☎ 020 8902 4220. Tube: White City.

Tennis

Wimbledon is synonymous with tennis in London (see Chapter 71). If you want to apply for seats for the Championships in June/July, send a stamped addressed envelope to the All England Club at PO Box 98, Church Rd, Wimbledon, London SW19 5AE for an application form (available from the previous September), and return it by 31 December. You will then be placed in a ballot. If that is unsuccessful you had better get to the courts by 07.00 on the day, when you may be lucky enough to get a seat for the Centre or No. 1 Court or at least one of the outside courts, where you can still see top-seeded players during the first week. If it rains all day your money will be returned.

Alternatively, you can try the Queen's Club, where the **Stella Artois** men's championship is played in early June: the application form for their ballot must be returned by 30 September, but a higher proportion of seats are made available at 10.00 on the day.

All England Lawn Tennis and Croquet Club, Church Rd, Wimbledon, London SW19 5AE. Tickets ☎ 020 8946 2244. General information ☎ 020 8944 1066. www.wimbledon.org. Tube: Southfields.

Queen's Club, Palliser Rd, London W14 9EQ. ☎ 020 7385 3421. Tube: Baron's Court.

Where to participate in sport

Most London parks have facilities for the obvious sports, in particular tennis, football, cricket, sometimes putting, and so on: you will find notices about such arrangements in the parks concerned, and can also phone the Leisure Department of the borough council (numbers in Yellow Pages). Here are some other ideas, sport by sport.

Fitness centres

Most local authority leisure centres offer gym facilities and fitness classes and many private fitness clubs around London, including *Cannons*, *Fitness First*, *Holmes Place* (for all, see www.cannons.co.uk) and *LA Fitness* (www.lafitness.co.uk), offer short-term membership. See *Yellow Pages* under Leisure Centres, and see Swimming below.

Golf

There are quite a few **public courses** within Greater London, where you do not need to be a member and can play a round for about £15. Alternatively, you can practise at a driving range or a putting green in a park. For more details, contact the *Golf Foundation*, ☎ 020 8367 4404.

Regent's Park Golf School, ☎ 020 7724 0643.

Metro Golf Centre, Hendon. ☎ 020 8202 1202.

Coombe Wood Golf Club, Kingston (see Chapter 64). ☎ 020 8942 6764.

Harrow Hill Golf Course (see Chapter 65). ☎ 020 8864 3754.

Horse riding

It is possible to hire horses and ride in central London (accompanied in Hyde Park) and in more outlying areas. Try the following:

Hyde Park Richard Briggs Stables, ☎ 020 7823 6422. Ross Nye Riding Stables, ☎ 020 7262 3791.

Richmond Park Kingston Riding Centre, ☎ 020 8546 6361; Richmond Park Stables, ☎ 020 8546 8437.

Ice skating
Broadgate, Broadgate Circus (outdoor—see Chapter 4). ☎ 020 7505 4068.
Queen's Ice Bowl, 17 Queensway. ☎ 020 7229 0172.
Sobell Leisure Centre, Hornsey. Tube: Holloway Rd. ☎ 020 7609 2166.
Streatham Ice Rink. ☎ 020 8769 7771. Station: Streatham (from Charing Cross).

Swimming
The following are general public facilities, variable in quality and price, sometimes with fitness centres attached. Phone for complete details.
Ironmonger Row, EC1. ☎ 020 7253 4011. Tube: Old Street.
Oasis, Endell St (outdoor). ☎ 020 7831 1804.
Porchester Spa, Queensway. ☎ 020 7792 3980.
Queen Mother Sports Centre, Vauxhall Bridge Rd. ☎ 020 7630 5522. Tube: Victoria.
The Sanctuary, Covent Garden (women only). ☎ 020 7420 5151.

In addition, there are numerous public pools run by borough councils. Phone them or Sportsline above.

 # Shopping

'*L'Angleterre est une nation de boutiquiers*' ('England is a nation of shopkeepers') Napoleon is said to have said, presumably not intending a compliment. Any visitor to London today would initially agree with him, although a little research would demonstrate that many of the shopkeepers and their shops are international rather than English. Whatever their pedigree, London is certainly bursting with shops and markets, and during your visit you will want to sample at least some of this rich variety. We survey them by both district and type of merchandise.

Shopping hours In the West End, few shops open before 09.30, but they are staying open later and later Monday to Saturday, until at least 18.00, and on **Thursdays** later still. Unlike in warmer climes, no one would dream of closing for lunch, which indeed is one of the most crowded times of day. If you want to find the shops at their least busy, go between 10.00 and 12.00 early in the week. Most shops also open on Sundays, but they are restricted to six hours of business, normally 11.00–17.00 or 12.00–18.00.

Antique shops open more selectively, and Saturday is usually the best time to visit them. Street markets also operate at variable times—see below. **Food supermarkets** are open late in the evenings, and sometimes 24 hours Monday to Saturday, but not (unaccountably) in Central London.

Sales Sales occur with increasing frequency and in some cases seem to continue throughout the year. But the official sales in the main shops are in **January**, sometimes starting as early as 26 December (Boxing Day), and in **mid-summer**. Except during sales, you will find the summer clothes ranges in February to May and the winter ranges arriving in August. Christmas goods begin to appear in September.

Taxes The prices of most items (not food or books) include Value Added Tax (VAT) at 17.5per cent. There are facilities for non-EU visitors to obtain a refund of this percentage through the Retail Export Scheme, but only if the shop in question participates. The fact will be displayed if they do. Contact the British Consulate in your country or the British Tourist Authority for more details. Note that the scheme does not apply to hotel bills and the like.

Where to go?

Oxford Street has to be Europe's most famous shopping street, but you will find it for that reason extremely full and pushy. It harbours mainly clothes shops, but there is plenty more to be seen and bought besides. Much the better shops are to be found in the western half. Oxford Circus marks the crossing with **Regent Street**, more congenial in many ways, with equally distinguished stores. **Carnaby Street**, struggling to recapture its 60s heyday, is just to the east of Regent Street. **Bond Street**, running south from a point half-way between Regent Street and Marble Arch, is more distinguished still.

The whole ensemble makes a fascinating walk (outlined in Chapter 21). The stores to be encountered include the department stores *Selfridge's*, *John Lewis*, two branches of *Marks and Spencer*, the music stores *HMV* and *Virgin Megastore* (all Oxford Street), the clothes store *Fenwick's* (Bond Street), and *Dickins and Jones*, *Liberty's*, *Hamley's* (for toys), *Aquascutum* and *Austin Reed* (Regent Street), and countless branches of well-known chainstores for clothes and other necessities. In Oxford Street itself there have also appeared a few dodgy premises, where apparent bargains of known brands are auctioned at rock-bottom prices. These are sometimes run by crooks: beware of tannoy messages inviting you in. Not to be missed are the enclave of **St Christopher's Place** to the north and **Gray's Antique Market**, with South Molton Street, to the south.

Piccadilly (Chapter 18) is slightly different in tone, as are Old Bond Street and Jermyn Street close by. There are no big stores here, but a greater preponderance of traditional names, such as *Fortnum and Mason*, *Cordings*, and *Lillywhite's* for sportswear. Numerous traditional suppliers display their 'by appointment to' royal warrants, and there are several large bookshops. **Jermyn Street** is famous for shirts, including *T.M. Lewin*, *Hilditch and Key* and *Thomas Pink*, and has *Paxton and Whitfield* for cheese. **Burlington Arcade** and similar spaces can also be enjoyed. St James's Piccadilly has a small market, at its best on Tuesdays.

Covent Garden (Chapter 10) is another story altogether. It is a close-knit jumble of small shops, market and street performers, with an atmosphere that long outlasts normal shopping hours: when Oxford Street has gone to sleep, Covent Garden is a-buzz. The mainstream clothes chains are all here, such as *Hobbs*, *Monsoon*, *Jigsaw*, *Accessorize*, *Next*, *Oasis* and *Whistles*, and inevitably *Gap* and *French Connection* as well as some rarer names, especially in Floral Street. Everything is kept small, in accordance with the original Covent Garden style. For maps and travel books, *Stanford's* in Long Acre is a must. In the original market, using the old Apple Market stalls, are a range of craft goods and clothes, and in Jubilee Market to the south more of the same, including antiques on Mondays. It is worth exploring north into Neal Street and Earlham Street for *Carluccio's* Italian grocer, *Neal's Yard* cheese shop and similar 'alternative' variants.

Going west, **Knightsbridge** (Chapter 16) is famous for two of the biggest names of all: *Harrod's* and *Harvey Nichols* stores. Prices are high but so is the quality and the range of goods is huge. There are branches of most other familiar names as well, all within a compact, crowded area. If you make your way south down Sloane Street, the quality and price rise further and the crowds diminish.

It is not a long walk from Knightsbridge down to **Sloane Square**, where the character changes again; *Peter Jones*, a big department store within the John Lewis Partnership, has been recently revamped. Also, close by are some very attractive furnishing shops such as *David Mellor* for kitchens and the *General Trading Company* for just about everything else. **King's Road** stretches away to the west; not quite as fashionable as it once was, it is great to explore even so. Many of the mainstream chains inevitably appear. (Sloane Square and King's Road are covered in Chapter 34.)

Not far away are the stores of **Kensington High Street** (Chapter 36), a kind of mini-Oxford Street, but pleasanter in many ways. There is a good selection of antique shops to the north up Kensington Church Street.

The largest places for bargain antiques are the **Portobello Road** (Chapter 38), especially on a Saturday, and **Chelsea**, at 131–141 and 243–253 King's Road. Haggling over price is possible, but you are unlikely to get more than 10 per cent off. Another popular general indoor antique market is *Alfie's*, next to the outdoor market in Church Street off Edgware Road. More specialist is **Camden Passage** in Islington (Chapter 43), best on a Wednesday or Saturday, but with many stalls open daily. For the expert, the place to go is **Bermondsey Market** on the corner of Long Lane and Bermondsey Street at crack of dawn on a Friday, where dealers from the other places go to replenish their stocks: it is all over by 11.00. An interesting secret is the London Silver Vaults at 53–64 Chancery Lane, with scores of silver dealers in an underground bunker.

Blue Guide readers will be interested in bookshops, and will probably know well enough that the greatest concentration is in **Charing Cross Road** (Chapter 22). Here are not only big branches of two major London chains, *Waterstone's* and *Books Etc*, but also *Borders*, the American chain that pioneered the excellent idea of coffees in bookstores; *Blackwell's*, a university supplier; and the unique, traditional, one-branch-only, *Foyles*. 84 Charing Cross Road, immortalised by Hélène Hanff, is no more, but there is no shortage of second-hand and high-quality remainder suppliers. Some stores combine new and second-hand stock. Of particular interest may be *Zwemmer's* (no. 80), for art, and *Henry Pordes* (no. 58), for art, history etc.

Food shopping

The giant food supermarkets, of which the leading names are Sainsbury's, Tesco, Safeway and Waitrose, have become a type of suburban paradise, superseding churches as providers of solace and joy in their product range and offering a weekly mecca for every individual and family. But these names only manifest themselves in the centre of town and the hotel districts in the form of mini-branches such as *Tesco Metro* or *Sainsbury's Central*, and there are only a few of them. There are smaller supermarkets, sometimes ethnic, sometimes open for long hours: some operate as chains (Europa, Food and Wine, Cost-cutter), but they must be acknowledged as pretty basic.

If you can afford it, it is better to do your food shopping at branches of *Marks and Spencer*, or the food halls of *Selfridge's* or *Harrod's*. You will also do well at Italian delis in various places, or in Chinatown, Soho. For fruit and vegetables in inner London you can not beat a street market—there are plenty (see below)—

but you will have to think of shopping in the morning and be prepared to carry it around all day.

For **special foods**, delicious and excellent **presents**, London is first class. Buy chocolates at any branch of ***Thornton's*** or other, more up-market chocolatiers such as ***Charbonnel et Walker*** in Old Bond Street and the Royal Exchange. Teas and coffees are good from ***Whittards***, or better still from the tiny ***Twining's*** shop in Fleet Street, or ***Fortnum and Mason's*** in Piccadilly. Also very acceptable as 'London' gifts are herbs and spices from branches of ***Culpeper*** (Covent Garden), ***Crabtree and Evelyn*** (branches) or ***Penhaligon's*** (Covent Garden), or even the ubiquitous but worthwhile ***Body Shop***; or the National Trust shop in Victoria (see Chapter 17). Excellent organic meat is sold at ***Lidgate*** on Holland Park Avenue and fish at ***Steve Hatt*** in Islington; ***Paxton and Whitfield*** in Jermyn Street and ***Neal's Yard*** in Covent Garden sell excellent cheeses.

Farmers' markets are increasing in popularity and many include growers from France, not surprisingly given London's proximity to the Channel. Information on these is available at www.farmersmarkets.net.

Street markets

As one of the competitor guidebooks has it, 'you haven't really got to grips with London until you've rummaged through the junk at Brick Lane or haggled for a jacket at Camden'. Street markets are historic in many cases, certainly traditional to this city, and now enjoying something of a renaissance for people exhausted by the sheer repetition of chainstores. We have mentioned those dealing with antiques above. Here is a selection of others: mornings (from about 10.00 to lunchtime) are the best time to go.

For fruit and vegetables (no haggling)
Berwick St, Soho (not Sun)
Brixton (see Chapter 53)
Chapel Market, Islington (not Mon)
Lower Marsh, Waterloo (not Sun)
Portobello Road (not Sun)
Leather Lane, Hatton Garden (not Sat or Sun)

For general foodstuffs (no haggling)
Borough Market, London Bridge (Fri pm and Sat am)
Spitalfields (Sun am)
Leadenhall, City (Mon–Fri)

For plants (try haggling)
Columbia Road (Sun am)
East St, Walworth Rd (ditto)

For clothes (always haggle)
Petticoat Lane (mainly Sun am)
Whitechapel Road (Mon–Fri)
Chapel Market (see above)
Camden Lock (see Chapter 40)

For anything (ditto)
Camden Lock (see above)
Brick Lane (see Chapter 45)
Greenwich (Sat and Sun only—see Chapter 49)
Walthamstow (not Sun—see Chapter 67)

Children's London

Take no notice of the conventional wisdom about Mediterranean countries being friendlier to children than the cold northerners. This used to be true, but children are given a pretty free rein everywhere in Britain, and the only places in London where they may seem unwelcome are the top restaurants. In the important historic homes they need to be kept under control, but even in many of these—Syon is a fine example—there are a number of attractions specifically for children.

Even so a list of suggestions may be helpful to concerned parents or grandparents, aunts or uncles desperate for ideas. The following attractions are grouped by type, and can be reclassified by area by turning up the page reference to seek other, different, activities nearby. Refer to the main text to make judgements about suitable ages. Most local history museums (see above) also have child-orientated sections or displays.

Museums

BBC Experience (p 273)
Bethnal Green Museum of Childhood (p 384)
Cutty Sark (p 397)
Golden Hinde (p 304)
HMS Belfast (p 299)
Horniman (p 414). Many activities aimed at children specifically.
Kew Bridge Steam (p 434). Especially good when 'in steam'.
Legoland, Windsor (p 495). A certain winner.
London Aquarium (p 315)
London Canal Museum (p 288)
London Dungeon (p 299). Not for young or nervous children.
London Planetarium (p 265)
London Transport (p 160)
London Zoo (p 270)
Madame Tussaud's (p 264)
Museum of London (p 121)
Musical Museum (p 435)
National Maritime Museum (p 400). For children aged around 10 and older.
Natural History Museum (p 330). Activities and events for all ages.
North Woolwich Old Station Museum, ☎ 020 7474 7244
Old Royal Observatory (p 401). Stand astride the meridian line.
Pollock's Toy Museum (p 276). Old-fashioned displays.
Ragged School Museum (p 385)
Royal Air Force Museum, Hendon. ☎ 020 8205 2266. Tube: Colindale. For children aged 10 and older.
Royal Mews (p 223). For the horses.

Science Museum (p 332). Activities and events for all ages.
Shakespeare's Globe (p 250). For children aged 10 and older.
Syon Butterfly House (p 436). See also Snakes and Ladders below.
Theatre Museum (p 160). Make-up and dressing-up sessions may appeal.
Tower of London (p 103)

Outdoor places

Victorian or suburban parks always have slides and swings and often more exotic play areas. For wild country, visit Richmond Park, Hampstead Heath, or Wimbledon Common. Try a river trip (see Chapter 74) or a boat on the lake in Regent's Park, the Serpentine in Hyde Park, or elsewhere. For rides on double-decker buses the upstairs front seats are best. Also try to go in the front seat when travelling on the Docklands Light Railway.

London Eye (p 314)
Battersea Park (p 422). Children's zoo and boating lake.
Golders Hill Park, Golders Green. Animal and bird enclosure.
Holland Park (p 344). ☎ 020 7603 2838. Organised playgroups.
Coram's Fields (p 286). Animal pens (adult must be accompanied by a child).
Wetland Centre (p 432)
Chessington World of Adventures, Chessington, Surrey. ☎ 01372 727227.
Freightliners City Farm (p 373), Islington. ☎ 020 7609 0467.
Hackney City Farm, ☎ 020 7729 6381.
Kentish Town, ☎ 020 7916 5421.

Mudchute City Farm (p 395),
Docklands. ☎ 020 7515 5901.
Stepping Stones City Farm (p 385),
☎ 020 7790 8204.
Surrey Docks City Farm (p 410),
☎ 020 7231 1010.
Vauxhall City Farm, ☎ 020 7582 4204

Theatres

Booking necessary in all cases.
The Bull, Barnet. ☎ 020 8449 0048.
Little Angel, Islington. ☎ 020 7226
1787 (Sat and Sun).
Lyric Hammersmith. ☎ 020 8741 2311
(Sat am).
Polka, Wimbledon. ☎ 020 8543 4888.
Puppet Theatre Barge, Little Venice.
☎ 020 7249 6876 (on the Thames in
summer).

Tricycle, Kilburn. ☎ 020 7328 1000
(Sat).
Unicorn Arts, 6–7 Great Newport St.
☎ 020 7836 3334.

Indoor play centres (if all else fails)
Bramley's Big Adventure, 136 Bramley
Rd, White City. ☎ 020 8960 1515.
Tube: Latimer Rd.
Discovery Centre, Clapham Junction
Shopping Centre. ☎ 020 7223 1717.
Fantasy Island, Wembley. ☎ 020 8904
9044. Tube/station: North Wembley.
Playhouse, Highbury Grove School,
Highbury Grove. ☎ 020 7704 9424.
Snakes and Ladders, Syon Park,
Brentford. ☎ 020 8847 0946.
Spike's Madhouse, Crystal Palace National
Sports Centre. ☎ 020 8778 9876.

Communications and media

Post offices

These are open usually 08.30–17.30 Mon–Fri, and some main post offices may
be open on Saturday mornings. The branch in William IV Street near St Martin's-
in-the-Fields is open 08.00–20.00 Mon–Fri and 09.00–20.00 Sat. Avoid going
at lunchtime and the end of the afternoon, when long queues form. Post offices
are not indispensable to the visitor, and you can often obtain stamps and even
post parcels from small newsagents, although only during the hours above, or
buy stamps for postcards from your hotel.

Postcodes This system divides London into districts unrelated to local
government boundaries. In inner London, an old designation of districts
into compass points still applies: W for west, NW for northwest, EC for east
central and so on. This is followed by a number sub-division, e.g. NW10.
This part of the code has long been a shorthand for the district itself. Further
out from the centre, the code represents the first letters of the main sorting
office, e.g. 'TW'. This example indicates not only Twickenham but, by number e.g. TW8, each of the surrounding areas. Such is the power of fashion
that house prices are affected by these postcodes. The second part of the
code, a digit followed by two letters (e.g. TW8 4LY), simply indicates the
delivery route within the district, but you must make sure you include it.
Mail with an incomplete postcode is treated as second-class, even if it carries
a first-class stamp.

Letters and postcards can often be posted from hotels, but the standard **post-box**, or pillar box—bright red and displaying the monogram of the monarch reigning when it was installed—will often catch the eye. The last post from these boxes is often as early as 17.30.

1st class post (currently 27p) means delivery next working day, 2nd class (19p) takes two or three days. Sending postcards to Europe currently costs 36p (or the stamps will be marked 'E'); to the USA, Canada, South Africa, Australia or New Zealand it costs 40p. For more information, ☎ 08457 740 740.

Telephones

Calls are cheaper **'off-peak'**, i.e. 18.00–08.00 Mon–Fri and all day at weekends. There is now competition between the former public monopoly, British Telecom, and private service providers, in particular for calls overseas (see the advertising on the Tube). Public **phone boxes** provided by both can be found, mostly taking cash (10p, 20p, 50p, £1 and £2 coins), credit cards or phone cards. Phone cards (for £3, £5, £10 or £20) can be obtained from newsagents, supermarkets and post offices. The phone in your hotel will charge at a steep mark-up, at all times of day or night. Also, beware of high-charging premium numbers, which begin 09. (Numbers beginning 0800 are free and those beginning 0845 charge at local rates.)

Telephone **directories** in call boxes have become rare, although post offices and your hotel should still provide them: the easiest way to find a number in the UK is to dial directory enquiries, but there will be a charge. For commercial enquiries you can use Yellow Pages.

Directory enquiries, ☎ 192
International directory enquiries ☎ 153
Operator services ☎ 100
International operator services ☎ 155

All London **telephone numbers** have eight digits, beginning with 7 (central London) or 8 (outer London). If you are dialling London from outside the city, precede the eight-digit number with 020. If you are dialling London from abroad, precede the eight-digit number with the country code, 44, and 20 for London (omitting the first 0). If you are dialling abroad from London, dial 00 followed by the national code, as shown, then the number.

USA, ☎ 00 1   *South Africa*, ☎ 00 27
Canada, ☎ 00 1   *Netherlands*, ☎ 00 31
Australia, ☎ 00 61   *Republic of Ireland*, ☎ 00 353
New Zealand, ☎ 00 64

If bringing your **mobile phone** to the UK, contact your service provider first to set up a roaming facility with a British company. You will need a dual- or tri-band phone. You can also hire a pay-as-you-go mobile service from a provider in Britain, on arrival.

Internet access

Many hotels and youth hostels now provide internet access, as do local **libraries**, and there are a number of **internet cafés** where you can log on and collect email. The five *easyInternetCafé* branches are open 24 hours and all are central (Strand, near Trafalgar Square; Oxford Street, opposite Bond Street station; Tottenham Court Road, southern end; Wilton Road, opposite Victoria Station; and Kensington High Street). Access costs from £1. www.easyeverything.com

Media

Visitors from overseas are sometimes startled by the assertiveness of the British press (see Chapter 8), but it is well worth buying the papers to find out what is going on in London, in terms of both news and events. *Time Out* has already been recommended for details of the great majority of activities in London (see p 40). The **broadsheet newspapers** (*The Times*, *Daily Telegraph*, *Guardian* or *Independent*), especially the Saturday editions, will add informed reviews and specialist articles to enrich your appreciation of London's culture. This is also true for some of the Sundays, notably the *Sunday Times*, *Observer* and *Sunday Telegraph*.

There is only one **central London newspaper**, called the *Evening Standard* but on sale from lunchtime. It is another excellent source for details of all events, and on Thursdays has a very useful supplement, *Hot Tickets*, with specific listings. *Metro* is available free at stations in the mornings. There are **local papers** for the various areas of London, such as the *Ham and High* (for Hampstead and Highgate) and the *South London Press*, which also carry listings.

Go into any newsagent to survey the vast number of specialist **magazines** on innumerable subjects. You will certainly find something for you. There are surprisingly few news weeklies, but try the *Spectator*, the *New Statesman* or the excellent *Economist*. For the availability of foreign publications, see p 63.

You can get plenty more information on **local radio**, such as London News Direct (97.3), Capital Radio (95.8 FM) or London Live (94.9 FM). The **national radio** stations are the prerogative of the BBC (see Chapter 26): the wavelength of most interest to visitors is probably Radio 4 (93.5 FM), with regular news bulletins and coverage, comedy, features and drama. There is plenty of commercial competition, but nothing to rival the BBC World Service (648AM).

The BBC is also responsible for two terrestrial **television** channels, BBC1 and BBC2. The chief commercial channels are ITV1 (effectively Channel 3) and the independent Channels 4 and 5. World news appears on BBC1 and ITV at 22.00. Local news is usually shown immediately after nationwide transmissions: for example, there is a full half-hour of London news after the 18.00 main news on BBC 1, Monday to Friday. There are satellite channels available from BSkyB and others and a growing number of cable channels. For news, tune in to CNN or BBC News 24.

Additional information

Banking services

Banks are usually open 09.30–16.30 Mon–Fri and sometimes Sat mornings in shopping centres and similar locations. The four big names are *Barclays*, *HSBC* (formerly Midland), *Lloyds/TSB* and *Natwest*; many of the biggest former building societies are now also banks and offer the same services (see p 11). Most bank branches have **ATM machines** outside, operating very much longer hours, if not 24 hours. Some have further machines inside. Most of these accept Visa, Mastercard, and many other cards. Sometimes a charge is made, but not if the bank concerned has an agreement with the card company.

It is best to go to a bank to cash **travellers' cheques**, where the commission will be less than at hotels or travel agencies and the rates of exchange probably better: take a passport or other ID. You cannot use travellers' cheques to pay for goods and services in shops and restaurants. If you need **non-British currency**, try a bank first. They may not have enough in stock, so be ready also to go to a **bureau de change**, of which there are many in the central streets and stations. The big names, again for better rates, are *American Express* and *Thomas Cook*. There is no exchange control in the UK.

Calendar of events and public holidays

There is something going on in London all the year round, but in case you want to plan your trip round a particular event, or if you want to know what will be happening while you are here, consult this calendar.

Bank Holidays

New Year's Day (1 January)
Good Friday (variable)
Easter Monday (variable)
First Monday in May
Spring Bank Holiday (last Monday in May)
August Bank Holiday (last Monday in August)
Christmas Day (25 December)
Boxing Day (26 December)

January

New Year's Day Parade (1 January).
  For information ☎ 0900 525 2020.
International Boat Show, Earl's Court
International Mime Festival

January/February

Chinese New Year celebrations,
  Chinatown, Soho

February

Clowns' Service and Show (first Sunday,
  16.00), Holy Trinity, Dalston
Fine Art and Antiques Fair, Olympia

February/March

Pancake Day Races (Shrove Tuesday),
  e.g. at Spitalfields Market 12.30.
Six Nations Rugby, Twickenham

March

Head of the River Race (29 March 2003
  at 14.00; 20 March 2004 at 15.00),
  Putney to Mortlake
Ideal Home Exhibition, Earl's Court
London Book Fair, Olympia
Chelsea Antiques Fair, Chelsea Old
  Town Hall

March/April

Oxford and Cambridge Boat Race,
  Putney to Mortlake

Easter

Easter Parade, Battersea Park, from 10.00

April

Flora London Marathon (third Sunday,
  start 09.00), Greenwich to The Mall
St George's Day (23 April)
  Shakespeare's birthday: service in
  Southwark Cathedral

May

May Day (1 May) Probable demonstrations in central London
Royal Windsor Horse Show
Chelsea Flower Show
Shakespeare's Globe outdoor theatre
  season begins (until end Sept)

June

Beating the Retreat Horse Guards
  Parade
Covent Garden Festival
Regent's Park open-air theatre season
  begins (until early Sept)
Trooping the Colour (2nd or 3rd
  Saturday) Horse Guards Parade
Spitalfields Festival
Coin Street Festival, South Bank,
  ☎ 020 7620 0544 (until Sept)
Derby Day (1st or 2nd Saturday)
  Epsom Races
Royal Ascot
Greenwich Festival
Gay Pride

Royal Academy Summer Exhibition
(until Sept)
Fine Art and Antiques Fair, Olympia
Squares Day (second Sunday)
The Fleadh, an Irish folk festival,
Finsbury Park

June/July

*All England Lawn Tennis
Championships*, Wimbledon
London to Brighton cycle race

July

Kenwood House Outdoor concerts,
☎ 020 7973 3427 (until Sept)
City of London Festival ☎ 020 7377
0540
Henley Royal Regatta
BBC Henry Wood Promenade Concerts
(until Sept)
Doggett's Coat and Badge Race, London
Bridge to Chelsea
Swan Upping (see p 494)

July/August

Cricket Test Matches at Lord's and the
Oval

August

Marble Hill Outdoor concerts,
☎ 020 7973 3427
Notting Hill Carnival (last weekend)

September

Open House (third weekend) Unusual
and inaccessible buildings open to
public, ☎ 020 7267 2070

October

Black History month
Trafalgar Day Parade (Sunday nearest
21 October)

October/November

State Opening of Parliament
London Fashion Week
Dance Umbrella Festival of
contemporary dance

November

Guy Fawkes' Night or Bonfire Night
(5 November) Fireworks displays
everywhere, bonfire in Battersea Park,
etc
London to Brighton Veteran Car Race
(1st Sunday)
Remembrance Sunday (nearest to 11
November) Two minutes' silence at
11.00
Lord Mayor's Show (2nd Saturday)
Fine Art and Antiques Fair, Olympia
London Film Festival
Christmas lights turned on in West
End

December

Christmas tree (sent from Norway) set
up in Trafalgar Square
Carol concerts at various churches—
see noticeboards
New Year's Eve celebrations in
Trafalgar Square and elsewhere

Crime and personal security

London is a comparatively safe place. The UK is not a gun culture, and we hope it never will be. Most police officers are still unarmed, and the American visitor, for example, will feel a lot more secure here than in the average city in the USA. Having said that, there are some dangers to be avoided.

Beware of **pickpockets**, especially on the Tube and in street markets, where crowds and noise create ideal conditions for them. Do not keep your wallet in a visible back pocket, use a bumbag, and be careful of people unzipping your backpack. Keep handbags in front of you whenever possible, not at your side.

Be especially vigilant near the large **railway termini** where there are two hazards: experienced muggers or thieves who can easily spot new and uncertain-looking arrivals in the city, and, separately, drunks and drug addicts who are more likely to congregate there.

Be selective with **beggars**, who have become something of a minor industry in big cities like London. You can help the genuinely homeless by buying a copy of the widely sold weekly *Big Issue* (£1.20, of which part goes to the seller).

Do not go down dark alleys or deserted courtyards, especially after dark. If you see people obviously the worse for drink or drugs, keep away. At night avoid empty carriages on trains or tubes. If in doubt, stay with the crowd.

Policemen in London streets—the helpful London 'bobby', in distinctive uniforms, although no longer always the traditional helmet—should always be consulted, before anyone else, in any sort of emergency, including being lost.

Electric current
In Britain electricity is supplied at 220–240 volts AC and appliances need rectangular plugs with 3 square pins. Adaptors are very widely available.

Emergency numbers
Police, ambulance or fire brigade ☎ 999
Textphone ☎ 18000
See also under Embassies and consulates, Lost property and Medical services, below.

Embassies and consulates
Australia Australia House, Strand, WC2. ☎ 020 7379 4334. www.australia.org.uk
Canada Macdondald House, 1 Grosvenor Square, W1. ☎ 020 7258 6333. www.dfait-maeci.gc.ca/london
France 58 Knightsbridge, SW1. ☎ 020 7201 1000. www.embafrance-uk.org
Germany 23 Belgrave Square, SW1. ☎ 020 7824 1300. www.german-embassy.org.uk
Ireland 17 Grosvenor Place, SW1. ☎ 020 7235 2171.
Italy 14 Three Kings Yard, W1. ☎ 020 7312 2200. www.embitaly.org.uk
Japan 101 Piccadilly, W1V. ☎ 020 7465 6500. www.embjapan.org.uk
Netherlands 38 Hyde Park Gate, SW7. ☎ 020 7590 3200. www.netherlands-embassy.org.uk
New Zealand 80 Haymarket, SW1. ☎ 020 7930 8422. www.newzealandhc.org.uk
South Africa South Africa House, Trafalgar Square, WC2. ☎ 020 7451 7299. www.southafricahouse.com
USA 24 Grosvenor Square, W1. ☎ 020 7499 9000. www.usembassy.org.uk

Lost property
At an airport
Heathrow, ☎ 020 8745 7727
Gatwick, ☎ 01293 503 162
Stansted, ☎ 01279 680 500
Luton, ☎ 01582 395219
London City, ☎ 020 7646 0000
On the Tube
☎ 020 7486 2496
On a train
Phone the mainline station.

On a bus
☎ 020 7222 1234
In a taxi
☎ 020 7833 0996
Lost or stolen credit cards
Visa, ☎ 0800 89 17 25
Mastercard, ☎ 0800 96 47 67
American Express, ☎ 01273 620 555

See also 'Embassies and consulates' and 'Medical services'.

Medical services

There are Accident and Emergency (A&E), or **casualty**, departments at several central London hospitals, including St Thomas's or the Royal London. Other major hospitals have Minor Injuries Units only. Emergency **dental treatment** can be obtained at the Royal London Hospital 19.00–23.00.

Charing Cross Hospital, Fulham Palace Rd, W6. ☎ 020 8846 1234.
Chelsea Hospital, Royal Hospital Road, SW3. ☎ 020 7730 0161.
Guy's Hospital, St Thomas St, SE1. ☎ 020 7955 5000.
St Thomas's Hospital, Lambeth Palace Rd, SE1. ☎ 020 7928 9292.
Royal London Hospital, New Road, E1. ☎ 020 7377 7000.
University College Hospital, Gower St (entrace Grafton Way), WC1. ☎ 020 7387 9300.

For further confidential advice you can also call *NHS Direct*, ☎ 0845 46 47.

Private medical services are increasing in Britain all the time. If you are uninsured or otherwise prepared to pay on the spot, the best approach is to visit the nearest hospital to your hotel (National Health or other), explain that you want private treatment, and take their advice on what to do and where to go. There is a long list of private general practitioners in the Yellow Pages under Doctors (Medical). You can reach a private doctor at any time at *Doctorcall*, ☎ 07000 372 255.

Newspapers

The *International Herald Tribune*, *USA Today* and many European papers are available at larger newsagents in central London (for example, at mainline rail stations), as are *Newsweek* and *Time*. Free magazines *TNT* and *Southern Cross* are good for backpackers. For the domestic press, see p 59.

Opening hours

Shops Usually open 09.00 or 09.30 to 17.30 or 18.00. In the West End shops may close 19.00 or 20.00 Mon–Sat. On Sundays, most shops are open 11.00–17.00, but some 10.00–16.00 or 12.00–18.00.

Banks See p 59.

Post offices See p 57.

Pubs Usually 11.00 or 11.30 for 12 hours to 23.00. Last orders are called ten minutes before closing, with 20 minutes 'drinking-up time'. Some still open 11.30–14.30 and 18.00–23.00. A few have licences to stay open later.

Restaurants Most have the same opening hours as pubs, but smarter establishments close in the afternoon, and often also on Sunday evenings.

Museums and galleries See p 36.

Business hours Usually 09.00–17.00 or 17.30. Nothing important closes for lunch, nor for any annual holiday, but not much is open on a Saturday morning and almost nothing on a Sunday or Bank Holiday.

Pharmacies

Staff in pharmacies (often called 'chemists') are well qualified to give on-the-spot advice, and to sell commercial treatments for most minor aches and pains. For anything serious a doctor's **prescription** will be needed, and you will probably have to pay a fee for it to be made up (currently £6.10). *Boots* is the biggest chain, but numerous smaller outlets are equally good. *Bliss*, 5 Marble Arch, is open 09.00–24.00 Mon–Sun.

Public toilets

It is recommended that you use the toilets in department stores, museums and fast-food restaurants rather than public lavatories in London. Facilities are also usually available for a small fee at main rail stations and a few Tube stations.

Religious services

The rich variety of religious belief existing in the capital gives a complex array of opportunities for participation. The best place to find out about church services in the centre of London is from the Saturday editions of *The Times* or *Daily Telegraph*.

> One day someone will write a special guide to the varieties of Christian practice available for consumption in Britain. One reason why this is important, quite apart from personal conviction or preference, is the growing inaccessibility of churches—often the most important piece of architecture in a town or village. Frequently the only way you will see a church interior is by going to a service. In London, this is increasingly the case. They used to be open all the time, and many still are, but vandalism, or the fear of it, has been the cause of the firmly locked doors which you will certainly encounter on many of the walks.

Roman Catholic masses are conducted at Westminster Cathedral at 08.00, 10.30, 12.30 and 17.30 Mon–Sat and and 08.00, 09.00, 10.30, 12.00 and 17.30 Sun. ☎ 020 7798 9097. The usual times for communion services at the **Anglican** churches in the centre of London is between 09.30 and 10.30, but for details it will be necessary to consult the notice boards outside individual churches. There are many weekday services at City churches, and often a mid-week service, as well as those on Sunday, in less central locations.

Non-conformist churches are almost always closed except for services. For centralised details of services, the following phone numbers may be useful: otherwise you must rely again on notice boards

Baptist, ☎ 01235 517 700. www.baptist.org.uk
Methodist, ☎ 020 7486 5502. www.methodist.org.uk
Quaker, ☎ 020 7387 3601. www.quaker.org.uk
Unitarian, ☎ 020 7240 2384. www.unitarian.org.uk
United Reform, ☎ 020 7916 2020. www.urc.org.uk

For places of worship for **other faiths**:

Buddhism, ☎ 020 7834 5858. www.thebuddhistsociety.org.uk
Hinduism, ☎ 020 8965 2651. www.swaminarayan-baps.org.uk
Islam, ☎ 020 8903 9024. www.mcb.org.uk
Judaism, ☎ 020 7543 5400. www.bod.org.uk
Sikhism, ☎ 020 8574 1902.

Time

In Britain a system of daylight saving, originating during the First World War, still applies. *British Summer Time* begins towards the end of March, when the clocks are put forward one hour, and ends at the end of October. Otherwise *Greenwich Mean Time* (GMT) is followed; this is 1 hour behind Continental European time, 5 hours ahead of US Eastern Standard Time, and 10 hours behind Australian Eastern Standard Time. For more on GMT, see Chapter 49.

Tipping

Tips are usually included in bills at hotels and increasingly at middle-grade and more expensive restaurants (as an 'optional' 12.5 per cent service charge). There is no need to add to this, unless you have received exceptional service and suspect that the person who provided it will not receive the tip in the bill. Do not tip in bars, pubs or coffee shops, unless the drinks are brought to your table.

It is usual to tip as follows:

Taxis and mini-cabs 10–15%
Cheaper restaurants 10% minimum
Hairdressers or barbers 10–20%
Cloakroom attendants 50p–£1 (unless a notice says 'Don't')
Porters, etc, in 4/5 star hotels £1

Tourist information

There are London Tourist Board offices at:

Heathrow Terminal 3 Open 06.00–23.00 daily
Heathrow Terminals 123 Underground station Open 08.00–18.00
Britain Visitor Centre 1 Regent St (near Piccadilly Circus)
Waterloo Station
Liverpool Street Station

None of these offices is contactable by phone.

Web directory

The following list is not exhaustive. Other addresses are given in descriptions of sites in the main text.

Entertainment, music and outings

Aquarium	www.londonaquarium.co.uk
Bookings (sites, events)	www.cityeventsonline.com
Children's outings	www.londonforkids.com
English National Opera	www.eno.org
Legoland, Windsor	www.legoland.co.uk
London Eye	www.ba-londoneye.co.uk
London Symphony Orchestra	www.lso.co.uk
Lord's Cricket Ground	www.lords.org
Notting Hill Carnival	www.carnival.com
Royal Albert Hall	www.royalalberthall.com
Royal National Theatre	www.nt-online.org
Royal Philharmonic Orchestra	www.rpo.co.uk
Royal Shakespeare Company	www.rsc.org.uk
Theatre guide	www.officiallondontheatre.co.uk
Ticket Master	www.ticketmaster.co.uk
Time Out	www.timeout.com/london
Wimbledon Lawn Tennis	www.wimbledon.org
Vinopolis City of Wine	www.vinopolis.co.uk
Zoo	www.londonzoo.org

Food, drink and shopping

Covent Garden Market	www.coventgardenmarket.co.uk
General listing (shops, restaurants)	www.streetsensation.co.uk
Hamley's toyshop	www.hamleys.com
Harrod's	www.harrods.com
Harvey Nichols	www.harveynichols.com
Liberty	www.liberty-of-london.com
Marks and Spencer	www.marksandspencer.com
Oxford Street	www.oxfordstreet.co.uk
Portobello Market	www.portowebbo.co.uk
Pizza Express	www.pizzaexpress.co.uk
Selfridge's	www.selfridges.com

Galleries

Barbican	www.barbican.org.uk
Courtauld	www.courtauld.ac.uk
Crafts Council	www.craftscouncil.org.uk
Dulwich	www.dulwichpicturegallery.org.uk
Estorick Collection	www.estorickcollection.com
Guildhall	www.guildhall-art-gallery.org.uk
Hayward	www.haywardgallery.org.uk
ICA	www.ica.org.uk
National	www.nationalgallery.org.uk
National Portrait	www.npg.org.uk
Queen's	www.the-royal-collection.org.uk
Queen's House	www.nmm.ac.uk
Royal Academy	www.royalacademy.org.uk
Serpentine	www.serpentinegallery.org
Tate Britain	www.tate.org.uk
Tate Modern	www.tate.org.uk
Wallace Collection	www.wallace-collection.org.uk
William Morris	www.lbwf.gov.uk/wmg
Whitechapel	www.whitechapel.org

Gardens and parks

Chelsea Physic Garden	www.cpgarden.demon.co.uk
Historic Parks and Gardens Trust	www.londongardenstrust.org.uk
Royal Botanic Garden	www.kew.org.uk

Government

City of London	www.cityoflondon.gov.uk
City of Westminster	www.westminster.gov.uk
Greater London Authority	www.london.gov.uk
Houses of Parliament	www.parliament.uk

Museums

Apsley House	www.vam.ac.uk
Banqueting House	www.hrp.org.uk
Bethnal Green Museum of Childhood	www.museumofchildhood.org.uk
British Library	www.bl.uk
British Museum	www.british-museum.ac.uk

Buckingham Palace	www.royal.gov.uk/palaces/bp.htm
Cabinet War Rooms	www.iwm.org.uk
Chiswick House	www.english-heritage.org.uk
Cutty Sark	www.cuttysark.org.uk
Design Museum	www.designmuseum.org
Dr Johnson's House	www.drjh.dircon.co.uk
Eltham Palace	www.english-heritage.org.uk
Geffrye Museum	www.geffrye-museum.org.uk
Gilbert Collection	www.gilbert-collection.org.uk
Hampton Court Palace	www.hrp.org.uk
Hermitage Rooms at Somerset House	www.hermitagerooms.com
HMS Belfast	www.iwm.org.uk
Horniman Museum	www.horniman.demon.co.uk
Imperial War Museum	www.iwm.org.uk
Jewish Museum	www.jewmusm.ort.org
Kensington Palace	www.hrp.org.uk
Kenwood House	www.english-heritage.org.uk
London Transport Museum	www.ltmuseum.co.uk
Marble Hill House	www.english-heritage.org.uk
Museum of Garden History	www.museumgardenhistory.org
Museum of London	www.museumoflondon.org.uk
National Army Museum	www.national-army-museum.ac.uk
National Maritime Museum	www.nmm.ac.uk
National Trust	www.nationaltrust.org.uk/regions
Natural History Museum	www.nhm.ac.uk
Royal Air Force Museum	www.rafmuseum.com
Royal Artillery Museum (Firepower!)	www.firepower.org.uk
Royal Observatory	www.rog.nmm.ac.uk
Science Museum	www.sciencemuseum.org.uk
Shakespeare's Globe Exhibition	www.shakespearesglobe.org
Sir John Soane's Museum	www.soane.org.uk
Somerset House	www.somerset-house.org.uk
Southwark Cathedral	www.dswark.org.uk
Theatre Museum	www.theatremuseum.org
Tower Bridge Experience	www.towerbridge.org.uk
Tower of London	www.hrp.org.uk
Victoria and Albert Museum	www.vam.ac.uk
Westminster Abbey	www.english-heritage.org.uk

Travel and tourism

Automobile Association	www.theAA.com
Avis car hire	www.avis.co.uk
Best Western Hotels	www.bestwestern.co.uk
Big Bus Company	www.bigbus.co.uk
British Tourist Authority	www.visitbritain.com
Budget Car Hire	www.budget.com
Car parking	www.ncp.co.uk
City Airport	www.londoncityairport.com
Coach travel	www.gobycoach.com
Disabilities—travelling with	www.holidaycare.com

Docklands Light Railway	www.dlr.co.uk
Eurostar	www.raileurope.co.uk
Gatwick Airport	www.baa.co.uk
Guides	www.london-guides.co.uk
Heathrow Airport	www.heathrowairport.co.uk
Hertz car hire	www.hertz.com
Holiday Inns	www.hiexpress.co.uk
Ibis Hotels	www.ibishotel.com
London Tourist Board	www.londontouristboard.com
London Transport	www.londontransport.co.uk
Luton Airport	www.london-luton.com
Marriott Hotels	www.marriotthotels.co.uk
Radisson Edwardian Hotels	www.RadissonEdwardian.com
Railtrack	www.railtrack.co.uk
Royal Automodible Club	www.rac.co.uk
Stansted Airport	www.baa.co.uk
Tours	www.britishtours.com/bt
Travelling in London	www.transportforlondon.gov.uk
Walks	www.walks.com
Work permits	www.fco.gov.uk
Youth hostels	www.yha.org.uk

BACKGROUND INFORMATION

London: an analysis

Character

What is London's defining characteristic? What simple quality, what aspect of its past, and its present, can be picked out? Or, if you like, what distinguishes London from Paris, New York, Rome, Sydney or any other great city?

The essence is conveyed in a single ordinary word: '**spread**'. London is spread out. Edmund Burke in the 1770s phrased it well, if not very colourfully: 'an endless addition of littleness to littleness, extending itself over a great tract of land'.

For most of its history, and all its modern history, London has spread, often out of control, along the River Thames in both directions, up and down the residual Roman roads, and then all over the intervening fields, swallowing villages whole, and even an entire county (it was called Middlesex). During the Roman occupation, and again briefly in the early Middle Ages, the City wall had some significance, but, for most of London's history, the wall as a retaining device was a hopeless failure.

Is there any kind of 'wall' or boundary today? Yes: it is known as the **Green Belt**, a ring of countryside roughly marked by the orbital motorway, the M25. Both these phenomena were invented in the mid-20C. The authorities, from monarchs to governments, notably Elizabeth I and Charles I, had long tried to stop the spread of London, and the Green Belt was the 1945–51 Labour government's attempt. It is successful for now. But for most of London's history, urban sprawl has crept unchecked over the countryside.

Unlike ripples on a pond, the spread is not even, but markedly sideways, west and east more than north and south. London is lemon-shaped. The reasons for this have been chiefly geographical and commercial—the river valley has terraces south and north, and was the focus of trade—but have become social and definitive. This horizontal spread, this single spectrum west to east, from rich to poor, leisure to work, culture to vulgarity, conveys sufficient dualities to give London its meaning. We do not recognise a North End or its opposite.

Population

Population changes and increases have broadly related to the city's spread. **Roman London**, crammed into its walls, was substantial, with 50,000 inhabitants at its peak. This was followed by a less-understood period when Saxons and Danes disputed the terrain, but after the Norman Conquest in 1066 London grew steadily, in the City and upmarket Westminster and the north bank between, as well as spreading east beyond the Tower. Around 1340, the population was again 50,000. And for the next 300 years the population grew, but was contained.

The growth of which we can still see evidence really got underway in the 17C, with new estates such as Covent Garden and Bloomsbury setting the trend. From 1600 to 1700 the population tripled from 200,000 to 600,000. The **Great Fire** did not halt progress in the least: on the contrary, it stimulated building in the west, a tendency which continued steadily during the 18C when one aristocratic landlord after another developed his leasehold estates to house the new and demanding middle class.

Yet even then population growth was steady rather than astonishing. By 1800 the total was near one million. London was the biggest city in the world, and the most important place in the world, too (Paris being in difficulties at the time), but the explosion of people was just about to happen. **Industrial development** was the cause, less marked in London than in Britain's northern cities, perhaps, but a profound movement nevertheless. First, jobs in agriculture declined as a result of new technology, so young people moved into towns where work was available. Second, the invention of **railways** enabled people to travel to work in London but to live out in newly built suburbs. Third, improvements in **public health** prolonged life. By 1900 London had really become what William Cobbett, the early 19C radical, had called 'the great Wen' (another word for a huge carbuncle), a giant conurbation stretching from Ealing to East Ham, and Edmonton to Croydon, with a population of 6.5 million—a great, broad, spreading, yet cluttered, vividly spinning hub for the British Empire.

Great Britain

'Great Britain' was a name coined by James I to signify the merging of the crowns of England and Scotland in 1603. It was less arrogant than it may sound. 'Great' meant 'greater' as opposed to 'smaller'—not 'great' as in 'I'm the greatest.' The English parliament did not like it, but the term became enshrined in legislation under the Act of Union in 1707. In a further Act of 1801 the full title of the nation became the United Kingdom of Great Britain and Ireland, the last modified to Northern Ireland after 1922.

Also in 1801, the national flag, the Union Jack, was devised, with the cross of St Patrick superimposed on those of St Andrew and St George. ('Jack' refers to the rod on a ship's mast to which a flag is attached). A very few clever people can sort out these elements and say when it is being flown upside down. Since the reign of Edward I, Wales has been no more than a territorial dominion: that is why under current devolution developments, Scotland has a parliament but Wales only an assembly.

1900 was in these senses, a peak. Until the Second World War the phenomenon of spread in fact continued, with suburbia, assisted by the 'Tube', creeping out into the fields of Ruislip and Cockfosters, and the population reaching 8.5 million in 1939. There were more people, but they were more healthily spread over more space. After the War, the **decline** in population numbers was quite significant. The reversal coincided with the establishment of the Green Belt, post-war austerity and the development of new towns and, gradually, inner-city deprivation. The trend has, however, been reversed again in the last 20 years: people are moving back into the centre; old offices are being turned into apartments; and, at the same time, new offices are being built, in Docklands and elsewhere. We are starting on a new period of growth. Watch out for the belt bursting soon.

Geography

'Spread' also reflects London's topographical character, its location in a **river valley**. London is where it is because the Romans found, opposite some decent rising ground on the north bank (the City), just sufficient in the way of a mound among the marshes on the south bank (Southwark) to create a crossing point. They built their settlement on the north side and in due course put walls round it, with the bridge to the south and a road network in key directions. Oxford Street, Edgware Road and the A10 to Cambridge, for example, still run along the Roman system. Generally, the terrain all around is level. The river threads its way through marshes lying east and southeast, and to a lesser extent in the west, with small tributaries from gently rising ground to north and south. Hills, at Hampstead, Highgate, Harrow in the north and Norwood and Anerley to the south, are rarities. In this sort of landscape there are few natural barriers to stop spread.

The very first instance of spread was actually a separate development, the Saxon monastic foundation of Westminster, on an island among the open marshland to the west. Edward the Confessor located his palace here in 1060, but meanwhile settlement had begun in the area in between. Then a series of magnificent ecclesiastical palaces began to appear along the riverside south of the Strand, with the temple of the Knights of St John (now the Inner and Middle Temple) and a royal palace at Bridewell completing the line up to the River Fleet and the boundary of the City. On the eastern side, in 1080, the new Norman king, William I, created his great fortress, the Tower of London, in a successful attempt to scare the local inhabitants into submission.

These patterns of nearly a millennium ago—abbey and palace in the west, military control in the east, commerce and people in the centre, with Southwark always a lesser settlement across the river—set the pattern not only of development, but also of character: government in one place, law in another, commerce in a third. London is still like this. The **City** is still a distinct entity. Although no longer the conglomeration of people in their trades, guilds, crafts and businesses which made up medieval and Tudor London—because for 150 years now people have commuted in to their work—it is still sharply separate from parliament and the monarchy. No monarch has lived at a palace in the City since the early 16C. Until the development of Docklands in the last 15 years, the centres for banking, insurance and the financial markets have all been in the EC2, EC3 and EC4 postcode areas and nowhere else. Likewise, since medieval times, national government has buried itself in Westminster, latterly in **Whitehall** specifically, so that the term 'Whitehall' itself has come to mean central administration in just the same way as 'the City' means finance.

Monarchs have been more mobile. They began happily at **Westminster**, and Whitehall too, but moved a little way to St James's, then to Kensington and finally to Buckingham House, while maintaining their river establishments at Greenwich, Richmond and Kew (once upon a time), at Hampton (for a while) and Windsor (still). Kings and queens have liked the river, as all Londoners do, and their palaces have mostly related to the narrowing Thames. But commerce has sought breadth, and the Thames downstream from London—the gateway to Europe and leading to the great oceans of the world—has been used for trade and by the navy.

It is kings and queens we must thank first—followed by Victorian public spiritedness—for the fact that London is not just buildings all over a river valley.

If monarchs had not commandeered land for hunting, and reserved it for that purpose, we would have no **royal parks**. The parks, too, show a western spread—St James's, Green, Hyde, Kensington, and Kew, Richmond and Hampton further upstream. Regent's Park lies north but its origin is the same. The royal desire to hunt gave way to recognition of a public need for open spaces, and the bequest of such areas for this purpose. The benefits of health, exercise, community and communing with nature in parks were obvious. Thanks to 19C planners, a further ring of spaces, from Hackney to Battersea, were saved, often with difficulty, from the depredations of speculative builders. These include some fine public parks still worth visiting today: they are perhaps a little seedy and very much given over to the great 20C preoccupation, sport, but they often conserve Victorian features. The same thinking has led to the conservation of Hampstead Heath, Wimbledon Common and Epping Forest. The spread of London happily contains many of these green bubbles.

Green 'lungs' cannot entirely disguise the endless acres of **housing**, yet even here the spread over place and time gives variety and range. There is hardly any of the medieval city left to see—the Fire accounted for that—but Staple Inn survives to give an idea. After 1666, we can see red brick give place to yellow stock brick, and after 1834, Classical give place to Gothic, then to Arts and Crafts, to garden suburbs and outer suburbia as a whole. The elegant Georgian terraces and squares which sprouted up in Westminster and the West End, first in brick and then in stucco, led onwards and upwards to Kensington, and outwards to Victorian speculations from Camberwell to Kilburn, and downwards to the slums of Wapping and Lambeth.

Nineteenth-century notions of charity brought housing improvements for the deserving poor (not all the poor were so regarded) through the work of such philanthropists as George Peabody, an American banker, and Sidney Waterlow, a former Lord Mayor and owner of a printing business. Then the idea of apartments or flats spread to the middle class. Terraces gave way to semi-detached houses and then returned as townhouses. Villas as seen in the Villages of Regent's Park spawned acres of imitative smart **suburbs**, such as Pimlico and Clapham. Local authority housing followed some of these examples, first the garden suburb, then the great apartment blocks, which in the postwar world became sharply vertical and modern. Twenty per cent of London's housing is local-authority owned, but today 56 per cent is owner-occupied, and 24 per cent privately let. All these varieties of home, their gardens carefully tended (as a rule), can be seen and studied, spreading over the land.

People

If spread defines London's spatial character, what about its personality? As a city, it is brisk, impatient, sometimes rude, conscious of its past and apparently traditional, but so keen on money and fashion that it is always modern and open-minded about change. Londoners have always been adaptable. In their time, they have seen upheavals and demonstrations, but never a revolution. Their city has caught fire and been bombed but never, since Rome, been occupied territory. The character of Londoners, 'Cockney' now incorporating all its newer residents as much as the old-timers, really is as perky, sharp and cynical as its stereotypes in TV and film suggest.

Cockneys

The word 'cockney' was originally an insult, meaning a feeble townsperson as opposed to a strong rustic character, but is now used more affectionately. True Cockneys are supposed to be born within the sound of the bells of St Mary-le-Bow, Cheapside: if this were construed accurately, they would today comprise a paltry number. But the term still applies more widely to both people and their accent.

Though they still have a strong accent, London's natives are now too diverse to retain their rhyming slang. This is something tourists often listen out for in vain, and of which little anthologies are published. The most obvious examples remain those which have passed into everyday speech ('loaf' for head—loaf of bread, 'titfer' for hat—tit for tat, 'butcher's' for look—butcher's hook, 'rabbiting on' for talking—rabbit and pork, and 'scapa' for go—Scapa Flow). Other, cruder examples, which the reader may briefly contemplate, include Jimmy Riddle (needing a ...), Khyber Pass (up the ...), Hampton Wick (gets on my ...), cobblers awls (nonsense).

London remains, on the whole, safe to travel and walk in. It accommodates rich and poor, without any apparent desire to equalise them. It now contains 7.2 million people, from 50 different **ethnic groups**, speaking 70 different languages. It may not be at the centre of Europe, but it is genuinely international.

Diversity

Spread has helped to achieve all this harmoniously, and has given London a rich collection of areas of separate character. The City, with a capital C, means finance. With New York and Tokyo, London is one of the three great financial centres of the world. That means markets for 24-hour dealing, international banks and fund managers; offices, and some churches, but little housing and no palaces; and today more telecommunications than personal visiting. It may have been rebuilt many times—after 1666, again virtually by the Victorians, again partially after the Second World War, and again partially in the 1980s and 1990s—but the City still reflects '**old money**'.

The 'new money' is in Docklands. It is trendier, smarter, brasher than the City, with a rash of exciting new architecture, colour and buzz. For business, it is competing with the City head-on. Yet you only have to walk out of Docklands for a half-mile (and in Chapter 48 you can) and you are in the old **East End**, where there is no glamour at all, just working-class grit and stoicism ('mustn't grumble'), still alive and struggling on.

London is a **capital city**—of England for 1000 years and of Great Britain since 1707—and 'capital' means Westminster. Parliament is here (and of 651 MPs, 74 represent London constituencies). The monarchy's main palace is here, and always has been—though the monarchs have moved around. The chief offices of the Church of England are here, or a river crossing away. There are 150 diplomatic missions and 18,000 diplomats, all in this area. And Whitehall, as we have noted, is a metaphor for the civil service.

The West End used to mean high-quality housing but now it means shops and theatres. So does Covent Garden. Since the 1860s South Kensington has been synonymous with museums. Since 1951 the South Bank, and now Bankside too, mean **culture** in a broader sense. As they have spread and changed, these inner areas have formed their own separate characters.

But so equally have outer areas. Coming in to London by train, or by bus or taxi from Heathrow, may give an impression of grey or red-brick uniformity, but that is misleading. The disparate **villages** which used to cover these 609 square miles, now the largest conurbation in Europe, have not been squashed out of existence. Their centres, churches, old pubs, and often their 18C villas and 19C terraces, still have unique visual character, distinct from each other, and their own separate meanings, some constant, some changing. Greenwich, for example, was a little old riverside town with a royal palace, later a magnificent naval hospital and the site of meridian 0.00: it still is. Dulwich was a genteel Jane Austen-type of village, with a famous school and the world's first purpose-built art gallery: it still is. Hampstead was full of impecunious poets and artists: it still is, but now they are richer. Muswell Hill had a giant Victorian exhibition centre and perfect Edwardian shops: it still has.

But other 'villages' have coped with startling **change**. Brixton was a prosperous 19C suburb: now it is the centre of a bracing Afro-Caribbean culture. Rotherhithe was first a place for boat building and embarkations to new worlds, then a great dock: now it has riverside housing, ornamental canals and parks. Notting Hill was all respectable Victorian terraces: now it is smart shops and restaurants, an antique market, a carnival and a film-set.

Travel

A spreading city needs good transportation systems, and in London new inventions for travel stimulated each tranche of growth. When London was of **walking** size, as when Dr Johnson's biographer James Boswell first arrived in 1762, he would leave his lodgings in Downing Street, proceed to Fleet Street, then call in at Covent Garden and spend the evening at Berkeley Square, covering several miles every day. There was no question of using a horse, to ride or to draw a carriage. Boswell could not afford to be carried in a **sedan chair**: only the rich employed chairmen. But this was no problem: the streets were a pleasure, and he could go by boat to Vauxhall, or cross the Thames by one of the new bridges.

But in the early 19C, as London expanded out into Kennington and St John's Wood, one needed a **horse** to get into the centre for work, or out of the centre for restoration of the spirits in the countryside. Islington became the destination for Sunday afternoon tea excursions, by chaise, not on foot. New middle-class terraces needed mews for grooms and carriages, stagecoaches departed from the main taverns, and the post raced out from Robert Smirke's new General Post Office. The London of Charles Dickens's *Pickwick Papers* had arrived: more villages had come within reach. The illustrator George Cruickshank cynically depicted the onward march of suburban housing, out towards Kilburn, Peckham and Holloway by now. Trade drifted gently back and forth on the new **canals**. Still dependent on the horse, in 1829, George Shillibeer copied Parisian precedent by introducing an 'omnibus' to ply between Paddington and the City.

The same year, a greater transport revolution broke. In 1829 the first London **railway**, with a steam engine, entered service from London Bridge to Greenwich. Euston mainline station opened in 1837. In 1851 the Great Exhibition in Hyde Park drew thousands of visitors, the great majority coming to London by train. By 1860, the termini and tracks into King's Cross, Liverpool Street, Victoria,

Waterloo and Paddington were all largely operative. And 1862 saw the opening of the Metropolitan Line, the first 'underground' track, hollowed out of the Marylebone Road from Paddington to Farringdon and covered over, now part of the Circle Line. The age of the rail commuter had begun.

The railways, not the car, were the cause of London's huge growth. The private **car** now clogs the city, poisoning it with fumes and blocking the streets, preventing buses and taxis from performing their public service. But the railway and Tube, whatever their current problems, are the lifelines which connect London together, the strands of its web, and the means by which it has spread.

For the visitor to this expansive and complex city, the transportation system is important, to get into the centre or out to places which matter, such as Hampton Court and Windsor, and others such as Kew and Greenwich in between. But in the centre, walking is often preferable. The architecture, any city's most obvious link with the past, is all around you and best seen on foot. Places in which to experience the contemporary culture—galleries, theatres, shops, museums, offices and public buildings, and venues for eating and drinking and other pleasures—although of course diffuse, as we have said, are accessible on foot throughout the long east–west centre, round the bend in the river, on both sides of it from the Tower to Westminster, and up to Hyde Park and the Zoo. Emulate Boswell: get around. If walking seems too much, use buses, especially routes 6, 8, 9, 11, 15, 19, 23 and 25 or take the Tube, or the DLR, or Silverlink trains. Or use the **black cabs**, normally driven by typical Londoners who are usually, but not invariably, chatty and always dogmatic.

Heart

This is the essential London, past and present, which you must discover, ingest and will inevitably come to love. To those of us who live here, and love it ourselves, this extract from a letter by Charles Lamb (one of us), written 200 years ago to his friend William Wordsworth (not one of us—a countryman), still captures the essence:

> *I don't much care if I never see a mountain in my life. I have passed all my days in London, until I have formed as many intense and local attachments as any of your mountaineers can have done with dead nature. The lighted shops of the Strand and Fleet Street; the innumerable trades, tradesmen, and customers, coaches, wagons, playhouses; all the bustle and wickedness around Covent Garden, the very women of the Town; the watchmen, drunken scenes, rattles; life awake, if you awake at all hours of the night; the impossibility of being dull in Fleet Street; the crowds the very dust and mud, the sun shining upon houses and pavements, the print shops, the old bookstalls, coffee-houses, steams of soup from kitchens, the pantomimes— London itself a pantomime and a masquerade ... the wonder of these sights impels me into night walks about her crowded streets, and I often shed tears in the motley Strand from fulness of joy at so much life ....*

London: a few key facts

Founded Soon after AD 43

Area 609 sq miles (1580 sq km) or 429,954 acres (178,000 hectares), the largest city in Europe

Population 7.2 million (8 million in 1961, 7.7 million forecast for 2021), the largest in Europe. Of these, 2.8 million live in inner London, 4.4 in outer London.

Average age 34.8

Numbers aged under 25 35% (national average 31%)

Ethnic proportions 25% non-white, 30% in inner London (national average 6.6%)

GDP £107billion (17% of national GDP)

Government 33 boroughs, including the City of London and City of Westminster

Governing body The Greater London Authority (established July 2000) is responsible for transport, planning, economic development, environment, police, fire and emergency services, culture and health

Elected representatives Mayor and members of the London Assembly

Parliamentary seats 74 (55 Labour, 13 Conservative, 6 Liberal Democrat)

Housing 3 million dwellings, of which 56% are owner-occupied (national average 67%), 20% local-authority owned, 24% privately rented

Work Main industries (as a proportion of GDP) are finance and business services (38.6%), other services (16.3%), distribution, hotel and catering services (14.2%), manufacturing (10.4%), transport and communication (10.3%), public administration (4.8%), other industries (5.5%).

Workforce 2.8 million, plus 670,000 commuting daily from outside London

Travel In the rush hour, 448,000 people and rising use the railways, 394,000 and rising use the Underground and DLR, 68,000 and falling use buses, 14,000 and falling use cars, 17,000 use coaches and 23,000 cycle or use motorbikes.

Airports Heathrow (62 million passengers per year), Gatwick (30 million), Stansted (10 million), London City Airport (14 million)

Chronology of London history

AD 43 Growth of London begins when invading Romans cross the Thames close to the site of the later London Bridge. Population approx. 30,000.

50 First London Bridge built and London established.

61 London is severely damaged in conflict between the forces of Queen Boudicca (Boadicea) and the occupying Romans.

200 London becomes a walled city in which trade flourishes. Population approx. 45,000–50,000.

410 Romans withdraw from London, which reverts to a farming community.

604	First St Paul's Cathedral founded.
834–1014	London regularly invaded by Vikings.
871	During the reign of Alfred the Great (Saxon) the office of alderman is created.
878	Lundenberg established by Alfred, in City.
1014	London continues to be coveted by warring factions and is stormed by Olaf, king of Norway. But stability returns, and soon London replaces Winchester as capital of England.
1060	Edward the Confessor becomes King and removes his court to Thorney Island, west of the City, having been refused monetary support. Westminster Abbey built on this site for the Benedictines.
1066	Norman Conquest. City besieged. William I crowned. A charter is established guaranteeing City's privileges. Population approx. 14,000–18,000.
1078	Building of White Tower (Tower of London) begins.
1097	Westminster Hall built by William II as part of the medieval palace of Westminster.
1100–1140	In return for supporting the Crown, the city is allowed to raise its own taxes and elect its own governors.
1123	St Bartholomew's hospital founded.
1176	London Bridge rebuilding in stone begins.
1189	Jews banned from coronation of Richard I and attacked. Henry FitzAilwyn chosen as first Mayor of London. Population approx. 20,000–25,000.
1215	As a reward for financial support King John recognises the authority of the Lord Mayor and agrees to the election of 24 aldermen. Dissatisfied, the city helps rebellious barons draft the Magna Carta.
1224	Westminster Hall becomes the chief law court of England.
1225	St Thomas's Hospital established in Southwark.
1245	New Westminster Abbey constructed.
1280	Old St Paul's Cathedral completed.
1290	Jews expelled from England.
1298	Recorder elected as City's senior law officer and judge.
1326	Riots against the king result from city squalor.
1338	Edward III makes the Palace of Westminster the regular meeting place of parliament.
1348	Black Death halves the city's population to 30,000.
1381	Peasants' Revolt. An army of labouring people wanting to end feudalism, led by Wat Tyler, occupies London for two days. Tyler is killed by the Mayor.
1394	Rebuilding of Westminster Hall begins.
1397	First of Dick Whittington's four terms as Mayor begins.
1399	City and Parliament combine to depose Richard II.
1400–1500	Increasing wealth of merchants begins to undermine feudalism. Guilds established. London becomes one of the great ports of the Europe.
1411	Construction of the Guildhall begins.

1450	Jack Cade leads Kentishmen in protest against the financial oppression and incompetence of Henry VI. They occupy London for three days.
1461	Edward IV, victor in the Wars of the Roses, knights many citizens of London in return for the city's support.
1476	Caxton sets up first printing press at Westminster.
1483	Murder of Princes in the Tower.
1499	Perkin Warbeck, pretender to the throne, hanged at Tyburn.
1500–1600	Financial expertise and a flourishing market establish London as a major trading port with the Continent.
1509	St Paul's School opens to provide secondary education.
1533	Closure of monasteries during the Reformation increases land available for building. Wealthy merchant families become the new gentry.
1553–1558	Period of instability under the fiercely Roman Catholic Queen Mary. Executions take place at Smithfield in the City.
1562	Elizabeth I forbids any new building within three miles of the City, in response to the growth of slums.
1572	First wave of Huguenot refugees reach London.
1599	Globe Theatre built by Richard Burbage on Bankside.
1600	New landed families begin to construct mansions on estates extending into the 'West End'.
1603	London begins to resent the autocratic style of the Stuart king, James I. But the king opens St James's Park to public.
1605	'Gunpowder Plot' to blow up Parliament and the royal family discovered.
1613	Globe Theatre burns down. New River opened to supply London with water from Hertfordshire.
1616	Queen's House, Greenwich, begins—the first classical building in Britain.
1630	First square in London built at Covent Garden.
1642	Civil War begins. London finances Parliament.
1649	Charles I beheaded in Whitehall. Commonwealth declared by Oliver Cromwell.
1650	Population approx. 350,000–400,000.
1652	First coffee-house open in St Michael's Alley, Cornhill; it becomes a centre for financial transactions and intelligence.
1656	Jewish families re-enter London.
1660	Reaction against fanatical religious egalitarianism leads London to support the return of Charles II. Royal Society founded.
1663	A theatre opens in Drury Lane. The 'King's Performers' are the only company allowed in London.
1665	The Great Plague kills up to 60,000 and causes a major exodus of wealthy families to outlying districts.
1666	The Great Fire begins in Pudding Lane and destroys most of the medieval city of London.
1667	The Act to allow rebuilding stipulates that stone or bricks

	should be used. London appoints commissioners to be responsible for sewers.
1675	Christopher Wren begins construction of the new St Paul's Cathedral. The Royal Observatory is built at Greenwich.
1685	Religious intolerance forces French Protestants to seek refuge in England, many settling in London.
1692	Chelsea Hospital, designed by Wren, is completed.
1694	Royal Charter establishes the Bank of England to pay for war with France.
1696	Howland Great Wet Dock (later Greenland Dock) constructed in Rotherhithe, the first wet dock in England.
1698	Whitehall Palace destroyed by fire.
1700–1750	Wren's rebuilding of the City completed and the skyline distinguished by the spires of 51 churches and St Paul's Cathedral. Villages to the west of London engulfed by spread of building. Gin becomes serious social hazard, repressed by higher duties. Population approx. 600,000.
1712	George Frideric Handel settles in London.
1720–1760	Many major London hospitals built: Guy's, London, St George's, Westminster and Middlesex.
1732	Covent Garden Theatre opens.
1733	City commissioners no longer prepared to dredge Fleet River, so plans are made for it to be arched over.
1739	London's second bridge constructed at Westminster.
1743	Riots against Act to control the sale of gin.
1749	Bow Street Runners set up to prevent crime in the vicinity of the legal centre of London.
1750	Population approx. 650,000.
1756	New Road from Marylebone to Pentonville.
1759	British Museum opens.
1768	Royal Academy of Arts founded.
1770	First canal in London completed from River Lea to Thames.
1774	Radical Whig reformer, John Wilkes, is elected Mayor.
1780	During the Gordon Riots, 850 lose their lives in protest against the repeal of anti-Catholic legislation.
1785	*The Times* newspaper first published (as the *Daily Universal Register*).
1787	Opening of first Lord's cricket ground.
1788	Bank of England's new building designed by John Soane.
1798	Demands for parliamentary reform are suppressed when members of the London Corresponding Society are arrested.
1799	During the next few decades various acts are passed to allow the construction of commercial docks. Traffic on the Thames remains in private hands.
1801	First census records 1,096,784 inhabitants, most of whom live outside the City boundaries. London continues to be a centre for reform agitation. River Police established.
1803	Surrey Canal completed from docks to Peckham.
1810	Riots in support of radical MP Sir Francis Burdett.

1811–19	Waterloo and Southwark Bridges designed by John Rennie.
1812	Regent's Canal joins the Grand Union to link London with Midland industries.
1812–27	John Nash develops Regent Street and Regent's Park.
1818	London still without effective local government. An Act establishes the system for voting in parish officers.
1820	The 'Cato Street conspiracy', a plot to assassinate the Cabinet, is uncovered. Earth removed from new docks helps to stabilise land around Belgravia.
1825	Buckingham House altered by Nash. London Bridge rebuilt to a Rennie design.
1826	University College—the 'godless institution'—founded in Gower Street.
1829	Metropolitan Police Force established, its area of operation excluding the City. First regular horse-drawn bus service begins along Marylebone Road. Construction of Trafalgar Square begins.
1831	Reform Riots in London. Sir Thomas Wilson begins his 40-year attempt to enclose Hampstead Heath. Opposition is based on free public access for local inhabitants.
1832	Construction of National Gallery begins.
1833	Police called to disperse reform protestors in Clerkenwell. First railway sanctioned by parliament to run between London Bridge and Greenwich. 10,000 die in cholera epidemic, leading to ban on burials within city boundaries.
1834	Palace of Westminster destroyed by fire.
1835	London exempted from Municipal Reform Act, so many pressing public health problems can not be dealt with effectively. The City establishes its own police force.
1836	University of London established.
1837	Geological Museum opens. London Bridge Station opens.
1838	Euston Station opens.
1840	Sir Charles Barry designs new Houses of Parliament in Gothic style.
1841	First station in City opens at Fenchurch Street. Isambard Kingdom Brunel designs Hungerford Bridge.
1843	First tunnel under the Thames from Rotherhithe to Wapping.
1844	Width of streets in the entire metropolis controlled by a new Act.
1848	Women students admitted to University of London.
1849	*Morning Chronicle* publishes Henry Mayhew's systematic survey 'London Labour and the London Poor'. Cholera kills 14,000. Harrod's opens as a small grocery store.
1850	Brunel designs Paddington Station.
1851	Great Exhibition held in the Crystal Palace, Hyde Park, afterwards rebuilt at Sydenham.
1852	Victoria and Albert Museum begins in Marlborough House. King's Cross Station opens, designed in functional style by Lewis Cubitt.

Monarchs since 1066

The Houses of Normandy-Blois
William I (the Conqueror) 1066–1087
William II (Rufus) 1087–1100
Henry I (Beauclerk) 1100–1135
Stephen 1135–1154
Henry II 1154–1189
Richard I (Coeur de Lion) 1189–1199
John (Lackland) 1199–1216
Henry III 1216–1272
Edward I 1272–1307
Edward II (deposed/murdered)
    1307–1327

The House of Anjou
Edward III 1327–1377
Richard II (deposed/murdered 1400)
    1377–1399
Henry IV 1399–1413
Henry V 1413–1422
Henry VI (murdered) 1422–1461
Edward IV 1461–1483
Edward V (murdered) April–June 1483
Richard III (killed in battle) 1483–1485

The House of Tudor
Henry VII 1485–1509
Henry VIII 1509–1547
Edward VI 1547–1553
Lady Jane Grey July 1553
    (for 9 days, executed 1554)

Mary I 1553–1558
Elizabeth I 1558–1603

The Houses of Stuart and Orange
James I (James VI, King of Scotland)
    1603–1625 (Scotland 1567–1625)
Charles I (beheaded) 1625–1649
Charles II (exile 1649/50 and
    1651/60) 1649–1685
James II (deposed) 1685–1689
William III and Mary II 1689–1702
    and 1689–1694
Anne 1702–1714

The House of Hanover
George I 1714–1727
George II 1727–1760
George III 1760–1820
George IV 1820–1830
William IV 1830–1837

The House of Saxe-Coburg and Gotha
Victoria 1837–1901
Edward VII 1902–1910
George V (House renamed Windsor)
    1910–1936
Edward VIII 1936
George VI 1936–1952
Elizabeth II 1952–

1855	Metropolitan Board of Works set up for London under new Act. First postbox installed in Fleet Street. Disreputable Bartholomew Fair, founded in 12C, finally closed.
1858	The 'Great Stink', outside the Houses of Parliament, results in a bill for creation of a sewerage system for London.
1859	Vauxhall Gardens, once elegant pleasure gardens, close.
1860–1880	Many refugees from Eastern Europe enter London. They tend to settle east of the City, in Aldgate, Whitechapel and Spitalfields.
1863	First underground railway opens (Metropolitan Line).
1865	Blackfriars Bridge, designed by Joseph Cubitt, opens on 18C site. St Pancras, Charing Cross and Broad Street stations open. St Thomas's Hospital moves to Lambeth.
1866	Riots develop when police try to break up a Reform League meeting in Hyde Park. Speaker's Corner is established as a result.

1867	Clerkenwell Prison bombed in an attempt to free Fenians (Irish radicals).
1868	Gothic-style hotel built at St Pancras.
1870	Victoria Embankment, covering sewer and railway line, opens. First tramcar service runs from Brixton to Kennington and Whitechapel to Bow.
1871	Hampstead Heath saved for the public.
1872	Bethnal Green Museum, part of the Victoria & Albert Museum collection, opens.
1873	Natural History Museum at South Kensington opens.
1874	Liverpool Street Station opens.
1880	Norman Shaw designs Bedford Park, Chiswick, which becomes the forerunner of the garden suburb.
1884	Toynbee Hall opens in the East End as the first 'university settlement'. Longitude 0° at Greenwich becomes prime meridian for the world.
1887	'Black Sunday'. Social Democratic Federation meeting in Trafalgar Square broken up by police, causing casualties.
1888	Series of murders in Whitechapel associated with 'Jack the Ripper'. New Unionism begins with a strike by badly paid women matchmakers.
1889	First London dock strike to protest at falling wages unites a traditionally competitive workforce. London County Council established.
1893	Tate Gallery (Tate Britain) construction begins on site of the old Millbank Prison.
1894	Tower Bridge opens. First Lyons tea shop opens in Piccadilly.
1897	Queen Victoria celebrates her Diamond Jubilee.
1899	Marylebone Station opens amidst controversy and local opposition.
1901	Population of London: Inner London 4,536,267, Greater London 6,506,889 and the City only 37,709.
1902	Water supply for London controlled by new Metropolitan Water Board.
1905	Aldwych and Kingsway opened.
1909	Selfridge's opens. Port of London Authority takes over running the docks.
1910	Privately owned powered motor vehicles begin to challenge horse-drawn public transport.
1911	Second London dock strike against insecurity of employment. Siege of Sidney Street, Stepney, against two Eastern European anarchists.
1915–18	German Zeppelins bomb London.
1926	General Strike.
1928	Science Museum opens on present site.
1932	Green Belt established around London to control spread of suburbs.
1933	London Transport created.
1936	British Broadcasting Corporation begins television broadcasts

from Alexandra Palace, north London.
At the Battle of Cable St, East Enders and anti-fascists prevent Oswald Mosley's blackshirts marching through mainly Jewish districts. Crystal Palace burns down.

1939	Population of Greater London reaches its peak at 8,615,050.
1940	City and East End severely damaged by bombs during the Blitz. Docks are targets for air raids. 30,000 lives and 130,000 houses lost.
1945	A mixture of private and public funds set aside for rebuilding of London.
1947	Legislation to protect buildings of historic and architectural importance begins.
1951	Festival of Britain on the South Bank helps revive the nation during postwar austerity. The Royal Festival Hall opens.
1954	Temple of Mithras discovered as the City is rebuilt.
1956	'Pea soup' fogs of London eliminated after the Clean Air Act is passed.
1958	Race riots in Notting Hill.
1960–1968	London becomes known as the 'Swinging City', as music and fashion develop.
1963	New Euston Station built, destroying Victorian entrance arch.
1965	Greater London Council formed as strategic planning authority.
1967	Conservation areas (now more than 300) identified and given statutory protection. Docks begin to close in response to declining traffic and economic pressure. Rennie's London Bridge sold and rebuilt in Arizona.
1968	Anti-Vietnam War demonstrations escalate into confrontation with police in Grosvenor Square. Ronan Point, a tower block, collapses after a gas explosion.
1969	Greater London Development Plan proposes housing, open space and major road works in and through London.
1974	Covent Garden market moves to Nine Elms, South London, but its existing buildings are saved for redevelopment.
1976	Museum of London opens. National Theatre company moves from the Old Vic Theatre to new South Bank complex.
1981	London Docklands Development Corporation created by government to co-ordinate use of derelict docks. Brixton Riots. First London Marathon.
1982	Billingsgate market moves to Docklands. Barbican Centre opens. Thames Barrier completed to prevent flooding of London. IRA bombs Hyde Park and Regent's Park bandstand.
1983	Population of London falls to 6,754,500. IRA bombs Harrod's. First woman Lord Mayor, Lady Mary Donaldson.
1985	London Regional Transport set up without GLC control.
1986	Greater London Council abolished.
1987	Docklands Light Railway opens. Heathrow Terminal 4 opens. Fire at King's Cross Underground station.

1988	Gatwick North Terminal opens.
1989	Gates erected at entrance to Downing Street.
1990	ILEA (Inner London Education Authority) abolished.
	Courtauld Galleries open in Somerset House.
1991	Sainsbury Wing of the National Gallery opens.
1992	Canary Wharf Tower completed. Leadenhall Market bomb.
	Windsor Castle fire.
1993	Bishopsgate bomb. Buckingham Palace opens to the public.
1994	Eurostar trains begin services to France and Belgium via
	Channel Tunnel.
1995	National Lottery launched.
1996	Isle of Dogs damaged by IRA bomb.
1997	Labour government elected with promise to reinstate a
	London-wide authority.
1999	Millennium celebrated at midnight on 31 December.
2000	Dome opens—and closes.
	New Mayor of London (Ken Livingstone) elected and Greater
	London Authority established. London Eye opens.

Further reading

There is a huge bibliography on London. Here are some suggestions for further reading, focusing on books in or only recently out of print but including some older publications and established classics.

History

Recent histories of London include Stephen Inwood, *A History of London* (1998); Roy Porter, *London: a Social History* (1994) and Francis Sheppard, *London: a History* (1998). All three are sound academically, but Porter is probably the easiest to read. More specialist histories include Nicholas Barton, *Lost Rivers of London* (1998 edition); Andrew Saint and Gillian Darley, *The Chronicles of London* (1994); Stephen Porter, *The Great Fire of London* (1996); and Stephen Halliday, *The Great Stink of London* (1999), the idiosyncratic and absorbing story of the sewage system. *London: the Biography* (1999) by the important London author Peter Ackroyd is part history and part imagination. *The London Enclycopaedia*, edited by Ben Weinreb and Christopher Hibbert (1992 edition), is properly encyclopaedic, although it does not include entries on individual Londoners. For a sense of the past and independently a joyful read, consider James Boswell's *Life of Johnson* (first published 1795), Boswell's *London Journal*, covering the years 1762 and 1763, and Samuel Pepys's *Diary*, which he kept for the years 1660 to 1669. There are abridged editions of these classics. Equally redolent of its period is John Stow's *Survey of London* (first published 1603): Stow was another Londoner who loved his city and deplored the way it was changing.

Art and architecture

Many of those who enjoy London's architecture today have been influenced by *Nairn's London* (1966): Ian Nairn inspired us to look at buildings with joy tempered by criticism. More serious sources are Yale's (formerly Penguin's) *The Buildings of England* series, named after their original author, Nikolaus Pevsner. All the original editions have or are being revised: *London I: The City of London* (1997) by Simon Bradley; *London II: South* (1983), *London III: Northwest* (1991) and *London IV: North* (1998) by Bridget Cherry; *London Docklands* (1998) by Elizabeth Williamson and *The City Churches* (1999) by Simon Bradley. The last two are in paperback. *London V: East* and *London VI: Westminster* are eagerly awaited in the next year or two. Other recommended books include Edward Jones and Christopher Woodward, *A Guide to the Architecture of London* (2000 edition); S.E. Rasmussen, *London: the Unique City* (1991, a reprint of a 1930s classic); and anything by John Summerson. Also useful are books in the Thames & Hudson *World of Art* series, such as *Victorian Architecture* and the biographies of Wren and Hawksmoor and, if you can find a copy, Ann Saunders's *Art and Architecture of London* (1983).

For paintings of London you are referred to the catalogues of the relevant galleries and that of the Museum of London, and in particular its *London in Paint* (1996). For art in London, the major gallery guides are recommended: *The National Gallery's Companion Guide* by Erika Langmuir, *The Tate Britain Companion to British Art* by Richard Humphreys and *The Tate Modern Handbook*.

Literature

London has featured in thousands of novels. The following list is a short, subjective choice of classics, compiled to reflect the immediacy with which London springs to life in their pages: Daniel Defoe, *Moll Flanders* (1722); Charles Dickens, anything except *Hard Times*, but especially *Great Expectations* (1860), *Little Dorrit* (1857) and *A Christmas Carol* (1843); John Galsworthy, *The Forsyte Saga* (completed 1922); George Gissing, anything but especially *The Nether World* (1889); George and Weedon Grossmith, *The Diary of a Nobody* (1892); Arthur Morrison, *A Child of the Jago* (1896). There are innumerable more recent fictional accounts, including Elizabeth Bowen, *The Heat of the Day* (1948); Joyce Carey, *The Horse's Mouth* (1944); Peter Carey, *Jack Maggs* (1997); Graham Greene, *The End of the Affair* (1951) and *The Ministry of Fear* (1943); Hanif Kureishi, *The Buddha of Suburbia* (1990); Rose Tremaine, *Restoration* (1989).

General

For reference purposes, besides *The London Encyclopaedia* mentioned above, you may find useful *The Times History of London* (1999 edition); *A History of London in Maps* (1990); *The Oxford Dictionary of London's Place Names* (2001); and *Discovering London Plaques* (1999), a guide to the blue plaques (see p 8). An up-to-date *London A–Z* or Collins *London Street Atlas* is indispensable. For further browsing, Paul Bailey's *Oxford Book of London* (1995) is recommended, as is David Piper's *London* (1980), now out of date in some respects but still a pleasure to read. *City Secrets* (2001) is a recent anthology of hidden treasures. For visual pleasure alone there are some excellent books of photographs of London by Jason Hawkes and Angelo Hornak.

In addition, there is a vast range of specialist guide books. Particularly useful are the individual Time Out guides to *Shopping*, *Eating and Drinking* and *London for Children*.

THE GUIDE

The City

The City is different, atypical. A distinct historic entity covering 677 acres, just over one square mile, it is older than any other part of London and still retains, against all the pressures to modernise, an ancient constitution and a rigid independence. Yet its character has changed completely, from centre of the capital (for about 1750 years) to solely a business centre (for the past 200 years). And because it is a business centre, the visitor has to work harder here than in an area like Westminster, for example, which consciously shows itself off to tourists. The City is reticent and secretive, its past has to be uncovered and its preoccupations—profit, tradition and independence of your or anyone else's opinion—have to be accepted.

The remains of the Roman and medieval walls somehow both confirm and symbolise this sense of separation, as do the narrow streets and the glowering offices. There are more tall buildings here than anywhere else in London except Canary Wharf, and even if not many are actually skyscrapers—the atmosphere is nothing like New York—they make a dark and forbidding architecture, entirely different from the West End. The feeling is confirmed by the closed doors of the livery companies, the silence at weekends, and the exclusive implications of terms like 'within the Square Mile' and 'something in the City', which seem to ignore the fact that this little area is surrounded by a great metropolis.

All this is very surprising because there has been plenty of change, some of it devastating. The Great Fire in 1666 and the Blitz of 1940–41 were two such disasters, bringing destruction and upheaval on a terrifying scale. Both were followed by vigorous new building programmes, of which the most distinctive memorials are, respectively, Sir Christopher Wren's churches and the Barbican Centre. Shifts of population, with or without such crises, have been continuous.

You might think that such upheavals would have changed attitudes. But despite new architecture, old customs were retained. The City is still a more sombre and serious place than elsewhere in London, especially on Sundays when no one is at work and few parishioners survive to attend the churches. Go to the Tower or St Paul's any day, but for the rest make it weekdays only, when by day especially the streets are more lively, with plenty of bars and restaurants buzzing and office workers spilling out onto the streets with their drinks.

- Use the City of London Information Centre in St Paul's Churchyard for up-to-the-minute details, especially on opening times. Open 09.30–17.00 Mon–Sun in summer; 09.30–17.00 Mon–Fri. 09.30–12.30 Sat in winter. ☎ 020 7332 1456.

1 • The central City

The centre of the City is the nameless seven-way crossroads with exits from Bank station on each corner. Such an important place needs a name: the Corporation of London should hold a public competition to decide on one. For the station itself, however, the name 'Bank' was an inspiration, unspecific but highly symbolic, and actually referring to the Bank of England. Our first walk will make a circle around this vital centre.

• Distance: 1 mile. Time: 1½ hours. Tube: Bank. Map 8, 9.

From Bank station (**Map 9,3**) take exit 3—toilets can be found *en route*—to the Royal Exchange. Reaching the daylight, turn round, stand for a while with your back to the ornate portico and observe the melée of taxis, buses, office workers: tourists are unlikely to be prominent here. Various public buildings can be picked out, including the Bank of England on your right, the Mansion House, and James Stirling's eye-catching No.1 Poultry. No church is visible, confirmation perhaps that despite the volume of Wren's oeuvre all around you, at its heart the City has become an entirely commercial and secular world. Beside you is a fine war memorial, and in Cornhill a new statue to **James Greathead**, whose deep-tunnelling techniques enabled the Northern Line and Waterloo and City Line to burrow under the Thames a century ago. In the foreground, Sir Francis Chantrey's equestrian statue of **Wellington** (1844) coolly oversees the battling traffic.

The **Bank of England**, on your right, is a key institution with no obvious means of identification. Thanks to Sir Herbert Baker's work between the wars, its appearance is bulky and anonymous rather than photogenic. Sir John Soane's curtain wall (*c* 1800), with its idiosyncratic Corinthian pilasters and columns with puffy bases looking soft as marshmallows, is all that remains of his master-piece. The windowless façade was a reaction to the Gordon Riots of 1780, when the old Bank was attacked. As we walk round the exterior, there is pleasure to be had from noting the rich variety of motifs Soane used to enliven the surface.

The Bank of England was founded in 1694 to co-ordinate the raising of capital for the war with France. Its operations began in the Grocers' Hall but the house of the first Governor Sir John Houblon, representing a small part of the present site, was taken over in 1732. The idea of a central bank came from William Paterson, a Scot and a prominent City merchant. The Bank's original powers were limited compared with the range it later developed, becoming the government's own bank, printer of banknotes and guardian of the currency, and overseer of the financial system generally. The Bank was a public limited company until nationalised in 1946. Its relations with government, before and after this, were always sensitive, and it hated to be thought of as merely Whitehall's spokesperson in the City. The Bank's dreams were fulfilled when in 1997 the Chancellor of the Exchequer Gordon Brown agreed to its independence, giving it authority to manage interest rates without constant reference to the Treasury.

The destruction of Soane's Bank to make way for Baker's changes has been described as the greatest architectural loss of the century. This is all very well, but what was a responsible public organisation to do? It could hardly preserve itself as a museum at public expense, regardless of operational difficulty. In reality

Baker's Bank is extremely respectful to Soane, reproducing many of his interiors, transferring the Court Room by Sir Robert Taylor (Soane's predecessor as Bank architect) to a new site on the first floor, and even, in 1989, reconstructing Soane's Bank Stock Office to house a museum. If the Bank of England fails as architecture it is because of all this compromise: the retention of the original exterior wall with Baker's massive pile sitting heavily inside was still wasteful of space. Note Sir Charles Wheeler's sculptures (*c* 1930), including a Britannia-like figure in the pediment, a reference to the Bank's nickname, the 'Old Lady of Threadneedle Street'. Kenneth Grahame rose from the position of clerk to Secretary of the Bank, leaving in 1908 just before the publication of his book *The Wind in the Willows*.

Keeping the Royal Exchange on your right, go up **Threadneedle Street**. The rear façade of the Royal Exchange is worth seeing: it repeats the fine tower of its predecessor, built on this site after the Great Fire by Edward Jerman. Note the large seated bronze of *George Peabody* (d. 1869), the American philanthropist whose apartment blocks still represent one of London's main strands of charitable housing (see p 321).

Cross Threadneedle Street and enter Bartholomew Lane, past the **Bank of England Museum**, which is well organised and lit and contains a fine collection of bank notes, silver and some Roman artefacts, as well as interactive displays to bring you into the 21C. Open 10.00–17.00 Mon–Fri. ☎ 020 7601 5545.

At the end of Bartholomew Lane, Throgmorton Street to your right reveals two tower blocks: the nearer is the **Stock Exchange** by Llewellyn-Davies and Co. (1969) and the farther is Tower 42 (see Chapter 4). Ahead of you is the former head office of NatWest Bank by Mewès and Davis (1921–32), with a handsome Classical façade. Continue to the left down Lothbury, past the energetic Venetian Gothic of the former Overseas Bankers' Club (1866), built as offices for the General Credit Company, to **St Margaret Lothbury**, a particularly worthwhile Wren church (1683–92, tower completed 1700).

The church exterior is quite modest but its south side runs confidently along the street, with a passageway on the east leading to a small garden. The tower, acquired with the second tranche of Coal Tax, as in many Wren churches, has a slender lead spire and contains the relatively grand pedimented porch. Inside all is dark, red and opulent with a comforting smell of polish. The furnishings are unusually rich, having in many cases been transferred from other Wren churches demolished in the 18C and 19C: the paintings came from St Christopher-le-Stocks and the amazing top-heavy screen and tester from All Hallows the Great. Crowded it certainly is, but St Margaret's remains one of the most appealing of City church interiors. ☎ 020 7606 8330.

As you leave and turn right, note a glum *Sir John Soane* by Sir William Reid Dick (1937) on the back of the Bank. The Tivoli corner on the northwest end of the Bank, where Lothbury meets Prince's Street and Moorgate, was based on the Temple of Vesta at Tivoli, which Soane had admired and drawn on his youthful travels, here recreated for foggy London. The pedestrian cut-through was Sir Herbert Baker's idea, a convenient vandalism. Look to the right up Moorgate to see some fine examples of 1890s City offices, absurdly pretentious now but a visual feast. Not much survives of the 19C interiors, here or elsewhere, because of the philosophy of 'façadeism'. To your left, out of sight on the west side of

City churches

The City still possesses nearly 50 places of worship, not a huge number when compared with the figure of over 100 before the Great Fire in 1666, but almost an embarrassment in one of the least populated areas of London.

Of those built by or under the supervision of Sir Christopher Wren after the Fire, 23 still survive plus the towers of six others. Although Wren's plan for a new city was largely abandoned (except for King Street and Queen Street), this integrated body of work from one coordinating mind is a unique collection in any city anywhere. The churches were built on medieval sites, hence their often irregular ground plans, and were financed by taxes on coal entering London under various Acts, the first in 1667, with an extra tranche to build the spires *c* 1700.

Some visitors with a collector's interest find it fun to pick off the churches one by one: nearly all are included in the walks that follow. Most are open Mon–Fri from 10.00 or earlier to around 16.00, and for services. In addition, there are several interesting pre-Fire churches.

Prince's Street, is the **Grocers' Hall**, the fifth on its site, rebuilt after a fire in 1965.

Cross Moorgate and go west along Gresham Street (**Map 8,4**) as far as Guildhall Yard on your right. You could detour briefly to the left down **Old Jewry**, so named from its tradition of Jewish residents. The tower of the demolished church of St Olave is visible on your right, converted by the cheeky Victorians into an office. Beyond that is Frederick's Place, built by the Adam brothers (1776) and a rarity in the City. Back in Gresham Street, at the traffic lights, King Street stretches away to the left, to be followed south by Queen Street down a gentle slope to Southwark Bridge. These streets were one of the few major pieces of re-planning carried out after the Fire, the king and queen in question being Charles II and his wife Catherine of Braganza. No 17C work remains.

Your attention should be caught by the spectacular east end of **St Lawrence Jewry** by Wren (1671–80, restored after war damage). The grand pediment and the swags of fruit and niches between the windows are motifs taken from the Banqueting House in Whitehall: these, and the careful symmetry of the south façade, show how much importance Wren attached to the site past which the king would process on his annual visit to the Guildhall. The interior is impressive in size and quality, as befits a church used chiefly for the performance of guild ceremonies. But before you form too unqualified an admiration for Britain's greatest architect take a look at the west end of St Lawrence's. The angles are mad: the door is off-centre, and the spire is askew against the tower, which in turn is out of line with the body of the church. ☎ 020 7600 9478.

Across the yard behind the church, and the rationale for the grandeur of the east end, is the **Guildhall**, headquarters of the City Corporation.

The Guildhall is an important building, parts of which may be visited. The site is naturally, after many deliberate changes and much bomb damage, a complex arrangement to accommodate a variety of functions but the central shape of the 15C hall, built by John Croxton, master mason, survives with surprising effect.

Open 10.00–17.00 Mon–Sat. ☎ 020 7606 3030, ext. 3780. For pre-booked tours of the crypt for groups of 10 or more, ☎ 020 7332 1463.

The Corporation of London

The constitution of the City is very ancient, self-contained and jealously preserved. In effect, it is simply the instrument for local government for the area, but it is worth trying to understand as a historical phenomenon, because the Corporation of London (as it still calls itself, as if London had no other districts) is the oldest municipal body in the world.

The Corporation consists of a hierarchy of a Lord Mayor, who holds office for a year, two Sheriffs, Aldermen, and the Common Council. The Court of Aldermen and the Court of Common Council are a kind of parallel of the House of Lords and House of Commons, in that the former acts as an upper house. Often they have behaved in that traditional manner, with the former defending established practice and the Common Council more open to change. The Lord Mayor is elected from among and by the Aldermen, and must previously have been a Sheriff. The Sheriffs are elected by the City Livery Companies (see below), one being already an Alderman and the other lay: Sheriff (shire-reeve) is the oldest office of all, dating back to 1132. Aldermen are elected for life by the City wards, who also elect annually Common Councilmen from among their freemen. The concept of freedom of the City dates back to the process of acquiring training in a particular craft through a guild, to a standard of proficiency which enabled the individual to become 'free' of that guild and free to practice in the City.

The eccentric entrance was added in 1788 by George Dance the Younger, the City architect, reflecting in a combination of Gothic and Hindu styles the City's medieval past and its new preoccupation with Indian trade. The hall behind is of considerable size (151ft x 48ft, and 89ft high) and in its heyday was inferior only to Westminster Hall. In the 19C it was given a similar hammerbeam roof, burned in the Second World War; the present roof is by Sir Giles Gilbert Scott, whose postwar restoration and improvements include the whole of the Corporation's offices to the north. It is used for meetings of the Common Council, ceremonies such as elections, and State banquets, including one in November when the prime minister makes an important speech.

Note the fine display of statuary, from a range of periods, including J.F. Moore's figure of **Lord Mayor Beckford** (1770), the particularly fine **William Pitt the Elder, Earl of Chatham** by John Bacon Senior (1782), and **Wellington** by John Bell (1856). As eye-catching as any is Oscar Nemon's seated bronze of **Winston Churchill** (1959). Note the limewood figures of **Gog and Magog**, mythical warriors supposed to have fought for Britain in a pre-Christian battle against Troy.

It is usually possible to see the **crypt**, which is the largest surviving medieval crypt in London. The entrance to the **Guildhall Library**, an excellent and user-friendly resource, is in Aldermanbury to the west, and contains a bookshop that specialises in London's past. Also worth a visit is the **Guildhall Clock Museum**. Open 09.30–16.30 Mon–Fri. ☎ 020 7332 1868.

Across the yard to the east is the **Guildhall Art Gallery**, housing the City's own domestic art collection. It contains some fine Pre-Raphaelite works and pictures from other periods, especially of London, as well as the overwhelming bequest of Sir Matthew Smith's studio (see p 120). The collection is hung in a fine new space, somewhat cramped in places because room had to be found for a monster work, *The Defeat of the Floating Batteries* by John Singleton Copley (1783), an over-the-top battle scene. During excavations for the art gallery in 1988–95, the remains of London's Roman amphitheatre were uncovered and incorporated into the basement, although not currently accessible to view.

Open 10.00–17.00 Mon–Sat, 12.00–16.00 Sun. Admission charge (free after 15.30 and Fri). ☎ 020 7332 1632. Recorded information ☎ 020 7332 3700.

Leaving the Guildhall complex, cross Gresham Street and walk south down Milk Street, the name an example of the market specialisation of medieval Cheapside. Turn left into Cheapside and cross the busy street. The tower of **St Mary-le-Bow** rises in grandeur, undwarfed by the surrounding office blocks.

> Often referred to as Bow Church, the name derives from Latin, 'de arcubus', and is presumed to refer to the bows or arches formed by the vaults in the crypt. Bow bells were a famous peal: it used to be said that only those born within their sound could truly call themselves Londoners.

The church features one of Wren's most ambitious steeples (224ft high) completed early, in 1679, financed from the initial rebuilding and costing nearly as much as the rest of the structure, from which it is almost detached. Allow your eye to ascend from the earth to the heavens. At ground-floor level, there are two grand entrances based on a Hardouin Mansart hotel in Paris, the destination of Wren's only visit abroad in 1665; then come strong, largely plain, storeys but with an iron balcony on the Cheapside façade; then Ionic pilasters surrounding the belfry; and then a series of pillared or decorated levels at each stage of the spire, culminating in a gold dragon weathervane. There is a statue to *John Smith*, governor of the Virginia colony, in the churchyard.

The interior of the church was badly bomb-damaged and was rebuilt by Laurence King (1956–64). There are interesting furnishings of this period, some a pastiche of the original but others startlingly different, such as John Hayward's stained glass (1964). Underneath is an important medieval crypt, functioning as a pleasant and very welcome café. ☎ 020 7248 5139.

Before leaving the area, look up and down **Cheapside**. In the Middle Ages this street contained London's chief market place, a fact confirmed by the presence nearby of many of the livery companies (Grocers, Mercers, Goldsmiths). This market was replaced by the Stocks Market on the site of the Mansion House and Cheapside, widened after the Fire, became a rather grand avenue of shops, houses and offices. In 1817 John Keats lived here, writing 'To a Grecian Urn'. Since the Second World War it has become a rather disappointing mixture, with only the tower of St Mary's to elevate the spirit.

On the east side of Bow Church is Bow Lane. Go down here to get an impression of the City's earlier appearance, hemmed in by alleys and dark, enticing corners. If after the Fire Wren had been able to make the clean sweep of the City streets embodied in his masterplan, this kind of area, which we find so attractive, would have been eliminated. As it is, here you still have a sense of the medieval city.

Turn left at **Watling Street** (Map 8,6) and note, on the right, **St Mary Aldermary**, Wren's excursion into Gothic (1679–82, tower 1701–4). The tradition is that the benefactor of the rebuilding specified that the church should be in the Gothic style, but it seems more likely that Gothic was chosen because of the more than usually extensive remains of the former church. As such it is a

---

Livery Companies and Wards

The City Livery Companies developed from the medieval craft guilds typical of other major cities in Europe, which made themselves responsible for training and standards in particular skills and trades, establishing a monopoly in each. The word 'livery' refers to their distinguishing uniforms. Now that the guilds have lost their monopoly powers over most of the crafts concerned, liverymen acquire that status by patrimony (inheritance), redemption (cash purchase) or apprenticeship (surviving a period of learning). The role of the livery companies is now largely social and educational: many run schools and charitable foundations. Today there are over 100 livery companies, some new, some extremely ancient, all absorbed with hierarchy. Their company halls include some of the City's finest, and least accessible, architecture. Dates of admission to the halls are released in early February of the previous year, so anyone wishing to visit in 2004 should apply in 2003. ☎ 020 7606 3030 and ask for City Information.

The City wards are geographical units, also of great antiquity, which in the old days had local responsibilities for the supervision of trade, sanitation, etc. Now their roles are solely electoral: the voters are those who occupy premises in the area as tenants or residents. Often wards maintain clubs for social intercourse. There are 25 wards, several still with evocative ancient names, such as Bassishaw, Cordwainer and Portsoken.

---

rare example of the late 17C approach to Gothic design. The name means 'older Mary', i.e. older than St Mary-le-Bow. ☎ 020 7248 4906.

Continue left and cross the busy road to follow Queen Victoria Street eastwards. Note the traditional oyster bar at the corner of the triangular Gothic block of the 1870s, a rare survivor of the original street layout. This street was a Victorian traffic-relief scheme to create, as had long been wished, a direct route from Blackfriars Bridge to the City.

Proceeding east, on the right, is Bucklersbury House, a vast, much-disliked, 1950s office slab. During its excavation, a **Temple to Mithras**, the deity popular with the Roman army, was discovered, taken up, and relaid, in accordance with contemporary archaeological practice (now viewed with abhorrence), in the shadow of the new building. The Roman ground plan foreshadows the development of the Christian church, with a nave, aisles and apse. Several items of sculpture were also unearthed and are now in the Museum of London.

Opposite are two significant office buildings of the 1990s. That on the left at 60 Queen Victoria Street is occasionally likened to a structure from Gotham City. More congenial to most eyes is James Stirling's **No. 1 Poultry**, to the right, completed in 1998. Although compared by Prince Charles to a 1930s radio set, the pink and orange stone of the building and its continually interesting and diverse façades and unexpected entrances should ensure it affection for a few decades.

The decision to implement Stirling's design was preceded by a 20-year conflict between the City and Lord Palumbo, who wished to erect on the site a posthumous block by Ludwig Mies Van der Rohe, the great Modernist who is otherwise unrepresented in London. Such an initiative was beyond the scope of City traditionalists, and many others regretted the passing of the 1870s Mappin and Webb building, in acute-angled Gothic, which had adorned the sharp corner for so long. But the final outcome is growing on everyone.

James Stirling

The work of James Stirling (1929–95), one of the most interesting architects of postwar Britain, is proving hard to label under the conventional epithets of Modern and Postmodern. His style has sometimes seemed perversely simplified, as in the Clore Gallery at Tate Britain, but elsewhere it is richly diverse, as at No.1 Poultry, which was completed just after his death. The Neuestaatsgalerie in Munich (1977) is thought of as his masterpiece.

We are now nearly back at the Bank crossing, but several important buildings must be noted first. Across Cheapside, or Poultry, as it is called here, note the head office of the former Midland Bank, now *HSBC*, a masterpiece of Sir Edwin Lutyens (1924–39). The façade contains many of Lutyens's trademarks including disappearing Doric pilasters. If you have time, cross over Poultry to see the interior, a grand luxurious space still retaining its counters, despite changes in banking practice, amid a forest of green Corinthian columns in African verdite.

Then go a short distance down Walbrook to see one of the most important of all Wren churches, **St Stephen Walbrook** (**Map 9,5**). The playwright and architect Sir John Vanbrugh was buried here in 1726, and its rector Chad Varah founded the Samaritans charity in the 1950s. The pretty spire (late, 1713–15) is almost Rococo and was clearly an afterthought to the church proper. Ascend the steps to give yourself the knock-out experience of the interior.

The design is full of subtleties and ambiguities. The ground plan is staked out by Corinthian columns: they demarcate a cruciform space, with a two-bay nave and single-bay transepts and chancel, all within a rectangular hall. As you proceed down the nave you see that the columns also denote another shape, a Greek cross, at the four corners of which they support in trios the superbly decorated dome. It is widely believed that Wren and his craftsmen used the construction of this dome as a trial for St Paul's, but in many ways its symmetry, balance and lightness make it more engaging than its more famous successor. To sit beneath the dome of St Stephen's, with its airiness and complexity of form, is uplifting. And although the decision to include a Henry Moore altar (1972) at the centre of the Greek cross, surrounded by refreshing light-oak pews, was controversial—emphasising the centrality of Wren's design and so upsetting its longitudinal elements—a visit to St Stephen's is still unforgettable. ☎ 020 7283 4444.

Leaving St Stephen's you will be aware again of the dominating presence of the **Mansion House**, George Dance the Elder's overweight but impressive public building (1739–52) for the Lord Mayor's occupation during his year in office. Note the Palladian references on the west side but go round to the front to admire the grand portico overlooking the Bank crossing.

Dance was the City's own architect, as was his son after him, but his design had to compete with others from such luminaries as James Gibbs, John James and Isaac Ware. The Mansion House project was a significant statement of civic pride, and followed similar initiatives in Dublin and York.

It is an odd building. Despite the removal of its transverse attic storeys, it still has the top-heavy look disapproved of by the Palladians who saw it as impure, while Londoners mocked it as the 'Mare's [Mayor's] Nest'. The pediment was carved by the young Sir Robert Taylor and shows the City celebrating its trading success.

The interior contains two fine spaces—the Saloon and the Egyptian Room—and many other offices and rooms for mayoral civic uses. The decoration reflects Britain's short-lived taste for Rococo. To arrange a free, 1-hour tour as part of a group, ☎ 020 7626 3500, giving six months' notice. www.cityoflondon.gov.uk

Moving to the right round the Bank crossing, you reach **St Mary Woolnoth** by Nicholas Hawksmoor (1716–27). The name derives from that of its Saxon founder, Walnuth. It is a generation later than the Wren churches in the City and indicates, we may say, a departure up a blind alley. The heaviness, sense of mass and angularity typical of Hawksmoor were soon to be rejected in favour of a more delicate Palladian Classicism, thus leaving his six London churches as the strange but invigorating survivals of a unique style.

Not that St Mary's is a typical Hawksmoor church: here in the City, he had to squash it into an uncharacteristically small site. It was, however, one of the 50 new churches planned under the Act of 1711 (p 388), an odd inclusion given the plethora of churches all around it. The assertive façade, softened only by the semi-circular porch, has a tower much broader than deep, like Christchurch, Spitalfields. In the 1870s, William Butterfield removed the interior gallery but, in a Postmodern manner, left the brackets in place. But the overwhelming impression inside is of Hawksmoor's centralised, all-embracing squareness. Like the architect's other churches, St Mary's is one of the murder sites in Peter Ackroyd's novel *Hawksmoor* (1985), and the 'dead sound' of its bells was noted by T.S. Eliot in 'The Waste Land'. ☎ 020 7626 9701.

Lord Mayor of London

The Lord Mayor is elected each autumn and holds office for one year. The first was in 1189: all have been men. The role has been upstaged for all practical purposes by the recently introduced policy of electing a mayor for the whole of London.

On the second Saturday of November each year, the new Lord Mayor of London processes to the Law Courts to take his oath of office before the judges of the Queen's Bench. The ceremony is an ancient one, dating back to King John's time, and has taken the form of a pageant for over 500 years, originally often travelling by river, but for more than 200 years now by road, using the Lord Mayor's coach designed by Taylor and kept in the Museum of London. Today the show takes the form of a procession from the Law Courts to the Guildhall in the City. Each Lord Mayor chooses a theme, usually relating to trade or contemporary issues.

Cross **Lombard Street**, the traditional street of banks, so-named to commemorate the financiers of the Italian Renaissance, and go through the passageway to the Royal Exchange. If you are visiting during banking hours, you could go through Lloyds Bank head office from one side to the other to admire the Beaux-Arts Classicism of the 1920s, another customers' shrine of marble columns. Then cross Cornhill, which rises gently to the highest point in the City, and finally you have returned to the front of the **Royal Exchange**.

It is the third on the site, the earlier buildings being by Sir Thomas Gresham (1566) and Edward Jerman (1667). Sir William Tite won the competition to build the Exchange in 1841 with this design, unfairly in the minds of some: 'the design marks the disintegration of the classical revival in England, [with] purity thrown to the winds for the sake of richness' (Pevsner). Be that as it may, as you walk round the structure, with its mixture of little shops, statues and multitudinous entries, there is a real sense of the warm Victorian city: in this sense, the 'impurity' helps, not hinders. Tite's interior courtyard, originally open, was roofed over in 1883 and a collection of history paintings commissioned from key artists of the day. After sundry vicissitudes, the interior is now in use again as a top-of-the-range shopping mall. You can take a lofty view of the art from the mezzanine level.

Having completed this walk you are overdue for some rest and refreshment. Maybe now is the time to follow City workers to one of the many sandwich bars, cafés or pubs nearby.

2 • EC3: Leadenhall, Lloyd's and the Monument

In this walk we shall explore the southeast section of the City, often known simply as EC3, its general postcode. All areas of the City had their specialist trades: this district near the Thames has traditionally been the home of insurance and shipping companies. Old and new mix more successfully here than in EC2.

- Distance: 2 miles. Time: 2½ hours, taking in the many churches. Map 9.

Again start from Bank station (**Map 9,3**), this time taking exit 4. Walk up **Cornhill**, named after an ancient cornmarket; it is not an ascent to leave you breathless but nevertheless leads to the highest point in the City. Take time to explore the tiny alleys and courtyards stretching away either side of Cornhill to get an impression of the crowded density of the Victorian City. Particularly evocative are the *George and Vulture* and nearby the *Old Jamaica* wine bar, which was arguably the first coffee house. Daniel Defoe, who ran a hosier's shop nearby, was pilloried here in 1703 for issuing a satirical pamphlet, and the poet Thomas Grey was born here in 1716.

Nearby, note **St Michael's**, a post-Fire church (1669–72) though not one of Sir Christopher Wren's own. The original tower was, of course, Gothic and in this case so was the rebuilt version of 1715–22, the top part being the work of Nicholas Hawksmoor. But the real Gothicisation was in 1857–60 when Sir George Gilbert Scott got to work, and his efforts are still widely visible despite feeble 20C attempts to lessen their effect. ☎ 020 7626 8841.

Higher up Cornhill, on the right, no. 50 is a spectacular Victorian bank, now (such are the times in which we live) a pub. Soon after that is the doorway of **St Peter upon Cornhill**, a re-building (1677–84) by Wren on a very ancient site, dating back to a Saxon church. The foundations of these earlier buildings were re-used after the Fire and their relative fragility may explain the absence of clerestory windows and why the roof of St Peter's is quite low. It is one of only two Wren churches with a screen (the other being St Margaret Lothbury) and this one was the model. Felix Mendelssohn played the organ here in 1840 and 1842. Go behind the church into the churchyard to see the steeple and for the best view advance to Gracechurch Street (widened after the Fire) where the 'show front' can be seen, with five grand windows in a line. ☎ 020 7283 2231.

Opposite is **Leadenhall Market** (**Map 9,5**) (open 07.00–16.00 Mon–Fri), a wonderful survival, even down to some of the original shops selling game, poultry and other foods. Wander through and enjoy the sights and smells. It was built in 1880 at the instigation of Sir Horace Jones, the City's architect, who was also responsible for Billingsgate and Smithfield. It covers part of the site of the Roman forum and basilica (AD 80–100), one of the largest structures in the northern part of the Empire. The pub in the centre, the ***Lamb Tavern***, contains a fine tiled picture (1889) showing Wren directing the construction of the Monument (see below).

Leave via Leadenhall Place to see Richard Rogers's famous **Lloyd's Building** (1976–86), the epitome of High-Tech architecture, radical by any standards and especially astonishing in a conservative place like the City. The site was once occupied by East India House where Charles Lamb and John Stuart Mill were at different times clerks.

> Throughout most of its history, Lloyd's has been a unique insurance market where underwriters—risk coverers—are liable to the fullest extent, that is, every penny they own. They still meet in a 'market' with brokers who persuade them to cover risks. As such the practice has hardly changed from the business established in the late 17C in Edward Lloyd's coffee house, which became known as a meeting-place for sea-captains, ship-owners and traders, and thus a natural venue for marine insurance. Lloyd's ceased to be a coffee-house in the 1770s and the business moved into the Royal Exchange. It came to EC3 in the 1920s, to a building by Sir Edwin Cooper, and an additional building in Lime Street, accessed by a bridge, was added in 1950–57. In the early 1990s the insurance market took major losses through a series of natural disasters and those covering the extra underwriting risks, known as 'names', suffered accordingly, many losing their homes and fortunes. Now, therefore, a system of limited liability has been introduced.

The keynote of the Lloyd's building is flexibility, an unquestionably modern virtue embodied in every part of the design programme. It is the rationale for the service functions—including toilets, staircases and lifts as well as electric cables, waterpipes and air shafts—being tacked on to the exterior rather than buried inside. Rogers's argument is that services change more than basic structure.

The interior, to which entry can rarely be gained but which can be observed from Lime Street and Lime Street Passage, is a 12-floor glass atrium criss-crossed by escalators. The central space, up to four floors high, makes up 'The Room', where underwriters and brokers do their daily business. In the middle sits the Lutine Bell, once rung to signify wrecks or losses, under a little tempietto from Sir Edwin Cooper's earlier building. Tucked away on the ninth floor is an exact rebuilding of Robert Adam's Saloon from the former Bowood House, Wiltshire, now functioning as Lloyd's

The Lloyd's Building

boardroom. This enclosed gem strikes an anachronistic note against the otherwise spectacular Modernism. There is also a war memorial by Sir Edwin Lutyens.

> ### Richard Rogers
>
> Lord Rogers (b. 1933) is one of Britain's most noted contemporary architects, whose work achieved an international reputation with the Pompidou Centre in Paris, designed with Renzo Piano. A committed urbanist, he conceived an integrated scheme for the regeneration of the South Bank, for which funds have not been forthcoming. His major new work in London is the development outside Paddington station, and he designed the Millennium Dome. The term 'High Tech' has been attached to his work, and the service elements of his buildings, by their separation from the main shell, have given the wrong sort of notoriety to his style. His importance and influence are unquestionable: if London had been left in his hands for the past twenty years it would be a greater city still!

Back in Leadenhall Street, note first the 28-storey block of the Commercial Union building and a smaller 12-storey counterpart for P&O: these modern glass boxes may once have been inspiring but now are vaguely depressing against the intellectual exercise of Lloyd's. Both were bomb-damaged in 1992 and have been refaced in their original form. For a spiritual uplift, turn right to see **St Andrew Undershaft** with its 15C tower (the upper stage is Victorian) and Perpendicular main church. The name refers to a maypole that used to be erected nearby each year. The interesting range of monuments inside includes one to John Stow, the famous commentator on Tudor London—he bemoaned the new developments (as one does) and thought the place was going to ruin. ☎ 020 7283 2231.

Behind St Andrew's is an important building site. Here stood the Baltic Exchange, a trading house for commodities: an undistinguished building, it was irreparably damaged by an IRA bomb in 1992. A skyscraper, already nicknamed the 'Gherkin', designed for a Swiss insurance company by Norman Foster, is being considered for the site and if agreed on will be the City's tallest building.

A little further along Leadenhall Street (**Map 9,4**) on the same side is **St Katharine Cree** (1628–31), a rarity in date though not particularly beautiful. St Katharine's was built in the period of religious upheaval which culminated in the execution of Charles I, and perhaps indicates this uncertainty in its apparent confusion of Perpendicular Gothic and Classical. Cree derives from 'Christchurch'. ☎ 020 7283 5733.

If you have time, and having first checked that it is open (☎ 020 7626 1274), it is worth turning left up Houndsditch and left again into Bevis Marks to visit the **Spanish and Portuguese Synagogue** (Map 9,4). This is the oldest surviving synagogue in Britain (1699–1701) and owes its obscure position to the 17C prohibition against Jews building in a high street. The architect was Joseph Avis, a Quaker. The furnishings and atmosphere inside at first sight resemble a Wren church but on closer inspection prove movingly different. The interior is beautifully maintained and is still used for worship. In 1813 the father of Benjamin Disraeli quarrelled with the synagogue's authorities with the result that his son was christened, and thus was able to become prime minister some 50 years later.

If you go only a little further east, under a few dangerous roads, and noting the child figures on Sir John Cass School, you are at the site of the medieval City's old eastern gate, the so-called Aldgate, demolished with the other gates in the 1760s. This is an opportunity to look in the church of **St Botolph-without-Aldgate** (1741–44). St Botolph is the patron saint of travellers, to whom gate churches are often dedicated. This is a work by the underestimated George Dance the Elder (compare Mansion House, St Botolph Bishopsgate, etc). The best view of it is from the south, down Minories, where we shall be going. The interior retains its gallery but in the 1880s was given a rather amazing bright blue Gothic ceiling by J.F. Bentley, architect of Westminster Cathedral. ☎ 020 7283 1670.

Retreat again into the subways and rise to walk down **Minories**—named after the Minoresses of a Franciscan convent which stood just outside the City walls (**Map 9,6**). This is a traffic-ridden and fairly unpleasant street, but after going under a railway bridge, make a detour through the London Guildhall University building on your right for two pleasant surprises. First you reach the housing south of America Square, known simply as **Crescent**, where George Dance the Younger, City architect like his father, built the first crescent and circus in London, based on the precedent of Bath: only a much-restored semicircle is left but it is a civilised oasis nevertheless. Second, down the slope near the entrance to Tower Hill station, you will find a substantial wedge of **Roman/medieval wall** in a sunken garden, which represents the ground-level in Roman times. Here there is a memorial, 'erected by his sorrowing widow', to Gaius Classicianus, the procurator who restored peace after the upheaval of Boadicea's rebellion (original in the British Museum); and a bronze statue with the head of Trajan. The inner side of the wall reveals the building method, with regular square ragstone blocks and triple courses of tiles exposing the rubble interior. The highest section of the wall is the medieval part (see Chapter 5).

Turn right along Tower Hill to Trinity Square Gardens. This now unpeaceful space was created by Samuel Wyatt (1797) to set off his **Trinity House**, which still stands, serious and plain, to the north, with alterations in keeping by Albert Richardson (1950). More dominant, unfortunately, is the former Port of London Authority's headquarters by Sir Edwin Cooper (1912–22), a survivor of Britain's last period of self-confidence, overwhelmingly superior in manner and festooned with vulgar statuary.

Trinity House

The early records of this curious, very ancient and still important body were entirely destroyed in the Great Fire, but its origins may go back as far as a guild of mariners established in the reign of King Alfred. For much of its history it has been responsible for the regulation of shipping from London to the mouth of the Thames, but its main role today is as the principal authority for lighthouses, buoys, pilotage and other navigational matters round the coast of Britain. Trinity House has had its headquarters on the east side of the City, orientated towards the sea, since records began. It is governed by ten Elder Brethren, who, on Trinity Monday each year, process for a service of rededication to St Olave Hart Street.

At the roadside of Trinity Gardens is the **Mercantile Marine Memorial**, a vaulted open passage by Sir Edwin Lutyens (1926–28), in the imperialist idiom of his Great War memorials in northern France. Behind it is an especially moving memorial to merchant seaman killed in the Second World War, by Edwin Maufe, architect of Guildford Cathedral. The huge number of recorded dead who sank with their ships—let alone the untraced—is heart-breaking. Occasional poppies are left.

Cross Byward Street/Tower Hill to see **All Hallows-by-the-Tower** (Map 9,6), founded as a daughter church of Barking Abbey (see Chapter 68). The only London church with any Anglo-Saxon work still visible, this pretty, mainly 15C building is a delight whether seen from the west, with the Tower behind it, or the east, enlivening the walls of office blocks. It was extensively rebuilt in the 1950s by Lord Mottistone who gave it strange, vaguely oppressive, perpendicular vaults of grey concrete, with odd lights within circles. From All Hallows tower Samuel Pepys watched the Great Fire consume the city: Sir William Penn, later founder of Pennsylvania, was christened here in 1644, and John Quincy Adams married here in 1797. It was also the birthplace of Toc H, a charity promoting peace and Christian fellowship, founded by a former rector after the First World War. Inside, among a fine collection of furnishings of various periods, is a gorgeous font-cover by Grinling Gibbons, with cherubs playing with flowers. The crypt houses tessellated pavements from the 3C Roman house on the site, and several Saxon crosses. Open 09.00–18.00 Mon–Fri (11.00–16.00 for audio guide and under-croft), 10.00–17.00 Sat, Sun (from 11.00 for audioguide). ☎ 020 7481 2928.

Next make your way by subway under Byward Street to **Seething Lane**, so-called from a medieval word for chaff, a reference to the existence here for many years of the Corn Exchange. There is a pleasant garden with a bust by Karin Jonzen (1983) of *Samuel Pepys*, who lived here in a house provided by the Navy. At the top is another fascinating church, **St Olave Hart Street** (Olaf fought with Ethelred the Unready against the Danes in 1014 and later brought Christianity to Norway), with a walled churchyard to the south. We are outside the line of the Fire here, so some medieval work remains, including the crypt. The main church is of the 1400s with later elements including a gateway of 1658. Heavily bombed and rebuilt, it retains its intimate feel. St Olave's has a wonderful collection of monuments, including a severe-looking *Mrs Samuel Pepys* by John Bushnell. This was the Pepys's church.

Samuel Pepys

Born in London, the son of a tailor, Pepys (1633–1703) went to St Paul's School and Cambridge University. His diary opens on 1 January 1660 and closes on 31 May 1669, when he thought, wrongly, that his eyesight was failing. His wife Elizabeth, whom he married at 22—she was 15—died later that year. Pepys continued his successful career in the Navy, being appointed Secretary to the Admiralty, but was forcibly retired after the Glorious Revolution in 1688. The diary tells us in memorable detail about such matters as the Plague, the Fire, and the work of the Navy Office as well as the author's private life. It was originally written fast in a form of shorthand, apparently as a private record, which accounts for its immediacy and zest. It was not deciphered into normal English until 1825.

Beyond the *Ship* pub to the west, you reach Mark Lane. Turn right to see, just past St Olave's church hall, the surviving tower of **All Hallows Staining**, dating from *c* 1450. The church collapsed due to excessive burials, but under the tower is the 12C crypt of the former church of St James in the Wall, a hermitage which once stood on London Wall. It can occasionally be visited.

Return down Mark Lane to Great Tower Street and Eastcheap, and walk westwards (**Map 9,5**). Take a brief turn up **Mincing Lane** (from a Saxon word for nuns) to see another startling recent office block, too 'Disney' to be comparable with the Lloyd's Building, but a real eye-catcher even so. The monastic notion is revived in the name of **Minster Court** by GMW partnership (1987–91), three separate Gothicky pink-granite towers enclosing a mass of escalators flying through open space, as in Lloyd's, with service facilities tucked up in the pointed gables. It is the gables which catch the eye from the river or Bankside.

Re-cross Great Tower Street and detour down Dunstan's Hill to see the elegant surviving tower of **St Dunstan-in-the-East**, with an open Gothic steeple by Wren, and a pleasant garden created in the bombed shell of the church. Then go west along St Dunstan's Alley to **St Mary-at-Hill**, another Wren church, altered (but not abused) by James Savage in the 1820s, seriously damaged by fire in 1988, but sensitively restored again. The plan is a variant on St Stephens Walbrook and St Martin Ludgate, with a shallow square dome supported by four free-standing columns. ☎ 020 7626 4184.

If you are still keen enough, you could now cross Eastcheap to note yet another Wren church, the relatively ordinary **St Margaret Pattens**, its name based on local makers of pattens (shoes), according to Stow. ☎ 020 7623 6630. Note the Gothic-Revival offices by Roumieu and Gough (1868) at 33–35 Eastcheap. The rest of Eastcheap can be omitted, so retreat downhill to look at some buildings in the now entirely unpleasant Lower Thames Street, where traffic thunders past in both directions. These include the **Custom House**, Sir Robert Smirke's rebuilding (1812–17) of a late 18C structure by David Laing, whose work collapsed, leading to his disgrace. Smirke's Long Room, austere but impressive, is closed to the public. The fine riverside façade, in which Smirke 'Grecianised' Laing's work, would look magnificent from the opposite bank but is obscured by anachronistic trees. The plain walls of yellow stock brick in Lower Thames Street, as against the stone used on the river side, reveal the relative importance of the building's main façades. Next to the Custom House is the original **Billingsgate** fish market by Sir Horace Jones (1874–78), now offices and a dealing floor. It is worth going down to the river by Old Billingsgate Walk to look at both riverside façades: then walk towards London Bridge.

Soon you reach a Wren church which is not optional, **St Magnus the Martyr** (**Map 9,5**). Its design is problematic and it is hard to be sure how much of Wren's concept is left, but undoubtedly the general dimensions and the complex tower (based on the Jesuit church in Antwerp) are the work of the master and his team. The gap underneath the tower was hollowed out in the 1760s to allow for road widening, when the houses on London Bridge were demolished. Alterations to the interior, which is described in Eliot's 'The Waste Land', have made the columns, aisle windows and clerestory windows misaligned but somehow it does not matter. The church contains a particularly rich collection of 17C woodwork, some of it successfully altered and extended in a 1924 restoration, and the tombs of Henry Yevele, architect of Westminster Abbey, and Miles Coverdale, 16C translator of the Bible. ☎ 020 7626 4481.

The incredible hulk of **Adelaide House** (1921–25) rises next to you and you may shudder at its glazed bricks. But if you go up the stairs next to the church, to the bridge, you will see that, although still grim, it is not quite so horrible as it appears from below. This may be a moment to explore **London Bridge** (see Chapter 6). It is certainly possible to get an impression of the way the 1830 bridge carried traffic over Lower Thames Street and bent its path firmly to the left up King William Street to the Bank and the centre.

Great Fire of London

The Fire was the most important event in the history of modern London, not excluding the Second World War. It began in a baking house just east of London Bridge around two in the morning on 2 September 1666. Fires were common and to begin with there was no panic. But this one, unusually, was fanned by southeast winds which spread it north and west at an alarming pace. An early casualty was the pump under London Bridge which was the main source of water, which hampered fire-fighting, and despite the practice of pulling down houses in its path, nothing could stop the Fire spreading for 72 hours without remission. The Guildhall, St Paul's, 13,000 houses, shops, 44 livery halls and 87 churches were destroyed, but only nine lives were lost.

The first reaction was that the Fire was an act of political terrorism: the French, Dutch and Catholics were blamed. But there was little rioting or looting and calm was soon re-established. New building regulations were introduced, involving less use of timber, straight-fronted houses and wider streets. A Commission, including Sir Christopher Wren, was established to oversee the reconstruction programme: established ownership of land was respected and early plans for radical redesign were dropped. By the late 1660s many of the livery companies had rebuilt their halls and in the 1670s many of the churches were reconstructed (see Chapter 1). By 1672 most aspects of life and trade were re-established but it took another 40 years to complete the new St Paul's.

A suitable climax to the walk is to view the **Monument** (Map 9,5), to your right as you leave the bridge or down Monument Street on the left, at the end of Eastcheap. Open 10.00–17.40 all year. Admission charge. ☎ 020 7626 2717.

Erected by Wren to commemorate the Fire in 1671–76, before most of the new churches and long before St Paul's, there was a plan for it as early as the Rebuilding Act of 1666. Wren was assisted by the scientist Robert Hooke, a friend but a prickly colleague on the Commission. The location was a former church, very close to the shop in Pudding Lane where the fire began.

The Monument is a single fluted Doric column of Portland stone, 202ft high, equivalent to the distance west to the bakehouse in Pudding Lane. If you can cope with the 311 spiral steps fine views can be had from the square balcony on top: Dr Johnson's biographer James Boswell regretted attempting the climb in 1763. Above the balcony, still visible from far around, is a cupola supporting a ball of gilt copper. Wren was said to have preferred the more Classical device of a statue of a monarch or female figure, but Charles II overruled him. Around the base are inscriptions commemorating the Fire—the earlier attribution of the disaster to 'the treachery and malice of the popish faction' was very properly obliterated in the 1830s. At the west side is a large relief by Colley Cibber of the ruins left by the Fire with figures of Architecture and Science standing ready to restore the City, which, with varying degrees of success, they did. They are directed by Charles II, the only figure in a wig—the fashion was only just beginning. 'Fire' lies miserably on the right-hand side, largely crushed but still flickering a little.

Charles II (1630–85, r. 1660–85)

Charles was a womaniser and an epicurean—the actress Nell Gwyn and sundry duchesses were his mistresses—but the 'merry monarch' tag is only part of the story. His actions after the Great Fire and his sponsorship of the Royal Society, a scientific body, demonstrate a concern for British social and cultural life. And he was not indifferent to religion and politics: he was subtler as a head of state than his unfortunate father Charles I, or wilful younger brother James II; he was ready to negotiate with Louis XIV or William of Orange (later William III) according to possible advantage; and he was shrewd at dealing with internal political intrigues like the Cabal and the 'Popish Plot'. Charles was an impressive monarch, and Rochester's judgement that he 'never said a foolish thing, nor ever did a wise one' was unjustified.

Go back up Monument Street, turn right and you are now at Monument station, communicating with Bank station where you started, completing your own circle to connect with the Circle Line.

3 • Tower of London

Going to the Tower is indispensable to any visit to London. A former advertising campaign used the slogan 'The Tower is London', which is nonsense, but you can see what was meant. This is the city's most important building. If you cannot spare a whole day, do only the quicker circuit round the Tower—made clear in the text—and omit Tower Bridge and St Katharine's Dock.

• Distance: 1½ miles. Time: 1½ hours + 2½ hours for the Tower. Tube: Tower Hill. Map 9.

From Tower Hill station (**Map 9,6**) descend the steps to go under Great Tower Street. You will immediately see on your left a section of Roman wall (see Chapter 2). Turn right and follow the signs to the Tower. A planted embankment stretches up to your right, and to your left, across the dry **moat** (there are plans to re-flood it) is the north face of the Tower—at ground-level Edward I's wall, behind that Henry III's wall, and rising from the centre William I's White Tower. Obtain your tickets at the end of this path. Before going in you might like to digest **Tower Hill**, scene of many past executions (see below) but now an entirely nondescript place with a depressing underground development of tourist shops. Above this, an occasional public speaker addresses an audience of two or three. There is an official **shop** for guidebooks and souvenirs.

Tower of London

Consider taking one of the **guided tours** by a Yeoman Warder, which are amusing, well-informed and thorough.

Yeoman Warders—or Beefeaters—of whom there are about 40, are all former army warrant officers with honourable service records, who have formed part of the Tower community as guards and prison officers since Henry VIII's time. Their duties today are entirely ceremonial.

- Open March–Oct 09.00–17.00 Mon–Sat, 10.00–17.00 Sun; Nov–Feb 09.00–16.00 Tues–Sat, 10.00–16.00 Sun–Mon. Admission charge. Cafés. Shops. ☎ 020 7709 0765. www.hrp.org.uk. Buy the excellent guide, or use the one you are now reading (see the list of monarchs on p 81).

History

William I (1066–1087), who believed strongly in castles as a means of control, began his largest building, the central White Tower, in the late 1070s, as both a warning to London's citizens that they were now under occupation and a defence against invaders from the river. The Roman wall protected it on the east and river sides and ramparts were thrown up on the north and west. About 100 years later the area round the White Tower was doubled, and Bell Tower in the southwest corner and the first moat were constructed.

Even more ambitious building work was carried out by the francophile Henry III (1216–1271), still with the primary objective of protecting himself if necessary from insurgent Londoners. This resulted in a further doubling of the area, marked out by a new defensive wall on the east, north and west sides punctuated by a series of D-shaped towers, the strongest (called Devereaux, Martin and Salt) at the corners. Henry's son Edward I (1272–1307) took the process even further by adding an outer wall on all four sides and surrounding it by a new moat. The western entrance by the Lion and Middle Towers, the conversion of St Thomas's Tower to royal lodgings, and the wharf and royal entrance from the river, all date from this time. The scale and extent of the whole range of buildings has remained largely as it was then, a genuinely medieval world.

It was at this time that the whole range of functions for the space was devised. It was a defendable royal residence, a prison and a site for many other activities which require secure premises—not just the protection of the Crown Jewels, but also for use as a mint, a zoo, an armoury and a store for confidential records. The Tower's role as a prison, and the many lurid stories arising from it, has become the chief source of its fame, but up to the 1470s it functioned mainly as a secure palace and the starting point for coronation processions. Associations with violence grew with the alleged murder of Henry VI in Wakefield Tower in 1471 and the disappearance of the boy princes, Edward V and his brother, in 1483.

The consequences of the Reformation, and the perceived need to establish firm control for the Church of England, gave rise to most of the notorious imprisonments and executions. Anne Boleyn (1536) and Catherine Howard (1542) both faced their executions in the privacy of Tower Green, but Thomas More, Bishop Fisher and Thomas Cromwell were beheaded more publicly on Tower Hill, just outside the walls. Lady Jane Grey was beheaded after nine days as queen of England. And Elizabeth I herself was imprisoned here as a princess in 1554: once she became queen the regular prisoners were more likely to be Catholics. Sir Walter Raleigh's imprisonment for allegedly plotting against James I occurred between 1603 and 1615.

Royal grip on the Tower was largely broken as a result of the Civil War, when the building was seized by the Parliamentarians. After the Restoration its use as either prison or royal palace declined, to be replaced by the very modern idea of displaying it and its contents as emblems of history. Any spare space came to be filled with buildings required for ordnance (these have all since been removed except for the New Armouries, and they are now a restaurant). By the 19C, the cult of medievalism became the determining idea. All 18C changes were removed and Anthony Salvin and his successor John Taylor set about renewing in Gothic form those parts of the Tower which had been brought up to date in the previous 200 years (in other words, Classicised). The Royal Mint moved to a site northeast of the castle in 1812, and from 1834 the menagerie moved to Regent's Park to become the nucleus of the London Zoo. In 1850 the official documents record moved to the Public Record Office in Chancery Lane. Although at the time of the Chartist riots (1848) a panicky Duke of Wellington saw a renewed role for the Tower as a place of defence, and implemented some military building including the Waterloo Barracks where the Crown Jewels are now housed, the Tower has essentially been a place of peace for 150 years. Today its role as a museum of its own past seems to be permanent. But who knows?

You enter at the former **Lion Gate**, so-called because it was the location of the royal menagerie, of which the only survivors here are the ravens whom you will encounter inside. The first tower to be seen is the **Middle Tower**, part of Edward I's work but refaced in the 18C: its entrance was originally guarded by portcullises. From the Middle Tower you will pass through **Byward Tower**, a gatehouse with two round towers which, despite interesting interiors, is not open to the public.

Outer Ward

Now you are in the Outer Ward of the castle. The inner wall to your left is mostly Henry III's work: 'Mint Street', where the royal mint was originally housed, stretches to your left and in front of you is **Bell Tower**, the oldest in the castle after the White Tower, a survival of the work of the 1190s and later the prison of Sir Thomas More. At the foot of Bell Tower you can see its original plinth, which faced the foreshore of the Thames. The path ahead of you through the outer ward is still known as Water Lane, a reminder of the time when the passageway could only be negotiated at low tide.

On the right, you soon reach **St Thomas's Tower** and **Traitors' Gate**, which Edward I inserted between the older work and the river. This structure represents the outermost part of the medieval palace and, with Wakefield Tower on the left (the bridge between them is 19C), constitutes the main residential component of the Tower for medieval kings from Henry III onwards. (The forbidding name of Traitors' Gate comes from the later Tudor period, when so many prisoners made their last entry here having been rowed from Westminster: before that it was the royal entrance for arrival by boat.) St Thomas's Tower has been altered many times since it was first built, but the present display illustrates the stages of its life with a most interesting indication of the archaeology of the structure. The second room was Edward I's private hall for dining and prayer.

Across the bridge to the interior you reach the **Wakefield Tower**, the second largest in the whole complex, built between 1220 and 1240 for Henry III's private use: like the Bell Tower, it then stood at the river's edge. The upper chamber

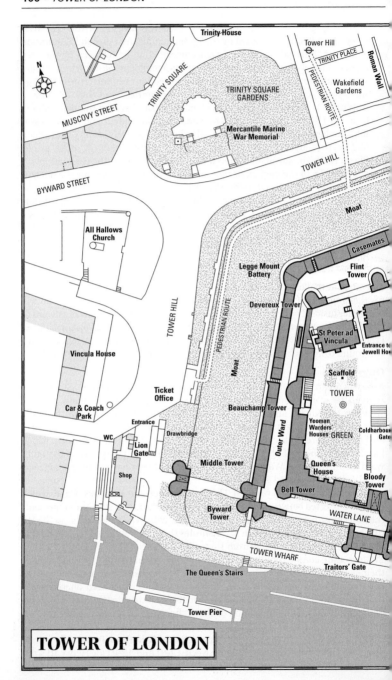

TOWER OF LONDON

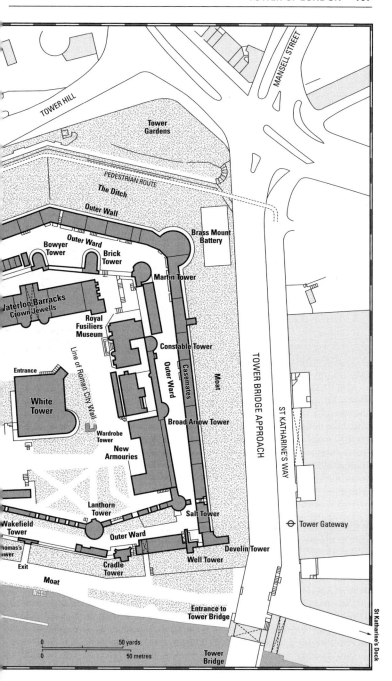

TOWER HILL

Tower Gardens

PEDESTRIAN ROUTE

The Ditch

Outer Wall

Brass Mount Battery

Outer Ward

Bowyer Tower

Brick Tower

Martin Tower

Waterloo Barracks
Crown Jewells

Royal Fusiliers Museum

Constable Tower

Outer Ward

Casemates

Moat

TOWER BRIDGE APPROACH

ST KATHARINE'S WAY

Entrance

White Tower

Line of Roman City Wall

Broad Arrow Tower

Wardrobe Tower

New Armouries

Lanthorn Tower

Salt Tower

Wakefield Tower

Outer Ward

Tower Gateway

Thomas's Tower

Exit

Cradle Tower

Well Tower

Develin Tower

Moat

Entrance to Tower Bridge

0   50 yards
0   50 metres

Tower Bridge

MANSELL STREET

St Katharine's Dock

has been furnished to recreate its appearance in the reign of Edward I, with a coronation chair copied from that in Westminster Abbey. By tradition the chapel is associated with Henry VI who, as a prisoner here, was allegedly murdered whilst at prayer through the actions of his rival Edward IV of York. Later this room housed the Crown Jewels.

Leaving Wakefield Tower by a spiral staircase, you enter the **Wall Walk**—in other words you are now standing on the wall of Henry III's improvements. It is a good point from which to look north into the Inner Ward. You can see the line of the original Roman wall of AD 200 marked in the grass, and directly beneath you is a stretch of the later Roman riverside wall. The White Tower was built within this space and its western side was closed off by a gatehouse whose outline can be seen in the ground to the left. The area now covered with grass, and often enjoyed by the ravens (legend has it that if the ravens left the Tower, the White Tower would crumble), was for centuries covered with a Great Hall for royal use, with other buildings running east to incorporate the **Lanthorn Tower**. All this was cleared away after the Lanthorn Tower was destroyed by fire in 1774 (it was rebuilt in the 19C and you can now proceed through it).

Further views can be had from the next piece of wall: note **Cradle Tower** to the right—built by Edward III as his water entrance—and Well and Devlin Towers beyond in the outer wall, with Salt Tower at the end of the wall on which you stand. Descend down a new flight of steps to ground-level where you can visit a shop, enjoy a coffee (outdoors only) or resume your explorations in Water Lane. Here is the exit from the Tower to which you will finally return.

If time is short you should now see the White Tower and Crown Jewels, but if not, it is worthwhile reascending the wall to the Wall Walk, which will take you through the **Salt Tower** (1240), prison of many Catholic priests in Elizabeth I's reign, some of whom inscribed their names on the walls.

After this you journey along the east side of the complex through Broad Arrow Tower, Constable Tower, where there is an excellent model showing the layout of the site *c* 1335, and **Martin Tower**, in which there is an interesting exhibition about the development of the Crown Jewels, which were housed here from 1669 for 200 years. The final stretch of Wall Walk to the west is not open to the public. It runs via the Brick Tower, Bowyer Tower (where the Duke of Clarence, brother of Edward IV, was drowned in a butt of Madeira wine after conviction for treason) and Flint Tower to the Devereux Tower, one of the strongest, built to withstand the potentially dangerous Londoners to the west. Descend the stairs of Martin Tower into the Inner Ward.

Inner Ward

Now is the moment to see the **Crown Jewels** themselves, an essential if slightly vulgar element in your visit. They are housed in **Waterloo Barracks** (built 1845), where they were installed in 1992–94. The route entails proceeding at the speed of the crowd, somewhat slowly, past sundry videos of royal occasions, notably the 1953 coronation of Queen Elizabeth II when the jewels were last publicly used. The collection dates almost entirely from Charles II's restoration in 1660 and subsequent coronations. Charles's orb and sceptre have been used on every such event since. Besides their historical and symbolic interest, the jewels incorporate some spectacular and priceless stones, including the largest top-quality diamond in the world, Cullinan I, the Koh-i-Noor, and others. A separate Jewel House shop may be visited.

The climax of the visit is unquestionably the **White Tower**, the oldest building in London (except for the remains of Roman wall). Begun in the 1070s, its designer may have been Gundulf, Bishop of Rochester, who completed many castles and churches for William I.

> ### *William I (r. 1066–87)*
> Despite continuous passing fashions in the teaching of history, 1066 is the one date that all English children seem to learn, as denoting the year of Britain's last invasion. But it appears probable that in 1051 William had received some kind of promise of the throne from Edward the Confessor, and took over the country, imposing the administration of Norman knights, in fulfilment of this plan, and eliminating the illegitimate claims of Harold Godwineson. Whatever the reading of such long-distant events, William, through the Domesday Book of 1086, endowed England with something it has never since lost, a structure of land ownership and municipal relationships more enduring than the depredations of any invading army.

The tower is largely square but has an odd, apsidal projection on the east to accommodate the altar of St John's chapel within. The Tower's name dates from Henry III's reign when the structure was whitewashed. There have been many alterations, but wooden steps up to the main entrance on the south façade reflect the ancient notion of a temporary staircase, removable in the event of attack. Only four windows—at top left on the south side—retain their original shape. The four world-famous turret roofs date only from Tudor times.

The White Tower at the Tower of London

The interior contains three floors above a basement (in effect at ground-level): each is split in two by the central wall. The first floor contains key items from the collection of the Royal Armouries, including armour made for Henry VIII. The next floor is more magnificent and, it is thought, may have been used by the monarch himself, whereas the floor below was more likely intended for assembly and receptions. It includes **St John the Evangelist's Chapel**, the oldest church in London: a complete and unadulterated Norman interior, a miniature Durham Cathedral, it is awesome in its simplicity. The yellow stone now reflects the sunlight, but was probably originally painted in bright colours. The top floor above (except where the chapel protrudes into the space) may have been added later in the medieval period.

The White Tower leaves a sense of climax, and could be a fitting place to end your visit. But there is plenty of interest left and you may like to explore **Tower Green**. From here you can enter **Beauchamp Tower**, one of Edward I's towers, more substantial than most as it had to face the troublesome west. It housed prisoners of high rank, including in Mary I's reign the Duke of Northumberland, who had tried to place his daughter-in-law Lady Jane Grey on the throne.

To the north is **St Peter ad Vincula**, a fine Perpendicular church originally built in 1307 but rebuilt in Henry VIII's time. It houses the tombs of Anne Boleyn (1536) and Catherine Howard (1542), both of whom were beheaded at the scaffold site outside, as was Elizabeth's favourite the Earl of Essex (1601). It is open only to those attending a service or as part of a Yeoman Warder's tour.

Elizabeth I (1533–1603, r. 1558–1603)

The Virgin Queen, a figure of almost mythical stature, was probably England's greatest monarch, giving her name to an age, like Queen Victoria, and re-establishing stability after the appalling upheavals of the reigns of Henry VIII and Mary I ('Bloody Mary'). Elizabeth's mother was Anne Boleyn and, with Henry VIII for a father, she had the advantage of parents devoid of those spiritual qualities that led to religious fervour. She pragmatically steered the Church of England between the twin dangers of reversion to Roman Catholicism and the blind alley of Calvinism. Some blood was spilt but it could have been worse. She survived plots on her life, plots to get her married, attempts to undermine her by Mary Queen of Scots and, triumphantly, the Spanish Armada of 1588. After this last event she embarked on the very modern practice of cultivating her own image and only then shrewdly nominating her successor, 'our cousin of Scotland', who became James I. In her reign poetry and music flourished, Shakespeare matured and performed and architecture was warm, local and comfortable. No wonder that in later, more dramatic periods dominated by European concerns, the England of 'Good Queen Bess' took on the status of a golden age.

Lastly, as you leave, you should see the **Bloody Tower** (originally St Thomas's Tower), built in the 1220s but altered in the 1360s by Edward III. Prisoners here included Archbishop Cranmer (1553–54), Archbishop Laud (1640–45), Judge Jeffreys (1688–89) and Sir Walter Raleigh (for 13 years from 1603), whose comfortable apartments can still be seen. The Bloody Tower was the last place where the 12-year-old Edward V and his 10-year-old brother Richard were heard of alive. Their murderer remains undetected.

You exit south, towards the river. It might be a relief to leave this bloodthirsty place, vital though it is, for the comparative peace of **Tower Wharf** and waterfront, where you can eat a sandwich, have a drink and admire Tower Bridge. The wharf remains a place for royal gun-salutes on special occasions, as well as a photo-friendly viewing-point for both the bridge and Norman Foster's new City Hall for the Greater London Authority (see Chapter 30).

When rested, walk left to the foot of **Tower Bridge**, designed by Sir John Wolfe Barry and Sir Horace Jones (1886–94) and ascend the stairs (**Map 9,8**). Opinion is largely in favour of this strange edifice, but it can be argued that it is an early piece of damaging Disneyfication in London, fake architecture, unfit to hold a place beside the historical reality of the Tower. The towers of the bridge support suspension cables and contain lifts to reach the high-level footbridge for use when the bascules or mechanical arms of the lower bridge are raised. This was intended to facilitate navigation (the bascules used to be raised once a day for two hours at high tide, but are now lifted only by arrangement). It is pure, indeed advanced, engineering, but all clad in an anachronistic Gothic outfit in deference to the Tower of London alongside.

The bridge contains a worthwhile **exhibition**, including working models, vivid commentaries and finally, on the south bank, a sight of the gleaming brass-work of the engineering triumph. From the upper bridge, there are magnificent views of the Thames, east and west. The tour lasts 1½ hours. Open 10.00–18.30 Mon–Sun. Admission charge. ☎ 020 7403 3761.

Return to the north side of the river, descend the steps to return to Tower Wharf, and walk through the passageway east to reach **St Katharine's Dock**. You will pass under the bulky *Tower Thistle Hotel* (1970–73) along St Katharine's Way and out into a vivid, overcrowded scene of 1820s warehouses, water, boats and modern shops and offices. This was a concept of the 1980s, euphemistically called 'mixed development', and that is what you get. It is a muddle.

St Katharine's Dock, designed by Thomas Telford, was the last and most west-erly of the great dock constructions of the early 19C, being finished in 1829 (see Chapter 48). It was the consequence of greed, the company having acquired the site by moving the former Hospital of St Katharine to the newly laid out Regent's Park and destroying a fine 14C church, as well as displacing many of London's poor from their modest homes. It soon failed, the dock proving too small for vessels of increasing size.

The most westerly **warehouse**, to your left facing onto the quay, is a semi-historical reproduction of the original, then new to London, copied from Liverpool, overcoming the need for separate transport of goods from ship's hold to storehouse. It has Tuscan Doric columns in cast iron and warehouses stacked above, but has been 'modernised' in various ways to make it anodyne and charming rather than heavy and industrial. To the right, dividing the two pools, is George Aitchison's original **Ivory House** (1858–60), the only genuine sur-vival to be seen. Walk past it round the dockside and over the bridges to the *Dickens Inn*, a complete fabrication that makes use of an old commercial ware-house, and complete the circuit by the dock entrance at the riverside, noting one other original, the **Dockmaster's House** (1828). The boats moored in this marina make an attractive sight, but whatever happened to industry?

Enjoy a coffee at one of the many pleasant cafés and reflect on the changes time has wrought. Return via the Tower Thistle Hotel and follow the signs under the road to Tower Hill Station.

4 • EC2 east: around Broadgate

To Londoners, the postcode EC2 conveys chiefly finance, a theme this walk will reflect in both positive and negative senses. The Broadgate development, centre-piece of our tour, still reflects the brash confidence of its 1980s origins both in its Postmodern architecture and even more in its forceful public sculpture, and is judged positively for the most part. Outside finance, there is a good sprinkling of churches, including some earlier than the Great Fire, to remind you of the more distant past.

• Distance: 2 miles. Time: 1½ hours. Tube: Bank. Map 9.

Start from the crossroads at Bank station (use Exit 2 or 3 from the station). Walk up **Threadneedle Street**, probably given its name due to the presence of the Merchant Taylors' guild, past the Bank of England, the Royal Exchange and the statue of *George Peabody* (see Chapter 1 and Chapter 33). Fork left down Old Broad Street. The undistinguished 1960s front of the **Stock Exchange** is on your left.

If you have time it is worth going a little way down Throgmorton Street to the left to look at the slightly absurd turbaned figures guarding the entrance to the **Drapers' Hall** (mostly 1866–70), a Victorian jewel case with sumptuous interiors. Note also, on the right, **Throgmorton Avenue**, a peaceful pedestrian retreat with heavy gates (closed at night) and a small private garden. From it you can see the attractive west façade of the Drapers' Hall and a delicious Arts-and-Crafts structure above the tunnelled entrance—as well as, just to the north, a good curved modern block of the 1970s by Richard Siefert, based on the shape of Centre Point in Oxford Street (see Chapter 22).

Return to Old Broad Street and go left: the first building of interest is the **City of London Club** on your right, by Philip Hardwick (1833–34), an underestimated architect. The building is in Palladian rather than Renaissance style (compare Charles Barry's Reform Club, Chapter 18), behind the fashion for its day—only to be expected for a City men's club. The Club was founded in 1832 for bankers, shipowners and wealthy merchants, and today is for principals of companies. Inside there are a fine staircase and rooms, if you can persuade the doorkeeper to let you look.

Turn back again and find a small passageway, Adam's Court, on your left from Old Broad Street, which will lead back to Threadneedle Street. Opposite you then, just to the right, is the **Merchant Taylors' Hall**, the only such hall with extensive 14C remains, left behind after the Great Fire but all subsequently built over. The Hall's two modest doorways in Threadneedle Street belie accommodation of great richness behind, a hall on the medieval site and a great kitchen on the site of a house which belonged to the king's tentmaker.

Turn left down Threadneedle Street to Gracechurch Street. On the left corner is the beautiful single-storey banking hall of the original **National Provincial Bank**, by John Gibson (1864). This bank merged with the Westminster Bank in the 1960s (hence NatWest); it has now become a formal space attached to Tower 42. We must be grateful that the grand corner façade with Composite columns, arched windows and Pre-Raphaelite statuary above has survived as a conference and exhibition centre. You can often get inside to see the brilliant Victorian decorative scheme, with plaster reliefs, by asking at the door.

Tower 42 (formerly the NatWest Tower, now the International Finance Centre and named for the number of its floors) lies behind and beyond and stretches over to Old Broad Street, to which you must return in the unlikely event that you wish to see it close-up. When built in 1970–80 the tower, designed by Richard Siefert, was Europe's tallest building at 600ft, a record held for ten years until the main tower at Canary Wharf was completed. The footprint of the tower repeats the NatWest logo, a fact entirely lost on the ground-based viewer. It looks best from a distance, where it may be said to symbolise the City of the 1980s and the Big Bang—the introduction of electronic share dealing and stock transfer in 1986: a greater bang in the form of an IRA bomb in 1993 left it somewhat shattered, after which NatWest moved out. Its offices are now let to a range of tenants.

In Bishopsgate cross over to St Helen's Place to see the atmospheric medieval church of **St Helen**, which survived the Fire and Second World War but was also much damaged by the 1993 bomb.

Helen, or Helena, was the mother of Constantine the Great, a connection important to the Benedictine nuns who founded the church and priory in 1210. The church is deeply committed to evangelical services, and after the bomb took the opportunity to build a new floor on one level, which offended those who had admired the previous lowered nave floors and higher chancel.

From the west, the twin-gabled façade is charming. The church's interior spaces are a reflection of its origins, as a chapel attached to the nunnery on the site, on to which a parish church was built in parallel. The collection of monuments, spread about like furniture in a room, is a wonder because of the numerous survivals from the pre-Fire period, including the tombs of the merchant, adviser to Elizabeth I and founder of the Royal Exchange, Sir Thomas Gresham (d. 1579) and of Sir John Crosby of the former Crosby Hall (d. 1475; see Chapter 34). A guide detailing all the tombs is available inside the church. ☎ 020 7283 2231.

Further down Bishopsgate, on the right, is **St Ethelburga's**, a tiny medieval church, the smallest in the City. It escaped the Fire but not the terrorist bomb, which largely destroyed it. Now it is slowly being reconstructed as a monument to reconciliation and peace.

Cross back over Bishopsgate and head north to see **St Botolph-without-Bishopsgate** (1727–29). This is earlier than St Botolph Aldgate (see Chapter 2) and was the work of a consortium including James Gould as designer and George Dance the Elder, the City's own architect. The handsome Wren-inspired stone west façade looks particularly grand from Houndsditch, on the opposite side of Bishopsgate. Some enrichments were made to the interior in the 19C, including an odd but attractive domed centre light. John Keats was christened here in 1795. The pleasingly proportioned former **school** (1861), with earlier figures of children, stands across the former churchyard, one of the first to be re-laid as a garden in 1863. ☎ 020 7588 3388.

Go through the garden and turn right, noting on the left an extremely odd Turkish former public lavatory, now the entrance to a restaurant. You are now opposite **Liverpool Street Station**. To your left, until 1985, there was another terminus, Broad Street, which is now the southernmost part of the Broadgate development which we are going to explore. It contrasts sharply with the station to your right, which looks Victorian, although this part is of exactly the same date as Broadgate. Only the red-brick *Great Eastern Hotel*, further to your right, and the yellow-brick building housing Macdonalds are authentically of the railway age (1880–84). The hotel had a similar purpose to other station hotels (St Pancras, Charing Cross), and gave visitors from East Anglia a grand start to their London experience. It now contains a state-of-the-art restaurant owned by Terence Conran.

The **interior** of the station, although mostly brand new, is a beautiful space, and worth wandering around. The brick twin towers by Nicholas Darbishire, between which you descend by escalator, are a Postmodern pastiche of the original terminus (1875), with a gallery at this level running round above an open concourse. From the gallery admire the great train shed by Edward Wilson, one of the last of the giants and one of the most ornate in its ironwork. Parts of it were rebuilt in the refurbishment and the eastern platforms closed off, but the replication is otherwise more or less exact. On your right is a magnificent war memorial. On descending to the concourse, you will see to the left a wide area stretching away, full of people, and behind you more people entering and leaving the Tube. Yet there is no scuffling: the uses of space here were well understood.

Go right and out into Bishopsgate again. Cross over and go down Devonshire Row a little way. In **Devonshire Square** a few substantial Georgian houses survive (nos 10 and 12). Next note **Cutlers' Gardens**, a 1980s conversion of the noble former warehouses of the East India Company, functional 18C accommodation for precious imports of tea, created by distinguished architects such as the Company's own Richard Jupp, Henry Holland and, later, S.P. Cockerell. The whole complex was revamped by Seifert and Partners, who retained for the most part the warehouses to the south and west, with new interiors, and rebuilt those on the east side. The original work is best seen in Jupp's Old Bengal Warehouse on the south side of New Street.

Return to Bishopsgate and walk north, noting the **Bishopsgate Institute**, a bouncy Arts and Crafts building designed by Charles Harrison Townsend (1892–94) for a late 19C educational foundation. Take a critical look across the road to Broadgate Exchange, the least successful of the development's offices but still bracing. Down Brushfield Street to the right you may catch a glimpse of Nicholas Hawksmoor's Christchurch Spitalfields (see Chapter 45), glaring at the vulgarity of its latest City neighbour. Cross back carefully—there is no pedestrian crossing—to enter the development 200 yards further north on the left at Primrose Street.

Broadgate (1985–91) was formed in the area of the tracks and platforms leading to the Broad Street terminus of the redundant North London Railway. It was an excellent co-operative project and entailed building a great concrete platform over the Liverpool Street tracks to form **Exchange Square** in front of Exchange House. This part of the project was co-ordinated by the Chicago firm of Skidmore Owings and Merrill (SOM), under its senior partner Bruce Graham, and Exchange House is very much in the 'Chicagoesque' idiom. The parabolic arch is exciting but really a decorative feature evoking a railway shed—though not Liverpool Street's. It is a pity the arch is composed of straight pieces. Exchange Square contains the most overwhelming of Broadgate's various sculptures, the *Broadgate Venus* by Fernando Botero (1990). Her weight makes one fear for the train passengers waiting below.

Walk west from Exchange Square between the other SOM buildings, Dashwood House and Hamilton House, to reach Appold Street (**Map 9,1**). Turn left and go south between further blocks to **Broadgate Circle**, where the arena in the centre conjures up visions of a ruined Roman London, with plants hanging from the surrounding balconies. But it is by no means a dead ruin: the centre is a skating rink—a direct reference to Rockefeller Centre, New York—and around it are tiers of shops and wine bars, pleasanter than the New York precedent. People circulate and congregate happily and traffic is altogether absent.

A similar, though less Mediterranean, atmosphere prevails in the third and final public space to the west, **Finsbury Avenue Square**. The concept and the surrounding buildings here were the work of Ove Arup Associates (1985–89). It is approached from Broadgate Circle via a darker corridor next to a round glass tower containing conference rooms. The hurrying group of commuters to be seen apparently toiling towards the station turn out on closer inspection to be a bronze by George Segal, *Rush Hour* (1983–87). Finsbury Avenue Square has a lower centre, popular with office workers at summer lunchtimes and on warm Friday evenings. Leave the square by going south into Eldon Street past the gaunt rusting iron slabs of *Fulcrum* by Richard Serra (1987), from which the passage-way into the station can be seen.

Cross over and walk south down Blomfield Street to London Wall, turning left to attempt an entry into **All Hallows on the Wall** (1765–67). This important little church established the career of George Dance the Younger after his bid to succeed his father as the City's appointed architect. He had returned from Rome imbued with the new theories of Neo-Classicism, namely the desire to return to the values of antiquity, by-passing the filtering process of the Renaissance. This pure approach shows itself at All Hallows in the simple exterior, but even more directly in the plain vaulted space of the interior, a basilica with a coffered apse, minimal entablature and unadorned surfaces. ☎ 020 7496 1680.

George Dance the Elder (1695–1768) and Younger (1741–1825)

This father-and-son team were successively appointed architects to the City. The older Dance designed the Mansion House and was involved in two of the churches dedicated to St Botolph. He was also responsible, with Sir Robert Taylor, for the modernisation of London Bridge in the 1760s. But it is the younger Dance who has achieved more fame. Having trained in Rome and won a prize at Parma, he returned home to his father's old job full of the new Neo-Classical philosophy. He seldom deviated from this idiom—plain, pure and austere—of which All Hallows on the Wall and the former Newgate Prison, where the Old Bailey now stands, are paramount examples. He was an enlightened planner, as Finsbury Circus still demonstrates. Sir John Soane, who was trained by him, always greatly admired his 'revered master', and the fulfilment of Dance's ideas can be identified in Soane's work.

Dance could design more than simply churches. Return along **London Wall**—so named, of course, because here it follows the path of the medieval city wall, just inside its northern line—past Blomfield Street, and turn right via Circus Place into **Finsbury Circus**. A small obelisk bearing a relief portrait of Dance greets you. This was his brainchild of the 1770s, although it was not imple-mented until 1815 by his successor William Mountague. There is no trace of the buildings of that period now and the great surrounding blocks of the early 20C have considerably altered the scale. Even so this is a lovely space, pleasingly oval, with a fine garden in which to circulate, as City workers do daily, with handsome and dignified commercial buildings looking on. The best of the offices is Salisbury House in the southwest quadrant, gorgeously French in Bath stone. On the opposite, southeast side is London Wall Buildings (1901–2), but the block most usually admired is Sir Edwin Lutyens's Britannic House in the northwest corner, recently refurbished and retaining the original circulating spaces inside.

Exit the circus into Moorgate and, if you are interested in Dance's planning ini-tiatives—they were far-reaching for their time—walk north for five minutes to glance at **Finsbury Square** (Map 9,1), an idea which the younger Dance inher-ited from his father, as a City parallel to the residential squares of the West End's aristocratic estates. No original houses remain and the garden itself is a deplorable mess. In the southeast corner was Lackington's bookshop (1778), known in its day as 'The Temple of the Muses' and one of the sights of London. There is also a plaque to commemorate the surprising fact that Anton Bruckner started work on his Second Symphony here.

There is one remaining treasure on this walk. Return down Moorgate, past Britannic House again and on the left the London Guildhall University (1900–3) by John Belcher, who should have known better, as we shall see. With dirty statuary decorating its upper floors, it has a slightly pathetic air. Cross London Wall and turn left down Moorgate Place to see the **Institute of Chartered Accountants**, also by Belcher (1890–93), covered in magical sculpture and playing with Classical motifs like a chess game. This is plastic architecture in the floppy and sensuous style of the Art Workers Guild, free and creative, mixing motifs and giving pleasure to all who stop to look at it. Note the hairstyles of the female figures. The ICA somehow managed to pick the right architect, Sir William Whitfield, to add a modern exterior in the 1960s. It is in complete contrast, yet lives happily with its elder sibling. It shows what can be done: why is that so rare?

Reflecting on these mysteries, you can now return up Moorgate to Moorgate station, or go south to Bank station, or seek enlightenment in one of the many nearby hostelries.

5 • EC2 west: London Wall and the Barbican

Here we explore the west side of the EC2 district, with the Barbican Centre as a cultural counterbalance to businesslike Broadgate. Why should culture and money be opposed? But they are. We shall also make an excursion outside the City 'walls', to illustrate the sharpness of the contrast, and finish with an outstanding museum.

- Distance: 1½ miles. Time: 3 hours, including the Museum of London.
  Tube: Moorgate. Map 8, 9.

City walls

Late in the 2C AD, the Romans built a wall round their city for defensive purposes. It was nearly two miles in length, enclosing some 330 acres, about half the area of the present City of London. The structure was 6–9ft wide and about 18ft high, built of Kentish ragstone which must have been brought by ship up the Thames, interspersed with red terracotta slabs. On the outer side was a V-shaped ditch about 10ft wide. The existing fort in the northwest had to be incorporated—hence the wall's odd shape in that area. Bastions were built at regular intervals and gates created, of which the later Saxon names survive in, for example, Aldgate, Ludgate and Cripplegate. In medieval times the wall was renewed in many places, but throughout the 18C and 19C it was steadily demolished in the course of urban redevelopment. Preserved sections can still be seen near the Tower, the Barbican and elsewhere. A signposted London Wall walk begins near Tower Hill station.

Begin at Moorgate station (take the Metropolitan Line exit), in a street with the ancient name of **Moorfields**, once an open space outside the walls (**Map 9,3**).

Here there was once a Roman cemetery, but by the 17C Moorfields was a pleasant spot for games or parades, and it later functioned as a tenter ground, an area used for stretching and drying cloth, which was spread out horizontally a couple of feet above the ground and hooked tightly to a frame (hence the expression 'on tenterhooks'). John Keats was born on the site of no. 85 Moorfields in 1795. In the 19C Sir Robert Smirke built the London Opthalmic Hospital here: the institution has since relocated but is still famous as Moorfields Eye Hospital.

First turn south, briefly, and take a look down **London Wall** to the right. This area of the City was almost completely destroyed by bombing in the Second World War. Today you can still see the 1950s conception of an ultra-modern urban space, with hints of Le Corbusier—tower blocks in sequence at an angle to the newly laid road (quite out of alignment with the old London Wall), from which pedestrians were supposed to be entirely banned, and still largely are. Until softened by Postmodernism it had a strangely bald, windswept feeling, a kind of bleak mid-20C 'city of the future'. This was all changed by 1980s developments such as Terry Farrell's Alban Gate straddling the street, with multiple variations of plane and texture, although it makes little difference to the inhuman scale and focus on traffic. Turn back, with relief, to walk north past the station. Note the station entrance (1900), on the right, with what look like sinister stone winged insects.

Turn left at Ropemaker Street (**Map 9,1**), so-named for its 18C role as a ropewalk. Here again Modernism has been tamed. The former Britannic Tower, the head office of British Petroleum, was the tallest building in the City when built (1964–67), another sharp slab within the same Barbican–London Wall plan: in 2000 it was made curvaceous and renamed **City Point**. It has become a more friendly, warmer, presence, with rounded corners replacing hard angularity.

Go past City Point's north side and turn right into Finsbury Street—the Merryll Lynch building (1987) is an example of High Tech—to cross Chiswell Street. To your left, on the south side of the street, is an excellent original 1980s block by Denys Lasdun's firm, in dignified green glass, a world away from his work on the South Bank (see Chapter 32).

Do not turn left but cross Chiswell Street and walk a few yards ahead to look at the green space behind the iron gateway. This is the **parade ground** of the Honourable Artillery Company, now a cricket field. It is the largest open space in the City, but is for the use of members only. The Honourable Artillery Company's headquarters, **Armoury House**, seen on the north side of the site, is a mixture of 18C and 19C but makes a very handsome façade. It is spoilt by recent developments either side.

The Honorable Artillery Company is the oldest regiment in England, incorporated in 1537. They were originally a body of archers, whose role was, as the HAC's has continued to be, the defence of London. The Company, which has some 2500 members, has participated with distinction in major wars, and has occupied its present grounds since the Civil War. One of the first full cricket matches, between Kent and the Rest of England, was played on their turf in 1774; ten years later the first successful ballon flight in England lifted off from the same spot.

Go back to Chiswell Street and turn right up **Bunhill Row**, where Milton finished *Paradise Lost* and *Paradise Regained*, and where he died in 1674. An odd orange-and-pink block (1980s) is on your right and an incongruous mixture on your left. Note the towering school building marked 1901—a late example of the distinctive building genre of the School Board for London, of which many examples can be seen in the inner suburbs. Keep going north up to the entrance to **Bunhill Fields**—formerly 'Bonehill', which explains their purpose—the famous burial place for Non-Conformists. It contains the remains of John Bunyan (d. 1688), Daniel Defoe (d. 1731), William Blake (d. 1827) and Isaac Watts (d. 1748), with George Fox (d. 1691), founder of the Quakers, in a separate burial ground in Banner Street to the north. If you penetrate east as far as City Road, you will be opposite **Wesley's Chapel** (1777) and **Wesley's House**, which functions as a museum. Wesley is buried behind the chapel. Chapel open 12.00–14.00 Sun. House open 10.00–16.00 Mon–Sat, after 11.00 Sun. Admission charge for museum. ☎ 020 7253 2262.

John Wesley

Wesley (1703–91) was a Christian of prodigious energy and influence. He began his work when at Oxford, when the term Methodist was first attached to his group of followers. He joined the Moravian Brotherhood, learned its techniques, and then embarked on a programme of almost ceaseless travel and preaching throughout Britain and the eastern USA, delivering 40,000 sermons—about two a day. His influence on the development of church-going, especially among the new industrial population, was enormous.

Retrace your steps through Bunhill Fields, across Bunhill Row and down Dufferin Street opposite. Make your way through buildings run by the Peabody Trust (see Chapter 33) to Whitecross Street (**Map 8,2**). Look right to the north end of the street, across Old Street, where closing the vista is the remarkable church of **St Luke**, a work by Nicholas Hawksmoor and John James (1727–33), now being restored; the extraordinary and discomfiting fluted obelisk spire remains. But our route is south, to explore the Barbican. We shall enter from the least attractive direction, but make allowances—none of the designers expected you to come this way.

As you cross Chiswell Street again, look left for an image going back 200 years, to **Whitbread's brewery** (18C). Some original buildings remain, including the Porter's House to the left of the main entrance, but much has been altered or rebuilt. It retains nevertheless an appealing period flavour. The brewery may only be visited as part of a group.

The Barbican

The Barbican (**Map 8,2**) was named after an outer fortification of the city including a watchtower, perhaps as long ago as the 13C. Today's Barbican represents the 20C at its most innovative and exciting, combining residential accommodation with a variety of public buildings, including theatres, a concert hall, art gallery and library as well as schools, public offices and a church. And it combines levels, textures, materials and spaces in exhilarating mixtures that you will not see repeated elsewhere in London.

The preoccupation with getting pedestrians off the street and on to their own car-free space above, an idea which dominated London's planning for some time, finds its most effective implementation in the Barbican development. The designers, Chamberlin, Powell and Bon, and the clients, the City Corporation, remained loyal to this idea of the early 1950s throughout the building period (1971–81), weakening only in the 1990s by attempting to soften some of the more brutal design features with extra statuary and colour. But it must be admitted that Londoners generally have not taken to the place. The later Broadgate (Chapter 4) is more popular with office workers, and flats in the Barbican, although always in demand, do not command the prices you would expect. The car has been successfully banished: it is just a pity we did not get better at finding our way around without streets.

It is hard to describe an ideal route through the Barbican Centre because, unlike any of our more conventional walks, we are here involved in three dimensions, vertical as well as horizontal. It is recommended that you walk around in various directions, inside and out, to get a feel for the space. To begin, go bravely down Silk Street, past a music shop on your right, into the **main entrance**, marked 'Barbican Centre' everywhere. Banish the feeling that you are entering an underground car park. Then, perhaps, take the lift or stairs to the top and work your way down.

The Barbican Centre

- **Barbican Centre**. Open daily 09.00–23.00.
  Barbican Art Gallery. Open 10.00–18.00 Mon–Sat (till 20.00 Wed); 12.00–18.00 Sun. Admission charge.
  Concourse Gallery. Open 10.00–19.30 Mon–Sat; 12.00–19.30 Sun.
  Conservatory. Open 12.00–17.30 Sun and Bank Holidays. Admission charge.
  Enquiries and tours of the building, ☎ 020 7638 4141; box office and art gallery information, ☎ 020 7638 8891; Searcy's restaurant, ☎ 020 7588 6008.

On level 3 is the entrance to the **art gallery**, which provides regular, unusual and always interesting exhibitions; items from Matthew Smith's studio collection, permanently on display, are guaranteed to stimulate the eye (see box, p 120). Also on this level you can find the entrance to the **conservatory**, a remarkable indoor garden, and the sculpture court.

Also at level 2 there is a bookshop and the library. Levels 2, 1 and 0 are part of the services complex for the **theatre** and a wonderful **concert hall**, the acoustics of which supersede both the Royal Festival and Royal Albert Halls. There are also cafés, shops and restaurants, although never quite enough people—even during a concert interval—to do justice to the architects' conception of the space. At lower levels are the **Pit Theatre**, for more intimate productions, a lecture theatre and a **cinema**.

Leave at level 2 and walk east, turning right over Gilbert Bridge to cross the water—the yellow line is there to guide you—and noting the view to the left, of more water surrounded by flats: the waterside here is private to the residents, on the same principle as a London square, but visible to you from above. Behind the Barbican Centre are three tower blocks of apartments, visible all over the London skyline, named after famous men loosely associated with the area—Shakespeare, Cromwell and Lauderdale.

Sir Matthew Smith

Sir Matthew Smith (1874–1959), who trained at the Slade School of Art but was above all part of the Fauve tradition, is prominent as a London artist because of the decision by his 'widowed' mistress to leave his studio's collection to the City Corporation. The provision was that some of his paintings should be permanently displayed at the Barbican Gallery—an arrangement which gives Smith perhaps more prominence than he deserves. But his strongly painted Matisse-like nudes and still-lives can often be remarkable and uplifting.

Descend on the right if you wish to see **St Giles Cripplegate**, a substantial Elizabethan church restored in both the 19C and in 1960 after bomb damage. Oliver Cromwell married here in 1620. It has an interesting collection of furnishings, mostly acquired from other churches. Bishop Lancelot Andrewes preached here and plaques record the burials of the martyrologist John Foxe (d. 1587), explorer Martin Frobisher (d. 1594), mapmaker John Speed (d. 1629) and John Milton. Pre-Raphaelite artist William Holman Hunt was christened here in 1827. ☎ 020 7638 1997.

John Milton

The reputation of Milton (1608–74) remains at the highest level, even if few read *Paradise Lost* or his other works in full, and in an age when the religious controversies which dominate his work seem irrelevant. Although he did not write about London, he was born, died, buried and spent most of his life in it. Walks round London continually produce connections that give not only his work renewed interest, but also small insights into his enigmatic and contradictory personality. Milton was born in Bread Street, off Cheapside, attended St Paul's School, lived later at Hammersmith (then a country village) before returning, after the Restoration and his third marriage, to live and work in what is now Bunhill Row, with intervals in the country at Chalfont St Giles.

Although visiting St Giles reminds you where ground-level is, re-ascend to walkway level and follow the yellow line south, turning right by *Pizza Express* inside Alban Gate, towards the Museum of London. Note as you go the remains of the **Roman wall**. On your right, down the steps, is a pleasant residential development on an old site, Monkswell Square, with the Barber-Surgeons' Hall (1969).

You will reach the Museum of London past a metal plate commemorating the place where John Wesley felt himself converted—on 24 May 1738: it quotes an extract from his diary which still has the power to move. A pretty garden slopes down inside the roundabout. The **Ironmongers' Hall** can be glimpsed to the north, a Neo-Tudor building of the 1920s, which Pevsner, referring to the red-brick ground floor with half-timbering above, calls 'riskily suburban'.

Museum of London

The Museum of London, built by Powell and Moya (1968–70), forms the western end of the London Wall scheme and the southwest corner of the Barbican, though it is earlier than the main development (**Map 8,4**). The contents are an amalgamation of the collections of the City, begun in 1826, and of the former London County Council.

- Open 10.00–17.50 Mon–Sat, 12.00–17.50 Sun. Garden open Easter to end Oct. Shop. Café. ☎ 020 7600 3699. www.museumoflondon.org.uk. Tube: Barbican.

As you enter, on your right there is an impressive **bookshop** with a wide range of material on London, both historic and contemporary. Past the paypoint there is a space for temporary exhibitions which also stretch to the right.

The galleries form two circuits—pre-history to 17C at first-floor level, more recent history below—around a square **courtyard garden**, which can also be visited in summer and displays a rather confusing history of the development of nursery gardens in London. The scale of the displays reflects the extent of the collection for each period: it is stronger on Roman than on Saxon London, for example.

The **Prehistoric Gallery** is full of imagination, a necessary element in picturing the London basin as open and undeveloped country. Amongst the artefacts are axes from 200,000 years ago, knives from 2000 BC, Bronze Age weapons and Celtic coins. The **Roman Gallery** recreates, with great effectiveness, life in the London of the Roman Empire, and very pleasant it looks, too: the wall decorations, sculptures and a fine mosaic floor from Bucklersbury indicate the prosperity of the city. A special window gives a sharp impression of the line of the Roman wall outside. A hoard of Roman coins found off Eastcheap in 2000 is a recent addition to the display here.

The display on **Saxon and Viking London** gives a sense of the much less secure and pleasant world in the trading town of Lundenwic, today's Aldwych. But after expelling the Danes, King Alfred reinstated Londoners in their original space, inside the walls, where prosperity was restored until the invasion of 1066.

The **Medieval Gallery** contains interesting displays on the Thames, trade, the Church, industry and the Black Death. There is a fine model of Old St Paul's. Statues from the Guildhall—*Discipline*, *Justice*, *Fortitude* and *Temperance*—trample on their corresponding vices. Comparatively, the **Tudor Gallery** is somewhat thin, but the expression on the face of *Sir William Hewett* (d. 1564), by Antonio Moro, shows that stress is not a quality new to the city. After this, the **Early Stuart Gallery** displays the Cheapside Hoard, a treasure trove from a former goldsmith's shop discovered in 1912, but buried in the 1640s. There are other significant reminders of the Civil War, and recalling the Restoration is a large panelled room from Wandsworth. An old-fashioned model, with flashing lights for flames, illustrates the Fire: children seem to enjoy it, but given its importance and the scale of the destruction, the display on the Great Fire is fairly minimal. You then descend a ramp, visiting the garden if you wish (on re-entering the museum, turn right and make your way back to resume the chronological route). There is more room at this lower level and as a result the 18C and 19C have larger, more vivid, displays, which have recently been extended to cover the period 1789 to 1914 under the title World City—the period was indeed London's finest hour.

The most eye-catching exhibit in the **18C Gallery** is the Lord Mayor's Coach, first used in 1757, designed by Sir Robert Taylor with paintings by the Italian artist Battista Cipriani, who had arrived in London in 1755 and was later to work at Somerset House. Other items of particular interest here include a doorway from Newgate Prison (with original leg-irons above), Pyke's clock of 1760 and some fine paintings, hung in insufficient light. A display highlights the fact that London's cosmopolitan atmosphere is nothing new: 250 years ago, blacks, Jews, Irish, Germans and Huguenots all enriched the bustling life of the streets.

The **World City** display begins with the proud pediment of the Pelican Life Insurance Company, which stood over its office in Lombard Street from 1797. It is made of Coade stone, a new material invented among the rush of new technology fostered by the Industrial Revolution. It was innovation more than anything that created London's world status, and the railways, from the 1830s, which turned it from city to metropolis. All this is brilliantly captured by the new displays, from J.C. Bourne watercolours of the railways under construction through a range of new inventions, culminating in the Great Exhibition of 1851, of which you can undertake a virtual tour.

The less savoury side of life, which came to worry the Victorians, poverty, dirt, disease and overcrowding, are not ignored, including the 'Great Stink' of 1858 when the smell of sewage in the Thames became unbearable. All this needs to be allowed for before we get too dewy-eyed about the 19C. But you will find it hard to resist the walk through a Victorian shopping street with a bank, a grocer, a tailor and a pub, with costumed guides around to help you. There are some evocative paintings too to add to the effect: *Bayswater Omnibus* (1895) by G.W. Joy, and *One Minute to Six at the GPO* (1860) by G.E. Hicks. Oral history is included, with East End characters, recorded in the 1970s, recalling their 1880s childhoods: 'I was only a kid, but I was wicious.'

By comparison, the **20C Gallery** fares less well although high points include Art Deco lift doors from Selfridges (1928), a 1940s Woolworths counter and a 1965 Ford Cortina. Rock and roll throbs out, restoring life to the 1950s. The two world wars are covered but with less immediacy than at the Imperial War Museum or the Cabinet War Rooms.

When you leave the museum, cross the bridge by the Wesley commemorative plaque and descend from the walkway into Noble Street. Here you can see another section of Roman wall and, on the same side, the church of **St Anne and St Agnes** by Sir Christopher Wren (1677–87). This is now run by the Lutheran Church and is not always open, but if you are lucky enough to get inside, enjoy the cosy interior with its centralised plan and dark woodwork. The outside reflects the same homely domesticated model, with red brick and a low stuccoed tower. It has been frequently restored. ☎ 020 7606 4986.

Turn right to cross over St Martins-le-Grand to look at **St Botolph-without-Aldersgate**, a City church of unusual date (1789–91), unassuming on the outside with a stuccoed finish, but concealing a rich and elegant interior with a fine collection of furnishings and monuments, many of them from the medieval church which preceded this one. ☎ 020 7606 0684.

The churchyard of St Botolph's is called **Postman's Park**, alluding to the headquarters of the General Post Office nearby. Inside Postman's Park is a display of tiled plaques commemorating acts of heroism, designed and built by the Victorian painter G.F. Watts and his wife: they are worth looking at closely— some of the deeds described still inspire. The former GPO lay to the south and east, a magnificent Greek-Revival building by Sir Robert Smirke, emulating the British Museum. The Post Office has now moved away even from the North Range which lies immediately south of Postman's Park, and behind the Edwardian façade a modern office has been constructed: the façade is said to be the largest in Europe to be retained in this hypocritical manner.

Cross back over St Martin's-le-Grand into Gresham Street and turn right into Foster Lane. On the corner is the magnificent **Goldsmiths' Hall** by Philip Hardwick (1829–35). The Goldsmiths are one of the oldest and richest of livery companies and Hardwick gave them a hall to reflect this. In style it represents the development towards exuberant Victorian Classicism, making free and eclectic use of a range of motifs, more liberal then Barry's Reform Club of the same date. The finest space is the livery hall on the eastern side of what is an island site.

Further down Foster Lane on the left is the church of **St Vedast**, a delightfully mixed Wren building, damaged in the Second World War but interestingly refur-bished. You can see the original pre-Fire stonework in the south wall. Wren's first rebuilding (1695–1701) itself burned down. The main feature is the tower and spire, done even later in the cycle (1709–12) and the most Italian-looking of all Wren's spires, with concave and convex alternation: you might almost be in Rome admiring the work of Borromini. The interior is arranged like a college chapel and the single aisle is tucked away round the corner. Through a door on the right as you leave a secluded and peaceful courtyard has Roman remains on view. ☎ 020 7606 3998.

After this, cross Cheapside to St Paul's station. The cathedral dominates your view, but a visit should not really be undertaken at the end of a walk of this length. It calls for stamina to do St Paul's thoroughly, and the building, Wren's and the City's greatest, deserves a chapter to itself.

6 • EC4: more Wren churches

This final City walk covers the southwest section as far as the former River Fleet (New Bridge Street). The City's boundary is higher up Fleet Street at Temple Bar, but its character changes at the path of the river. The route tries as much as pos-sible to avoid the concessions to traffic made by Victorian and 20C planners. Some big roads have to be endured, but there are plenty of Sir Christopher Wren's churches to make up for it.

- Distance: 2¼ miles. Time: 2 hours, taking in the many churches. Tube: Bank. Map 8, 9.

We begin again from Bank station. From the maze of exits take that signposted to **King William Street** and start down it towards the Thames (**Map 9,5**). The straightness and the name are clues to the street's origin, as a cut-through devised in the 1820s to link the new London Bridge with the crossing at Bank and named after William IV. At the bottom, where the road bears right to approach the bridge, there was originally a giant statue of the king, now to be seen in Greenwich Park.

Short detours are needed to both left (Clement Lane) and right (Abchurch Lane) to view two churches by Wren. The first is **St Clement Eastcheap** (1683–87), so-called because, before King William Street was built, Eastcheap used to stretch this far. It is small, stuccoed (though originally brick) and plain, both inside and out, with a gloomy interior. The best things in it are the original woodwork: note the fine pulpit and tester. ☎ 020 7283 2711.

St Mary Abchurch (1681–86), its name supposedly deriving from medieval 'Abbe' or 'Abbo', is a different case and you should try to gain entry if you can. The exterior is again modest but warm, in red brick with homely stone quoins, like St Anne and St Agnes or St Benet. Inside you find a perfect, intimate space with peaceful original 17C pews under a painted dome, unique among Wren churches. The dome is saucer-shaped, not so structurally ambitious as St Stephen Walbrook, but comfortable and informal, a characteristic enhanced by the painting done in 1708 by William Snow, but heavily restored after bomb damage in the Second World War. St Mary's has an enormous reredos by Grinling Gibbons himself, and other contemporary furnishings repaired or restored after the bombing. ☎ 020 7626 0306.

Grinling Gibbons

An Englishman born and trained in Holland, whose first language was Dutch, Gibbons (1648–1721) came to London soon after the Fire. He gradually established a large woodcarving workshop whose services were in constant demand by both the Crown and Wren. Gibbons became master carver to the Crown in the 1680s when his practice extended to include large-scale stone sculpture. His finest work, however, was in wood, often constructions of individually carved pieces of limewood which compose exquisite collages of leaves, shells flowers and fruit. These were applied to pulpits, altarpieces and chimney pieces. Many can be seen in the City churches, and also at St Paul's and Hampton Court.

Returning to King William Street, cross through Monument station, go out on to London Bridge and look back. You will see the Monument and Adelaide House on your right (see Chapter 2). On your left, best viewed from here, is the **Fishmongers' Hall** (1831–35) by Henry Roberts. Roberts later specialised in designing housing for the poor working class of London, but he was only 28 when he built the Fishmongers' Hall and no social conscience is apparent in the luxurious design, which shows the influence of Sir Robert Smirke, with whom Roberts had trained and who was responsible for the approaches to the new bridge. There are frequent guided tours of the building (see Chapter 1).

The Fishmongers' Company ranks fourth in the hierarchy of livery companies, the guild dating back to the reign of Edward I. It is one of the few that still regulates its trade and has several fishmongers among the livery. The religious significance of fish allowed it to gain its early importance.

The **London Bridge** (Map 9,5) you are standing on was built in 1967–72 by

Mott, Hay and Anderson, the engineers for several important postwar bridges, with Lord Holford as architectural adviser. It does not excite, but does its job perfectly well.

> The most famous London Bridge was the medieval one of *c* 1200 with 19 arches. From its early days it supported houses, a chapel and, at the south end, a drawbridge. The houses were demolished around 1760 and a new wider central arch inserted. The bridge was an object of enduring myth, part of which related to the rapid flow of water between the narrow arches, striking fear in the heart of river travellers. More elegant and much more effective was John Rennie's bridge of 1830–32, built some 30 yards west of the medieval bridge, and mainly level, thanks to the newly constructed high approaches. Traces of it can be seen near water level on the north and south banks, but the bulk of it was sold in 1968 and re-erected in Arizona.

Return and turn left down Cannon Street, on the whole a tedious line of offices. By contrast, it is well worth peeping down **Lawrence Pountney Hill** on your left to look at nos 1 and 2, with beautiful doorcases of 1703, giving an indication of how handsome the City must have looked around that date with its new streets and churches. Back in Cannon Street, look out for the **London Stone**, inserted into a wall opposite Cannon Street Station. An old landmark first referred to *c* 1100, its original purpose is unknown.

Note 80 Cannon Street by Arup Associates (1972–76), with its criss-cross steel frame, designed to provide a shaft for a proposed underground line, before the Jubilee Line extension along the south bank was agreed. **Cannon Street Station** was originally built in 1865 to deliver City commuters, and was intended to give the South Eastern Railway a competitive edge against the London Chatham and Dover Railway's initiative at Blackfriars. The only evidence of the original station is the twin towers overlooking the river bridge. Offices were inserted between these, over the tracks, in the 1960s and 1980s.

After passing the front of the station (**Map 8,6**), turn left down Dowgate Hill and admire the arcaded walls of London stock brick. Behind them, below the railway, was once the first cold store in Britain. At the bottom turn right along College Street to find **St Michael Paternoster Royal**, a photogenic Wren church (1686–94) with a particularly fine steeple, possibly by Nicholas Hawksmoor (1713–17). Some of the interior is taken up with offices of the Mission to Seamen, and the remainder is light new oak, postwar damage restoration, with some interesting original furnishings. The church's name derives from the manufacture of rosaries (paternosters) and a Gascon colony, La Reole, merchants from which occupied a nearby street. Dick Whittington, four times Lord Mayor, was buried in 1423 in the pre-Fire church, and is commemorated, with his cat, in one of the present windows. ☎ 020 7248 5202.

Though it is not essential, you could cross the horrible Upper Thames Street here to take a look at the river from **Southwark Bridge** (1912–21), a strangely small crossing, scarcely necessary it sometimes seems. It feeds its northbound traffic left and right into Upper Thames Street, giving us no chance whatsoever to ascend the only processional route the City acquired in its post-Fire building, up Queen Street and King Street to the Guildhall. The first Southwark Bridge, by Rennie (1814–19), was a daring three-arch structure of iron, but its delicate pale-green steel successor by Sir Ernest George takes five arches to cross the narrow stretch of river. It has nice lampposts, though. On the west side of the bridge is the **Vintners' Hall**, with some 17C work still to be seen inside, but a Postmodern portico facing the river. The Vintners' Company still shares, with the Dyers' and the Crown, ownership of all swans on the Thames, which are marked at Swan Upping each year (see Chapter 73).

Continue west along Upper Thames Street to another Wren church, **St James Garlickhythe**, the name a reminder of its riverside location in the days of sea-born trade. The tower is comparable with that of St Michael's nearby and was probably by the same designer. The interior is a simplified version of St Stephen Walbrook, attempting to combine a Latin with a Greek cross plan. As a result of insensitive road-widening, the south front outside looks naked against the street. ☎ 020 7236 1719.

Cross Upper Thames Street over a metal bridge. Looking to the west, you can see the handsome tower of **St Mary Somerset** by Wren (1695): the rest of the church was demolished in 1871. Descending the steps, follow the signs to the Thames Path, via Broken Wharf. Here is an opportunity, especially when the tide is out, to gain a sense of the historical river, and sometimes you can even get down to the foreshore and search for treasure like a mudlark. The Thames Path here leads west under Blackfriars Bridge to the Victoria Embankment, but follow it only as far as the Millennium Footbridge with Tate Modern opposite. Just beyond is the present **City of London Boys' School**, a building of the mid-1980s. The school itself dates back to the Carpenter Bequest of 1442 and is built on the site of the second Baynard's Castle

> Baynard's Castle was built *c* 1275 and rebuilt in 1429. The first was by the present Blackfriars Bridge. Founded by one of William I's Norman knights, it was an important place in medieval and Tudor London: Henry VIII used it extensively, and it became a permanent home for his fourth wife, Anne of Cleves. As a riverside building, the castle was destroyed by the Great Fire, although one turret survived until 1720. No trace of it is left today.

Turn right up the steps and gradually ascend to Queen Victoria Street. Keep looking back to admire the vista over the bridge to Tate Modern (see Chapter 31), but also look forward, for a primary view of St Paul's south transept. You will emerge into the street with the **College of Arms** (Map 8,6) across the road to your left. The College—the only royal building remaining in the City—is a handsome post-Fire construction by Maurice Emmett (1671–73), the master bricklayer to the Office of Works and therefore a colleague of Wren. The building is somewhat truncated, but still retains the civilised proportions of its period. The gates came from Goodrich Hall, Herefordshire, in 1956. Founded in 1484, the College's role is to maintain the records of coats of arms granted by the Crown to chosen persons and organisations; it can be consulted by the public. Open 10.00–16.00 Mon–Fri. ☎ 020 7248 2762.

Queen Victoria Street, a windswept, frankly uncongenial, highway, was cut through by the Victorians to create a long-needed direct route from the Embankment to Blackfriars Bridge and the centre of the City. After bomb damage, it is now the location for some unusually depressing buildings. Walk a little way to the right to see an exception, **St Nicholas Cole Abbey**, a Wren church on the north side, run by the Free Church of Scotland. The name may be a corruption of the medieval 'cold harbour', meaning a shelter. Note the fine compartmentalised ceiling rebuilt after war damage and the vivid postwar windows by Keith New. The spire is a pleasing novelty, again rebuilt after the Second World War. ☎ 020 7248 2513.

Go a few yards further to the suitably pink **Financial Times building** by Sir Albert Richardson (1955–59). This was the first postwar architecture to be listed and its modernisation in 1988–89 by Michael Hopkins respects the original. The next office block to the east is also important: the **Credit Lyonnais building** (1973–77) was the first anywhere to be encased in glass-fibre cement. It also emulates the acute-angled corner site of its Victorian predecessor, in a Postmodern manner early for its date.

Now return down Queen Victoria Street past the deplorable Faraday House (1932): even in the muddled 1930s there were protests that it wrecked the image of St Paul's from the south. To the left you can catch a glimpse of **St Benet Paul's Wharf**, another domesticated Wren design, isolated but pretty as a picture, now belonging to the Welsh Church (☎ 020 7489 8754). Near the foot of the slope, on the right, is **St Andrew by the Wardrobe** (1685–95), also by Wren. The wardrobe in question was the clothing store of the Crown, including arms and armour, which stood here until the Fire. The church was bomb-damaged and carefully restored, although its rich red brickwork is now pleasingly grubby again. It is sited in a dramatic position above the street. The aisles of the interior are used as offices for the important Churches Conservation Trust, whose role is to care for Anglican churches no longer in use but not in ruins, a critical architectural heritage which will present the 21C with increasing dilemmas. ☎ 020 7248 7546.

Turn right up St Andrew's Hill to explore the maze of streets, unbombed and therefore well endowed with smaller Victorian buildings, which lead up to St Paul's Cathedral. First, on the left, is the *Cockpit* pub (1865), on the site of an original cockpit with the gallery and viewing area recreated: the sport had been banned only as recently as 1849. Turn left into Carter Lane. Look left into Church Entry, running across the east end of the nave of the original abbey of the Blackfriars, the passage between the public area and the chancel consecrated to the Dominican friars (see Chapter 8). Carter Court, next on the left, is a good place to get a feeling for the old city; now a pleasing mixture of architecture from the 1800s, 1900s and (repro-Georgian) 2000 it seems peaceful enough, but actually represents the kind of close court that was common in 19C London. On the other side of Carter Court is the **Apothecaries' Hall**, dating back to 1670.

Turn right into Pilgrim Street and so into Ludgate Hill to take in one last Wren church today, and a good one, **St Martin Ludgate** (1677–86). Tucked into the busy street, it is thought it was carefully placed by its architect to reflect against the backdrop of St Paul's. Inside the door is a passage with a gallery above, insulating the church from the street. The interior is particularly rewarding, with excellent carved woodwork by William Emmett, brother of the builder of the College of Arms, and a handsome square plan demarcated by four Composite columns. ☎ 020 7248 6054.

Turn right out of St Martin's and take the first right to reach **Old Bailey** and the Central Criminal Court, built on the site of Newgate Gaol (**Map 8,3**). It is a fine Edwardian building by architect E.W. Mountford (1900–7), with all the exuberance and self-confidence of that doomed age. The dome refers no doubt to St Paul's, and its design is related to the Wren domes at Greenwich: the famous gilt-bronze statue of *Justice* on top is by F.W. Pomeroy, the sculptor of more heavily symbolic statues inside. Visitors over 14 admitted to most courts 10.30–13.00 and 14.00–16.30 Mon–Fri, space permitting. No drinks, cameras or mobile phones.

Among many famous trials held here were those of Oscar Wilde (in an earlier building), and, in the 20C, those of the murderer Dr Crippen, the traitor William Joyce, known as 'Lord Haw-Haw', and the East End gangsters the Kray twins.

Newgate Gaol

This was London's most famous, or notorious, prison from as early as the 12C. A new building was erected in 1672, grand on the exterior but appalling inside, where typhoid, corruption and murder were endemic. It was replaced in 1770–78 by an architecturally more notable prison by George Dance the Younger, with separate wings for male prisoners, females and debtors. This building was wrecked by the Gordon rioters in 1780 when many of the prisoners escaped. It was afterwards rebuilt more securely still and became a place to visit, or to see executions, which continued as a public spectacle until 1868. Newgate was demolished in 1902.

From Old Bailey turn right along Newgate Street and right again down Warwick Lane. On the right is Amen Court, with good 17C houses for the clergy of St Paul's. Beyond that, **Stationers' Hall** is a post-Fire building largely disguised from the front by a Neo-Classical façade by Robert Mylne (1800). This is one of the richer halls and the Company, which was founded in 1403, has a distinguished history, until 1911 nominally regulating all printing in Britain.

You then return to Ludgate Hill to find yourself in the shadow of St Paul's—go past it in the same direction for three minutes to reach St Paul's station. You could take coffee or lunch in the *Crypt Café*—it has an entrance separate to that of the cathedral. This is the point from which our guided tour of the cathedral begins.

7 • St Paul's Cathedral

St Paul's Cathedral ranks second only to the Tower amongst the sights you must see in the City of London. Christopher Wren's masterpiece is the cathedral of the capital, and thus in a sense the Church of England's most important building, a focus for spiritual as well as cultural values.

• Distance: a few hundred yards. Time: 2 hours at least. Tube: St Paul's. Map 8.

The best way to approach St Paul's is from the west, as Wren intended, up **Ludgate Hill** (Map 8,3), to see the west façade gradually filling out the view. The impression was until recently marred by post-Second World War office building, but this has recently been demolished in conjunction with new development to the north of the Cathedral: it is too early yet to form a view of its success.

• Cathedral open 08.30–16.00 Mon–Sat, between services Sun. Admission charge. Crypt and restaurant open 09.00–17.30 Mon–Sat, 10.30–17.00 Sun. Guided tours of the Triforium Gallery 11.30 and 14.30 Mon, Thur (to book, ☎ 020 7246 8319). Audio guide. ☎ 020 7236 4128. Free organ recitals at 17.00 on Sundays. www.stpauls.co.uk. **Note**. St Paul's is sometimes closed to tourists: check the diary published on the website.

Sir Christopher Wren

London's greatest architect would probably have been regarded as such even without the fortunate opportunities offered to him after the Fire. His work at Greenwich, Hampton Court, Chelsea and some churches outside the City are evidence of this. But the surviving City churches accompanied by St Paul's Cathedral represent a body of work under a single co-ordinating mind which cannot be found repeated anywhere else in the world.

The son of a clergyman, and of a conservative family, Wren (1632–1723) began as an academic, becoming professor of astronomy and mathematics at the University of Oxford at the age of 30. He visited Paris in 1665, and briefly met the great Baroque sculptor and architect Gian Lorenzo Bernini who was there to advise on rebuilding the Louvre. Wren was undeniably well-placed to become chief commissioner for the rebuilding after the Fire. In this capacity he developed, within a few days of the disaster, a comprehensive scheme for urban renewal—though this was not implemented—and oversaw the reconstruction of 51 churches, and their later towers, and submitted a succession of designs for St Paul's, culminating in what is, despite some faults, his masterpiece. He lived perhaps too long, and his last years were dominated by criticisms of his work by an important new generation whose values in both design and society were different. Nothing, however, can detract from the grandeur of the finished product.

History

Old St Paul's stood for nearly 600 years, from 1087, and had itself been preceded by earlier churches, the first one founded in AD 604. Tradition has it that the first building on the site, prominently raised above the rivers Thames and Fleet to the west, was a temple to Diana. The medieval cathedral, completed in 1240 and frequently altered thereafter, was the longest in England at 600ft and had a magnificent steeple and spire, until it was struck by lightning and collapsed in 1561.

The old cathedral was in a poor state by the time of the Great Fire. Thirty years before, Inigo Jones had 'Classicised' the nave transepts and the west front by rounding the windows, placing Corinthian pilasters along the aisle walls and piers on a massive scale (40ft tall) in a portico on the west front. It must have looked extremely odd. Furthermore, bad habits had been adopted: commercial traders were allowed to operate within the nave as well as all around the exterior. And then, during the Civil War, the Parliamentary army who were stationed there mutilated all the monuments.

Christopher Wren had been involved as a consultant on the restoration of the crumbling structure in 1663, and had begun to prepare plans for the replacement of the medieval crossing with a dome, an idea perhaps inherited from Jones, but clearly one that never left him. He was thus effectively the only possible choice for the rebuilding. But the project caused him much anguish and, as we shall see, after at least three false starts resulted in some slightly questionable architectural decisions.

It became clear, although only gradually, that the old structure could not be restored, and by 1669 Wren's first design was submitted: it was a strange affair with shops in the aisle space, to be accessible only from the exterior, and not surprisingly it was rejected. The second design, known as the Great Model—indeed there is a 20ft model of it in the Cathedral's collection in the Triforium Gallery—was uncompromisingly Classical, domed, based on St Peter's in Rome, and founded on the shape of a Greek cross. To Wren's great disappointment this was judged to be liturgically unacceptable. It is a great deal more 'purely' Classical than the finished result, slightly smaller, dignified, austere, cold: it would have set a very different tone for the City. The third, known as the Warrant Design, was a more conventional creation, Classical but firmly cruciform, with a spire over the crossing: it is perhaps a good thing that it was never implemented as drawn.

But the royal warrant which authorised this design allowed for alterations to be made as building progressed and from 1675 Wren, learning from experience, prudently erected scaffolding around the whole site so that no one could see, and second-guess him on, the work in progress. Money was obtained from the tax on coal instituted for rebuilding the City churches and stone obtained chiefly from Portland in Dorset, whence it was transported by sea and up the Thames. The cathedral was finished in 1710, when Wren was nearly 80. The total cost was £736,000. The project was judged to have gone so slowly during the last years of building that Wren had his salary cut by a half, and had to plead with Queen Anne to obtain the arrears.

Exterior

Look first at the **west façade**, made grander by being raised above the original medieval crypt up an imposing flight of steps. Its portico of 12 paired Corinthian columns, surmounted by a second level of eight further columns, this time Composite, is a reference to Claude Perrault's Louvre and also a compliment to Jones's earlier added-on portico. Wren would like to have repeated Jones's giant portico, but Portland could not provide stone of sufficient size.

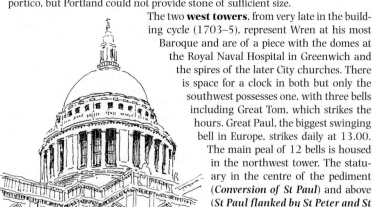

The two **west towers**, from very late in the building cycle (1703–5), represent Wren at his most Baroque and are of a piece with the domes at the Royal Naval Hospital in Greenwich and the spires of the later City churches. There is space for a clock in both but only the southwest possesses one, with three bells including Great Tom, which strikes the hours. Great Paul, the biggest swinging bell in Europe, strikes daily at 13.00. The main peal of 12 bells is housed in the northwest tower. The statuary in the centre of the pediment (*Conversion of St Paul*) and above (*St Paul flanked by St Peter and St James*) is the work of Francis Bird, an important sculptor who regularly worked for Wren. Bird also designed the statue of *Queen Anne* in the forecourt, although the present version is a Victorian replacement.

The dome of St Paul's

Walk round the cathedral to the left, clockwise. The cathedral is 510ft in length and 479ft wide at the transepts. You come first to an entry to the crypt where there is a **shop** and **restaurant**. On your left is the **Chapter House** by Wren (1712–14), similar in idiom to Marlborough House. Look up at the cathedral wall to your right and ask yourself how light can reach the nave at clerestory level: above the aisle windows there appear only to be niches for statues in an otherwise solid wall. The answer is that the upper part of the wall is only a screen, with nothing behind it but air, the nave being lit from a conventional buttressed clerestory out of sight across the open space behind. This design feature has troubled devotees of honest architecture ever since. Wren presumably fixed on it to give greater security and stability, and perhaps Classical ethos, to the exterior walls. There is no question about the magnificence of the masonry, where Grinling Gibbons forsook wood to complete a constantly inventive series of carvings beneath the windows, drawing on all his usual themes from nature. The balustrade at the top was added during Wren's lifetime but after his connection with the Cathedral was ended: he disapproved of it.

Go through the gate by the **north transept porch** into the garden. The porch is based on the design of Santa Maria della Pace in Rome which Wren had seen in engravings. Its Baroque quality is unique among Wren's work (although adopted by James Gibbs and Thomas Archer in their London churches). Beyond the north transept is **Paul's Cross**, a renewal (1910) of an ancient structure: in the days of Old St Paul's it was a key point for communication including speeches, announcements, ceremonies, burning Tyndale's Bible and 'preaching down' papal authority in Henry VIII's time. Thomas Carlyle called it 'the Times newspaper of the Middle Ages'.

Through the churchyard, you pass round the east end of the cathedral, where the spire of **St Augustine Watling Street** can be seen, all that remains of a small Wren church to which a new building for St Paul's Choir School was attached in 1960. To the southeast of the cathedral is a pleasant public garden from which the south façade can be admired and photographed. There is a good view of the **dome** and the lantern at the top apparently balanced on it, a Baroque conception to match the west towers, the whole structure 365ft high. Above is the gold ball and cross (1721). This dome is only visible from the exterior. Made of lead on a timber frame, it would create too lofty a space on the inside and could not structurally support the lantern. The lantern in fact rests on top of a brick cone inside the outer dome, which in turn provides the structural support for the whole, and inside which the inner dome can nestle. The thrust is spread down the heavy, solid interior piers and along those screen walls.

Beyond the southwest end of the churchyard you will see in the ground traces of the **cloister** of the medieval church. Glance over to your left to see the **Deanery**, in Dean's Court, the finest 17C mansion remaining in the City. Turn right to ascend the steps into the interior.

Interior

The first impression you will have looking down the nave is of awe, closely followed by a sense that, grand though it is, it is all more conventional than the exterior led you to hope. The design Wren finally adopted was that of a Gothic cathedral—cruciform, with nave, aisles, transepts, crossing and chancel—with an apse at the east end; somehow we feel marginally let down after the Classical extravagance outside. The nave is only three bays long.

But look around you. The atmosphere of the architecture is rich but ordered, perfectionist, cool. The massiveness of the piers which support the west door, and the framework of the chapels at the west ends of each aisle, give a feeling of sublimity, security and strength. There is also great richness and variety in the composition of the piers, the Corinthian pilasters of different heights and in the use of various types of stone in the nave construction—notably Portland for the framework, and Barnack (from Northampton) for the vaulting. It is worth remembering that in Wren's time, and to his annoyance (he did not want to alter his church for 'a box of whistles'), the Father Schmidt organ would have been placed across the chancel entrance, cutting off the choir and blocking your view of the altar, as at Westminster Abbey. For this opening up we must thank the Victorians. The organ was played by George Frederic Handel and Felix Mendelssohn.

On your immediate left, before the paypoint, is **All Souls' Chapel**, dedicated to the memory of the First World War Field-Marshal Lord Kitchener. Next to it is the larger **St Dunstan Chapel**, dedicated to Dunstan, Bishop of London and Archbishop of Canterbury 1000 years ago. The chapel on your right, which you can visit when you exit, was dedicated to the Order of St Michael and St George in 1906.

Walk down the centre of the nave but make detours here and there into the aisles. On your left, between the nave and the north aisle, is the only piece of statuary in the nave arches, the dominating **Wellington memorial** by Alfred Stevens (1912), finished long after the great Duke's death. Wellington, covered in dust, sits on horseback at the summit: his remains are in the crypt below. As you reach the crossing you will see that the arcading of the nave is succeeded by solid wall, part of the secure support for the dome.

Then sit in the crossing to digest the sight of the **dome** above (it is 218ft up to the crown of this inner space) and its complexities. You can see James Thornhill's grisaille paintings of the *Life of St Paul* on the ceiling, somewhat garishly set off below by mosaics and figures added in the 1890s. Although he did allow that the cathedral could be much more richly decorated than his churches, Wren would probably not have approved of these figures of saints and prophets. But they are quite significant works: one is by Stevens, completed while he was at work on the Wellington monument, two are by G.F. Watts and the remainder are by W.E.F. Britten. Above the cornice the Whispering Gallery, famous for the quirk of its acoustics, runs round the base of the drum (see below). The windows in the drum provide the main lighting, punctuated by a Victorian statue in a niche in lieu of every fourth window. The light through the oculus of the dome comes from invisible windows in the outer dome, a Baroque effect.

Let the eye travel down through the spandrels to locate where the thrust of the mass is carried, and it will be seen that the structure is almost unpleasantly massive and weighty. Elegant it is not. This is partly structural conservatism and partly necessity. Whereas the nave, transepts and chancel carry four large arches, the intermediate arches of the aisles are narrower and have therefore been filled in with lower segmental arches, adding strength no doubt, but a minus aesthetically. The lower arches create triangular spaces above, which were filled with gold mosaics in the 1890s. It is all too much—too much masonry and too much colour.

Look beyond to the wonderful Gibbons carvings of the **choir stalls** and the

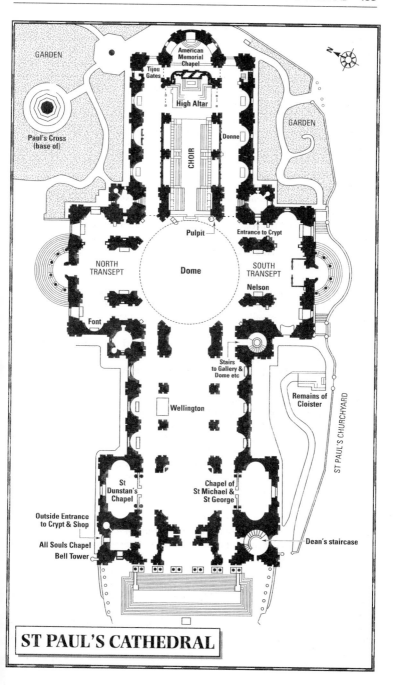

ST PAUL'S CATHEDRAL

organ case. Each stall is different, every flower and leaf design and the expression on every cherub's face unique. Unfortunately it is not usually possible to examine them closely unless attending a service. The pulpit, although in Wren's style, is quite recent, by Lord Mottistone (1964).

In the **north transept** hangs the famous painting *The Light of the World* by William Holman Hunt (a later version, finished 1900). The font, by Francis Bird (1700), requires a block and tackle to lift the lid.

Enter the **chancel** on the north, left-hand side. In the north choir aisle is a marble *Mother and Child* by Henry Moore (1984), a modern shock in these Classical surroundings, but meltingly beautiful. The iron gates are the work of Jean Tijou, a French craftsman whom Wren often employed. The east end of the cathedral was the one area damaged by bombs, hence the visibly new woodwork in the apse and high altar. The imposing **altar**, reminiscent of Bernini's in St Peter's, Rome, but on a smaller scale, was a creation of the 1950s: this may strike you as incompatible with Wren's simplicity, but a drawing of such an altar was found among Wren's papers. The stained-glass windows—of which Wren would certainly not have approved—are also of 1958 although they look older. The east end functions as the **American Chapel**, dedicated to US servicemen who gave their lives in the Second World War; on the high altar itself is a memorial to Commonwealth dead of both World Wars.

Over the ceiling of the choir is an extravagant programme of **mosaics** by Sir William Blake Richmond (1890), representing the *Creation* with *Christ in Majesty* in the apse. Wren's architecture has been gilded to conform to the rich colour scheme.

As you return down the south chancel aisle note the **tomb monument of John Donne** (1631–32), poet and Dean of St Paul's, the only monument to survive the Fire. The design, showing him upright, snugly wrapped in his shroud, was his own, carved by Nicholas Stone. This is also a good place to look closely at Gibbons's limewood decorations to the rear of the choirstalls: the structures of leaves, stems and petals can be examined at close quarters.

Returning to the crossing and the transepts, it is worth admiring some of the monuments here. The first to arrive were the four in each corner: *Dr Johnson* (d. 1784), rather uncomfortable in Roman dress, in the northeast; *John Howard* (d. 1790) the prison reformer in the southeast; the now forgotten *Dr William Jones*, an educationalist in the southwest (all these are of the 1790s by John Bacon the Elder); and in the northwest *Sir Joshua Reynolds* (d. 1792) by John Flaxman (1803–13). Flaxman was also the sculptor of the magnificent yet tender **monument to Nelson** (1808–18), on which Britannia points out the Admiral as role model to two young sailor boys, accompanied by a despondent but still growling lion.

Next, if you have the energy, ascend the stairs at the southwest corner of the

John Flaxman

John Flaxman (1755–1826) was a sculptor of international renown, a British artist in his time more appreciated than any other. He was most notable for his reliefs, on memorials and elsewhere, and was a precursor of the most austere Neo-Classicism, of which the religious elements set the tone for Victorian religious revivalism. But the noble style of Nelson's monument at St Paul's shows that he could achieve massive grandeur as well.

crossing to reach the galleries of the dome. The **Triforium Gallery** (guided tours only) contains a number of interesting artefacts relating to the history of St Paul's, including Wren's model. There are 259 steps to the **Whispering Gallery**, where, if you face the wall and whisper, you can be heard by someone at the other side of the dome. At this level the view is naturally vertiginous but remember you are only halfway up. You ascend a further 119 steps through smaller staircases to reach the **Stone Gallery** stretching round the drum of the dome. Another 152 steps, offering a chance to see and marvel at the brick cone, take you to the **Golden Gallery** round the base of the lantern. On a fine day the views are spectacular—less so than those from the London Eye, but whereas that moves, here you can stay for as long as you want.

Returning to ground-level, it is worth leaving the cathedral via the **crypt**, entered from the south transept. It is an ancient space, dating back to the medieval cathedral, but now full of additional supporting columns and countless monuments. The eastern space houses the **OBE Chapel**. Turn right at the foot of the stairs to see the earliest monuments, under the south aisle, including Wren's own.

> In the late 18C there was great debate as to whether Wren should be commemorated with a statue but in the end a plain slab was erected by Robert Mylne, the surveyor of St Paul's, with the famous line *Circumspice si monumentum requires* ('If you seek a memorial, look around you')—the phrase came from Wren's son's account of his father's life.

Honours

It has been said of the honours system that there is very little system. It is an accumulation of practices developed by whoever is in power, from Monarch to democratically elected government, to reward its favourite people. In Britain the range of peerages (see House of Lords) has been used for centuries but life peerages are now by far the more usual. Knighthoods (Sir) are still common, but baronetcies (Sir–Bt) most unusual. A sign of democracy was the growth in the 20C of Orders, Commanders and Members of the British Empire (OBE, CBE and MBE) but the British Empire Medal (BEM) for general workers still effectively signifies the British pre-occupation with social class. Some ancient honours, such as the Garter (dating to Edward III) and the Order of the Bath (George I) still carry weight, as do honours for bravery (Victoria Cross and George Cross), which for a nation of military prowess were introduced surprisingly late (Queen Victoria and George VI).

Nearby are memorials to some other architects and artists of the period and throughout the crypt there are a vast number of 19C monuments, grouped by profession. Amongst many notable names are William Blake, Turner and Constable, in the area known as 'Painters' Corner', Sir Edwin Lutyens and Florence Nightingale. There is a remarkable relief-group of the *Redemption* by J. Singer Sargent (d. 1925).

The graves of Nelson (d. 1805) and Wellington (d. 1852) have pride of place under the crossing. Nelson's sarcophagus was that originally intended for the ashes of Cardinal Wolsey, made by Benedetto da Rovezzano (1524), and revamped by Robert Mylne in 1806. Wellington's tomb (1858) by F.C. Penrose is an allusion to Napoleon's in Les Invalides in Paris, soldierly and dignified, and a fitting partner to Stevens' great memorial in the nave above. Many other distinguished military figures are commemorated nearby.

Often interesting exhibitions are arranged in the crypt. The **Treasury** shows ecclesiastical vestments and plate belonging to the Cathedral and items on loan from elsewhere in the diocese. Beyond, you exit into a public area, which can be entered separately from outside without an admission charge, housing the shop, toilets, a café and a pleasant restaurant serving lunches. Recover here.

You leave St Paul's by the northwest corner, opposite the Chapter House. Turn right for St Paul's station.

North Bank: along the Strand

'North Bank' is a rarely used term but deserves wider adoption as a description of the critically important area of London linking the City and Westminster. It is separate from the West End, in character and history, with few residents but a huge number of daily visitors, and has its own distinctive personality. Logically it should be paired with its opposite number across the water, the South Bank.

The area's history reflects its topography as a bankside location between the more important places to east and west. It has been convenient for people wishing to travel the short distance in either direction, and as a base for the legal, marketing and transportation services required by the City's or Westminster's varied residents. For centuries it was the location of rich, elaborate Thameside palaces and gardens, established by ecclesiastical houses in the Middle Ages and redistributed to Henry VIII's aristocratic friends after the Dissolution of the Monasteries. Most of these survive only in streetnames (including Northumberland Avenue, Durham House Yard, Essex Street) or newer designations (the Savoy, the Temple); in one case, at Somerset House, the site survives fully, indeed magnificently, in 18C form.

The defining geographical feature is the spine of the Strand, once reached from the east from the valley of the Fleet up the long riverbank of Fleet Street, and from the south up a steep slope from the muddy shores of the Thames, which has now been embanked for more than a century. At the eastern end (described in Chapter 8), we are still within the boundary of the City, though in an area different in character. At the western end (Chapter 11), Trafalgar Square and Charing Cross have gradually formed their own distinct entity as a location in some ways more 'central' than their more historic neighbours either side. The measurement of distances from London is taken from here, and for many years the policy for numbering houses in streets placed no. 1 at the house nearest to Charing Cross.

8 • Blackfriars to Temple

This is quite a short walk but the area it covers is dense with historical associations, especially to the law. Lawyers settled in this area from early times, before which the best land was owned by the Knights Templar. The press dominated Fleet Street for a while, and then left. The climax of the walk is the Royal Courts of Justice, one of London's most spectacular but underestimated buildings. Go on a weekday: some buildings are closed on Saturdays and Sundays.

- Distance: 2 miles. Time: 2½ hours. Tube: Blackfriars. Map 8, 15.

Start at **Blackfriars Station** (**Map 8,5**). If arriving by Tube on the District/Circle Line, first go up the escalator to the Thameslink rail station to see the remains of an exotic façade showing destinations which could be reached, in theory at least, by the former London, Chatham and Dover Railway. Where else could you find Sheerness twinned with Vienna? Then leave the underground by exit 4 or 5 to look at **Blackfriars Bridge**. This wide and impressive arched bridge—the work of Joseph Cubitt—was opened in 1869 by Queen Victoria, whose statue stands at the centre of the road. Note the giant columns of Aberdeen granite, the ornate capitals with pelicans, and the rich cast-iron balustrades. Its predecessor, an even finer Neo-Classical structure by Robert Mylne (1760–69), was only the third bridge in central London and originally was to be called Pitt Bridge, after William Pitt the Elder, the admired prime minister of the day.

> The Black Friars (named from the colour of their habits) were a Dominican order, originally in Holborn, who established their monastery here in 1278, having been given Baynard's Castle which was rebuilt to the east of its old site (see Chapter 6). The Black Friars used stone from the castle and the city wall to build a huge church, 220ft by 95ft, on the rising ground. They were always an influential order and their monastery was the site of important events, including the condemnation of John Wycliffe's heresies in 1382 and the divorce case between Henry VIII and Catherine of Aragon in 1529. Parliaments were also held there. The monastery was dissolved in 1538. Later in the century the refectory was used as the Blackfriars Playhouse, now marked by Playhouse Yard, where the Burbages acted before moving to the Globe (Chapter 31) and where Shakespeare's plays were performed. Both he and Ben Jonson lived in the area.

As you stand on the bridge looking north along New Bridge Street to Ludgate Circus, your eye is following the line of the **River Fleet**, which entered the Thames here. It was once an important waterway but became polluted and was covered over to create an approach to the bridge. On your left is the imposing and confident Unilever House (1932) with odd repetitive statues above and fierce horses at the corners, all by Sir William Reid Dick. Further left is the former City of London Boys School (1881), now the façade of an office, and next to it **Sion College**, an eye-catching brick Gothic building by Sir Arthur Blomfield (1886).

> Its style must be a reference to Bridewell Palace, built by Henry VIII near this site. Edward VI gave Bridewell to the City which turned it into a hospital, workhouse and prison—in turn launching Bridewell as a name for other prisons. The building was burned in the Great Fire and rebuilt twice, and finally demolished when the new bridge was opened.

Return via the station to leave at exit 1—do not try to cross the road above. Note, standing alone, the *Black Friar*, an Arts and Crafts pub, with a complete decorative scheme of the 1890s including lots of beaten copper and tiles. Then walk north along New Bridge Street to **Ludgate Circus**, laid out in the 1860s but recently raised to reduce the gradient of Ludgate Hill, with the Thameslink railway track running underneath.

> Lud Gate was one of the ancient city gates, allegedly built by the mythical King Lud in 66 BC, but probably of Roman origin. Like other City gates it was demolished in 1760.

Ahead of you now is the bright-red **Holborn Viaduct**, part of a Victorian traffic-improvement scheme to span the Fleet valley, opened by the Queen on the same day as Blackfriars Bridge.

Turn left (west) up **Fleet Street** and then look back: Sir Christopher Wren intended you to see the needle-sharp point of the spire of St Martin Ludgate (Chapter 6) in contrast with the great, softly curvaceous dome of St Paul's Cathedral (Chapter 7). Note on the right the former offices of the *Daily Express*, by Sir Owen Williams, the first curtain-walled building in London (1931) and still a glamorous piece of Modernism. Beyond it is the *Daily Telegraph* building, by Elcock and Sutcliffe, of the same period but much more dated, in Art Deco Egyptian style.

Fleet Street and the press

The British press is still referred to by the collective term 'Fleet Street', where many national papers were based until the 1980s, but its earliest associations were with books. Caxton's pupil Wynkyn de Worde set up a press here *c* 1500 and it has been home to printers, bookbinders and booksellers. These in turn attracted many writers, from Samuel Richardson and William Cobbett to Raymond Chandler and Evelyn Waugh, whose novel *Scoop* satirised the Fleet Street press through the fictional *Daily Beast*.

London's first newspaper, the *Daily Courant*, was published on Fleet Street from 11 March 1702; *The Times* was established in 1788 and it and others have proved remarkably resilient. British newspapers are now grouped into the 'broadsheets' (the respectable *Times* and *Daily Telegraph*, the more radical *Guardian* and relatively new *Independent*) and the 'tabloids' (the scandalous, or entertaining, *Mirror*, *Sun* and *Daily Star*). The *Daily Mail* and *Daily Express* take the middle ground but are also tabloid in format. These divisions reflect the main fault-lines in British society: social class, education, postcode and political viewpoint.

In response to developments in printing technology, newspapers have now largely abandoned Fleet Street for premises in Wapping and elsewhere. Only a few of their buildings remain but in their heyday the big dailies were glad to be placed strategically between London's financial and political centres.

On your left, through a courtyard cut in 1824, you will see the famous steeple of the church of **St Bride** (from St Bridget), 1671–78, the 'wedding cake', at 226ft the tallest of all Wren's steeples, finished in 1701–3 (**Map 8,3**). The body of the church was bombed in the Second World War and remodelled on the lines of Wren's interior by Godfrey Allen in the 1950s. Although beautiful, the interior is too heavy and autocratic to feel like Wren's work, with Tuscan double columns, collegiate woodwork and a painted apse. The crypt is of exceptional interest, showing that beneath the church there was a Roman house overlooking the River Fleet, on top of which a Saxon church was built, and on that the Norman church that the Fire destroyed. It is absorbing to see the hierarchy of periods revealed, including a Roman pavement. There is also a permanent and interesting exhibition on the history of the press. Samuel Pepys and his siblings were baptised here, and the early novelist Samuel Richardson buried here. ☎ 020 7427 0133.

Return to Fleet Street and continue up the hill, noting Carmelite House by Sir Edwin Lutyens (1939) next door to the church—it is no great beauty, but Lutyens's work should always be pointed out. In Salisbury Square to the south is a startling statue of *St George and the Dragon* by Michael Sandle (1987). Cross **Whitefriars Street**, a reminder that the Carmelite Friars, who wore a white mantle over a brown habit, established their monastery here in the 13C.

> The Whitefriars were originally a group of hermits who lived on Mt Carmel in the Holy Land and were brought back to England by a brother of Henry III during the Crusades. They became a mendicant order and worked in cities among the people, with whom they were always popular.

Cross Fleet Street and go up Bolt Court, which twists and bends, into Gough Square, where **Dr Johnson's House** at no. 17 makes for a worthwhile visit. Johnson (see box, p 140) lived here from 1746 to 1759 while working on his *Dictionary*, which he compiled on the attic floor assisted by six clerks. His wife died here in 1752. The late 17C house is furnished with 18C items and many portraits and mementoes of the great man and his associates, including the painter Sir Joshua Reynolds, actor David Garrick, and the playwrights Oliver Goldsmith and Richard Brinsley Sheridan. The shop contains many rare printed pamphlets and shorter works, as well as James Boswell's biography of Johnson.

Open May–Sept 11.00–17.30 Mon–Sat; Oct–April 11.00–17.00 Mon–Sat; closed Sun and Bank Holidays. Admission charge. Shop. ☎ 020 7353 3745. www.drjh.dircon.co.uk. Tube: Blackfriars or Chancery Lane.

Walk back again to Fleet Street. You could refresh yourself at *Ye Olde Cheshire Cheese* (entrance at 145 Fleet Street): Johnson and his friends met here, as did the Rhymers' Club including W.B. Yeats and Oscar Wilde in the 1890s, and later John Galsworthy, Dylan Thomas and G.K. Chesterton. Part of the 14C crypt of the Whitefriars monastery survives in the basement.

Continue up the north side of the street (**Map 15,2**) to **St Dunstan in the West**, where Izaac Walton was a vestryman in the 17C. The church harmonises so beautifully with the street, where it picturesquely curves, that you could be forgiven for thinking it was medieval. The tower was indeed copied from a medieval church, All Saints Pavement in York, but the date is 1830: the architects John Shaw Senior and Junior rebuilt the church after street widening. There is a statue of *Queen Elizabeth* (1586) on the exterior, from the former church, to which it had been transferred from the Lud Gate, like the statues of *King Lud and his Sons* in the vestry porch underneath. The wonderful clock (1671) with figures to strike the hours also comes from the old church: these are the eponymous chimes of Dickens's second best 'Christmas Book'. Inside, the church is octagonal, with several chapels containing icons, some brought from Bucharest in the 1960s. There are memorials to Lord Baltimore (d. 1632), the founder of Maryland, and to Daniel Brown, the first Anglican clergyman to be ordained in America, in 1723. ☎ 020 7242 6027.

By way of contrast, opposite is the contemporary and amazingly restrained **Hoare's Bank**, by Charles Parker, 1829. Uniquely it is still a family concern, with a dignified banking hall and garden court beyond.

Now we must re-cross Fleet Street to explore one of London's secrets, including some serious architecture. But first note beyond you, past Chancery Lane (**Map 15,2**), the formal entrance to the City, marked by a fierce and spiky griffin on top of a high plinth replacing **Temple Bar**, the grand gateway by Wren (1672) now mouldering away at Theobalds in Hertfordshire. It is rumoured to be returning for reconstruction as part of the St Paul's precinct. Even today when the sovereign attends City events on state occasions, she fulfils the custom of obtaining permission from the Lord Mayor to pass this point. The present structure was erected in 1880: bronze reliefs show Queen Victoria passing through the old Temple Bar.

Dr Johnson

Samuel Johnson (1709–84) somehow stands in relation to 18C London as Charles Dickens does to the 19C. He can be sensed especially in Fleet Street and the area round his house in Gough Square, and in Johnson's Court where he lived later. He was born in Lichfield and spent his early life as a teacher in Birmingham, coming to London with Garrick, his former pupil, in 1737. His literary output was prodigious—he wrote much journalism as well as biographies, novels and poetry—but he is now best remembered for his *Dictionary* (published 1755). Johnson's great, broad personality, by turns melancholy and exuberant, and the still brilliant aphorisms and one-liners of his rich conversation, have come down to us through his companion Boswell, whose *Life of Johnson*, published in 1791, many feel is still the finest biography in English.

Johnson both loved and hated London. He published a poem on the city in 1738, soon after his arrival, deploring its vices and affectations and the oppression of its poor. But he uttered one of the most famous of all quotes about the place. Boswell recalls: 'I suggested no doubt, that if I were to reside in London, the exquisite zest with which I relished it in occasional visits might go off, and I might grow tired of it.' Johnson replied, 'Why, Sir, you find no man, at all intellectual, who is willing to leave London. No, Sir, when a man is tired of London, he is tired of life; for there is in London all that life can afford.'

The Inner and Middle Temple

Find Inner Temple Lane or Falcon Court to gain access to the Temple. These entrances are sometimes closed at weekends, when you can reach the Temple from the east gate in Tudor Street. The entrance at Inner Temple Lane is a fine half-timbered work of the late 16C. The space on the first floor inside, known as **Prince Henry's Room** after the elder son of James I, has oak panelling. Open 11.00–14.00 Mon–Sat. Admission free. ☎ 020 7936 4004.

The Temple

After Jerusalem was captured by Christian forces in 1099 the notion of going there on pilgrimage became fashionable. It was a dangerous journey and a group of knights pledged themselves to the protection of travellers. Their headquarters were established in the building in Jerusalem known, probably incorrectly, as the Temple of Solomon. Branches of this group—the Knights Templar, answerable only to the pope himself—were established in many European cities, including London, where the Temple marks the area where they built their second church and monastery (the first, long gone, was in Holborn). Templar churches had round naves, based on the Dome of the Rock in Jerusalem. That in London was large and richly endowed. It comprised an outer, a middle and inner areas—hence Middle and Inner Temple, the Outer having been built over long since.

Both royalty and citizenry were naturally jealous of the Knights and resented their freedom from local law: France acted first, but London followed and in 1308 the Knights were accused of various heresies and consigned to the Tower. Their property was taken over by the Knights Hospitaller (see Chapter 29), but the Temple was soon reallocated to lawyers to form two of the Inns of Court.

Through here you reach the grounds of the Inner Temple, and the **Temple church**, which also serves the Middle Temple immediately to the west. It has a round nave and a larger, rectangular chancel, all much restored in the early 19C and again after bomb damage in the Second World War. Even so the church (built around 1185) represents a most unusual and interesting point in the history of medieval architecture, at the transitional stage between Norman and Gothic. Norman can be seen in the portal at the

Temple church

west end, Gothic in the circular interior where important supporters of the Knights Templar were buried. The monuments include those of William Marshall, Earl of Pembroke (d. 1219), his sons, and Geoffrey de Mandeville (d. 1144): as Crusaders, their legs are crossed. The chancel (1240) is an even finer space, built as a hall with aisles of the same height. Oliver Goldsmith, who lived nearby, was buried here in 1774 but his gravesite is unknown. ☎ 020 7353 3470. Tours of the church and Inner Temple Hall at 10.30 can be pre-booked on ☎ 020 7797 8421.

Leave the church to explore the buildings around, all within the Inner and Middle Temples. Turn left (east) across Church Court, through an alley to reach **King's Bench Walk**. This fine space is spoiled by its use as a car park, but is inspiring even so. Former residents include H. Rider Haggard, Harold Nicolson and his wife Vita Sackville-West. On the east side, a fine but much-restored row of houses of the late 17C is unconvincingly associated with Wren: even so they give a good idea of how a London street of that period must have looked. If it seems familiar, remember how popular it is with filmmakers. Nos 2, 3 and 7, and the porch of no. 5, are all beauties. From no. 8 onwards the work is of 1814, and south of Paper Buildings opposite all is 'Gothick', but the mixture holds together wonderfully well, helped by the green space and the sense of the river nearby. Paper Buildings itself is solemn stuff by Sir Robert Smirke (1838), architect of the British Museum.

Inns of Court

There are today four surviving Inns of Court—the Middle and Inner Temple, Lincoln's Inn and Gray's Inn. Originally there were many more, including Furnival's Inn and Staple Inn, which comprised the Inns of Chancery and now exist only in name. The Inns of Court were always the more senior. Entirely independent bodies still, they were established in the later Middle Ages as accommodation for trainee lawyers during their apprenticeship. Each is still governed by Benchers (Masters of the Bench), who alone have the power to call successful students to the bar (as barristers). Readers (senior barristers) give regular lectures, but until very recently the only formal requirement the Inns imposed on students was that of dining there three times per term for 12 terms. The layout of the Inns is collegiate but the Oxbridge atmosphere you feel is misleading: there is little sign of students of any sort, but plenty of practising barristers quietly lurk in their chambers. The effect is peaceful but, in its way, unsettling.

Return west along Crown Office Row, rebuilt since Charles Lamb was born there in 1775: he and his sister Mary later lived in Mitre Court nearby. **Inner Temple Gardens** are on your left but you will not be able to get in unless accompanied by a member of the Inn. The gardens illustrate how the banks of the Thames must have looked before the 17C, with the lawns of great houses sloping down to the stream. To the west there was a whole series of such houses but the riverside feeling is now crudely severed by the Victoria Embankment. W.M. Thackeray used the gardens as a setting in his *History of Pendennis*.

From Crown Office Row you can go through into Middle Temple Lane. Turn right and immediately on your left is **Middle Temple Hall** (1570) with a wonderful oak hammerbeam roof and screen, Elizabethan tables and numerous royal portraits. Shakespeare's *Twelfth Night* was first performed here on 2 February 1601. Open usually 10.00–12.00 and 15.00–16.00 Mon–Fri. Admission free. ☎ 020 7797 7768.

Opposite, in Brick Court, Goldsmith lived and wrote *She Stoops to Conquer*; later residents included Thackeray and Anthony Hope, author of *The Prisoner of Zenda*. **Fountain Court** is straight ahead. Many London locations appear in Dickens's novels but one of the most appealing and realistic is the scene set here in *Martin Chuzzlewit*, when John Westlock meets Ruth Pinch. **New Court** at the western end of Fountain Court is a street by Nicholas Barbon (1675), the great post-Fire speculator, which typically he sold to the Middle Temple at a thumping profit. To the left is **Middle Temple Gardens**, where, tradition and Shakespeare have it, the fateful quarrel took place which led to the Wars of the Roses. Open May, June, July and Sept 12.00–15.00 Mon–Fri.

Leave the Temple via the **Middle Temple Gatehouse** at the top of Middle Temple Lane (**Map 15,2**). This fine gateway is by Roger North, an obscure but entertaining contemporary of Wren, and a Bencher of the Inn: it looks best from across the Strand. You may as well cross over at this point because we are not yet finished with the law: the climax is coming now.

Royal Courts of Justice

You will certainly have noted already the vast Gothic pile stretching west on the north side of the street: this houses the Royal Courts of Justice, nearly always called the Law Courts.

- Open 09.00–16.30 Mon–Fri. Closed Aug and Sept. Admission free. ☎ 020 7947 6000. Tube: Holborn or Temple. **Note**. No cameras are allowed inside (the jewellery shop across the road will very kindly look after your camera.)

The Law Courts designed by Sir John Soane survived the fire at Westminster in 1834 but were never particularly popular with lawyers, being cramped and too few in number. It was a long-term aim to centralise the civil courts in one location and, after an unsatisfactory competition and dithering over the site, this one was chosen: it is hard to realise now, but the scheme also presented the opportunity to eliminate some serious Victorian slums. The Royal Courts of Justice are George Edmund Street's masterpiece, and were completed in 1882, the year after his death which was caused, it was said, by the frustrations of the project.

British legal system

Law in Britain today is principally made through parliamentary Acts, but a vast body of case law also exists, based on the precedents of decisions made in the courts over time. The latter is especially important in civil law, the subject matter of the Royal Courts of Justice and the High Court. Criminal law, defined by statute, is handled by Crown courts and magistrates' courts throughout the country, and by the Central Criminal Court in the Old Bailey for major cases (Chapter 6). Appeals can be made against the decisions of both courts, and these are heard at the Royal Courts of Justice and, if necessary, ultimately in the House of Lords.

There are three divisions of the High Court: Chancery, dealing with land disputes, trusts, insolvency; the Queen's Bench, for cases of debt, contract, libel; and Family, for divorce, adoption, etc. The Royal Courts of Justice deal with all these, as well as judicial reviews and injunctions.

You are represented in court by a barrister, whom you meet via your solicitor. The two are quite separate. Solicitors may not speak in court, whereas barristers' work is confined to the courts. A Queen's Counsel (QC) is a senior barrister who wears a silk robe (hence the name 'silk'). Barristers and judges wear wigs in court. The judge, seated on a raised dais (bench), hears the cases for and against, and delivers the verdict, sometimes assisted by a jury. At the Royal Courts of Justice juries tend to be confined to libel and slander cases.

Examine the **exterior** first from opposite the main entrance in the Strand, towards the western end. (Stand on the island where there are public toilets:

St Clement Danes is on your left.) In front of the entrance, Monday to Friday, there may well be press cameras hoping for shots of happy or disappointed litigants. Street's building came towards the end of the Gothic Revival and represents its full maturity: it is an invigorating mixture of International Gothic forms, imaginatively collected into a kind of catalogue of the style—pointed arches, mouldings, tourelles, lancets, spires, with occasional statuary and, as so often, a dominating clock-tower. It was the Victorians who made us time-conscious. There is some symmetry round the entrance but none as the eye travels eastwards.

Now go inside, past a bag-check. You now stand in Street's great **central hall**, extravagant in conception and use of space, off which run sinister-looking spiral staircases to the various courts. Originally there were 19 courts, but since then extensions in different directions over the site, including into the basement, have increased the number to over 80. Barristers resplendent in traditional dress fit well with the grandeur and sense of superiority conveyed by the architecture. Gothic can make you feel small, and in the courts this may be intentional: if the law was anxious to proclaim its majesty, Street's building certainly delivered.

The interesting display and video in the central hall is worth looking at and documents may be available describing a **walk** round the building. This is recommended if you have time, and if you do not find the whole experience too oppressive. Most of the courts when sitting are open to the public and you can therefore enter one and sit in the gallery. Note, at least, Armstead's fine statue of *G.E. Street* (1886) himself on the east side of the hall near the entrance: it is rare for an architect to be so honoured.

> ### George Edmund Street
> A noted Victorian architect, Street (1824–81) was, as you might have expected, serious, scholarly, a follower of John Ruskin and resolutely Gothic. He began as a designer of churches: in London, his notable works include St James the Less, Pimlico, and St Mary Magdelene, Paddington. But his greatest success came with the competition to design the Royal Courts of Justice in 1866. Although the original design changed several times, the finished product remains one of the finest, and final, examples in London of the application of High Gothic principles to secular architecture.

You can leave the Royal Courts of Justice on the north side but it is best to return to the Strand again. There is just time for another church, prominent on your right, but first cross the road to see the riotous tiling in the branch of Lloyd's/TSB at No.22, built originally as a restaurant and surviving as a triumph of the Doulton porcelain factory's skills: the tiles were designed by John McLennan in 1883 and made across the river in Lambeth. *Twining's* nearby is not only supposed to be the narrowest shop in London but also the oldest business still on its original premises and doing what it was set up to do, in this case, to sell tea.

Wren's work at **St Clement Danes** (1679–82) was not a rebuilding after the Fire, which never reached this far west, but was a continuation of an uncompleted work from the traumatic 1640s. James Gibbs finished off the steeple (1719–20) and the main body of the church had to be rebuilt again in the 20C after war damage. It is a bit of a mixture but is unique among Wren churches (apart from St Paul's Cathedral) in having a double-apsed east end. This may represent a continuation of the original medieval plan which, with the name, is a reminder of the antiquity of this area. 'Danes' refers, it is thought, to the Viking invasions and the existence of a Danish community here before Alfred's Saxon triumphalism removed them. The church is now dedicated to the Royal Air Force. ☎ 020 7242 8282.

From the west end of St Clement's you can walk down Arundel Street to Temple station (closed on Sundays), or round Aldwych and up Kingsway to Holborn. There are plenty of buses going to the West End.

9 • Aldwych and Somerset House

This walk explores the area around Aldwych. The distances are not great, but there are two unforgettable sites, Lincoln's Inn and Somerset House. The latter contains three important galleries and has distinguished architecture, so allow plenty of time to study it. There are a number of pleasant places for refreshment on the way and at Somerset House itself. If you plan to visit the Hermitage Rooms at Somerset House, note the point about timed tickets.

• Distance: nearly 2 miles. Time: 1 hour + 3 hours for the galleries. Tube: Temple. Map 7.

Aldwych was a name adopted by the Edwardians, derived from *ald wic*, meaning an ancient settlement in the Saxon language and referring to that period, *c* AD 800. Recent research has indicated that the Saxon invaders did not base their main town in the Roman city but here, on the high ground west of the Fleet river, overlooking the Thames, which they partially embanked in the sweeping concave bend near Charing Cross. They called their settlement Lundenwic. It was abandoned at the time of the Viking raids. King Alfred is traditionally supposed to have given the area over to occupation by the defeated Danes—hence St Clement Danes (see Chapter 8).

We start at Temple station (**Map 7,8**); it is closed on Sundays, when you should use Charing Cross. Go up the steps from the station, turn left past the Howard Hotel and then right up **Surrey Street**. This area first belonged to ecclesiastical houses in the Middle Ages, and then was the site of two great aristocratic establishments—Arundel House and Essex House—that stretched, with their fine gardens, from the Strand down to the banks of the Thames. They were demolished as part of the post-Fire building boom, and there is no trace of them today, but the beauty of their world is conveyed in literature and art collections. Edmund Spenser wrote his *Prothalamion* to celebrate a double wedding which took place at Essex House in 1596, ending each stanza with the evocative line 'sweet Thames, run softly till I end my song'. At Arundel House next door Thomas Howard, Earl of Arundel, who enabled Inigo Jones to study Italian architecture, built up his collection of Classical statuary, the first great British collection, which was passed by a descendant to Oxford University.

Take a small alley to the left half-way up Surrey Street to see, just beyond a serious outbreak of terracotta, the so-called **Roman bath** in Strand Lane. You can only glimpse it through a window (switch on the light). It is a plunge bath, 15½ft by 6½ft, but although built of red bricks it has yet to be proved authentically Roman (it may be 17C). Open by appointment May–Sept 13.00–17.00 Wed. Admission free. ☎ 020 7641 6254.

Just above it, up the hill, do not miss a perfect Regency verandah—its view of the river before the embankment was built must have been delightful. Back in Surrey Street the familiar plum-coloured tiles of the early Piccadilly Line can be seen on Aldwych station, which was closed in 1982.

At the top of the hill you join an Edwardian world, fiercely punctuated by contemporary traffic. Have no regrets: from 1905 the whole layout of **Aldwych** and Kingsway was designed to accommodate increasing traffic. The architecture itself is from another era. The buildings opposite you—Australia House to the right, Bush House to the left, behind St Mary-le-Strand church—and the swirling roadway were conceived in that confident Imperial era, when Britain was just ceasing to be Great but had not yet realised it.

> ### Edward VII (1841–1910, r. 1901–1910)
> Edward had to wait until he was 60 years old before getting the job he was born to, and during that time his lifestyle gained for him a dubious reputation. Disrespectful of the values of his parents—a great sin to Victorians—he enjoyed gambling, the turf and women. His Danish queen, Alexandra (see Chapter 66), turned a blind eye to most of this and they were not unhappy. Moreover he was never unpopular with the public and was quite a successful king, proving unafraid of political involvement during a turbulent period. His reign has come to be seen as an Indian summer before the onset of 20C horrors, but in fact the signs of impending international upheaval were already visible, literally so, perhaps, in the provocative imperialism of Edwardian architecture.

Cross at the pedestrian lights and make your way through Melbourne Place straight ahead. **Australia House** (1912–13, by Marshall Mackenzie) on your right is in the grandest Beaux-Arts style, with a sculpture collection by Harold Parker (1915–18) to match. Glimpse the gilded marble entrance hall—very much to Dame Edna's taste. On your left—turn left first to see it properly and to cross the road at the lights—is **Bush House**, built as a trade centre by an American, Irving T. Bush, but taken over by the BBC Overseas Service in 1940. The building is by the American architect Harvey W. Corbett (1919–35), but no less imperial for that. It is at its grandest on this north side, facing up Kingsway. It was considered too American at the time, but now suits the atmosphere of Aldwych well. The somewhat chauvinist dedication, 'To the friendship of the English-speaking peoples', originating in the sentiment of American–English relations, turned out to be appropriate for the BBC broadcasts overseas. The sculptures of *Great Britain* and the *USA* as male figures were executed in the USA by Malvina Hoffmann (1925).

Cross to the northeast side of Aldwych and make your way up Houghton Street, home of the **London School of Economics**, through Clements Inn Passage and Grange Court into Carey Street. The great Gothic building on your right is the Royal Courts of Justice (Chapter 8). Note on your left, first, a memorial to the martyr Sir Thomas More and then the *Seven Stars* pub (1602), which must be London's tiniest; the name refers to the seven provinces of the Netherlands. Beyond, the archway to Lincoln's Inn contains *Wildy's* bookshop (1830), one of the oldest in London. Towards the end of Carey Street, on the left, is a fine 17C house, now occupied by the President of the Law Society. Beyond it is another example of a new London phenomenon, a bank turned into a pub.

You now reach historic **Chancery Lane**, named from 'Chancellors Lane', after the residence of the Lord Chancellor and the maintenance here of the Rolls of Chancery from 1311 (**Map 7,6**). To the right you can see the **Law Society's Hall** with a noble Greek-Revival portico, built by Lewis Vulliamy (1831) as a club for solicitors, with an interesting Edwardian extension (1902) by Charles Holden, of later Tube station fame. Opposite is the Gothic-Revival former Public Record Office by John Nash's son-in-law, James Pennethorne (1856), now the library of King's College, London.

Turn left (north) up Chancery Lane. On your left note Chichester Rents, with nice little shops, and beyond it Star Yard with a genuine Victorian gentlemen's convenience, no longer in use. On your right is the pleasing enclave of Quality Court, with Quality House and a little further, at Southampton Buildings, the **London Silver Vaults**, endless basements full of silver, all for sale, and well worth exploring if you have time and money.

Lincoln's Inn

If you have neither, turn left through the Gate House into Lincoln's Inn (**Map 7,6**), one of the Inns of Court (see Chapter 8), to appreciate a rich collection of architecture, all immediate and free, though not all of it open. The **Gate House** (1518) leads into Old Buildings (1524–1613) and the **Old Hall** (1489–92), where hangs William Hogarth's painting *Paul before Felix* (not a success), and where the Court of Chancery used to sit. It is here that the interminable but unforgettable case of Jarndyce v. Jarndyce is heard in Charles Dickens's *Bleak House*.

The very late Gothic **chapel** (1619–23) lies above the open undercroft, used for legal consultation. The chapel contains a magnificent stained-glass window. Every night, at 21.00, the chapel bell tolls 60 times: it also chimes when a Bencher dies. One distinguished preacher at the Inn was John Donne, who laid the foundation stone and whose resonant line 'Send not to ask for whom the bell tolls: it tolls for thee' can thus be linked to this place. Open 12.00–14.30 Mon–Fri.

Beyond, the Inn opens up into **New Square**, a fine group of late 17C houses put up by the Bencher and speculator Henry Serle, not originally intended for lawyers but now exclusively occupied by them. The square is still lit by gas lamps. To the north—explore into the garden—on the left lies the neo-Tudor New Hall and Library by Philip Hardwick (1845), magnificent in red brick and black diapering, a reflection of the style of Old Buildings. On the right, in ruthless Classical contrast, are Stone Buildings by Sir Robert Taylor (1774–80).

Leave Lincoln's Inn by the western gateway into **Lincoln's Inn Fields**. This open space is really too large to be read as a square, and has a somewhat different history. The members of Lincoln's Inn, although not the owners, always wanted it to remain open as their equivalent of Temple Gardens (Chapter 8) or Gray's Inn Walks (Chapter 23), and in the early 17C reached agreement with a developer, William Newton, to confine the houses to the edge. Only one such early house now remains, Lindsey House (nos 59–60) on the western side, the design of which is linked to Inigo Jones, but past residents included John Milton, Nell Gwyn and Alfred, Lord Tennyson. **Sir John Soane's Museum** is close by on the north side and could be included in this tour, although to digest it with Somerset House would perhaps be too much, hence its inclusion in the walk round Holborn (Chapter 23). Walking along the south side you pass the **Royal College of Surgeons**' fine portico, by George Dance the Younger (1806), retained when Charles Barry reconstructed the building in 1835. Inside is an unusual museum, containing chiefly the anatomical collection of John Hunter, the distinguished 18C surgeon. It is slightly gruesome, but extremely interesting. Open 10.00–17.00 Mon–Fri, with a free guided tour Wed at 14.00. Admission free, donations encouraged. ☎ 020 7869 6560. Tube: Holborn.

Note also the harmoniously modern structure of Cancer Research UK (formerly Imperial Cancert Reseach Fund) (1960). Just at the western end of Lincoln's Inn Fields turn briefly down Portsmouth Street to reach Portugal Street, which contains the *Old Curiosity Shop*, unlikely to have been Dickens's inspiration but nevertheless reputed to be the oldest shop in London (1567).

Turn left down **Kingsway**. This windswept thoroughfare has lost some of its grandeur but the original concept was part of that early 20C splendour to which we now return; the king in question was Edward VII. As you walk south Bush House postures at the bottom before you, and the former tram subway disappears underneath to the Embankment; since 1964 it has been an underpass for traffic from Waterloo Bridge. Across Kingsway, to the west and tucked away behind the street façade, is the fine modern tower block of the **Civil Aviation Authority**, in the Centre Point idiom (see Chapter 22), with concrete frames.

Turn right into Aldwych again. The magnificent *Waldorf Hotel* (1908) dominates the north side, and it is worth crossing the street, though at risk to life, to inspect from a distance the delightful sculptures at penthouse level, of putti turning head-over-heels. On the south side is **India House** by Sir Herbert Baker (1930), with little reliefs of Indian subjects all over the walls. Cut through India Place, past a bust of *Pandit Nehru*, to the Strand.

Immediately on your left is **St Mary-le-Strand** by James Gibbs (1714–17), one of the fifty new churches erected under the 1711 Act (see Chapter 45) and the architect's first public building in London. If the word 'pretty' can ever be applied to a church it must be to this one, which used to feature on the cover of the *Strand* magazine. Delicate but elegant, Italianate with its little urns, it is not at all Londonesque. It stands alone, exposed to traffic on both sides, a factor of which Gibbs took account by making his ground-level window spaces blind with niches, and leaving the clerestory to provide the light. The design does not take Nicholas Hawksmoor's approach to the Baroque but relates to its Italian origins, which John Summerson traces to the building formerly in Rome known as Raphael's house. Gibbs added the ultra-refined rectangular steeple a little later, after a plan to erect a column to Queen Anne was abandoned. The round portico is a reference to Sir Christopher Wren's transept porticoes at St Paul's. The interior is slightly oppressive because of the high windows, perhaps not so pretty but equally interesting as a design, with a patterned ceiling, apsed east end and tulip-shaped pulpit. ☎ 020 7836 3126.

Before crossing the road outside St Mary's, look to the left to see **King's College**, founded in 1832 as a Christian rival to the godless institution of University College in Bloomsbury (Chapter 27). The Strand front is uncompromisingly modern (1966–71), but within are buildings by Sir Robert Smirke (1830s). More important, however, immediately in front of you is the climax of this walk, Somerset House.

James Gibbs

A bachelor, a socialite, a Roman Catholic and a Tory, Gibbs (1662–1754) was by no means a typical architect but he produced church buildings that were to prove highly influential, both in Britain and the USA. He was a Scot trained in Rome, features which, like his religion and politics, probably told against him. St Martin-in-the-Fields and especially St Mary-le-Strand are churches which reveal his Italian education. Gibbs found a way of developing Wren's generalised Classicism into something more formal, more humane than Hawksmoor, and distinct from the more hidebound principles of the Palladians.

Somerset House

Somerset House was built to provide two things, accommodation for certain learned societies and offices for the navy. Only recently has it become a great deal more, with art galleries, restaurants, cafés, a river terrace, a remarkable public space for concerts and a skating rink in winter; and there are still government offices, today for the Inland Revenue, who just won't go away. Nor should they, because it is the long residence there of government that has conserved Somerset House so perfectly. Architecturally this is one of the finest, most complete and unaltered historic buildings in London.

History

The site was always important. After the Dissolution of the Monasteries (from 1539), it had been taken over by Edward Seymour, Earl of Somerset, who had a house built for himself. As the brother of Jane Seymour, Henry VIII's third wife, Somerset was therefore uncle and 'Protector' of the boy-king Edward VI. He was beheaded in 1552 for treason, and the house that bore his name became a royal palace. It was a distinguished building, one of the first in England in a Renaissance style, including a river frontage and chapel by Inigo Jones. On the riverbank were a formal garden and terrace.

By the 18C the place had become neglected: in 1774 George III agreed to its demolition and redevelopment as offices for the navy, regarded after the recent war with France as Britain's most important service. After a shaky start under another architect, in 1775 the project was placed in the hands of Sir William Chambers, already distinguished for his work at Kew Gardens and elsewhere, as the author of a historical treatise on architecture, and as the treasurer of the newly established Royal Academy. His connections with George III undoubtedly enabled him to pull a few strings, which must have helped the Academy in acquiring space in the prestigious Strand wing of the new building. The challenge was to integrate into a single entity accommodation for three learned societies as well as innumerable small offices for government clerks, in a scholarly Classical style (he would tolerate no less), on a site with a narrow front widening and sloping sharply down to the river. Seeing the building today, you are not conscious of any of these difficulties. Chambers levelled the site by including extensive vaults for government records and other storage, placed the societies in more refined architecture at the Strand entrance, and located the offices round a courtyard with a formal south front incorporating a great arched entrance from the Thames.

The building was finished in 1806, a few years after Chambers had died.

The societies stayed there until the mid-19C but found themselves other homes (the Royal Academy at Burlington House from 1869, the Society of Antiquaries likewise, and the Royal Society now at Carlton House Terrace), and government offices filled the entire place. Until a few years ago the courtyard was a car park. The most famous tenants were the Probate Registry and the Registrar of Births and Deaths, and the huge records of these departments filled the vaults for decades. To the west, in Lancaster Place, is an extension put up by James Pennethorne in the 1860s, called the New Wing.

We enter from the Strand, through the triple archway. Besides the Inland Revenue, Somerset House today contains the Courtauld Galleries and the Courtauld Institute of Art—these are on your immediate right and left respectively—and, in the south wing overlooking the river, the Hermitage Rooms and the Gilbert Collection. This walk will take you round the exterior but *en route* covers the three public galleries, which you may want to tackle separately. To appreciate Chambers's work fully you need to see both the interior of the Courtauld (for which you have to pay the gallery entrance charge) and the south wing (which is free).

Courtauld Galleries

The Courtauld Galleries—a delicious mixture of art from early medieval to early 20C, particularly strong in Impressionism and Post-Impressionism—come first.

• Open 10.00–18.00 Mon–Sat, 12.00–18.00 Sun and Bank Holidays. Admission charge, except 10.00–14.00 Mon (excluding Bank Holidays). Joint ticket available with Gilbert Collection. Café. Shop. ☎ 020 7848 2526. Tube: Temple or Charing Cross.

The nucleus of the collection reflects the prescient taste of Samuel Courtauld, who was chair of the famous textile company and who also, with Lord Lee of Fareham, founded the Courtauld Institute of Art. He took to buying Impressionist paintings in the 1920s before anyone else was interested, and left them to London University, of which the Institute is a part, as a memorial to his wife. After the Second World War several bequests augmented the collection, including in 1978 that of Count Seilern, an Austrian, with its rich resources of work by Rubens and Tiepolo. The result provides a gallery visit of perfect length and variety, in rooms of ideal proportions: a feast for eye and mind.

On admission look around the **entrance hall**. This was the original entrance for Royal Academy members and visitors. The room on the right, **Gallery 1**, was where the Academy's students assembled to draw from the nude model. Now it holds the early medieval collection, including magnificent ivory miniatures. Look up and down the **stairwell**: Chambers was a genius at staircases. His semicircular flight here is matched by an exactly similar flight on the eastern side of the block, originally reserved for the Royal Society and Society of Antiquaries (now part of the Institute, it can be seen if an exhibition from the separate world-class drawings collection is in progress—ask at the desk). The original plan was for the first Keeper of the Royal Academy to live in the basement and to access his front door via the strange internally rusticated doorway which now leads to the café and cloakrooms. Go down for refreshment or just to see it. The Keeper did not like it, understandably enough: this is one of Chambers' rare infelicities.

Sir William Chambers

One of the two most important architects in London in the second half of the 18C, Chambers (1723–96) was born in Sweden and travelled extensively in the Far East before training in architecture in Paris and Rome. This background might have made him cosmopolitan, and certainly enabled him to design for the Prince of Wales some exotic garden buildings at Kew, such as the Pagoda. But his temperament was conformist, correct, academic, dependent on Palladio and France, and his London masterpiece, Somerset House, reflects these qualities. Even here, though, the imaginative stamp can be seen in the staircases and what is left of the basements and river façade. Chambers was the first treasurer of the Royal Academy and, with his connections to George III, self-consciously the establishment architect of the day in contrast to the Adam brothers' more blatantly commercial mentality.

Next ascend the staircase to the main floor. Enjoy the decorative scheme as you rise in a journey through the orders, via Ionic and then Corinthian, growing in enrichment as the architect intended. Enter **Gallery 2** ahead, containing works of the Early and High Renaissance. Mariotto Albertinelli's *Creation and Fall of Man* (1510–15), with several scenes in one, is as vivid and full of action as a strip cartoon. There is a movingly beautiful wooden *Virgin and Child* of the late 15C.

Gallery 3, the former Committee Room of the Royal Society, overlooks the courtyard. It contains mostly High Renaissance and Mannerist works, notably Parmigianino's delectable *Virgin and Child* (1524), Palma Vecchio's large, and less delectable, *Venus in a Landscape* (1520) and Giovanni Bellini's savage *Assassination of St Peter Martyr* (1509).

In **Gallery 4** we proceed through the 16C via Northern Europe. Note Lucas Cranach's *Adam and Eve* (1526), diet-conscious compared with the Italian beauties in the previous room, but all-too-convincingly human, he full of doubt and she of tempting suggestion. There is a *Landscape with the Flight into Egypt* by Pieter Bruegel the Elder (1563), and Hans Eworth's strange portrait of *Sir John Luttrell* (1550), up to his waist in sea-water and dripping with symbols.

Gallery 5 was originally the meeting room of the Society of Antiquaries. It contains mostly works by Peter Paul Rubens from the Seilern collection. Especially compelling is the early portrait of the painter *Jan Bruegel and his Family* (1613), prosperous, respectable, amused but on their dignity, and *Landscape by Moonlight* (1635–40) from Rubens's maturity. There is also his set of designs (1611) for the *Descent from the Cross* in Antwerp Cathedral.

The next room, **Gallery 6**, opposed architecturally to Gallery 3, was the meeting room for the Royal Academicians, for whom Chambers provided a much grander ceiling than he gave to the scientists: the plasterwork is by Thomas Collins and the marble fireplaces by Joseph Wilton, two of his regular associates. Here are paintings of the mid-17C, including memorable portraits such as Sir Peter Lely's *Sir Thomas Thynne* and the mysterious William Dobson's *An Older and a Younger Man* (1640s).

More portraits are to be found in **Gallery 7**, including *Don Francisco de Saavedra* (1798) by Francisco Goya—such surprises are one of the pleasures of viewing personal, as opposed to national or committee-led, collections of art—and Thomas Gainsborough's tender, humane image of his wife (1778).

Now climb up a steeper flight of stairs—consider why they are steeper—to the main exhibition room. The stairs are actually dangerous, especially when you descend, and were from the start the subject of much satirical humour, including Thomas Rowlandson's print of the 'Great Stare Case', showing dignified ladies and gents tumbling embarrassingly down. At the top, the luxury of the decorative plasterwork is at its height and you can gaze down at the perfect symmetry of the semicircular flight.

Ahead of you, in the **Ante Room** (Gallery 8), are world-beating early Impressionists, including Camille Pissarro's *Lordship Lane Station* (1871), souvenir of his sojourn in London to escape the Paris Commune, Pierre Auguste Renoir's *Le Loge* (1874) and Edouard Manet's sketch for *Le Dejeuner Sur l'Herbe* (1867). Claude Monet's *Autumn Effect at Argenteuil* (1873) and Renoir's *Seine at Argenteuil* (1874) epitomise the Impressionists' capturing of the moment, as does Edgar Degas' *Two Dancers on the Stage* (1874).

Pass into the **Great Room** (Gallery 9), where once, at the Academy's annual exhibitions, the paintings hung from floor to window without an inch of wall space between. Now, with suitable space between and with smaller crowds, you can enjoy Impressionist and Post-Impressionist masterpieces of the 1880s and 1890s, including Manet's *Bar at the Folies Bergère* (1881–82) and Vincent van Gogh's *Portrait with a Bandaged Ear* (1889)—perhaps the most famous of all the images in the Courtauld collection. The riches also include Paul Gauguin's *Te Rerioa* (1897) and *Nevermore* (1891), both of them threatening and discomfiting, several of Georges Seurat's detached and impersonal Pointilliste experiments, and several intellectual works by Paul Cézanne, including the *Man with the Pipe* (1892), *Mont St-Victoire* (1887) and the *Card Players* (1892–95). In the centre of the space are several of Frank Dobson's dumpy yet compelling figures of the 1920s.

Beyond, in the smaller **Galleries 10 and 11**, are some relative curiosities by Roger Fry, C.R.W. Nevinson and Percy Wyndham Lewis, and by significant French artists of the early 20C, including Pierre Bonnard and the Douanier Rousseau. There are often very imaginative temporary exhibitions in **Gallery 12**.

Now we return for a while to the architecture. As you enter the main **courtyard** of Somerset House pause and look around. Behind you is the rear of the Strand front, where Chambers has spelled out the orders in his own academic fashion: heavy vermiculated rustication at basement level; Doric for the ground floor (see the evidence in the entrance archway); mezzanine next; Ionic above, where the learned societies had their most important rooms; and then Corinthian. Above that, where we might have expected a pediment, as purists of the 1780s were quick to point out, there is a rectangular projection above the cornice, to accommodate the Great Room. It has Diocletian windows to give better light. The statues in front represent the four continents, with America second from the left belligerently holding a spear: there was a war on in the 1770s.

Then turn to examine the east, west and south wings. These are fully rusticated, to indicate that they are **offices**: the precedent was William Kent's Treasury (see Chapter 12). Chambers believed that the Composite order, a combination of Ionic and Corinthian, was subordinate to Corinthian, so his use of it for the offices of mere civil servants on the upper floors distinguishes them from the quarters of the more significant royal societies.

The naval connection is confirmed by statuary of mermen and catches from the sea to either side of all the entrances. The bronze statue of *George III* by John Bacon the Elder (1789), with the prow of a Roman galley as well as the usual lion, underlines the message, and the significance of the Thames as a trading route from the sea is indicated by the river god below, pouring riches from his cornucopia. (Bearded gods of English rivers can be seen on the Strand façade, too.) The fountains in the centre of the courtyard—another watery symbol—were installed in 2000 and give displays at 13.00, 18.00 and 22.00, with short displays on the hour and half-hour 10.00–23.00 (stopping earlier in winter). For ice skating here, ☎ 020 7845 4600.

You may feel that the **south wing** is the least successful, with the pediment awkwardly placed behind the balustrade and the dome above somewhat diminutive, but the overall dimensions and semiotics of the courtyard create a wonderfully integrated space. If the weather is fine take some refreshment outdoors from the café in this wing and study it all at leisure.

Next enter the south wing, under the dome, to see the former **Seamen's Hall**. Here Chambers created a fine, perfectly proportioned waiting area for seamen attending the bureaucrats in the offices: Horatio Nelson must have waited here (but not for long presumably, in view of his reputation). Take the corridor to the right, past café, restaurant and shop and continue through doors to see the **Navy Stair**, one of Chambers's finest achievements with breathtaking plastic architecture, an oval space with the two outer flights merging to fly across the centre. You may ascend it.

Hermitage Rooms

Return via the ticket room for the Hermitage Rooms, which are located off the Seamen's Hall on the eastern side. This changing loan exhibition offers an introduction to the treasures of the State Hermitage Museum, housed in the Winter Palace in St Petersburg.

• Open 10.00–18.00 Mon–Sat, 12.00–18.00 Sun and Bank Holidays. Entry by timed ticket (advance booking, ☎ 020 7413 3398 or on-line at www. ticketmaster. co.uk). ☎ 020 7845 4630. Café nearby. Shop. www.hermitage rooms.com

   Remember, these confined spaces, now with brilliant marquetry floors and ornately painted ceilings based on designs from the Winter Palace, were intended merely as offices. They can therefore become very cramped, so understandably entry is by timed ticket. You can buy these in advance (see above) or, in limited numbers, at Somerset House on the day.

Exit to the **terrace**, where coffee is available in summer. Here you would have a fine view of the river if it were not for two intrusions, the Victoria Embankment and the superfluous trees planted on it. Towards Waterloo Bridge there is an interesting view through the space between Chambers's west wing and Pennethorne's 1860s building. Note how windows pose as doors at your level, when ground-level is some two floors below (the space is taken up by a wretched neo-Georgian staff canteen). This former 'street' was another of Chambers's problems, a public right of way down to the river, over which he dramatically placed a Piranesian arch, now above your head.

There is one more sight to see, accessible either down the steps at Waterloo Bridge, or inside the south wing and down in a lift, or even via the Stamp Office stairs, a utilitarian staircase in the southeast corner accessed from the courtyard.

You will reach an information display on Somerset House itself and the entrance to the Gilbert Collection. Adjacent to the entrance—and not to be missed—is a short staircase down to the old river level where you can see a former **King's Barge**, a rare surviving example of the type of craft which used to ply the Thames for formal trips in the 18C, 'moored' at the point under Chambers's great river arch where waterborne entry to the premises was effected.

Gilbert Collection

Enter the Gilbert Collection on the east side of the Embankment entrance. This new museum (opened in 2000) may sound rather specialised, even dull, but be assured it is full of amazingly beautiful objects of unbelievable workmanship and, being new, it displays everything superbly. Again, as in the Courtauld Galleries, there is a special pleasure in inspecting the collection of a single individual as against a national or committee-based series of choices.

- Open 10.00–18.00 Mon–Sat, 12.00–18.00 Sun and Bank Holidays. Admission charge, except 10.00–14.00 Mon. Joint ticket available with the Courtauld Galleries. Café nearby. Shop. ☎ 020 7420 9400. www.gilbert-collection.org.uk

> The individual in this case was Sir Arthur Gilbert (d. 2001), an Englishman who lived in California from 1949 and amassed substantial wealth, much of which he invested in collecting. The results of this he generously decided to bequeath to Britain, so London is the honoured beneficiary of Sir Arthur's idiosyncratic, sometimes odd, invariably interesting, taste. The chief glories of the collection are gold and silver, but it also contains many items of micro-mosaic and hardstone as well as many portrait miniatures.

Use of the audio-guide with Gilbert speaking is strongly recommended. The first area contains furniture and pictures in Florentine **hardstone**, or *pietre dure*, a rather hard and unsympathetic material. Then ascend the disconcerting new staircase to the main gallery area—you are now immediately under the terrace above, so there are fine views of the river. Ahead of you lies case after case of **silver and silver-gilt** objects—walk slowly through and enjoy.

Even greater, **gold** treasures lie up a few steps to the right, in suitable semi-darkness. Particularly mind-blowing is a gold ewer of 2500 BC from Anatolia in Turkey. But the most perfect might be said to be the gallery of snuffboxes, including six belonging to Frederick the Great.

At the same level are the collections of **micro-mosaics**—less harsh than the hardstones and ostensibly a practice requiring immense skill, resulting in some remarkable, if slightly impersonal, objects—and of **portrait miniatures**. Finally, head downstairs again for similarly luxurious items of furniture from India and China.

And so the walk ends. If you turn left on the Embankment you will soon reach Temple station. To reach Charing Cross, ascend the steps at Waterloo Bridge and make your way along the Strand, whose somewhat different pleasures await you in Chapter 10.

10 • Strand and Covent Garden

This walk covers two of London's most famous and currently popular areas, both examples of transformation. Whereas the City and Westminster convey in varying degrees a strong flavour of their pasts, in contemporary Covent Garden, full of 21C buzz, it is quite hard to experience history, although our tour will attempt to explain something of this. These are crowded, lively places today; with the exception of the Adelphi, the main themes are shopping and the theatre.

- Distance: 1¼ miles. Time: 1½ hours + 2 hours for museums.
  Tube: Embankment. Map 15.

We begin at Embankment station (District, Circle, Northern and Bakerloo lines), a stone's throw from Charing Cross, which was indeed the station's former name (**Map 15,3**). As you exit, either into Villiers Street or onto the Embankment itself, turn first into **Embankment Gardens**. Note the pleasant bandstand where deckchairs area spread for lunchtime concerts in summer.

This beautifully planted space is land 'reclaimed' from the river bed, built over and embanked from 1868 to 1874 by Joseph Bazalgette, the Metropolitan Board of Works' Chief Engineer as part of the Victoria Embankment project. The construction was a major technical achievement and had long been hoped for and discussed, but it took Victorian energy, and the pressure to improve public health by the creation of a new main sewer, to achieve it. Killing three birds with one stone, Bazalgette installed under the road the sewer, a tunnel for cables and similar services, and a tunnel for the District Line. Here at Charing Cross there was a wide mud bank in the bend of the river which created the space for a garden between the road and the former riverbank where the buildings, on firmer ground, begin. It would all have been much more elegant if the gardens could have overlooked the river, with the roadside plane trees within them: then perhaps the Thames would have been green and beautiful again. But the Victoria Embankment, with the roar of traffic—it is an important by-pass—puts paid to any such pleasant notion.

Meanwhile the gardens are still beautiful, with many moderately interesting statues, notably those of **Sir Arthur Sullivan**, with the embodiment of Music in mourning, by W. Goscombe John (1903), and **Henry Fawcett**, the blind Postmaster-General and campaigner for female suffrage with his wife Millicent, by Mary Grant (1886). Nearby, on the Embankment, is a bust of Bazalgette himself by George Simonds. The gardens have good flower displays in summer. A particular delight is the **York Watergate** (1626), tucked away at the back, a fortunate but nevertheless now humiliated survival from the great days of the river. It was once the main entrance for visitors arriving by boat at York House, home of George Villiers, Duke of Buckingham and friend of Charles I, whose only, but significant, memorial is in the names of streets all around: George Street, Villiers Street, Duke Street, Buckingham Street and even Of Alley (now York Place). Outside the gardens and across the Embankment, by the river, stands **Cleopatra's Needle**, a now-famous landmark, 60ft high and weighing 186 tons, brought to London with great difficulty in 1878.

It is by a long way the oldest outdoor object in the entire city, having been cut from the granite quarries in Aswan around 1475 BC for erection at Heliopolis, and is dedicated to the Pharaoh Tethmosis III. Cleopatra became associated with it when it was moved to Alexandria, where later still it collapsed. It was given to Britain by the Turkish Viceroy in Egypt after the Napoleonic Wars, but was too enormous and heavy to ship to London for another 60 years. Buried beneath it is a collection of memorabilia of 1878, including a railway guide and portraits of beautiful women of the day.

After exploring the gardens and looking at the Needle, leave via the Watergate and make your way up Buckingham Street or York Buildings to John Adam Street. Turn right into Robert Street and look out over Adelphi Terrace. Below you lie the gardens. You have ascended the riverbank to the level of the Strand, built up in this way by the Adam brothers from 1772 as a small but grand residential development for their own profit, the **Adelphi**. The name was part of their brilliant marketing plan: it is Greek for 'brothers'. The objective was to provide wharfing and underground mooring for river trade, with middle-class housing above, thus furnishing a double income. The housing comprised a fine riverside terrace, backing onto a similar terrace (deprived only of riverside views) in the street behind, with suitable flanking terraces, all streets being named after members of the Adam family. Robert and James, among many other famous residents, lived in the development at 1–3 Robert Street.

Robert Adam

Robert Adam (1728–92), Britain's best-known 18C architect, has given his name to a particular kind of fireplace and other schemes of interior decoration. Although a Scot who later in life completed perhaps his finest work in that country, he nevertheless made a great impact on the buildings of London. After training in Rome—and soon joined by his brother James—Robert established his practice in London and, spurred by a powerful ambition, captured many important commissions, usually for the conversion and refurbishment of older houses then in the countryside, notably Osterley and Kenwood, and 20 Portman Square, Portland Place and Fitzroy Square in London. The Adelphi project nearly ruined them financially. Adam's special qualities were an extreme sensitivity to the aesthetic of Neo-Classical forms and their application to the enhancement of domestic comfort.

Only a few remnants of this ambitious and brilliant scheme survive: the main housing terrace was demolished as recently as 1936 and replaced by monster offices with fascist-style sculpture. You can still gain a sense of the Adelphi's grandeur by peering about and looking over into basement wells, or by visiting the **Royal Society of Arts** building in John Adam Street, with its Great Room and frieze by James Barry. Guided tours, given on the first Friday of each month at lunchtime, should be booked in advance, ☎ 020 7451 6874; or visit on the first Sunday of the month 10.00–13.00. Admission free. www.rsa.org.uk

The Royal Society of Arts was founded in 1754 as a body to sponsor the commercial development of new design and inventions: throughout its history its principles have remained consistent with the first enthusiasms of the 18C industrial revolution.

Go along John Adam Street, turn left into Adam Street, noting at no. 7 another, frequently filmed survival of the original scheme, and then turn right into the **Strand**.

This great street is now a pale, or rather tawdry, shadow of its heyday around 1900, when its theatres, music halls and restaurants reflected the glittering prosperity of the Edwardian elite. Even in Benjamin Disraeli's time he could describe it as 'perhaps the finest street in Europe'. That is hardly a fair description now, but it is still always lively. The roadway itself is of very ancient origin, being the riverside path between the two centres of London, the City and Westminster, and from it in the Middle Ages great houses stretched down through exquisite gardens to the river. Now there is little left of interest in this part of the Strand; the more important architecture east of Waterloo Bridge is covered in Chapter 9.

It is fun to look at the apparently vandalised statuary on **Zimbabwe House** (no. 429), built as new offices for the British Medical Association in 1907: the nude figures representing the *Ages of Man*, by Jacob Epstein, were strongly objected to. But the *London Encyclopaedia* says that actual vandalism is unproven, quoting a report to the effect that the sculptor had mistreated the grain of the stone, rendering parts of the figures unsafe, so that the only course was 'cutting away their projections'. Poor things.

You could explore the Strand as far east as Aldwych. Look out for the *Savoy Hotel* on the right, an Edwardian dream with, if you hunt for them, traces of Art Nouveau ironwork. The Grill Room is an outstanding restaurant (the hotel's first chef was Auguste Escoffier) and the forecourt is the only street in the entire British Isles where traffic must keep to the right. The **Savoy Theatre** next door was part of the same 1880s initiative by Richard D'Oyly Carte, who built it specifically to produce Gilbert and Sullivan operas: his company perform them there to this day. It was the first public building in London to be lit by electricity. The recently restored interior in Art-Deco style is by Basil Ionides (1929).

Gilbert and Sullivan

There has never been anyone quite like this duo—in England at least: Rodgers and Hammerstein might be parallels. W.S. Gilbert (1836–1911) was born in this area, in Southampton Street, and attended King's College in the Strand. After an unsuccessful start as a lawyer, he turned to comic verse (inventing the word 'topsy-turvy' to describe the world it conveyed) followed by dramatic works in the same vein. Sir Arthur Sullivan (1842–1900) was born in more humble circumstances in Lambeth, but was an outstanding musical student and a serious composer who would have preferred to be remembered as such. His name is in fact connected indissolubly to that of Gilbert, whom he met in 1869. Their joint success dates from 1874, when Gilbert met Richard D'Oyly Carte: it began with *Trial by Jury* and ended 20 years later with *The Grand Duke*, their only failure.

Just beyond is *Simpsons-in-the-Strand*, a traditional British restaurant, now something of a rarity. First opened in 1848, it serves roast beef and Yorkshire pudding—mouth-watering but today eaten only by the brave. Besides its real clients, Sherlock Holmes and Dr Watson favoured it.

Just down Savoy Street on the right is the **Savoy Chapel** (originally of 1508), which has fine pews. It is the dedicated chapel of the Royal Victorian Order. Open 11.30–15.30 Tues–Fri and for services Sun; closed Aug, Sept. ☎ 020 7836 7221. The entire site was originally the Savoy Palace (1246), yet another noble riverside home, royal rather than ecclesiastical, bequeathed by Henry III to his wife's uncle, the Count of Savoie. It had a grand but chequered history, and the site was finally cleared in 1820 for the building of Waterloo Bridge.

Perhaps now is the moment to explore a little further east by turning right down Lancaster Place and walking out onto **Waterloo Bridge**. The distinctly Art-Deco structure—by engineers Rendel, Palmer and Tritton (1937–42), with Sir Giles Gilbert Scott as architect—is very fine (**Map 15,4**). It replaced an even finer bridge by John Rennie, opened in 1817 on the second anniversary of the great battle, thus giving its name to a railway station and an area of the South Bank (see Chapter 32). If you advance out over the Embankment to half-way across the stream, you will encounter some of London's finest views, both right to Westminster and left all the way past the City to Docklands—exhilarating on a windy day, and even better at night.

Covent Garden

Now return to the north side of the Strand and go up into Covent Garden (**Map 15,1**). If you can see one, do this via one of the 19C courts, once narrow and smelly but now harmless enough (though still occasionally smelly) and evocative: otherwise use Bedford Street or Southampton Street. Linking these two is Maiden Lane, where the painter J.M.W. Turner's father owned a barber's shop and where *Rules*, London's oldest restaurant (established 1798), which once served Edward VII and his mistress Lillie Langtry, can still be enjoyed.

Proceeding north, you will soon find yourself drawn by the hubbub in the so-called **Piazza**, where at most times of day there is plenty going on—street theatre, cafés, stalls selling gifts and crafts and, all around, a general zest for life, very much present tense.

History

The area's history is nevertheless worth telling. Covent Garden was once the garden of the abbey, or convent, of Westminster, given on the Dissolution of the Monasteries to John Russell, 1st Earl of Bedford. His grandson built Bedford House, one of the magnificent houses on the Strand already referred to. It was the 4th Earl who decided, against royal wishes, to develop part of the estate as a profit-making housing speculation. He took advice from Inigo Jones, who designed for him terraces of arcaded houses round three sides of a brand new square, called from the start the 'piazza': it was the first proper square in London, and modelled on those Jones had seen on his Italian travels; there was also a resemblance to the Place des Vosges, which had been completed in Paris some 20 years before. The houses, which had the best rooms on the first floor and pleasant gardens behind, soon became the height of fashion, and although none still exists a good idea of their appearance can be gained from the small red-brick and stone section on the northwest side of the Piazza, put up by Henry Clutton in 1877.

It was thought necessary to include a church within the housing scheme. The Earl, preferring the rents from housing, was not keen, and is said to have asked the architect for nothing more than a barn, to which Inigo Jones replied, 'Sire, you shall have the handsomest barn in all England.'

Whatever the Earl thought of it the church of **St Paul** remains a very significant, if somewhat odd, building, with its Tuscan portico, based on Vitruvius' most simplified order, glaring baldly out over the square, with no visible door or entrance and crude wooden eaves and pediment. The church burned down in 1795 and was re-erected according to its original design, allegedly, although in engravings the old church looks less squat than the present one.

It is worth going inside, for which purpose you will have to make your way along Henrietta Street or King Street and turn into the delightful little churchyard garden. The church has always been associated with the theatre and many famous actors and others are buried or commemorated inside. Among them are the sculptor Grinling Gibbons (1648–1721) and Thomas Arne (1710–78), composer of 'Rule Britannia'. John Wesley preached here. The portico is the setting for the opening scene of George Bernard Shaw's *Pygmalion* (which became the musical and film *My Fair Lady*), where Eliza Doolittle attempts to sell her violets. ☎ 020 7836 5221.

As time went by, the market stalls that had initially supplied fruit and vegetables to the residents became more and more intrusive and their businesses expanded. This in turn reduced the desirability of the houses, which gradually became run-down and dilapidated. In the 1830s the 6th Duke of Bedford decided to re-establish family authority by the construction of a purpose-built market structure designed by Charles Fowler, abandoning any great pretence that the area was residential but sponsoring a really successful format for the now-established purpose. There was—and still is—a retail avenue at the centre, running east–west, and wholesale areas to either side, north and south, with cellar space below for storage and means of delivery at various points. You can still see, and may trip over, the ramps. At the eastern end, a plethora of columns confirms the original formal entrance.

This was a most successful market development, but the wholesale traders were still unhappy. They, after all, were still out in the rain while their retail partners were safe and dry in their shops, so they petitioned the Duke for improved facilities. Finally, in the 1870s, iron roofs were inserted, their columns standing clear of the stone structure. At the same time other market buildings were erected on the edge of the site: the Floral Hall, by E.M. Barry (1860), next to the Opera House, and the Flower Market (1870). The Jubilee Market (1904) to the south of the Piazza was built to celebrate Queen Victoria's 60-year reign and was intended for imported flowers.

And so Covent Garden continued as an odd combination of market and opera until the late 1960s, when the fruit and vegetable trade moved to Nine Elms near Vauxhall, where it remains as the New Covent Garden Market. After much controversy and public debate, it was decided to restore the fabric of the original market to its state in 1870, when the iron roofs were erected (alternative dates included 1830 and 1630), and to re-let it in small units as specialist shops, cafés and restaurants, with stalls for a new craft market. The cellar area of the southern wholesale market was opened up but otherwise all is as it was: a complete delight. Enjoy it for as much time as you have.

In the southeast corner of the piazza, housed in the former Flower Market, is the **London Transport Museum**. Open 10.00–18.00 Sat–Thur, 11.00–18.00 Fri Admission charge. Café. Shop. ☎ 020 7379 6344. www.ltmuseum.co.uk. Tube: Covent Garden.

This delightful museum takes full advantage of the Flower Market's glass roof, which makes the exhibits, especially the buses and trains, sparkle. The layout is broadly chronological, beginning with the first horse-drawn buses to the latest in underground technology. 'London Transport' is to be interpreted as including buses, trams, trolleybuses and the Tube, but not cars, bicycles or national rail services. It starts with George Shillibeer's Omnibus, an idea copied from Paris and introduced in 1829 on a route along the New Road from Paddington to the Bank. There are frequent special exhibitions, excellent (i.e. never embarrassing) actors to demonstrate exhibits, some guided tours and plenty of hands-on opportunities for children. Of particular interest are the Art-Deco poster designs of E. McKnight Kauffer, and early versions of Harry Beck's now iconic Tube map.

Covent Garden spreads away from the Piazza in different directions. Do not miss James Street to the north, with its enterprising selection of street performers; but then move east down Russell Street. On your right is the **Theatre Museum**, run by the Victoria and Albert Museum, charting the history of the English stage. Open 10.00–18.00 Tues–Sun. Admission charge. Shop. ☎ 020 7943 4700. www.theatremuseum.org

It is an odd mixture, part of the content strongly and very successfully child oriented and other parts quite sophisticated. There are often temporary exhibitions on the ground floor with scope for pushing knobs and pulling strings (or puppets, for example). Then you descend the ramp to two underground galleries in the lower of which is a studio theatre where it is often possible to participate in workshops and/or live performances. There are practical demonstrations of theatrical make-up and costume. For the more serious taste, the museum has a fine collection of paintings, photographs, memorabilia and films relating to the London theatre and its star performers over 400 years.

Then to the real thing. First, peeping into view straight ahead, is the **Theatre Royal Drury Lane**, much altered but still with a Regency feel about the foyer and frontage. The present building was constructed in 1811–12 to the designs of Benjamin Wyatt, and the navy-blue colonnade, for alighting from carriages out of the rain, in the 1830s using columns from John Nash's Regent Street. It is the successor to other theatres destroyed by fire. In the first, Nell Gwyn made her debut in 1665. In the second (designed by Sir Christopher Wren), David Garrick made his first appearance in 1742, and later became owner and manager, being succeeded in 1776 by Richard Brinsley Sheridan. And, in an interior designed by the Adam brothers, John Kemble made his debut as Hamlet, in 1783. In the 20C Drury Lane became famous for an almost unbroken series of long-running musicals, a tradition that continues. Backstage tours of the theatre begin at 14.15 and 16.45 Mon, Tues, Thur, Fri, Sun and 10.15 and 12.00 Sat. Book in advance ☎ 020 7494 5091.

To the right, down Wellington Street, you can see the **Lyceum**, another important theatre (built 1834), now restored to its former glory and again a venue for musicals. Throughout the 20C it had a rather chequered existence, functioning as a dance hall and the venue for Miss World competitions.

David Garrick

Garrick (1717–79) came from Hereford but not from an acting family, being the son of a recruiting officer. He was educated at Lichfield, becoming for a time a pupil of Dr Samuel Johnson and moving with him to London. After a brief period in the wine trade he took up the stage and was an immediate and lifelong success. Equally versatile in tragic and comic roles, Garrick was also a writer of plays, a producer and director. He became a distinguished presence in the Club, the dining society to which Johnson, Sir Joshua Reynolds, Oliver Goldsmith and others belonged. He married a dancer, Eva-Maria Violetti, who long outlived him, dying in 1822. Later in the 19C a theatre, private club and street were all named after him.

The Royal Opera House lies to your left, up **Bow Street**. This curving highway was famous as a residential street in the 18C, and later for its magistrates court from which the Bow Street Runners, predecessors of London's police, operated. The novelist Henry Fielding was a magistrate at the court (1749–54), followed by his blind brother John. Garrick and the actress Peg Woffington lived at no. 6 in the 1740s. Now the **Royal Opera House**, an internationally famous institution and in the old days an unremittingly high-flown presence among the fruit and vegetables all around, is all-dominant.

There have been two opera houses on the site before the present one: the first, built in 1732, was burned down in 1808 and its successor, London's introduction to Sir Robert Smirke's minimalist Greek-Revival style, was also destroyed by fire. Many of George Frideric Handel's operas were premiered here. So were Goldsmith's *She Stoops to Conquer* (1773) and Richard Brinsley Sheridan's *The Rivals* (1775). It has seen great performers (Kemble, Edmund Kean, Mrs Siddons, Adelina Patti) and performances, including the first English production of Richard Wagner's *Ring*, conducted by Gustav Mahler, in 1900. Rows over seat prices have become endemic: beginning with riots in 1763, they are still a problem.

The present structure, with a relief by John Flaxman from the previous building under the portico, was built to the design of E.M. Barry (1858–61). It was closed in 1997–99 for a huge refurbishment and is now grander than ever. Productions are of equal grandeur, and unquestionably a visit to the opera at Covent Garden would be an unforgettable highlight of any London visit. For details of the current programme ☎ 020 7240 1200. There are three guided tours per day Mon–Sat, including backstage. ☎ 020 7304 4000.

Plenty of the interior space is open to view during the day without the need to attend a performance, or even a tour. You can enter the **foyer** and sense the luxurious atmosphere, and mount the stairs to the half-landing, from which you can stare into the Crush Bar above. Straight ahead is the former **Floral Hall**, rebuilt as part of the refurbishment but reusing the original iron structure. It is the perfect place for a coffee or lunch. Open to all 10.00–15.30, but in the evenings to opera-goers only.

You can ascend the escalator to a further restaurant area above, and look out from the open **balcony** over the Piazza below, dreaming you are in Florence. This architecturally exciting extension is the work of Jeremy Dixon and Edward Jones, who are also responsible for the somewhat similar project at the National Portrait Gallery (Chapter 11).

After the Royal Opera House, turn left along Floral Street, on its north flank, and at James Street turn right, past the Tube station. Cross Long Acre and go down the slope of **Neal Street**. There are many small, interesting shops here and in the streets either side. Return to Long Acre and proceed west to further explore the range of shops. Of unique interest is *Stanfords*, the seller of maps and travel books, at nos 12–14. You will soon reach Leicester Square station; or you can return to the Tube at Covent Garden. If you have the stamina, you may fancy taking in the bookshops along Charing Cross Road (see Chapter 22).

11 • Trafalgar Square

The geographical centre of this walk is the Square itself, but the cultural centre is the National Gallery. Its almost-as-important sibling, the National Portrait Gallery, comes at the end. The walk as such is not long but provides some physical antidote to the slow motion of gallery visiting. Of course both galleries can be given as much time as personal preference suggests, from an hour to a lifetime.

• Distance: ¾ mile. Time: ½ hour + 3 to 5 hours for the galleries. Tube: Charing Cross. Map 15.

We start from **Charing Cross Station**—or you may prefer its companion under the arches, Embankment (**Map 15,3**). The mainline station was a similar venture to Cannon Street, by the same engineer, John Hawkshaw, and was opened in 1864 as part of the Victorian railway companies' constant struggle to out-do each other in providing convenience of access to the North Bank. In this case, the South Eastern Railway Company brutally commandeered Isambard Kingdom Brunel's suspension footbridge over the Thames, **Hungerford Bridge**, built to enable pedestrians from the South Bank to shop in Hungerford Market, over which the station was then built. The piers of the original footbridge remain, and badly needed new pedestrian walkways are now being added either side of the tracks. But above all it is a railway bridge.

The hotel at the front of the station, built at the same time by E.M. Barry, has a dreary exterior with iron fancy bits, though it was one of the first London buildings to be faced with artificial stone and has some lavish interiors. But the dominating presence now, although invisible from the north, is Terry Farrell's **Embankment Place** (1980s), which integrates station, arches and hotel into a green-and-yellow Postmodern collation of offices, quite an eye-catcher and best seen from Waterloo or Westminster Bridge, or the South Bank.

In front of the hotel is a replacement by E.M. Barry of the original **Charing Cross**, located a short distance west, where Charles I's statue now stands, which had marked the last resting place of the body of Eleanor of Castile, Queen of Edward I. Deep underneath Charing Cross station, on the Northern Line platforms, David Gentleman's tiles (early 1980s) vividly commemorate the construction of the original cross.

Opposite, across the Strand, lies all that was done of John Nash's West Strand improvements of 1831, still handsome and refined. The pepper-pot corner blocks denote the triangular site of **Coutts Bank**, founded in the Strand in 1692 and still bankers to the Queen. The Victorian philanthropist Angela Burdett-Coutts was the heir to the family fortune. Nash's scheme (see Chapter 25) was London's most ambitious piece of town planning, designed to stretch from Westminster up to Regent's Park, and here you see the southeastern tip of it. In the 1960s the interior of this block was entirely rebuilt with anomalous escalators and indoor plants, but it is well worth going in to see Sir Francis Chantrey's sculpture of *Thomas Coutts* (d. 1822) and other interesting reminders of past grandeur. At least the shops at street level were reinstated to appear as they did in the 1830s. To your left is St Martin-in-the-Fields, to which we shall return.

Edward I (r. 1272–1307) and Queen Eleanor

Edward I was tall and strong, a fine rider and swordsman. He was known as the 'hammer of the Scots' for his continual military objectives in that direction. His devotion to his first wife, Eleanor of Castile, who bore the first Prince of Wales, was legendary. When she died near Lincoln, in December 1290, while accompanying him to Scotland he returned grief-stricken to London with her body, ordering that a cross of the finest workmanship should be placed at every point where the bier rested, 12 in all. The best-preserved ones are at Hardingstone, Northamptonshire and Waltham Cross, Hertfordshire. Eleanor's tomb in Westminster Abbey shows her tender, fragile beauty.

Meanwhile turn left out of Charing Cross Station forecourt, or go round the corner from Embankment station, to locate **Craven Street**. The side dominated by the railway arches contains original houses of *c* 1730, with the elegant proportions of that civilised age, even if varied in the details. Red brick surrounds the windows, brown elsewhere: these pre-date London's rash of yellow stock bricks. Benjamin Franklin lived at no. 36 when he was the representative in London of the colony of Pennsylvania; the house may open to the public by the end of 2002. ☎ 020 7930 9121.

Half-way down Craven Street, cut through Craven Passage on the right to **Northumberland Avenue**, built on the site of the great 17C mansion Northumberland House. The street, by Sir Joseph Bazalgette, was itself cut through in the 1870s from his new Victoria Embankment to Trafalgar Square. The recommended *Sherlock Holmes* pub, with exclusive memorabilia of the great detective, is on the right. More than anywhere else in central London, Northumberland Avenue is reminiscent of Baron Haussmann's Paris, with tall blocks of apartments, originally hotels, and gloomy trees, all in a ruthlessly straight line. The date suggests that Bazalgette (whose grandfather was French) must surely have been influenced by the developments in Paris. The **Playhouse Theatre**, at the eastern end, is a fine late Victorian affair, but is often dark. Beyond it, across the Embankment, is Bazalgette's own memorial.

Trafalgar Square

Proceed along Northumberland Avenue to Trafalgar Square (**Map 15,3**)—this is not an entry to the Square that was originally intended but it is a good one from which to take in the topography and ask yourself: does it succeed as a major public space?

History

Although very central—perhaps better placed than any other spot to signify the heart of London—it is by no means ancient, unlike the squares at the centres of many major capitals, having been conceived as part of Nash's town plan around 1830. By this time St Martin-in-the-Fields was already in place, and another area was occupied by the Royal Mews, which had become derelict. The magnificent church was given some extra steps and a superior corner all to itself, and the National Gallery (1832–8) was designed to fill the chief north façade and close the vista from Whitehall, a role which it has been felt insufficiently noble to achieve. The square lies on a steepish slope, which Sir Charles Barry, who laid it out following Nash's death, levelled by erecting a terrace on the north side (1840). The other buildings—which will be described—were arranged higgledy-piggledy around the circumference.

The square was named after the Battle of Trafalgar (off Portugal) which the British, led by Admiral Horatio Nelson, had won in 1805: using the name 25 years later was a patriotic excuse to commemorate that vital naval triumph, along with Nelson himself, on his off-centre column (see below).

Trafalgar Square thus earns a high mark for character and atmosphere but a low one for planning and aesthetics. It is used for occasional political speeches and demonstrations, and for celebrations at Christmas and New Year, but mainly for tourists to feed pigeons, an unaccountable desire which the Mayor of London plans to terminate.

Trafalgar Square's entrances are in very asymmetrical places, except for Whitehall running grandly to your left, with the ultra-grand Mall squeezed in next through Admiralty Arch, then Cockspur Street to the west and Duncannon Street to the east ignoring the square altogether, and Charing Cross Road (like Northumberland Avenue, an improvement of the 1880s, cutting through slum areas) curling away to the north past St Martin's.

On a small traffic island immediately in front of you, as you stand at the top of Northumberland Avenue, the oldest object in sight is Hubert Le Sueur's bronze statue of *Charles I* (1633), cast during the King's lifetime for a garden at Roehampton. It was triumphantly erected here after the Restoration in 1675, on the site of the original Eleanor Cross which the Commonwealth citizens had destroyed. The poor stone plinth is terribly weather-beaten, but Charles still looks pretty good.

Cross into the centre of the square—by no means easy (another planning deficiency)—in particular to examine the reliefs and sculpted lions at the base of the **Nelson Column**.

The column was designed by William Railton and erected in 1839–42. It is 145ft high, of Devon granite, with a bronze Corinthian capital and E.H. Baily's 17ft-high stone figure of the Admiral himself on top, a perch for the over-fed pigeons. The reliefs around the base, usually defaced by the birds, depict Nelson's various victories, and the lions, designed by Sir Edwin Landseer, were added in the 1860s. The fountains behind, modified by Sir Edwin Lutyens in 1939, begin to play at 10.00 daily.

Around the square stand four plinths for statues. In the northeast corner is a rather sedate equestrian bronze of *George IV*, by Chantrey (1834). In the two southern corners are the otherwise forgotten military heroes *Sir Charles Napier* (by George Canon Adams, 1855) and *Sir Henry Havelock* (by William Behnes, 1861), now under threat of removal. The northwest plinth has been vacant since first erected and there is an ongoing debate as to who or what should occupy it. Various modern sculptures have been displayed here for short periods. For the latest position visit www.rsa.org.uk/fourthplinth. It is an important matter: this is an ideal location for public sculpture. Three busts of naval men are lodged in the north terrace wall, as well as the official imperial measures of inch, foot and yard, placed here in 1876.

Horatio Nelson

With the possible exceptions of Wellington and Winston Churchill, Horatio Nelson (1758–1805) may be elevated to the title of Britain's greatest hero ever. He was one of eight children of a Norfolk clergyman, but his uncle, Comptroller of the Navy in the 1770s, was able to ensure the successful beginning of his career. He was a natural risk-taker whose talent was always recognised, and his promotion was steady: he became an Admiral in 1797. His great victories during the French wars at the Nile, Copenhagen and above all Trafalgar, where he was killed, were retold to generations and were certainly decisive in ensuring British domination of the sea—though the war was not ended until Wellington won ten years later at Waterloo. Nelson treated his injuries, including the loss of an eye and an arm, with indifference. He had a craving for love and in 1801 left his blameless wife for the anything-but-blameless Emma Hamilton, by whom he had two daughters. His death was mourned equally by navy and nation alike.

It is suggested you proceed round the square clockwise. Return, using the subway, to the exit leading to the Mall. Note **Admiralty Arch**, the masterpiece of Sir Aston Webb (1910), finer than his Buckingham Palace façade, with three imposing curved arches and a heavy attic above. Though built as a memorial to Queen Victoria, the building has no role at present.

Then use the crossing over Cockspur Street to pass, on your left, what is now **Canada House** (originally the Union Club and converted to its current use in the 1920s) backing on to the former Royal College of Physicians, all by Sir Robert Smirke (1824–27). The north porch is Smirke at his purest Greek, with not a hint of ornament to be seen, just six great Ionic columns. What a pity it does not face the square—presumably the plans for that had not matured sufficiently to allow it. Before crossing to the north side, take in William Wilkins's National Gallery façade (1832), with Robert Venturi's Sainsbury Wing (1991) to the west.

National Gallery

The National Gallery, founded in 1824, houses the national collection of Western European painting, one of the finest and most representative in the world. Its coverage goes up to 1900: for later work, visit Tate Modern (Chapter 31).

- Open 10.00–18.00 daily, 10.00–21.00 Weds. Café. Restaurant. Shop. Admission free. Audio guides to the collection, and three shorter themed guides (including one for children) are available from Soundtrack desks, as are audio guides for visitors with visual or hearing impairments. Free guided tours at 11.30 and 14.30 daily (also 18.30 Wed) leave from the Sainsbury Wing information desk. Family talks 11.30 and 14.30 Sat. ☎ 020 7747 2885. www.nationalgallery.org.uk

Wilkins, Venturi and the National Gallery

William Wilkins (1778–1839) was, like Smirke, a leading Greek Revivalist. Unusually he came from an academic background, and as a young man travelled in Greece with a learned, but perhaps too pedantic, eye. His design for Downing College, Cambridge (1806) was the forerunner of both Grecian styles and of campus university colleges, but his works in London, University College and the National Gallery, seem to reveal a mind more preoccupied with parts than the integrated whole. Even so he deserves more fame than architectural history accords him.

Wilkins had endless trouble with the Trustees of the National Gallery, who quibbled with his estimates, designs and plans, and posterity has never admired this building much. John Summerson cruelly described the central portico with its dome and the subsidiary pavilions either side as 'like a clock and vases on a mantelpiece, only less useful'. Wilkins had to make use of Henry Holland's columns from the then recently demolished Carlton House so he had to use the Corinthian order, although it was probably appropriate architectural language for a temple of art.

The long narrow site necessitated a long narrow building which the national art collection soon outgrew, and various enlargements occurred. A major extension was planned after the Second World War and a radical modern building was proposed, famously described by Prince Charles as 'a monstrous carbuncle on the face of an elegant and much-loved friend', probably the highest compliment Wilkins's building had ever received. That plan having been dropped, Robert Venturi, the famous American Postmodernist, was invited to design an extension that the Sainsbury family were to sponsor. Venturi came up with a jokey and very appealing answer, with numerous references to Wilkins's work randomly applied on the exterior, and inside a fine ground-floor space, shop and a great, imposing staircase that is a joy to ascend. The Renaissance galleries are above.

Around the turn of the 18C/19C many European countries were considering making national collections of art, but Britain was one of the last to do so. It was not until the 1820s that two private collections which had been bequeathed to the nation, and the purchase of the collection of John Julius Angerstein, were combined to form the nucleus. Even then there was opposition from the Treasury. All this was greeted with great amusement in Paris, where the French royal collection had been open to the public for 200 years.

Note. Our tour of the National Gallery begins at the Sainsbury Wing entrance, rather than the central portico, on the assumption that a chronological route will be preferred.

Sainsbury Wing: painting 1260–1510

As you enter, there is an extensive and well-stocked shop on your left, where you are recommended to buy the excellent *Companion Guide*. There are toilets halfway down the stairs. Temporary exhibitions (admission charge) are often held in the basement galleries. The restaurant and **micro-gallery**—a free computerised database where you can research every picture in the collection, plan your visit and even print out an itinerary—are half-way up Venturi's lovely staircase.

Our tour starts at the top of the stairs, turning left: in Gallery 51, Leonardo da

Vinci's **Virgin of the Rocks** (1508) will sink you immediately, whatever your beliefs, into a mood of spirituality and contemplation. There is an earlier version of the same subject in the Louvre. You are strictly meant to see this painting last, as a bridge between works of the Early Renaissance here and those of the High Renaissance in the west wing. But here it is before you, so contemplate it now.

Galleries 51–66 in the Sainsbury Wing cover painting from 1260 to 1510; the works are hung in broadly chronological order, starting in Gallery 51 with the collection's oldest work, Margareto's **Virgin and Child Enthroned** (1260s). Gallery 52 contains Italian works before 1400, including two by Duccio. In Gallery 53, you must not miss the **Wilton Diptych** (late 14C), which was commissioned by Richard II for his own devotion: he is shown in the left-hand panel, the first English king to be recorded in a portrait (there is a larger picture of him in Westminster Abbey). Look for uses of this king's special symbol, the white hart, often also encountered in pub names.

In Gallery 54, you will want to see Masaccio's **Virgin and Child**, with her throne shown in heady perspective, and his **St Jerome and St John the Baptist** (both early 15C) and Sassetta's **Stigmatisation of St Francis** (c 1440). Paolo Uccello's chivalric **Battle of San Romano** (c 1450) will catch your eye in Gallery 55, with its crashing horses and knights in the foreground, although there is no blood, and curious little incidents take place in the hills beyond; also Fra Filippo Lippi's tender **Annunciation** (1448). Do not miss the northerners, including Jan van Eyck, in Gallery 56, in particular his **Arnolfini Marriage** (1434) famous chiefly because of the artist's early use of oil to define, with undreamed-of precision, a whole range of surfaces from dog's hair to polished brass and the glass in a mirror. If you do not much care for the couple themselves, examine their clothes. The **Man in a Turban** (1433) may be Van Eyck's self-portrait

Turn back into Gallery 57 for works by Carlo Crivelli, Cosimo Tura and images of the **Agony in the Garden** by both Andrea Mantegna (c 1460) and Giovanni Bellini (c 1470), which are instructive to compare and contrast. In what ways did Italian painting advance in those ten years?

Going back in a straight line you enter Gallery 58, where the star is Sandro Botticelli, with examples of his old-fashioned resistance to the naturalistic trends in contemporary Florentine painting: the secular **Venus and Mars** (1480–90) and the **Mystic Nativity** (1500), with angels up to all sorts of tricks. Gallery 59 is dominated by the Pollaiuolo brothers' brutal altarpiece of the **Martydom of St Sebastian** (1475). Somewhat more consoling is Piero di Cosimo's **Satyr Mourning over a Nymph** (1495), with its preoccupation with dogs, wildlife and the natural world.

High spots in Gallery 60 are Raphael's **St Catherine** (1507–8), leaning on her wheel and elegantly contemplating the heavens in a pose which takes us from Early to High Renaissance, and the same artist's **Madonna and Child with St John the Baptist and St Nicholas of Bari** (1505), the four heads parallel but gazing in varied directions, which confirms his genius.

Cross over into Gallery 61 where contemporary works from Venice include Bellini's **Doge Loredan** (1501–4) and his pupil Cima's **Incredulity of St Thomas** (1502), incredible indeed in its colouring. Then we travel north, in Gallery 62, to the more solemn and awkward, yet also more human, Netherlandish artists, such as Hieronymus Bosch with **Christ Mocked** (1490–1500) and Gerard David with **Virgin and Child with Saints and Donor** (1510). Even more solemn

Germans congregate in Gallery 63, including the newly acquired, tiny and exquisite *St Jerome* (1495) by Albrecht Dürer. There is another recently acquired masterpiece in Gallery 64, the Spaniard Bartolomé Bermejo's *St Michael* (1468).

In Gallery 65, note Lorenzo Costa's delightful *Concert* (1488–95), in which the lead singer follows the music and the others beat time to follow him. In Gallery 66 the Early Renaissance ends with the dreamiest of all its artists, Piero della Francesca, whose *Baptism* (1450s) and unfinished *Nativity* (1470s) exhibit both peacefulness and human frailty.

Cross back through the Sainsbury Wing to Gallery 51, where before leaving you should look at Leonardo's cartoon of the *Virgin and Child with St Anne* (1507) in the darkened room behind the *Virgin of the Rocks*. Then cross the link into the Wilkins building to continue the chronological tour.

West Wing: painting 1500–1600

The handsome gallery which you now enter is the Wohl Room, part of E.M. Barry's extensions to the gallery in 1867, largely invisible from the outside. It contains chiefly large Venetian works of the 16C, most notably Titian's *Bacchus and Ariadne* (1522) and, from his famous maturity, when his fingers had largely replaced his brushes, the *Death of Actaeon* (c 1560). Also to be seen are his *Vendramin Family* (1543–47), Veronese's *Family of Darius before Alexander* (1565–70) and Tintoretto's moving *Christ washing his Disciples' Feet* (c 1556).

Go next to Gallery 8, for Rome and Florence. The masterpieces, Michelangelo's early unfinished altarpiece of the *Entombment* (1500) and the so-called *Manchester Madonna* (mid-1490s) and Raphael's *Pope Julius II* (1511), will of course catch your eye. But it is also fascinating to trace the moves towards Mannerism apparent in Jacopo da Pontormo's *Joseph with Jacob in Egypt* (1518) and the uncomfortable *Allegory with Venus and Cupid* (1540–50) by Bronzino. Sebastiano del Piombo's *Raising of Lazarus* (1517), the first item acquired from the Angerstein collection, has the privilege of being number 1 in the National Gallery's catalogue.

El Greco's *Agony* (late 16C) cries out to you in Gallery 7, more vividly perhaps than the portraits in Gallery 6. It is all the more startling, in Gallery 4, to see what the early 16C was producing in Northern Europe, with the astonishing colour of Albrecht Altdorfer's *Christ Taking Leave of his Mother* (1520?), the blatant eroticism of Lucas Cranach's *Cupid Complaining to Venus* (1530s) and the portraits by Hans Holbein. Much studied and admired today, in pride of place at the end of the room, is his *Ambassadors* (1533), a double portrait on the face of it, but also a catalogue of the cultural pursuits of the age with, famously, a *memento mori* in the foreground. The portrait was set in London and the paving is derived from the Cosmati marble in Westminster Abbey (see Chapter 13).

Gallery 2 contains mostly Correggios and Parmigianinos, generating a slight feeling of lassitude after Holbein and company. Back in Gallery 5 are works from Ferrara, through which you pass to the over-powering Veronese allegories in Gallery 11. Turn left into Gallery 10 to continue this brief return to Venice, with Giorgione's *Sunset* (1506) and Titian's *Noli me Tangere* (1510–15) and *Portrait of a Man* (1512).

Retrace your steps to Gallery 12 to the earthy Netherlandish work of Pieter Bruegel the Elder's *Adoration* (1564), with ugly kings and citizens, and similar characters to be seen in close-up in the portraits of Mabuse (Jan Gossaert). This is the real world, against Italian idealism.

For refreshment go through the little Gallery 13, down the stairs of the National Gallery's main entrance, and below to the basement **café**. The jokey mosaics on the floor, laid in the 1950s by Boris Anrep, seem out of keeping.

North Wing: painting 1600–1700

Next we go to the North Wing for art of the 17C. There are a score of Rembrandts in Gallery 23 and other marvels. For Dutch genre go to Galleries 16 and 25–28; for French painting, see Galleries 18–20; for Flemish artists, including Rubens, Gallery 29; for Spain, Gallery 30; for Italian art, Gallery 32; and for English work, Galleries 31 (Van Dyck) and 15. The choice is yours: a logical tour of the North Wing is more difficult to lay out.

Gallery 15 is not a bad place to start because, as the *Companion Guide* says, the inclusion of paintings by J.M.W. Turner alongside Claude Lorrain's **Embarkation of the Queen of Sheba** (1648) not only fulfils the request in Turner's will for this comparison to be available to us, but also immediately elevates landscape to the high plateau it still holds in English art.

The Rembrandts in Gallery 23 include **Woman bathing in a Stream** (1654), one of the National Gallery's earliest gifts, from the collection of the Rev. Holwell Carr, one of the two original donors. It was thought to depict the artist's mistress, Hendrikje, but although she is the model, the true subject is the biblical Susannah. There are also several major portraits, including the **Self-portrait at Age 34** (1640), to be compared with the Titian in Gallery 10, and **Belshazzer's Feast** (1636).

The Claudes in Gallery 19 include a **Landscape with Aeneas at Delos** (1672). There are several cerebral works by Nicolas Poussin in Gallery 20: the **Adoration of the Golden Calf** (1634), **Triumph of Pan** (1636) and the **Finding of Moses** (1651), as well as one of his haunting landscapes.

Not to be missed, of course, are the paintings by Peter Paul Rubens which appear in the elongated Gallery 29. The most notable works include **Peace and War** (1629) and **Samson and Delilah** (1609), but to many visitors, others will be more appealing, such as **Susanna Lunden** (1622) in her super hat, and the magical **Autumn Landscape with a view of Het Steen** (1636), a morning view intended to be paired with **Landscape with a Rainbow**, the afternoon image to be seen in the Wallace Collection (see Chapter 24).

For Spanish art, go to Gallery 30. Here is El Greco's **Christ driving the Traders from the Temple** (1600), violent action on the left and guilty reaction on the right. You can also see an unctuous **Two Trinities** (1675–82) by Bartolomé Murillo and the same artist's harder **Self-portrait** (1670). The more challenging Diego Velazquez is represented with the meltingly beautiful **Rokeby Venus** (1647), the ambiguous **Kitchen Scene with Christ in the House of Martha and Mary** (1618?), and the apparently meticulously correct **Philip IV in Brown and Silver** (1631–32): the brushwork of the costume is free as air.

Do not miss the equestrian portrait of **Charles I** (1637) by Antony van Dyck in Gallery 31: the subject is a little precise person made to look like a great hero, but the likeness to the statue outside is startling. Nearby stand the same artist's offensively self-confident **Lord John and Lord Bernard Stuart** (1638)—enough to make you support Cromwell. Just back through the Spanish gallery are the rich Italian paintings in Gallery 32, including Caravaggio's **Supper at Emmaus** (1601), with all its incredulous gestures, and many equally vigorous but less satisfying images—although both the subject and interpretation of Guido Reni's *Lot and his Daughters* (1615) find a response in the modern mind.

East Wing: painting 1700–1900

Finally, you reach the East Wing, and the period 1700 to 1900. Some of the post-1860 paintings may look radical, but as the *Companion Guide* explains, they, and the contents of Tate Modern (which follow them in an unbroken chronology), are all securely based in the artistic and visual framework the collection has already established.

Begin with the dignified, elegant 18C in Galleries 33–40. France very properly comes first, with images of a somewhat stifling world in Gallery 33. But we are still charmed by the *House of Cards* (1736) by J.-B.-S. Chardin, attracted by Elisabeth Vigée le Brun's *Self-portrait* (1782) and scared by Jean-Germain Drouais' *Madame de Pompadour* (1763). Get some fresh air with the English in Gallery 34, where John Constable will take you out under cloudy skies to *Weymouth Bay* (1816) or into the fields of *The Hay-Wain* (1821); or with Thomas Gainsborough join *Mr and Mrs William Hallett taking their Morning Walk* (1785). And, to really blow the city away, see Turner's *Fighting Téméraire* (1838) and *Rain, Steam and Speed* (1844). The countryside still looks lovely even if under ownership, as the sitters proudly confirm, in Gainsborough's *Mr and Mrs Andrews* (1748) in Gallery 35. William Hogarth's series *Marriage à la Mode* (*c* 1743) shows the sordid side of town life. Serious portraits by Sir Joshua Reynolds and Sir Thomas Lawrence adorn Gallery 36.

It is pleasing to contrast all the native Englishness with Canaletto's view of the same world in *Eton College* (*c* 1754) in Gallery 38, where the scene is given an order and correctness it surely never possessed. Did he do the same to Venice, in the *Stonemason's Yard* (1726)? A comparison with Antonio Guardi can be made in Gallery 39, but not with Tiepolo in Gallery 40, where we are back in the unreal world of the spirit.

At last, for the 19C, return via the Sackler Room (Gallery 34) to Gallery 41, to commune again with the French, *Louis-Auguste Schwiter* (1826) by Eugène Delacroix, and, less interestingly, *Madame Moitessier* (1856) by J.-A.-D. Ingres. But the heart will lift when you reach the Impressionists in Gallery 43, in the sun on Claude Monet's *Beach at Trouville* (1870) or, closer to home, in *The Avenue, Sydenham* (1891) with Camille Pissarro. Joy continues with Pierre Auguste Renoir's *Boating on the Seine* (1879) in Gallery 44 and, more downmarket but more monumental, with Georges Seurat's *Bathers at Asnières* (1884). Paul Cézanne's *Bathers* (1900) and Vincent van Gogh's *Yellow Chair* (1888), with Paul Gauguin's *Faa Iheihe* (1898), recently swapped with Tate Modern, take you to the brink of the 20C. The effect is continued with Edgar Degas' *After the Bath*, (1880s) and Claude Monet's *Water Lily Pond* (1899).

Turn left out of the main entrance to continue this walk. As you proceed towards the church, note the one or two interesting statues: Grinling Gibbons's version of the rarely-celebrated *James II* (1686), and a bronze replica of Jean-Antoine Houdon's diminutive *George Washington*, the original being at Richmond, Virginia.

Leave the north side of the square and cross to **St Martin-in-the-Fields (Map 15,3)**. This church is exceptional in many ways: for its imposing site (the name refers back to the medieval foundation in the fields north of Westminster Abbey), its connections with the Hanoverian royal line (George I was a churchwarden), and as a trend-setting design and James Gibbs's masterpiece in London.

It was built 1722–26 and followed Gibbs's earlier, even more original, design for a circular church. If you look at the portico from across the road, at the corner of the National Gallery, you will probably, and rightly, admire its grandeur: your eye will travel up the magnificent tower and spire above, based on Sir Christopher Wren's designs but richer, reflecting Gibbs' Italian experience. Then think: is it logical, even for the sake of symmetry, to have a temple portico, the epitome of a grand entrance, with a church tower immediately behind it sticking up through the roof and, at ground-level, psychologically blocking the way in? Architectural connoisseurs have always found the idea troublesome. But since no one else ever lost a wink of sleep over the matter, the St Martin's design was repeated throughout the 18C all over England, Scotland and the eastern USA.

The rest of the exterior continues to reflect Gibbs's monumental preoccupations and is wonderfully integrated. Note his blocks of rustication round the windows, known ever since as 'Gibbs surrounds'. The interior is equally fine, with a lovely barrel-vaulted ceiling, the work of Italian plasterers Bagutti and Arturi, whom Gibbs brought back with him from Italy. Note the royal boxes, diagonally placed at gallery level between nave and chancel—so that royalty could not only see the altar but be seen themselves. Actress Nell Gwyn, cabinet-maker Thomas Chippendale, and painters Reynolds and Hogarth are buried here. The pews are mid-19C, and the fine early 18C pulpit was brought in from elsewhere at that time. The organ is new. The church gives frequent candlelit **concerts** of Baroque music at 19.30 Thur–Sat (admission charge) and lunchtime concerts at 13.05 Mon, Tues, Fri (free). Choral evensong 17.00 Sun. ☎ 020 7839 8362.

In the **crypt**, also worth visiting, there are an excellent café, a shop and a brass-rubbing centre. Open 10.00–18.00 Mon–Sat, 12.00–18.00 Sun. ☎ 020 7930 9306. Outside, within the original railings, there is a lively crafts market and behind the churchyard, in Adelaide Street, an approachable new sculpture of *Oscar Wilde* by Maggi Hambling.

Before you turn north, note **South Africa House** which overlooks Trafalgar Square from the east side. This was designed by Sir Herbert Baker in the 1930s, and inside shows his facility, developed in that country, for Cape Dutch style. To enquire about admission, ☎ 020 7451 7299. This completes our circuit of Trafalgar Square.

Return past St Martin-in-the-Fields to start up St Martin's Lane. Note further parts of the Nash scheme, including a National School, on the right, facing the north façade of the church. In St Martin's Lane, on your right, is the **Coliseum**, with luscious Edwardian interiors by Frank Matcham (1904)—go in to the foyer to admire them. It now the home of the English National Opera, a great company, which sings the works in English. Box office, ☎ 020 7632 8300.

Further north on the right, peep up Goodwin's Court, a little alley with bow-windowed shop-fronts; opposite stands the *Salisbury*, a real Victorian pub popular with gay Londoners. Cut through to Charing Cross Road and turn left. (The main area for bookshops is the northern half of Charing Cross Road, above Cambridge Circus—see Chapter 22.) Finally, return south past the statue of

Edith Cavell by Sir George Frampton (1920), on an unnecessarily tall plinth, to enter the National Portrait Gallery on the right.

National Portrait Gallery

The National Portrait Gallery is a uniquely British institution. This country's favourite form of art (apart perhaps from paintings of horses and landscapes) has always been pictures of its citizens, a long tradition which stretches back to Tudor times.

• Open 10.00–18.00 daily, 10.00–21.00 Thur, Fri. Admission free. Café. Restaurant (reservations ☎ 020 7312 2490). Shops. Musical performances 19.00 Fri. Free lectures 13.00 Tues, Thur. ☎ 020 7306 0055. www.npg.org.uk. Tube: Leicester Square.

The idea of a gallery devoted exclusively to portraits was, needless to say, a Victorian one, proposed in 1856 with the approval of Prince Albert. But it was not until 1895 that the present building was erected, to designs by Ewan Christian. It was extended sideways and upwards in 1999, by Dixon and Jones, to provide a small amount of additional hanging space and a substantial and very popular restaurant, overlooking the rooftops around Trafalgar Square.

A tour of the gallery is best done chronologically, which means taking the long escalator to the second floor and then following a route through the galleries in numerical order. Galleries 1–3 cover the **Tudors**, flamboyant in their gorgeous clothes but often rather mean and calculating in expression. This is clearly not true of *Sir Thomas More* (1593) and his family and descendants, who look as respectable and nice as can be imagined. But *Henry VIII as a Young Man* (1520), in Gallery 1, looks notably thin and calculating and the Dacres (1559) in Gallery 2, particularly grasping and selfish. It was an age when self-preservation ruled.

The **Stuarts**, in Galleries 4–8, look a great deal more reflective, *James I* (1621) and *Anne of Denmark* (1612) in Gallery 4 especially so. In Gallery 5 *Charles I* (1631) by Daniel Mytens also looks more subdued and anxious than Van Dyck presents him in the National Gallery, and Robert Walker's fine portraits of the Commonwealth leaders show them as the stressed and assertive individuals they must have been.

In Gallery 6, *John Bunyan* (1684) looks more *bon viveur* than Baptist, but the compelling image here is that of the now relatively unknown *Samuel Butler* (*c* 1665), author of *Hudibras*. *Samuel Pepys* (1666) turns crossly and uncomfortably towards us in Gallery 7, wearing the Indian gown he hired to pose to John Hayls. Opposite *Charles II* (1680), looking debauched and exhausted, sits crumbling in Sir Thomas Hawker's fine image. In Gallery 8, Sir Peter Lely's *Mary II* (1677) comes over as the Diana-type beauty she undoubtedly was, the future *James II* (painted *c* 1665) seems a great deal pleasanter and gentler than history has left his reputation, and *Queen Anne* (1705) simply looks cross.

Gallery 10 contains portraits of the artists and writers of the period, including *Christopher Wren* (1711), sprightly at 79, a complacent *Lord Burlington* (*c* 1717) and a vivid self-portrait of *Michael Dahl* (1691). There are politicians and public men in Gallery 11, along with a smug *John Wesley* (1766) by Nathaniel Hone and a villainous-looking *Robert Walpole* (1740). Later 18C culture is represented in Gallery 12 with numerous vivid characterisations by Reynolds, including *Mr and Mrs David Garrick* (1772), an odd *Laurence Sterne* (1760) and the romantic **William Beckford, aged 22** (1782). A wonderful happy-looking group, **The Sharp Family** (1779), is by John Zoffany. More serious, but no less impressive, people appear in Gallery 13, including **Lady Mary Wortley Montagu** (1717) by J.B. Vanmour, Hogarth's **William Jones** (1740) and thoughtful studies of the great engineers Boulton and Watt. Britain in the world, seen to be getting more self-conscious and pompous, can be explored in Gallery 14, with much agonising going on in **The Death of the Earl of Chatham** (1779– 81) by J.S. Copley. The hang makes less impact in this gallery, as it is in Gallery 17, where Britain's heroes of the French wars (1789–1815) are celebrated.

But wonders continue in Galleries 18–20. **William Blake** (1807) looks curiously worldly in Thomas Phillips's portrait. Benjamin Haydon's thoughtful vision of the elderly **William Wordsworth** (1842) contrasts oddly with his own bluff portrait by his pupil Georgiana Zornlin (1825). In Gallery 19 a special joy is **The Fourdrinier Family** (1786), with the urn of a deceased member inscribed 'JF aet. 51 Her good qualities were known to you all. Follow her example and be happy'. In these later galleries, media extend to engravings, wax models and sketches, as well as oils and busts.

The climax on this floor is the large carpeted Gallery 20, where the leading names of the Regency return our gaze benignly. **George IV** (1815) is flattered by Lawrence. The little pink eyes of **Sir John Soane** (1828) by John Jack twinkle back at us, Henry Perronet Briggs's **Sydney Smith** (1840) cannot repress his mirth, and William Beechey's **Thomas Hope** (1799) shows off his Greek outfit.

Descending to the first floor, the excitement wanes a little. First you need to process down the new Gallery 32, with icons of the 1960s, out of chronological order, and looking distinctly unimpressive, in order to reach the Victorians. There the Queen herself, appearing both confident and apprehensive at the same time, looms large in Gallery 21, in Sir George Hayter's famous coronation portrait (1838). **Prince Albert** (1859) by F.X. Winterhalter is cool and dignified—no wonder she loved him. A particular delight is H.N. O'Neil's group scene of **Princess Alexandra arriving at Gravesend in 1863**. But generally the Victorians in Galleries 22 to 29 are a dull collection, heavily pompous and solemn. The authors and artists are not much better. But there are some delights, for example Jules Bastien-Lapage's vivid, abandoned attempt to capture an image of **Henry Irving** (1880)—he walked out.

Galleries 30 and 31 redeem the 20C to some extent. Some startling images of famous names have the power to make us reassess their reputations. In particular Gallery 31, called 'The Armistice to the New Elizabethans' (1920s to 1950s) reveals an unforgettable parade. Among musicians alone, we can survey Vaughan Williams, Benjamin Britten and Peter Pears, Arthur Bliss, Gustav Holst, Frederick Delius and William Walton. A special memory is the vigorous self-portrait of **Anna Zinkeisen** (1944).

Pass quickly through the poor collection of contemporary royal portraits on the first-floor landing and enjoy the special changing exhibitions (some with admission charge) on the ground floor. The Gallery has an enormous collection of **photographs** on which temporary exhibitions often draw: you can research this collection by appointment. At mezzanine level there is a useful **IT gallery** where you can trace images of any Briton you may be curious about, even if his/her portrait is not on display. There is a good bookshop and café in the basement, and a gift shop to the right of the main entrance.

Leaving the gallery via the basement, turn right to go back through Trafalgar Square to Charing Cross Station, or left for Leicester Square. Whether or not this is the centre of London, it is certainly the centre of Britain's art.

Westminster

Crucially important, steeped in the past, redolent with monarchy it may be, but so far as the history of the capital is concerned, Westminster is a suburb of the City. Edward the Confessor's decision in the 1060s to shift his palace to a location next to the abbey church on Thorney Island, at the mouth of Tyburn Stream, was similar to that of Louis XIV's to relocate from Paris to Versailles, inspired by a desire to escape the urban mobs and muddle, the usual suburban motive.

Westminster was a separate, exclusive community, on marshy ground too shallow for shipping, with space for ambitious dignitaries of church and state to build subsidiary palaces. From the start, it developed a rather high-class tone. The Abbey and old palace (of which Westminster Hall, where the Houses of Parliament began, is the magnificent surviving evidence) attracted to the area William Caxton and his printing press. The presence of the court and the rich houses that located themselves along the riverbank also drew a number of trades to support them. By the 15C, Westminster had become a noisy bustling area in its own right, with a crime problem exacerbated by the Abbey's policy of giving sanctuary to fugitives. Westminster gained its bridge in 1750, which opened it up to the South Bank, but before then royalty had left the area for healthier, higher ground in Kensington and Windsor. In the 19C, the area of Victoria to the west became respectably residential, filled with London's first flats.

Edward the Confessor's move was of deep significance and had long-term effects, dividing government from commerce and trade. The geographical hiatus between Britain's administration in Westminster and its chief area of wealth creation, the City, has remained a feature of the nation's character ever since, critical elements of life, permanently opposed. 'Westminster' and 'Whitehall' are terms now synonymous with the political strands of British life, and the Abbey remains a key spiritual focus.

The area is much simpler to understand than the City, and can be covered in three main walks (Chapters 12–14). They contain some of London's finest buildings—the Houses of Parliament, the Banqueting House and Westminster Abbey itself—and scores of other important historical places. Two walks starting from Victoria are also included (Chapters 15 and 16): although in style they have more in common with the West End, most of the areas they cover belong administratively to Westminster and SW1, and there are other geographical links. Although refreshments are harder to come by than in the City, Westminster generally is more accessible and friendly to visitors.

12 • Whitehall

This short but concentrated walk explores Whitehall in a leisurely manner, from north to south, diverting east and west from time to time. You might find the changing of the Horse Guard occurring conveniently at about the half-way point.

• Distance: 1½ miles. Time: 1 hour + 2 hours for visits. Tube: Charing Cross. Map 14, 15.

Charing Cross Station (**Map 15,3**) is the best starting point. Turn left from the front facing the Strand, cross Northumberland Avenue and go over to Charles I's statue on the island site of the original Eleanor Cross (see Chapter 11). This is effectively the northern terminal point of **Whitehall**. Look south from here.

The wide thoroughfare, now crammed with buses and taxis, has been a busy street since medieval times, completing the link via the Strand and Fleet Street to the City. Originally it terminated halfway down, at Holbein Gate (long since demolished) just beyond the Banqueting House, south of which the area was constricted and crowded. The old Palace of Whitehall, developed by Henry VIII from York Place, the London seat of the Archbishops of York, lay to the left, facing the river. As at Hampton Court, Henry ousted Cardinal Wolsey to gain possession. He married Anne Boleyn and later Jane Seymour here, and died here in 1547. St James's Park, where Henry also developed leisure facilities for himself and his court, lies through Admiralty Arch to your right (see Chapter 17). The name Whitehall refers to Henry's palace: it may have had pale-coloured stonework but more likely this is an example of the general term 'White Hall', used in the period to signify a festive location.

We begin in the area to the east. Cross back to the left-hand side of the street and walk past the touristy shops. There are two or three pleasant pubs here, though unprepossessing from outside, including the *Old Shades* with its original 1890s exterior. Detour briefly up the cul-de-sac of Craig's Court to see a fine façade of 1702, formerly Harrington House, and then return to turn left down **Great Scotland Yard**. There is now no trace of the houses built here for occupation by the kings of Scotland when in London, dating back as far as the 10C. In 1829 a police station was established here which later gave its name to New Scotland Yard to the south.

Cut through Scotland Place, to the right, to Whitehall Place, turn left and then right. On the opposite corner, past a new monument to the Royal Tank Regiment by Vivian Mallock from a design by G.H. Paulin, is the **National Liberal Club** by Alfred Waterhouse (1884). The club is full of glazed tiling that caused Lord Birkenhead to admit he was surprised to find it was 'a club as well as a lavatory'. Next to it, to be gazed at in admiration, is **Whitehall Court**. This utterly wonderful building, a landmark from here, from St James's Park and even more from the river, is unknown by nearly everyone, though its staggeringly rich and imaginative use of French Renaissance motifs should make it world-famous. It was built as apartments in 1884 by the firm of Archer and Green—much of it is now offices and clubs, but it still offers a joyful antidote to the Classical bureaucracies all around.

Keeping the National Liberal Club on your right, continue down Whitehall Place to **Victoria Embankment Gardens** and walk through them (for the

Embankment itself, see Chapter 10). From here you can obtain a good view of both the river frontage of Whitehall Court and statues of almost forgotten heroes like General Sir James Outram and Sir Bartle Frere (now not seen as a hero at all) and, in another league, *William Tyndale* by Sir Joseph Boehm (1884). At the end, cross Horseguards Avenue and note in the garden beyond, behind a bronze of *General Gordon* looking thoughtful, by Hamo Thorneycroft (1887), **Queen Mary's steps**.

These are all that remain of a riverside terrace Sir Christopher Wren built in 1691 for Queen Mary II. Whitehall Palace still existed at that time but King William never liked it, and after the Queen's death he moved to Kensington. Only a few years later, in 1698, the entire palace except the Banqueting House was destroyed by fire.

There are statues commemorating figures from the Royal Air Force beyond: *Viscount Portal of Hungerford*, looking at the sky, by Oscar Nemon (1975); and *Air Chief Marshal Viscount Trenchard* by William Macmillan (1961).

Inigo Jones

Jones (1573–1652) burst on to the architectural scene in 1616 with the Queen's House at Greenwich, which must have looked more revolutionary to contemporaries than the most startling Postmodern structure looks to us. He was born in Smithfield, the son of a clothworker, and spent his early career as a designer of costumes and scenery for masques at James I's court. But after two visits to Italy, in 1603 and 1613, he succeeded in influencing the royal family into choosing the then novel Classical style, based on the work of Palladio and buildings in ancient Rome.

The Queen's House, a version of one of Palladio's villas, was built for James I's queen, Anne of Denmark and finished for Charles I's wife, Henrietta Maria. Just as radical were the Banqueting House at Whitehall, begun in 1622, the Queen's Chapel at St James's Palace, and the church of St Paul, Covent Garden. It was equally original of Jones, and almost perverse from this distance of time, to line the walls and west front of old St Paul's Cathedral with Classical columns: but the precedent was of key importance to Wren when he designed the new cathedral a generation later.

You must now return towards Whitehall to see the Banqueting House. As you go, note on your right the forceful architecture of the old War Office (1899–1906). On the left, the **Ministry of Defence** by Vincent Harris (1936–55) looks as if it had dropped in from Central Europe: not a pretty sight. Outside it stands a statue of *Field-Marshal Viscount Montgomery of Alamein* by Oscar Nemon (1980).

Banqueting House

The civilised Banqueting House (**Map 15,5**) now comes into view on your left. Students of architectural history might want to analyse its façade (1622) against that of Horse Guards (1750s) across the road ahead, and identify resemblances and differences.

• Open 10.00–17.00 Mon–Sat. Admission charge. ☎ 020 7930 4179. Tube: Westminster.

Why is this building so important? The answer is that it introduced London, and therefore Britain, to Classical architecture. Jones had, admittedly, started the Queen's House at Greenwich a few years before (see Chapter 49), and the nativity of British Classicism is strictly there. But that was a small villa on private land whereas this, although part of Whitehall Palace, was in a public street in a centre of the capital. Londoners must have been amazed. The Banqueting House's lofty appearance in early paintings and prints confirms its then spectacular presence. Now, of course, because of our familiarity with Classicism, it seems ordinary and quite diminutive, and it is hard to realise what a revolutionary building it once was.

Look at the Whitehall façade, which repays careful attention (you may need to get to the island in the road, or even cross, for the best view). It was originally faced with stone from three different areas of England, but in 1829 was repaired and refaced by Sir John Soane in Portland stone only. The basement is plain, rusticated, with small windows, but at main-floor level the strict formalism is spelled out. The three central bays project forwards and are marked by Ionic columns, with balconies to the windows. The outer bays have pilasters, paired at each end for emphasis. The windows have alternately segmented and triangular pediments. Above the entablature is a Corinthian attic floor with a frieze of swags and carved heads, the capitals appearing as Composite. A balustrade runs along at roof level. Jones thus presented a rich Italianate frontage to his new building, using a range of motifs from Palladio and other Italian precedents.

Interior The interior is a double cube, 100ft x 55ft x 55ft. It is assumed that the building was intended to be part of a range, with a grand entrance from at least one side, probably the north, whereas you now slip in through what is no more than a side door. Underneath, accessed from ground-level, is an extensive brick-vaulted basement, where you can see a video introduction to the building's history. As you see, the unfinished route to the hall above is quite unimpressive—go up some stone stairs and suddenly you are inside.

You will probably be struck first by the great paintings on the ceiling, and by the light flooding in from the generous windows. Nearly as compelling is the forceful motif of the scrolled brackets supporting the first-floor **balcony** and emphasising the Ionic columns. All this grandeur encases so much emptiness, and yet emptiness was the architect's intention. This space is like a stage, waiting to be set for whatever activity is thought appropriate—not, usually, a banquet ('banqueting house' had a different meaning; see the Glossary)—but more likely the performance of a masque or a grand reception. The main furnishing would have been tapestries, even if that meant blocking up some windows. The throne at the southern end, on a dais, would have been removed for masques.

Peter Paul Rubens's **ceiling paintings** were commissioned by Charles I during a diplomatic visit made by the painter to England in 1629. The diplomacy, in which Rubens was as adept as painting, was successful and the artist departed with a knighthood and an order for a comprehensive programme of canvases to depict the glories of the reign of Charles's father James I, who had died in 1625, with a subtext to emphasise the divine right of kings to rule. It is sobering to reflect that his fixation with this latter principle would lead to Charles's death, in front of this very building, 20 years later in 1649.

Charles I (1600–49, r. 1625–1649)

From the distance of the 21C Charles I—the only English king to be involved in civil war and to be executed—looks to have been, not an evil or dangerous character, but a wilfully perverse one. He seems to have been insensible to the strong opinions of the time in relation to parliament, religion, taxation and international affairs, and naïve in his belief in the divine rights of monarchy. His pragmatic father James I and son Charles II would certainly not have got themselves into such a mess.

Having failed to gain a Spanish bride he was influenced first by the Duke of Buckingham into foolish manoeuvres against Spain, the wrong enemy. Then, with his French Catholic queen Henrietta Maria, he tried to work without a parliament and later to bend it to his will, despite its obvious sponsorship of a powerful and independent standing army. He could not be trusted in negotiations. He was a gifted patron of the arts, and a collector whose acquisitions form the core of the royal collection to this day; in other relations of life these gifts of insight entirely deserted him.

Rubens never came back to England but the canvases were delivered in 1635. After their installation, the perceived purposes of the room become more serious, and masques were banned. The programme of the paintings is as follows:

(i) at the north end, over the entrance—the *Union of England and Scotland*, with Hercules representing strength, on the left, and on the right, Minerva representing wisdom.

(ii) in the centre—the *Apotheosis of James I* with, to either side, triumphal processions of rejoicing putti.

iii) at the south end, over the throne—the *Benefits of James I's Government*, with Wise Government on the left and Royal Bounty on the right.

You might expect that the powerful symbolism of these paintings would have led to their destruction in Oliver Cromwell's time but they survived unharmed and remained in place throughout the long years from 1698, when the Banqueting House functioned as the Chapel Royal, Whitehall. From 1890 to 1964 the building was an army museum. With its significant architecture, art and dramatic changes of use, the obviously vacant Banqueting House today seems in a provisional state, awaiting some new role.

Leaving the Banqueting House, cross Whitehall and go north again briefly to look at the **Old Admiralty**. The screen in front is the first London work by Robert and James Adam (1759–61), through which you can see the main building of a generation earlier by Thomas Ripley (1725–28), not admired by the experts but nevertheless of noble 18C proportions. Ian Fleming, creator of James Bond, worked for Naval Intelligence here. Next to it, coming south, are Admiralty House and the Paymaster General's Office, also 18C buildings, plain and simple.

The next important, and exceedingly beautiful, structure to study is the **Horse Guards** (1750–58), headquarters of the Household Division of the cavalry. It is always attributed to William Kent, but was mostly built after his death by John Vardy (1750–58). It is an original concept—Classical but no longer in homage to Palladio, or to Jones. From Whitehall you can see the very distinctive clock tower, the varied setting of the individual elements, and the narrow passageway through to the parade ground. The mounted guards sit motionless on either side, to the delight of the tourists: those in blue tunics are Blues and Royals, those in red Life Guards.

Go through to **Horse Guards Parade**—if you are lucky with your timing the Horse Guard may be formally changing (11.00 Mon–Sat, 10.00 Sun), always an impressive sight. In June, Trooping the Colour takes place here on the Saturday nearest the Queen's official birthday, with rehearsals on the two preceding Saturdays. Tickets for the event (not needed for the rehearsals) are sold by lottery to those who apply to the Brigade Major, HQ Household Division, Horse Guards, Whitehall, London SW1A 2AX (send an SAE).

St James's Park is beyond, but turn round to examine the Horse Guards' west façade. Here the restless sense of movement is even more marked, with blocks receding and projecting and of a great variety of heights, yet all precisely symmetrical. The symmetry is Palladian, but for the rest you feel that Kent was fighting to say something else.

> ## William Kent
> Kent (1675–1748) was an ordinary Yorkshireman who somehow managed to travel to Italy to train as an artist and designer. He was taken up by Lord Burlington, who sponsored his career on his return and employed him at Chiswick and elsewhere. In his lifetime Kent was equally at home as an architect, painter, designer of interiors and furniture, or of gardens, but he is now admired chiefly as an architect and even more as an innovator in garden design. The Horse Guards is based on his masterpiece, Holkham Hall in Norfolk. Its façade conveys the satisfying sense of movement developed by the Adam brothers, though they did not acknowledge Kent's influence.

Before returning through the passageway, look to your right. The heavily rusticated block facing you is also by William Kent: known as the **Old Treasury** (1733–36), it is still part of the Treasury complex. It was built on the site of Henry VIII's cockpit. To the right of it and slightly behind, in red brick, is the back of 10 Downing Street—this is a view of the famous Cabinet Room also designed by Kent (see below). Between it and Horse Guards you can see the back of Dover House by James Paine (1755–58). In the foreground are fine equestrian statues of two controversial figures from the Boer War, *Field-Marshal Earl Roberts* by Harry Bates (1923) and *Field-Marshal Viscount Wolseley* by Sir William Goscombe John (1920).

Go back through the arches into Whitehall and turn right to pass the front of **Dover House**, now the Scottish Office, a very beautiful addition by Henry Holland (1787). Across the road, in yellow brick, you can see Gwydyr House (1772), now the Welsh Office, and behind it the horrible Ministry of Defence offices. Underneath them lies Henry VIII's wine cellar, ingeniously re-installed from the former Whitehall Palace. To the right of them, **Richmond Terrace** by George Harrison (1822–25) looks as if it has escaped from Nash's terraces in Regent's Park. Beyond it are the enterprising Home Office buildings by William Whitfield (1988).

Staying on the west side of the road, go south past the front of the former Treasury by Sir Charles Barry (1845), now the Cabinet Office, and look along **Downing Street**. You are unlikely to be able to get past the iron gates (1990), so stare through like a prisoner and see what you can make out.

'Downing' comes from George Downing, an astute speculator who acquired the lease of this piece of land in 1680. It was he who built the terrace of houses, some of which you can still see. James Boswell was a resident. Out of sight behind No. 10, and now attached to it, is a larger 18C building which used to house the German ambassador: this was given by George II to Robert Walpole, who suggested that it should be used by future prime ministers when in office. William Kent made some alterations at the time he was working on the Treasury next door, including the setting up of a large domestic space now known as the Cabinet Room. Since 1856 the Cabinet has met here. There are also fine rooms in No. 10 designed by Sir John Soane in the 1820s.

No. 10 Downing Street

Much of the plasterwork and other decoration is original but changes have been made by most prime ministers during their respective occupancies. No. 11, similarly, is the official home of the Chancellor of the Exchequer, and No. 12 of the Government Chief Whip.

South of Downing Street are the enormous complex of the **Foreign and Commonwealth Office** by Sir George Gilbert Scott (1868), and the former India Office by Matthew Wyatt (1867). Pamphlets about the British Isles can sometimes be acquired from inside the Whitehall entrance of the Foreign Office and you may be lucky enough to penetrate further.

The design of the Foreign Office, you will see, is Classical. The choice of style was the subject of a prolonged dispute between the architect and the government, most notably the prime minister, Lord Palmerston. Scott was unfortunate. A strong supporter of A.W.N. Pugin and a church builder himself, he wanted Gothic. His reasons for caving in reveal the sordid dilemmas of the professional: he would like to have stuck to his principles and resigned, but that meant giving up an opportunity 'which Providence had placed in the hands of my family', so career came first. He should not have worried: the building is suitably magnificent as it is. And Scott was to achieve his great Gothic opportunity at St Pancras; see Chapter 28.

Cabinet War Rooms

Turn right into King Charles Street and walk to the end (**Map 14,6**) to visit the Cabinet War Rooms. This excellently presented, if politically biased, piece of history is run by the Imperial War Museum. It is incredibly evocative, an effect enhanced by tapes of air-raid warnings, all-clears and Winston Churchill's speeches.

- Open April–Sept 09.30–18.00; Oct–March 10.00–18.00. Admission charge. Audioguide recommended. ☎ 020 7930 6961. www.iwm.org.uk. Tube: Westminster.

These underground rooms were hollowed out in the 1930s when things looked ominous and, in August 1939, one week before war was declared, they became operational. The leaders of Britain's wartime government and armed forces worked and slept here throughout the air attacks on London. When the Second World War ended, the rooms were sealed up and left untouched until some were opened as a museum in 1981. More rooms will be opened in the near future.

Nothing has been changed, and that may be why the whole experience seems so real: it is real. Churchill's presence permeates the space like a spirit—you hear his voice and see his notes, drafts of his speeches, his bedroom and the desks used by his long-suffering secretaries, looking as if they had just popped out for a moment. You fear the phone will ring in their absence and you will have to answer it. This is a special place—don't miss it.

Winston Churchill

Churchill (1874–1965) has to be classified as Britain's greatest prime minister and most inspiring orator: he was a towering personality and, as is often forgotten, winner of the Nobel Prize for Literature. Born at Blenheim Palace, Oxfordshire, to an American mother, he was a grandson of the 7th Duke of Marlborough. His early life contained innumerable romantic and courageous exploits, as a soldier and war correspondent. He enjoyed wars and fought, briefly, in the trenches in the First World War.

Churchill entered politics in 1900 as a Conservative, but became a Liberal and at an early age filled Cabinet posts. At the Admiralty, he was credited with the foresight to have the fleet in readiness for the outbreak of war in 1914, and he served at various points in Lloyd George's coalition government. Rejoining the Conservatives in 1924 he became Chancellor of the Exchequer, unwisely returning Britain to the gold standard. He was not popular at this time, opposing the General Strike in 1926 and losing his seat in 1929. During the 1930s, from outside parliament and against popular opinion, he opposed both the abdication of Edward VIII and policies of appeasement.

But when war against Hitler came, Churchill proved a man of destiny. Returning first to the Admiralty, he soon replaced Neville Chamberlain as prime minister. As war leader he was ruthless, impetuous, single-minded and inspirational. His sole aim was to defeat Nazi Germany, and he recognised this could not be done without American help. He largely ignored the Home Front, but even so was adored and respected as the architect of victory. Such popularity did not prevent his party being defeated, however, when Clement Attlee's great reforming government was elected in 1945. His voice continued to be heard internationally, drawing attention to the 'Iron Curtain' descending across Europe. Churchill returned as Conservative prime minister in 1951 and led a very successful government, retiring in 1955.

He was devotedly married to Clementine—evidence of their affection can be seen in the Cabinet War Rooms displays. He painted well and wrote major histories of his times.

Return to Whitehall. At the southern end, overlooking Parliament Square (see Chapter 14), is the building now used as the **Treasury**, but built as offices for the

Ministry of Health by J.M. Brydon (1909). It is a fine example of Edwardian Imperialism, like the War Office mentioned above. (If you travel on the London Eye, look at this building from above. Inside is a great circular colonnaded space, of which there is no hint from Whitehall: it shows what we miss.)

Parliament Street, at 130ft the widest street in London, was laid out in the 19C. Opposite are some ornate, non-government buildings of the same period, including a fine pub, the *Red Lion*. In the block to the south, note one surviving 18C brick house crouching nervously among its taller stone and stucco neighbours. In the middle of the road is an important monument by Sir Edwin Lutyens, the **Cenotaph** (1919–20), the national memorial to the 'Glorious Dead' of the two 20C world wars. 'Cenotaph' means empty tomb: it has no religious symbolism. On Remembrance Day, the Sunday nearest to 11 November, the date of the Armistice in 1918, a memorial service attended by the Queen is held here, with a two-minute silence at 11.00.

> ### Sir Edwin Lutyens
> Lutyens (1869–1944) is thought of as an Edwardian architect because the height of his career coincided with that extravagant decade. But his Classical buildings are today less appreciated and recognisable than the smaller 'Arts and Crafts' country houses he built in the Home Counties, often with gardens designed by Gertrude Jekyll. Of his work in London, the little former Midland Bank in Piccadilly, playfully reflecting Wren's church of St James behind it, or the Cenotaph, are more appealing to today's taste than the luxurious Classicism of Britannic House, Finsbury Square, or the offices of HSBC in Poultry. Lutyens's several war memorials have the same solemn emotional power as Edward Elgar's music.

At the foot of Whitehall, cross from west to east to reach Westminster station. This Tube station was rebuilt by Michael Hopkins in 1999 to accommodate the Jubilee Line and is buried deep within his new parliamentary offices, **Portcullis House**, built at controversial expense but to the highest quality. Behind it, facing the river, you can catch a glimpse of the former **New Scotland Yard**, once the Metropolitan Police headquarters, built by R. Norman Shaw (1890) and now named after him. A fine example of that architect's style, with Arts and Crafts overtones, it too now provides office space for MPs.

13 • The Houses of Parliament

The Houses of Parliament are London's finest building and therefore have the bulk of a chapter to themselves. Our walk takes you round the exterior, tells the building's history and covers the interesting little area beyond, within the sound of the division bell. Sometimes you can get inside and it is worth making every effort to do so: this chapter describes the 'line of route' for tours. The arrangements are complicated (see below) but opportunities are improving.

- Distance: 1¼ miles. Time: about 1 hour + 1½ hours for a tour of the interior if arranged. Tube: Westminster. Map 15.

Visiting the Houses of Parliament

- Parliament in session mid-Oct to Christmas, Jan to Easter, June, July. **House of Commons** open 14.30–22.30 or later Mon–Wed, 10.30–19.30 Thur, 09.30–15.00 Fri (if sitting). **House of Lords** open 14.30–20.00 or later Mon–Wed, 15.00–20.00 or later Thur, 11.00 till end of business Fri (if sitting). Commons information ☎ 020 7219 4272. Lords information ☎ 020 7219 3107. www.parliament.uk

- It is possible to attend **debates** in the Commons or the Lords by queuing at St Stephens' Porch (see below). The queues for the Commons will be long at peak times, in the afternoons—these include **Prime Minister's Questions** at 15.00 Wed, which can be more interesting than debates. There is usually no problem after 17.30 Mon–Thurs, or when the House sits in the early morning, or when visiting the Lords.

- To bypass the queue, apply for a **ticket**, up to eight weeks in advance, by writing to your Member of Parliament (if you are a UK citizen), or to your Embassy or High Commission, unless you are from North America in which case write to the Commons' Education Unit, House of Commons Library, Westminster, London, SW1A 2TT. This is the best way to be sure of getting in to Question Time.

- To be put on a **guided tour** of the building, allowing you to examine the architecture, write to your Member of Parliament or ☎ 020 7219 3000, if you are a UK citizen. If you are not, write or phone your Embassy in London and make the same request.

- There are sometimes **public tours** when the House is in recess (July, Aug and Sept) which can be pre-booked via Ticketmaster ☎ 020 7219 4272/3107. To find out the current position, or to ask any other questions, visit www.parliament.uk and locate 'visits' in the site index.

From Westminster station (District/Circle or Jubilee Lines) take the exit under Bridge Street to ascend under the shadow of the clock tower—or Big Ben as it is invariably but wrongly called (see below). Then walk half-way out on to Westminster Bridge and look back at the river façade and the clock tower itself. Take time—this is a rich **view**.

As architecture, not least of the great strengths of the Houses of Parliament is its magical relation to the river. Only Somerset House and Wren's buildings at Greenwich show the same sensibility to the river view; but Somerset House is disfigured by the Embankment and plane trees, and Greenwich is out of town. The view of the Palace of Westminster (as it is still curiously called) from the Albert Embankment at Lambeth (Chapter 33) is one of the great sights of London, worth crossing Lambeth Bridge, or the world, to see. You can get some idea of its magnificence by starting this walk towards the south side of Westminster Bridge.

History

There has been a palace at Westminster since before 1066, occupied by royalty until Henry VIII abandoned it for Whitehall Palace in 1512. Its use for parliaments (see below) was originally a royal concession, beginning in the reign of Edward I, when the 'model' parliament met in Westminster Hall. Thereafter the Lords were able to use the palace and the Commons had to manage as best they could, often in the Chapter House of Westminster Abbey.

St Stephen's Chapel, the palace's own chief place of worship, was secularised at the Reformation and became a convenient meeting place for the Commons. It was here, occupying the choir stalls arranged opposite one another for antiphonal choral music, that over time the members divided themselves into two opposing 'parties'. Thus, architecture effectively determined the development of the two-party system of British government.

So matters continued until 1834 when the chapel and nearly all the rest of the medieval palace were destroyed by a fire, intended to burn old tally-sticks but which got totally out of hand. Various suggestions for rebuilding had been made in the intervening 300 years but had come to nothing. Now there was no alternative. A parliamentary committee announced that designs for a completely new Houses of Parliament were invited, 'in the Gothic or Elizabethan style', consciously rejecting two centuries of Classicism. This design specification was partly a reference to the parts of the old building, including Westminster Hall, which had survived, and to Westminster Abbey nearby, but also reflected the then growing perception of Gothic or Tudor as a national style.

The designs of Charles Barry and A.W.N. Pugin won the competition, Barry's focusing on planning and construction management and Pugin's on decoration and ornament. Work began in 1837: the House of Lords was completed in 1847 and the Commons in 1852. Some of the later parts took an unduly long time, and the ventilation system caused particular difficulty.

Special trouble was taken over the decoration of the interior, not only through Pugin's countless individually designed features, from stained glass to inkwells, but also in the provision of paintings and sculpture. Prince Albert took a personal interest and chaired the Select Committee, pressing on the designers the value of fresco, incompatible though the technique was with English weather. The symbolism of the art, needless to say, is the celebration of British government, with its mixture of monarchy and democracy.

In 1940–41 most of the House of Commons was destroyed by bombs, and was later rebuilt by Sir Giles Gilbert Scott. Scott did not attempt to replicate the Victorian detailing and the Commons is a much more utilitarian space than the interior of the House of Lords, which remains Pugin's unforgettable masterpiece.

As you stand on Westminster Bridge, look first at the **clock tower**, properly called St Stephen's Tower, and allow your eye to travel up it. Its sheer familiarity as an image—pointing to the heavens with the grey foggy Thames in the foreground—makes us forget how spectacular is the detail of the projecting clock faces surmounted by concave sections of spire punctuated by tiny windows.

The tower is 316ft high and 40ft square and was completed in 1858. The clock face projects slightly, to create what has become an internationally recognised symbol. The clock faces were designed by Pugin. There are four quarter bells ('Westminster chimes') and an hour bell, weighing 13½ tons, called 'Big Ben', perhaps after Sir Benjamin Hall, a six-footer who was the First Commissioner of Works when the bell was hung. At the first stroke of each quarter-hour, the clock is accurate to within one second, and this is checked and adjusted three times a week. A light in the clock tower signifies that parliament is in session.

Houses of Parliament

Also look along the riverside **terrace** to the left, the first part a meeting place for Members of the Commons, and beyond that a separate terrace for the Lords. The projecting block at the corner in front of you is the **Speaker's Residence**: you may be able to glimpse in through the windows.

Sir Charles Barry

A versatile and wholly successful Victorian architect, Barry (1795–1860) built Neo-Gothic churches in Islington and elsewhere and the Neo-Renaissance Travellers' and Reform Clubs in Pall Mall. While working on the Reform he won, with Pugin's help, the competition for the new Houses of Parliament with a design which is Georgian in the tidiness of its planning, but Gothic in the richness of its skyline and resulting romantic allusions—a model combination which has given London its primary architectural image. His son, Edward M. Barry (1830–80), although lesser-known, was also important in London building; he designed the present Royal Opera House and the Charing Cross Hotel.

The cast-iron **Westminster Bridge** itself is impressive. It was built just as the Houses of Parliament were being finished (1854–62), with Barry as architectural consultant, to replace the bridge of 1750, which had been only the second bridge to cross the Thames in London and which inspired William Wordsworth's famous poem. Look across the impressive width to the statues at either end: the Coade-stone lion in front of County Hall (Chapter 32) and *Queen Boudicca*, scourge of the Romans, with her daughters in a chariot above Westminster pier, made in the 1850s by Thomas Thorneycroft but not unveiled until 1902.

Now walk down Bridge Street towards Parliament Square and turn left. **New Palace Yard** is on your left. Peer through the railing to note St Stephen's Cloisters, also partial survivors of the 1834 fire, with Barry's new building attached behind them: in Tudor times there was a fountain here, but now it is the main entrance for MPs. There is a curiously formal garden in the centre, like the square in a French town. On the right, unobtrusive from this angle, is Westminster Hall.

As you walk down St Margaret Street there is a bronze of *Oliver Cromwell*—a figure in British history no less unpopular than Charles I—by Hamo Thorneycroft (1899), with the obligatory, significantly patriotic, lion below. Cromwell is perhaps slightly lucky to be here, having had his remains brutally dug up from the Abbey across the road. But it is good to see him, because most of the statuary on this entirely political building is of kings and queens, not politicians: there was little in Pugin's scheme of decoration to remind the observer that Britain was by then a democracy.

Oliver Cromwell

Cromwell (1599–1658) has been a powerful but strangely ambiguous figure in English history, judged today neither hero nor villain. No other private person before him had taken power in a European kingdom, let alone tried the sovereign in lawful process and seen him publicly executed like a criminal. But Cromwell has had no successors in this country and left no movement behind: his daring has never even been attempted again.

A minor provincial gentleman, his greatest success was as an army general. After early victories over the royalists, he reformed the army on the New Model, and became not only its commanding officer but also its political representative. Following victory in the Civil Wars and the death of Charles I, he led campaigns in Ireland brutal in their degree of repression, and after personally rejecting the Rump Parliament in the 1650s drafted constitutions which led to the appointment of a Lord Protector, a post for which he himself was the obvious choice. His aim was to create a godly nation, but too few shared this vision. By 1660, the mood of the people seemed to favour, instead of a state army and high taxes, a pragmatic restoration of the monarchy.

You now reach **St Stephen's Porch**, where you can queue for the public gallery or enter if you have a ticket. Otherwise continue down Old Palace Yard, past the highly romantic bronze statue of *Richard I* made by Baron Marochetti (1860): he stands defiant in front of Barry's great south window to Westminster Hall. At the foot of **Victoria Tower** is the sovereign's entrance, on the same site as that in the old palace. At 336ft the Victoria Tower is even taller than the clock tower, a massive object that was the largest structure in Europe when it was completed in 1860. It houses parliamentary records.

Tour of the Houses of Parliament

The journey through the building undertaken by the Queen when she comes to open parliament is known as the line of route, and is the same as that followed by public tours. It begins by entering the **Norman Porch** at the foot of the Victoria Tower, where it was originally planned to erect statues of the Norman kings. In fact the statuary consists of busts of prime ministers who have sat in the House of Lords. The richly gilded vaulting in the chamber at the top of the stairs gives a foretaste of what is to come.

The route turns right, into the **Robing Room**, an interior of extraordinary richness, overwhelmingly red and gold, with portraits of Victoria and Albert either side of the throne. The theme of the frescoes on the walls and the bas reliefs below, by William Dyce and H.H. Armstead respectively (1860s), is the life of King Arthur, chosen as a subject because the Victorians perceived that as the legendary starting point of British national history. This room is also the starting point of the crowned and robed monarch's route into Parliament.

She proceeds first into the **Royal Gallery**. Here, in a space less comfortable bu no less rich than the Robing Room, are portraits of recent monarchs as far back as George III, under a giant beamed ceiling with pendants. The eye is mainly taken by the two huge frescoes, completed with great difficulty by Daniel Maclise, who was sent to Berlin by Prince Albert to learn the technique. The subjects are *Wellington's Meeting with Blücher* (1862) and the *Death of Nelson* (1865). In display cases there are important documents in constitutional history, including the 1689 Declaration of Rights, and a model of the old Palace of Westminster. The Minton tiles that cover the floor require constant renewal. When not used for processions, the Royal Gallery comes in handy as a space for parliamentary receptions for visiting heads of state.

The next room reached is the **Prince's Chamber**—a name inherited from the old palace—where there is an elaborate and brilliant scheme of full-length portraits of Tudor monarchs, specially painted by students at Prince Albert's newly-established Royal School of Fine Art. They were allegedly based on original works, the research of which was one of the causes of the foundation of the National Portrait Gallery in 1856. Below the portraits is a series of bronze bas-reliefs by William Theed. The room is dominated—'dwarfed', said the *Builder* critically in 1856—by John Gibson's 8ft-tall group of *Queen Victoria* throned above Justice and Mercy. Beneath her are reliefs of Commerce, Science and a steam engine and a telegraph cable, what the Victorians called Technological Progress. The type of furniture in the Chamber was designed by Pugin for use throughout the House of Lords: he was responsible for every detail including the inkstands. To either side are passageways to the Lords Library and Committee Rooms.

A.W.N. Pugin

Pugin (1812–52), whose work is one of the keys to the Victorian psyche, was an exciting, radical, workaholic designer who became a Roman Catholic and developed unshakeable principles about Gothic (especially 13C Gothic) as the only appropriate style for building. He detested Classicism, basing his arguments on tradition and on function. Through his work with Charles Barry in the design of the detail of the Houses of Parliament he achieved sufficient fame to publish tracts that enabled his views to become widely read, and thus influential on other church builders and patrons of the day, including the Ecclesiologists, and on John Ruskin and William Morris.

As Pugin went on to become an even more committed Gothic Revivalist, he came to feel that the Houses of Parliament had been an unsatisfactory compromise: 'All Grecian, Sir: Tudor details on a classic body.' But Pugin died before the building was finished, and although features such as Barry's axial plan and formal fenestration are in many ways Classical in spirit, the two towers, asymmetrically placed, are inspirationally Gothic.

House of Lords

The climax of the monarch's route is reached. Entering either left or right, go in and stand in front of the monarch's throne and canopy, Pugin's masterpiece. From it, the Queen addresses parliament at the State Opening. The shape of the throne is, as you would expect from Pugin, based on precedent—the coronation chair in Westminster Abbey—and its elaboration set the standard for the chamber as a whole. Painting here is reduced to a few dim frescoes high up at each end, and the eye is blinded by the mass of red and gold.

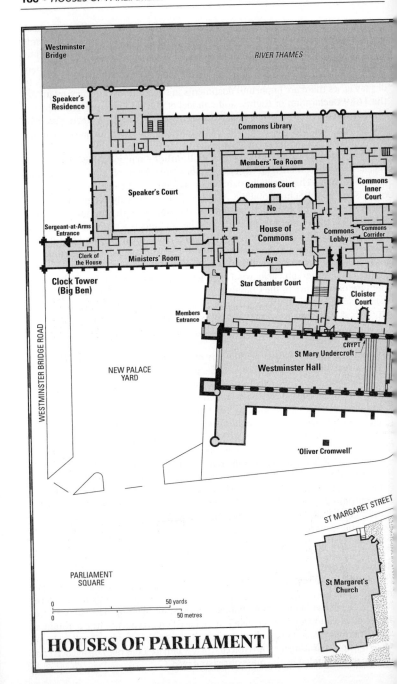

Westminster
Bridge

RIVER THAMES

Speaker's
Residence

Commons Library

Members' Tea Room

Commons Court

Speaker's Court

Commons
Inner
Court

No

Sergeant-at-Arms
Entrance

House of
Commons

Commons
Lobby

Commons
Corridor

Clerk of
the House

Ministers' Room

Aye

Clock Tower
(Big Ben)

Star Chamber Court

Cloister
Court

Members
Entrance

CRYPT
St Mary Undercroft

WESTMINSTER BRIDGE ROAD

NEW PALACE
YARD

Westminster Hall

'Oliver Cromwell'

ST MARGARET STREET

PARLIAMENT
SQUARE

St Margaret's
Church

0   50 yards

0   50 metres

HOUSES OF PARLIAMENT

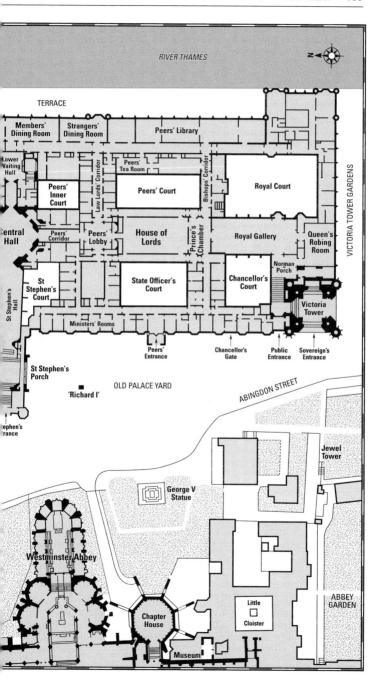

The Upper House of the two Houses of Parliament dates back to the Great Council of the Norman kings. Over its long history its importance relative to the Commons has progressively diminished—although its architecture would lead you to think otherwise. This process continues with the recent removal of voting rights for hereditary peers and more changes are planned. The members, currently numbering around 700, comprise 'lords spiritual' (archbishops and a few bishops) and 'lords temporal' (peers, hereditary and life) who can represent the interests of any political party or be independent. The Lords can delay legislation or send it back to the Commons, but not money bills such as the budget, which can go direct to the monarch for royal assent. The Lords is also the highest court of appeal in the legal system, as represented by a panel of Law Lords.

Although the term 'peers' implies equality within the group, there is in fact a rigid heirarchy. Dukes, often people of royal blood, are at the top, marquesses next, then viscounts, earls and finally barons. Viscounts, earls and barons are all conventionally called Lord ('Lord Smith'). Only a hereditary peer's eldest son or daughter is addressed with the first name included ('Lord John Smith') and they are not peers. Younger children can use the title Honorable ('The Hon. Mary Smith').

Face into the chamber, with the throne behind you, to see it all from the Queen's viewpoint. On your right sit the government peers, with the 'lords spiritual' on the benches at the front nearest the throne. The opposition peers sit on the left and independents on cross benches, behind the **Woolsack**, an ancient symbol of British prosperity. On this object sits the Lord Chancellor, who acts as Speaker in the House of Lords, although he does not use the firm control customary in the Commons. For the State Opening of Parliament, MPs from the Commons come to stand at the Bar of the House behind the cross benches. Far above is the Strangers', or public, Gallery

Pugin's decorative scheme is everywhere, in the woodwork of the panelling, the tables, benches, the ironwork, the stained glass, the programme of statuary and the embellishment of the ceiling. It may all seem too much. It certainly did to some members of the Commons when first planned and constructed, and some stinging criticisms had to be fended off by Robert Peel, prime minister in the 1840s. The lavishness of the quarters for the unelected Lords, compared with those of the elected Commons, is still hard to stomach.

You leave by the north entrance, leaving the monarch behind—she never gets this far—via the **Peers' Lobby** where Pugin again indulged himself, in a similar colour scheme. In the **Peers' Corridor** beyond, the struggle for democracy is reflected in the subjects depicted in the art—less of royalty and more of the people, as well as less of the Middle Ages and more of the 17C. In this, the corridor between the two Houses, the scenes are carefully balanced to present both sides of the coin. The artist was C.W. Cope, who completed the series in 1867.

Thus you reach the **Central Lobby** midway between the two Houses, a buzzing public space. People queuing to hear debates pass through here, others come to lobby (this is where the verb comes from) their MPs, others simply to look. The vaulted ceiling is decorated with the rose and portcullis emblems seen throughout the building. The mosaics, done after Pugin, show the four national saints of the United Kingdom, George (England), Andrew (Scotland), David

Wales) and Patrick (Northern Ireland). St Stephen's Hall is to your left—we shall return to it—and the corridor to your right leads to stairs (where there is a statue of Barry, worth trying to see), committee rooms and the river terrace. But we press on into the Commons.

Parliament

The origin of parliament was as a means for the monarch to hear the opinions of his most powerful subjects on key matters. It evolved into the chief instrument of government, reducing the monarch to a figurehead.

It has always been divided into lords and representatives of the community ('commons'), who have sat in different chambers. Gradually the Commons have been chosen more and more democratically, currently by a franchise for all registered citizens over the age of 18. The Lords, or peers, or Upper Chamber, either inherited their titles or are appointed by the government in power. Hereditary peers can no longer vote on legislation.

An elected government from the Commons provides the monarch with a list of bills they wish to introduce. She then announces them annually at the State Opening of Parliament. Each bill is 'read' (i.e. debated) in the Commons three times, and in between is amended by a parliamentary committee. After the third reading a vote, or division, is taken. A similar process then occurs in the Lords, with possible further amendments, although some bills by-pass the Upper Chamber. It usually takes at least six months for a bill to obtain royal assent (effectively nominal) and so become an Act of Parliament, and law.

House of Commons

The Commons Corridor leads to the **Commons Lobby**, where forceful bronzes of *Winston Churchill* by Oscar Nemon (1966) and *David Lloyd George* by Uli Imptsch (1963) guard the entry to the Commons chamber. This area was rebuilt in the 1950s after bomb damage, and the shattered stones of the arch were retained for effect. Churchill's bronze foot has been burnished to brightness by the superstitious touch of many fingers, of MPs and others seeking supernatural advantage.

The tour will probably take you first to the right, through part of the Commons Library, with volumes of Hansard (verbatim records of parliamentary debates) on the shelves, and then the **Division Lobbies**, used for members voting 'Aye' or 'Noe' in debates. You then enter the **House of Commons** from the north, behind the Speaker's chair. You will see that it is not just plainer architecturally than the Lords, sober green against rich red, but, following repairs after the 1941 bombing, is in the stylistically sober mid-20C Gothic style of Sir Giles Gilbert Scott. References to tradition here are not in accordance with the medieval philosophy of Pugin and the Victorians, but safer, easier, kinder and, we may say, duller. This is a working chamber, not a showcase, now very familiar from television images, and when you are in it, surprisingly small. It is far too small for all MPs to be seated and was designed on the premise that, first, they would hardly ever all be there at once and, second, a shortage of seats would be an incentive to attend early. The red line in the carpet marks the point beyond which an MP may not advance. Again, looking at it from the Speaker's angle, the government is on the right and the opposition on the left.

You then return through the Lobbies to **St Stephen's Hall**, rebuilt by Barry on the exact site and in the idiom of the 13C/14C St Stephen's Chapel, which serve as the Commons' chamber from 1547 to 1834 (see above). The medieval chape under St Stephen's, also known as St Mary's Undercroft, survived the 1834 fir and was redecorated *à la* Pugin in the 1860s. E.M. Barry provided a baptister These spaces are not normally on view.

Westminster Hall

The climax of the visit is seen on leaving St Stephen's Hall, or glimpsed whe coming through from the other direction, namely the great historic space Westminster Hall, which also escaped the fire and gave the Gothic rationale t the new building.

William II first constructed it in 1097–99, with timber supports for the roo It was then the largest hall in Europe. In the 1390s Richard II renovated th Hall to the designs of the mason Henry Yevele, and replaced the suppor with the new technology of the hammerbeam, which enabled the full span t be covered: the carpenter was Hugh Herland.

The Hall became the seat of the law courts and, occasionally, of parli ments, and even housed small shops. Edward II abdicated (1327) an Richard II was deposed here (1399); Charles I was tried here (1649); Willia Wallace (1305), Sir Thomas More (1535) and Guy Fawkes (1606) were co demned in the Hall; and the bodies of monarchs and other leaders lay in stat Its significance in English life may be reflected in Shakespeare's setting scen from *Henry IV* and *Henry VI Part 3* here.

The space was adorned with statues of kings, some of which, rather battere can still be seen in niches above the top of the steps and on the sills of the ea wall. This noble interior now lacks a real purpose but is occasionally used fc state occasions. It ought to be opened from the north, quite independent of a the palaver of getting into Parliament, to show off its roof—still the fine hammerbeam ceiling in England—and for historical exhibitions.

You exit, past a state coach, into New Palace Yard and resume your progre south—past Cromwell, Richard I and the Victoria Tower as already describe Turn left beyond the corner of the Tower to Black Rod's Garden, which forms th northern part of **Victoria Tower Gardens**. The gardens and Houses Parliament project into the river, as it were forming the launch pad for th Victoria Embankment to the north (Chapter 10). The public gardens are nothir special but this is a good place to admire the river. There is first a bronze of th suffragette leader *Emmeline Pankhurst* by A.G. Walker (1930), to which a med of her daughter *Christabel Pankhurst* by Peter Hills was added in 1959, and copy (1915) of Auguste Rodin's *Burghers of Calais*. The pretty Gothic drinkir fountain of 1868 was erected by Charles Buxton to mark the ending of slave in 1834, in which his father, the MP Sir T. Fowell Buxton, was a prime mov with William Wilberforce. Across the water are good, though undeserved, viev of St Thomas's Hospital, and of the more deserving Lambeth Palace (Chapter 3

At the foot of the gardens is **Lambeth Bridge** (**Map 15,7**) of 1929, with ey catching red and brown paint, a little, unimportant and therefore rather charmir bridge, like that at Southwark. It is worth walking on to it for the views. Th Archbishop of Canterbury owned a horse ferry here, until it was made redu dant by Westminster Bridge, and the memory is retained in Horseferry Road.

Shudder at the 1920s government buildings either side of the roundabout. Return up Millbank and turn left into Dean Stanley Street. Opposite you is one of London's oddest churches, **St John Smith Square**, now a concert hall. It is the work of Thomas Archer (1713–28): Pevsner called it 'one of the boldest manifestations of the English Baroque in London, spectacularly independent'. The Greek cross plan is made more Baroque by the concave bays at each corner. The four towers with their ogee tops, the pediments and the rest of the roof-line make an extraordinary show. There are a restaurant and toilets in the crypt. Details of concerts may be obtained there, or ☎ 020 7222 1061. Restaurant ☎ 020 7222 2779. www.sjss.org.uk

The surrounding streets are composed of small-scale, very attractive 18C houses, much favoured by MPs and parliamentary people who wish to be within the sound of the division bell. Make your way up Lord North Street, cross Great Peter Street and go up Cowley Street to the back of Westminster School at the top of Barton Street, the two comprising an attractive Georgian development. T.E. Lawrence once lived at 14 Barton Street. If it is a Tuesday, Wednesday or Thursday, take the opportunity now of visiting the **Abbey Garden** via nearby Dean's Yard (Chapter 14). Turn right along Great College Street and back across the grass in Abingdon Street, where MPs can often be seen uttering soundbites on television. On the lawn stands *Knife Edge* by Henry Moore (1967).

Ahead of you is the **Jewel Tower**, a survival from the old palace, the repository of the king's valuables, gold, silver, furs and jewels until the reign of Henry VIII. It dates from 1365 and was probably designed by Henry Yevele, chief architect of Westminster Abbey. There will be more of him in the next chapter. Open April–Sept 10.00–18.00 daily; Oct 10.00–17.00; Nov–March 10.00–16.00. Admission charge. Shop. ☎ 020 7222 2219.

You enter via the remains of a garden overlooking a moat. There is a shop on the ground floor, with other remains of the old palace and an amazing Saxon sword found on the site. Then, on the first floor up a spiral staircase, there is a good exhibition on the history of parliament, useful if you cannot see the interior of the House. On the second floor, a 30-minute video on how parliament works is similarly instructive. In the 19C the Jewel Tower became the Board of Trade Standards department: all this is explained in a further display.

Beyond the Jewel Tower is **Old Palace Yard**, the site where Sir Walter Raleigh was beheaded, now a curious if very handsome Georgian intrusion. It is a survivor from an earlier uncompleted scheme of rebuilding by John Vardy (1750s), the man who built Spencer House (Chapter 18). Next is a solemn *George V* on an enormous pedestal, by Sir W. Reid Dick (1947)—and then Henry VII's Chapel in the Abbey and Parliament Square.

Walk back to Westminster station, or take a bus up Whitehall. Westminster secular is over: next is Westminster spiritual.

14 • Westminster Abbey and its environs

This short walk chiefly covers the Abbey but has other ecclesiastical connections. The minster west of London gave the area its name and origin and, as we have noted, was the magnet which drew the palace. Abbeys themselves created communities around them, and Westminster's environment is no exception.

- Distance: ⅔ mile. Time: 15 minutes + 1½ hours for the Abbey.
  Tube: Westminster. Map 15.

From Westminster station, walk down Bridge Street away from the river to **Parliament Square (Map 15,5)**. The architecture is a rich, unforgettable ensemble: the Houses of Parliament are on your left, St Margaret's and the Abbey behind it are across the square and Whitehall extends to your right. Cross into the square if you can, to get a feel for the space. Laid out in 1868, it was part of Charles Barry's scheme to set off his masterpiece, the Houses of Parliament, but the traffic wrecks it and makes it quite unsuitable as a site for statuary. Even so the bronzes of *Benjamin Disraeli* by Mario Raggi (1883), *Jan Smuts* by Jacob Epstein (1958) and *Winston Churchill* by Ivor Roberts-Jones (1973) are worth looking at. On the west side of the square note the startling rash of carving on the former **Middlesex Guildhall** (1906–13), now the Crown Court: it is a history lesson, including Magna Carta, Henry III and Lady Jane Grey.

> ## Church of England
> There has been a Church of sorts in Britain since Roman times but the proper establishment of Christianity here dates from the 7C, when Aidan brought the faith from Ireland to Northumbria and Augustine from Rome to Canterbury. Until 1534, Britain was then part of the European Church. The break from papal authority and towards royal supremacy was brought about by Henry VIII's anxiety to divorce Catherine of Aragon, but this was simply the culmination of growing public disenchantment with the wealth and dominance of the medieval Church. It was not until Elizabeth I's reign, later in the 16C, that the Church of England was formally established and the Book of Common Prayer and Thirty-Nine Articles launched.
>
> Supremacy, or the divine rights of kings, did not suit the English sense of liberty, however, and the 17C became a period of religious upheaval. Numerous Protestant sects emerged, and most were excluded from the Restoration settlement; Roman Catholics were also suppressed. From the 18C onwards, although enshrined in the monarchy and in parliamentary procedure (26 bishops still sit in the House of Lords), the Church of England has never represented the people as a whole as a national church. Yet it is, in another sense, international. Its head, the Archbishop of Canterbury (Augustine's successor), oversees 450 dioceses comprising a worldwide communion, represented at conferences held every decade. The Church of England can also claim to be the pivotal religious institution in Britain, with a system of parishes administering key buildings in every area, an architectural and musical heritage of enormous richness, and, even if numbers attending church services are small, providing an imprecise but genuine cultural identity within the national character.

Cross on the south side to the Westminster parish church of **St Margaret** (1485–1523), warm, wide and comfortable, as Perpendicular Gothic always is. The rebuilt tower (1735–37) is an example of 18C Gothic. There are some small but interesting monuments and other furnishings inside. The exciting modern windows in the south aisle are by John Piper (1966), but the window at the east end will catch your eye first: made in Holland to celebrate the betrothal of the future Henry VIII's elder brother Arthur to Catherine of Aragon, it was not installed until 1758.

Although St Margaret's was built quite independently of the Abbey, at this date still monastic, the original builders were the Abbey masons. Sir Walter Raleigh was buried here following his execution for treason in Old Palace Yard in 1618: a tablet nearby reminds us, 'Should you reflect on his errors, remember his many virtues, and that he was mortal.' John Milton and Samuel Pepys were both married here in the 1650s. Printer William Caxton and artist Wenceslaus Hollar, who recorded the topography of London before the Great Fire, are buried here.

St Margaret's nestles in the shadow of Westminster Abbey's north façade (**Map 5,7**), and this great building we must now explore, starting with the north façade of the exterior.

Westminster Abbey

Today Westminster Abbey is two things: first, a great Gothic church, extensively renewed; and second, a national exhibition of sculpture. It is important to be aware of both aspects as you tour round: do not let either put you off the other.

Open 09.20–16.45 Mon–Fri, 09.20–14.45 Sat. Admission charge. Vergers' tours (recommended) at extra charge at 10.00, 11.00, 14.00, 15.00 Mon–Fri (additional tour at 14.30 Fri) and at 10.00, 11.00 and 12.30 Sat. Shop. ☎ 020 7222 5152. www.westminster-abbey.org. The Chapter House, Museum and Pyx Chamber are operated separately by English Heritage. Chapter House open April–Sept 10.00–18.00 daily; Oct 10.00–17.00; Nov–March 10.00–16.00. Museum and Pyx Chamber open 10.30–16.00 daily. Small additional charge. ☎ 020 7222 5897.

History

There has been an abbey on this site since at least AD 960, when St Dunstan established a group of Benedictines here, probably in a Saxon church. The more important church was the initiative of Edward the Confessor, who built it at the same time as establishing his palace nearby, next to the river, in 1065. He was buried in front of the high altar. William I, having successfully established himself as king, was crowned in this church in 1066, and the coronation of every monarch since (except Edward V and Edward VIII) has taken place in the Abbey. Many kings and queens are buried here, but it was the tomb of Edward the Confessor, canonised in the 12C, which drew pilgrims throughout the Middle Ages. The interior was crowded with them then, just as it is now with tourists.

Henry III sank large sums of royal money into rebuilding the Abbey and in 1269 organised the rededication of the sanctuary to his hero Edward the Confessor. Only the first five bays of the nave were completed by the original designer, Henry of Reyns, but when work was resumed in the 1370s under Henry Yevele the same design was repeated and extended to the west end. The self-contained Henry VII Chapel was begun by that monarch in 1503 as a resting place for his uncle Henry VI, who in fact was never buried there.

Exterior

We cannot complete a circuit round the building because of surviving or restored monastic buildings on the south side, and we will see the west front at the end of the tour. It is important to realise that restorations and rebuildings characterise much of the exterior of the Abbey and that as you view it you are observing work of a wide range of periods.

The **north transept** faces you outside the west end of St Margaret's: here you will enter the interior. It is appropriately grand, because this was the royal entrance to the Abbey, but everything you see here now is Victorian, the work of Sir George Gilbert Scott and J.L. Pearson (1875–90). The form of the statuary and decoration is English, but overall Westminster is the most 'French' of all English abbeys and cathedrals, with a high nave, the highest in England, and a series of apsed chapels at the east end. This is because the main sponsor of the present building was Henry III, who, although he had lost any claim to French possessions, was steeped in the culture of that country and promoted its influence here.

Henry III (r. 1216–72)

Henry was the first English king to come to the throne as a minor—he was nine years old—and of all that have done so, survived longest. He was extremely pious and in appearance 'thickset, with a narrow forehead and a drooping eyelid'. If this sounds unattractive, he certainly proved a major influence on English culture. Besides sponsoring the rebuilding of Westminster Abbey, in emulation of the achievements of his brother-in-law Louis IX of France in the Sainte-Chapelle in Paris, he set up the royal menagerie at the Tower, acquiring England's first elephant. Famously he died from eating 'a surfeit of lampreys' (a kind of local eel). He was resolutely Francophile in both political policy and personal lifestyle.

From the north transept look right (west) to note the height of the exterior, with flying buttresses supporting the nave roof. The different phases of building in the 13C and 14C are visible at various points, for example at clerestory level in the window design and in the size of saints' statues at aisle-roof level.

Walk to the left (east) a little way to look at the two rounded projections formed by the chapels on the north side of the original east end, from Henry III's building: they conform with the nave. An innovation from France were the triangles with concave sides seen above the lancet windows. The mason responsible is known only as Henry of Reyns, thought to mean Reims, where similarly shaped windows of exactly the same date are to be found. Then feast your eyes on the later **Henry VII Chapel** which projects beyond, a masterpiece of the Perpendicular style. Note the restless movement within each window bay, becoming more acute in those at the east end, and the way the functional buttresses are made a prime decorative feature. This is Gothic at its most ornate, refined or (A.W.N. Pugin might have said) decadent. The Perpendicular style is to be found only in England—see also St George's Chapel, Windsor (Chapter 73).

Interior

Now explore the interior. The ticket offices are at the north transept entrance, so this must be your point of entry. Visitors have to follow a set route round the Abbey, as described here.

The north door may be royalty's entrance, but a more vivid impression would be given by entry at the west door, allowing you to take in the architecture, which we cannot fully examine until we reach the nave at the very end of the tour. As

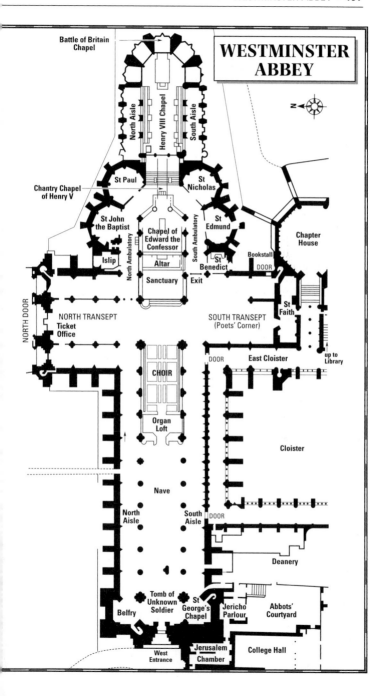

WESTMINSTER ABBEY

N

Battle of Britain Chapel

North Aisle

Henry VIII Chapel

South Aisle

St Paul

St Nicholas

Chantry Chapel of Henry V

St John the Baptist

St Edmund

Chapter House

Islip

North Ambulatory

Chapel of Edward the Confessor

South Ambulatory

St Benedict

Bookstall

DOOR

Altar

Sanctuary

Exit

St Faith

NORTH DOOR

NORTH TRANSEPT

Ticket Office

SOUTH TRANSEPT (Poets' Corner)

DOOR

East Cloister

up to Library

CHOIR

Organ Loft

Cloister

Nave

North Aisle

South Aisle

DOOR

Deanery

Tomb of Unknown Soldier

St George's Chapel

Jericho Parlour

Abbots' Courtyard

Belfry

West Entrance

Jerusalem Chamber

College Hall

it is, immediately confronted by a mass of statuary, you might have difficulty in absorbing the uniquely French Gothic character of the building. So step forward to peep down the nave to the right. It is over 100ft high, with piers of distinctive Purbeck marble from Dorset and yellowish-grey Caen stone, imported by Henry III from Normandy at great expense—it would originally have been richly painted. If you have visited other English Gothic cathedrals, Westminster may strike you as surprisingly small, but this impression is partly due to the quantity of contents, and partly to its 'French' character.

North transept The north transept does provide a view across to the south transept with its rose window, renewed *c* 1890 but of original dimensions. The rose window above your head, which you looked at from the outside, received the same treatment, but the glass is of 1722 to a design by Sir James Thornhill. Many of the statues here are of statesmen, including on the left (east) side *Benjamin Disraeli* by E. Boehm (1881), *William Gladstone* by Sir Thomas Brock (1898) and *Robert Peel* by John Gibson (1850), and on the right the huge memorial to *William Pitt the Elder, Earl of Chatham* by John Bacon (1778), which set the trend for many others. It is worth going behind this monument into the west aisle of the transept to see another substantial monument, to *Lord Mansfield*, developer of Kenwood (see Chapter 41) by John Flaxman (1801), in which Death is shown as a naked figure with an extinguished torch. Compare this representation with that in the famous monument to *Elizabeth Nightingale* by L.F. Roubiliac (1761), in the transept's east aisle, with Death as a skeleton coming out of the tomb to point a lance at poor Mrs Nightingale. You have to go round the monument to Robert Peel to get into this aisle, where there are also early monuments to *Sir Francis Vere* by Maximilian Holt (1609), with four knights supporting his armour, carved piece by piece, and to *Sir George Holles* by Nicholas Stone (1626). At the entrance to the east aisle is another giant memorial, to *General James Wolfe*, by Joseph Wilton (1772).

North ambulatory Now we proceed round the ambulatory, where two 15C tomb brasses lie on the floor to your right. Also on the right, high up, are the important **royal tombs** which can be seen properly only on vergers' tours of the sanctuary. The first, in the Sanctuary, is that of *Aveline, Countess of Lancaster* (d. *c* 1273). Next come those of *Aymer de Valence* (d. 1324), with small sculptures; and *Edmund Crouchback, Earl of Lancaster* and son of Henry III (d 1296). After that, Edward I (d. 1301); see below.

The first chapel to be seen on the left of the ambulatory is **Abbot Islip's Chapel**, on two floors: he died in 1532. Then we immediately reach the two radiating chapels we saw from the exterior. The first, the **Chapel of St John the Baptist**, is entered via the tiny Chapel of Our Lady of the Pew. Within, you will notice there is a wall passage running in front of the windows, another French feature, taken from Reims. There are many monuments, most noticeably the tallest in the whole Abbey, to *Lord and Lady Hunsden* (1596). In the centre of the chapel is the tomb of *Thomas Cecil, Earl of Exeter* (1623) and his first wife, with space left for the second, who refused to accept this inferior position and decided to be buried in Winchester Cathedral. Good for her.

There are many more monuments next door, in the **Chapel of St Paul**. An interesting one is that of *Dudley Carleton, Lord Dorchester*, by Nicholas Stone (1640), probably the first in England with the effigy semi-reclining. Until then effigies always lay flat, as you see here in the monuments to *Sir James and Lady*

Fullerton (1632) and *Sir John and Lady Puckering* (1596), with their children kneeling against their tomb-chest.

Opposite these chapels, in the **Chapel of St Edward the Confessor** high up to your right (see below), are the beautiful tombs of *Edward I* (d. 1307), his father *Henry III* (d. 1272) and Edward's first wife *Eleanor of Castile* (d. 1297). Edward was over 6ft tall, as the size of his tomb indicates, although there is no effigy beside that of his beloved wife (see Chapter 11). The effigies of Henry and Eleanor were cast in the 1290s by William Torel, in an inimitable style giving the faces expressions not regal but full of human tenderness. Note also the ironwork grille and surviving painting on Eleanor's tomb.

Henry VII Chapel Continue up the steps into the Henry VII Chapel. First, turn left into its **north aisle** to see the monument to *Elizabeth I* by Maximilian Colt (1603). She shares it with *Mary I* (d. 1558), her Roman Catholic half-sister, with the inscription 'Consorts both in throne and grave, here rest we two sisters, Elizabeth and Mary, in the hope of one Resurrection.' This union was James I's idea: it seems unlikely either of the deceased queens would have cared for it. Beyond is **'Innocents Corner'** with monuments to James I's infant princesses; one, three-day-old *Sophia*, is shown in an alabaster cradle by Colt (1606). In the wall above, in 1678, the alleged bones of Edward V and Richard, Duke of York, murdered at the Tower, were located and re-interred here.

Now go back to enter the main part of the Henry VII Chapel (1503–19), via original oak doors plated with brass panels and covered in the emblems repeated elsewhere. The chapel was planned as a shrine to Henry VI, whom Henry VII was for political purposes trying to promote as a saint: in the event it became his own burial place. A 13C Lady Chapel was demolished to build it. The chapel consists of a nave with aisles—you have seen the north aisle—and five radiating chapels at the east end, replicating the effect at the east end of Henry III's Abbey. The fanciful shapes of the windows are even more attractive in here than they were when seen from outside, and an additional wonder is the huge programme of sculpture decorating the walls beneath, and inside the radiating chapels and aisles. The overwhelming glory is the **vaulting**; ostensibly fan vaulting, in fact the 'fans' are pendants extended from the cusping of the vaults. In the apse, the pendants appear to form the petals of a flower, with a smaller pendant at the core surrounded by gilded insignia.

The painting on the altar is by Bartolommeo Vivarini (*c* 1480): beneath it Edward VI (d. 1553) is buried and in the floor before it George II (d. 1760) and his family are interred. Behind the altar, in the centre of the floor space, is the **tomb of Henry VII** (d. 1509), shared with his queen Elizabeth of York (d.1503); James I (d. 1625) lies in the same vault. The screen around it is beautiful in its detail and of a piece with the Tudor architecture all around. The tomb itself is another matter. This object is the birthplace of the Renaissance in England. The effigies of the king and queen lying together on top are traditional enough, but everything else is in the new taste, with pilasters, niches, medallions, putti and many other harbingers of Classicism. The sculptor was the Italian Pietro Torrigiano, who had been a student with Michelangelo (and had famously broken his nose in a fight): he was in England 1511–19. Even if Classical architecture in this country had to wait for Inigo Jones, Classical sculpture began here a century earlier.

> ### *Henry VII (r. 1485–1509)*
> The founder of the Tudor dynasty and initiator of a long period of stability
> for the throne itself, Henry VII was not a colourful personality. His claims to
> kingship were not incontestable but, as a Lancastrian who married Elizabeth
> of York and defeated the Yorkist Richard III at Bosworth, he effectively
> brought to an end the War of the Roses and, despite other challengers, held
> tight. Of his three sons, only Henry VIII survived and was able to embark
> on a prosperous reign as a result of his father's financial prudence, a great
> rarity among English monarchs. The chapel at Westminster was Henry VII's
> architectural legacy, a fitting resting place for the man described by Francis
> Bacon as 'a sad serious prince, full of thoughts'.

The chapel stalls are of the same date (*c* 1520), with many entertaining
misericords, most in the mainstream tradition. One, on the south side and to the
left of the second stair, is 13C. The colourful banners above the stalls are those of
members of the Order of the Bath, whose chapel this has been since 1725.

Look also at the five **apsidal chapels**. The central or easternmost has been
known as the Battle of Britain Chapel since 1947. A plaque records the fact that
Oliver Cromwell was originally buried here in 1658. In the others, note the monument to the *Duke and Duchess of Lennox* (1639) by Hubert Le Sueur, the vivid,
semi-reclining figure of *John Sheffield, Duke of Buckingham* (1721), for whom
the first Buckingham House was built, and the tomb of *George Villiers*, the 1st
Duke of Buckingham and James I's favourite, also by Le Sueur (1628). Above
them is a new east window donated by Lord Harris (2001).

Now go to the **south aisle** of the Henry VII Chapel. *General Monk, Duke of
Albemarle*, the military leader who sponsored the Restoration, is buried to the
left of the altar, with a monument designed by William Kent (1730), beneath
which are buried the monarchs Charles II (d. 1685), William (d. 1702) and Mary
(d. 1694), and Anne (d. 1714). The tomb of *Mary, Queen of Scots* by Cornelius
and William Cure (1605–10) is very prominent, and grander in some ways than
that of Elizabeth I: it was the choice of James I, Mary's son. *Margaret, Countess
of Lennox*, whose tomb is of similar style and date, was his grandmother. The
most important monument here is an earlier work by Torrigiano, the first from
his few years in England, and commemorates the mother of Henry VII, *Lady
Margaret Beaufort* (d. 1509): there are incipient signs of the Renaissance here,
too, and brilliant characterisation.

South ambulatory   Leaving the Henry VII Chapel you descend the stairs to
the south ambulatory. Directly ahead of you, high up, is the **Chapel of Henry V**
(1422), a chantry cleverly fitted into the space; it is not usually possible to visit.
Currently on display in front of it is the **Coronation Chair**, made to order for
Edward I (1296) to enclose the Stone of Scone, which he had captured but which
was returned to the Scots in 1996. The chair has been used for every coronation
since that of Edward II (1308).

Beyond the chantry, high up and to your right from the ambulatory, are the
Chapel and Shrine of St Edward the Confessor, once a powerful place of pilgrimage. The shrine was originally in three parts, a decorated stone base, a gold
coffin for the saint and a canopy which could be raised to reveal the shrine. It has
been much damaged, especially since the Reformation, but the canopy has been
restored.

Edward the Confessor (r. 1042–66)

Important in his time, and elevated to cult status later, this monarch was involved in extremely difficult problems of succession. He had no children and the claims to the throne of his wife's brother Harold were surely less strong than those of his mother's nephew William I, who invaded and conquered England after Edward's death. He was pious and committed, qualities for which he was given great acclaim by the Normans in their propaganda and which were endorsed further by Henry III for similar francophile purposes. The title 'Confessor' was part of this image-creation.

More royal tombs, currently to be seen only on vergers' tours, surround the shrine, those of *Philippa of Hainault* (d. 1369) and her husband *Edward III* (d. 1377). The faces of the effigies are less tender but more characterised than Torel's work a couple of generations earlier; see too the little weepers round Edward's tomb. Next to them are *Richard II* (d. 1400) and his queen *Anne of Bohemia* (d. 1394)—Richard looks edgy and apprehensive (as well he might; see Chapter 29).

On the left side of the south ambulatory are two more chapels to match those seen earlier. The Percy family, still the only family with the right to be buried in the Abbey, have a vault in the **Chapel of St Nicholas** (only ashes are interred there now). There are many more interesting monuments in the **Chapel of St Edmund**: note, for example, the use of alabaster for the monument to *John of Eltham* (d. 1337), second son of Edward II (whose own tomb in Gloucester Cathedral is in this material, then considered precious), and the extravagant gestures of the little weeping figures.

South transept Light comes via the rose window that we saw when we entered and from the twelve lancet windows beneath. Look up—with binoculars if you have them—at the south wall to note the carvings between the upper set of lancets, with angels prominent at either end. These are among the finest 13C sculptures left anywhere in England, certainly the best in the Abbey. Beyond, through the door, is the **Chapel of St Faith** (reserved for prayer) and to either side are huge, late 13C wall paintings showing the *Incredulity of St Thomas* and *St Christopher*, perhaps by Walter of Durham.

This area is known as **Poets' Corner**. The first was *Geoffrey Chaucer* (d. 1400), who found a place in the Abbey because he had been a court official, not because he was a poet. His tomb is later (16C). Others buried here include Edmund Spenser (d. 1599), Ben Jonson (d. 1637), John Dryden (d. 1700), Samuel Johnson (d. 1784), Robert Browning (d. 1889) and Alfred, Lord Tennyson (d. 1892). Many of the other monuments are by notable sculptors, especially those to *William Shakespeare*, designed by Kent and carved by Peter Scheemakers (1740), and to *George Frideric Handel* by Roubiliac (1761), on the opposite wall. These and others are visually wonderful but all the plaques on the floor seem overdone. You cannot possibly miss the huge monument by Roubiliac to very much a non-poet, the *2nd Duke of Argyll*, on the south wall (1748). The figure of Fame is recording the Duke's name and titles but has stopped half-way, as if in shock.

Turn back towards the crossing to examine the **sanctuary**, if entry is possible. If not, you can often sit here for services, to enjoy the music and the spiritual experience within the architectural space. The reredos and high altar are

Victorian, by Sir George Gilbert Scott. Sometimes on display is one of the Abbey's greatest treasures, the Cosmati pavement (1268). The Cosmatis were a family of Italian craftsmen who laid tiny pieces of marble in intricate patterns, like mosaic. Henry III commissioned them for this work and for the decoration of Edward the Confessor's shrine, which is less well preserved. From the steps you can see the paintings in the canopy of Richard II's tomb. Anne of Cleves, fourth wife of Henry VIII, is buried nearby, with Edmund Crouchback and others, mentioned above.

Note the four huge columns of Purbeck marble which denote the **crossing** and the powerful sense of verticality they induce. It is in the centre of the crossing that the Coronation Chair is placed for the monarch. The choir stalls, extremely rich and absolutely in keeping, are by Edward Blore (1828), an underestimated Victorian.

Cloisters The prescribed tour now takes you round the cloisters, begun 1245–50 and completed a century later. Shrewd observers will have noticed that the east wall of the cloister is incorporated into the south transept as its west aisle—an odd medieval space-saver and a means of taking a stair from the dormitory above into the Abbey. Brass rubbing can be undertaken in the north cloister, where a rather draughty cup of coffee is available.

Off the east cloister, the Chapter House, Museum and Pyx Chamber are accessible for a small additional admission charge (for opening times, see above). The **Chapter House** in particular is worth seeing, both for the effect as you walk through cloister, outer and inner vestibules into the brilliantly lit arched space, and for its own architectural purity. It was one of the first parts of the Abbey rebuilt by Henry III and it, too, incorporated ideas from France, this time from Amiens and the Sainte-Chapelle in Paris. It had a critically important role as an administrative space in which the abbot and monks met daily to discuss business and policy. The House of Commons also used it until 1547.

The shape of the Chapter House is an octagon, with an entrance in one side and windows in six of the others. Although much restored by Scott in the 19C, the architecture probably looks much as it did in 1250, with rich clusters of columns between the windows and a central compound pier which lightly and perfectly supports the complex vaults above. The windows are 19C and later, but their shape and effect can be seen as original. To either side of the main entrance arch life-size sculptures (1253) represent the *Annunciation*, with Gabriel on the left and Mary on the right. On the backs of the *sedilia*, or priests' chairs, are some important wall-paintings showing the *Last Judgment* and *Apocalypse* (both late 14C) and *Beasts* (c 1500). The tiled floor, providentially covered up by boards for much of the Chapter House's life, is original medieval work.

The **Pyx Chamber** and the **Museum** next door are spaces that date back to Edward the Confessor's abbey, having formed the undercroft of the dormitory which was located above. You might guess this from the simplicity of the structure compared with the ornate decoration you have seen elsewhere. The pyx was the box which held standard pieces of gold and silver, and the space was used as a treasury in the 13C. The Museum contains some rather macabre figures, royal funeral effigies that were placed on top of the coffin in full regalia for viewing until the moment of burial. They are surprisingly life-like, and, if they are also accurate, somewhat chastening in their mere humanity.

Leaving the Museum, keep going away from the main cloisters through Dark

Cloister to peep at the **Little Cloister** and a peaceful private garden and, if it is open, the **Abbey Garden** (1374). This space is rarely visited, and largely unpublicised, but is in fact the oldest surviving garden in London, with a collection of herbal plants consistent with the original planting by the Benedictines. Open 10.00–18.00 (16.00 in winter) Tues, Wed, Thur. Admission free. Then return and complete your circuit of the cloisters to reach the nave.

Nave In the nave at long last, you can get your mind round Henry Yevele's architecture. His decision to complete the building of the Abbey in the style chosen by his predecessors was a remarkable act of professional deference. The result is that the architecture of the nave is an integrated whole, interrupted only by the insertion of the choir and the pulpitum or screen before it. The height will surely now impress, stretching up the Purbeck piers, from each of which a stone shaft rises through the gallery level and clerestory to support the ribs of the quadripartite vaults. Much pleasure can be had by studying the changes introduced as they went along by Henry III's successive architects, minor ones in the first four bays west from the crossing, and then, from the fifth bay onwards, Yevele's work of the 1370s. Although he adhered to the brief, Yevele made many changes—for example, to the windows, the shields above the arcading in the aisle walls, the diapering, the bosses in the vault, and the vaulting methods.

Henry Yevele

Yevele (d. 1400) became a freeman of the City in 1353, and later mason to the Black Prince, to the king and to Westminster Abbey. Not much is known about his life that might help us to understand better the role of the master mason and patron in relation to national architecture, though he seems to have been a man who owned a good deal of property. The nave of Westminster Abbey is usually attributed to him, and he was responsible for the rebuilding of Westminster Hall in 1394. His readiness to continue largely unchanged the model of his predecessor at the Abbey 100 years before shows a self-restraint most unusual in an architect.

While your eyes are raised, note the modern chandeliers. Next turn to the sculpture of the nave, dominated by the two major works in the **pulpitum**; on the left is *Sir Isaac Newton* (1731) and on the right *Lord Stanhope* (1733), both designed by Kent and executed by John Rysbrack. Above the pulpitum, out of sight, is the **organ** console, the pipes very visible either side: it is a reminder of the Abbey's powerful musical tradition and its many distinguished organists and choirmasters, including Henry Purcell, John Blow and Orlando Gibbons.

Henry Purcell

Some say Purcell (1659–95) was the greatest English composer. Certainly he was the one most strongly connected with London, where he was born and died, tragically young. The music he composed for the funeral of Mary II was played, soon afterwards, at his own. He was adept in every field— church music, theatre music, court odes, songs and instrumental—and was open to the Baroque influences from Europe, thus embodying a stronger emotional range than the English musical temperament usually allows itself.

There is another sensational Roubiliac monument in the south aisle, to *General Hargrave* (1757), pyramids collapsing above him while he calmly steps out of his tomb. Playwright William Congreve (d. 1729) is commemorated on the south wall. Among a great many other works of interest, hanging on a column at the west end of the south aisle is the portrait of *Richard II* (1396), the first known contemporary likeness of an English monarch. There are many more monuments in the north aisle.

At the west end is the **Chapel of St George**, now dedicated to the dead of the two World Wars. Behind it, and accessible only on tours, are the **Jericho Parlour** and **Jerusalem Chamber**, where Henry IV died in 1413 after praying at the shrine. Stained glass of 1735 floods light down on the west entrance and the grave of the **Unknown Warrior**. This became an important 20C shrine, where many visiting heads of state still pause: it covers the body of one of countless unidentified soldiers of World War I, brought back from Flanders in 1920 and reburied here. Nearby is a stone commemorating *Winston Churchill* (d. 1965), war leader, and over the west door is a huge statue of *William Pitt the Younger* by Richard Westmacott (1806).

West Front As you leave the Abbey turn to examine the west front and twin towers, perhaps from a slightly more distant point near the free-standing column—a memorial by Sir George Gilbert Scott (1859) to former pupils of Westminster School killed in the Crimean War. Most of the lower parts are Yevele's work, but you can catch out your friends by testing them on the date of the **towers** above. This world-famous pair, symbolising London nearly as potently as Tower Bridge or the Houses of Parliament, are no more genuinely Gothic than those other two impostors, having in this case been designed by Nicholas Hawksmoor in the 1730s. Hawksmoor's Gothic is reasonably convincing, at least until you look at it closely. Just above the clock you will see a telltale segmental pediment straight out of a City church—in fact rather more Baroque than a City church.

Below the west window, in niches, are a series of brand-new statues, done in an entirely traditional way, to commemorate **20C Christian martyrs**. The Abbey guidebook tells us there were more martyrs in this century than in any previous period. Amongst those represented—again binoculars are useful—are Martin Luther King, Dietrich Bonhoeffer and Oscar Romero. The statues were unveiled by Queen Elizabeth II in July 1998.

Abbey precincts

Finally, after perhaps a glance in the bookshop by the west door, explore the Abbey precincts. First, cross the busy **Broad Sanctuary**, where there are public toilets. Of two interesting public buildings here, that on the right is the **Queen Elizabeth II Conference Centre** designed by Powell and Moya (1986) and built on the site of the former Westminster Hospital—it is impressive in a modern, monumental way. On the left is the exuberant **Methodist Central Hall** by Lanchester and Rickards (1905–11), Edwardian but also French Beaux-Arts in pedigree, as this firm so often preferred. This is the headquarters of the Methodist Church. The first meeting of the General Assembly of the United Nations took place here in 1946.

Cross back and go through the **Sanctuary Arch** into Dean's Yard. The name 'sanctuary' refers to the Abbey's medieval role in giving protection to the oppressed. Although this right of refuge ended by the 18C, that did not prevent the area continuing as a serious slum and a magnet for the criminal fraternity. It was cleaned up by Scott (1853), with the gatehouse and surrounding houses employing to full effect his asymmetrical principles for terraces. Would that other Victorian builders had done as much.

Dean's Yard is a green space with a variety of structures round it, most notably Sir Herbert Baker's Church House (1935–39) at the south side. The unobtrusive buildings of the famous **Westminster School** are here and through Little Dean's yard to the left. Famous pupils have included Jonson, Dryden, Christopher Wren, George Herbert, Edward Gibbon and Peter Ustinov. The school buildings in Little Dean's Yard include the beautiful **Ashburnham House** by John Webb (1662), built on the foundations of the former Prior's Lodging, and therefore obliged to ignore the contemporary requirements for symmetry.

At the southeast corner of Dean's Yard, you pass the 20ft precinct wall of the **Abbey garden** (see above).

Finally go down Great College Street to reach Millbank. Turn left, past the Jewel Tower (Chapter 13) to return to Westminster station.

15 • Victoria and Pimlico

This area was once a marshy triangle between Westminster, the royal parks and Chelsea, and until the 19C was regarded as dangerous and unhealthy. All that was changed, however, by the development of Buckingham House (see Chapter 17), stimulating the building of ultra-respectable Belgravia and lesser Pimlico, which in turn was to be transformed again by the advent of Victoria Station. This walk is not in itself a specially interesting journey but passes some significant individual buildings and climaxes at the great Tate Britain.

- Distance: 3 miles. Time: 1½ hours + 2 hours for Tate Britain, perhaps including lunch. Tube: Victoria. Maps 14 and 18.

We start at **Victoria mainline station** (Map 14,7 or 18,3). That this station appears to be in two halves is due to the fact that it was developed by two separate railway companies, first the Brighton Line (always to be pronounced in Lady Bracknell's astonished tone) in 1860, and soon afterwards by the Dover and Chatham Line, to bring to the capital travellers from Europe. The Brighton Line was the first to cross the Thames, the Grosvenor Bridge being built for it by John Fowler, taking trains up the course of the by-then disused Grosvenor canals to platforms 1–8. The once luxurious and still spectacular *Grosvenor Hotel* by J.T. Knowles (1860), now the Thistle Victoria, was one of the first of London's big terminus hotels, with medallions of the famous among its decorations. The canopies over the bus park and taxi rank still have an enclosed Victorian air.

Go out of the station to the north, past the buses, and the clock called Little Ben (the name is self-explanatory) first erected here in 1894, into **Victoria Street**. This road improvement was cut through the Westminster slums between 1852 and 1871 and provided London's first examples of middle-class flats or apartments on a grand scale. The venture was slow to succeed, because of the Victorians' perception of flats being suited primarily to accommodate the poorer classes. (This social prejudice has guaranteed that London has never become a city of apartments like Paris.) In Victoria Street, however, few of these early flats survived the greed of 1970s developers and slab blocks of considerable tedium now line this part of the street. Don't worry, it gets better.

Westminster Cathedral

Make your way east until you reach an opening on your right which reveals the enticing Mediterranean forecourt of Westminster Cathedral. This remarkable Byzantine pile, in red brick and white stone, is properly called the Cathedral of the Precious Blood, and is the chief Roman Catholic Church in England.

- Open 07.00–19.00 Sun–Fri, 08.00–19.00 Sat. Admission free. Journeys by lift to the top of the campanile 09.00–17.00 Thur–Sun (small additional charge). ☎ 020 7798 9055. www.westminstercathedral.org.uk

There has been a Catholic Archbishop in England only since 1850 and it was not until 1894, under Cardinal Vaughan, that building of the cathedral began, to the designs of J.F. Bentley. Vaughan's predecessor, Cardinal Manning, had commissioned a plan from Henry Clutton but this had been rejected on grounds of expense. Even Bentley's design has been beyond the Church's means and in 1903 it was decided to leave the completion of the decoration of the interior to future generations, who, it must be said, have failed to stump up much so far. But that is part of Westminster Cathedral's special atmosphere.

The interior is in fact well worth exploring. Naturally it at first seems Italian in atmosphere and decorative idiom, and some of the materials, such as that of the fine baldacchino over the altar, come from that country. The technology of the 1890s enabled the nave to be the widest in England. The chapel of the Blessed Sacrament, to the left of the altar, has mosaics by Boris Anrep (1956–62). Cardinal Basil Hume, who died in 1999, is buried in the chapel of St Gregory and St Augustine towards the main entrance, where there are more impressive mosaics. So much richness against the uncovered, incomplete, stock-brick walls leaves an odd impression: a spiritual dualism, perhaps, between riches and poverty, over which the Church has always had to agonise. Do not miss the *Stations of the Cross* by Eric Gill (1913–18), on the piers.

Westminster Cathedral is a greatly underestimated enrichment to London's architecture. If you still have doubts, look back at the **campanile**, nave and east end, as you walk down Ambrosden Avenue, to the right as you leave. To be seen beyond the eastern apse of the Cathedral are several further buildings by Bentley, including the Archbishop's House and the Choir School. They are all in the same half-Byzantine, half-Italian style, but less stripy and more consciously Arts and Crafts, with semicircular forms and small domes. On the opposite side of the street, and in Thirleby Road, are long ranges of unusual flats of the same date, in prominent red-and-white stripes like the Cathedral. Eyecatchers themselves, they are a distraction from Bentley's masterpiece.

Turn left in Francis Street and right down Emery Hill Street. As you cross Greencoat Place (**Map 18,4**) look for the little court at no. 55, a rare survivor of a common type. When you reach Rochester Row, turn left. Across the road is the church of **St Stephen** (1845), a gift of Baroness Burdett-Coutts to convert the poor of Westminster; the architect was Benjamin Ferrey, a follower of Pugin.

> ### Roman Catholic Church
>
> Roman Catholicism in Britain was repressed following Henry VIII's Reformation, and again with greater ruthlessness under Elizabeth I. Despite some small relaxations in the 17C and 18C and the growing practice of 'quietist' Catholic practice, there were periodic anti-Catholic scares. These, and in particular the brief reign of James II, the later Scottish-initiated attempts to restore the Catholic Stuart line to the throne and the Gordon Riots of 1780 delayed any real progress towards Catholic emancipation. Roman Catholics were forbidden to hold public office or to stand for parliament, let alone have their own churches and schools. This was finally changed by the Catholic Emancipation Act of 1829, although even this was introduced chiefly to deal with problems in Ireland. The Catholic hierarchy, reuniting Roman Catholicism in England with the European community, was not restored until 1850, and it took another 40 years to get started on a national cathedral. The Act of Settlement of 1701, forbidding a Catholic monarch, still stands.

Opposite are some 19C almshouses replacing an earlier establishment founded by Emery Hill in 1708.

At the end of Rochester Row is a busy traffic interchange, with the rebuilt **Greycoat School**, with figures of 18C charity children, on the right. At the top of Artillery Row, in Victoria Street, is the *Albert*, a fine traditional pub. 'Artillery' refers to butts established here in the 16C. As you pass, note the startling Westminster Palace Gardens (1887), with lots of late Victorian decoration. Further east, in Strutton Ground, is a small street market with several pubs.

If resisting all these enticements, turn right down Greycoat Street. On the corner with Elverton Street is the **Royal Horticultural Society's New Hall**, an interesting piece of early Modernism by Murray Easton (1923), based on Swedish precedents. It is often open for special exhibitions and retains a strange between-the-wars atmosphere.

> The Royal Horticultural Society was founded in 1804, but came to prominence under Prince Albert's initiatives in South Kensington, when it developed a garden in the centre of what is now the museum complex. The RHS is also responsible for mounting the Chelsea Flower Show each May (Chapter 34). Its main garden today is at Wisley, Surrey. Open 10.00–18.00 daily (10.00–16.30 in winter). Admission charge. Restaurant. Shop. Garden centre. ☎ 01483 224234. Trains: Waterloo to West Byfleet or Woking.

Go left to see, at the top of Elverton Street, in Horseferry Road, the building for TV company Channel 4 by Richard Rogers (1994). Go right to reach **Vincent Square**, a large green field which the boys of Westminster School use for sport. Walk round the square clockwise and admire the plane trees. As a piece of land it must be worth millions. There are some pleasant houses here and there around the circumference—especially nos 84–85 and no. 86—and a nostalgic prewar cricket pavilion, looking as if dropped in from the village green. If you are keen on the work of Edwin Lutyens, at the corner make a short detour down Fynes Street to Page Street opposite, and then Vincent Street to the south to see his Grosvenor Estate, where he adopted an odd check pattern of brick and plaster, a freakish combination of Lutyens and Modernism.

Leave the square at the south corner via Osbert Street and cross the windswept Vauxhall Bridge Road to see **St James the Less** (1860–61) by G.E. Street, architect of the Royal Courts of Justice (Chapter 9). This is one of his most important churches and reflects the lessons he taught himself on his Italian travels, distinguishing it from the contemporary work of William Butterfield and J.L. Pearson. Like St Stephen's a little way back, the objective of this church was to bring Christianity, High Anglicanism in this case, to the poor of Pimlico. At the time, the *Illustrated London News* described it as rising 'as a lily amongst the weeds'— rude to the surrounding environment, but still true to a degree, even if the weeds are now 1970s flats. The interior is gripping, with stout granite columns, brilliantly carved capitals and multi-coloured brickwork all around. The painting over the chancel arch is by G.F. Watts. ☎ 020 7630 6282.

From the church, turn right down Moreton Street, across Belgrave Road (**Map 18,6**), to reach Lupus Street, at the heart of Thomas Cubitt's **Pimlico Estate**. This was Cubitt's most extensive project, street after street of stuccoed houses (some today needing a lick of paint), modest, respectable, never so ambitious or fashionable, then or now, as Belgravia, but very pleasing in their own regular way. To the west, at the foot of St George's Drive, is a good bronze of the developer, wielding a spirit level (1996). Turn left down Lupus Street past St Saviour's Church (1864) with Cubitt's St George's Square stretching south to the river. Just before is the Pimlico School, in very advanced modern glass.

Thomas Cubitt

Cubitt (1788–1835) stands out as London's most successful, and most architecturally distinguished, speculative builder. Within the industry, his major innovation was the general trades contract, employing all the various building trades equally on a permanent-wage basis, replacing the chaotic system of one-off deals from which London had always suffered.

Bloomsbury, Belgravia and Pimlico were areas built by him or his firm; there are more in Clapham and elsewhere. His brothers Lewis, architect of King's Cross Station, and William, of Cubitt Town, Isle of Dogs, were also his partners.

Make your way past Pimlico station back to Vauxhall Bridge Road and turn right. **Vauxhall Bridge** by Sir Alexander Binnie (1895–1906) is spectacular—arched, wide and fast, with bronze figures. It replaced an earlier iron bridge by John Rennie (1816), opened even earlier than his stone masterpiece at Waterloo. Near the bridge in Millbank is another bronze, abstract this time, *Locking Piece* by Henry Moore (1968). Across the stream are the **MI6 building** by Terry Farrell (1980s), green and cream, a Postmodern extravaganza, and the spectacular new apartments of St George's Wharf (2000). Ponsonby Terrace and Place, on the left, are attractive, and beyond them is the former Royal Army Medical School, being prepared for its future role as an art college.

Until Pimlico's housing was developed in the 1820s, **Millbank**, down which you should now turn, was a lonely riverside path, named after Westminster Abbey's original mill. In 1809 Sir Robert Smirke began work on the Millbank penitentiary, a famous prison in its day, and one of the first buildings in London to be constructed on a raft of concrete—Smirke's invention—to give stability in the muddy ground. It was demolished in 1890, and the main landmark today is

The MI6 Building

Millbank Tower by Ronald Ward and Partners (1960–63), an impressive early 'skyscraper' built for the Vickers Group but now sub-let. Tenants include the Labour Party: in the Tony Blair era, the term 'Millbank' has come to denote unwelcome central control.

Tate Britain

What you have chiefly and finally come to see lies this side of Millbank Tower (**Map 18,4**). A handsome, if modestly sized, river-related portico surmounting a formidable flight of steps announces Tate Britain.

- Open 10.00–17.50 daily. Admission free (charge for special exhibitions). Café. Restaurant open 10.00–15.00 Mon–Sat, 12.00–16.00 Sun (reservations ☎ 020 7887 8825). Shops. ☎ 020 7887 8000 or 8725 (information). www.tate.org.uk. Tube: Pimlico.

The original building is the work of Sidney Smith (1897), but there have been several extensions, first under Sir Joseph Duveen and his son Lord Duveen, and second, the Postmodern Clore Gallery, designed by James Stirling (1987) to house the paintings J.M.W. Turner left to the nation and which had for the most part shamefully remained in a vault. The initial collection was that of Sir Henry Tate, sugar refiner, who founded the gallery, but this was greatly enriched by bequests from the Duveens and enlightened purchases over the years. By the 1990s it comprised an impossibly large group of works covering the whole history of British art and an outstanding collection of international 20C art. The decision was taken to split the collection into two separate groups, and in 2000 the modern works were transferred to Tate Modern at Bankside (Chapter 31). A smaller new extension on the south side was opened in 2001.

The best place to enter is straight ahead, up the steps: alternatively, go to the new Manton entrance in Atterbury Street, to the left, which provides direct access to special exhibitions at the lower level, or through the garden to the Clore Gallery at the right, past three more Henry Moore bronzes. The steps lead to the main **information desk**, shops and restaurant. Pick up a plan and make your way straight ahead to Gallery 1. This tour covers only the permanent collection, which has recently been redisplayed, and focuses on highlights.

Your route goes through the Duveen Galleries, which usually have displays of sculpture from the Tate collection. Particularly wonderful is Jacob Epstein's *Jacob and the Angel* (1936–41), a massive and inspiring alabaster.

Part One: 1500–1900

Gallery 1 opens the current hanging of the British collection, 'Different Britains 2002–1500'. The reason for the odd juxtaposition of dates becomes immediately clear: the present is only accessible from the past. The storyboards explain this well, and it is worth reading each one before examining the works concerned. In Gallery 1 is proposed the idea that English art had its virtual beginning at the Reformation, when iconoclasm and cultural reform had the effect of strangling former artistic instincts but at the same time stimulated the literary sensibility for which British culture has become renowned.

This contentious notion appears to be confirmed in the rather inhibited 16C portraits in Gallery 2, such as Marcus Gheeraerts the Younger's *Captain Thomas Lee* (1594) and *The Cholmondely Ladies* by an unknown artist (1600–10). Such curious works as these, naive yet charming, show how much English art of the period was waiting for the civilising influence of the Renaissance. In Gallery 3, we can see how European painters as well as native artists such as William Dobson developed **portraiture** to a naturalness and presence unknown in the reign of Elizabeth. The change, through Sir Antony van Dyck (from Antwerp), to Sir Peter Lely (from the Netherlands) and Sir Godfrey Kneller (from Germany), left their subjects with a new elegance and self-confidence which has made 'face-painting' a lasting British speciality. Look for Dobson's royalist portrait of *Endymion Porter* (1642–45), with his gun and Classical busts, illustrating the uniquely English dual preoccupation with art and sport.

Gallery 4 is devoted to **William Hogarth** and the 'theatre of life'. The Tate has a good Hogarth collection, including his portrait of six servants (1750–55) and the self-portrait, *The Painter and his Pug* (1745). There are good representations of Hogarth's contemporaries in this room, and an absorbing scene of *Covent Garden Market* by Balthazar Nebot (1737). Gallery 5 is given over to **miniatures**, another English speciality, not much appreciated today but often as revealing and informal as passport photographs.

The theme in Gallery 6 is **Britain and Italy in the 18C**, underlining the importance of that country to the formation of British taste and culture. The process worked in both directions, with Italian artists coming to work in England—including Antonio Verrio, the decorator of Hampton Court, and the plasterers of James Gibbs's churches—and young aristocrats and artists seeking training on Grand Tours to Rome and elsewhere. The Italian influence was very widespread and is illustrated here by Thomas Gainsborough's *Giovanna Baccelli* (1782), a ballerina in a delicious pose; Joseph Wright of Derby's frightening vision of *Vesuvius* (1776–80); and Sir Joshua Reynolds's *Holy Family* (1788–89), based on Raphael but with noticeably Reynolds-type children.

English art has always been preoccupied with **landscape**—not just local countryside but more violent terrain discovered through colonisation, and public landscapes opened up as society expanded. This tradition is explored in Gallery 7. There are several works by George Stubbs, showing beautiful horses but an idealised vision of contemporary labour, to be contrasted with Wright's *Sir Brooke Boothby* (1781), reclining in his woodland estate with a book by the progressive Jean-Jacques Rousseau. Gallery 8 focuses on **William Blake** and

Gallery 10 on **George Cruickshank**. Between them, grand Gallery 9 is filled with contemporary representations of **history**, from which you can see the growth of Britain's overconfident view of itself in the 19C. There are some iconic works here, such as the *Death of Chatterton* by Henry Wallis (1856) and the *Boyhood of Raleigh* by Sir John Everett Millais (1870), in which the wonder in the boys' eyes is magically expressed.

If all this strikes you as somewhat heavy, relief is at hand in Galleries 11–13, where you can enjoy the refreshing outdoor breezes in the paintings of **John Constable**. Constable took much longer to establish his reputation than J.M.W. Turner, who has a whole set of galleries to himself at the Tate (see below). These three galleries are particularly interesting in the way they illustrate the transition in Constable's works from outdoor sketches to outdoor masterpieces such as *Flatford Mill* (1816). *Chain Pier, Brighton* (1826) offers a direct comparison with Turner; and note the desolate sketch of *Hadleigh Castle* (1828). London enthusiasts can stare for a long time at the *Opening of Waterloo Bridge*, an event of 1817 (painted in 1832); it makes one realise what a loss the destruction of this great bridge was.

In Gallery 14 there is a good display of the strange visions of **John Martin**, which are perhaps of limited appeal; of much wider interest will be the marvellous illustrations of **Victorian society** in Gallery 15. Amongst the riches here, and indicative of the period's self-confidence and sense of moral purpose, are William Powell Frith's *Derby Day* (1856), Augustus Egg's *Past and Present* (1858) and Millais' *Christ in the House of his Parents* (1849), against which Charles Dickens's absurd reaction is described in the accompanying label. From later in the period come some fine portraits by John Singer Sargent and James Whistler and several of James Tissot's stifling scenes of social decorum.

The influence of France on British art is explored in Gallery 17, from which you can return to the central corridors. At this point you may want to find refreshment or stay in the 19C with the work of Turner.

J.M.W. Turner

Turner (1775–1851) was not only perhaps Britain's most exciting artist, but his character—more than Dickens, more than Dr Johnson—conveyed the paradoxes of the Londoner: a down-to-earth Romantic, but also a proponent of a radical change in style, who survived and prospered within a highly traditional institution, the Royal Academy.

Born in Covent Garden, he was essentially self-taught, but was admitted to the Royal Academy schools in 1789, becoming a full Academician at the exceptionally young age of 27. At this stage his work was topographical and chiefly in watercolour. He was always drawn to Classical antiquity and established influences such as Claude Lorrain. In the early 1800s Turner began to travel extensively in Italy, Switzerland, Germany and France, producing work for discerning patrons and amassing a collection of his own which he planned to leave to the nation, and which now forms the basis of the Clore Gallery displays. He was way ahead of his time, and although absorbed by the past also embraced what we now see as modernity.

Clore Galleries

Go straight through Galleries 19 and 20 to enter the Clore Galleries, which are largely given over to the work of J.M.W. Turner. A wander through these rooms might convince you that he was the greatest British artist: the Tate is in a particularly good position to argue the case, having been chosen as the location for Turner's studio collection which he left to the nation.

The nature of the hang in the main galleries changes fairly often to reflect different aspects of the collection and offer varying perspectives on Turner's art: prints and drawings are shown separately upstairs in Gallery C10. If they are on show, you may wish to see the masterpieces in the collection, including *Snowstorm: Hannibal and his Army crossing the Alps* (1812), *Shipwreck* (1805), *Norham Castle, Sunrise* (1845)—illustrating Turner's proto-modernist reputation—and *Snowstorm—Steam-Boat off a Harbour's Mouth making Signals in Shallow Water and Going by the Lead* (1842): Turner was very fussy and precise about his titles!

Part Two: the 20C

The work of Turner may interrupt the chronology of the tour, but in stylistically bypassing Victorian culture he also helps to connect what came before and after. Galleries 18–33 follow a more or less continuous route through the 20C although the hang changes fairly frequently, and the curators regularly come up with new ways of seeing modern British art. The following remarks offer recommendations for specific periods, movements or artists for you to investigate.

The devastation and psychological trauma of **World War I** led artists to reject the 19C in wholly different ways. The war itself was commemorated either as a tragic waste and an appalling mistake, or as heroic. Both responses, perhaps especially the latter, are visible in war memorials located in London streets and squares. In the Tate collection the first response is the more obvious, and is followed by an atmosphere of bleak emptiness in the 1920s. Look for Mark Gertler's *Merry Go Round* (1916), Winifred Knight's *The Deluge* (1920) and the sculptures of Gill and Epstein. Sculptures also draw on Britain's cultural history, making use of traditional materials: this can be seen in the work of Moore and Barbara Hepworth, mergers of modern form with established technology.

By the 1930s Britain was inevitably affected by the revolution of **abstraction**, accompanied by the resolutely Modernist notion of constructivism, which sought to bring science, art and architecture into step. The geometrical works of Ben Nicholson and Naum Gabo illustrate the search for new artistic utopias. Herbert Read's description of abstract art helps our interpretation: 'the art of pure form, composed of harmonies of form and colour which are not beautiful relatively, but always naturally and absolutely'.

In parallel with this cold, clear purity, something much more uncomfortable developed, to be seen in the work of Edward Burra and Francis Bacon, whose international reputations are perhaps unequalled among British artists. Bacon's *Three Studies for Figures at the Base of a Crucifixion* (1944) vividly demonstrate both his individuality, even if this was based on past precedents such as Velazquez and Picasso, and his familiar sense of pain and physical violence.

Another kind of brutality emerged in the 1950s, a kind of postwar **realism**, which had its effect on architecture as well as fine art. The freedoms of abstraction came to be accompanied by images from popular culture. The works of Richard Hamilton, David Hockney, Peter Blake and Gilbert and George include a return to figurative painting, but no restoration of comfort or consolation. Equally, the portraits of Stanley Spencer and Lucian Freud are wholly figurative but never in the least cheering.

The final galleries are likely to be showing contemporary, or at least recent, British art, including photographic and video works. At the end of this space are galleries for **special exhibitions**, which each autumn include the shortlisted artists for the Turner Prize, now seen as the apogee of new British artistic production.

It is difficult to recommend an ideal end to this walk. Descending Tate Britain's steps, you are somewhat remote from civilisation. You can walk to Westminster station up tedious and windswept Millbank, or return to Pimlico station, or wait for a 77a bus to Charing Cross, or take a cab (the best option). But your head should be sufficiently full of powerful images to generate indifference to a little discomfort.

16 • Belgravia and Knightsbridge

Belgravia's stucco terraces and Knightsbridge's glamorous shops still signify a life of wealth and ease, which this walk generously covers. If you catch an occasional surprising sniff of vulgar newness—compared with Mayfair's solid-gold aristocratic squares—remember that Belgravia was created out of wet and marshy ground only in the 19C, while at that time Knightsbridge was little more than a village with the odd new estate nearby. There are no museums or galleries on this walk but several churches and some nice pubs.

• Distance: 2¾ miles. Time: 1½ hours + 1½ hours for the shops. Tube: Victoria. Maps 13 and 17.

Start at Victoria Station (**Map 17,2**) and leave it next to Platform 14 to see Victoria Place, one of the more successful shopping arcades with which major stations have become endowed. You emerge on Eccleston Bridge, with Colonnade Walk opposite continuing the shops and offices over the railway tracks. Turn right, across Buckingham Palace Road, into Eccleston Street.

Belgravia

Crossing Ebury Street establishes the tone for what is to come. (Further to the south Ebury Street almost runs into Chelsea, and down at no. 180 is the house where the eight-year-old Mozart composed his first symphony in 1764.) Note Ebury Mews to left and right: mews were a key component in the Belgravia ethos, and as will become clear, these little streets, with garages and no space for servants, have become very desirable locations for a contemporary lifestyle.

The Grosvenors

The Grosvenor family, since 1874 the Dukes of Westminster, still own the two wealthiest areas of London, Mayfair and Belgravia. They used also to own Pimlico. All three come from ancient holdings of land acquired by individuals culminating in the 'infinitely rich' Hugh Audley in the 17C, who left them to his nephew Alexander Davies, a scrivener. In 1677 Davies' 12-year-old daughter Mary was snapped up by a Cheshire baronet, Sir Thomas Grosvenor. The Grosvenors' wealth has since grown exponentially. Their names occur frequently in both areas, especially Belgravia, with 'Audley' and 'Davies' to be found in Mayfair. Belgrave itself is a village near Leicester where the Grosvenors also had an estate.

Turn right into Chester Square, long and thin, and cut in two by Eccleston Street. Now you are in Belgravia, architecturally speaking at the quietest end.

Belgravia was the name given almost from the start to the marshy area west of the newly royal Buckingham Palace which Thomas Cubitt, working for the Grosvenor family, developed as a housing estate from the 1820s. It aimed, in style and marketing, for a similar clientele to Regent's Park, with rich stucco terraces as opposed to Mayfair's 18C brick, but its layout was quite original. Belgrave Square is the only square square, as it were, and there is a 19C desire, even within Classicism, to emphasise variety rather than regularity.

Mary Shelley died at no. 51 Chester Square; Mathew Arnold lived at no. 2; and in 1940–45 the court of Queen Wilhemina of the Netherlands occupied no. 77. At Lower Belgrave Street turn left and go past the top of the larger and even longer **Eaton Square** (Eaton Hall in Cheshire was home to the Dukes of Westminster): note the variety of Classical orders in the porches. The church of **St Peter**, on the right, is usually open. Built in 1824 as the estate church, its exterior is by J.H. Hakewill. According to the rules of Classicism, the portico should close the vista, but as you see it has to stand to one side—a classic compromise. The interior, burned out in 1987, has been beautifully reconstructed and is full of light and joy.

Continue up Upper Belgrave Street, noting all the time the use of varied motifs in the terraces—each group is conceived differently, and the balance within each composition is varied, too. You soon enter **Belgrave Square** itself, where the scale becomes rather less congenial, even larger and grander, although the variety is maintained. The architect of the central terraces was George Basevi (1825). The trees in the square are so tall, and its dimensions so large, that it is almost impossible to read it as a square at all, and the road entries in the corners exacerbate this difficulty. Moreover, the fast-moving traffic—exclusively taxis and large cars—makes it a challenge to cross to the centre: the garden is in any case private. It is better to walk round the outer pavement, to the left. The large houses at each corner are very fine, each by a different architect of the day and varied accordingly. There are statues of **Simon Bolivar** and **Christopher Columbus** in the eastern and southern corners of the garden: the presence of numerous embassies here may explain these choices of subject.

Proceed to the western exit, Halkin Place, and go down West Halkin Street (**Map 13,7**). Slotted in on the right, a Presbyterian Gothic chapel of the 1860s is now a lunch club run by chef Anton Mosimann, and just beyond that is Halkin Arcade, through which you proceed to Motcomb Street. Although you will see by the houses that we have come down a peg or two, nevertheless you face one of Belgravia's landmarks, the **Pantechnicon** by Seth Smith (1830). It is only the front façade of what was, until burned in 1874, two acres of warehouses, stables and wine vaults, a huge service area for the bourgeois residents of the squares. Go through the portico: the sculpture beyond is *The Fountainhead* by Geoffrey Wickham (1971), and the covered area effectively softens the 1970s Modernism.

Turn right, past Kinnerton Street, and go through Belgrave Mews North and across Wilton Crescent into Wilton Row. Follow it left to reach the *Grenadier*, an especially pleasant pub at which it may be opportune to take some refreshment (although there are more to come shortly). Take the footpath to the right of the pub and turn left through the open gates into Wilton Place (**Map 13,5**).

On your left is the church of **St Paul**, another estate church by Thomas Cundy Junior (1840–43); this time the style is Gothic, but not the sort of which A.W.N. Pugin would have approved. Even so, it is rather grand inside, if you succeed in entering, with decorations and glass of 60 years later by G.F. Bodley. There is a series of beautiful tiled memorials. Cross over to look at **Kinnerton Street**, pretty as can be: it was clearly designed to provide more estate services, as it may do for you in the *Nag's Head* or the *Wilton Arms*, both small, intimate pubs. There is no way out so return to make your way north up Wilton Place into the noise and hubbub: you are leaving staid, 1830–50 Belgravia for rumbustious 1880–1900 Knightsbridge.

Knightsbridge

Turn left, and across the road the giant *Hyde Park Hotel*, which was originally built as apartments, will demonstrate what this transition means, with turrets, balconies, and every fanciful detail you can think of: it is by Archer and Green (1888) and has the same overwhelming self-confidence as their Whitehall Court (Chapter 12). Its guests have included Mahatma Gandhi and Rudolf Valentino.

On the corner are Knightsbridge station and **Harvey Nichols** (invariable spoken of as Harvey Nicks), a vivid and exciting fashion store with great food available on the fifth floor.

> It was originally run by Benjamin Harvey, a local draper whose little shop, founded in 1813, did well out of the 1851 Great Exhibition across the road in Hyde Park. He left the shop to his daughter who went into partnership with Colonel Nichols, a silk buyer. The store is now part of the Debenhams Group.

There are many more top-name shops stretching down Sloane Street to the left. People come to Knightsbridge to shop and in fame one store stands out above all. You will find **Harrod's** about 200 yards further down Brompton Road, on the left.

> Nearly as long-established as Harvey Nichols, the store began life on this site as a grocer's, founded in 1849 by Henry Charles Harrod. In 1860 Mr Harrod's son Charles Digby, aged 20, took over the business and gradually built it up, expanding into perfumes and stationery and progressively buying adjoining properties. In December 1883 the whole store was destroyed by fire and Charles wrote to his customers, 'your order will be delayed in the execution by a day or two', but still met everyone's demands by Christmas. The fire and Charles's promptitude doubled Harrod's business.

The present building is by C.W. Stephens and was begun in 1894, with predictable exuberance, which still extends throughout the interior today. It must be toured through, whether or not you purchase anything—look out for the new Egyptian Hall with its escalators (Harrod's installed the first such in Britain in 1898, with an assistant waiting at the top with smelling-salts), the memorial fountains, and the Food Hall, with remarkable hunting scenes in Doulton tiles designed by W.J. Neatley. As you leave through the Hans Road exit, note Stephens's sensational treatment of doorways down this façade.

Across Hans Road, it cools the blood to catch sight of two severely restrained but entirely original Arts and Crafts houses, no. 12 by Arthur Mackmurdo (1894) and nos 14–16 by C.F.A. Voysey (1891), their asymmetry and horizontality creating a deliberate and self-conscious opposition to all that surrounds them.

At the end of Hans Road, turn right into Walton Place leading to Walton Street. Poor St Saviour's church, recently converted into a millionaire's mansion, was by George Basevi (1840), but now confirms the apparently permanent triumph of Mammon. It is slightly cheering to reach Pont Street, where **St Columba** (Church of Scotland) by Sir Edward Maufe (1950–54), architect of Guildford Cathedral, pushes its coldly pure white stone tower to the heavens.

Turn left and after about 100 yards right into **Cadogan Square**. The buildings all around you, tall red-brick mansions of the 1880s, were pejoratively labelled by architecture critic Osbert Lancaster 'Pont Street Dutch'. The style continues to be the design ethic for Cadogan Square (**Map 13,7**), but rebellion has been simmering, as some houses on the west side of the square confirm. All were designed for the seriously rich, but nos 62, 68 and 72 by Norman Shaw push the Dutch idea a long way further, and no. 52, by Ernest George, goes right over the top into Flemish Renaissance.

Sir Hans Sloane

Sloane (1660–1753) was an Irish physician and plant collector, and later president of the Royal Society. He returned from Jamaica with 800 specimens which he set out in a catalogue dedicated to Queen Anne, who was one of his patients. In 1712 he bought the manor of Chelsea and endowed the Chelsea Physic Garden (Chapter 34) in 1722. His manuscripts, library and collections formed the nucleus of the first British Museum in 1759.

The Cadogan estate and its square, and the neighbouring Sloane estate—all then farmland—were joined in 1717 when Charles Cadogan married Elizabeth, daughter of Sir Hans Sloane. The names of many of the streets in both areas reflect these family connections.

After Cadogan Square, like the early escalator-travellers at Harrod's, you too may now be in need of smelling-salts. Proceed gently south to Cadogan Gardens and make your way east to Sloane Street. Help is at hand: first, to be glimpsed on the left in Sloane Terrace, is the perfect white stone oriental façade of the **First Church of Christ Scientist** by R.E. Chisholm (1908), an architect who had mainly worked in India. You are unlikely to get inside. But you probably will be able to see inside the final treat, at the end of Sloane Street, **Holy Trinity** by J.D. Sedding (1888), the outstanding Arts and Crafts style church in London. This kind of interior left the Gothic Revival behind, spiritually and spatially: wide, light, open, it is essentially enlightened in feeling, Late Gothic moving towards the Renaissance. One of the windows is by Edward Burne-Jones and William Morris and many other leading Arts and Crafts practitioners contributed towards the furnishings. Note the marble pulpit and Art Nouveau-like screen, altar rails and lectern. There is beaten copper everywhere, windows full of saints and a gorgeous font.

Also on this street is the *Cadogan Hotel*, where Oscar Wilde was arrested and where Lillie Langtry, mistress of Edward VII, lived. You are now close to Sloane Square station. Sloane Square itself is covered in Chapter 34.

Arts and Crafts

This movement, which in architecture put paid to the Gothic Revival and stimulated the love of hand-made artefacts which survives to this day, was born out of a reaction against the Great Exhibition of 1851. Its chief principle was resistance to machine-made production, in building and furnishing, and its early proponents were John Ruskin and William Morris, and later Norman Shaw. It was influential in both Europe and the USA, and in Britain on many early public housing estates as well as some churches, notably Holy Trinity, Sloane Street and St Cyprian, Clarence Gate (Chapter 25). Bedford Park was one of its chief manifestations in domestic housing (Chapter 57).

West End

The West End has been perceived as a distinct entity since the early 19C, when the term itself was first used. It is architecturally somewhat older than the East End to which it is opposed, in another London dualism. The extensions of this opposition are well known—money versus poverty, upper class versus working class, leisure versus trade—and the pattern has been for the west always to win; there is little immediate prospect of this changing, although Canary Wharf is a rising star in the east.

The original 'West End' comprised the aristocratic estates of Grosvenor, Cavendish-Harley, St James's and others , developed as leasehold property investments by wealthy landlords from the 1660s onwards. Each had its own central square and terraces of housing. The estates were developed around Crown land which had never been handed over or sold to noble families: for centuries this constituted the royal parks and became ideally suited for fashionable parade, on foot, by carriage or on horseback.

Where there is money, there will always be consumption, and for the last 200 years the area's most famous feature has been its shops, originally for the rich local residents but now for all Londoners and millions of visitors, too. In the 20C, the West End has also denoted theatres and entertainment of all sorts. This seems likely to remain the case in the 21C until we all buy on-line only, and the attention of most visitors, and Londoners too, is focused on the main streets—Oxford Street, Regent Street, Piccadilly and Shaftesbury Avenue—and on Soho.

These walks integrate the past glories of residential occupation with the parks and the shopping areas, so you can enjoy whatever appeals. One walk (Chapter 20) is set entirely in a park, stretching far over into the west for those with stamina, and assumes the weather is fine. Another (Chapter 21) deals entirely with shopping.

17 • St James's Park and Buckingham Palace

This is a lovely walk, showing London at its most colourful and dignified, especially on a fine summer day. If you want to see inside Buckingham Palace in August or September, make sure that you book a ticket (see below).

- Distance: 2¼ miles. Time: 1 hour + 1 hour for all the museums + 1½ hours for Buckingham Palace. Tube: St James's Park. Map 14.

If you arrive at St James's Park station (**Map 14,8**) by Circle/District Line, exit at Palmer Street and turn left. Caxton Street is named after William Caxton, who in the 1470s set up his first printing press nearby. It contains two interesting buildings. On the north side, past the gloomy *St Ermin's Hotel* (1887), is **Caxton Hall** (1878), a former town hall which achieved fame as a Registry Office when such places were risqué. Opposite, a little further west, is the **Blewcoat School**, a delicious survival from 1709. The Ten Commandments, to guide the children, are still there above the fireplace. It functions as a National Trust shop, selling ideal gifts. Open 10.00–17.30 Mon–Fri, 10.00–19.00 Thur. Closed Sat and Sun.

Return up Palmer Street to Petty France. Try to ignore the modern concrete monster housing the Home Office, on the north side at 50 Queen Anne's Gate. To the east, in Broadway, are the **London Transport Headquarters** by Charles Holden (1927–29), LT's favourite architect and creator of such groundbreaking modern buildings as Southgate station. Here his style remained semi-Georgian, but there are some remarkable sculptures by Jacob Epstein built into the walls and easily visible, as well as, higher up, figures representing winds by other notable sculptors including Eric Gill (north side, west wing and east side of the north and south wings) and Henry Moore (north side, east wing).

> ### Jacob Epstein
> Epstein (1880–1959) was born in New York, trained in Paris, and settled in London in 1905. His baptism of fire was the series of statues he produced for the British Medical Association building in the Strand (1908), which soon afterwards were apparently vandalised and remain so to this day (but see Chapter 10). After that almost every one of his new commissions was greeted with uproar, and it worked out that Epstein bore the brunt of anti-Modernist feeling in Britain throughout the first half of the 20C; but perhaps he thus enabled greater sculptors like Moore and Barbara Hepworth to be accepted more calmly.

Cross Petty France, once a location for French wool merchants, and go up **Queen Anne's Gate**, the initial L-shape a largely complete ensemble of early 18C houses, brown brick with stone bands, dignified, solid and quiet (**Map 14,6**). It continues east with some later, and more mixed houses, but apart from a shocking intruder at no. 36, the home of the National Trust (1909), is still very attractive. Jeremy Bentham, utilitarian philosopher, owned no. 40, and prime minister Lord Palmerston was born at no. 20. The statue of the eponymous queen was first noted in 1708. Go straight on down the narrow slope into **Birdcage Walk**, so named as the home of James I's aviary. St James's Park faces you, but before crossing and entering you may like to see the **Guards' Chapel** and Museum, to the left at the front of Wellington Barracks. The impressive chapel designed by Bruce George (1963) replaced an interesting 19C building hit by a flying bomb during a Sunday service in June 1944, causing 121 deaths.

The **Guards' Museum** is below ground nearby. The museum, opened in 1988, covers the history of the Foot Guards, that is, five of the seven household regiments of whom the Queen is Colonel-in-Chief. Their familiar names are Grenadier, Coldstream, Scots, Irish and Welsh. The guard at Buckingham Palace, which changes daily at 11.30, is drawn from these regiments. The museum displays will help you tell which is which from the uniforms. Open 10.00–16.00 daily (sometimes closed Jan). Admission charge. ☎ 020 7930 4466, ext. 3271.

St James's Park

Now for the delight of a walk in St James's Park (**Map 14,6**). Cross Birdcage Walk and enter wherever you like, making your way across to the bridge over the lake. Bands play at the bandstand on summer weekends; deckchairs are for hire April–Sept. It is a place to relax.

St James's Park obtained its name from the site of a medieval leper hospital here which was dedicated to the saint. It was taken over by Henry VIII in 1532 to become the grounds of his new St James's Palace and is thus the oldest of London's royal parks. It was James I who first developed it as a park (his son Charles I walked to his execution at Whitehall across it) but much more significantly Charles II had the grounds laid out in the French style, creating a canal. Most enlightened of all was his opening of the place to the public. Sometimes violent characters entered and Charles's brother (later James II) queried whether he was wise to walk in the park alone, as he often did: Charles bluntly replied 'They won't kill *me* to make *you* king!'

Throughout the 18C, the park formed an important meeting and walking place for Londoners, featured in plays and poems, and was a location for such as James Boswell to consort with 'ladies of the town'. In the 1820s, George IV commissioned John Nash to replan the canal as a lake and replant the surroundings in the 'picturesque' mode, which the park still retains.

From the bridge pause to look west to Buckingham Palace and east to Duck Island, created for bird watching, with the magical towers and spires of the Horse Guards and Whitehall Court behind. To the right of these is the Foreign Office, encircled by the inescapable London Eye. All around are more than 30 species of waterfowl, including the pelicans which were a gift from the Russian ambassador in James I's time; they are fed at 15.00 daily.

On the north side of the lake, turn right—refreshments are available at a kiosk—to reach the gaunt **Guards' Memorial** facing Horse Guards Parade, which commemorates those who fought in the First World War. The lonely detached bronze figures representing the five regiments, cast from German guns taken by them, are by G. Ledward and stand in front of a stone cenotaph designed by H.C. Bradshaw (1926).

Horse Guards Parade lies in front of you. If you cannot manage the Whitehall walk (Chapter 12), now is the moment to go through the arches of Horse Guards and look at Whitehall, especially the Banqueting House opposite. Otherwise, or afterwards, turn north towards the **Citadel**, a freak survival from the Second World War, built to house the Admiralty's communications centre and very ugly, even when covered by a creeper. To its right are the Admiralty block (1894–95) and the back of Admiralty House (1786), startlingly plain in brick. Ahead of you is Nash's noble Carlton House Terrace, across the **Mall**.

> For the past 100 years the Mall has had a different character from that of its earlier foundations. The game 'pell mell' was once its *raison d'être*: Charles II laid out a large avenue just here for the sole purpose of playing it. The avenue ran parallel with the carriage road to St James's Palace, which threw dust on the players, so from the 1660s the road was re-aligned to the north as Pall Mall (Chapter 18). Later pell mell fell out of favour, but not the avenue in which it had been played, and this became 18C London's most fashionable place to promenade. It was sidelined in Nash's scheme but found renewed importance from the time of Edward VII.

The Mall's current appearance, a fine wide boulevard, the most formal and processional street in all London, dates from the death of Queen Victoria and the decision to commemorate her with Admiralty Arch in the east and the Victoria Memorial in the west. It is wonderful for parades but somewhat bald otherwise, especially when contrasted with the picturesque landscape of the park.

Carlton House Terrace replaced Carlton House, the Prince Regent's London home which had been built for him by Henry Holland (1790s) and then conceived as the southern terminus of Nash's great scheme taking Regent Street up to Marylebone and Regent's Park. When he became king, George IV lost interest in Carlton House: it was demolished and replaced by Nash's terraces and the Duke of York's steps (1820s). This is a shame, although the terraces and steps are magnificent (**Map 14,4**). Eminent Victorians Lord Palmerston, William Gladstone and Earl Grey all lived in the Terrace.

In the eastern terrace you will find the unobtrusive **Institute of Contemporary Arts** (ICA), founded by Herbert Read and Roland Penrose in 1947. It presents exhibitions of avant-garde art and films, and is a social centre with an interesting bookshop selling appropriately radical titles. Open 12.00–01.30 Tues–Sat, 12.00–22.30 Sun, Mon; art gallery open 12.00–19.30 daily. Admission charge. Café. ☎ 020 7930 0493. Further along to the west are the more conventional **Mall Galleries**, normally showing changing exhibitions from arts societies and others. Open 10.00–17.00 daily. ☎ 020 7930 6844.

Do not bother to ascend the **Duke of York's Steps**: the **Duke of York's Column** is better seen from below. Frederick, the 'Grand Old Duke of York' was the second son of George III and a popular Commander-in-Chief of the army—until, on his death in 1827, a day's pay was stopped for every soldier to pay for this memorial. It is 136ft high, and the work of Benjamin Wyatt; the figure is by Richard Westmacott (1834). There was much agonising as to whether the Duke should face up Regent Street or down towards Westminster, not an easy decision. At least, now, he is facing you.

Walk west along the Mall, or return to the park to take a more winding and picturesque route. You may wish to look at St James's Palace (Chapter 18), in which case turn right into Marlborough Road. At the end of the Mall, Green Park stretches away to your right and Buckingham Palace lies ahead. In approaching from the east you have the grandest view of the Palace's façade, but in the foreground you cannot escape Queen Victoria's memorial, which must be examined before we discuss the Palace; cross over to safe ground to do so.

The **Queen Victoria Memorial** forms the climax of Sir Aston Webb's grand scheme to link Trafalgar Square with the Palace via Admiralty Arch and a widened Mall (**Map 14,5**). It is reached via the memorial gardens which stretch either side, now usually a mass of flowers but originally intended as plain lawns. Parts of St James's Park and Green Park had to be taken to form them. The magnificent gate to Green Park is on the right. The memorial itself, by Sir Thomas Brock (1911), comprises 2300 tons of marble representing not only Queen Victoria but also what Osbert Sitwell politely called 'tons of allegorical females ... with whole litters of their cretinous children'. What is more, there are prows of boats, reliefs, and grim bronzes round the circumference. The quality of the workmanship is superb.

Buckingham Palace

The late Victorian/Edwardian east front of Buckingham Palace seen through the gates, so prominent and famous, was really an afterthought completed by Webb at the same time as the Victoria Memorial. The chief monarch to be associated with the building as a whole is its sponsor, George IV, who somehow dominates the interior.

George IV

George IV (1762–1830) was the most flamboyant English monarch since Charles II, the most cultured since Charles I—and one of the least popular of all time. A man of powerful worldly appetites, for women, drink and luxury, his exploits had always been a worry to his ultra-respectable parents, for example, his secret but fairly successful marriage to Mrs Fitzherbert in 1785 and his official but immediately failing one to Caroline of Brunswick ten years later. During the final ten years of George III's illness, he acted as Regent and pursued the projects which still bear that name, the Park and Street. His interest in them was abandoned when he became king in 1820.

Having decided that Carlton House (see above) was inadequate for him as king, George IV took over Buckingham House, originally built by the Duke of Buckingham, which was convenient but outside the official boundaries of Westminster and the City. It had been latterly occupied by the Queen Dowager, and George intended Nash to transform it into something suitably magnificent. In the end the budget was wildly exceeded, Nash dismissed and disgraced, and George died before the Palace could be occupied. Although when he died *The Times* said 'there never was an individual less regretted by his fellow-creatures', Wellington described him as possessing 'a medley of opposite qualities, with a great preponderance of good'.

Architecturally the front is grand but characterless, with none of the exuberance of Admiralty Arch, nor the restraint to be found in Nash's original conception. The ornamental **gates** (1913) to Webb's forecourt are quite an interesting period piece by the Bromsgrove Guild, steeped in the Arts and Crafts tradition.

This façade covers a Victorian east wing, built by Edward Blore (1847) to make the Palace habitable for Queen Victoria's growing family. Blore's wing replaced Marble Arch, which was removed to where it stands today (Chapter 21). Nash's palace for George IV, built in the 1820s, still largely intact but invisible from where you are standing, comprised south, west and north wings of surprising modesty (given the tastes of their sponsor) though still built at hideous expense. Nash's work can be seen if you turn the corners either side of the front façade.

Tour of Buckingham Palace

After comprehensive reworkings in the reigns of Victoria and Edward VII the interior today makes a wonderful tour, and the gardens which you see as you leave are as beautiful and picturesque as any in England—a reminder that, at heart, this is not really a palace at all, but a large English country house.

• Open 09.30–16.15 daily Aug, Sept and maybe early Oct. Admission charge (entry by timed ticket). Advance booking ☎ 020 7930 4832. Credit card bookings ☎ 020 7321 2233. Recorded information ☎ 020 7799 2331. Shop. www.royalresidences.com. Tube: Green Park. **Note**. In quieter periods the ticket may be timed for immediate use, but is more likely to be for some hours, or even days, ahead, so this must be considered when planning.

The ticket booth for purchasing or collecting tickets is at the foot of Green Park, opposite the Palace. Entry is via the Ambassadors Court, through an odd little side door with irregular Ionic piers, round the left-hand side of the front façade. It takes you almost immediately to the south side of the interior **Quadrangle**. This is the area, almost invisible from the front railings, into which cars sweep, bearing the great and good. It is only from here that we can appreciate the three stages of the architecture, from Nash, via Blore, to Webb. Nash's meltingly rich Bath stone inner frontage, which used to be that seen from the Mall, draws you into the Louvre-inspired portico of double columns.

You now proceed into the **Grand Hall** behind, dug down to a lower level to add grandeur to the height. All is plush and polished, the carpets a royal crimson. From this you ascend, like royalty's own visitors, by a complex internal manoeuvre, the grand double staircase of Carrara marble to process through the Green Drawing Room to the **Throne Room**, where the monarch is traditionally photographed on Coronation Day. This route, staircase, guard room, drawing room to throne room, is all that survives from the French *enfilade*, which in Versailles had led visitors through a score of rooms to reach Louis XIV and even at Hampton Court took six rooms to reach William III. All around are sumptuous furnishings, paintings, porcelain and sculpture, much of it collected by George IV.

From the Throne Room you turn left into the room that runs like a spine through the state apartments, the **Picture Gallery** designed by Nash, top-lit for better scrutiny of the paintings. Here are some of the finest works in the Royal Collection, most notably *Charles I and Henrietta Maria with their Two Eldest Children* (1632) and *Charles I with M. de St Antoine* (1633) by Sir Antony van Dyck, *The Music Lesson* (1670) by Jan Vermeer and *Agatha Bas* (1641) by Rembrandt.

From the Picture Gallery we move through a series of smaller rooms to another magnificent suite developed by Victoria and Albert, who found the Nash layout too cramped for their large family and for entertaining. Queen Victoria employed James Pennethorne (Nash's son-in-law) to furnish other parts of the building to a new standard of lavishness, through which the visitor now wonderingly proceeds. These begin with the East Gallery and proceed through the magnificent **Ballroom** (1853–55), the Cross and West Galleries, the **State Dining Room**, the **Blue Drawing Room**, the **Music Room**—a bowed space at the centre of Nash's garden façade—to the **White Drawing Room**. This still seems a more private space where, as the excellent guide book quaintly puts it, 'the Royal Family gather before meeting their guests'.

Descent from the first floor is via the Minister's Staircase and out, through the ground-floor Bow Room, into the **gardens**. This replicates the route taken by thousands of garden-party guests each summer. Leave via the garden and an excellent shop, into Grosvenor Place.

It is unlikely that we would have the opportunity to follow this magnificent progression through the state apartments if royalty had not, first, needed money to effect repairs after the Windsor Castle fire in 1992, and second, felt in need of improved public relations after the embarrassing and internationally absorbing marital failures of the same period. The important consideration now is that these openings should continue, and be extended to a longer period of the year—if not all year on certain days of the week. Otherwise the conduct of the tour should not change: the guiding is unobtrusive but well-informed and the opportunity to go at one's own pace in uncrowded conditions most welcome.

Proceed down Buckingham Gate past the **Queen's Gallery**, to be re-opened in May 2002 after refurbishment, with an exhibition of 450 outstanding works from the Royal Collection to celebrate the Queen's Golden Jubilee. Open 10.00–17.30 daily. Admission charge (entry by timed ticket). Information ☎ 020 7839 1377. Advance booking ☎ 020 7321 2233. www.royal.gov.uk

You soon reach the **Royal Mews** built by Nash (1824–25). Open Aug–Sept 10.30–16.30 Mon–Thur; Oct–July 12.00–16.00 Mon–Thur. Admission charge. Shop open 09.30–17.00 all year. ☎ 020 7930 4830. www.royalresidences.com. Tube: Victoria. This is the place to see the royal horses and carriages and related equipment. The horses are lined up, face forward, in their stables so it is difficult to get much of an impression of them, but the collection and variety of coaches is interesting, especially Sir William Chambers's over-the-top State coach (1762), still used for coronations.

As you leave the Royal Mews turn right down Buckingham Palace Road. Cross Grosvenor Place: if you feel in need of refreshment, the *Bag O'Nails* pub is on the corner. There is one more small architectural treat before the walk ends. On the right, turn into **Victoria Square**, built by Matthew Wyatt in the 1840s, and still largely intact despite its startlingly central location: it is all white stucco and Corinthian pilasters, a gem born to blush unseen. A few yards further on, cross at the traffic lights to join the melée at Victoria Station.

18 • Piccadilly and St James's

This is a civilised walk with some grand architecture and finishing in green and pleasant surroundings: it shows London at its most polite, in the 18C sense of that term.

- Distance: 2¼ miles. Time: 1½ hours + extra time for galleries. Tube: Piccadilly Circus. Map 14.

Piccadilly Circus, where we begin, is far from 'polite', in any sense (**Map 14,4**). This crossroads, unaccountably a tourist spot, was not always deplorably vulgar. It was laid out by John Nash as part of his Regent Street development, as a circus

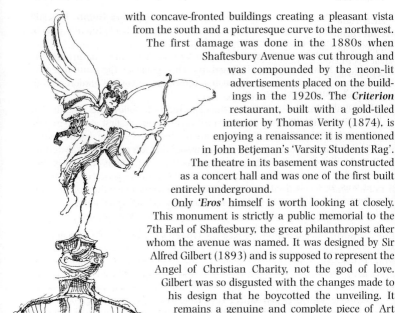

'Eros' at Piccadilly Circus

with concave-fronted buildings creating a pleasant vista from the south and a picturesque curve to the northwest. The first damage was done in the 1880s when Shaftesbury Avenue was cut through and was compounded by the neon-lit advertisements placed on the buildings in the 1920s. The *Criterion* restaurant, built with a gold-tiled interior by Thomas Verity (1874), is enjoying a renaissance: it is mentioned in John Betjeman's 'Varsity Students Rag'. The theatre in its basement was constructed as a concert hall and was one of the first built entirely underground.

Only *'Eros'* himself is worth looking at closely. This monument is strictly a public memorial to the 7th Earl of Shaftesbury, the great philanthropist after whom the avenue was named. It was designed by Sir Alfred Gilbert (1893) and is supposed to represent the Angel of Christian Charity, not the god of love. Gilbert was so disgusted with the changes made to his design that he boycotted the unveiling. It remains a genuine and complete piece of Art Nouveau in London, full of curves and froth, yet somehow repellent, as Art Nouveau so often is.

Do not delay here but proceed past the former London Pavilion, the Trocadero next door and similar amusements, to turn right down **Haymarket**. You cannot miss the remarkable crazed-horse fountain on the corner or, looking up, bronze divers descending on you from the roof. Haymarket was once exactly as it sounds, supplying hay and straw for the Royal Mews that used to be located where Trafalgar Square now is. It has also been a street focusing on entertainment in one form or another since the 17C. On your left at no. 24 is a former tobacconist's (1750s) which is worth going inside; it now sells souvenirs. Further down on the left is the main branch of *Burberry's* (more detail is given in Chapter 21). Next comes the *Haymarket Theatre* by Nash (1821), with a portico intended to be seen down the vista from Charles II Street. Oscar Wilde's plays *A Woman of No Importance* and *An Ideal Husband* were first staged here in the 1890s.

Take the first left after it, Suffolk Place, and go round to the back of the theatre to **Suffolk Street**. This little area is a rare survival from Nash's great Regent Street project, and gives a good idea of its grandeur and sense of purpose, with big, bold Doric columns and delicate wrought iron, and everything covered in cream-painted stucco.

Retrace your steps to Haymarket. Opposite is the monster of *Her Majesty's Theatre* by C.J. Phipps (1897), and **New Zealand House** by Robert Matthew (1963), a rare example of successful Modernism in central London with fine views from the occasionally accessible top floor and at ground level the popular *Sports Café*.

Turn right along **Pall Mall**: immediately on your right is **Royal Opera Arcade**, again by Nash (1816). This was London's first shopping arcade, and is completely preserved with Regency shop fronts. It was so-called because the old Royal Opera House stood on the site of Her Majesty's Theatre before moving to Covent Garden.

> We shall return to Pall Mall later but it is worth noting here its importance as a thoroughfare. The name comes from the Italian *pallo a maglio* ('ball to mallet'), a proto-croquet game that became a craze in France and is thought to have been brought from there to Scotland by Mary, Queen of Scots. As 'pell mell' it was popular in London from her son James I's time, and became even more so after the Restoration of Charles II. The Mall (Chapter 17) was constructed so that Charles and his court could play but it was the parallel street that was given the name. Nell Gwyn lived here in those days and, more respectably, so did a large number of the fashionable aristocracy. It is odd to think that the name of countless shopping malls throughout the world stems from the Italian for 'hammer'.

Cross Pall Mall at the pedestrian crossing to get to the **Institute of Directors** at no. 116, formerly the United Services Club, now for business leaders. Yet another building by Nash (1827–28), it was altered by Decimus Burton in the 1850s and again in 1912 by Walford and Thompson. It contains the original staircase from Carlton House, which stood on this site, as well as other rooms of great magnificence. Carlton House was the Prince Regent's private palace, demolished when he became George IV in 1820 and his fancy was taken by Buckingham House nearby. Beyond and to the left is **Waterloo Place**, which leads south to the Duke of York's Steps (Chapter 17). Here are some fine bronze statues, the most notable being those to *Edward VII* by Sir Bertram Mackennal (1922) and *Captain R.F. Scott* by his widow, Kathleen (1915). On the other side of Pall Mall, spectacularly dominant, is the **Guards' Crimea Memorial** by John Bell (1859), fronted by statues of *Florence Nightingale* and her greatest ally, *Sir Sidney Herbert* by Arthur Walker and John Foley respectively. It is all very patriotic around here, so it comes as a slight relief to behold the broader values implied in the civilised profile of the club on the western side, the **Athenaeum**, a highly cultivated Greek-Revival building by Burton (1829–30). On the porch is a gilt *Athene* by E.H. Baily (1829), the sculptor of Nelson in Trafalgar Square, and above her a lovely parthenaic frieze by James Henning on a vivid blue ground. This has always been a club for literary men (and recently women), including William Makepeace Thackeray and Anthony Trollope.

Clubs

In the 18C coffee houses and assembly rooms became fashionable, and from them developed the club. The heyday of clubs was the 100 years following the 1820s, and is reflected in the literature of that period, beginning with Thackeray and ending with P.G. Wodehouse. They still exist but, with their dress codes and male chauvinism, seem to most people an anachronism; to anyone under 30, going clubbing today means something very different.

Pall Mall and St James's Street are the place for clubs. Next after the Athenaeum is the **Travellers' Club**, an early commission by Charles Barry

(1828), which was a ground-breaking building at the time, since it revived the Florentine Renaissance. Barry and A.W.N. Pugin were later to set in train the much more significant Gothic Revival with their work on the Houses of Parliament. Next is the same architect's **Reform Club** (1841), founded for supporters of the great electoral legislation of 1832: here the Italian Renaissance style is practised on a larger scale and with even greater confidence. Pevsner called it Barry's masterpiece, appearing, after the Travellers', as 'maturity after lovable youth'. Beyond on the left is the **Royal Automobile Club** by Mewès and Davis (1910), too large for the scale of the street, and soon after that **Schomberg House** (façade 1698), a rare survival from Pall Mall's earliest days, where the painter Gainsborough died.

> ### Thomas Gainsborough
> Gainsborough (1727–88), like Sir Joshua Reynolds, arrived in London in 1740 to train as an artist while acting as a painting restorer for dealers. He developed an early preference for landscapes, but it is as a portrait painter that his reputation was made, and having established his own studios first in Ipswich and then Bath, he returned to London in 1774 to establish his practice in Pall Mall. His superior painting technique has allowed his work to survive better than Reynolds's, and he was more skilled at catching a likeness, but he never gained the honours that came to his rival despite being preferred by both the royal family and leaders of fashion.

Cross Pall Mall and go north into **St James's Square** (**Map 14,4**), perhaps to take a rest in its garden and admire the statue of *William III* by John Bacon, father and son, placed here in 1808. Under the horse is a bronze molehill to commemorate the cause of the King's fatal riding accident—'the gentleman in black velvet'. St James's Square is the centrepiece of an early London housing estate, and was the first proper West End square.

> The developer was Henry Jermyn, Earl of St Albans, a friend of Charles II and connected (some say intimately) with Charles's widowed mother Henrietta Maria. Soon after the restoration in 1660 Jermyn acquired leave from the Crown to develop the area. The estate was planned in a very un-English, symmetrical way, as in France or Italy, with entrances to the square halfway along the west, north and east sides joining it to the main streets round the boundary (St James's, Jermyn Street and Haymarket). The first houses, none of which survive, were grand detached red-brick mansions, but by the 18C these had been gradually replaced by the more typical, and by then fashionable, terraced housing. But there was no diminution in the square's high standing: in the 1720s, six dukes and seven earls lived there.

Today we see a mixture of architecture, all of a pleasing scale though now institutional rather than residential. Some 18C survivals can be seen in nos 4, 5, 9–11 and above all 15, in the northwest corner, an exquisite Palladian townhouse by James 'Athenian' Stuart (1763). Nos 20 and 21 by Robert Adam (1775–89) copied its principles. No. 14 houses the London Library (for members only), founded in 1841 at the instigation of Thomas Carlyle: it featured in the Booker prizewinning novel *Possession* by A.S. Byatt. No. 16 is the former East India United Service Club, with appropriate elephants in the frieze. During the

Second World War, General Eisenhower and the Allied headquarters operated at no. 31.

Leave the square by Duke of York Street (named after he who was to become James II) to the north. You may wish to visit the ***Red Lion***, an authentic Victorian pub. Note, too, at the top of the street, the south façade of Sir Christopher Wren's church of St James Piccadilly (see below), which is correctly oriented west–east and therefore incapable of effectively closing the vista, although the architect once had a door in the centre of this façade and even now the central bay window has a cherub keystone and scrolling brackets at the foot.

Jermyn Street runs east and west and is worth exploring if you want to buy smart shirts from ***Hilditch and Key, T.M. Lewin*** or ***Thomas Pink*** or other up-market menswear; or cheese at ***Paxton and Whitfields*** at no. 93 (founded 1740); or to admire several fine examples of in-filling architecture of *c* 1900. Cross the street and enter **St James Piccadilly** (1683–84) from the south. It is surprisingly capacious for an estate church (built to serve the new district being developed by St Albans), and we know from Wren's own words that he saw it as something of a model for church design. The five bays' broad width and the galleries enable 2000 people to be seated. The interior is in the form of a basilica, nave and aisles without a chancel, with all parts visible at once. There is a spacious curving gallery which, at the west end, has the organ at the centre. The organ was originally built by Renatus Harris for James II's Catholic chapel in Whitehall Palace, but was transferred here at the request of Queen Mary in 1691, when it was installed by Father Schmidt. It thus has associations with both the great figures of 17C-organ building. The fine marble font and limewood reredos are by Grinling Gibbons. The satirical cartoonist James Gillray was buried here.

The church was much damaged in the Second World War but was carefully restored by A.E. Richardson, who gave it a new lead spire which you can see by exiting from the North Door into the **market** usually assembled in the churchyard—it sells antiques on Tuesdays. The church is a venue for regular concerts and there is a pleasant coffee shop at the west end. It is a place to linger before exploring Piccadilly. ☎ 020 7734 4511.

Very ancient, curving slightly to the south, **Piccadilly** at one time contained further great houses, larger than those in St James's Square, such as Burlington House and Melbourne House (now Albany).

> It was first called Portugal Street, in honour of Charles II's queen, Catherine of Braganza, but soon acquired its very distinctive title. The name is supposed to originate from a form of collar in vogue at the time of the Restoration, made in large quantities by Robert Baker, who brought the land out of his profits. Like the rest of the area it soon became the height of fashion, and landlords such as Robert Boyle, 3rd Earl of Burlington developed both their own houses and built estates around them.

As you leave the church, note the pretty little bank on the west side of the churchyard, Edwin Lutyens's pastiche of Wren. To the right is the former ***Simpson's*** store, now a Waterstone's bookshop, in a good modern building (1935). Opposite is the overbearing ***Meridian Hotel***, built by Norman Shaw (1905–8) in the style of the exuberant Edwardian Classical Revival. Just to the right is ***Cording's***, with a startling over-the-top shop front, unchanged because Cording's commissioned it.

Cross over and walk west along the north side of the street. Note **Albany** on your right, Sir William Chambers's stock-brick mansion (1770), built for Viscount Melbourne but soon converted by Henry Holland into apartments for city bachelors, now women as well as men; it is known as The Albany after the second owner. There have been many famous residents, including more recently Graham Greene and Edward Heath. Opposite is *Fortnum and Mason*, the grandest of grocers (it sells clothes too), founded by a footman of George III in the 1770s. It is famous for afternoon tea (bookings ☎ 020 7734 8040) and for the modern clock (1964) on the Piccadilly façade—good fun on the hour. Next door is *Hatchard's*, a bookseller founded in 1797 a few doors away on Piccadilly which moved to its current premises in 1801.

The **Royal Academy** in Burlington House soon comes into view on the right, duly signed along its over-elaborate 1860s street façade (**Map 14,3**). The statue in the courtyard is of its first president *Sir Joshua Reynolds* by Alfred Drury (1931).

> The building was formerly a Palladian mansion in the purest taste, developed from 1716 by Lord Burlington, who championed the style in England (see Chapter 57), with the help of Colen Campbell and James Gibbs. Some changes were made in 1816, but when the Royal Academy arrived in the 1860s, it proceeded to destroy all Palladian purity, adding a third storey and putting up wings either side of the courtyard to house other learned societies. The Sackler Wing designed by Norman Foster was opened in 1992; among current developments, a building by Michael Hopkins will link Burlington House to Burlington Gardens (see below); and the car park will be relocated beneath the courtyard.

This is an exciting location for loan exhibitions and the Academy has a fine collection of art of its own, including Michelangelo's *Taddei Tondo* (1505). From 2003 the Fine Rooms will be open to the public permanently. There is an excellent self-service restaurant and shop accessible without the need to buy tickets for the current exhibition. Open 10.00–18.00 daily (10.00–22.00 Fri). Admission charge for special exhibitions. Restaurant. Shop. Free tours of the Fine Rooms at 13.00 Tues–Fri. Recorded information ☎ 020 7300 5760. www.royalacademy.org.uk. Tube: Piccadilly Circus or Green Park.

Royal Academy

The Academy is the most prestigious association of British artists and the sponsor of major exhibitions, including its own Summer Exhibition, the largest in the country open to amateurs and professionals alike. It was established in 1768 with the indispensable patronage of George III, who helped to fund it after earlier unsuccessful attempts to form a co-ordinated group of artists for the purpose of training and self-promotion. Thanks to the initiative of its first treasurer, Sir William Chambers, it began its life in the newly rebuilt Somerset House, holding its exhibitions in the Great Room there. In 1837 it moved into the National Gallery's new building, but transferred to its own premises at Burlington House in 1868. With art education still one of its major aims, it also runs the Royal Academy Schools.

Next door to the Royal Academy is the **Burlington Arcade** by Samuel Ware (1815–19), with its long run of good-looking and expensive shops. Go through it to emerge at the back into Burlington Gardens. To the right is an eye-catching piece of Victorian Classicism, built for the University of London by James Pennethorne (1866–69), encrusted with statues of famous Britons. It backs on to the Royal Academy which will be extending into it from 2005. You should now turn left to reach Bond Street.

Strictly speaking this is **Old Bond Street**, filled not with clothes but with art-dealers: they include *Agnew's* at no. 43, *Colnaghi* at no. 14 and the *Redfern Gallery* at 20 Cork Street (for Sotheby's, see Chapter 21). The street was developed in the 1680s by Sir Thomas Bond: New Bond Street was started in the 1720s. There is not much noteable architecture left here, although see *Cartier* at nos 175–77, but there are plenty of windows to gaze in—a habit as popular in Georgian times as now, and in the years in between, as the High Victorian façade of *Asprey's* at nos 165–69 New Bond Street confirms.

Return to Piccadilly and cross over, looking back at the imaginative turn-of-the-20C blocks on the north side with terracotta, balconies, tiles, sunflowers, hope and exuberance everywhere. To your right is the *Ritz*, by Mewès and Davis (1906), designers of the Paris Ritz which this openly emulates with its Louis XVI interior and Rue de Rivoli arcade. The Ritz has the distinction of being the first steel-framed building to be erected in London, although you would never know as it is covered in Norwegian granite. This is another place to go for an expensive afternoon tea (☎ 020 7493 8181); note that 'smart dress is preferred'.

Averting your gaze from the hideous corner block go down **St James's Street**, a handsome thoroughfare, wide and distinguished—you are back on the Earl of St Albans' estate. Here there are more clubs: first, on the right, what was **Crockford's** at no. 50 (now St James's Casino), built by Benjamin and Phillip Wyatt in 1827 and altered in the 1870s. Opposite at nos 37–38 is **White's**, perhaps the most distinguished club of all: George IV, William IV and Edward VII were all members, as were every prime minister from Walpole to Peel, and Jonathan Swift, Joseph Steele, John Gay and Alexander Pope. White's has been largely a gambling club, but its origins in 1693 were as a chocolate house owned by an Italian called, yes, Bianco. The present building of 1755 was also altered in the 19C: note the Classical figures in relief and the Greek motifs added to the central bow window.

Further down on the left at no. 28, in brown brick with a fan-surrounded Venetian window, is **Boodle's** by the architect John Crunden (1775–76), named after its first manager. Boodle's was similar in tone to White's and had many of the same members, but is much better looking architecturally. Opposite, at no. 60 on the right-hand side, is **Brooks's** by Henry Holland (1788), in shabby-looking white brick with fine Corinthian pilasters, another gambling club associated in its heyday with the Whigs: both Charles James Fox and William Pitt were members. On the left, note Alison and Peter Smithson's brutalist offices for **The Economist** (1960s): critics call them intrusive but in fact they are easy to miss altogether. This is more than can be said for 66 St James's Street, on the right, looking like a couple of torpedoes waiting to be launched. How can this sort of thing ever have been allowed, even in the liberal 1980s?

Peep down Blue Ball Yard on the right to see some comforting early 19C stables, with flats reached from a balcony on wooden brackets. You may also want to explore **St James's Place**, where the torpedoes are. In 1848 Frederick Chopin stayed in a house on the right (see plaque) and left it to give his last public performance. On the left look down Duke's Place for a feeling of silent luxury. St James's Place widens at the end to reveal **Spencer House**, a perfect Palladian house by John Vardy (1756–65), with some interiors by James Stuart. The house was built for John Spencer, heir to the Duchess of Marlborough, who became Earl Spencer in 1765: he was an ancestor of Diana, Princess of Wales. It is now owned by the Rothschild organisation. Open 10.30–17.30 Sun only; closed Aug, Jan. Charge for obligatory guided tour. ☎ 020 7499 8620.

You will see the façade facing Green Park shortly but meanwhile return to St James's Street. Opposite is King Street, where you will find the auction house **Christie's**. For information on sales and previews, ☎ 020 7839 9060. This is another area of art dealers, including Frost and Reid at nos 2–4, Spinks at no. 21 and Cox at 37 Duke Street.

Continuing downhill on St James's Street, note the **Carlton Club** at nos 69–70 on the right, by Thomas Hopper, in perfect Palladian style although as late as the 1820s, and beyond that the enormous former **Conservative Club** by George Basevi and Sydney Smirke, of the more exuberant 1840s. The Club was founded in 1832 to oppose the Reform Bill and every prominent Conservative since has been a member, from William Gladstone, Benjamin Disraeli, Winston Churchill and Anthony Eden to Edward Heath. Opposite, looking quietly subservient, are the hatters *Lock and Co.* at no. 6 and wine merchants *Berry Bros. and Rudd* at no. 3, old businesses in old houses, still meeting the needs of the wealthy.

You now reach St James's Palace, but at the end of the street take a look at the last two buildings. Both are by Norman Shaw for the Alliance Assurance, and show how his style changed—for the worse—as he moved with fashion between 1880 and 1905. The building on the left is in a lovely rich Arts and Crafts style, but by the time we get to that on the right (no. 88), Shaw is in the thick of the Classical Revival.

Although the name is familiar, **St James's Palace**, used to accommodate various members of the Royal household and the Lord Chamberlain's office, is surprisingly secret (**Map 14,6**). One of the difficulties is that it is very hard to see anything—there are no opening arrangements comparable with Buckingham Palace—and so it is impossible to appreciate the interior, which contains much distinguished work by Wren. No monarch has lived here since the early 19C and it seems inappropriate that there is never an opportunity for public visits.

St James's Palace was the home of English monarchs for 300 years. It was built by Henry VIII while he was pursuing higher ambitions at Whitehall Palace, and the comfortable red-brick resemblance to Hampton Court is obvious. Queen Mary I died here in 1558, bitterly unhappy, and Queen Elizabeth I and James I held court here. George III and IV were married here. From 1698 the official London residence of the sovereign, it was the setting for all court functions and foreign ambassadors are still accredited to 'the court of St James'.

The red-brick gatehouse which you have been looking at all the way down St James's Street has been a London landmark for 500 years, and is the oldest building in the area. Behind, and invisible, is the **Chapel Royal**, also Tudor but redecorated in 1836, most famous for its connections with English church music; Tallis, Byrd and Purcell were all organists there. Just to the left, visible by peering down a driveway marked 'private—keep out' is **Marlborough House** (1709–10), built next-door to St James's by Wren for Sarah, Duchess of Marlborough, courtesy of her friend Queen Anne. She wanted it to bear no resemblance to Blenheim Palace in Oxfordshire, which John Vanbrugh was building for her husband at very great public expense. The house has been altered many times, and has housed a range of occupants; it is currently used by the Commonwealth Secretariat.

Continue down Marlborough Road to see the **Queen's Chapel**, or at least the exterior—again the interior is open only for services. This is by Inigo Jones (1623), and like most of his work now seems revolutionary. It was the first church in the Classical style in England and is 'of a simplicity and beauty rarely matched in the more ingenious and complex designs of Wren' (Pevsner). It was built as a Catholic chapel for Charles I's intended Spanish bride, but when she did not materialise it became a chapel for Henrietta Maria. Built of brick and cemented over to look like stone, an early 'stucco' treatment, it has pediments at each end and the east end displays Britain's earliest Venetian window. In the wall, on the left, do not miss Alfred Gilbert's delicious if disturbing Art Nouveau **memorial to Queen Alexandra** (1926), who lived in Marlborough House after Edward VII's death. Gilbert must have felt better about this than 'Eros'. It is audibly a fountain but the waterworks are virtually hidden from view.

When you reach the Mall and its lovely trees, turn right and pass **Clarence House**, just visible over the top of the wall, fence and hedge which successively rise to obscure it. It was built by Nash (1825) for the Duke of Clarence, later William IV. It is currently the home of the Queen Mother. Pass Stable Yard Road on your right. Buckingham Palace is ahead and on your right, on the corner, is **Lancaster House**, built as York House by Benjamin Wyatt (1825–29) for the Duke of York (he of the steps), another brother of George IV. It was a prominent venue for royal social events in the 19C where the famous could glitter on the magnificent staircase. In 1912 it was acquired by Lord Leverhulme, who renamed it Lancaster House and generously gave the remainder of the lease to the government, who to this day use it for hospitality and conferences. Again, it is a small scandal that there is no public access.

Turn right into **Green Park** at Queen's Walk, named after Caroline, wife of George II, for whom it was laid out (1720). Make your path to the left if you wish the rich green of the grass and canopy of trees to be the last stage of this tour (**Map 14,5**). The grass here seldom dries up in summer unlike that in Hyde Park—perhaps because the Tyburn runs in pipes beneath it—and with nothing in the way of entertainment provided it always feels peaceful. Charles II designated this land a royal park and it was his habit to walk around in it mingling with the public. Here he built a 'snow' house to cool drinks (the first in England), the mound of which can still be seen at the northern side. As you ascend the path, you will see the fine façade of Spencer House on your right.

Reaching Piccadilly again you may like to explore the rest of it to the west—some of which is covered in the next chapter—but Green Park station makes a handy termination.

19 • Mayfair

Mayfair—the most expensive place on the Monopoly board, its name redolent of wealth and luxury—may seem quite ordinary to walk through, especially compared with outwardly more opulent environments like St James's Park or Regent's Park. But secretly it retains its wealth and, despite the advent of up-market offices and hotels, you can still feel this in the antique shops, the parked cars, and general ambience. Our walk contains one or two detours so as to cover the whole of the area, but these can be omitted if time is short.

- Distance: 3 miles including detours. Time: 1½ hours + 2 hours for museums. Tube: Hyde Park Corner. Map 13, 14.

We begin at **Hyde Park Corner**, and look first at the central island amid the maelstrom of traffic (**Map 13,6**). To get to it you must negotiate carefully the nightmare system of pedestrian exits. First choose Exit 2 (toilets are at Exit 1).

That Hyde Park Corner is famed for its traffic is fair enough: it has always been perceived as a key gateway to London, and various architects over time have proposed grand entries. The result today may be a muddle but it is composed of good individual parts. To the north Decimus Burton's **screen** (1825) is placed across the entry to the park and must be read as a gateway for royalty coming up Constitution Hill from the palace. It seems too grand for such a wide-open public space, which otherwise has minimal fencing.

Behind you is the so-called Constitution Arch, or **Wellington Arch**, also by Burton (1828), which originally marked the top of Constitution Hill and one entry to the palace—Marble Arch once marked the other. On top there was to be a giant statue of the Duke of Wellington by M. Cotes Wyatt, now at Aldershot. In 1883 the arch was moved to where you now see it and in 1912 the remarkable bronze *Quadriga of Peace* by Adrian Jones was erected on top. Its driver defiantly faces northwest, whence no enemies have ever come throughout the entire history of these islands. The arch is worth visiting as an unusual monument and gives some invigorating views. Open 10.00–18.00 Wed–Sun (10.00–16.00 in winter). Admission charge. Shop. ☎ 020 7930 2726.

Also on the traffic island, on the west side, are **First World War memorials**. That to the Royal Regiment of Artillery, with fine bronze gunners and a grimly terrifying stone howitzer, is by C. Sargeant Jagger. Behind it is the *Lanesborough Hotel*, formerly St George's Hospital by William Wilkins (1820s). In the northeast corner stands the memorial to the Machine Gun Corps, in a totally different idiom, with a bronze and virile *David* holding a sword, by Francis Derwent Wood (1925). Facing Apsley House there is a large bronze of the *Duke of Wellington* on his favourite horse, Copenhagen, by J.E. Boehm (1888)—indeed the whole of Hyde Park Corner is itself something of a memorial to the great Duke.

Apsley House
Return underground and now leave by Exit 1 (stairs or ramp) to ascend to Apsley House, the Wellington Museum. This is a museum of some magnificence, worth visiting for three things, its architecture, its contents and its associations.

- Open 11.00–17.00 Tues–Sun. Admission charge. Shop. ☎ 020 7499 5676.

This fine house was built in brick by Robert Adam (1771–78) for Lord Chancellor Henry Bathurst but was bought in 1807 by the Duke of Wellington's elder brother, who in turn sold it to the Duke on his return from France in 1817. It became known as 'No.1 London' as the first house encountered when approaching London from the northwest. In the 1820s the Duke used funds voted to him by a grateful parliament to encase the house in stone and make considerable improvements and extensions, including installing the great statue of Napoleon by Antonio Canova. His architect was his former secretary, Benjamin Dean Wyatt, designer of the Drury Lane Theatre and the Duke of York's Column.

Duke of Wellington

Arthur Wellesley, 1st Duke of Wellington (1769–1852), general and prime minister, was the third surviving son of an obscure Irish peer. At Eton he was thought too dreamy and introspective to be suitable for anything except the army, which thus became his first career. After early experience in the Low Countries he established his reputation with victories in India and confirmed it as a defensive general in Portugal during the Peninsular War. But he proved equally resourceful in attack, as victories at Salamanca and Vittoria showed, and of course most famously of all, at Waterloo in June 1815. As a soldier he despised popularity and had no illusions about war: 'Next to a battle lost, the greatest misery is a battle won.' From 1815 he enjoyed a career as a diplomat and Conservative MP, becoming prime minister in 1828. He alienated ultra-conservatives by agreeing to Catholic emancipation and liberals by opposing reform, which in the end he pragmatically accepted. In his later years he was a venerable elder statesman, whose death in 1852 was followed by national grief and a colossal funeral at St Paul's, where he is buried (see Chapter 7).

You enter via an **Outer Hall** with various busts, mainly of Wellington, including that by Sir Francis Chantrey (1823). There is also a painting of the 1836 Waterloo Banquet: these spectacular occasions for the officers who had served him were organised by the Duke at Apsley House annually from 1820 to his death in 1852. In the **Inner Hall** is the moving *His Last Return from Duty* by James Glass (1853), showing the Duke's final departure from his office at Horse Guards.

To the left of the Outer Hall is the **Plate and China Room**, housing the Duke's collection, re-set here in 1981. The most remarkable object is perhaps the Waterloo Shield designed by Thomas Stothard (1822), showing scenes from Wellington's various victories. Return through the Inner Hall to the staircase where the nude statue of *Napoleon* dominates. It was commissioned from Canova by Napoleon in 1801, finished in 1806, first seen by its subject in 1811 and disliked—he said it was too athletic), and bought by the British Government in 1816, to be presented by the Prince Regent to Wellington.

The staircase itself and the apsed **Piccadilly Drawing Room** entered above, left, are fine examples of Adam's work: in the latter the frieze, doors, ceiling design and marble chimney-piece are all his. The paintings are mostly a fine collection of Dutch genre, but the eye is caught by David Wilkie's *Chelsea Pensioners reading the Waterloo Despatch* (1822), which the Duke commissioned.

Proceed right to the Portico Drawing Room with a further Adam fireplace and then into the opulent **Waterloo Gallery**, added to the house by Wyatt in 1828 to hold the Duke's collection of paintings, over 200 of which had been captured from the Spanish royal collection in 1813 and subsequently presented to him, and to accommodate the by-then highly fashionable and therefore somewhat gross Waterloo Banquets. There are masterpieces here, including the *Waterseller of Seville* by Diego Velazquez (1620), *Queen Mary I* by Antonis Mor (1554), in a frame designed by Wyatt, as well as works by Correggio (whose *Agony in the Garden*, 1520s, was the Duke's favourite), Guercino, Peter Paul Rubens and Sir Antony van Dyck. Francisco Goya's equestrian portrait of the *Duke of Wellington* was made in 1812.

In the **Yellow Drawing Room** are more fine pictures, including Wilkie's portrait of *William IV*, indicating how the epithet 'Silly Billy' might have been conjured up (although it was a gift from the King to Wellington in 1833 and he hung it where you see it now). After this comes the **Striped Drawing Room**, decorated by Wyatt after Adam's Etruscan Dressing Room. The paintings here are military, including many fine portraits: note William Allan's *Battle of Waterloo* (1843), showing the moment of Napoleon's last unsuccessful attempt to break the British lines. The Duke is said to have commented when he saw it: 'Good, very good—not too much smoke.'

Last on this floor is the **Dining Room**, with more portraits, but the showpiece here is the centrepiece of the table service presented to the Duke in 1816 by the Portuguese. The four dancing figures were originally linked by garlands of silk flowers. Before leaving you may like to see the small exhibition of memorabilia in the basement, where there are rather splendid toilets but sadly no café.

On leaving Apsley House, locate to the left the subway under Park Lane, which is uncrossable at ground level. (If you want to explore the Park, turn right from Apsley House and follow Chapter 20.) You find yourself crossing Hamilton Place built for rich occupants (1865–70), at the top of which lie the *Inn on the Park* and the *Intercontinental Hotel*. Our route now explores the western end of Piccadilly (see Chapter 18 for the rest of this famous street). Green Park is on your right.

Immediately on the left is the *Hard Rock Café*, a notable tourist spot, but noisy and disagreeable. You may prefer the *Rose and Crown* in the next street, Old Park Lane. Note that Piccadilly is descending: the lowest point marks the route of the Tyburn, an ancient tributary of the Thames, long since buried underground but still flowing. On the left in Down Street there is a collector's item, the maroon tiled entrance to a disused station on the Piccadilly Line. After that the Edwardian opulence of the *Park Lane Hotel* and no. 106 Piccadilly look proudly out over Green Park. This whole stretch of Piccadilly was in Regency times one of the most fashionable addresses in London, but the traffic gradually drove the rich away and their houses became clubs. Most of these have now been replaced by hotels or offices but the **Naval and Military Club**, otherwise known as the In and Out from the signs on its gateposts, survives.

Turn left into White Horse Street to explore at random the little turnings of **Shepherd Market**. This area was built in the 1730s (and re-arranged in 1860) as a market for the residents of Mayfair and Piccadilly by Edward Shepherd, the main designer of Grosvenor Square. It is still charming, with many small cafés and the *Grapes* pub, and reminds us that supplies of food and other necessities for the grand houses and extensive urban terraces of Georgian London continued to be acquired through traditional, even rural, types of transaction.

Make your way north into **Curzon Street**. Now you are in Mayfair proper. The name comes from a spring fair held annually from the 17C until suppressed by the rich residents who moved in over the next hundred years. To the left of Queen Street is Crewe House, a typical example of the larger detached villas of which the area originally had many: it was built by Shepherd (1730) but in 1816 altered to what you now see. It is now the Saudi Embassy. Further to the left is **Chesterfield Street**, with complete 18C brick terraces. Opposite is the authentic **Curzon Cinema** by the distinguished Sir John Burnet, Tait and Partners (1935), proof that Art Deco was not the only style for cinemas of the period.

Walk back east down Curzon Street, past no. 10 where Nancy Mitford lived, *Trumpers*, royal barber, and then the Third Church of Christ Scientist by Lanchester and Rickards (1910), grandiloquently facing down Half Moon Street. Turn left up Fitzmaurice Place into Berkeley Square (**Map 14,3**).

A short detour is possible a little way up **Charles Street** to the left—there are several good 18C houses here (nos 48, 39–41, 16, and 21 with a lovely iron porch and balconies), and some spectacular later buildings, such as Dartmouth House. William IV as Duke of Clarence lived at no. 22. At the far end, uniquely, is a weatherboarded wall and, as a reward, a peaceful pub, the *Red Lion*.

Berkeley Square, the first of the three great Mayfair squares, must be accepted as relatively disappointing. Nightingales no longer sing here, or if they did you would not notice for traffic.

The beautiful 200-year-old plane trees remain the square's finest surviving feature. It was discovered early that this tree, *platanus x hispanica*, with its distinctive flaking trunk and large palmate leaves, was resistant to pollution and the hybrid was planted in many European cities, but we are proud to call it affectionately the London plane.

At this southern end stood Lansdowne House, a great Adam work, but now replaced by an office block. On the west side there are some fine Georgian houses (nos 43–46), especially no. 44, designed for Lady Isabella Finch by William Kent (1744). It possesses 'the grandest staircase and grandest drawing room of any 18C private house in London' (Pevsner): we will never know, as it is now an even more private club. No. 50 is allegedly haunted.

Before proceeding north, decide whether you want to explore east, across the square via Hay Hill to **Dover Street**: at no. 37 is a Palladian beauty by Sir Robert Taylor (1772), built for the Bishop of Ely. To the north in **Grafton Street**, nos 3–6 are quieter houses by Taylor (1760).

Turn right into Albemarle Street to see the **Faraday Museum** (see box, p 236) in the basement of the Royal Institution, founded in 1799. It is notable for a really dense run of Corinthian columns along the street, added to three houses in 1838 when the Institution took them over. Besides Faraday, other famous professors have included T.H. Huxley and Lord Rutherford.

The museum includes the great man's original notebooks and other items of interest in the history of science. Open 10.00–17.00 Mon–Fri. Admission charge. ☎ 020 7409 2992.

From the Faraday museum retrace your steps via Berkeley Square. Go past Bruton Street off the eastern side, where there are many art dealers to explore if you are interested. Leaving the square to the north, via Davies Street, turn right into **Bourdon Street**. Note Bourdon House on your left, altered but originally (1725) an example of the fine detached mansions erected in the area. Bourdon Street (**Map 14,1**) is typical of the network of mews created to provide services for Mayfair's middle-class—note the horse-high garage doors. Opposite is a 19C galleried block of working-class flats.

Michael Faraday

Faraday (1791–1867) is indissolubly associated with the Royal Institution, and would otherwise be taken entirely for granted as he refused all public office and titles. Faraday went there in 1813 to work for Humphrey Davy. His lectures were riveting and his scientific work, on the nature of electricity, magnetism and light, was profoundly influential, leading to the establishment of both the electricity industry and field theory in physics.

At the end of the street, cross New Bond Street and go down Maddox Street to **St George Hanover Square**, designed by John James (1713–24). The portico spills confidently over onto the pavement, as at St Martin-in-the-Fields, but this church was designed even earlier and must therefore be said to be equally influential. Inside there is a complex pattern of vaulting, confused compared with St Martin's but still dignified and calm. There is also some horrible stained glass, and behind the altar a large painting of the *Last Supper* by William Kent. ☎ 020 7629 0874. The church is a concert venue and hosts the Handel Festival each spring; for information, ☎ 020 8761 3311.

St George Street was laid out—in a funnel-shape to emphasise the portico of the church, an effective and unusual device—at the same time as the area of **Hanover Square** (1715), which took its name from the new royal family. The square, on a south-facing slope, is still pleasing and has a few original houses, among them no. 24 with distinctive pilasters of red brick. The statue of *William Pitt the Younger* is by Chantrey (1831).

George Frideric Handel

Handel (1685–1759) was born in Halle, Germany, in the same year as Bach, but whereas Bach was a stay-at-home, Handel travelled. First, escaping parental opposition to a musical career, he went to Hamburg, thence to Italy, where he developed skills in choral work of an Italian style, then back to Hanover. He came to London in 1712 and never left, becoming a naturalised Englishman in 1726 and enjoying royal patronage (among the results of which were his 'Water Music' and 'Music for the Royal Fireworks'). Over the next 20 years he composed 30 operas, turning then to oratorios, of which 'The Messiah', written in 23 days in 1741, has been judged his masterpiece, becoming the most popular of all English choral works. He is buried in Westminster Abbey.

Return from the southwest side of Hanover Square along **Brook Street**. Immediately on the right at no. 4 is a mad, late 19C extravaganza from an Elizabethan architect's pattern book. At no. 25 on the left, is the **Handel House Museum**. The house has been restored as a typical 18C London residence with particular reference to Handel, who lived there from 1723 until his death. Open

10.00–18.00 Tues–Sat (10.00–20.00 Thur), 12.00–18.00 Sun. Admission charge. ☎ 020 7495 1685 (the number is a nice touch, corresponding with the date of Handel's birth). www.handelhouse.org

Continuing the musical connection, unconsciously one assumes, Jimi Hendrix lived at no. 23 in 1968–69. By the 19C much of Brook Street was being converted from houses into hotels large and small: the most famous example is *Claridges*, further along on the left, founded here in the 1850s by William Claridge, a butler in an aristocratic household who had carefully saved his wages. The vivid red makes you feel almost unwell. The Savile Club at no. 69 was an important literary club in Victorian London: founded in 1868 it moved to this street in 1927.

Turn left at Davies Street and make your way down to **Mount Street** on the right (**Map 13,4**). It is a spectacular demonstration of later Mayfair, although the name signifies a much older historical connection, to one of the forts erected around London by anti-monarchist rebels in the 1640s, which came to be known as Oliver's Mount. Pevsner's description of the area as a 'paradise of pink terracotta' is perhaps a contradiction in terms: see especially Lupus House (1887) on the left. Much of this is by George and Peto, notably extravagant architects of the period (see also Cadogan Square, Chapter 16).

Turn left past the *Connaught Hotel* into the peaceful green space called Mount Street Gardens, past an entrance to the **Church of the Immaculate Conception** by the important Roman Catholic architect J.J. Scoles (1844–49), with a high altar designed by A.W.N. Pugin himself. It contains much other interesting hardware and many later chapels. The front of the church leads out into Farm Street, but it is best to return through the north door and go west through the gardens, with their public library, fountain and school, all of the 1890s.

At the end, in South Audley Street, is another gem, the **Grosvenor Chapel** built by Benjamin Timbrell (1730) as part of the Grosvenor Square scheme. Dainty and delightful, it is a reminder of New England: not surprisingly it has an organisation of American Friends. Inside, its perfect simplicity was somewhat wrecked by Sir Ninian Comper's enrichments (c 1900), although these are consistent with the wealth of Mayfair all around.

From the chapel, turn right, up to **Grosvenor Square**. This is the largest of Mayfair's squares, indeed the second largest in London. The United States Embassy at the western end by Eero Saarinen (1956–60) wilfully refuses to conform with its surroundings. But no attempt to conform was really to be expected, as any Georgian unity the square may once have possessed had long disappeared. Only lovely no. 9 in the northeast corner and no. 38 on the south (beaten up in the 19C) are original. John Adams, later President of the USA, lived here when ambassador in 1745. The garden has been forced towards formality: the old freestanding trees are disciplined by the south–north paved way and diagonal paths, all seeming to lead to Sir William Reid Dick's statue of *F.D. Roosevelt*, unveiled in 1948.

Leave the square on the north side into **Duke Street**, where there is more northwest Mayfair Victoriana: you may develop a taste for it in time and, if not careful, will come to see Georgian Mayfair as rather stiff and dull, as the Victorians did. On the right is a typical late 19C church by Alfred Waterhouse, architect of the Natural History Museum, with lots of characteristic yellow terracotta and red brick: it was the **King's Weighhouse Chapel** (now the Ukrainian

Catholic Cathedral). Opposite is a strange raised terrace with odd domed structures at each end, constructed in 1905 for electricity supply. All around, if you look, are red-brick working-class flats put up in 1888 on the Grosvenors' land by the local authority—contemporary versions of the Bourdon Street mews.

You have now reached Oxford Street (the shops are described in Chapter 21). Bond Street station is two blocks to the right.

20 • Hyde Park and Kensington Gardens

This is simply a stroll in the park, with fresh air, plenty of space, not too many people, but trees, horses, some flowers, a few statues, and water (you could include Kensington Palace, covered in Chapter 36). These two open spaces comprise a large area, however, so prepare yourself for quite a lot of walking, on grass or asphalt paths. Outside summer months, it can be bracing; but in summer you can recuperate in a deckchair, or swim, or take a boat in the Serpentine.

• Distance: 6 miles. Time: 2 hours. Tube: Hyde Park Corner or Marble Arch.
  Map 11, 12, 13.

Hyde Park
A start from Hyde Park Corner is suggested, perhaps after visiting Apsley House (Chapter 19), but it would also be feasible to begin at Marble Arch (Chapter 21). Leave Hyde Park Corner station (where toilets are available) by Exit 1 and enter the park (**Map 13,6**). Open 05.00–24.00 daily. Bands play in summer. ☎ 020 7298 2100.

> Yet another gain to the Crown at the Reformation, yet another hunting ground for Henry VIII and Elizabeth I, and a venue for military reviews, Hyde Park's 360 acres and the 275 acres of Kensington Gardens developed under royal management, each with its own, still distinguishable character. James I opened Hyde Park to the public, and although the Commonwealth government planned to build on it it was returned to royal hands at the Restoration and the Ring or Carriage Drive around which it became fashionable to parade was developed. Samuel Pepys tried it on a hired horse, 'looking mighty noble he felt, but his mount got out of hand and he had to withdraw discreetly to avoid being noticed by King Charles II and his mistress, Lady Castlemaine.
>
> Rotten Row, from *route de roi*, came into being in the late 17C, when William and Mary decided to move their palace from Whitehall to Kensington. In William III's time, Rotten Row was the first highway in England to be lit by night, by 300 oil lamps, but even this did not deter highwaymen. To this day it is exclusively for horse and rider.

Get your bearings first. To the right is **Queen Elizabeth Gate**, a Postmodern curiosity by David Wynne and Guiseppe Lund, opened by Queen Elizabeth, The Queen Mother in 1993. Beyond is the Achilles statue (see below) and behind to the right is Apsley House. Immediately on your right is Decimus Burton's **Screen** (1825), designed as a formal entry to the park from Buckingham Palace, down Constitution Hill. Rotten Row stretches away to the left, up a picturesque slope, and to the extreme left is Knightsbridge (see Chapter 16).

Parts of the route we shall follow are also designated part of the **Diana Princess of Wales Memorial Walk**. These are denoted by plaques designed by Alec Peever, with a rose emblem etched in aluminium. For more information on the 7-mile walk, which also extends into Green Park and St James's Park, and an accompanying book, ☎ 020 7298 2000.

Go past the Queen Elizabeth Gate and inspect the statue of *Achilles* by Richard Westmacott (1822). This 20ft-high bronze warrior, bar fig-leaf, was the first nude public statue in England. It was cast from captured French guns and 'erected by the women of England' in honour of the Duke of Wellington and 'his brave companions in arms'. Facing the Duke's Apsley House, the figure was described by a contemporary as 'manifesting the most furious intentions of self-defence against the hero whose abode it is looking at'.

Set off to the north up **Lovers' Walk**. Lovers would have to be fairly desperate to choose this particular path which has, close by on the right, dreadful traffic-choked Park Lane and its equally ugly hotels; but try to imagine dignified carriages in front of the grand Mayfair residences (Grosvenor House, Dorchester House and Londonderry House) which used to line the street. Or you can walk up the parallel **Broad Walk**, where Pepys lost control of his horse, although here you may encounter rather too many rollerbladers or joggers. What would Pepys have made of this phenomenon? To the left, across the grass, you can see the tower block of **Knightsbridge Barracks** designed by Basil Spence (1970): it houses the Household Cavalry, which exercises its horses in the Park 06.00–08.00. The tower with the green dome is part of Imperial College.

At Marble Arch, if it is a Sunday, you may find **Speakers' Corner** in action. Here, since 1866, anyone has been able to address the public on any subject he or she wishes, provided the words used are not obscene and do not cause a breach of the peace. Heckle speakers if you wish; or, if you have something to say, make your own speech. Most of those participating tend to be more concerned about helping you to the next world than improving your life in this: in other words, religion is more popular than politics here.

Cross southwest towards the trees over the flat area, still used sometimes for reviews or parades. Signs will lead you to the Reformers' Tree, now only a memorial of the place where supporters of the great Reform Bill of 1832, which widened the electoral franchise, met in the early 19C. Behind it is the Old Police House, a dignified Neo-Georgian building, and next door the Ranger's Lodge. Go down to the water, called the **Serpentine**. Here you can hire a boat: to save queuing on a fine day, you can reserve a boat by phone, ☎ 020 7262 1330.

Walk west by the lake as far as the second boathouse and then turn up the slope to the **Norwegian Navy Memorial** (placed here 1978), a free-standing piece of stone, 'shaped for thousands of years by the forces of nature, frost, running water, rock, sand and ice until it obtained its present shape', as its inscription says. Further up the gentle slope stands *Rima* by Jacob Epstein (1925), part of a memorial to the naturalist W.H. Hudson, the author of *Green Mansions*, who died in 1927; it was daubed with paint by anti-Modernists in its early days but it is hard to see what their problem was. Behind it is a nursery of plants.

Walk west and cross the North Ride (sandy, for horses) and West Carriage Drive (asphalt, for cars) to enter Kensington Gardens.

Kensington Gardens

The character of the environment subtly changes here.

The Gardens, unlike Hyde Park, have been carefully planned and planted, both by royalty and later management. William III, and Queen Anne after him, extended the grounds of Kensington Palace into Hyde Park, reducing public access, and Queen Caroline, wife of George II, took a good deal more, creating the Long Water and the Serpentine with water from the River Westbourne. These interventions have made Kensington Gardens more formal in tone than Hyde Park, and the criss-crossing paths, at first seeming similar, actually create a focus on the Palace at the western side, set off by the Round Pond. All this was done by Queen Caroline's garden designers, Henry Wise and Charles Bridgeman, in the 1720s and 30s.

Turn right along Buck Hill Walk. This was Queen Caroline's original boundary, which is demonstrated by the partial restoration of the ha-ha and bastion at the northeast corner. Follow the path round towards Marlborough Gate. A pets' cemetery, interesting but rarely open, is on your right, followed by **Queen Anne's Alcove**, so-called because Sir Christopher Wren designed it as a summer house for her occupation in Kensington Palace; it was moved here in the late 19C.

To the left now is a large paved courtyard with four fountains overlooked from an Italianate **summer house**, said (but unlikely) to have been designed by Prince Albert in imitation of the Petit Trianon at Versailles. The fountains are also overlooked, rather miserably, by a bronze of *Dr Edward Jenner* by W. Calder Marshall (1858); Jenner introduced vaccination against smallpox.

Go down the right-hand side of the fountain courtyard. Soon, in a dell, you discover the famous statue of *Peter Pan* by Sir George Frampton (1912), the gift of J.M. Barrie. Thought not of today's taste, either in sentiment or style, it is beautiful nevertheless.

Sir James Barrie

Barrie (1860–1937), now almost forgotten, was a literary man of great fame in the first half of the 20C, being knighted and awarded the Order of Merit. Born in poverty in Scotland, he nevertheless went to Edinburgh University and came to London chiefly to write plays. *The Admirable Crichton* (1902) and *Dear Brutus* (1927) were great successes. But his reputation rests on *Peter Pan* (1904), the play from a story he made up for the five sons of his friends, about the 'boy who would not grow up'. Barrie's brand of whimsy seems far from current fashion.

Turn right up the slope to another statue, similar in date but very different in mood; *Physical Energy* by G.F. Watts (1904) is a duplicate of the image he created for the Cecil Rhodes Monument in Cape Town. It is not at all beautiful, but extremely assertive. Behind you are good views of the **Serpentine Bridge** (1826), designed by the two sons of the great John Rennie, George and Sir John (knighted for his work on London Bridge). It is a fine structure: father would have been proud. In the foreground is the Queen's Temple, originally by William Kent (1730s), where Queen Caroline could contemplate the same view, minus bridge. Turning north you will pass the **Speke Memorial**, a mysterious gaunt obelisk marked simply 'In Memory of Speke: Victoria, Nyanza and the Nile 1864'. The explorer John Hanning Speke 'discovered' these places, including the source of the Nile itself.

Cross over the grass to the northwest corner of Kensington Gardens, crossing the Broad Walk (**Map 11,1 and 3**), where more rollerbladers have to be negotiated. There is a refreshment kiosk of modest quality and, more important, an ambitious **children's playground** (some of the play equipment inside really is only for ambitious children) dedicated to Princess Diana, and a further part of her memorial opened in 2000. Next to it is the **Elfin Oak**, a quaint ruined tree in which elves, witches, fairies, and so on, have been carved—it is rather creepy.

Go south down the Broad Walk, which was once lined with trees but is now windswept. Note the backs of houses for the seriously rich in Kensington Palace Gardens. Soon you reach the **Orangery** of Kensington Palace, where some delightful refreshments may be had, as well as the Palace itself (all fully described in Chapter 36). In front of the palace is the **Sunken Garden**, surrounded by pleached limes; it is locked but has squints through which you can look and admire. Just to the south is a fine statue of *Queen Victoria*, done by her daughter, Princess Louise (1893).

Opposite is the **Round Pond**, and south of it the bandstand. To the right, discernible through the trees, is the Albert Memorial (Chapter 35). The **Flower Walk**, which extends in both directions either side of it, is often beautifully planted, and a mass of colour and fragrance. Walk along it, returning in a north-easterly direction, to reach the **Serpentine Gallery** (**Map 12,5**), originally built as a tea-room by Henry Tanner Junior (1934). Since the 1970s this has been the location for regular exhibitions of quite radical contemporary art, and has an excellent art bookshop. It is an institution astonishingly out of character with the traditional atmosphere of Kensington Gardens, and is not to be missed. Open 10.00–18.00. Admission free. Shop. ☎ 020 7402 6075. www.serpentinegallery.org

Then re-cross West Carriage Drive to re-enter Hyde Park. Note behind you the iron gates, cast in Coalbrookdale, which originally marked the entry to the Great Exhibition of 1851 (see box, p 242) in the Crystal Palace. The great palace itself was constructed on the area of grass now in view to your right, where a bowling green and tennis courts are located.

If you managed to get past the Orangery refreshments, you may now like to visit the Park café to the left, overlooking the Serpentine. Then stay by the water, walking past the **Lido**, where swimming is possible May–Sept 10.00–18.30. The cordoned-off section of water was a socialist inspiration of the 1930s, promoting healthy exercise for all. At the end of the lake, a recent elegant urn commemorates Queen Caroline's sponsorship of this beautiful stretch of water, although, remember, she did not do it for us.

Beyond is another pleasant place for refreshments, and behind that is the **Dell**, a cascade formed from the damming of the River Westbourne and prettily planted, which you should explore. Within it is a strange upright stone, origin unknown, and outside but nearby, a Holocaust memorial. The grass area to the north is called Nannies' Lawn, and you can still see nannies sitting there, prams neatly parked and children playing nicely: some aspects of comfortable Kensington never change.

Go eastwards, finally, through the **Rose Garden**, which is wonderful in June. On the left, across the drive, is the fearsome **Cavalry memorial** by Adrian Jones

(1924) showing St George triumphant over an unusually nasty dragon. At last, you leave the Rose Garden and return to the Queen Elizabeth Gate. Hyde Park Corner station is on your right.

> ### Great Exhibition
>
> If the Festival of Britain (1951) was good but austere, and the Dome (2000) a flop, the Great Exhibition of 1851 was a staggering success. It opened in May and closed in October, having received six million visitors, many transported to London by the new railway system. Queen Victoria herself visited it over 30 times. The exhibits, from all over the world, celebrated manufacturing above all, although many were handmade or precious, including the largest pearl ever found and the Koh-i-Noor diamond. The profits from the exhibition were used to found the museums at South Kensington.
>
> As a design the iron and glass Crystal Palace was a last-minute choice, over 230 more conservative brick-based offerings having been rejected, and had to be erected in six months. The architect was Joseph Paxton, who had built the Duke of Devonshire's glass conservatory at Chatsworth in Derbyshire. At the end of the exhibition the building was taken down and re-erected at Sydenham, in south London, where it stood until destroyed by fire in 1936. Today, 'Crystal Palace' survives only in the names of the surrounding park (Chapter 52), which still shows concrete prehistoric animals from the original exhibition, and a First Division football team.

21 • Oxford Street and Regent Street

This walk can be treated as a shopping expedition covering all the main retailers in London's central West End, but you will find plenty of buildings of interest along the way.

• Distance: 2¼ miles. Time: 1 hour + as much time as you want to spend on the shops. Tube: Marble Arch. Map 5, 6.

Start at Marble Arch station, on the Central Line (**Map 5,7**). There are a multitude of exits. To see Hyde Park (Chapter 20), use Exit 10 and negotiate various nasty corridors to reach Exits 8 and 9 into Speakers' Corner. To do the Bayswater walk (Chapter 37) take Exit 12. To see Marble Arch itself, use Exit 3.

> Long before Marble Arch's arrival, and until 1783, this was the site of Tyburn gallows, where over the centuries 50,000 people were hanged. The gallows were large enough to hang 21 people at once, and until it was moved to Newgate Prison, the event always attracted large crowds.

Marble Arch is quite handsome—drawing on the Arch of Constantine in Rome—despite the pigeons fighting for space on top of the sculpted heads. It was designed by John Nash (1828) to stand in front of his new Buckingham Palace. There it stood until Edward Blore's improvements (1850–51), when it was moved to where you now see it; it was islanded in 1908. The equestrian statue of George IV which surmounted it fared better and was placed in Trafalgar Square (Chapter 11). The Arch once had a tiny police station inside.

Oxford Street

Set off down Oxford Street to the east. It is unpromising to start with, but rapidly improves.

> You are walking along a road of great antiquity which in Roman times led west to Bath and Silchester, with the northern turning (now Edgware Road) leading to St Albans. Oxford Street, under various names, has been the main route west throughout London's history, but it does not lead to Oxford; the name comes from Edward Harley, 2nd Earl of Oxford who developed the estate on the north side of the street in the 18C (Chapter 26).

At this end there are a number of major chain stores that have innumerable branches in other parts of London and elsewhere; the Oxford Street branches are not necessarily larger and there is no particular advantage in visiting them except for convenience. That is not the case with **Marks and Spencer** on the corner of Orchard Street. Opened in 1930 to designs by Trehearne and Norman, this is the largest and most variously stocked of all its branches. The chain originated when Polish emigré Michael Marks established a market stall—his 'Penny Bazaar'—in Leeds in 1884. He was joined by Thomas Spencer in the 1890s.

Across Orchard Street you reach the long and dominating façade of **Selfridge's**. The entrance to the Food Hall is here, but other entrances occur along Oxford Street, with the most spectacular at the centre. Selfridges is worth walking through, at least: it is now beautifully laid out, more comfortable than Harrod's, and has nearly as wide a range of stock at lower prices.

> Gordon Selfridge was an American who worked at the Marshall Field store in Chicago. Keen to set up on his own but reluctant to compete with his old employer, he came to Europe and brought with him to London the idea of the department store, which was already to be seen in Paris but had not been copied hitherto. Selfridge's opened in 1909 in the massive temple it still occupies today (completed 1928), behind giant Ionic columns, in a design emanating from Daniel Burnham of Chicago. The 11ft-high figure under the clock, the **Queen of Time**, is by Gilbert Bayes.

Opposite, on the south side, are more of the major chains. At the east end of Selfridges you reach Duke Street, which has some pleasant cafés and leads up to the Wallace Collection, if you feel like an injection of culture (see Chapter 24). Look out carefully, on the north side, for the tiny entrance to **St Christopher's Place**: it is easy to miss, opposite Bond Street station. Explore up here for a range of designer shops, pleasant cafés and the more humane architecture of former terraced houses now converted into commercial premises. The largely pedestrianised area stretches up to Wigmore Street.

So far the architecture of Oxford Street is pretty dreary, except for Selfridge's, but the branch of the chemist Boots near Bond Street station has a fine 19C façade. On the north side is the more obviously handsome **Stratford Place**, a small enclave of 18C houses, with, at its head, Stratford House, built by Richard Edwin in 1773. Now the Oriental Club, it was originally protected from Oxford Street by gates, of which only one pier remains with a Coade-stone lion on top. Next door, to the left, a giant HMV record store occupies premises built as the famous shoe shop of Lilley and Skinner.

You will see that Bond Street station lies in a dip in the main street. This was created by the former Tyburn stream, which rose in Hampstead, crossed the Regent's Canal by an aqueduct, and flowed past Regent's Park where it was used to fill the lake. It went on to fill the lake in St James's Park before reaching the Thames at Westminster.

Immediately after Bond Street station, bear right, away from Oxford Street, down **South Molton Street**, where William Blake lived at no. 17. It is now pedestrianised and delightful, with trendy boutiques which are more designer-orientated and more expensive than the Oxford Street chains. On the corner of Davies Street is a huge antiques supermarket called Gray's. At its foot, South Molton Street reaches Brook Street where the Handel House Museum has recently opened at no. 25 (Chapter 19).

Turn left and then right down **New Bond Street**, keeping to the right-hand side. Everything is higher quality here, the shops, the prices, and the architecture above. Opposite, *Fenwick's* puts up a fine show with its Ionic colonnade: it is a high-quality clothing and accessories store, with a restaurant and a *Carluccio*'s café in the basement; you will come back past it in a minute.

Near the Versace store, explore down the alley called Lancashire Court into **Avery Row**, recently renovated to form a most attractive little group of shops and restaurants—an object lesson in how to restore life to otherwise undistinguished back streets. Back in New Bond Street a growing number of antique shops and art dealers can be seen, including the Fine Art Society at no. 48 with rather stuffy Edwardian architecture.

There is no need to go further south than Bruton Street. On the east side is **Conduit Street**, the name of which commemorates a water supply taken from the Tyburn centuries ago by the City Corporation. Now return up New Bond Street on this side to pass a branch of *Burberry's*, whose main shop is in the Haymarket. It is still the best shop for coats. Thomas Burberry began the business at Basingstoke in 1856, moving with his sons to London. His breakthrough came with clothing requirements for the motor car, and for polar and mountaineering expeditions. The chequered lining used for the clothes has become recognisable world-wide.

Returning up Bond Street, do not miss no. 31, Fior, to see what façades here looked like before the Edwardians introduced their grandiose ideas: it is of plain, dirty stock brick and has large but simple, reassuring windows. Next you reach *Sotheby's*, the famous art and antique dealers. Founded in 1744 in Covent Garden, Sotheby's have been here only since 1917: the London sales account for about half their international revenue. ☎ 020 7293 5000.

Cross Maddox Street: on the next corner is the very elaborate F. Pinet shop and after that the music publishers Chappell's. Next come Calvin Klein and after that Fenwick's again. The northern part of New Bond Street can then be tackled from this side of the road. There are still chains here but they are much more exclusive and expensive. Among the architecture on the east side, the red-brick and stone mixture at no. 68 is particularly delicious. Enjoy the statuary of science, commerce and art above no. 70, the vigorous grapes on no. 74, and the curving Edwardian Classicism above no. 80. On the west side, note the attractive oriel windows on no. 101.

Now you have returned to Oxford Street (**Map 5,8**). To the left Marylebone Lane, an ancient street, creeps in on the north side. Further up it becomes **Marylebone High Street**, with attractive food and other shops aimed more at locals than visitors (see Chapter 24). Next to Marylebone Lane is *Debenham's*, a middle-range department store and the flagship of a bigger chain. William Debenham set up his little drapery shop in nearby Wigmore Street in 1813 but despite numerous acquisitions and mergers (absorbing Freebody, Marshall and Snelgrove and Harvey Nichols) his name lives on. On the south side are branches of smaller chains with rather dreary façades above, but note *Thornton's* chocolate shop beneath an exuberant piece of Edwardiana. Nos 335–37, though very ordinary shops, similarly have High Victorian architecture above.

Now cross the road to the north side at Vere Street. A little way up it is St Peter's (1721), a brick church by James Gibbs (described in Chapter 24). Turn right to continue along Oxford Street. Next is *D.H. Evans*, an historic name among department stores, like Debenham's, but now part of the House of Fraser group. The architecture is European by Louis Blanc (1930s), but the founder was the son of a farmer from Llanelli, Wales. D.H. Evans is still chiefly a medium-quality clothing emporium. Opposite, after New Bond Street, come the usual names. Harewood Place leads down to Hanover Square (Chapter 19).

Do not miss *John Lewis*, which is popular with English middle-class shoppers for everything a department store can provide, and very price-conscious: all their delivery vans used to proclaim 'Never knowingly undersold'. The John Lewis Partnership is an interesting and unusual organisation that has absorbed numerous other stores including Peter Jones in Sloane Square, and Waitrose supermarkets, and continues to be owned by its staff, who are all called 'partners'. John Lewis started the company in 1864, but the present building is an example of reasonably accomplished Modernism by Slater and Uren (1958–60), with a Barbara Hepworth sculpture on the east wall (1963).

After Holles Street there is a towering modern block which contains the **London College of Fashion**, and at street level various chains including a large branch of *BHS* (British Home Stores), a competitor of Marks and Spencer but with its own distinct niche. Then we reach Oxford Circus and Regent Street. This space, and Piccadilly Circus, were the key crossroads for Nash's new route to Regent's Park (Chapter 25).

Look at the four concave segments which comprise **Oxford Circus**: traffic, buses and people are everywhere, and the shops are familiar and accessible but hardly in the Bond Street class. The shape is probably what Nash intended, but three out of the four fronts are 1920s versions of Classicism: the fourth is modern. And yet it is all quite effective, busy but with style. The view to the north is brilliantly conceived with **All Souls Langham Place** both completing the vista and pointing round the corner to indicate the way ahead up Portland Place (Chapter 26). If regulation could be brought in to give some conformity to the shopfronts it would look quite sophisticated. Parisian it is not, but it does try.

There is no need to go far to the east, as Oxford Street fairly soon degenerates into cheaper, downmarket stores. Although the odd block reveals some interesting late 19C design, tat prevails, especially on the south side (in Martin Amis's novel *London Fields*, one character falls prey to those touting fake perfume here). But, on the north side, in the block preceding another large branch of HMV, are the former premises of furniture store Waring and Gillow, in amazing Hampton

Court Baroque style (1905). Opposite is a large branch of Marks and Spencer occupying the site of the **Pantheon**, the great domed assembly room that launched the career of James Wyatt in the 1770s. After many changes of fortune, fire and rebuilding, the Pantheon was demolished in 1937, when Marks and Spencer took over the site. The black granite façade is by Robert Lutyens (1938), son of Sir Edwin.

Regent Street

The areas to the south of Oxford Street are worth exploring (covered in Chapter 22) but go south, now, from Oxford Circus to enjoy Regent Street.

The name comes from the period 1811–20, when the future George IV acted as Regent during George III's final illness. He was a prime mover in the scheme to develop Regent's Park to the north (Chapter 25) and its new processional way to his own Carlton House, with links east to the Strand. In the event the southern axis was superseded by Waterloo Place (Chapter 18). John Nash was the presiding genius for the whole concept.

Regent Street was based on Parisian precedents, such as the Rue de Rivoli laid out under Napoleon, but was entirely English in its sinuous shape, reflecting the aesthetic principle of the picturesque. It made use of the existing Portland Place by Robert and James Adam in the north, but employed curves and bends to link its way from these via Oxford Street down to Piccadilly Circus southwards. The original shops were located in a series of individually designed blocks, with a great colonnade, the Quadrant, curving into Piccadilly Circus. The shops were rebuilt from about 1900 to the 1920s, but the shape survives and so does much of the grandeur.

As you go down the gentle descent, ***Dickins and Jones*** is on your left; this is another House of Fraser store in a building by Sir Henry Tanner (1920s), architect of the Oxford Circus 'corners'. Dickins and Jones have been occupants of this site from the construction of the original Regent Street. Across Great Marlborough Street, you can see and enter the Disney-esque half-timbered frontage of ***Liberty's***. The timber-framed northern façade of the store and the wood-panelled area of the interior were constructed in 1925 out of two wrecked ships, enhanced by Liberty's own craftsmen. Go through the store via the bridge over Kingly Street, and you find yourself in an oriental-classical world. But also look up at the third-floor exterior overlooking Regent Street, where a bizarre but vigorous collection of sculptures, including a camel, elephant and Britannia herself, occupy themselves energetically on top of a concave colonnade. The effect is startling if, on the whole, repellent. The architects of both parts were the brothers E.T. and E.S. Hall—proto Postmodernists.

It is difficult to overestimate the influence of this shop on English taste. Arthur Lasenby Liberty opened his own shop after the 1862 Exhibition, having already become an expert on oriental shawls and other imported goods. Besides being a prominent member of the Arts and Crafts movement, he also showed great commercial enterprise, buying up adjacent properties in Regent Street and pioneering the commercial success of William Morris and related fabrics and artefacts. It is to be hoped that this eclectic mixture, always in perfect taste unlike the shockingly tasteless architecture of the shop itself, will be maintained today, as Liberty's has recently been sold out of family control.

On the west side of Regent Street all is quieter and duller, including the shops, although some are under a handsome symmetrical façade. It is more interesting to stay on the eastern side to reach *Hamley's*, one of the world's great toy shops, originally opened by William Hamley in Holborn in 1760 as 'Noah's Ark'. Inventors of games came first to Mr Hamley with their ideas: one idea was called Cossima—not an easy brand to market, it was felt—so it was re-named Ping-Pong. A few doors down, trying to compete, is a Warner Bros. store.

After Tenison Court, jewellers Mappin and Webb appears under attractive Art Nouveau detail. There are useful facilities in the British Airways Travel Office further down.

Now we reach the **Quadrant**, still an exciting architectural experience, although now more overpowering than Nash ever intended, with the back of the ultra-dominant *Meridien Hotel* by Norman Shaw (1905–8) on the south side blocking the light. Even so, it is a beautiful sweep of alternating colonnades and arched spaces, not quite symmetrical, but of such prodigious length that you do not notice. In the middle, at no. 69, is the *Café Royal*, which first opened here in 1876. Its long list of distinguished patrons before its rebuilding in the 1920s included Oscar Wilde, Max Beerbohm, James Whistler and the future king Edward VIII.

Opposite, on the convex side, are *Aquascutum* (like Burberry's, makers of high-class coats) and several smaller but high-quality outlets in the Quadrant Arcade. You may notice that **Air Street**, a survivor from the street layout preceding Regent Street's construction in the 1820s, still runs across from an arch in the Norman Shaw building, and slips away on the other side of the road through a matching arch, part of the Café Royal.

Finally, walk to Piccadilly Circus. On the left is a 1920s version of Nash's County Fire Office, designed to close the vista to the south, which it still does. Opposite, Tower Records is in the building created for Swan and Edgar, a once-famous store. As described elsewhere (Chapter 18) Piccadilly Circus is a pretty dreadful place, but *Lillywhite's*, an excellent sports store on the south side, is worth visiting.

After this journey it is hard to imagine that you have any credit left on your cards, so perhaps it is best to slip silently away down one of the entrances to Piccadilly Circus station.

22 • Soho

Characterised by its many bars, restaurants and cafés, the centre of gay, media and sex-shop London, Soho is a distinct and identifiable entity, dense and enclosed, so that you are aware when you have left it. The Victorians could not grasp this point and drove Charing Cross Road and Shaftesbury Avenue straight through the middle—perhaps deliberately, to break up slum areas. But Soho's boundaries are wider than these two thoroughfares, and our zig-zag walk goes east to cover St Giles and Seven Dials.

• Distance: 1½ miles, plus twists and turns. Time: 1 hour. Tube: Oxford Circus or Tottenham Court Road. Map 6.

The origin of the name is said to be a hunting-cry, 'So-ho': if this sounds far-fetched in the present surroundings, remember how much London land was acquired by Henry VIII at the Dissolution of the Monasteries for his own pleasures, not least of which was hunting. These fields north of Whitehall Palace must have been ideally placed for such excursions.

We start from Oxford Circus station (**Map 6,7**) and immediately turn down **Argyll Street**. On your right is the *Argyll Arms*, a real Victorian pub and perhaps a good place to get into the Soho mood. This street was once the location of Argyll House, the 3rd Duke of Argyll's London property, built in 1735. It was replaced by the **London Palladium**, a theatre designed by Frank Matcham (1910); its Corinthian portico makes it the most handsome building in sight. The American writer Washington Irving lived next door when in London. Nearby, in Little Argyll Street, stood the Argyll Rooms, extremely fashionable among Regency beaux and later the place for concerts at which Franz Liszt Carl Weber and Felix Mendelssohn all independently played. Now the site is covered by the Dickins and Jones store (see Chapter 21).

At **Great Marlborough Street** turn left—note Liberty's opposite, and on your left an Art Deco monster by distinguished American architect Raymond Hood (1928), in black with gold along the skyline. You might prefer the well-proportioned ex-magistrates' court next door, designed by J.D. Butler (1913). Immediately turn right into **Carnaby Street**, shrine to 1960s fashion. It was pedestrianised then and still has character, with interesting little streets either side and many charming examples of how the original houses looked. At Broadwick Street, on the left, is a giant mural. At the end is Beak Street (where Canaletto lodged 1749–51); turn right and left down Upper John Street to reach **Golden Square**.

This is quite a tiny space by the standards of London squares, developed first in 1668, when Soho became fashionable partly through an influx of the homeless middle class seeking new property outside the City after the Great Fire. It was very respectable for a time and members of the nobility lived here, including the Duke of Chandos, Viscount Bolingbroke and Charles II's mistress, the Duchess of Cleveland. Gradually the centre of fashion moved further west and by the 18C it was occupied by embassies and artists such as Angelica Kauffmann, the first female member of the Royal Academy, who lived at no. 16. In Charles Dickens's *Nicholas Nickleby* the villainous Ralph lives here.

Nos 21 and 24, although somewhat altered, give an idea of what the square looked like originally. The boring gardens include a statue of *George II* by John Nost (or Van Ost, 1731), erected here by the Duke of Chandos in 1753.

Continue past booksellers *Bernard Quaritch* and turn left down **Brewer Street**, named after breweries that once stood on the north side. The street still has much character, but little interesting architecture. Turn right into **Great Windmill Street**. There have been no windmills here since the 17C but note Soho Parish School on the left in pretty yellow stock brick. Further on the left, still with its sign outside, is the former **Windmill Theatre**, built as a cinema but more famous for its risqué revues.

In the 1930s these ran non-stop from 14.30 until midnight. A certain type would stay here hour after hour. The show went on all through the Second World War, the Windmill being the only London theatre to be open continuously, leading to the proud claim and advertising slogan 'We never closed'. It was a predecessor to the current Comedy Store, and many comedians cut their teeth there, including Jimmy Edwards and Tony Hancock.

Beyond it, on the same side of the road, is a dreary crimson, five-bay façade, now the side of the **Lyric Theatre** but formerly the front of the house of Dr William Hunter, distinguished Scottish physician, who practised as a surgeon in London and lectured on anatomy here. The residence included a museum, library, lecture theatre and dissecting rooms designed by Robert Mylne (1766).

Cross Shaftesbury Avenue, to which you will return, and go down a grim arcade to turn left into Coventry Street. You are following the outside walls of the **Trocadero**, an entertainment centre which has been on this site since 1851. It has gone through various permutations, from a notorious dance hall, to a music hall, to J. Lyons's premier Corner House restaurant, to what it is now, with low-quality, pompous Edwardian architecture and tacky shops.

Keep going east into Leicester Square, past what was the Swiss Centre, an outrageous 1960s' original with a remarkable clock, now in terminal decay. On the left up Leicester Street, note the delicate Dutch façade of the former hospital, now a pub.

Leicester Square

Love it or hate it, this space is one of the most historic London squares (**Map 6,8**).

The gardens of Leicester House—built by Robert Sidney, 2nd Earl of Leicester (1631–45)—were developed as a public square in the 1670s. In the 18C the place was very famous and fashionable, with artists such as William Hogarth and Sir Joshua Reynolds and many aristocratic families among its occupants. The gardens were formal and correct. In the 19C there was a period of decline and although important theatres and places of entertainment were built around the edge, the gardens fell into disuse and the whole area took on the *demi-monde* air of the rest of Soho to the north. The extraordinary 'Baron' Grant, an MP who had made a fortune by dubious means, restored it to some kind of order in the 1870s and commissioned the central Shakespeare fountain and busts of former residents Hogarth, Reynolds (see box, p 250), Hunter and Sir Isaac Newton (who in fact lived nearby), which can still be seen at the four corners.

Sadly, today Leicester Square is rather a mess—although free of traffic and with a pleasant but very crowded garden, it is surrounded by uninspired buildings. Occasionally there is a lively funfair, and there are often street performers. The cinemas here are important for their size and the film premières they host. Some, including the *Empire* (1884), were once historic theatres; others, like the *Prince Charles*, put on interesting programmes. Like Covent Garden it is another site of transformation, far less successful at present but containing the possibility of a future miracle.

Go along the north side: you will see at the end of Cranbourn Street the spectacular Hippodrome, with horse and rider aloft, another former theatre by Frank Matcham. It is now a club. Turn left before it up Leicester Place. On the right is the modern, highly original, though not altogether likeable church of **Notre**

Dame de France by Hector Corfiato (rebuilt 1955), with a glass dome and stickily sentimental altarpiece, but good stone carvings outside and murals by Jean Cocteau in the Lady Chapel. It is the French Roman Catholic cathedral. At the top note the street name, 'New Lisle Streeet MDCCXCI', proudly proclaimed in an original pedimented vista. ('Lisle' was a family name of the Earls of Leicester.)

Sir Joshua Reynolds

Reynolds (1723–92) came to London from Devon in 1740 and, apart from travels in Italy and Holland, never left. He was responsible for the development of painting as a profession and became the first president of the Royal Academy when it was established in 1768. The series of learned discourses he gave to its members over the next 20 years established the principle of combining contemporary observation with a learned study of the antique. His huge output of portraits illustrates his practice of this ideology, but his disdain of passing fads induced many more fashion-conscious sitters to prefer to have their likeness taken by Thomas Gainsborough (Chapter 18).

Turn right. You are now unmistakably in London's Chinese quarter (**Map 6,8**) Go to the end and turn left, and left again to enter **Gerrard Street**, originally a project by the 17C developer Nicholas Barbon. Aristocrats once lived here, then came coffee houses and taverns, then artists (George Morland, John Sell Cotman and later small hotels and restaurants. In the 1950s—Soho's heyday, many would argue—the street was all coffee bars and 'night clubs' charging exorbitant prices

Now it teems with new life as the main street of **Chinatown**, with remarkable archways in Gerrard Place and in Macclesfield Street, and telephone boxes with pagoda roofs: only the 1936 Post Office building jars. There are several surviving 18C houses and an unbelievable selection of Chinese restaurants. Exit at the western end into Wardour Street and turn right, again crossing Shaftesbury Avenue

Shaftesbury Avenue, named after the great philanthropist commemorated by 'Eros' at Piccadilly Circus, was cut through in 1877–86, partly to improve traffic flow and partly to improve the quality of housing in an area of appalling slums. It was perhaps not so destructive of Soho as this sounds, as, like Charing Cross Road (a similar contemporary improvement) it followed the lines of certain existing streets. The avenue immediately became '**Theatreland**' and between 1888 and 1907 the Globe (renamed the Gielgud in 1996), Lyric, Apollo, the original Shaftesbury (bombed) and Queen's theatres all opened here, as did the Palace at Cambridge Circus. Although architecturally undistinguished the picturesquely curving street always seems a vibrant place. The architecture of the Apollo, with spectacular female figures at attic level, raises eyebrows.

Continue up **Wardour Street**, traditionally associated with furniture-making but with a modern role as a centre for film production companies. On the right is all that remains of the church of **St Anne**, a building by Sir Christopher Wren long-ruined but retaining a remarkable yellow-brick tower by S.P. Cockerell (1802–6)—with a strange, bulbous lead top stage to house the clock—and pleasant garden all around. The **Intrepid Fox** pub was allegedly named by its owner in 1784 as a gesture of support for Charles James Fox in the elections that year. Cross Old Compton Street, a centre for social life among gay Londoners.

Note **Meard Street** on the right, according to Pevsner 'the most rewarding of all Soho streets', referring to the well-preserved early 18C houses on the south side. Turn left into Peter Street and immediately right into **Berwick Street** enjoy the street market, held here since the 18C (not Sundays), when local shop-keepers began moving their counters out on to the pavement.

Turn right at **Broadwick Street**, where William Blake was born at what is now no. 74, and cross east again via St Anne's Court to **Dean Street**, which also has several fine 18C houses. The best are to the south—it is worth going to see nos 67 and 68, with original porches, nos 78 and 79, and above all the unique Rococo shop front at no. 88. Karl Marx and his family lived in great poverty at no. 28 in the 1850s: three of Marx's children died here. In the 1950s the Colony Club at no. 41 was frequented by London artists including Francis Bacon, Lucian Freud and Frank Auerbach. The members-only Groucho Club at no. 44 is a rela-tively recent but now famous haunt for those in the media and arts. During the Second World War the *French House* pub at no. 49 became the headquarters of the Free French and has souvenirs of famous Frenchmen on the walls. Nearby, in Frith Street, is *Ronnie Scott's*, a jazz club. At the northern end of Dean Street, take the right turn into Carlisle Street to reach **Soho Square**.

This square, the first part of the area to be developed, was laid out in 1680 on land which by then belonged to the Duke of Monmouth, Charles II's most prominent illegitimate son. His house lay on the south side. None of the orig-inal houses remain, and with its heavy trees the space can seem somewhat claustrophobic, but in the garden a contemporary statue of *Charles II* by Caius Gabriel Cibber (1681) reminds us of past associations. (Ignore, if you can, the weird half-timbered summerhouse in the centre.)

The buildings around the square include several of interest. Note the **French Protestant Church** in the northwest corner, built to look like offices but very much of its period (1893), as is demonstrated by the quantity of terracotta. Inside it is more churchy but still distinctive. It is an early work of Sir Aston Webb, who went on to design Admiralty Arch and the front of Buckingham Palace. The French Protestant Church was originally in the City but Soho is a more appropriate place, as it was for centuries a favourite location for Huguenot émigrés and other Continental groups. On the east side is the church of **St Patrick**, very Italian inside and out, of the same date. It was built on the site of Carlisle House, an important assembly room in the 18C. Just to the south is no. 1 Greek Street, the **House of St Barnabas**, a near perfect building of 1750. It is open occasionally for tours; see the notice in the window or ☎ 020 7437 1894.

Leave the square down **Greek Street** at the southeast corner. The *Pillars of Hercules* is a fake timber-framed pub, with more of the same at the *Three Greyhounds* further south. The famous pub, however, is at no. 29: the *Coach and Horses* was favoured in 1950s Soho by Bacon (see box, p 252), writer Daniel Farson and their circle, and still has the same ambience.

At Moor Street, fork left into **Cambridge Circus** (Map 6,8), a true circus unlike Piccadilly, and named not as a counterpart of Oxford Circus but because it was opened by the Duke of Cambridge in 1887. The **Palace Theatre** by Collcutt and Holloway (1888), a curved red terracotta triple-decker, glows over the scene.

Charing Cross Road stretches north and south, and now is the moment to decide if you want to explore its bookshops. The street was laid out at the same time as Shaftesbury Avenue, and with the same objectives: there is some dreary charitable housing for the working class just south of the circus. Turn left for the big chain bookstores, and the unique *Foyle's*, which has been here since 1913. The bookshops to the south are more specialist, including **Zwemmer's** (art), **Collet's** (left-wing), and several second-hand dealers. At no. 84 used to stand Marks and Company, immortalised in Hélène Hanff's *84 Charing Cross Road*.

> ### *Francis Bacon*
> The most notable British artist of the 20C, Bacon (1909–92) was a shocking and alarming personality whose art, once seen, is unmistakable and impossible to forget. He was born in Ireland and was entirely self-taught, beginning his career in the 1930s as an interior designer. His best period seems to have been the 1950s and 60s and arguably the staggering promise of those decades was never fulfilled. His work can be seen in Tate Modern. Somehow the atmosphere of Soho gives the sensational drinking, sexual and gambling exploits of his heyday some sort of permanent life.

Go east from Cambridge Circus down Earlham Street (**Map 7,7**). On the right, in Tower Street, is an ambitious early London Board School (1874), now offices. Soon you reach **Seven Dials**. This odd road junction dates back to the late 17C and was the centre of an estate laid out by Thomas Neale, Master of the Mint, who hoped to compete with Soho and Covent Garden. The area was never as fashionable as its rivals and by the 19C was a terrible slum: even today it lacks the buzz of either neighbouring district, but there are fascinating little courts and alleys all around to explore, and the pleasing Art Deco **Cambridge Theatre**.

Proceed north up **Monmouth Street** to St Giles High Street where much traffic appears. The Shaftesbury Theatre (1920s) is on your right. Turn left to see **St Giles-in-the-Fields**, a fine Palladian structure by Henry Flitcroft (1733), Lord Burlington's favourite architect. The relief carving on the gate dates to 1687.

> The foundation is extremely ancient, dating back to 1101, when Queen Matilda (wife of Henry I) established a leper colony in these remote fields, well away from the city walls. St Giles was the patron saint of the homeless and underprivileged. Ironically it was in this parish that the great plague of 1665 started, and the number of burials in the former churchyard was excessive. Quite apart from the great bulge in the records in 1665, the burial register includes some most interesting names, including poet Andrew Marvell, painter Sir Godfrey Kneller and architect Sir John Soane. In the 19C the area round about, known as the Rookery, was one of the most feared slums of all.

Continue down St Giles High Street to Tottenham Court Road station (**Map 6,6**). There are two interesting modern phenomena to note before we finish: the tower block and the station itself. **Centre Point** by Richard Seifert and Partner (1963–67), with 36 storeys but actually quite restricted in floor space, was hated for the first 30 years of its life because the public did not like Modernism and because it was left empty by the developers for years for economic reasons. What looked like a white elephant has today become an admired structure, and is listed for conservation.

Finally you enter **Tottenham Court Road station**. Squashed and pushy, it is one of the Underground's busiest. The claustrophobic effect is enhanced to the point of neurosis by Sir Eduardo Paolozzi's mosaics, installed in the 1980s. But is a fittingly jazzy end to a walk in Soho.

Sir Eduardo Paolozzi

The work of Scottish artist Paolozzi (b. 1924) is visible in various key locations in London—his Blake/Newton figure in the forecourt of the British Library (see the cover of this Guide), an office at the top of Chancery Lane, and the mosaics in Tottenham Court Road station. Paolozzi's is an easily identified personal style relying on blocky, fractured representations of human figures of robotic types or on abstract designs for a machine age.

---

23 • Holborn

It must be admitted at the outset that there is nothing special about Holborn as such. The attractions of this walk are the places, including a variety of churches, you see as you go and, near the end, one of London's most secret and special museums. There are also several good pubs to visit along the way.

- Distance: 3 miles. Time: 1½ hours + 1½ hours for the museums.
  Tube: Tottenham Court Road. Map 6–8.

Start at Tottenham Court Road station (**Map 6,6**), described at the end of Chapter 22. Take Exit 3 and set off east along **New Oxford Street**. Centre Point is on your right. The street, never very attractive, was laid out in 1847 to connect Oxford Street with Holborn, bypassing the notorious slums in St Giles to the south.

At Dyott Street (no name is visible—look out for Jacob's camera shop), turn left. Just ahead of you, on the corner of Streatham Street, is **Parnell House**, a historic building by Henry Roberts (1849) proudly inscribed 'Model Houses for Families'. It represents one of the first Victorian attempts to provide housing for the poor of the area, but only the 'deserving poor', under a charitable foundation succinctly named the Society for Improving the Condition of the Labouring Classes. The architect became a pioneering specialist in working-class housing. It is now cleaned up and enclosed.

Beyond, on the left, is an equally innovative modern building, **Congress House** (1953–57), the Trades Union Congress (TUC) headquarters designed by David Aberdeen in 1948, before even the Festival Hall was built. Through the glass you may be able to see Jacob Epstein's war memorial of 1955, in the form of a pietà, against a huge blue mosaic slab. Go to the right along Great Russell Street (**Map 7,5**), over busy Bloomsbury Street: *Unsworth's* is an interesting bookshop. Cross Coptic Street, noting the pretty dairy, now *Pizza Express*, and turn right into Museum Street. The British Museum is just to your left: if you have time to spend an hour or so there (admission is free), you could consult the list of highlights in Chapter 27, but it is better to spend a day there. Museum Street has some interesting but expensive second-hand bookshops. Turn left into Bloomsbury Way.

On your left is a treat, the church of **St George Bloomsbury** by Nicholas Hawksmoor (1716–31), typically compelling and absorbing (**Map 7,5**). This was one of the earliest porticoed churches in London (St George Hanover Square was the very first), and one of the most grandiose. Virtually separated from it is the equally eye-catching tower at the west end. You need to crane your neck to see the upper section, a remodelling of the mausoleum of Halicarnassus as described by Pliny—Hawksmoor was something of an archaeologist—surmounted by a statue of George I, on whose head pigeons frequently land. Inside, the altar is placed on the north side opposite the portico entrance, but in Hawksmoor's day it had to be in the east. The original layout of the church was designed to accommodate this, as the location of the paired columns confirms. The peeling paint is part of the church's gloomy appeal. ☎ 020 7405 3044.

Continue along Bloomsbury Way to **Bloomsbury Square**, now very disappointing, with terrible 1970s planting covering an underground car park, but also a fine bronze of *Charles James Fox* by Richard Westmacott (1816). Once the height of fashion, the square was developed by the 4th Earl of Southampton in the 1660s as the centrepiece of his new housing estate, in the early days of the genre, with detached houses built by individual lessees served by various trades in the smaller streets round about. It was known as the 'little Towne' and was much visited by tourists of the day. Southampton Place, to the south, contains later, elegant Palladian terraces by Henry Flitcroft (1750s). **Sicilian Avenue**, a little way further to the southeast, is a pretty invention (1905).

Walk through Bloomsbury Square to the north side. On the northwest corner is John Nash's first work in London, an imposing house in his Regent's Park style but done 50 years earlier, in 1777. It is marked 'The Pharmaceutical Society of Great Britain' in large confident lettering, although no longer having that purpose. Look up **Bedford Place** to the north. This is typical of James Burton's dignified Bloomsbury terraces (1820s), which the Victorians found so tedious. You may agree. Burton, oddly enough, was later to be Nash's main building contractor. (Bloomsbury proper is explored in Chapter 27.)

Walk east along Bloomsbury Place into Southampton Row, a busy street of traffic and hotels (**Map 7,3**). Note, on your right, the former Liverpool Victoria Insurance building, 'fascist' architecture of the 1920s, but in its alarming way quite impressive (now being refurbished). Cross Southampton Row and walk north, turning right into Cosmo Place, which can be hard to spot. You soon reach **Queen Square** (1708–20), named after Queen Anne and once very fashionable. The novelist and diarist Fanny Burney lived here and admired the then open aspect to the north, where she could see 'the delightful prospect of Hampstead and Highgate'. None of the original houses survives, although the church of St George the Martyr on your right, with a silly spire, was part of the original scheme, even if later Victorianised, and there are two good 18C houses on the south side, nos 42–43. William Morris lived and worked at no. 26 (1865–81): the Art Workers' Guild he helped to found in 1884 is now at no. 6. The square is full of medical buildings, and as you proceed east you enter a now famous 'medical' street, Great Ormond Street. Note on the right Barbon Close, named after the original developer.

Nicholas Barbon

The son of Praisegod Barbon, or Barebone, an eminent Puritan MP during the Commonwealth, Barbon (*c* 1640–98) trained as a doctor in Holland, returning to London in 1669. He never practised medicine but became famous, and widely feared, as the most enterprising and assertive building developer London has ever seen. He also laid the basis for fire insurance as we have come to know it, and was the author of economic tracts. As a businessman he was highly dangerous, convincing but untrustworthy. His developments in London included Red Lion Square, Bedford Row, New Court in the Temple, and the sites of Essex House and York House, off the Strand.

On the left is the internationally famous **Great Ormond Street Hospital for Sick Children**. The buildings are mostly modern, although it was founded in 1851 as the first children's hospital in Britain, nearly 200 years after the first in Paris. Author J.M. Barrie gifted copyright of his play *Peter Pan* to this hospital. Go on to find St Christopher's Chapel on the ground floor, with a sensational Byzantine interior by E.M. Barry (1876). In 1992 it was moved, literally, boxed up and slid on runners, to its present position. It has little pews for the intended occupants. Take a look at the notes in the Intercession Book.

After the hospital you reach a crossroads with **Lamb's Conduit Street**. Turn right, but first look to the left to see, or even visit, an authentic Victorian pub, the *Lamb*, with original brass-rails and snob-screens (so that you can drink in the private bar without being seen by nosey-parkers in the public bar). The conduit was made by diverting a tributary to the River Fleet in 1577, on the initiative of William Lamb. There is no sign of it now, except for a statue of a water-carrier at the northern end. The street is very pleasant and lively, with attractive 19C shop fronts and one or two interesting shops, a rarity in this area. There are some good 18C houses in Dombey Street on the right.

When you reach Theobald's Road, cross into Red Lion Street and take an immediate right fork down Lamb's Conduit Passage to look at **Red Lion Square**. (Another good pub, the *Dolphin*, is on the left-hand corner of the passage.) Red Lion Square was laid out in 1684 by Barbon. His builders had to fight with lawyers from Gray's Inn who wanted their fields to remain open but, typically, Barbon kept going and won. None of his houses remains. A plaque commemorates John Harrison, inventor of the chronometer, who lived and died here (see his amazing clocks at Greenwich, Chapter 49); another notes the residence at no. 17 of Pre-Raphaelites Dante Gabriel Rossetti and Edward Burne-Jones. After all the churches this guide has pointed out, you may find it refreshing to see in the northeast corner **Conway Hall** (1929), headquarters of the South Place Ethical Society, a humanist organisation founded in 1839. It holds occasional chamber concerts April–Oct on Sun. ☎ 020 7242 8032.

Turn left into Princeton Street and walk east until you reach **Bedford Row**. Here at last we can see some of Barbon's houses still *in situ*, and the others, which are later and restored, are equally handsome in this wide and civilised street (Map 7, **4 and 6**). Barbon's houses have windows flush with the wall, a practice forbidden by early 18C fire codes, which demanded a recess: they are nos 42, 43 and perhaps 36. The brass name plates on many of the doors reveal we are venturing into barrister country.

Walk north to Theobald's Road, turn right and walk until you reach the open space of **Gray's Inn**—enter the gardens on the right, via Jockey's Fields. Open in summer 12.30–14.00 Mon–Fri. This is the most northerly of the Inns of Court (see Chapter 9), and the least famous, although it ranks equally with the other three. It was much bomb-damaged but was sensitively restored by Sir Edward Maufe, architect of Guildford Cathedral and in London of St Columba's (Chapter 16).

The gardens are known as the Walks. The 16C philosopher and statesman Francis Bacon, treasurer of the Inn, laid them out in the early 16C, at the same time as extensive rebuilding. It was Bacon who argued, 'When Ages grow to Civilitie and Elegance, men come to Build stately, sooner than to Garden Finely: as if Gardening were the Greater Perfection.'

The point is not demonstrated in this somewhat windswept space, but you see it at less than its best: it was once popular as a place for promenading, and as a convenient location for duels. The very plain terraces of barristers' chambers either side were built in the early 19C.

At the south end lies Field Court, where you turn left through a passage into **Gray's Inn Square**, similar in scale, purpose and date to New Square at Lincoln's Inn, but less warm. Briefly turn right into South Square: there is a bronze statue of *Francis Bacon* by F.W. Pomeroy (1912) in the garden. Most of the building here is postwar, by Maufe, although there is one house dated 1759. The Common Room, tucked away on the right as you enter, is interesting as the last work of Raymond Erith (1970–72), a Neo-Georgian architect whose reputation has since grown.

Back in Gray's Inn Square on the right is the Hall of the Inn, scene of many notable events, including the first performance of Shakespeare's *Comedy of Errors* in 1594. It is not usually open, but you can peer through the coats of arms in the windows. Beyond it lies the chapel, rebuilt in 1689 and much restored since, simple and austere but with fine late-Victorian stained-glass windows. Open 10.00–18.00 Mon–Fri.

Leave Gray's Inn through the passageway to the east, marked 'Out'. Cross Gray's Inn Road, turn right past the Geographers' A–Z shop and go down Brooke's Court on the left, where you reach **St Alban the Martyr**. This was originally a church by William Butterfield (1856–62) to be considered in the same bracket as the unforgettable All Saints Margaret Street (Chapter 26), but bomb damage saw to most of it, except for the tower and clergy house (1858–63), which still exhibit the crushing Butterfield manner. The interior by Adrian Scott (1960) is worth seeing—light, fresh and un-Butterfield though it is. There is a major mural by Hans Feinbusch (1966) over the altar.

From the church, turn left down Dorrington Street to reach Leather Lane (**Map 8,3**), where there is a street market on weekday mornings. Turn right and then left into Greville Street, across **Hatton Garden**, centre of the diamond trade. The erstwhile garden belonged to Sir Christopher Hatton, Elizabeth I's favourite chancellor. Go on part way down the hill towards the valley of the former river Fleet and turn right into Bleeding Heart Yard, commemorated for ever in Charles Dickens's *Little Dorrit*.

Return to Hatton Garden, turn left and at Holborn Circus left again, and then left again, to reach Ely Place (**Map 8,4**), historic site of the Bishop of Ely's London house from the 13C until 1772, with an important surviving Roman Catholic church, the former 13C chapel of the house. This is **St Etheldreda**: the saint was a 7C Abbess of Ely, one of whose hands is allegedly retained inside the chapel as a relic. The building has two storeys—as 13C private chapels often did (compare St Stephen's in the Palace of Westminster and the Ste-Chapelle in Paris), the main one above, with important windows unblocked during a restoration in 1874. There is brilliant glass by Joseph E. Nuttgens (1952) in the east window and fibreglass statues of English martyrs (1962–64). ☎ 020 7405 1061.

At the foot of Ely Place is **Holborn Circus**, cut out as a traffic roundabout in 1872 around an equestrian statue by Charles Bacon (1874) of *Prince Albert* cheerily raising his hat to us passers-by. To the east is Holborn Viaduct, part of the same traffic improvement scheme, crossing over the Fleet valley. Opposite is a Wren church—never miss one of these.

Although it feels a long way from the City, **St Andrew** was the largest of all Sir Christopher Wren's City churches. That he rebuilt it (1684) was due not to fire damage but because it was falling down. He kept the 15C tower but refaced it (1703): some see the hand of Hawksmoor in the design. There are statues of children from the former parish school on the exterior. The site had plenty of room and it was therefore no problem to create a symmetrical seven-bay church, with vestibules either side of the tower, all on the apparently standardised pattern of St James Piccadilly or St Clement Dane. Without the odd sites left by the Great Fire, you feel, Wren's work might have become a little stereotyped.

Go back west, across Holborn Circus: there is a curvaceous new block by Norman Foster on the corner (2000); and opposite, on the north side of High Holborn, the red-brick and terracotta Gothic of the former **Prudential Assurance building**. The early part is 1879 and architect Alfred Waterhouse (of the Natural History Museum) kept faith with Gothic for the later work of 1899–1906. You can walk into Waterhouse Square, opened up as public space in a 1990 restoration, with a large flowing bronze war memorial by F.W. Blundestone (1922). As you come back to Holborn peep through the windows either side to see the amazing tile patterns of the former offices. The building stands on the site of Furnival's Inn, one of the Inns of Chancery (Chapter 8), where the young Dickens lived and began to write *Pickwick Papers*.

On the south side of the road, at Chancery Lane station, your eye is certain to be caught by an extraordinary survival, the timber-framed exterior of **Staple Inn** (1586). Pre-Fire London was full of exactly this kind of housing, but now you have to go far into the country—to Chester, Stratford or Ludlow—to find anything like it. Nor can this example be given a certificate of authenticity, having been heavily rebuilt more than once, most recently after bombing in World War II. Like Furnival's Inn, Staple Inn was an Inn of Chancery. It is worth going through into the pleasant courtyard (**Map 7,6**). The rebuilt hall of the Inn on the right houses the Institute of Actuaries. Continue through to Chancery Lane and turn right, back to High Holborn. Opposite on the right is a recommended pub, the *Cittie of Yorke*, with a bar of prodigious length.

Turn left (west) and soon left again into the alley of Great Turnstile, which takes you into **Lincoln's Inn Fields**. (This is separate from Lincoln's Inn, described in Chapter 9.) Before you leave High Holborn, note on the other side of the road an impressive new office block, Mid City Place, by Kohn Pedersen Fox (2001), with yet another curvy top. Then, as you enter the square, note *Camdonian*, a sheer iron shape by Barry Flanagan (1980). Turn right and go along the north side to reach Sir John Soane's Museum.

Sir John Soane's Museum

The museum is exactly as Soane left it when he died in 1837 and is therefore remarkable not only for its contents but also for its own antiquity. It may look closed but is definitely open at the times stated. If necessary, knock/ring at no. 13.

• Open 10.00–17.00 Tues–Sat; also 18.00–21.00 first Tues in the month. Admission free. Guided tours 14.30 Sat (for a small charge). ☎ 020 7405 2107. www.soane.org.uk. Tube: Holborn.

Soane bought no. 12 Lincoln's Inn Fields in 1792 as a family home, with an office at the back, and lived there when in London. (He also maintained a country house at Pitshanger Manor in Ealing.) In 1813, he bought no. 13 next door, converting that into a home and museum to house his collection, which he opened to the public and finally left to the nation. Later he also acquired no. 14, into which the museum was extended.

Sir John Soane

Soane (1753–1837) was in some ways Britain's most unusual and radical architect, and his house and collection at Lincoln's Inn Fields survive to prove it. The son of a Reading builder, he trained under George Dance the Younger and Henry Holland, winning a scholarship to Rome. This auspicious beginning was fulfilled with his appointment as architect at the Bank of England, leading in turn to his masterpiece, the single storey, top-lit Bank, extending its severe and idiosyncratic brand of Classicism over a site so huge that it could not hope to survive in the competitive world of 20C commercial land values. You can still see the outside wall (Chapter 1). Elsewhere in London, besides Lincoln's Inn Fields, Soane's work can still be admired at Dulwich Picture Gallery (Chapter 52), or at Pitshanger Manor, Ealing (Chapter 60).

We follow the route Soane advised. It is worth going slowly, as although the place is small, it is densely filled and quite disorientating. Right, off the hall of no. 13, you enter the **Dining Room**, lit from a small court on the left, opening up into the **Library** to the front of the house. The Soanes used these rooms for entertaining. Mirrors are used to expand the sense of space. Above the fireplace is a fine portrait of *Sir John Soane* by Sir Thomas Lawrence (1828).

You then go through two tiny rooms—a study and dressing room—into the corridor, a tall narrow space lit through a yellow-glass skylight and filled with marbles and casts acquired by Soane over the years. He threw nothing away, and often bought extra antiquities when they came on the market. You are now in the filled-in courtyard of house no. 14, which enabled the **Picture Room** to the right to be lit from above. Here Soane could display William Hogarth's *Rake's Progress* (1733) and *The Election* (1754), the original paintings from which engravings were made. Behind the door is a portrait of Mrs Soane, with a sad expression. The walls of the Picture Room can be opened out to display further items from the collection.

Leaving the Picture Room, turn right and descend to the basement. On the left, under the Picture Room, is the so-called **Monk's Parlour**, with a grave visible in the remaining yard outside. Soane called this the grave of Padre Giovanni, but in the shrine are actually the remains of Mrs Soane's dog Fanny. This elaborate joke was intended to amuse Soane's many guests and other visitors to his museum. Laughter fades as you explore the **Crypt**, spreading through the courtyards of nos 13 and 12. Here are numerous memorials to the more important dead, including the sarcophagus of Pharaoh Seti I (d. 1279 BC), one of the most important Egyptian antiquities ever discovered, bought by Soane in 1824 after the British Museum had turned it down. The words on the model of Soane's tomb for his wife, who died in 1815 and was buried in Old St Pancras churchyard (Chapter 40), are extremely moving.

Return up the narrow stairs to the Colonnade and Dome. Here are countless further Classical remains, many regrettably unlabelled, all under the watchful eye of a bust of Soane by Sir Francis Chantrey (1829). You then find yourself in the **New Picture Room**, built over the outer courtyard of no. 12 in 1890, where three great Canalettos hang. Books relating to Soane and the Museum are on sale here.

Return right into the older (from Soane's point of view) breakfast room of no. 2, where he had also constructed a ceiling in a starfish design, very much his own trademark, but emanating from his master Dance. Both men used it in several of their public buildings. Retrace your steps and turn right into the small **Breakfast Room** of no. 13, where Soane implemented what he called 'those fanciful effects which constitute the poetry of architecture'. A canopy is formed by an additional ceiling containing coloured glass and pieces of mirror, and views are constructed of the Monument Court and the Dome. It is magical but at the same time solemn.

Finally, it is possible to go to the first floor of no. 13 and see the **Drawing Rooms**, which are less idiosyncratic, except for the extension at the front, built out over the basement area. J.M.W. Turner's fine painting *Admiral von Tromp's Barge Entering the Texel* hangs here. Soane's projecting stone façade was an improvement which present-day planners would never allow, and even in his time was criticised. In these rooms are more fascinating items from the collection, including a portrait of Soane's two sons, with whom their parents quarrelled bitterly on account of Soane's disappointment that they did not follow him into the same profession. He was a great architect but an unsatisfactory parent, a difficult but fascinating man, whose prickly personality seems still to haunt this equally fascinating place.

The museum has an extensive **Library**, which includes the architectural drawings of Robert Adam and George Dance the Younger, bought by Soane, and much other absorbing material. This can be accessed by appointment. A recently opened extension holds regular exhibitions on architectural themes.

Leaving the museum, turn right to the end of Lincoln's Inn Fields and on to Kingsway (Chapter 9). Holborn station is to your right, but if you have any energy left you may like to go down **Great Queen Street** opposite, for two reasons. Firstly, this street of the 1630s was one of the first formally designed streets in the entire capital—linked to Covent Garden nearby (Chapter 10)—and still contains some fine early 18C houses on the north side. The second reason is the **Freemasons' Hall**, the headquarters of freemasonry in England, on the left, designed by Bros. H.V. Ashley and Winton Newman (1927–33), in staggeringly luxurious Art Deco style, it is the third Masonic hall on this site. If your timing is right, you may be able to get in to see the museum, or even join a guided tour into the Temple, as it is called, but if you try this after the Soane you may suffer serious architectural indigestion. Open 10.00–17.00 Mon–Fri. Admission free. Tours at 11.00, 12.00, 14.00, 15.00 and 16.00, but first ☎ 020 7831 9811. Tube: Holborn.

Return to Kingsway to find Holborn station to the left, or continue into Long Acre to locate Covent Garden station.

New Road: from Marylebone to Clerkenwell

Whereas 'North Bank' is a neologism made up for this Blue Guide, 'New Road' is an archaism revived. It was the original name for a by-pass constructed from Paddington to Islington in 1757, so that cattle could be driven from the west to Smithfield avoiding Oxford Street and the valley of the Fleet. It was an inspired piece of town planning and serves its purpose as a by-pass to this day—though cars have replaced cows. In times between it was used by carriages above and then by trains beneath. George Shillibeer started his omnibus service along the New Road, from Paddington to the City, in 1829; and the first Metropolitan Line with the world's very first underground railway (its tunnels now used by the Circle and Hammersmith and City Lines, and the Metropolitan Line going on northwest into the country), was constructed on the 'cut and cover' principle under the New Road in 1860. In fact parts of the road had been renamed Marylebone Road, Euston Road and Pentonville Road in 1857.

The New Road was originally conceived as a metaphorical boundary for London, as the M25 is today. The railways had to struggle in over the new canal but made no attempt to cross the New Road. The suburbs beyond it were more countrified, and the 18C estates south of it saw the road as their northern limit. As it rose to higher ground in the east, the road formed a look-out point south over the old City, and marked a cluster of wells and ponds where, before it reached you in pipes, you could imbibe fresh water to cleanse your system from the ravages of soot and grime.

All the areas covered in the six walks that depend from the New Road, from Marylebone to the Angel at Islington, take some of their character from it. They have little else in common: Marylebone and Fitzrovia (Chapters 24 and 26) were and still are, smart if slightly decaying; Regent's Park (Chapter 25) is a separate green entity; and Bloomsbury (Chapter 27) is entirely distinct in its own right. The stations in Chapter 28 are different again and the Clerkenwell walk (Chapter 29) taking us downhill into the City picks up some of its commercial flavour.

24 • Marylebone

'St Mary by the Bourne' once described St Mary's church by the stream of Tybourne or Tyburn. Now Marylebone denotes a pleasing area of mostly 19C houses with some fine squares, Georgian churches and historical connection. On this thorough walk you will be able to digest the character of the area and include either of two remarkable London attractions catering perhaps for opposing tastes, the Wallace Collection and Madame Tussaud's.

• Distance: 2¾ miles. Time: 2 hours for the walk + 2 or 3 hours for either of the attractions. Tube: Marylebone. Map 5.

Start from **Marylebone Station** on the Bakerloo line (**Map 5,5**). The last major terminus to reach London, built for the Great Central Railway by H.W. Braddock (1899), it was controversial to the residents of St John's Wood to the north by was still part of the great era of railway display. The sunny little station has the atmosphere of a country town terminus, with the initials GCR proudly displayed in its ironwork.

The hotel opposite by Robert Edis, of the same date and with much terracotta to prove it, is reached under a glass porch from Marylebone Road. It is much grander than the station, especially at the front, and even more so inside, with palms in a spectacular atrium. After functioning for generations as offices for the nationalised British Rail, it is now restored to glory as the *Landmark Hotel*.

Turn left out of the station to look at **Dorset Square**, site of Thomas Lord's first cricket ground between 1787 and 1811 and the source of the name of the world-famous Marylebone Cricket Club (MCC). The houses were built immediately after Lord had moved his ground out to St John's Wood (see Chapter 39), and the square named after the Duke of Dorset, an early cricketing enthusiast. It retains the dignity of its period. George Grossmith, co-author of *Diary of a Nobody*, lived at no. 27 on the left-hand corner, and Charles Babbage across the other side, where he developed the first computer in 1834.

Turn right down Balcombe Street and note **Marylebone Town Hall** (1912–18) and **Library** (1938–39) across the Marylebone Road. Both are by Sir Edwin Cooper and, as Pevsner points out, looking from one to the other you can see how the Edwardian architect felt obliged to adapt to the ideology of the 20C. In Marylebone Road on your left is **Marathon House**, a nicely proportioned and beautifully maintained slab-and-podium block of the 1960s: if only all its products looked as good, we might love Modernism more.

Cross the fearsomely busy Marylebone Road to reach Upper Montagu Street. You now join the pleasantly proportioned streets of an early 19C estate. At York Street turn right. Go as far as Sir Robert Smirke's fine and dignified church of **St Mary** (1821–24) noting on the right the typically and commendably respectable 'Ladies Residential Chambers' (1892). The church has an attractive semi-circular porch, as Greek as a church can be, closing the vista to the south. Go in this direction through the elongated **Bryanston Square**, built by former chimney-sweep David Porter (1812) and named after the Portman family's county estate in Dorset (**Map 5,7**). The end blocks are stuccoed for emphasis. At the bottom turn left to pass **Montagu Square**, parallel to the east, also built by Porter and named in honour of Mrs Elizabeth Montagu in gratitude for her having helped him establish himself as a builder. Montagu Square is much more heavily decorated with unnecessary bay windows. Between the squares are good examples of mews housing.

After Montagu Square you reach forbidding Gloucester Place. Turn right and carefully cross to reach the north side of **Portman Square**, built earlier (from 1764). Here, on the site of the *International Hotel* on the right, was Mrs Montagu's house, built for her by James 'Athenian' Stuart and one of the richest residences in London at the time. Mrs Montagu was a notable hostess described by Fanny Burney as 'brilliant in diamonds, solid in judgment, critical in talk'. On the opposite corner—turn left round it—stands **Home House**, built by Robert Adam (1773–76): though uninteresting from the outside it has magnificent original interiors, with a wonderful flying staircase and walls decorated by Antonio Zucchi. These are usually inaccessible as Home House is now a private club, but tours are occasionally arranged, ☎ 020 7670 2000.

Continue along the north side of Portman Square, cross Baker Street and go down Fitzhardinge Street to the pleasant **Manchester Square** (1770–88). On the north side, spoiling the proportions, is the later, unprepossessing façade of Hertford House (**Map 5,8**). But joy awaits you inside.

Wallace Collection

You have reached one of London's greatest gems, the Wallace Collection. There is an attractive restaurant in the courtyard—a little grand and slow, perhaps, but of high quality (not a bad summary for the whole collection).

- Open 10.00–17.00 Mon–Sat, 14.00–17.00 Sun. Admission free. Restaurant (reservations ☎ 020 7563 9505). Shop. ☎ 020 7935 0687. www.wallace-collection.org.uk. Tube: Bond Street.

The name refers to the illegitimate son of the 4th Marquess of Hertford, Sir Richard Wallace. The collection was more than simply that of Wallace: it also included those of earlier marquesses, among them his father and grand-father. The 4th Marquess had lived in Paris as a recluse but bought consistently the then unfashionable French art of the 18C. He had inherited, but kept in London, the collections of his own father, the 3rd Marquess, a famous rake and a specialist in Sèvres porcelain and 17C Dutch paintings of interiors. Wallace added his own interests—armour, firearms and Renaissance metal-work—and the result is a mixed but overall stunning display. At Wallace's wish his widow, who was French, left the entire collection to the British nation on her death in 1897, on condition that it should always remain here in central London, so this is the only place where you will ever be able to see a number of internationally famous masterpieces. The collection was opened as a museum in 1900.

It is perhaps best to start your tour to the left of the entrance hall, via the shop: the cloakrooms are some way off within—ask for directions. In the **Entrance Hall** is a mixed collection of English paintings and some marble busts (*Queen Caroline* by John Michael Rysbrack (1739) makes you realise what an impressive woman she was): a grand staircase stretches upwards. Collect a free 'Visitors Directory' and use it to get your bearings. The following description will ensure you see all the highlights. The best come towards the end, but you should try to cover them all. The shop leads to the Billiard Room, not the most exciting but undoubtedly a representative space, with a great wardrobe and cabinet by André-Charles Boulle (d. 1732), dripping luxury, and 18C French paintings. There is more of the same in the **Dining Room**, with François Boucher nymph over the doors, two quiet portraits by Jean-Marc Nattier and lots of horrible pictures of game (with which the Wallace is peculiarly well endowed: this is not a current taste, as the Curator acknowledges by skying them virtually out of sight). Come back into the Entrance Hall and pass under the stairs to see contemporary busts of the 4th Marquess and Sir Richard and Lady Wallace. In the Back State Room there is more game but also some more appealing Rococo furniture and cases full of Sèvres porcelain.

There is more Sèvres in the **Front State Room** and some interesting portraits such as Sir Thomas Lawrence's of the *3rd Marquess of Hertford* (c 1824) and socialite *Lady Blessington* (1822) and, especially attractive, Thomas Sully's early portrait of *Queen Victoria* (1838) at the time of her coronation, looking coyly a us over her shoulder. Go round the corner into the long and rather dreary **16C Gallery** showing the collection's Renaissance holdings, which include Limoges enamels, French bronze figurines, *The Young Cicero Reading* by Vincenzo Foppa (1464), and the little, tense *St Roch* by Carlo Crivelli (1493). In similar vein, the **Smoking Room** has majolica plates, medals and 16C furniture from Burgundy, restored in the 19C. That this was indeed Sir Richard's smoking room can be confirmed by the Minton tiles (which did not absorb smoke, unlike draperies or wallpaper) of outrageous design.

Then come three consecutive galleries devoted to Sir Richard Wallace's particular interest, arms and armour from all over Europe. The next gallery is similar but the armour is oriental in origin, and some French 19C Orientalist paintings have been hung here. In the **Housekeeper's Room** beyond are several works by the extremely interesting R.P. Bonington (1802–28), a Keats-like figure who, had he lived, would have rivalled J.M.W. Turner. Most of these works are small popular history paintings, worth examining carefully; alongside them is hung a picture in the same idiom by Eugène Delacroix, whose studio Bonington shared when in Paris. There are also some evocative coastal scenes by Bonington.

Go up the grand staircase next for a similar circuit, though here the richness of the painting and furniture becomes particularly apparent. Boucher's *Rising and Setting of the Sun* (1752–53) lighten your ascent. The landing looks out over the square. Turn right into the **Boudoir**, which contains more 18C French work, mostly weary-looking females by J.-B. Greuze but also Sir Joshua Reynolds's little *Miss Bowles* (1775) sparkling among them. In the corridor to the **Study** are some gold boxes (though no competition for the Gilbert Collection in Chapter 9). In the Study, there is more Sèvres, furniture, Jean-Honoré Fragonard's *Pierrot* (c 1760) and Elisabeth Vigée Le Brun's vivid *Madame Perregaux* (1789). The Oval Dining Room is often closed so you are likely to return to the **West Room**, where the real joys of the collection begin: here is Boucher's *Madame de Pompadour* (1759) and a gilt-bronze clock by Louis-Simon Boizot (1771), with figures of the river Rhône and its tributary the Druance sexily communicating their union.

In the **West Gallery** come lashings of French 18C pleasures: Fragonard's *Swing*, *Schoolmistress* and *Souvenir* (1760s), Jean-Antoine Watteau's *Lady at her Toilet*, a *Fête in a Park* and *Music Party* (c 1715–20), works by J.-B.F. Pater, Nicholas Lancret and Boucher, and furniture of the period by Antoine Gaudreaux and Bernard van Risambergh. There is some decline in quality in the 19C Gallery, but none in enjoyment. Taste may have lapsed in 19C France but there is still plenty of delight to be had in front of Horace Vernet's *Judah and Tamar* (1820s), she with leg and breast exposed but lips demurely covered, and the *Temptation of St Hilarion* by D.-L.-F. Papety (1840): this saint needed counselling.

In the **Great Gallery**, running the length of the north side of the house, are the unmissable *Landscape with a Rainbow* by Peter Paul Rubens (1638), the portrait of *Titus* by Rembrandt (1657), *Dance to the Music of Time* by Nicolas Poussin (1638), and *Lady with a Fan* by Diego Velazquez (c 1640). There are more works by Rembrandt and Rubens, a Titian, a famous Frans Hals, several by Bartolomé Murillo and Antony van Dyck, a painting by Claude Lorrain to compare with one by Salvator Rosa, and some great English portraits. You may enjoy contrasting the three images (by Reynolds, Thomas Gainsborough and George Romney) of *Mrs Robinson*, the 18C actress named Perdita after her performance in *The Winter's Tale*. Is she acting a different role for each artist? Or, try to relate the Rubens landscape to its pendant in the National Gallery. Or, discuss why Hals *Laughing Cavalier* (1624) was so popular for so long, why Lord Hertford should have bid up to six times the reserve price to buy it in 1865, and why it is now relatively ignored again.

The Great Gallery is a hard act to follow, and the **East Galleries** have a different theme entirely, the 2nd Marquess's collection of Dutch landscape and genre. Here you can indulge in a different, smaller-scale visual experience, with paintings by Aelbert Cuyp, Meindert Hobbema and Jacob van Ruisdael; Jan Steen's *Harpsichord Lesson* (1660); two peaceful courtyard scenes by Pieter de Hooch and the more exuberant work of Nicolaes Maes and the boors of Adriaen Brouwer and Adriaen van Ostade, rough country next to the civilised world of 18C France.

Pass through the less interesting East Dining Room to reach the **Small Drawing Room**: here there are six views of Venice by Canaletto and two by Francesco Guardi. The Large Drawing Room has Sèvres and furniture reminiscent of that on the ground floor. Go back downstairs finally to see some of the interesting temporary displays on the lower-ground floor, only recently exposed to view as part of Rick Mather's ingenious project to cover the courtyard. Particularly recommended is the **Reserve Collection** which includes a stimulating display of fakes and forgeries. Can an honestly made copy be interpreted as a forgery? The gallery's notes say that it all depends on the maker's intention, but surely it all depends on us?

Out in the square, turn left up Spanish Place, then right and left into Thayer Street. You pass on your left the Roman Catholic church of **St James**, a good late Gothic Revival building by Edward Goldie (1890). Thayer Street leads immediately into **Marylebone High Street**, a pleasant, almost villagey, street of small shops and restaurants continuing the original Marylebone Lane, which in turn follows the path of the original bourne or burn (**Map 5,6**). Go up the High Street as far as Paddington Street on the left: there are nice pubs and restaurants all around and few tourists. In Paddington Street are more quaint old shops, and many minor architectural pleasures are to be found in the street façades. On the left of Paddington Street is a **public garden** which was the original burial ground for the parish. It is hard to imagine, but there were once 80,000 graves here: the only one still to be seen is a mausoleum built in 1759.

To the north, up Luxborough Street, are the gaunt 1970s piles of the University of Westminster. Proceed in this direction to reach Marylebone Road and cross it to visit Madame Tussaud's and the Planetarium (**Map 5,5**).

Madame Tussaud's and Planetarium

For some reason, although one of London's most popular tourist attractions, Madame Tussaud's is seldom visited by Londoners themselves.

• Planetarium and waxworks open 10.00–17.30 Mon–Fri, 09.30–17.30 Sat and Sun (sometimes open 09.00). Admission charge (high). Timed tickets available for the waxworks alone or the Planetarium and waxworks combined are bookable in advance for an extra charge, ☎ 0870 400 3000. These are recommended as queues can be lengthy. Café. Shop. www.madame-tussauds.com Tube: Baker Street.

The lay-out of **Madame Tussaud's** waxworks puts famous contemporaries in the first section, where most visitors take the opportunity to photograph themselves alongside their favourites. The next section, '200 years', contains heads and limbs of a range of famous individuals of the 19C and 20C, arranged in a macabre manner on shelves. The Grand Hall displays statesmen and royalty over an even longer period, together with presidents of the USA and other international figures. But of course the most famous section is the Chamber of Horrors, which fully lives up to its name, if only in the sense of being in shockingly horrible taste. The final part of the show is the 'Spirit of London', a short and rather obvious tour through London's history.

Madame Tussaud's is of some historical interest. Tussaud fled the French Revolution to arrive in London in 1802. She first toured England with her exhibition of wax figures before settling at Baker Street in 1835. The show soon became an institution and was regularly visited by the curious and the famous, including Charles Dickens and the Duke of Wellington, who used to contemplate thoughtfully the effigy of Napoleon. The waxworks were moved to their present site in 1884.

The **Planetarium** was first opened in 1958 and houses a Zeiss projector to reveal 9000 stars: its main offering is a 20-minute visual presentation of the history of astronomy.

Head back across the windy Marylebone Road going east, to see **St Marylebone** parish church, built on this site to the design of Thomas Hardwick (1813–17) to replace the former parish church just to the south (**Map 5,6**). It is a handsome building, generously proportioned and with some interesting monuments. The church itself is often closed but in the crypt there is a pleasant café. ☎ 020 7935 5066.

When John Nash was designing Regent's Park (see Chapter 25) he hoped the new church would form the centrepiece of the circus planned for what is now Park Crescent, but the Duke of Portland insisted that the church should be on his own land to the west. Nash, never blind to opportunity, took advantage by laying out York Gate to the north as a grand entry to the park, with the church closing the southern vista. Robert Browning and Elizabeth Barratt were married here in secret in 1846.

It is worth exploring behind the church to see its odd shape on the south side. Just to the south, off Marylebone High Street, you will find the site of the earlier parish church, now laid out as a little **garden**, where the tomb of Charles Wesley (d. 1788), the hymn writer, can still be seen. Also buried here were James Gibbs the architect, J.M. Rysbrack the sculptor, and Allan Ramsay and George Stubbs, painters. You may be interested in the *Conran Shop* opposite, selling artefacts of expensive but high-quality design.

Back on Marylebone Road is the **Royal Academy of Music**, the oldest such institution in England, founded in 1822. The present building is by Sir Ernest George (1912). A museum has recently been opened in the Nash building alongside. Open 12.30–18.30 Mon–Fri, 14.00–17.00 Sat–Sun. Free. Shop. ☎ 020 7873 7373. Turn right to reach Devonshire Place and continue down the long and tedious straight line of Wimpole Street. In 1891 Arthur Conan Doyle had his consulting rooms at no. 2, where he wrote two of the Sherlock Holmes stories. Look at no. 7 (1896), surely designed as a blast against conformity. No. 50 Wimpole Street (since rebuilt) is famous as the address from which Elizabeth Barratt eloped with Browning on 12 September 1846.

Elizabeth Barratt Browning

The eldest of 12 children of a tyrannical father, Elizabeth Barratt (1806–61) was an invalid languishing in Wimpole Street from 1838. She was highly intellectual, publishing poems from the 1820s, and friendly with a similar circle including the Carlyles and John Ruskin. Robert Browning courted her from 1845 and the following year they married secretly and left for Italy, living for the rest of Mrs Browning's life in Florence. Fiercely political, she supported Italian liberation. When non-political William Wordsworth died in 1850 she was widely canvassed as poet laureate, but was probably too controversial. She died in Browning's arms in 1861.

Also associated with poetry is no. 67, home of the historian Henry Hallam, whose son Arthur was the friend of Alfred, Lord Tennyson and the subject of the great poem *In Memoriam*. Of the outside Tennyson wrote, 'The dark house by which once more I stand, Here in the dark unlovely street': still an apt summary. Most of the houses are late 19C, some very impressive and grand, and most are associated with the medical profession, as in Harley Street running parallel to the east.

At the south end of Wimpole Street you join Wigmore Street (**Map 5,8**). Just to your right is the **Wigmore Hall**, London's most cultivated venue for music recitals, with a restaurant below. The building (1901) was the initiative of Friedrich Bechstein to supplement his piano showrooms next door at no. 38. The Hall became public space in 1917 after Bechstein, as a German, was ejected from the country and his stock of pianos sold off. It predictably sprouts terracotta (as do many of the façades in this area) but possesses an almost perfect acoustic: even if the decoration is slightly uncomfortable, if you close your eyes the musical experience can be unforgettable. For details of recitals, ☎ 020 7935 2141.

Opposite is the spectacular no. 33 Wigmore Street, built as a department store (1907–8). It should certainly be used for something grander and more public than private apartments. Cross Wigmore Street and continue to the foot of Wimpole Street. Not in any sense forming a vista is the east end of the chapel of **St Peter Vere Street**, a brick miniature by Gibbs (1721) of St Martin-in-the-Fields, with a cosy feeling. It now houses the Institute of Contemporary Christianity, who create interior warmth with coffee and a bookshop.

The chapel was built to serve the Cavendish-Harley estate developed in the 1720s, of which **Cavendish Square** was the centre. Go east to locate it; the backs of large shops (Chapter 21) are on your right. On your left, the scary 20C Classicism of the Royal Society of Medicine will give you the shivers. A place of many distinguished associations, Cavendish Square is now of little architectural interest. Traveller and writer Lady Mary Wortley Montagu lived at no. 5 between 1723 and 1738, and Nelson in 1791. The north side contains two wings of a house started for the Duke of Chandos in the 1720s by Edward Shepherd, designer of the Grosvenor estate. The centre block was never completed but in a bridge across the gap, over the entrance to a convent, is a *Madonna and Child* by Jacob Epstein (1953). On the south side of the square is a statue of *Lord George Bentinck*, MP and horse-racing enthusiast (1802–48), by Thomas Campbell (1851).

Leave at the northeast corner up Chandos Street. On the corner at no. 5 is an important house in a curious grey stone by Robert Adam (1771): it should be restored. Turn right into Portland Place with the *Langham Hotel* (1864), an ultra-grand piece of Victoriana where Mark Twain and H.W. Longfellow once were guests, on your right. The BBC stands opposite (Chapter 26). To your left stretches the last fine avenue of this walk, **Portland Place**, laid out by Robert and James Adam from 1778 (**Map 5,6**).

> Magnificent in proportion and scale, it was once seen as the grandest street in all London, and not surprisingly Nash perceived it as the grand final section of his processional route up Regent's Street from Westminster to the park. Its noble width was a happy accident, the result of a legal wrangle whereby Lord Foley, who occupied a house at the south end where the Langham Hotel now is, was awarded the right to retain an uninterrupted view to the north. Nash was able to place All Souls at a picturesque angle on the necessary bend, and continue the straight line north as the Broad Walk in the park (Chapter 25).

In the 20C Portland Place was cruelly abused. It is fun, if also depressing, to look out for surviving pieces of the Adams's work as you walk along: there are some doorcases and cornices and even at, no. 59, part of a pediment. On the right look out for the headquarters of the **Royal Institute of British Architects**, an authentic Art Deco building by Grey Wornum (1934), with an excellent book-shop and an upmarket café. Exhibitions are held in the new hall 10.00–21.00 Tues–Fri, 10.00–17.00 Sat. ☎ 020 7307 3770. www.architecture.com.

Enobling the street, there are also monuments to *Quintin Hogg*, founder of the Polytechnic, by Sir George Frampton (1906), and, by the RIBA, to the soldier *Sir George White*, who twice won the Victoria Cross; the statue is by John Tweed (1922).

At the northern of Portland Place you reach **Park Crescent** (1812–22) which was originally to have been a circus with a church in the centre but which now makes a very successful, grand opening to Regent's Park. Regent's Park station is round the corner and Great Portland Street station just to the right.

25 • Regent's Park

In the context of Green London, this walk is a partner to Chapters 17 and 20: if the Park is your only or primary interest, it will make a delightful two-hour stroll. London Zoo occurs *en route*, a visit to which turns two hours into a day trip.

- Distance: 4 miles. Time: 2 hours for the walk + as much time as you want to spend at the Zoo. Tube: Baker Street, Regent's Park or Great Portland Street. Map 4, 5.

From Baker Street station (**Map 5,5**), where there is a bronze statue of *Sherlock Holmes* (by John Doubeday, 1999), walk north, with the Abbey National bank's head office on the left. This is the building which covered 221B Baker Street—famous as Holmes's residence. No. 239, a little way to the north, has been renumbered 221B and contains the **Sherlock Holmes Museum** (see box, p 268). Open 09.30–18.00 daily. Admission charge. Shop. ☎ 020 7935 8866. www.sherlock/holmes.co.uk

Before turning into the Park, go a short way further to discover on the left, at the top of Glentworth Street, St Cyprian's Clarence Gate with a stunning interior by Sir Ninian Comper (1902–3). Then return to enter Regent's Park at **Clarence Gate**, denoted by a little Doric lodge. This is one of several located at the Park's

> ### Sherlock Holmes
> Many people believe Holmes to have been a real person, an early London detective, and he received many letters during his 'lifetime' at 221B Baker Street—so many that allegedly a clerk at the Abbey National was employed just to deal with them. But of course he was the fictional creation of Sir Arthur Conan Doyle (1859–1930). Wanting to concentrate on more serious work, Conan Doyle made more than one attempt to kill Holmes off, but had to resurrect him by public demand. For many people the stories of Sherlock Holmes and Dr Watson catching trains to Surrey and hailing cabs through foggy gas-lit nights to mysterious suburban locations epitomise late 19C London more vividly even than its surviving architecture.

main entrances and reminds us that when first constructed it was a private place, to which non-residents would be refused admission.

- Park closes at dusk. Boats for hire April–Sept. Children's boating pond. Bands play July–Aug at lunchtime and around 17.00 (15.00 at weekends). Other events posted on notice boards at the entrances. ☎ 020 7486 7905.

Regent's Park is unique among London's parks in being largely of a single period (1811–27) and originally had a very specific agenda. The land had belonged to the Crown since Tudor times but had remained undeveloped until estate growth in the surrounding areas at last prompted some official interest. The proposal by the Commissioner of Woods and Forests, John Fordyce, was that development of housing should be accompanied by a new through-road to Westminster. This was the birth of London's only successful attempt at town planning, a route from the New Road via Portland Place and Regent Street to Trafalgar Square and Whitehall, or, as was originally intended, to the royal residence at Carlton House. It is to John Nash we attribute the dynamic management of the project, and the designs of most of the terraces. But there were many other contributors, such as the government commissioners who supervised the project, the chief builder, James Burton, and his young son Decimus, who became a distinguished Victorian Classicist.

Reaching the Outer Circle and facing the Park, **Clarence Terrace** (1823) is on your left and **Cornwall Terrace** (1820–21)—particularly grand with its caryatids—stretches away to your right. Both are early works of the 21-year-old Decimus Burton. It was planned at one stage that the residents of Cornwall Terrace should have a private garden across the road in the greensward, which at this location remains largely unplanted.

Walk to the left, noting the way Clarence Terrace's façade signifies, not a row of town dwellings, but an English country house, part of the illusion the ideology of the 'picturesque' sought to achieve. You soon reach **Sussex Place** (1822), now the London Business School and one of Nash's most exotic designs, with hints of the Royal Pavilion at Brighton, another of the Prince Regent's extravagances. It originally comprised 26 terraced houses, a fact again disguised and now detectable only by observing the party-wall chimney ridges punctuating the roof. The finest of the houses were at each end: the first of these is occupied by the Dean of the Business School.

After this is the more recent and quite unobtrusive Royal College of

Obstetricians (1960). Turn left into the garden of **Hanover Terrace** (1822–23), its stagey statuary mass-produced by George Bubb's workshop. Here the identity of the individual houses is not disguised but proudly proclaimed with cast-iron entrance stairs. The block is still private residences. H.G. Wells and Ralph Vaughan Williams lived here at different times. It is worth peeping round the back of the terrace to see the mews for the earlier residents' carriages, with grooms' accommodation above. Opposite is the back of Kent Terrace, the most modest of the terraces and, therefore, the only one which faces away from the Park: the grander houses were to have the finer views.

John Nash

Nash (1752–1835) has a special place in London architecture as the mind behind its only serious scheme of town planning, Regent's Park and Regent Street. The Park Villages to the east of Regent's Park, Nash can also be said to have been the creator of the notion of a garden suburb, the influence of which, as any Tube journey to the current edge of London will confirm, has been vast. Nash's gifts were for picturesque effects on a large scale—for example, All Soul's Langham Place, positioned to make a scenic gem out of an awkward corner, or the Quadrant curving north from Piccadilly Circus, enticing you to see where it leads. Nash's career did not end in a knighthood or glory, however: after the death of his chief patron, George IV, he was sacked from work on Buckingham Palace and died on the Isle of Wight, his reputation under a cloud. Yet, after Sir Christopher Wren, he was the chief maker of London.

Retrace your steps and cross the Outer Circle into the Park proper. You can glimpse to the right **The Holme**, built by Decimus for his father James Burton (1816), picturesquely positioned beyond the lake and surrounded by trees. Nash would have appreciated the way this original planting pattern has been maintained. Walk left by the side of the lake, noting to the left the **London Central Mosque** by Sir Frederick Gibberd (1972–78). Open 09.30–17.00 Mon–Fri. Women should wear a headscarf and dress sensitively. ☎ 020 7724 3363.

Now cross two bridges over the lake. There are many waterfowl to be studied. Then, passing the boathouse on your right, follow the path with the railing to your right—the Zoo's Mappin Terraces adorn the horizon to your left—to another bridge, cross that and proceed to reach the **Inner Circle**.

If you wish you can walk clockwise to see **St John's Lodge**—built by John Raffield (1817) but extended by Charles Barry (1846) and again by Robert Weir Schultz (1892)—and its newly restored Victorian garden. Going anti-clockwise and turning left through the elaborate iron gates (1935) you can enjoy the even greater pleasure of **Queen Mary's Rose Garden** (named for George V's queen). This was originally the garden of the Royal Botanic Society before it moved to Kew. There are evening performances between April and September at the **Open Air Theatre**: to book in advance, ☎ 020 7486 2431. Information ☎ 020 7935 5796. Two productions each summer are of Shakespeare's plays. There is a pleasant café to the left.

On the east side of the Inner Circle, find Chester Road and proceed along it for a quarter of a mile, then turn left into **Broad Walk** (the more horticulturally exciting part, developed by architect W.E. Nesfield in the 1860s, lies to the south).

This straight path originally marked the continuation of the great scheme from Regent Street up Portland Place into the Park, to reach the Prince Regent's *guingette*—a summerhouse for royal relaxation, never built—at a spot roughly identical with the site of the Victorian Gothic fountain. Unless visiting the Zoo, bear right here across the grass and cross the Outer Circle to reach Gloucester Gate (see below). If you want to fit the Zoo into this walk, turn left when you reach the road. The main entrance appears soon on your left.

London Zoo

If you have children with you, London Zoo is almost certain to be on your itinerary. If you have a concern for conservation and the future of wildlife on the planet, again, the Zoo should be visited. And if you are interested in an eclectic collection of architectural ideas, some oddly unsuitable, others quite brilliant, all set in creatively planted gardens, then the Zoo is for you, too.

• Open March–Oct 10.00–17.30 daily; Nov–Feb 10.00–16.00. Admission charge (high but good value). Events include feeding the pelicans at 13.30 (daily) and the snakes at 14.15 (Mon, Fri only). Cafés. Restaurants. Shops. ☎ 020 7722 3333. www.londonzoo.org. Tube: Camden Town. Bus: 274 (Camden Town–Baker Street). Waterbus from Camden Lock or Little Venice (see Chapter 39).

The Zoological Society of London was founded in 1826 and its 'gardens', the first in the world set up for the purpose of study, laid out the next year after the decision was made to build no more terraces in Regent's Park. Although the 'zoo' was open to members from 1828, the public were not admitted until 1847. In recent years the emphasis has shifted sharply away from animals as entertainment to conservation, breeding and, if they can be adequately protected, returning species to the wild. The zoo's motto is now 'Conservation in Action'.

The main site is a triangular space of 24 acres south of the Outer Circle, from which the zoo was to be entered—most visitors arrived by carriage. Later some land was also acquired north of the Regent's Canal, to be accessed over attractive iron bridges: tunnels were built under the road. So the whole is enclosed in a pleasingly varied space, delightfully arranged so that it seems much larger than it really is. Its history explains its odd location as part of the Regent's Park complex of housing, open space and entertainment, off the public transport map. Most visitors today seem to arrive by car, for which there is ample parking. Walking across the Park, as we have done, remains the most pleasing way to arrive.

It is suggested you enter at the main gate and follow the recommended route marked with green signs. This will take you first through the tunnel to the **giraffes and antelopes**, still housed, and very comfortably it appears, in a Decimus Burton building (1836–37). From here go to the Charles Clore Small Mammal House, a lively collection of **nocturnal animals** who are fooled into thinking it is night so that you can observe them by day. Opposite, across the canal, note Lord Snowdon's **aviary** (1961–65), a visionary piece of engineering. Return to the main area through the east tunnel, and perhaps refresh yourself at the rather average restaurant in a pompous neo-Georgian structure of the 1920s. Next to the fountain you can see Burton's clock tower and what remains of his camel house, one of the earliest buildings (1828). Next to it are the attractive Sobell Pavilions for **apes and monkeys** (1972), but you should make your way to the left, through the gardens, to see the Lion Terraces (1976) and an exhibition on conservation called the Web of Life. Nearby are the Bird House (1883), always a joy, and the beautifully managed **Children's Zoo**, which provides opportunities to feed and stroke. In front is Berthold Lubetkin's famous **Penguin Pool** (1934), amazing abstract architecture with curvilinear geometric forms—an icon of Modernism, although the **penguins** never look very thrilled with it. Nearby is the Casson Conder Partnership's Elephant and Rhino Pavilion (1962–65), the height of Brutalism: the form of display is based on the Hanbury principle, with no railings and more space (the elephants have moved out to Whipsnade, the Zoo's country park in Bedfordshire). The other main sight at Regent's Park is the Mappin Terraces by John Belcher and J.J. Joass (1913–14), strange artificial rock outcrops constructed for antelopes but now populated only by **bears**; the Aquarium is underneath.

After the Zoo, return clockwise round the Outer Circle to reach **Gloucester Gate**, the last to be completed (1827). Note the giant Ionic pilasters, twice as big as they should be due to a builder's mistake—Nash never concerned himself with details. If you have time, explore Park Village West, one of two groups of semi-vernacular cottages and villas which Nash designed at the end of the project, and still a delicious eclectic mixture. Nash was perhaps even more radical here than he knew, setting a standard for suburban development and the notion of the 'garden suburb' which was to affect British housing design for a century or more.

Off Albany Street is the church of **St Katharine** by Ambrose Poynter (1826–28), formerly the chapel of St Katharine's Hospital. It now belongs to the Danish Church in London. It is part of **St Katharine's Hospital**, transferred and rebuilt following the excavation of St Katharine's Dock in 1826. Nash was said to be angry at the choice of stock brick and a simplified 'Gothick' style, but some have found it a refreshing change after the acres of stucco.

Return to the Outer Circle and on the left enter the drive for **Cumberland Terrace** (1826), with the grandest theatrical façade: you can see just how theatrical in the free-standing pediment, blatantly breaking one of Classicism's golden rules. It is surmounted by a further supply of Bubb's patent statuary. Cumberland Terrace residents have their own fine private garden between the drive and the road, but a short detour to the rear will demonstrate that the grandeur is skin-deep only, for there the grimy London stock bricks of the towering rear walls look out over the original market area on the other side of Albany Street. Only servants and tradespeople were supposed to behold this view, whereas the luxurious front façade was intended for the fastidious eyes of the Prince Regent, indulging himself in his *guingette*.

Walk south to the end of Cumberland Terrace. Note as you go the 'triumphal arch' devices leading through to the service areas, and the range of lamp-posts and bollards with the monogram of the monarch for the period of their manufacture. Continue down **Chester Terrace** (1825), the longest of them all, with separate blocks denoting the two wings—a misunderstanding, it seems, of Nash's design by the builder James Burton. The large sign proclaiming to the world 'Chester Terrace.' is a delight for its blue background, period lettering and pedantic full stop.

At the south end of Chester Terrace, rejoin the Outer Circle. On your left is Cambridge Terrace, a Nash oddity, followed by **Cambridge Gate** by Archer and Green (1875), a vivid demonstration of how Victorian designers were not prepared to ape an earlier style just because it had set the trend. Next on the left, less discordant but as radically different, is Sir Denys Lasdun's **Royal College of Physicians** (1961–64), proud, clean and functional in its Modernist assertiveness. Finally you reach **St Andrew's Terrace** (1823), a miniature gem with a cobbled drive, Regent's Park at its most irresistible.

Now you have a choice. To complete the circuit, turn right, and note first **Park Square**, heavily enclosed for its residents' private use, and then Ulster and York Terraces. Their private gardens preclude front doors, which are therefore oddly located in the street behind. York Terrace is split at York Gate by the grand vista of St Marylebone parish church by Hardwick (see Chapter 24), which Nash was able providentially to incorporate in his scheme. See how many blind windows you can spot in these terraces. Turn left towards the church, then right past Madame Tussaud's to Baker Street station.

Alternatively, from St Andrew's Terrace you can continue south past the reconstructed **Diorama**: it was designed by A.C. Pugin for Nash and in 1823 was opened by Jacques Mandé Daguerre to present moving pictures operated by a special mechanism. **Park Crescent** is reached last on this walk but was intended as the grand introduction to the Park (**Map 5,5**). It was the first terrace to be started in 1812: in the original scheme, it was to have formed a whole circle, or circus, but even as a crescent it makes a most harmonious climax. Regent's Park station is now to your right, and Great Portland Street to your left. If you go left, enjoy a church by Sir John Soane, **Holy Trinity** (1826–28): it is balanced, somehow non-religious as architecture, but in good shape as a Christian bookshop (SPCK) selling new and second-hand titles.

26 • Fitzrovia

The term 'Fitzrovia' has died out in recent years but used to denote the area round Fitzroy Square and its arty, progressive but not really radical inhabitants. This easy walk explores the inheritance of richer days, including some unusual churches, one of them unforgettable, a fine square and streets of character.

- Distance: nearly 2 miles. Time: 1½ hours. Tube: Oxford Circus. Map 6.

We begin at Oxford Circus station (**Map 6,5**) and go north, up the northernmost part of John Nash's Regent Street. On the left is part of the University of Westminster. Straight ahead, stylishly placed on Langham Place with its round portico facing you and leading the eye round the bend in the road, is **All Souls** by Nash himself (1822–24). Nash, always versatile, here turned necessity to advantage, as explained in Chapter 24. Above the Greek porch is a pointed Gothic spire, a ridiculous combination if you think about it—his contemporaries ridiculed the architect—but looking great if you don't. The barn-like interior has a large gallery to pack in the masses. The church was built under an 1818 Act sponsoring the construction of 600 new churches, a reaction to the perceived worsening of public morality, loss of Christian faith and growing influence o

Non-Conformity after the Napoleonic Wars. Carefully rebuilt over an enlarged crypt after bomb damage, All Souls is a popular and crowded place for Evangelical worship on Sundays. ☎ 020 7580 3522. There is a bust of Nash in the porch.

North of All Souls' entrance, projecting south like the prow of a ship, is the headquarters of the British Broadcasting Corporation (BBC), know to older generations as **Broadcasting House**. By G. Val Myers (1932) it is very Art Deco, as befits the era, and the exterior is unchanged even if technology has moved on in the studios inside. The contemporary sculpture facing All Souls, at first sight religious, actually represents *Prospero sending Ariel out into the World* and is by Eric Gill. The building was bombed twice during the Second World War, but broadcasting never stopped. Here you can visit the **BBC Experience** which tells more of broadcasting history and gives insights into the world of radio: you can test yourself as a sports commentator, or construct a radio drama, or perform in front of the cameras. Tours (it is best to pre-book) from 10.00–16.30 daily. Admission charge. Café. Shop. ☎ 0870 603 0304. www.bbc.co.uk/experience

---

British Broadcasting Corporation

Still regarded as the voice of Britain, as its founders in 1922 intended, the BBC was conceived as a publicly funded and publicly controlled institution, both independent of government and relatively free of commercial pressures. In 1936 the BBC was also given management of television, again to be paid for by individual licences bought by viewers. Despite changes in the direction of commercialism after the Second World War the BBC is still expected, perhaps unrealistically given the increasing pressure from new modes of communication such as cable and satellite, to be impartial in its reporting and maintain high standards of public broadcasting.

Return down Portland Place and after All Souls turn left down Riding House Street. (The Langham Hotel opposite is covered in Chapter 24.) Turn right into Great Portland Street and go south as far as the *Cock*, a mad-looking Victorian pub. You are now nearly at Oxford Street but turn left into Margaret Street. Cross Great Titchfield Street to reach, on the left, the sharpest possible contrast in church building to All Souls (even the name makes a contrasting point), **All Saints**.

This tightly constructed jewel by William Butterfield (1849–60) is on a tiny site, yet packs in a choir school and a vicarage either side of a courtyard entered from the street, with the church at the rear. The 227ft spire, based on a German precedent in Lübeck, soars above. The design is Gothic Revival in style, with asymmetric windows, polychromatic brickwork, symbolic sculpture, and an extreme emphasis on verticality.

The initiative came from a philanthropist and later MP, Beresford Hope, who sought to re-establish the Church in this then poor area. The doctrinal position was unequivocally High Church, or Anglo-Catholic, and remains so. John Ruskin admired it, and G.E. Street thought it 'not only the most beautiful but also the most vigorous, thoughtful and original' of all Gothic Revival churches; it certainly influenced his own in Pimlico and Paddington.

When the eyes adjust to the initially dark and mysterious interior, it is seen to be a rich mass of colour and detail over every surface, floor, walls, piers and ceiling. Despite his many arguments with Hope, Butterfield was responsible for the decorative scheme throughout and to him should go the credit for its overall effect. His are the pulpit, the screen, the font and the decorations. The stained glass is by French brothers H. and A. Gerente, the tiled panels on the north aisle by Alexander Gibbs, and the structure which serves as a Lady Chapel is by Sir Ninian Comper (1911). (Sir Laurence Olivier was a choirboy here.) ☎ 020 7636 1788.

William Butterfield

One of the big names of Victorian architecture, to be mentioned in the same breath as Street and George Gilbert Scott, although a narrower specialist, Butterfield (1814–1900) worked only on ecclesiastical and educational buildings. He was much approved of by the *Ecclesiologist*, the journal which set the standards in mainstream Gothic Revival architecture. Besides All Saints in Margaret Street, he produced two other great London churches, St Mathias, Stoke Newington and St Alban, Holborn; both were largely destroyed by bombs in the Second World War.

Turn left from the church—there are some former ecclesiastical buildings opposite—then left again into Wells Street. At the top turn left and immediately right to reach an attractive crossroads between Foley Street and Great Titchfield Street, with a former dairy and public loo, now a studio. Why are there not more bits of London like this? Artists Henry Fuseli and Sir Edwin Landseer lived at no. 37 and 33 Foley Street respectively. Turn right along Foley Street and look down Candover Street, where there is a little assembly of Arts and Crafts offices and apartments, partly stretching round the corner on the left into Riding House Street, with lovely colours and shapes.

If you can face a short detour, go into **Middlesex Hospital** via the entrance in Mortimer Street and turn left inside to locate the chapel—a hidden treasure of the 1890s, Byzantine and covered in marble and mosaics. The architect was the important J.L. Pearson. The chapel was left behind when the hospital was rebuilt in the 1920s, and is now threatened again.

Otherwise, turn off Foley Street into Ogle Street: here there is another Victorian church, **St Charles** (1862), with the interior now rearranged for a particular kind of Roman Catholic service. Opposite the top of the street, in New Cavendish Street, is the University of Westminster's School of Engineering, an example of heavy 1960s Brutalism with the main lecture theatre cantilevered dramatically over the street.

Walk along to Cleveland Street and turn left (**Map 6, 3**). You are as close as can be to a now-famous London landmark, the 620ft-tall **British Telecom Tower**, still unloved to a great extent but also unknown, designed by Eric Bedford (1964). The revolving restaurant at the top, opened with great ballyhoo when the tower was built, closed after a bomb scare in 1975: no one has been inside it since.

Turn left up Cleveland Street, right into Maple Street, and left into Conway Street where there are some good 18C houses with pretty balconies. Now you are in **Fitzroy Square**, the heart of Fitzrovia. It is a pleasure for two reasons, first because the square is a creation of the Adam brothers, and second because of its associations with 19C and 20C artists, writers and other cultural types.

Gothic Revival

There have been two Gothic revivals: one, in the 18C, was light-hearted, based on fashion, and commemorated in such buildings as Horace Walpole's Strawberry Hill (Chapter 63); the other, in the 19C, was based on deeper feelings and only its products really matter as considered architecture. Part of the rationale for the 19C revival were literary sources, 'romantic' interpretations of medievalism in Keats' poems and Sir Walter Scott's novels, which renewed a sense of the nation's historical past. A.W.N. Pugin added a religious element, quoting the churches of medieval England as his inspiration, and greatly advanced the cause with his work on the new Houses of Parliament with Charles Barry in the 1830s (see Chapter 13). Gothic, it was argued by Pugin, and later by Ruskin, was the only appropriate style, for reasons of nationalism (England's medieval and Tudor past), religion (Classicism was pagan) and function (Gothic was flexible, whereas Classicism was locked into proportion and symmetry). In church architecture it became a pure and unbreakable doctrine for a new generation of Anglo-Catholics in the 1850s and 1860s and was also widely applied to civic buildings such as the new Law Courts and Manchester Town Hall. But it was overtaken, through William Morris, by preoccupations with craftsmanship *per se* rather than the Gothic style, and by the incompatibility of medievalism with technology.

The sponsor of the development in the 1790s was the 1st Baron Southampton, a descendent of Henry Fitzroy. 'Fitzroy' was the family name of the Dukes of Grafton. As the name implies, Henry began life as an illegitimate son, of Charles II and Barbara Villiers, Duchess of Cleveland. This was no disadvantage: Henry married the heiress of the Euston estate in Suffolk and also acquired the manor of Tottenham Court next door.

The artists' community in the late 19C included Ford Madox Brown at no. 37, the Stephens (parents of Virginia Woolf and Vanessa Bell) and G.B. Shaw at no. 29; and in the early 20C Roger Fry's Omega workshops at no. 33. The term 'Fitzrovia' came to be used pejoratively by non-residents. The artistic trend continued into the mid-20C, via the 'Bloomsburys' (Chapter 27) who were quite close neighbours, and it bore practical fruit in the establishment of the Euston Road School of painters. This group founded an art school at 314–16 Euston Road in 1938, and sought to re-establish objectivity in realist painting. It was short-lived, being dispersed by the Second World War, but its ideas took root in teaching subsequently done elsewhere. Its main participants were Claude Rogers, William Coldstream and Victor Pasmore.

The architecture of the east and south sides of the square is that of the Adams at the end of their careers (Robert died in 1792)—plainer, more rational than the decorated surfaces of Kenwood and the Adelphi, with motifs emphasising centrality—tripartite windows and lunettes—imaginatively displayed. The façades are worth studying carefully. The generous doors and fanlights somehow invite you inside. The square itself has been ruthlessly pedestrianised and the gate of the round garden, designed it seems as a giant saucer, is locked. The north and west sides of the square are later.

Leave the square by the southeast corner, down Fitzroy Street, to reach

Charlotte Street (Map 6,4). Named after the queen of George III, it was also a artists' quarter: George Morland lodged here, and Richard Wilson lived at no. 8, Joh Constable at no. 76 and Daniel Maclise at no. 85. Now it has many pleasant sma restaurants and pubs. The *Fitzroy Tavern* was a meeting-place for many writer (often working at the BBC) and artists in the 1920s and 1930s, including Dyla Thomas, George Orwell and Augustus John.

When you get to Tottenham Street, turn left. On the corner of Whitfield Stree and Scala Street, to the right, is **Pollock's Toy Museum**, a small but attractiv and atmospheric collection of Victorian toy theatres and puppets crammed in period house, with an interesting shop. Open 10.00–17.00 Mon–Sat. Admissio charge. Shop. ☎ 020 7636 3452. Tube: Goodge Street.

Continue down Tottenham Street to **Tottenham Court Road**. Opposite i *Heal's*, a business dating back to 1810 and on this site since 1840. The preser building is by Smith and Brewer (1912–17), 'the best commercial front of it date in London' according to Pevsner. It is an elegant furniture shop to explor along with *Habitat* next door. Furniture shops are a tradition in this area.

Go south down Tottenham Court Road. To the left, from Chenies Street to Stor Street, is **Alfred Place**, with little crescents north and south originally laid ou in 1810 by George Dance the Younger, the introducer of crescents into Londor though none of his work is visible here. In South Crescent is the **Buildin Centre**. Open 09.00–17.30 Mon–Fri, 10.00–16.00 Sat. Admission free. Shop Library. ☎ 020 7692 4000. The design firm Imagination has converted tw buildings into an awe-inspiring internal atrium.

Tottenham Court Road led, of course, to Tottenham Court, latterly a Fitzro property but as old as the Domesday Book. It lay in the countryside the other sid of Euston Road and in the 18C became a popular spot for Sunday excursion. Now the whole street is moderately awful, with shops selling acres of electroni goods, but at the southern end are a few final curiosities. One is the pub at no. 4 the *Rising Sun*, by the famous pub architects Treadwell and Martin (1896 covered with pseudo-Art Nouveau and Gothick bits and pieces.

Look to the right down Hanway Street, an oddly surviving little enclave wit the former 'Westminster Jews Free School', as inscribed over the door in Hanwa Place. Opposite, across Tottenham Court Road, is the *Horseshoe Hotel* (1875 another Victorian pub extravaganza, next to the *Dominion Theatre* (1929), popular venue for musicals. Just to the south are Centre Point, Charing Cros Road and here, under your nose, claustrophobic Tottenham Court Road statior

27 • Bloomsbury

Bloomsbury today is the campus for London University, the British Museum an other institutional bodies; a quiet area of Georgian squares, still run on the prir ciple of a residential estate, with virtually no pubs or shops; and a huntin ground for traces of the Bloomsbury Group. This walk explores it in a clockwis direction, with several small museums *en route*, ending with the big one. Unles you decide to visit the British Museum separately the outing therefore lasts a da you could have lunch in the Museum before you tackle the contents.

• Distance: nearly 2 miles. Time: 1½ hours + 3 hours for a tour of the Britis Museum's highlights. Tube: Tottenham Court Road. Map 7.

egin at Tottenham Court Road station (**Map 6,6**), exit 3. Walk briskly past the
ominion Theatre—the immediate area is wretched—and turn right into Great
ussell Street, then left up Adeline Place, crossing Bedford Avenue. 'Russell' and
3edford' tell you that you are on another of this family's estates, like Covent
arden, and the names of their Devon and Bedfordshire properties—Tavistock,
ndsleigh, Torrington and Woburn—are celebrated in street names throughout.

You now reach **Bedford Square**, one of London's finest and most complete 18C
quares. It was designed by Thomas Leverton and others (1775–80). The four
des are not equilateral but each is designed to look like an integrated set piece
/ith a 'palace front' at the centre—that is, the central houses in the terraces on
ne north and south sides are stuccoed and made prominent with a pediment
nd paired front doors. Inside they are no grander than the rest. This idea came
om Bath. Each house has a distinctive doorcase of Coade stone with regular
ermiculated blocks and a bearded head at the keystone. The fanlights form a
chly varied series. The window rhythm is irregular, indicating that the plans of
ne interiors vary. It is a shame that you can not get into the garden of the square,
nd unreasonable when most of the occupants are no longer private individuals
ut offices. There is too much space for pedestrians but this does help to reduce
ne effect of traffic. The **Architectural Association** at nos 34–36 has a good
ookshop and café open 10.00–19.00 Mon–Fri, 10.00–15.00 Sat.

Leave the square at the northeast corner and walk up **Gower Street**. The
'ictorians found this sort of Georgian street tedious—and so may you. But John
uskin, calling it the '*ne plus ultra* of ugliness in street architecture', was over-
oing it. Look out for no. 7, where the Pre-Raphaelite Brotherhood was founded
 1848, and no. 10, where between 1908 and 1915 Lady Ottoline Morrell
ntertained her circle of 'Bloomsburies' as well as other literati of the day (see
elow). Architect George Dance the Younger (1741–1825) lived and died at no.
1, and Charles Darwin lived in 1838–42 in a house on the site of London
niversity's Biological Department.

Pre-Raphaelite Brotherhood

The Pre-Raphaelites formed themselves as a 'Brotherhood' in 1848 with the
objective of re-establishing in art the moral and visual truthfulness which
they felt had been lost from Raphael onwards. Of the original seven the most
famous were Dante Gabriel Rossetti, William Holman Hunt and Sir John
Everett Millais. Ruskin encouraged them, which helped to overcome the hos-
tility with which works like Millais' *Christ in the House of his Parents* (Tate
Britain) were originally received. The Pre-Raphaelite Brotherhood's early
landscapes still retain a magical sense of sunlight, achieved largely through
a particular technique, but their later mystic medievalism is more alien to
taste today.

At Torrington Place a big *Waterstone's* store functions as the university book-
hop, in a remarkable building by Fitzroy Döll (1900). Keep going past University
ollege on the right until you reach the lodge gates. Opposite is the former
niversity College Hospital, built by Alfred and Paul Waterhouse
 1896–1906) as a massive Gothic X-shape to provide maximum light and venti-
tion in all wards, not caring a jot for the Georgian conformity of Gower Street
r the College opposite. George Orwell was married and died here in 1950.

Enter the lodge gates on the right to explore the quadrangle of **University College London** (UCL), as you would a college in Oxford or Cambridge. The giant ten-column portico and the range either side as far as the corners were designed by William Wilkins (1827–29), and intended to house a new University of London founded on radical principles of religious toleration. The University itself was separately constituted in 1836, after the foundation of its Anglican rival King's College. UCL is now the largest within the university and a centre of excellence.

To the north of the portico, and part of UCL, is the **Slade School of Art**, founded in 1871. It has produced, and still does produce, a succession of students who became famous in British art, including Augustus John, Gwen John and William Orpen in the 1890s, and later Stanley Spencer, David Bomberg, Roger Hilton, Matthew Smith and William Coldstream, who became the Professor in 1949. Inside the College, entered via the door to the right of the steps, is the **Strang Print Room** which houses the College art collection. In the Flaxman Gallery you can see casts of the great sculptor's chief church monuments, acquired by the College after his death. In a glass case is preserved the fully dressed body of Jeremy Bentham, philosopher and one of the earliest supporters of the College, shown as he requested in his will, sitting 'as when I am engaged in thought'. Open 13.00–17.00 Weds–Fri (term time only). Admission free. ☎ 020 7679 2000. Tube: Euston Square.

To the south—and hard to find, but worth the trouble of negotiating your way through a series of doors and corridors—is another UCL museum, the **Petrie Collection** of Egyptian archaeology, donated by Sir Flinders Petrie in 1932: it contains, remarkably, the world's oldest dress. Open 13.00–17.00 Tues–Fri, 10.00–13.00 Sat. ☎ 020 7679 2000.

Exit into Gordon Street and cross **Gordon Square**, which may be quite heavily populated with students: the garden is often a mess, but it is a good location from which to view later Bloomsbury estate housing (**Map 6,4**). Look at the east side. To the left the building is in dignified yellow stock brick, with stone dressings including creamy pilasters and the restrained balconies of the Regency. But to the right, 30 years later, you see the greater exuberance and excessive decoration of the 1850s, with extra floors and larger porches. Both earlier and later parts are the work of Thomas Cubitt, whom we encounter also in Pimlico, Belgravia and Clapham, here employed by the Bedford Estates and responding to their requirement for long thin squares, more brick and less stucco.

Walk down the east side of the square, past no. 46. There is a plaque to economist John Maynard Keynes, but before his occupation this was the chief sanctuary of the Bloomsbury Group. In the southeast corner of the square is another small university museum, the **Percival David Foundation of Chinese Art**, an awe-inspiring collection of Chinese ceramics and other artefacts. Open 10.30–17.00 Mon–Fri. ☎ 020 7387 3909.

The church in the southwest corner of Gordon Square is an oddity, the former first **Catholic Apostolic Church**, a movement founded in the 19C by Edward Irving. The architect was Raphael Brandon (1853). It later became the university church but now seems to be out of use. It is in good Gothic Revival style, if you can get in, with strange details relating to the rituals of its original patrons, whose services called for a large number of officials acting as Apostles.

Bloomsbury Group

The Bloomsbury group evolved from the meetings of friends at the home of the Stephen sisters, Virginia and Vanessa, at no. 46 Gordon Square. It came to include J.M. Keynes, who later lived here, biographer Lytton Strachey, living at no. 51, novelist E.M. Forster and the artist and art critic Roger Fry. Virginia Stephen married Leonard Woolf and her sister Vanessa, Duncan Grant, forming a separate coterie of artistic people at Charleston in Sussex. The 'Bloomsburies' believed art and culture were the only things in life which mattered, an attitude which, although criticised as dilettante and elitist, nevertheless profoundly affected the development of the avant-garde in art and literature in 20C Britain.

Cross over from the church and go down Malet Street. On the left, after a little way, a large block with a rather terrifying tower in the centre, all encased in white stone, begins to loom behind heavy railings. This is the main building of London University, called **Senate House**, a work by Charles Holden (1932–37) with none of the lightness and inspiration of his contemporary Tube stations at the farther reaches of the Piccadilly Line. George Orwell used it as the model for the Ministry of Truth in *1984*, perhaps partly because during the Second World War it had housed the Ministry of Information which had censored his own writing. Go through and explore, especially to the right (south). It is all as heavy and serious as the exterior leads you to expect, rather a depressing experience.

Leave the building on the north side and keep going east. The new **Brunei Gallery** of the **School for Oriental and African Studies** (SOAS) on the right has a bookshop, and sometimes special exhibitions. ☎ 020 7898 4915. The SOAS building itself is again by Holden (1940), happily in a more restrained mood. The library extension by Sir Denys Lasdun (see Chapter 32) should be seen as part of a scheme with his more important **Institute of Education** (completed 1976) straight ahead, with a stepped spur facing you. There were originally to have been five of these spurs, creating an enormous megastructure, but funds would not run to it. Nevertheless, the one which was achieved is vigorous and exciting.

Turn right into **Russell Square** (Map 7,3), the largest and most central of all Bloomsbury squares, laid out in 1800 by Humphry Repton. There are some original houses on the west side by James Burton, father of Decimus Burton the architect, who was the contractor in this period for all the Bedford family's estates. The Sedleys and the Osbornes lived here in W.M. Thackeray's *Vanity Fair* 1848). On the north and south sides Burton's houses were decorated with terracotta when the craze for that material was at its height in the 1890s. The fantastic, unmissable terracotta building in the northeast corner of the square is the *Russell Hotel* by Fitzroy Döll (1898). The tower of Senate House on the west wrecks the proportions of the surrounding area. The garden of the square is being carefully restored to Humphry Repton's original plan.

British Museum

Now, finally, you reach the British Museum (Map 7,5). You can go in from the north side in Montague Place, into the Edwardian wing, but the effect of entry— exciting and ennobling in itself, as the architect Sir Robert Smirke intended—is best enjoyed from the south. So go down Montague Street and turn right, and right again into the main outer courtyard. A forest of Ionic columns stretches out on either hand.

• Galleries open 10.00–17.30 Sat–Wed; 10.00–20.30 Thur, Fri (main floor Egypt and Ancient Near East galleries only). Great Court open 09.00–18.00 Sun–Wed, 09.00–23.00 Thur–Sat. Admission charge only for special exhibitions. Tours of Museum (90 minutes, admission charge) at 10.30, 13.00 and 15.00; tours of specific galleries (50 minutes, free) on the hour and half-hour 11.00–15.30, except 12.30. Café. Restaurant. Shops. ☎ 020 7323 8000 www.thebritishmuseum.ac.uk. Tube: Tottenham Court Road or Holborn.

The origin of the British Museum was a suggestion in the 1753 will of Sir Hans Sloane (see Chapter 16) that parliament should buy his works of art, antiquities and natural history collections for a price far below what they had cost him. The deal was done, and the Cotton and Harley collection of manuscripts purchased at the same time. To this nucleus a vast number of further purchases and bequests have been added since, including the Elgin Marbles and George III's library.

In 1759, the museum was opened in Montague House, Bloomsbury, with restricted admission. The attitude of the 19C was more enlightened, sponsoring the present building by Smirke (1823–47), and in 1879 free unrestricted access. The Reading Room was added to the central courtyard to the design of Robert's brother, Sydney Smirke (1852–57), and the Edward VII galleries on the north side in 1914.

The British Library moved to St Pancras in 1998, vacating the Reading Room and other space and in 2000 the central court was covered by a glazed canopy by Norman Foster and Partners.

There is so much in the British Museum that you have to decide on your approach before visiting. What is your focus? How much time have you got? The main themes are as follows (and there are often special temporary exhibitions):

Ancient Near East	Galleries 6–10, 51–59, 88, 89
Asia	Galleries 33, 34
Britain and Europe	Galleries 37, 40–50
Egypt	Galleries 4, 61–66
Greece and Rome	Galleries 11–23, 69–73, 77, 78, 82–85
Japan	Galleries 92–94
Ethnography	Galleries 25, 26, 27
Money	Galleries 68, 69a
Prints	Gallery 90
Special Exhibitions	Galleries 1, 2, 5, 24, 35

The following route will take you on a tour through the entire Museum, focusing on famous highlights from the whole and taking about three hours. If you have only an hour, visit Galleries 4, 18, 41, 49, 50 and 62–3 to see the highlights mentioned below in those places. Use the floorplan available from desks in the Great Court to find your way around.

First go straight through into the **Great Court**. Only since 2000 have we been able to enjoy this magnificent space, from which various temporary storerooms have been cleared away, and coffee bars, information desks, shops and toilets assembled under a remarkable glazed canopy. Admire Smirke's porticoes, revealed for the first time since the 1850s: the one on the south wing had to be rebuilt and there has been a controversy over the quality of the stone. Nevertheless it all works brilliantly. Wander about to absorb the space and decide where to start.

Smirke intended the original open courtyard to function as a botanical garden. When the specimens did not grow, the **Reading Room** was added. This circular, domed space enjoyed 140 years of fame as the centrepiece of the British Library and the haunt of Karl Marx, H.G. Wells, George Bernard Shaw and countless other readers. It has been restored and now functions as an **information centre**, which has books and computerised databases of information on the British Museum's collections, accessible to visitors from 12.30 daily.

Sir Robert Smirke

Smirke (1780–1867) was, with William Wilkins, the leading Greek Revival architect in London. The son of a Royal Academician, he first trained unsuccessfully with Soane and then travelled extensively, returning home fired with conviction about the purity of ancient Greek architecture. It was his Doric opera house in Covent Garden, later destroyed by fire, which launched the movement in London, demonstrating the dignity and grandeur it was capable of achieving, and he went on to illustrate the principle even more clearly in the General Post Office (also destroyed) and above all the British Museum. He had a distinguished, if stuffy, career culminating in knighthood and a long retirement.

While enjoying a coffee in the Great Court, take a look at some 'tasters' from other galleries located here, notably *Hoa Hakananai'a*, an Easter Island statue of sometime between the 11C and 17C: his expression will never leave your memory.

West wing, ground floor

Gallery 4 Our route takes you first into Gallery 4 of the west wing, among awesome Egyptian sculpture. On the right is the upper half of a statue from Thebes, of *Rameses II of the 19th Dynasty* (13C BC), weighing seven and a quarter tons and brought here in 1816. Its arrival prompted Shelley to write the famous lines

'My name is Ozymandias, King of Kings:
Look on my works, ye mighty, and despair'.
Nothing beside remains. Round the decay
Of that colossal wreck, boundless and bare,
The lone and level sands stretch far away.

Now turn left and go south down the sculpture gallery. Towards the end, on the right, is the **Rosetta Stone**. This object, dated 196 BC, is a decree issued at Memphis during the reign of Ptolemy V. Its importance arises from its use to interpret the hieroglyphics and thus understand the language of Ancient Egypt. The stone was found by Napoleon's army at El-Rashid (Rosetta) in 1799, before their defeat by the British, and then given to the Museum by George III.

Galleries 7, 10 The end of Gallery 4 runs into Gallery 6. Turn right and right again through the parallel Galleries 7 and 10 to see reliefs of *Assyrian lion-hunts* (7C BC). Assyria, in what is now Iraq, possessed its own species of lion—now extinct—which was ritually hunted by the king. These reliefs are from King Asturbanipal's palace at Nineveh.

Gallery 23 Now turn left in Gallery 23, straight across 17 into 18, to jump two centuries from Mesopotamia to Ancient Greece. Here are the Parthenon sculptures (447–432 BC), known as the **Elgin Marbles** after Lord Elgin who, as British Ambassador at Constantinople, acquired them in 1801–3 from the Turkish government which at that time occupied Greece. His motive was conservation, as the Parthenon was in a state of serious deterioration following a gunpowder explosion a century earlier. In 1816 Elgin sold the sculptures to the British government for £35,000, far less than he had spent getting them here. The sculptures comprise a portion of the Parthenon frieze, showing the processional festival in honour of the goddess Athene, some pieces from the east pediment and 15 metopes from the south façade depicting a battle between Centaurs and Lapiths. The Greek government now seek the return of the marbles to combine with those which have survived in Athens; the attitude of the British government is that the sculptures were legitimately acquired. This dispute and the principles underlying it on both sides, as well as the statues' intrinsic worth, make them unmissable in a London visit. There is a good audio-guide if you want to spend more time in this gallery.

Gallery 17 Return to Gallery 17 to see the **Nereid monument** from the area of Turkey once known as Lycia. After Lycia was captured from Greek occupation by the Persians (545 BC), a style of ornate funerary monuments developed, mostly built as decorated chests on the tops of tall pillars. The Nereid monument (c 400 BC) is larger and was brought in ruins from Xanthos in Lycia in the mid-19C and reconstructed in the Museum.

Galleries 19–23 Note in Gallery 21 the remains of one of the Seven Wonders of the Ancient World (although less uplifting than the Parthenon), the **Mausoleum of Helicarnassus** (modern Bodrum, Turkey) (c 350 BC). This great temple—on which Nicholas Hawksmoor based his design for the spire of St George Bloomsbury in Chapter 23—was found in ruins in 1856 and several portions of it brought to London. Next door in Gallery 19 and alongside in 23, 22 and 21 are many further famous works from the Greek or Hellenistic worlds. In Gallery 22, for example, is a portion from another of the Seven Wonders, a marble column drum from the **Temple of Artemis at Ephesus** (324 BC); and the *Spinario*, a Roman copy of a Greek sculpture of a boy taking a thorn from his foot (3C BC).

Galleries 11–15 You have now 'completed' the west wing on the ground floor but if the Classical world is your chief interest, explore Galleries 15, 14 and 13 for red- and black-figure vases and 12 and 11 for the Mycaenean and Cycladic cultures which preceded Greece.

West wing, lower ground floor

Galleries 82–88 If you want more Classical sculpture, now is a convenient moment to explore the lower floor: return to Gallery 23 and go down the stairs in Gallery 10 to the right, passing between a pair of human-headed winged bulls of c 700 BC from Khorsabad in Assyria: there is more Assyrian art in Galleries 88 and 89 to the right at the bottom of the stairs. The Classical collections are in Galleries 82–88: particularly recommended are the sculptures (mostly Roman) collected by Charles Towneley and acquired by the Museum in 1805, including the *Discobolos* and the *Towneley Greyhounds*; and in Gallery 85 shelves full of marvellous Roman portrait busts, commemorating unidealised faces and expressions still to be seen all around us.

Upper floors

Continuing on the tour of the Museum's highlights, make your way via Gallery 21 or 9 or 4 to the west stairs. This is quite a climb: in Smirke's day visitors must have been fitter. Supervising your ascent is the Chinese **Amitabha Buddha** (585 AD), whose 20ft height takes him up through the stairwell.

Galleries 69–73 At the top are some more Classical artefacts arranged by period—the extent depends on you—through Galleries 73–69. The highlight to be sought out is the **Portland Vase** in Gallery 70. This extreme rarity, a cameo-glass vessel from antiquity (?1C BC), was owned by the Dukes of Portland, lent to the museum in 1810, smashed in 1845 but stuck together again. The base is a separate cameo-glass disc but was attached in antiquity, perhaps after an earlier accident. Generations of Wedgwood and other imitations of this famous vase have been produced.

Galleries 36–50 While you are passing through this end of the Museum you may be interested in the Money Galleries, 69a and 68. Continue through Gallery 37 (pre-history) and 36 for European culture, starting in Gallery 40, Britain first. To keep it chronological, turn left in Gallery 49 and 50 to see the Bronze and Iron Ages, and Roman and Celtic periods. Do not miss the **Snettisham Horde** in Gallery 50, the largest deposit of gold and silver from Iron-Age Europe; it was probably a tribal treasury of Celtic gold torcs, many discovered as recently as 1990 near a village in Norfolk. A torc is a heavy ornamental neck ring worn by both men and women.

Nearby is the **Battersea Shield**, a Celtic work in decorated bronze of *c* 300 BC, found in 1857 in the Thames near Battersea, where it was perhaps thrown as part of a funerary rite. The Thames also gave back the winged Waterloo Helmet (*c* 150 BC), shown in a case nearby. Even more vivid are the remains of **Lindow Man**, affectionately christened Pete Marsh because he was found in a peat marsh near Wilmslow, Cheshire in 1984. Pete's is the oldest face to have survived from British history, a 25-year-old murdered around 150 AD and thrown into the bog, the acids of which preserved him.

Go back into Gallery 49 for archaeological finds from Roman Britain. There are many interesting items, but none more than the earliest known **representation of Christ**, beardless and open-faced with carefully arranged hair. It is part of a mosaic pavement (4C AD) discovered in 1963 in a field near the village of Hinton St Mary in Dorset. More human is the collection of correspondence from **Vindolanda**, a Roman fort near Hadrian's Wall, Northumberland, written on thin wooden strips. It includes not only military papers such as intelligence reports and marching orders, but also a birthday party invitation from the wife of one fort commander to another. There are also two startlingly rich **treasure hoards** from Mildenhall and Hoxne (Suffolk), with fine silver table-ware.

Now return to Gallery 41 and go round the circuit through 42 to 48. In the first, it is worth spending some time getting your mind round the 7C **Sutton Hoo Ship Burial**, again from Suffolk. Who was this noble Anglo-Saxon buried with his own 90ft ship? The most likely candidate is Raedwald, king of the area south of the Humber. Whoever he was, the find in 1939 greatly extended our knowledge of Anglo-Saxon culture and recognition of its art: see, for example, the exquisitely beautiful shoulder clasps. The art of this period has been seriously under-estimated: never again can this period be called the 'Dark Ages'.

Continuing round the circuit the collections are less extensive but in Gallery

44 is a great array of clocks ticking away. Do not miss the 12C **Lewis Chessmen**, made of walrus ivory, or the 14C **Royal Gold Cup** made in Paris for Charles V of France, acquired and passed to Henry VI, then given by James I to a Spanish duke, thence to a convent of nuns in 1610 until sold in Paris in the late 19C. Gallery 48 contains a small but interesting 20C collection.

Galleries 51–60 Now head back through Galleries 49 and 50 to the Ancient Near East, country by country, or civilisation by civilisation, proceeding from Gallery 51 (Syria) via 52 (Iran), 53 and 54 (Anatolia–Turkey), 55 and 56 (Mesopotamia–Iraq) and 57–59 (The Levant–Turkey). Particular highlights are the survivals from Babylon (700 BC) and from the Royal tombs of Ur in Mesopotamia (2600 BC) famously excavated by Sir Leonard Woolley in the 1920s, full of people, and the **Oxus Treasure** in Gallery 52. The remains from the Levant date from the Neolithic (8500 BC) to the Phoenicians (300 BC).

Galleries 61–66 The Ancient Near East galleries will be relatively empty compared with our next destination, Galleries 61–66, Egypt. Here burial rites achieved a unique glamour. Begin in Gallery 61, which sets the scene. The spectacular stuff in Galleries 62 and 63, along with the most eye-catching **mummies**, is from the period of the New Kingdom (c 1500–1000 BC).

> The principle of mummification was to preserve the body of the deceased in order to ensure eternal life. The process was gradually perfected over 2000 years, during which it was recognised that the internal organs (apart from the heart) needed to be removed and separated, dried in special canopic jars. Some 70 days after death, during which time various treatments were applied, the body was wrapped in bandages, with jewellery inserted, and placed, with the canopic jars and their contents, in a wooden coffin with a painted lid or stone sarcophagus.

The museum has many such bodies, from Thebes (modern Luxor) and elsewhere. In the late to Roman periods (500 BC–AD 400), the portrait on the coffin lid became increasingly and amazingly lifelike, for example, that of Artemidorus in Gallery 62. He died around 100 AD and his mummy was brought to the museum around 1888, but the face looks as if he might have been alive yesterday, one of us. His funeral inscription in Greek reads, 'Fare Well, Artemidorus': he has, comparatively.

In Galleries 64 and 65, earlier Egyptian burial practices can be traced. In the pre- and Early Dynastic periods, burial took place in the sand, which also preserved the body pretty effectively, as the reconstructed **grave pit** with its typical individual occupant (sometimes known as Ginger from the red tints in his hair) and his grave goods shows. Dating from 3400 BC, he makes Artemidorus, and Pete Marsh, for that matter, seem like novices: but Ginger is one of us, too.

Gallery 67 After these dramatic sights, peace can be restored by going a half-flight down the north stairs to Gallery 67. The **Korea Foundation Gallery** contains an important collection of Korean artefacts and features a house constructed *in situ* by Korean master craftsmen. Sadly, you can not enter it.

Galleries 90–94 Now keep going up to the **Prints and Drawings** collection in Gallery 90, where there are changing exhibitions from the three million works on paper in the Museum. Then go up further (or take a lift) to the **Japan galleries** at the top of the Museum in Galleries 92–94, with a Japanese teahouse and special exhibitions. Again peace descends.

North wing, ground floor
Gallery 33 Take the lift back down to the main floor and enter the substantial **Joseph Hotung Gallery**. A lacquer Buddha from Burma (18C) greets you across the space. To the left are artefacts from **India**: several highlights (explained in a separate pamphlet available in the gallery) include, at the far end, Buddhist sculpture from the stupa at Amaravats. Elsewhere images of Vishnu, Shiva and Parvati take you into Hinduism. To the right are the displays on **China**, with a separate introductory guide again available in the gallery. Here is an even richer range, from 4000 years of culture, China having, as the guide reminds us, 'a greater coherence over a longer period than any other civilization'.

Galleries 26, 27 Unless you wish to return to Gallery 34, on **Islamic art**, go up one flight of stairs, through Gallery 33 and turn right at the end into Gallery 33b (with temporary exhibitions) and back downstairs, past an early 19C red cedar totem pole from Canada, through Galleries 27 and 26. These galleries continue with ethnography from the **Americas**, the northwest coast and Mexico, which are to be extended into Gallery 24. There are stairs down to fascinating new displays on **Africa** in three separate galleries all under Gallery 25 at lower level. Return to the Great Court.

This tour covers the entire permanent Museum. The first part of the building to be finished in 1836, and arguably the finest interior after the Great Court, is the **King's Library** (Gallery 1). At the time of writing it is largely empty but is due to reopen in 2003 on the 250th anniversary of the foundation of the Museum. There is another shop in Gallery 2. There may also be further temporary exhibitions, up the stairs of the Great Court in Gallery 35, or in Gallery 5 at the south-west front. If you feel in need of the restaurant, go up the Great Court stairs.

Exhausted, you will find Holborn station not far away down Southampton Place (Chapter 23), or you can return along Great Russell Street to Tottenham Court Road station.

28 • Euston, King's Cross and St Pancras

This circular walk covers more than just the railway stations—although they are important, interesting to compare, and should not be missed. One of London's most civilised new venues, the British Library, is preceded by some under-visited rarities—St George's Gardens, Dickens's House and the Canal Museum. If you include them all, with detours, it is quite a lengthy walk, although individual sights are not particularly time-consuming.

• Distance: 3 miles. Time: 2 hours + more time for stops. Tube: Euston, King's Cross. Map 6 and 7.

Begin at **Euston Station**, emerging from the underground into the hall of the national rail station, an airport-like space of the 1960s, functional enough but barren and desolate to many of us. It replaced something more important (**Map 6,2**).

The original Euston, named after the landowning Duke of Grafton's country house, Euston Hall in Suffolk, was the first and finest of all London's termini, built by Philip Hardwick (1837) for the London and Birmingham Railway.

This noble structure's great Doric arch and magnificent ticket hall were demolished, despite widespread protest, to make room for the modern platforms, offices and ticket hall: originally spacious, these are now crowded out with little shops of the usual variety.

Go out to the south, past a statue of the railway's engineer *Robert Stephenson*, by Baron Marochetti (1871), to cross the New Road, now called Euston Road. **Friends House**, headquarters of the Quakers, is a Classical design by Hubert Lidbetter (1926) in deference to the station arch that once stood opposite. It has a pretty garden on the east. Further down Euston Road is the **Wellcome Trust**: its award-winning museum of the history of medicine is currently undergoing refurbishment although the library is open. For information ☎ 020 7611 7211. www.wellcome.ac.uk. The Two10 Gallery holds exhibitions on related issues. Open 09.00–18.00 Mon–Fri. ☎ 020 7611 8651.

Go through the garden of Friends House to Endsleigh Gardens and turn left. At the end is the frigid Greek façade of **St Pancras** parish church, by the Inwoods, father and son (1819–22). The son visited Greece in 1819 and was inspired by the Erechtheion and its supporting caryatids. Sometimes you can go inside, where the Greek theme continues: you can understand why A.W.N. Pugin, champion of Gothic, found it objectionable.

Turn south down Upper Woburn Place into a corner of Bloomsbury (Chapter 27), then left into **Woburn Walk**, London's first pedestrianised street (1822), to discover a great rarity, two rows of complete Regency shop fronts, gently Greek Revival in style, placed here by the builder Thomas Cubitt because the Bedford Estate allowed no shops. Return and continue down Upper Woburn Place. Note the British Medical Association building on your left, with the main hall at the back built by Sir Edwin Lutyens for the Theosophists (Lady Lutyens was one) but taken over and completed for the British Medical Association in 1938. **Tavistock Square**, on your right (**Map 6,4**), is a beauty, with a fine Cubitt terrace (1826) on the west side. Charles Dickens and Virginia Woolf once lived and wrote here. There is a statue of *Ghandi* by Fredda Brilliant (1966) in the middle; the Mahatma stayed near here when in London.

At Tavistock Place, turn left. After a short distance you reach a monument to the Arts and Crafts architectural style by A. Dunbar Smith and Cecil Brewer (1895–97), the former Mary Ward Centre, founded in 1890 by the novelist known as Mrs Humphry Ward as a play and social centre. Pevsner calls it 'one of the most charming pieces of architecture designed at that time in England', which is high praise because many lovely things were created in the aftermath of the Gothic Revival, and before Classicism bullied its way back. The building is now the National Institute for Social Work Training. Go on to the traffic lights and cross to turn right down Marchmont Street. You soon reach an entirely novel modern structure, the **Brunswick Centre**, a pioneering housing scheme of the 1960s by Patrick Hodgkinson. The flats descend in two straight lines of terraces overlooking the miserable and windswept shopping street: no cars can be seen—they are all parked underneath, a 1960s mania. A good cinema, the *Renoir*, can be found within. Turn left out into Brunswick Square, laid out by S.P. Cockerell (1800) and named after Caroline of Brunswick, the unhappy queen of George IV: no original housing remains. Go round the edge of the open space known as **Coram's Fields** (**Map 7,3**).

This was the site of the Foundling Hospital, an important 18C charity founded in 1739 by Captain Thomas Coram, who was scandalised at the number of deserted children he found in the London streets. His initiative was supported by William Hogarth, G.F. Handel and other well-known figures of the day and the rather gaunt Classical buildings stood on these grounds until the 1930s. The charity still exists, and its school is now at Berkhamsted, Hertfordshire.

It has recently been decided to open the art collection of the **Foundling Museum** at no. 40 Brunswick Square to the public in 2004. For information, ☎ 020 7841 3600. In Coram's Fields there is a playground, out of bounds to adults unless accompanied by a child. Circuit the Fields to reach **Mecklenburgh Square**, named for George III's queen, Charlotte, who was formerly Princess of Mecklenburgh-Strelitz. Built to match Brunswick Square, it has a good deal of original housing. Exit on the east side and walk south, across Guilford Street, to reach no. 48 Doughty Street (**Map 7,4**), now the **Dickens House Museum**. This is the author's only surviving London address, where he finished *Pickwick Papers* and wrote *Oliver Twist* and *Nicholas Nickleby*. It has a rather cheerless atmosphere but some interesting exhibits. Open 10.00–17.00 Mon–Sat, 13.00–17.00 Sun. Theatrical shows May–Sept 19.30 Wed. Admission charge. Shop. ☎ 020 7405 2127. www.dickensmuseum.com. Tube: Russell Square.

Charles Dickens

Dickens (1812–70) is the archetypal London writer, both in his manner of production and in his subject matter. He was born in Portsmouth in humble and deteriorating circumstances; his family came to London in the 1820s. His father was imprisoned for debt and Dickens, aged 12, was put to work in a blacking factory, an experience he later recalled incessantly. His irrepressible personality prevented any lengthy disposition to melancholy, however, and by the age of 18 he had become a shorthand reporter at the House of Commons; he was soon a widely published journalist, writing primarily on London and its types. It was a decision of genius to turn this fecundity of prose into fiction, and to publish it in the journalistic form of monthly instalments, beginning with the *Pickwick Papers* in 1836 when he was 24, and continuing through 14 great novels to *Our Mutual Friend* in 1864. Play-readings, public readings of his novels, continuing journalism and editing made for a life so busy that it wearies one to read of it. His family life was unhappy and in his later years the actress Ellen Ternan became his mistress.

All the novels except *Hard Times* are centred on London and seem to capture perfectly the essence of Dickens's times. But it would be wrong to see the London in his work as consistent: it changes its character from the sparkling and cheerful Georgian stage-coach world of Mr Pickwick, where nothing stays very serious for long, to the darker, railway city of mid-century when poverty, complexity, dirt and fog oppressed the spirits of the people, including Dickens himself. No other author on London has come so close to penetrating its heart.

At the top of Doughty Street continue into Mecklenburgh Street, turning left into Heathcote Street to see briefly **St George's Gardens**, the burial ground of the churches of St George Bloomsbury (Chapter 23) and St George the Martyr, and hygienically located in 1713 at the emptier northern edge of the paris (**Map 7.1**). There are nice winding paths between the monuments. Leave a Sidmouth Street on the north side, noting **Regent Square** to the left; before th Second World War it was moderately grand with a fine Greek Revival church o the east side. Turn right to reach Gray's Inn Road.

You must toil up this dreary street but it will be worth it in the end. At the to on the right, after Britannia Street, a taster is provided in a building by Hart an Waterhouse (1910), a joyous mixture of old styles. Fork right and cross shabb Pentonville Road to go up **Caledonian Road**, laid out in 1826 (off **Map 7.1**): th name comes not from the railway to Scotland but from one of the original build ings here, the Royal Caledonian Asylum for the children of exiled Scots. On th right is an amazingly pretty little development, Keystone Crescent (1845).

Continue up Caledonian Road and turn left into Northdown Street, acros Wharfedale Road into New Wharf Road to locate the **London Canal Museu** (off top of **Map 7**), housed in the former ice house of Carlo Gatti (d. 1878), th man who introduced ice cream to the mass market. He also sold ice, and store it in a huge pit in the centre of the museum. But the main purpose of th museum is to tell the story of London's canals, their development, their boa and the people who worked on them. It is a fascinating and necessary counter part to the London Transport Museum in Covent Garden. Open 10.00–16.3 Tues–Sun and Bank Holidays. Admission charge. Shop. ☎ 020 7713 083(www.charitynet.org/~LcanalMus. Tube: King's Cross.

Beyond, and worth exploring briefly, is the canal basin of **Battlebridge** on th Grand Union, here part of the Regent's Canal (see Chapter 39). Then eithe return down York Way to King's Cross or, for an atmospheric detour, go up Yor Way to turn left down Goods Way. On your right are the now listed gasholder which may or may not survive plans to bring the new Eurotunnel rail link in t St Pancras. They date from the 1880s. In this environment the **Camley Stree Natural Park**, a peaceful reserve for birds and wildflowers, comes as a complet surprise. Open 09.00–17.00 Mon–Thur, 11.00–17.00 Sat, Sun (10.00–16.0 in winter). Admission free. ☎ 020 7833 2311. www.wildlondon.org.uk

Turn left in Pancras Road. Walk back down it to note, on the left, Stanley Building among the oldest surviving flats for the working class in London (1864), wit cast-iron balconies off a central exterior staircase, an approved model. Final you reach King's Cross hotel and station. Be aware that this is a red-light distri and you may not want to linger around the station too long, especially at nigh

King's Cross and St Pancras stations

Look at **King's Cross Station** (**Map 7.1**) from the front first. It was built by Lew Cubitt (1850–51) as the terminus for the Great Northern Railway, servin Lincolnshire and Yorkshire. The line was designed by William Cubitt and his so Joseph (1846–50). Euston had been opened only a few years before, its overpow ering Classical portico a grandiloquent welcome to the trains getting up stea within. Here at King's Cross there is a welcome, but no disguises, no romance— simply twin arches constructed with yellow stock bricks, reflecting the two ope arches of the train shed behind, a plain modernist statement of function wa ahead of its time. Between them a clock tower reflects the popular 1840s idio of the Italian villa: it is a pity about the 1970s structure in front of the statio To the left, and quite separate to differentiate its function from that of the railwa erminus, is Cubitt's hotel, curved to follow the old line of Pancras Road, and gain in bright yellow bricks with stone dressings.

It is a certainty, however, that during your survey of King's Cross your eye will ave been incapable of resisting a look at the multicoloured, frilly Gothic masses f **St Pancras**, to the left, flaunting themselves along the Euston Road. The combined view of these two buildings forms an almost moral architectural dilemma, etween the functional and the blatantly decorative. The building fronting the tation was originally the Grand Midland Hotel. The architect was Sir George ilbert Scott (1865–74). He is sometimes said to have used designs rejected for he Foreign Office years before (Chapter 12), although all there is proof for is cott's extensive study of European Gothic. But no one could say that this is simly an academic exercise. The richness of the motifs, materials and ideas constiite what is now seen as one of London's great buildings. The interior (occasionlly open) is disappointing only on account of its dilapidated state, which may be ransformed if it receives the same care recently lavished on the exterior 1991–95). This may happen when the Eurotunnel link goes ahead. Then it will e possible to see the grand staircase, the coffee room and even perhaps the adies Smoking Room restored to their former glory.

Sir George Gilbert Scott

Scott (1811–78) was the most prolific of Victorian architects, and typifies what later generations criticised in High Victorian Gothic: they thought it complacent, slick, over-decorated and uninspired. Scott trained as a builder of workhouses but, himself an evangelical, turned to church architecture and obtained commissions to build or ruthlessly restore innumerable examples, including many described in the 'village' walks in this guide, as well as Westminster Abbey. His most famous work is the St Pancras Hotel, which he suggested might be 'too good for its purpose', his pleasure in it deriving partly from the chance to complete a major secular building in Gothic after being forced to adopt a Renaissance Classicism for his Foreign Office building. The Albert Memorial (Chapter 35) perhaps exemplifies all that is best about Scott and his period.

Go up the steps to the St Pancras forecourt and through to the platforms ehind. This area is equally magnificent, but for totally different reasons. Here a uge span of 240ft was constructed by the London Midland Railway's engineer .H. Barlow in cast iron. It was originally painted entirely sky-blue and fully lazed so that the effect aimed at invisibility, though it was soon made filthy by team from the engines. The shed is 20ft above ground level, a functional decion in several respects: first, learning from the problems at Euston, it allowed igineers to make a level track away to the north; second, it enclosed tie bars to ipport the roof; and, third, it stored hundreds of barrels of beer from Burton on rent to quench Londoners' legendary thirst.

After exploring the train shed, the Gothic ticket office to the west (find the railay navvies commemorated in the carved capitals), and the cab route with its rnate vaulted roof, turn right across Midland Road for the last stop on this walk, ie inspiring British Library.

British Library

You enter across an open public courtyard, with mixed levels, gardens, steps and statuary. Note the grand **entrance gate**, alluding to the original doors to the King's Library in the British Museum, and Sir Eduardo Paolozzi's statue after William Blake, *Newton as the Ancient of Days*, designed to signify literature and science and quietly forgetting the critical sense of Blake's original engraving. Before you reach the main entrance in the left of the two wings, note the rich use of orange and red as a compliment to the St Pancras building towering above, with green for the window sunshades and white stone inserted for contrast.

- Open 09.30–18.00 Mon, Wed–Fri, 09.30–20.00 Tues, 09.30–17.00 Sat, 10.00–17.00 Sun and Bank Holidays. Admission free. Reading rooms require a ticket; public access to events in the conference centre and theatre. Bookable tours at 15.00 daily (not Thur), also 18.30 Tues, 10.30 Sat, 11.30 Sun. Café. Shop. ☎ 020 7412 7332. www.bl.uk

In 1998 the British Library opened on this site, having moved from the British Museum. The gestation of the new library building was long and painful: the architect Colin St John Wilson was appointed as early as 1962. Thanks to government meanness or the indifference of private patronage (depending on your politics), the finished library, after a generation of hesitation and cutbacks, is half the size originally planned. In time this may be a source of bitter regret, since the object of the library is to collect every printed text published in the United Kingdom. But if, as some forecast, the role of the book is to decline and give place to the website, there may be enough room after all. In any case there is space within the site for expansion upwards and downwards, if necessary.

Inside, all is open and light, the sun shining through. A fine shop is on your left and comfortable stairs lead up to the **John Ritblat Gallery** exhibition spaces housing among other treasures the Magna Carta (1215), a copy of the Gutenberg Bible (1455), the First Folio of Shakespeare plays (1623) and work in the handwriting of the famous from Leonardo da Vinci to Sir Paul McCartney.

The British Library on Euston Road

The **Tower of Books** comprises the original King's Library (the gift to the nation by George IV of his father's collection), accessible on request but meanwhile presented as a design statement.

The British Library has a wondrous interior, and gives the lie to the theory that a painful project, and shortage of funds, must imply a disappointing building. Whatever the future of the book, this building has done it justice for the present.

he Library ends this walk. Continue west along Euston Road to Euston or
uston Square station, noting the caryatids above the entrance to the burial
rypt of St Pancras New Church. On the right there is a delightful Art and Crafts
re station, one of several such in London.

9 • Clerkenwell

his walk is a slow descent from the 'heights' of Islington through the former
illage of Clerkenwell into the City itself, just outside the original walls and the
each of the Great Fire. We shall see good evidence of the past and of the medieval
orld in particular. Note the details for pre-booking tours of St John's Priory and
ie Charterhouse.

Distance: 2½ miles. Time: 2 hours + more to study the churches. Tube: Angel.
Maps 7 and 8 (starts off map).

tart at Angel station on the City branch of the Northern Line. Ignoring the
ttractions of Islington (Chapter 43) turn left down to the traffic lights and cross
ver to walk west along **Pentonville Road** (1750s). This represented the final
tretch of the New Road and was developed at this eastern end by Henry Penton
om 1770. Some original early 19C terraces remain visible on either side at this
oint. The **Crafts Council Gallery** is housed in a former chapel of 1818, part of
ie then-new developments, from which the original railings survive in front. Go
rough the Ionic porch. The Gallery has changing exhibitions, a picture library,
hotostore and reference library. Open 11.00–18.00 Tues–Sat; 14.00–18.00
un. Admission free. Café. Shop. ☎ 020 7278 7700. www.craftscouncil.org.uk
    Go back to the traffic lights, turn right down St John Street and right into
osebery Avenue, a cut-through organised in the 1890s and named after Lord
osebery, first chairman of the London County Council. Note on the right the
ecently reopened *Sadler's Wells Theatre*, mainly for dance productions. In
683 wells were found in the garden of Thomas Sadler's music hall, which soon
ecame a tourist spot noted for its pleasant gardens and water features. The first
ieatre was built in 1746.
    On the left is the once revolutionary new housing of the **Spa Green Estate** by
erthold Lubetkin and Francis Skinner (1946–50), two partners in the Tecton
rchitectural practice. Soon the imperialistic former headquarters of the
letropolitan Water Board come into view on the right, just after the Modernistic
aboratory Building of 1938. All this is known as **New River Head** and is now
nostly flats, but was once the terminal point of the whole operation. Inside the
920s building is the Oak Room, with woodwork by Grinling Gibbons and 17C
astering, a remnant from the original New River Head buildings which lay
ightly to the north.

This New River, flowing from mid-Hertfordshire to Islington, is neither new
nor is it a river. Opened in 1613, it was constructed by private capitalists, of
whom the leading light was Sir Hugh Myddelton, and backed by the City, to
bring and sell fresh water to Londoners. Fairly soon it became an indispensable public service as the water of the Thames became increasingly polluted,
and for 200 years, pure water from storage ponds or reservoirs here flowed
through elm pipes down to the City. As an overground aqueduct, it also had—

and still has in many places, including Great Amwell in Hertfordshire and Gentleman's Walk, Enfield—much picturesque visual appeal.

Next, on the left, is the jolly exterior of the former Finsbury Town Hall (1895). Behind it, in a separate building, is the **Family Records Centre**, where you can research your British ancestors. Open 09.00–17.00 Mon–Sat (19.00 Tues and Thur). Admission free. ☎ 020 8392 5300. www.pro.gov.uk/. Tube: Angel or Farringdon.

Turn left down Rosomon Street and right into **Exmouth Market**, a quaint mid-19C street with cafés, pubs, second-hand shops and a small street market (**Map 7,2**). The name commemorates Lord Exmouth who in 1816 bombarded Algiers as part of the British anti-slavery campaign. The purely Italian church of the **Holy Redeemer** on the left, by J.D. Sedding (1887), is spectacular but you are unlikely to get inside.

At the end of Exmouth Market is a substantial crossroads, on the other side of which is the even more substantial **Mount Pleasant** main sorting centre for the Post Office (**Map 7,4**). One third of the country's entire mail passes through here, much of it by van but also by 'mail rail', a self-contained automatically operated track running underground from here to London's other sorting offices. Tours morning and afternoon (mail rail shown only in afternoon) Mon–Fri. Admission free. No children under 12. Book 2–3 weeks ahead. ☎ 020 7239 2311.

At the end of Exmouth Market, turn left into Pine Street to see one of the sacred sites of the Modern movement, the **Finsbury Health Centre**, the first public commission of Lubetkin and Tecton (1935–38). (See more of their work at Highpoint, Highgate, in Chapter 42.) This building pre-dates the National Health Service and was a pioneer both in architecture and public health, aimed at providing a service for those in the overcrowded housing all around. It looks a little shabby today, but the light of its brave new world still shines. Turn left down Northampton Road to visit the **Metropolitan Archives**—there is no public museum, but access to many important documents relating to London's history. Open 09.30–16.45 Mon, Wed, Fri; 09.30–19.30 Tues and Thur. Admission free ☎ 020 7532 38202. www.cityoflondon.gov.uk/archives/lma. Tube: Farringdon.

Otherwise turn right to **Farringdon Road**. Close by, at no. 94, is the *Quality Chop House*, a rare surviving old-time working-class restaurant, still with wooden benches. Go down the hill. There are plenty of reminders that this was a poor area of slums around the smelly Fleet valley on which was imposed working-class charitable housing such as the huge Peabody building (1883) on the left. When this comes into view turn left down Pear Tree Court, then right down Clerkenwell Close with St James's church on your left. Clerkenwell's history is distinct and needs to be understood.

The waters of the Fleet once made it delightful, and its springs and wells served several monastic establishments (the area's name derives from 'Clerk Well', clerks being monks). After the Reformation, many of the new property owning aristocrats built mansions here and in the 18C the wells and spa among them Sadler's Wells and Spa Fields, became popular venues for weekend entertainment. Small firms of watch-makers, jewellers and gin distillers set up their businesses, attracted by the water supply—Booth's and Gordon's gin both began here. Overcrowding gradually polluted the waters and created slums, made worse by the Victorians driving new roads through the den housing. Clerkenwell gradually became infamous as a centre of 19C radical-ism and a breeding-ground for the Chartist movement of the 1840s and related riots and demonstrations. The area still has its radical connections: the British Communist Party and its newspaper had offices in Farringdon Road, the *Guardian* does still, and the *Big Issue*, the newspaper sold by the homeless, is also printed here. But in the 1990s Clerkenwell also became one of the most fashionable areas in which to live as City workers followed artists in converting warehouse spaces into apartments.

It may be possible to make an appointment to see the original Clerk's Well through Finsbury Lending Library; ☎ 020 7527 7960 and ask for Local History. The church of **St James** was built on the site of St Mary's nunnery by a local architect, James Carr (1788–92), who gave it an eye-catching spire similar to that of St Martin-in-the-Fields (**Map 8,1**). The interior is often open, up the tall steps: it is plain but pleasing. To the east lie Woodbridge Street and Sekforde Street, a more or less complete early 19C estate—a lovely stuccoed Savings Bank breaks the brick terrace in Sekforde Street.

To the south, past the recommended *Crown Tavern*, you reach Clerkenwell Green, with office-workers in evidence but also plenty of 18C atmosphere. On the west side is the Middlesex Sessions House by Thomas Rogers (1779–82), and on the north the **Marx Memorial Library**—evidence of Clerkenwell's radical-ism—which was built in 1738 as a Welsh charity school. In 1902–3 Lenin had an office here, which can still be seen, as can a powerful Marxist mural advocat-ing revolution, done in 1935. The Library itself was opened in 1933 to celebrate the 50th anniversary of Marx's death. Open 13.00–18.00 Mon; 13.00–20.00 Tues–Thur; 10.00–13.00 Sat. Closed Aug. Admission free. ☎ 020 7251 4706.

Go south into Clerkenwell Road (another Victorian cut-through) and walk east to a small crossroads. To both left and right are remains of the **Priory of St John**, former headquarters of the Knights Hospitaller. The church, on the left, was rebuilt after the Second World War by John Seely and Paul Paget; the key sight here is the crypt, an original 12C space. (If it is closed, try booking a guided tour as described below.) You can see evidence of mid-12C work in the unaisled western section and a more elaborately decorated later 12C development at the altar end.

Knights Hospitaller

Less controversial than the Knights Templar (see Chapter 8), the Knights Hospitaller were established after the First Crusade to support pilgrims and care for the sick. Their first priory in England was in Clerkenwell. They fol-lowed the Augustinian rule—the Templars were Cistercian—and formed mixed communities of knights, doctors and chaplains. When the more unpopular Templars were suppressed, the Hospitallers took over most of their property, although not in London.

To the south lies the gatehouse of the former Priory, now the **museum**. Open 10.00–17.00 Mon–Fri; 10.00–16.00 Sat. Admission free. Guided tours (charge, not recommended) of Chapter Hall and Church at 11.00 and 14.30 Tues, Fri and Sat. ☎ 020 7324 4000. Tube: Farringdon.

The original Priory was burned down during the Peasants' Revolt (see below); the early 16C building has been restored many times, most recently by J.O. Scott, son of Sir George Gilbert Scott, but still has a fine medieval flavour. The museum tells the story of the Knights and also of their modern counterparts, the St John's Ambulance Brigade, founded in 1877 to provide a voluntary first-aid service to the public.

Continue down St John's Lane to join St John Street, at the end of which you reach **Smithfield Market** (Map 8,1). It is worth making a circuit round this important-looking structure, perhaps down Grand Avenue and back up Poultry Avenue. It was built by Horace Jones (1866–67), the City's architect, later to do Billingsgate and Tower Bridge; this was his first big scheme. In the 1990s it was extensively renovated and modernised to comply with modern hygiene regulations and, as if to make up, repainted in such bright colours that even a Victorian would blink. It all works pretty well, and when the great slabs of meat are lying around you feel, first, that the 19C would have strongly approved of all this blood and lusty consumerism and, second, that it can't last much longer.

Smithfield's association with animals goes back to the Middle Ages when, as a 'smooth field', it was ideal for a horse market. Bartholomew Fair, a notoriously rowdy event, was held here from 1133 until 1855. From the 17C a cattle market was held here despite the great problem of driving the live cattle through the ever more built-up streets of north London—although the New Road helped—and the subsequent ghastliness of the slaughter. For 400 years Smithfield was also the place of execution of criminals, 'witches' and especially of heretics, including the Protestant martyrs burned under Mary I.

Peasants' Revolt

Smithfield is also important as the location of the climax of the Peasants' Revolt in 1381. This was the first large-scale uprising by English people, beginning in Essex and Kent, when angry mobs marched on London. The causes were greater poverty in the years following the Black Death of 1348 and, more immediately, an imposed poll tax of one shilling per head. The rebels seized and executed the Archbishop of Canterbury and other officials, and in London caused great destruction. Under Wat Tyler's leadership they assembled to present their radical demands to the 14-year-old Richard II at Smithfield. The King, whose attitude was moderate, coolly heard the complaints, but Tyler was stabbed by the Lord Mayor. With some courage, Richard nevertheless led the protestors north into the fields of Clerkenwell where they dispersed. He never had such a success again and is the only English king to have his throne usurped. And poll taxes still seem to madden the British.

If you are undertaking this walk on a Wednesday in spring or early summe you may want to join a tour of the **Charterhouse**. Pre-booked tours April–Ju only at 14.15 Wed. Admission charge. ☎ 020 7251 5002.

The Charterhouse was founded in 1370 as a Carthusian monastery, built o the burial ground of 50,000 victims of the recent Black Death. Carthusia live silently in isolated cells, a group of which was built for them here, wi other monastic buildings, by Henry Yevele (see Chapter 14). The Carthusia resisted the Reformation and were accordingly slaughtered. The Charte house was often visited by the later Tudor monarchs and taken over by th aristocratic favourites but in 1613 it was purchased by Thomas Sutton, 'the richest commoner in England', who set up a school and a hospital for poor gentlemen. And so it functioned until the late 19C, when Charterhouse School moved to Surrey.

The pensioners are still there and, despite bomb damage, so is a remarkable series of surviving buildings, both medieval and Tudor/Jacobean. Since they are largely invisible from the street, a tour is the only option if you are interested in seeing them.

Happily, the last two buildings on this walk, part of a single foundation, are properly open, and lie just south of Smithfield Market. Cross West Smithfield, a square containing a circular underground space built to link the market with the Metropolitan Line, and look out for a gateway in the southeast corner (**Map 8.2 and 4**). This leads through to **St Bartholomew the Great**, after the chapel in the Tower the oldest church in London.

It is necessary to understand that, as you walk to the church down the pathway, you are walking down the south aisle of what was once a huge abbey. To your left, instead of the present raised churchyard, was the nave and beyond that the north aisle. The west wall ahead of you was erected as recently as the 1890s by Sir Aston Webb (of Admiralty Arch fame), who was responsible for the entire, very effective, restoration of that date. St Bartholomew's had been another casualty of the Reformation, when the bulk of the abbey was demolished and only the former choir and crossing, and the Lady Chapel, were handed over as a parish church.

One of the original bays of the north side of the nave survives across the churchyard: you can walk over to it and at the same time glance at the beautiful street façade of **Cloth Fair**, laid out in 1590 on abbey grounds—there are several good 18C houses and shop-fronts and, at nos 41–42, a complete 17C merchant's house. Return to look inside the church.

You enter through the base of a brick tower (1628). To your right you immediately see the entry to the east walk of the cloister, all that survives from an extension of 1405. To your left and ahead, the interior of the church opens up to reveal the crossing of the abbey and its choir, formed of massive 12C piers: a restored ambulatory curves around behind the altar, off which a double-apsed chapel projects to the south. There were once similar chapels to the north and east, before the Lady Chapel was built in the 14C, when a craze for these extensions developed. Most of the present chapel is by Webb, but there is an early 16C crypt below. As you return through the church, there are some fine monuments. The most important is to Rahere, the Augustinian founder of both abbey and hospital:

St Bartholomew the Great

he died in 1144, but the tomb is part of the remodelling of *c* 1405. Another, the early 19C, in the north aisle, is on behalf of a couple and records touchingly

> *She pre-deceased him,*
> *He a little tried*
> *To live without her,*
> *Liked it not, and died.*

There is much Victorian woodwork: stalls, screen, organ case and galler; Webb was responsible for the pulpit, lectern and the wrought-iron screens. Th odd altar dates from the 1950s. ☎ 020 7606 5171.

Finally, leave the church and cross over to see **St Bartholomew's Hospit**; (known universally as Barts), the oldest charitable institution still on its origin; London site (**Map 8,3 and 4**).

> It has now been spared demolition, or at least replacement as a hospita. There was a similar scare when Henry VIII dissolved the monastery and wa prevailed upon to re-open the hospital only on his death-bed after pleas from the City. His statue (18C) appears over the gatehouse between figures *Lameness* and *Disease*, about which he cared not a rap. William Harvey, di coverer of blood circulation, was chief physician here 1609–43.

Go through the Baroque gateway (1702) to discover the church of **S Bartholomew the Less**, once the hospital chapel but for many centuries now parish church. The octagonal building—unusual in itself—was originally th work of the ever-inventive George Dance the Younger (1789), later altered b Thomas Hardwick (1823–25). The tower and west vestry date back to the 15 and there are some monuments from those days, including a brass in the vestr

Further in lies the 18C central quadrangle of the hospital with north, east an west wings by James Gibbs (1730–50), originally in Bath stone but refaced i Portland stone by Philip Hardwick in 1850. Hardwick provided the fountain The South Block, or George V building, is 20C. Gibbs's blocks are very handsom and are unusual for their date in being detached from each other as a safegua* against both fire and cross-infection. In the fine staircase of the North Wing a* William Hogarth's paintings of the *Pool of Bethesda* and *Good Samaritan*, don for free, in line with his similar contributions to the Foundling Hospital (Chapt 28)—they were important in the struggle to introduce history painting into pu lic places in England. Hogarth had been born in Bartholomew Close in 169 Tours of the North Wing leave from the gatehouse at 14.00 Fri. ☎ 020 7601 815 and ask for the archivist.

A walk around the hospital will show other architecture (19C and 20C), but you began back in Islington and have made it this far, you deserve a rest. *Cl Gascon* (next to St Bartholomew the Great) is recommended, and there are le expensive places to eat towards St Paul's and its Tube station close by.

South Bank: Southwark to Vauxhall

The two banks of London's river have strongly opposing characters, even more than in Paris. From the chance way the Thames bends at Waterloo Bridge, it happens that Westminster and the 'North Bank' area take up 75 per cent of the riverside, and to the east the City was dominant from the start: so the stretch along the southern bank from Southwark to Vauxhall has always had a sense of its inferiority.

For centuries, apart from the settlement of Southwark itself, Bankside and the South Bank generally were places for recreation and entertainment, free from the City's restrictions. The area was close enough for the population of London to cross the river easily, over the bridge or by ferry, and procure some pleasure in the theatre, or bear pit or brothel or, later, at Vauxhall Pleasure Gardens upstream. But the South Bank had other features. The cathedral of Southwark, though of course smaller than St Paul's, gave the Church a strong presence, reinforced by the Bishop of Winchester's Palace (of which only a small ruined section survives) alongside. At Lambeth, the Archbishop of Canterbury's London palace served its purpose from the 12C.

For many generations, nothing lay between these ecclesiastical goal posts but marsh, gradually superseded by a long line of riverside wharves, boat-builders and barge houses, then terraced houses criss-crossed by railway tracks. Then, after the Second World War and widespread bomb damage, a gradual change occurred, starting with the Festival of Britain in 1951, which effectively extended the notion of entertainment along the whole strip of southern riverbank.

The four walks which are included here give full weight to the South Bank's wide and still growing range of entertainments and cultural institutions, from the oldest to the newest, including the London Eye and Tate Modern. They try also to keep in the frame those traces of the past, sometimes conserved in museums (such as the Old Operating Theatre) or repackaged and re-presented (such as the Globe) and sometimes retrieved by archaeology (such as the Rose Theatre), which gave the South Bank its particular distinction.

30 • Shad Thames to Borough

The hardest part about this walk is getting to the starting point: after that it is full of interesting and unusual sights, resonant of old Thameside London, dirty, foggy, Dickensian, but inevitably smartened up by modern money.

• Distance: 2¾ miles. Time: 2 hours. Tube: Bermondsey or London Bridge. Map 9.

The best route is to walk from Bermondsey station (Jubilee Line) west along Jamaica Road as far as Dockhead (off **Map 9**). It is a tedious tramp and will take 10 minutes at least. If you can't face it, do the walk in reverse, starting at London Bridge—but the overall distance will be further.

Dockhead refers to the inner terminus of St Saviour's Dock, which was originally the mouth of the long-invisible River Neckinger, now flowing underground. The eye-catching church on the corner is **Most Holy Trinity**, a Roman Catholic church by H. Goodhart-Rendel (1960), with the detailed brickwork of

Art Deco cinemas. Take a look up the dock from the main road. Although now flanked by office redevelopments of the 1980s, it still conveys the feeling of the warehouses which were once filled from it, mostly housing grain, peas, wheat and barley in this area of Bermondsey.

Turn up Mill Street towards the river. You are now walking through the area known as **Jacob's Island** and notorious in the 19C as the worst slums in all London, described with horror by journalists and novelists such as Charles Dickens (Bill Sykes meets his death here in *Oliver Twist*). All is now respectable new flats and offices. The block to the immediate left is called Vogan's Mill (1987–89).

Cut through at the end of Mill Street on the left to New Concordia Wharf, a pioneering forerunner (1981–83) of the prestigious warehouse conversions which have extended like ribbon development down the Thames. When you get out to a view of the river, you can see to the right **China Wharf**, not a conversion but a new Postmodern structure by CZWG (1986–88) with bright colours, original shapes, jokes, and references to its surroundings. To the left is a beautiful footbridge glinting against the water and warehouse walls, by N. Lacey and Partners (1995). Opposite, one of the last to be converted, is the eastern section of Butler's Wharf.

Cross the bridge and take the riverside path to join **Shad Thames**: 'shad' is supposed to be a corruption of St John, a reference to the original ownership of this land by the Knights Templar. A remarkable sculpture, *Exotic Cargo* by Peter Randall-Page (1995), precedes the **Design Museum**, built in a converted 1950s warehouse by Conran Roche in 1989 (**Map 9,8**). The brainchild of Sir Terence Conran, the Museum has regularly updated displays from its permanent collection of modern objects and presents changing exhibitions on historical and contemporary themes. Attached to it is the *Blue Print Café*, one of Conran's earliest and smallest restaurants. There is an interesting shop and a pleasant café overlooking the river. Open 11.30–18.00 Mon–Fri; 10.30–18.00 Sat–Sun. Admission charge. Café. Shop. ☎ 020 7940 8790. www.designmuseum.org

This is a good place from which to admire Tower Bridge from the east (Chapter 3). Turn left to follow Shad Thames westwards. Although all the buildings have been converted from warehouse use, you can still get a vivid impression of what the area was like originally, smelling of spice and sprinkled with the spillages of innumerable sacks. Many of the iron bridges linking the riverside warehouses to landward storage are still in place. Now most of the warehouses are offices or flats, but at ground-floor level there are many pleasant cafés and shops. Note on the left Cayenne Court, a too-suburban development.

Cut through at some point—there are several openings—towards the river. Here along the riverfront Terence Conran has developed a series of attractive restaurants, with **Butler's Wharf** (originally 1871) towering above, all beautifully converted. Where you see old timber, do not assume it was always in its present location—but at least ancient materials were used in preference to new.

Keep on by the riverside, under Tower Bridge—this is where you can enter to see the gleaming engineering (see Chapter 3)—into an area now under intensive redevelopment. It was known as Potter's Fields and until demolition was a mass of relatively unimportant small buildings, not the grand warehouses of the eastern side. A piece of exciting architecture is rapidly taking shape on the site, the new **City Hall** building by Norman Foster Associates, known already as the

'Helmet'. Built to house the Greater London Authority, it is surprisingly modest in scale but compelling in shape and location. Public access to the walkway round the interior will be possible when the building opens around June 2002. www.london.gov.uk.

Greater London Authority

This new body was set up in spring 2000, when London voted into office its first ever Mayor, Ken Livingstone. (The ancient office of Lord Mayor has responsibility only for the City of London, and its holder is not democratically elected.) The new Mayor appoints an advisory cabinet and works with a separately elected group, the London Assembly. Together they are responsible for eight areas of administration in London: transport; planning; economic development; environment; police, fire and emergency services; culture; and health.

For earlier forms of local government in London, see p 315.

In the stream is **HMS Belfast**, a cruiser and museum administered by the Imperial War Museum, which is a recommendation (**Map 9,8 and 7**). Open March–Oct 10.00–18.00; Nov–Feb 10.00–17.00. Admission charge (children free). Café. Shop. ☎ 020 7940 6300. www.hmsbelfast.org.uk. Tube: London Bridge.

The vessel is well worth a visit, perhaps especially for children but also for war-enthusiasts: it makes a pair with the Cabinet War Rooms (Chapter 12). *Belfast* was launched in 1938 and at 11,000 tons was the Royal Navy's largest cruiser. She served in the Second World War and the Korean War and is the last survivor of the huge fleets of armoured warships built for the Navy for the two world wars. Tours of HMS *Belfast* are self-guided and fascinating. You clamber up and down narrow ladders, and are liable to bang your head, but the four decks open to visitors are well signposted and described. As you explore the gun turrets above and the boiler rooms below you gain a real sense of what it must have been like to be involved in naval warfare in the mid-20C.

On the riverbank, you pass Southwark Crown Court, boring in brown brick, but soon reach the more exciting **Hay's Galleria**. Alexander Hay founded a wharf and warehouses here as long ago as 1651; it was the oldest wharf in the Port of London and in the 1860s pioneered cold storage. Until the 1970s, the area was a small dock surrounded on three sides by warehouses erected in the 1860s, following a disastrous fire in Tooley Street in 1861. In the 1980s the dock was drained and covered and the warehouses converted into offices. A glass roof was constructed to enclose, in effect, a shopping mall, quite distinctive and pleasant to wander round. The *Navigators*, a Heath-Robinson-type ship sculpture and fountain, seems too fussy.

You can go through Hay's Galleria to Tooley Street, or through Cottons' Centre next door. **Tooley Street** is not at all beautiful, the whole of the south side being taken up with the infrastructure of London Bridge Station's railway tracks (**Map 9.7**), but it is historic, its name allegedly being a corruption of St Olave's Street ('Stoolaf'), after a church founded here in the Middle Ages and the Viking invader who successfully demolished an early London Bridge. John Harvard (founder of the university) spent his boyhood here.

Across the street is the **London Dungeon**, a popular tourist venue cultivating the legend of Jack the Ripper and similar grisly episodes, now including the Fire of 1666. This is entertaining if you like that sort of thing, which many do. Open 10.00–17.30 (17.00 in winter). Admission charge. Café. ☎ 020 7403 7221. www.thedungeons.com

A few doors east from the Dungeon is another new-ish museum, **Winston Churchill's Britain at War**, housing in the characteristically dilapidated premises of a reconstructed Tube air-raid shelter a collection of artefacts from the Home Front. Newsreels and soundtracks contribute to the atmosphere, which is quite effective though not in the same league as the Imperial War Museum (Chapter 33). Open 10.00–17.30 (till 16.30 in winter). Admission charge. ☎ 020 7403 3171. www.britainatwar.co.uk

Opposite, on the north side of Tooley Street, is **St Olaf House**, a rarity in London inter-war architecture in that it attempted the International Modern style. It is, like the church at Dockhead, by H. Goodhart-Rendel (1929–31), who was also a distinguished architectural writer (his *English Architecture since the Regency* of 1953 remains a classic); he called it 'hard and cornery'. Its river frontage, which can be seen from London Bridge, is even more eye-catching.

If you detour to look at St Olaf House from bridge level, your eye will be taken by a spiky Postmodern giant at the southeast corner of the bridge. If you enter this building and descend the escalator—it is a public right of way during office hours—you can exit into the old part of Tooley Street and see, on the land to your right, a surviving arch from John Rennie's 1832 London Bridge, its voussoirs noble and secure. Beyond is Southwark Cathedral (Chapter 31).

Turn left to find Tooley Street proper and the London Dungeon across the road. Next to the Dungeon is Stainer Street, dark and spooky under the London Bridge tracks. Go through to reach St Thomas Street. This is where St Thomas's Hospital originally stood before the development of the station moved it to Lambeth (see Chapter 33). Its first dedication to St Thomas à Becket was amended at the Reformation, for political reasons, to St Thomas the Apostle.

Thomas à Becket

Becket (*c* 1120–70) was a tricky and controversial Archbishop of Canterbury, a Londoner who began life as an office clerk and, although not a monk, was most unusually appointed archbishop by Henry II on the strength of loyalty he had shown as a courtier. As archbishop he persistently made life difficult for Henry, himself a controversial king of unique energy and drive. Henry spent much of his time in France, and it was four French knights who, acting officially or otherwise, murdered Becket in Canterbury Cathedral on 19 December 1170. The crime scandalised Europe. It led almost immediately to Becket's canonisation and the growth of one of the most powerful cults of all time, lasting until the Reformation and beyond, attracting, among others, Geoffrey Chaucer's fictional pilgrims 200 years later.

The line from **London Bridge Station** to Greenwich was the first to open in London, in 1836, and the structure of the station is particularly historic, but at track level it has been rebuilt many times and is not worth a detour to see.

On the opposite side of St Thomas Street is **Guy's Hospital**, originally founded in 1726 by a rich bachelor, Thomas Guy, on land he had acquired opposite St Thomas's Hospital; his statue by Peter Scheemakers (1733) stands in the courtyard. Guy's was, and is, famous as a pioneer in medical research and surgery.

Bright's Disease, Addison's Disease and Hodgkin's Disease were all discovered here and named after Guy's practitioners. The old hospital buildings (1721–25) still surround a pleasant courtyard, with further wings built by Richard Jupp (1774–77). In the west wing and always open is the chapel, a miraculous survival with a monument to Guy by John Bacon (1779), described by Pevsner as 'one of the noblest and most sensitive of its date in England'.

Across St Thomas Street is the church of St Thomas (1702–3) which houses, up very narrow, steep stairs, the novel **Old Operating Theatre Museum and Herb Garret**. Open 10.00–17.00 daily. No disabled access. Admission charge. Shop. ☎ 020 7955 4791. www.thegarret.org.uk. Tube: London Bridge.

This has been described as London's strangest museum. Being located in the roof of a church is unusual, but it makes sense when you realise that the establishment was once part of St Thomas's Hospital, whose old wards directly abutted the church tower. Some enterprising person concluded that a hole could be driven through the wall of the tower into the church roof to create both an operating theatre for patients and a pharmacy for herbal treatments. The original operating theatre dates to 1828 and was rediscovered in 1956, over a century after the hospital had moved away to Lambeth. The operating table and benches for spectators are all intact. Gruesome but, in the context of modern medicine, it makes existence in the 21C most reassuring. The herb garret is full of interesting remedies.

Keep going west along St Thomas Street to **Borough High Street**. This ancient street, once the main road from the south, has always been packed with pubs, which once included Chaucer's Tabard Inn, where pilgrims assembled on account of the area's connection with Becket.

Geoffrey Chaucer

Chaucer (?1343–1400) is one of the earliest English authors whose work is still regularly read and referred to, largely on the basis of the *Canterbury Tales* though his overall production was much wider. He was an accomplished and successful administrator in public service, who travelled in France and Italy and married the sister-in-law of John of Gaunt, who became his patron thereafter. He was also a Londoner. The prologue to the *Canterbury Tales* sets the scene in the Tabard Inn in Southwark where a group of individuals meet up *en route* to Canterbury as pilgrims to the shrine of Thomas à Becket. Their host at the inn suggests they should reduce the tedium of the journey by each telling a story to the others as they ride along, and he will award a free supper to the best.

The Tabard stood on the site of Talbot Yard until 1876. Many other pubs survive in the streets either side and are worth exploring, including the *King's Head* and the *White Hart*, but only the *George* is original (1676). The last galleried coaching inn left, it is owned by the National Trust and presents occasional theatrical productions in the yard. 'Coaching' was the reason for the inns' existence: coaches became too large to cross old London Bridge and terminated at inns in this street.

Walk south down Borough High Street. Mermaid Court, on the left, is built on the site of the first Marshalsea Prison, a notorious gaol mostly for debtors. It was relocated a little further south in the 19C (to a site now marked by Angel Place) and it was here that Charles Dickens's father was held for debt in 1824; the novelist later immortalised its long-term inhabitants in *Little Dorrit*. Nearby also once stood the King's Bench Prison, also for debtors.

About an eighth of a mile south you reach Borough station (Northern Line). Before ending the walk there, take a look at the church of **St George the Martyr** by John Price (1734–36), a fine, strong and handsome building, looking good from all angles. The design is based on Sir Christopher Wren's for St James Piccadilly, which the great man had recommended for copying. Dickens has Amy Dorrit and Arthur Clennam marry here.

Not far away is the **London Fire Brigade Museum**. To get to it (if booked), turn right up Marshalsea Street to Southwark Bridge Road where, turning left, you will find it inside a handsome building which was once the headquarters and residence of the Chief Fire Officer of the Brigade (**Map 8,8**). It has one of the most comprehensive collections of fire-fighting equipment in the country as well as uniforms, medals, photographs and paintings. Tours at 10.30, 12.30 and 14.30 Mon–Fri (must be pre-booked). Admission charge. Bookings ☎ 020 7587 2894. Shop open 09.00–17.00 Mon–Fri.

31 • Bankside

This historic area is another which has been regenerated in recent years. With a cathedral, several museums, the Globe and Tate Modern it has become popular among tourists and, being small in scale in places, can seem crowded. But even with much late 20C building it is full of character—although not the brothels and bear-baiting of its dissipated past—and it is worth exploring off the beaten track to which this walk on the whole adheres.

- Distance: 1¼ miles. Time: 1 hour + 3 hours for the cathedral and Tate Modern. Tube: London Bridge. Map 9.

Start at London Bridge station (**Map 9,7**) and go towards Southwark Cathedral, crossing the busy road and going down steps on the left. You will immediately find yourself in a fruit and vegetable market under a Victorian iron canopy (1850s). **Borough Market** is allegedly the oldest in London: in the 13C it was reported as spreading to the southern end of old London Bridge. It is a rich muddle, with characteristic shops round the edge selling wholesale early each day. On Friday afternoons and Saturday mornings from 10.00 till lunch there are up-market food stalls comprising a 'Farmers Market'. It is well worth a special visit on these days.

Just south of Borough Market is Southwark Street. To the right, past the Hop Exchange, a fine building of 1866 by R.W. Moore, a short detour takes you to the unusual **Bramah Tea and Coffee Museum**, recently relocated here. This interesting if slightly quirky museum tells the story of tea- and coffee-importing, which was crucial to London trade in its time. Tea, in particular, is a huge element in the British psyche. Every aspect seems to be covered, including the locations of all the 18C coffee houses in London. The founder, Edward Bramah, comes from a distinguished family of former tea and coffee importers. Open 10.00–18.00 daily. Admission charge. Café, with excellent coffee and tea! Shop. ☎ 020 7403 5650. www.bramahmuseum.co.uk

But our main route is north of Borough Market to Southwark Cathedral.

Southwark Cathedral

Just to the north of the market is the impressive pile of Southwark Cathedral, which contains, in the choir and retrochoir, the earliest purely Gothic architecture in London.

- Open 08.00–18.00. Admission free. Refectory 10.00–17.00 daily. ☎ 020 7367 6700. www.dswark.org.uk

Its foundation allegedly dates back to the 7C, like St Paul's. For most of its life it has not been a cathedral, but was first a priory and, after the Dissolution, the parish church of St Mary Overie ('over the water'): it became a cathedral in 1897. The present building is the fourth on the site, the earlier ones having been destroyed by fire, and was begun in 1220, making it the first Gothic church in London (St Paul's building at that time was still Romanesque). The oldest part now visible from the outside is the tower, of which the two upper stages are 14C–15C and the pinnacles date to 1689.

Although left alone during the Civil War, the church was not well looked after and retained the area's negative associations with theatres and general depravity. The major restorations were done by George Gwilt Junior in the 1820s and further changes were made in the 1830s in conjunction with the rebuilding of London Bridge. The decision in favour of cathedral status was preceded by a major rebuilding of the nave in the 1890s by Sir Arthur Blomfield. The latest renovations took place in 1999/2000, so what you see now is as up-to-date as can be and makes a rewarding tour. The new buildings on the north side are brash and cheerful, encouraging a warm welcome. Coffees, lunches and teas are available to restore flagging energy after a tour of the interior.

Entering from either south or north, you will find yourself at the western end of the **nave**. Under your nose is the font by George Bodley (1890s), 'with all the stops out' (Pevsner). Stretching away to the east are the nave and aisles, virtually all rebuilt by Blomfield but still with plenty of interest. Immediately to the left of the south entrance is a memorial to the victims of a disaster on the Thames in 1989, when 51 people attending a party on the river boat *Marchioness* were killed in a collision with another boat. Next to it is some surviving 13C **arcading** which Blomfield incorporated in his new wall. Continue down the south aisle to find at the end the Shakespeare Memorial by Henry McCarthy (1911), celebrating the nearby Globe Theatre and the burial in the church of Shakespeare's brother Edmond, a 'player'. Southwark holds an annual service commemorating the playwright.

In the **south transept** there are several attractive monuments, for example the half-figure of John Bingham, saddler to Elizabeth and James I. Opposite are the arms of Cardinal Beaufort, who sponsored the restoration of the south transept in 1420, with his hat on top. In the south chancel aisle, do not miss the tomb of the great Lancelot Andrewes (d. 1626), the last Bishop of Winchester to live in the palace nearby.

From here you can enter the **choir** to see its original Early English architecture. It is very plain with relatively low arcades surmounted by quartets of lancets at triforium level, each with a passage behind, and triple arcading in the clerestory. The great stone reredos was erected in 1520 but its (by then offensive) statues were covered in the 17C: when the covering was taken away, most had disappeared and those you now see date from 1905. The 20C decorations are by Sir Ninian Comper.

Behind the high altar is the 13C Early English **retrochoir**, again very plain, spacious, and lower than the choir. The four altars and screens are by Comper. On the north side is a particularly beautiful piece of furniture, the **Nonesuch Chest** of 1588, given by Alderman Hugh Offley, who had been treasurer of St Thomas's Hospital. Go back down the north choir aisle, where there is a wooden effigy of a knight (1275) and the particularly likeable Trehearne monument (1618), showing that baldness is nothing new: even one of the mourning sons below has receding hair. To the right is the **Harvard Chapel** dedicated in 1907 to John Harvard, founder of the university, who was born in Southwark in 1609. It has a tabernacle by A.W.N. Pugin first shown in the Medieval Court of the Great Exhibition of 1851.

Now you reach the **north transept**, with the somewhat comical Lockyer monument (1672)—he was a quack doctor—and the much more refined Austin monument (1633), full of meanings to be adduced by the intellectual visitor. Finally walk down the north aisle, where the monument to the poet and friend of Geoffrey Chaucer, John Gower, shines prettily (1408 but much restored). Exit by the north door, through the shop, refectory and temporary exhibitions.

From the Cathedral, walk westwards, skirting orange-brick offices of the early 1980s, to see the **Golden Hinde**, a reconstruction of the ship in which Sir Francis Drake circumnavigated the world (1577–80), moored in the ancient St Mary Overie Dock. It too sailed around the world before settling here. Open 10.00–17.00 (phone first). Admission charge. Overnight stays for children (with accompanying adult) can be arranged. ☎ 020 7403 0123. www.goldenhinde.co.uk

You now take Clink Street, opposite the ship, to pursue a riverside walk through an area rich in character. On the right are the remains of 19C riverside warehouses, and on the left the much older remains of the **Bishop of Winchester's Palace**—in its day (12C–17C) it rivalled the Archbishop's Palace at Lambeth. All that survives now is the framework of the great hall, beneath which was an undercroft, with a magnificent rose window outlined in the west wall, dateable to the early 14C.

The Bishops of Winchester owned all the land in this area but their reputation was mixed: their tight regulation of the local brothels for their own income simply encouraged yet more prostitution. Offenders were cast into the Clink prison, next to the Palace, of which no trace now remains although its memory survives in the phrase 'in the clink'.

These unhappy times are recalled in the **Clink Prison Museum**, underground on the same site, consisting largely of torture instruments poorly displayed. Open 10.00–18.00. Admission charge. ☎ 020 7378 1558. www.clink.co.uk

Soon after this you find yourself going under Cannon Street railway bridge (Chapter 6), where many of the arches are taken up by **Vinopolis**. This new, very slick but quite pricey museum tells the history of wine in a novel and interesting way. It gives a region-by-region tour of the international wine trade, including for example, a scooter ride through Chianti and an aeroplane trip over the Australian vineyards. The admission charge allows you to taste five wines, the audio-guide is good and there are, predictably, many opportunities to purchase Open 11.00–18.00 Tues–Fri and Sun; 11.00–20.00 Sat and Mon (except i

Dec). Admission charge. Restaurant (bookings ☎ 020 7940 8333). Wine bar. Wine warehouse. ☎ 0870 4444 777. www.vinopolis.co.uk

Then return to the riverside where the *Anchor* pub still offers a warm welcome to its dark, late 18C interior, or on a fine day to tables overlooking the Thames. The path then winds under Southwark Bridge (Chapter 6), past some eye-catching new apartments, to reach the Globe. Bear Gardens to the left was the location of a contemporary theatre, the Hope, which opened on the site of a bear-baiting arena; and it is well worth detouring briefly down the new Globe Walk and turning left into Park Street to find the site of the **Rose Theatre**. A vivid light-and-sound presentation is shown on this, the original archaeological site, bringing to remarkable life the atmosphere of the earliest of the Bankside theatres, built in 1587 by Philip Henslowe. Shakespeare acted here. Open 10.00–17.00 (from 12.00 in winter). Admission charge. ☎ 020 7593 0026. www.rosetheatre.org.uk

Shakespeare's Globe Theatre

Then return to the Globe Theatre, which, while a great deal more spectacular than the Rose, is a wholly new creation, about 200 yards from its original site, now buried under Southwark Bridge Road.

Exhibition and tours (hourly Mon–Sat) open May–Sept 09.00–12.00; Oct–April 10.00–17.00. Plays performed May–Sept. Box office ☎ 020 7401 9919. Admission charge. Café. Restaurant (reservations ☎ 020 7928 9444). Shop. ☎ 020 7902 1500. www.shakespeares-globe.org

The original Globe theatre was built by Richard Burbage in 1598–99. The vision behind its reincarnation was that of Sam Wanamaker, an American actor who first came to London in 1949 and was appalled at the paltry attention given to the theatre's origins, and above all Shakespeare's activities, in this area. He became friendly with Theo Crosby, co-founder of Pentagram, a design and architectural practice, and the result of their co-operation was the Globe community we see today, opened in 1996 but still developing.

The central wooden 'O' was recreated as a 20-sided polygon, based on archaeological research into the original. The shape is outlined on a brick plinth with oak timber sills above bearing the oak framework. Within the frame, which is held together by pegs, laths and staves are fixed to support the plasterwork, which is finished with limewash. The roof is thatched, as was that of the original Globe, which was the cause of a fire in 1613. The rebuilt version, which lasted until 1642, had a tiled roof.

Shakespeare's Globe Theatre

Plays by Shakespeare and contemporary authors are performed in the Globe from May to September. Also on the site is an educational centre and an exhibition about the building and the way Shakespeare was originally performed. A separate small theatre, in which indoor productions will be possible, is based on a design by Inigo Jones (1617), never originally built but found amongst his drawings now kept in Worcester College, Oxford.

William Shakespeare

Shakespeare (1564–1616), the world's most famous dramatist, voted England's man of the millennium, and surely the most studied writer in literature, was born in Stratford, Warwickshire, on 23 April 1616 and died on the same date 52 years later. After education at the grammar school he married Anne Hathaway in 1582. The couple had three children and brought them up in Stratford, where in due course Shakespeare became a person of property. But his working life was always in London. He seems to have joined a theatre company around 1587 and was an established playwright by the early 1590s. The three parts of *Henry VI* and their sequel *Richard III* seem to have been written first, then many of the comedies (but also *Romeo and Juliet*), and the rest of the histories except *Henry VIII*. The chief tragedies belong to the period 1599–1609. *The Tempest* was perhaps written last, in 1611. He was buried in the local church at Stratford.

In London, lodging in Bishopsgate and elsewhere, Shakespeare became a leading member of the theatrical company called the Lord Chamberlain's Men from 1594, which became the King's Men in 1603. They performed at the Globe and in winter at the Blackfriars. It was during only the third performance of *Henry VIII* that the original Globe was burned down in 1613.

Leaving the Globe and resuming the riverside path you will see on your left nos 49–52 Bankside, dateable to the early 18C. A plaque on no. 49, called Cardinal Wharf, indicates that Sir Christopher Wren lived here, but this is most unlikely. Ahead of you across the river stretches the **Millennium Bridge** by Norman Foster Associates and Ove Arup, which opened for three days in 2000 before being closed due to undue vibration. It has been stabilised and reopened, so you can cross over to St Paul's Cathedral (Chapter 7).

Tate Modern

And now, looming up formidably on your left, is Tate Modern, which was the destination of five million visitors in its first year of opening.

• Open 10.00–18.00 Sun–Thurs; 10.00–22.00 Fri–Sat. Admission free. Additional paying exhibitions and numerous tours and audio-guides. ☎ 020 7887 8000. Information ☎ 020 7887 8008. www.tate.org/modern

History

In the late 1980s the Trustees of the Tate Gallery realised that the 1900 building on Millbank, even with James Stirling's additional Clore Gallery of 1982 (Chapter 16), could not be extended sufficiently to house its collection. They therefore decided to find a site for a second gallery in London, and to split the collection into two—British art and international 20C art.

That much was orthodox planning. What was inspirational was to identify and select Bankside Power Station for the new gallery. The power station (1957–60) was the last to be built in London, burning oil instead of coal to provide electricity for the City. The architect was Sir Giles Gilbert Scott, designer of Waterloo Bridge and the red telephone box, not to mention Liverpool Cathedral, and of the earlier power station at Battersea. By the 1970s most of Bankside Power Station was redundant, and remained derelict, a decaying landmark, until the Tate Trustees discovered it. They saw it as a fine if severe building, a mass of brick, symmetrical, with minimal decoration and a glowering chimney and, above all, it was available.

Swiss architects Jacques Herzog and Pierre de Meuron won a hotly contested competition on the basis of their manipulation of the interior space, respecting the integrity of Scott's building and using it as a framework for the new gallery. The other designs, it was felt, ignored the power station ethos and simply fitted a gallery into a shell: Herzog and de Meuron, however, integrated the two forms.

Responses to the architectural experience have been varied. It is recommended that you enter through the **west entrance**, down the ramp, so that you can experience the powerful sense of space in the former Turbine Hall. Visiting the galleries you will see how the additional light-beam inserted at the fifth and sixth floors, odd-looking though it is from the outside, and the retention of the existing windows, illustrate the architectural philosophy, as well as wonderfully presenting the art.

The originality continues with the hanging of the art, which is divided not chronologically or nationally, nor by artist, but according to four themes: the human body, human society and history, still life and object, and the environment that we inhabit. The names of the galleries indicate their themes. Since the hang changes fairly often at Tate Modern, it is important to note these names and to read the storyboards before examining the art. A current copy of the free Tate plan is necessary to supplement this tour: this can be obtained from the desks at the bottom of the ramp in the Turbine Hall; the lifts are to the left. Straight ahead up the stairs on Level 1 is the **Clore Study Room** where you can learn about the collection and access its website and video links.

If there is a problem with Tate Modern, it is simply that visitor numbers can make the relatively small galleries crowded, but this will settle down.

Level 4

Nude/Action/Body At the door is Auguste Rodin's *The Kiss* (1901–4), signifying as it were the end of the Classical traditions. There is, within the theme, a chronological progression of sorts, and a representational one, so that in the first gallery, 'Naked and Nude', this initial opposition is revealed. Among the exhibits here are likely to be works by Henri Matisse, four studies of a back (1908–1931) and the *Snail* (1953), celebrating pure colour; Henry Moore, including his *Recumbent Figure* (1930) and *Reclining Figure* (1951); Alberto Giacometti, from his Surrealist to his existentialist phases; and Barnett Newman's *Adam* (1951), permissible within this section only through its title.

In another gallery a video by William Kentridge, Steve McQueen or Sam Taylor-Wood may be playing continuously. Works by David Hockney and Graham Sutherland and Pablo Picasso's *Weeping Woman* (1937) or *Three Dancers* (1925) are likely to be on display.

The important thing, rather than to seek out the work of specific artists, is to experience the journey of representations of the body from the refined and perfected nude, via the naked figure and then its deconstruction, abstraction and performance, to a dispassionate record on film of apparent reality. There is a bookshop at the end of the galleries in this section.

History/Memory/Society Then you can pass through the chimney stack to the end of the next section. To experience it from the beginning—and as before there is a kind of progression—go back to the main landing and enter past Naum Gabo's **Head No.2** (1918). The first gallery is called 'Manifestos', and again because of frequent changes, look at the plan and the storyboards to understand where you are going.

'History', 'Memory', 'Society' are all fine words but within such a grouping 20C art essentially refers to politics, or the moral guidelines by which we choose to live. 'Manifestos' are typical, as is the preoccupation with technology and destruction. But a broader reduction is apparent from the age of heroes and great pasts which earlier painters celebrated to the perception of history as small, local, individual and uncertain. Illustrations of this progression, or regression, appear in Piet Mondrian's own route from Fauvism to his abstract grids in primary colours, in the minimalism of Donald Judd or Dan Flavin, and in the fierce abuse of advertising media in the work of Jenny Holzer and Barbara Kruger.

The painful journey we took to reach this simplification and focus on personal responses rather than governments can be seen in Georg Grosz's **Suicide** (1916) and the carvings of Georg Baselitz, including **Untitled** (1982), as well as the more overtly political works of Picasso and Boris Taslitzky. Appropriately perhaps, Andy Warhol's tacit acceptance of capitalist production comes last in the succession of rooms.

Level 4 also contains **temporary exhibitions** with an admission charge.

Level 3
Still Life/Object/Real Life The 'permanent' display continues on Level 3, where the next section is introduced as it were by Claes Oldenberg's **Giant 3-Way Plug** (1970). Still life represents one of the easier routes through the minefield of 20C art movements. Cubism is most easily understood in terms of the break-up of a simple object into its respective planes. It leads on via Dada to Surrealism and Pop, through all of which the changing treatment of objects can be quite easily traced. 'Real Life' means incorporating real objects as such into the work of art, a phenomenon reaching its peak in the 1960s.

Start at the room titled 'Desire for Order'. The still lifes of Paul Cézanne are likely to appear early, to be followed by the Cubist approaches of Picasso and Georges Braque, with, later, the first appropriation of real objects, such as a piece of newspaper, into the painting. From this it is not far to the inclusion of ready-made objects, as in the work of Marcel Duchamp, even if such objects are arranged in ambiguous or unclear ways, to constitute Surrealism. A famous example is Salvador Dali's **Lobster Telephone** (1936), making the ordinary somehow wholly distasteful, and conveying meaning accordingly.

Some of the art works in this category require a lot of space, and it is in such arrangements that the limitations of Tate Modern become apparent. There simply is not enough room to appreciate, for example, Bill Woodrow's **Elephant** (1984) or Rachel Whiteread's work. Damien Hirst's **Pharmacy** (1992) is itself room. Nevertheless our contemporary preoccupations with materialism and our absorption with ideas which confuse the virtual with the actual make this section of the gallery seem especially relevant.

Landscape/Matter/Environment Pass behind the chimney again, or go back to the main landing, for the fourth section. It has an easier theme than the other three, perhaps because of the survival of 'nature' in one form or another in even those environments most damaged by mankind. The Impressionists after all, as represented here by Claude Monet's *Water Lilies* (1916), reflected society's enjoyment of the natural world. It was Cézanne's deconstruction of landscape to planes of colour which had a more radical effect.

In one gallery, Monet is contrasted, or should we say combined, with Richard Long's constructed landscapes, including *Slate Circle* (1979) on the gallery floor, its very mobility a reminder that the 'natural' school of landscape artists recognise their work to be temporary, impermanent, and within the changing environment.

Other galleries remind the viewer of longer perspectives. Mark Rothko's great canvases imply unlimited space, infinite distance: his *Seagram series* (1958) has also been interpreted with a more humanistic meaning. Against the abstractions of Rothko and Jackson Pollock, photography as shown in the work of Jeff Wall or Andreas Gursky—whose *Montparnasse 1993* dominates the landing on Level 3—returns us to the immediate. Reality, not poetry, is where this section takes us, and this indeed is the effect of Tate Modern as a whole. Viewing the art here is unsettling, discomfiting: it makes you feel you should take action, do something, about the modern world. But what?

Perhaps you will find the answer in the excellent and extensive **bookshop** at ground level in the Turbine Hall. Or alternatively forget the question, and find some refreshment, either up on Level 7—where you should take in the view, a real landscape, across the Thames—or less spectacularly on Level 1, above the bookshop. You can leave at this level, giving out on to the riverside path again, or via the west entrance. If you choose the latter, go round to the south side of the building just to complete the experience. This south wing still functions as a switching station. In time, the Tate may acquire it for yet more hanging space. They need it: you will agree, now you have seen it, that this collection demands room to live.

After all this spectacle, you may feel sated with art. But a few yards further along the river bank is the very demure **Bankside Gallery**, which specialises in water-colours and small exhibitions for enthusiasts. Open 10.00–20.00 Tues; 10.00–17.00 Wed–Fri; 11.00–17.00 Sat, Sun. ☎ 020 7928 7521.

Go through the 1970s flats which incorporate the Bankside Gallery into their ground floor, and make your way down Hopton Street. Just west of here the largest of Bankside's 16C theatres, the Swan, was located. On the left is a remarkable loft conversion by CZWG, building on a former warehouse—it was visible from the west entrance of Tate Modern curving up into the sky. This form of development, loft living, remains unusual in London but here works with excellent effect. Beyond it are the diminutive **Hopton Almshouses** (1752), restored and happily performing their original intended function. Past them you reach Southwark Street, of interest as an example of Victorian street planning: it was cut through in 1872 by Sir Joseph Bazalgette, the Metropolitan Board of Works engineer, to link two more ancient streets, Blackfriars Road and Borough High Street. As such, it is remarkably unchanged and still retains several of its original 1870s' office blocks.

Cross Southwark Street and go down Burrell Street under the railway, to reach Blackfriars Road (**Map 8,7**). Opposite is the humble brick church of **Christ Church**, rebuilt after the Second World War. On your left is a nice white restored terracotta office. Turn left: under another railway bridge on the right is Southwark station (Jubilee Line), or turn right to go over Blackfriars Bridge.

32 • South Bank

The term 'South Bank' has developed its resonances—culture, music, 'difference'—chiefly over the last 50 years, since the Festival of Britain in 1951. The phrase is often used to refer to the arts centre of that name between Waterloo and Hungerford Bridges, but in 1951 it meant the somewhat larger area where the Festival was laid out. Before that, the wider neighbourhood had music halls and the Old Vic theatre tucked in amongst modest working-class houses and market gardens, criss-crossed by railways snaking out from the termini at Waterloo.

This walk includes the best selection of modern architecture you will find in London, including two masterpieces. If you plan to ride on the London Eye—and it is strongly recommended—book in advance as described below. This is an easy walk, but designed to provoke thought.

- Distance: 2¼ miles. Time: 1½ hours. Tube: Blackfriars or Southwark. Map 8, 15

> ### *Festival of Britain*
> The idea of the Festival held in 1951 was to boost Britain after five years of postwar austerity. Unlike its more distinguished predecessor, the Great Exhibition of a century before, it was planned to run at a loss—an outcome in turn accepted more readily by the public than in the case of the Dome in 2000. The Festival brought life to the South Bank and cheered up a nation. Its temporary buildings contained some remarkable structures, including the Dome of Discovery and the 290ft-high Skylon. The layout was also planned in a radical way, with no central axis or grand avenues, but informal and asymmetrical—a thoroughly 'modern' approach at the time. Battersea Park was developed as a pleasure garden as part of the Festival.

Start from Blackfriars station (**Map 8,5**) and immediately cross the bridge t reach the river path on the south side, or go to Southwark station (Jubilee Line and walk north to the river, to arrive at the same point. **Blackfriars Bridge** (opene 1769) and Road were part of the same mid-18C inspiration, designed to open u the area to middle-class housing and create a fine entry to the City for visitor arriving from Europe at the Kent ports. Today the road is a mess and its origina promoters would be appalled.

Pick up the riverside path under Blackfriars Bridge. There are some interestin tile displays showing G.B. Piranesi's imagined representation of its constructio (1764); the designs for the original bridge by Robert Mylne and others (1769); i replacement—the present structure—and its grand opening in 1864. It wa widened (1907–10) to accommodate trams and as such is the widest of Londons bridges. If you look along the path a little to the east, towards Tate Modern, you will see the Thameslink railway bridge (1884) alongside, part of the former Holborn Viaduct Railway's investment, now cleverly engineered to take trains across London from north to south, a dream the Victorians did not achieve. A relic of the bitter competition between the early railway companies are the piers between the two remaining Blackfriars Bridges, all that survives of the London, Chatham and Dover Railway's line.

Go west along the river path. The first structure is a noisy pub called **Doggetts**, after the 18C promoter of an annual boat race, still held on the first of August, in which the winner receives a coat and badge. Next are mixed blocks of moderately horrible housing and offices—Sea Containers House, the King's Reach development and so on—by Richard Seifert (1970 onwards). The delightful **Oxo Tower** is an excellent conversion of a former warehouse by A.W. Moore (1928) into co-operative housing, small craft shops—sadly these often change, as visitors are reluctant to go up to the first and second floors—and restaurants. The Tower displays 'OXO' in its ventilating louvres, originally cocking a snook at the advertising ban imposed between the wars by the London County Council. Go into the Tower to explore: take the lift to the eighth floor, where you can go brazenly through a passageway in the restaurant (without needing to be a customer) to get onto the viewing balcony. From there you can see a fine panorama of the north bank from Somerset House to St Paul's, with Temple Gardens sweetly green in the middle.

Keep going along the river. The next site, after Bernie Spain Gardens, is **Gabriel's Wharf**, a mixture of little shops and restaurants. A Georgian street façade was once painted on the blank east-facing wall, but is now peeling a little. It is all quite grubby but charming in its way. This site, the Oxo Tower and Bernie Spain Gardens are all administered by the Coin Street Community Builders, who originally resisted office development here in the 1970s, and still do.

Next comes London Weekend Television's boring 1970s' tower, but it is followed by a lovely office building, the **IBM Central Marketing Centre** by Sir Denys Lasdun (1979–83), an object-lesson in architecture, elegant in scale and proportion, dignified and civilised in conception (**Map 15,4**). Look inside if you can.

Sir Denys Lasdun

Lasdun (1914–2001) was the most notable practitioner of Modernist architecture in London, giving us the National Theatre, the IBM building next door—they make perfect neighbours—the Royal College of Physicians in Regent's Park (Chapter 25), and the Hallfield Estate, Paddington (Chapter 37). His place in architecture is an important one: he drew the best of the radical inter-war ideas emanating from Walter Gropius and the Bauhaus design school, in which London is so poorly represented, into the postwar age, but avoided its extremes. 'Difficult Denys' was a man who stuck to his architectural principles, objecting to Postmodernist pretence.

National Theatre

You may have been wondering what has happened to the promised culture and arts, but now they make their entry. The National Theatre is first: recently lightly extended and cleaned, it is essentially the same self-confident, intellectual but concrete, blocky shape that first startled Londoners in the 1970s. It is worth examining carefully and comparing with its near-contemporary, the Barbican (Chapter 5), the atmosphere of which is quite different.

- For details of performances, ☎ 020 7452 3400. Box office ☎ 020 7452 3000. Bar. Restaurant. The NT's public spaces are closed Sun.

The idea of a national theatre was proposed as far back as 1848, ten years after the opening of the National Gallery—itself a latecomer; its realisation took another 130 years. Serious proposals were developed earlier in the 20C, with productions of Shakespeare especially in mind. A site in Cromwell Road, at first closely considered, was abandoned after the Second World War and the focus moved to the South Bank, originally to a site next to County Hall. The theatre company was formed under the leadership of actor Sir Laurence Olivier and began productions at the Old Vic (see Chapter 33). Building began at last on the present site in 1969 and the first production—*Hamlet*, with Albert Finney—opened in March 1976.

There are three theatres in the complex: the **Olivier**, with an open stage, seating 1160; the **Lyttelton**, a proscenium stage, seating 890; and the **Cottesloe**, with a separate entrance and flexible seating for up to 400. From the river bank, the building projects outwards as it rises and the mix of levels, struts and angles is startling. There is a regrettably obvious service area in the northeast corner, and it is best to let the eye rise above this through an exhilarating series of architectural ideas to the daring skyline, dominated by the Olivier's flytower. The entrances are in the projecting section towards the river; the shop is a recent extension, to which Lasdun strongly objected.

Go in to savour the **interior**. You will immediately find that the complexity of spatial division is as marked here as it was in the exterior view, but now you are within it, being taken diagonally. Around you is raw concrete with the timber shuttering marks ingrained on it: above is heavy concrete coffering. Although dark, it is not oppressive, and generates a real excitement. This is especially true when you arrive for a play, whether in summer, when the river glints behind you in the sun, or winter when the wind rustles the bare plane trees on the path: the architecture recaptures, in modern form, our first childhood excitement at the theatre's door.

As you emerge, take in the view of **Waterloo Bridge** (see also Chapter 10). It looks especially exciting from the river bank, north or south (whereas to cross it is blandly flat, despite the exhilarating panorama). Look between the line of piers for a visual kick.

Waterloo, of course, has nothing to do with London but is the village in Belgium where the Duke of Wellington defeated Napoleon in 1815. It was obvious to patriots of the time that the battle should be commemorated, and the name became attached to John Rennie's new Strand Bridge, which opened in 1817. The small area of housing at the southern foot of the bridge began to develop and in 1848 the train station was built and given the same name. Rennie's bridge must have been magnificent: Antonio Canova, the great Italian sculptor, claimed it was worth crossing the world to see. The new version is pretty good as well.

Secondhand books are often sold under the bridge, but there are better selection in Charing Cross Road. Underneath the arches on the bank—again note how the bridge is far longer than the width of the river (Rennie's pre-embankment Waterloo Bridge was even longer)—the **National Film Theatre** shows a rich programme of classic and contemporary films from around the world in its three cinemas. Run by the British Film Institute (BFI), it is also the focal point of the London International Film Festival in November. Box office ☎ 020 7928 3232. www.bfi.org.uk/nft. The BFI's **Museum of the Moving Image** covering the history of film and television is currently closed, but may reopen in 2003 on a new site if the redevelopment of Jubilee Gardens goes ahead (see below).

Before continuing along the river, retreat south between the bridge and the National Theatre, across Upper Ground (with conveniently placed branches of *Chez Gérard* and *Pizza Express*), to see the **BFI IMAX cinema**, opened in 1999, with a huge screen so that the image seems all around one. It fills the centre of a traffic roundabout, which the cinema's cylindrical purity greatly enhances, visually at least. For details of current programmes, ☎ 020 7902 1234.

Return via the pathway on the further side of the bridge. The **Royal Festival Hall** is now visible on your left—the fine south façade has recently been attractively opened up to the street. You now need to ascend one of the odd white staircases to reach the **Hayward Gallery**—with exhibitions usually of modern or contemporary art—and beyond it the **Purcell Room** and **Queen Elizabeth Hall**. The three are connected in concept and the two concert halls linked in interior space: all are the work of the GLC Architects Department, including Leslie Martin and others (1965–68). These buildings are at the time of writing under threat, and debate is underway as to their value. They have never been popular with the British public who disliked 'Brutalism' from its inception—indeed British architectural opinion is generally very traditionally biased. The two concert halls work well inside, and the Gallery quite well, but better facilities would replace them, so the issue is how valuable they are as architecture. Hayward Gallery open 10.00–18.00 Mon, Thur–Sun, 10.00–20.00 Tues, Wed. Admission charge. Shop. Café. ☎ 020 7261 0127. www.sbc.org.uk

Then we reach the **Royal Festival Hall**, the sole survivor of the Festival of Britain, by Sir Robert Matthew and Leslie Martin (1949–51); cheery resonances of the 1950s can still be sensed in features of its design. It is a period piece, but a very interesting one, and in its use of interior space a radical building. You have already seen the south side, with its contemporary blue lettering. The riverside façade was altered by Sir Hubert Bennett (1962–65) and so is rather less authentic. It is best to enter on the east side, the original main entrance, as you come through from Upper Ground.

At first-floor level you have the first glimpse of marvellous spatial freedom. An open area for dancing or exhibitions is immediately revealed and, a few steps up, a performance/promenade space, a bar, and room for shops and cafés stretching towards the river. Stairs ascend either side. It is worth going up to see how views of the river from various balconies are integrated, and to visit exhibitions, the *People's Palace* restaurant or the **Arts Council Poetry Library** on the fourth floor, open 11.00–20.00 Tues–Sun. ☎ 020 7921 0664.

All the while the **concert hall** itself seems suspended in space alongside you, analogous, its architects said, to an Easter egg in its box. If you have occasion to go into the hall itself for a concert or performance, you can complete the experience, noting the way the decoration of the interior seeks a compromise between the Modernist desire for unadorned surfaces and the necessity for acoustic facilities and all the paraphernalia of an international orchestra. Only the lighting in the entirely enclosed space of the concert hall is depressing, with none of the magic to be found outside on the stairs and balconies. For information on concerts in all the South Bank concert halls, ☎ 020 7960 4242. www.sbc.org.uk

Leave the Festival Hall by the riverside entrance on the first or ground floor and turn left towards **Hungerford Bridge**. This was once an exclusively pedestrian bridge, erected by Isambard Kingdom Brunel in the 1840s to provide access to Hungerford Market on the north bank, but it was rebuilt except for the brick piers by the South Eastern Railway in the 1860s to take their trains to Charing Cross. A very uncomfortable pedestrian passageway was added as an afterthought, but handsome new ones are now under construction to either side. On this walk you do not cross the bridge, however, but turn left, back to Upper Ground. There is a giant bust of *Nelson Mandela* by Ian Walters (1985), erected by the Greater London Council while the great man was still incarcerated. Turn right in Upper Ground under the bridge. On your left is the **Shell Centre** (1956), a much-disliked lump of Portland stone with little windows, though it contains excellent facilities and some artworks for the staff inside to enjoy. There is an interesting modern fountain by Franta Belsky (1961) in the forecourt.

You will have been unable to avoid catching sight of the **London Eye** by Julia Barfield and David Marks (2000) in your progress along either bank of the river. Now it is in full view to your right, across Jubilee Gardens. Open Nov–April 09.30–20.00 daily; May–Oct 09.30–22.00 (often closed for maintenance in Jan). Admission charge. Booking advised on ☎ 0870 5000 600, where pre-recorded details of availability are given; expect queues anyway. Café. Shop. www.ba-londoneye.com. Tube: Waterloo or Westminster.

The British Airways London Eye was erected in 1999 to celebrate the Millennium and opened to visitors in February 2000. It is by any standard a piece of remarkable engineering, 135m in diameter and 1900 tonnes in weight. It was assembled laying flat on the surface of the river from parts made in various places in Europe and delivered up the Thames by boat. The rim is connected by steel cables to the hub and spindle, which are held on A-frame legs founded deep under Jubilee Gardens on the bank. The last step in construction was the attachment of the 32 capsules, each able to hold 25 passengers, who step on and off during the continuous movement.

A full circle takes 30 minutes. Views are affected by weather but on a fine day it is possible to see 25 miles in any direction. The sun can be blinding: take dark glasses as well as a camera and binoculars. There is a commentary in the capsule to help you identify the sights, but the official guide book is also useful for this purpose. It is easy to walk around in the capsule to view in all directions. It is possible to understand the ground plans of buildings much more vividly from here—for example, those in Whitehall (see Chapter 11)—but bear in mind that architects never intended you to look at their work from above.

Some original and invigorating views are to be had from the Eye, but most of us are not on the Eye, and there misgivings set in. It is a huge structure to have placed in the centre of the capital and it bullies its way in to your perspective most forcefully. Furthermore, what does it symbolise? Its sponsors claim it 'represents' the wheel of time, celebrating London's past and looking forward to its future. Is this really a coherent argument? To most people it is just a vehicle for entertainment and as such it bears little relation to the cultural resources of the South Bank, and none at all to most of the buildings juxtaposed to it. You may be on the ground looking up at a fairground wheel: but the Eye, as you will never be allowed to forget, is looking down on you.

The Eye's nearest neighbours are **Jubilee Gardens**—laid out in 1977 to celebrate the Queen's Silver Jubilee but currently a wasteland awaiting a decision on proposals to relandscape—and **County Hall** (1912–33).

A fine structure in its day, County Hall was the masterpiece of Ralph Knott (1871–1929). Until 1986 it was the headquarters of the Greater London Council (GLC, see below). The prime minister, Margaret Thatcher, hated it and all it stood for, and when the GLC was wound up ensured that the building should not fall into other government or bureaucratic hands. So it is now a mixture of hotels, flats, the Eye ticket office, an aquarium, a populist art gallery, a McDonalds and an amusement arcade.

Not much of the old dignity remains but the *Marriott Hotel*, at the south end, has been diligent in conserving several of the interiors and maintains an excellent restaurant in the former library. On the other side are some new apartments, stylistically referring to the Edwardian building, flanking a dignified piazza and exposing to view an ancient and derelict lying-in (maternity) hospital of the 1830s, scandalously neglected.

London County Council and Greater London Council

These bodies, both now defunct, were all-powerful in the administration of London for most of the 20C. The LCC was established in 1888 as successor to the Metropolitan Board of Works, which had looked after roads and drains since 1855. The democratically elected LCC was given much wider powers: its 126 Councillors were responsible for the housing, transport, health, welfare and education of 3.2 million Londoners, and for the city's open spaces. From 1922 it occupied County Hall. Perhaps its finest monument is the nearby Royal Festival Hall, its contribution to the 1951 Festival of Britain.

In 1965 a major reorganisation of local government in Britain saw the establishment of the Greater London Council, which superseded the LCC and covered the far greater area over which London had expanded. Its responsibilities were similar, although education was run by a separate body, the Inner London Education Authority. The GLC was abolished in 1986 and until the establishment in 2000 of the GLA (see Chapter 30), the capital had no strategic authority to oversee the work of its 33 boroughs.

On the river side, the **London Aquarium** is certainly of interest. It contains three basement floors of tanks, some large enough to accommodate small sharks, and others open at the top to enable visitors to touch the fish, if the fish—rays, for example—are agreeable. Open 10.00–18.00. Admission charge. ☎ 020 7967 8000. www.londonaquarium.co.uk

Next door to the Aquarium is a somewhat tacky exhibition of the works of **Salvador Dali**, or works related in some way to the controversial Spanish Surrealist. Some have spaced themselves on the embankment outside, but there are plenty more within. Open 10.00–17.30. Admission charge. Café. ☎ 020 7620 2720. www.daliuniverse.com

Proceed past the river frontage of County Hall to Westminster Bridge, noting the **Coade-stone lion** by W.F. Woodington (1837) above. He used to mark the entrance to the Lion Brewery, on the site now occupied by the Festival Hall. (Coade stone, an artificial substance manufactured in Eleanor Coade's factory on this site in the later 18C and early 19C, can be seen carved and constructed elsewhere in many London buildings of the period.) There are fine views across the river to the Houses of Parliament, Portcullis House and the former New Scotland Yard.

Turn left down Westminster Bridge Road and left into York Road for Waterloo Station: alternatively cross the bridge for Westminster station.

33 • Lambeth

'The Lambeth Walk', a dance made popular in the 1937 Cockney musical *Me and My Gal*, was named after an actual street in Lambeth, once a vivid market. This route covers a number of interesting areas and buildings that convey a real sense of the past: it also takes in the finest view in London and a world-class museum.

- Distance: 2½ miles. Time: 3½ hours, including the museums. Tube: Lambeth North. Map 8 and 15.

Start from Lambeth North station (Bakerloo Line) and cross over the two roads opposite to walk down Hercules Road (**Map 15,8**). On your left, dominating the crossroads, is the surviving tower of **Christ Church Congregational** (1873), founded by Samuel Morley MP and a very fine Gothic Revival building. The eye-catching stars and stripes in the decoration of its spire denote that the funds came from the USA. Morley's name was also given to the college just to the south—which has a good 1950s frontage and a small art gallery—although the initiative for its original work came from Emma Cons, of whom more later.

At no. 23 Hercules Road (now demolished but marked by a plaque on the wall of the flats there), lived William Blake and his beloved wife Catherine; this was for the Blakes the most enduring of their various London addresses. They would sit naked in the garden or the summerhouse, reciting verses from *Paradise Lost*. Somehow this area still reflects, more than the north side of the Thames, the special bleak quality Blake saw in London.

William Blake

Entirely a Londoner, Blake (1757–1827) has been seen as one of the most gifted and versatile artists and poets that Britain has ever produced. He trained as an engraver, but from his early years he possessed a powerful spiritual side which informed both his artistic vision and his writing. It is not always easy today, in a materialist age, to empathise with such strongly metaphysical sentiment. Blake published his own work in a variety of media, but is best known for a technique of illuminated printing whereby both text and design were engraved on copper plate with the rest of the surface etched out. Most of his life was spent isolated from the rest of the cultural world, neither understood nor admired. Except for three years in Sussex (1800–3) he lived in various parts of London, having been born in Marshall Street near Oxford Circus. He found it a joy to escape from the centre to the then rural environment across the Thames in Lambeth.

Take Centaur Street on the right, under the railway, and keep going up Royal Street to Lambeth Palace Road. Opposite is **St Thomas's Hospital**.

Founded in 1106 at Southwark (Chapter 30) and some time afterwards dedicated to St Thomas à Becket, it was closed by Henry VIII at the Reformation but soon re-opened, now dedicated less controversially to St Thomas the Apostle. Much development occurred in the 19C at the time of Thomas Guy's establishment of a sister hospital next door, but the site of St Thomas's was acquired in 1859 for London Bridge Station and the hospital rebuilt where you see it today. The long series of blocks by the river was built by Henry Currey (1871) in accordance with the principles laid down by Florence Nightingale—separate buildings to avoid cross-infection, with plenty of windows for fresh air—who also established her training school for nurses here. Later W. Somerset Maugham was a student doctor here; the hospital appears as St Luke's in his novels *Cakes and Ale* and *Of Human Bondage*.

After bomb damage and in response to development needs, there has been much more recent building, including the north wing (1969–76) by Yorke, Rosenberg and Mardall, with a fountain by Naum Gabo (1976) in the sunken garden, visible from Westminster Bridge.

The **Florence Nightingale Museum** housed in the hospital is accessed from Lambeth Palace Road. The displays trace the life and work of Nightingale not only in the Crimea but throughout her life. There is a warm welcome and an interesting video. Open 10.00–16.00 Mon–Fri; 11.30–16.00 Sat, Sun, Bank Holidays. Free 20-minute tours at 14.00 and 15.00 daily. Admission charge. Shop. ☎ 020 7620 0374. www.florence-nightingale.co.uk

Florence Nightingale

A woman of great versatility and charisma, Nightingale (1820–1910) was born the second daughter of a well-to-do gentleman. There was no reason why she should not have had the comfortable life of a Victorian lady, but she developed, from nowhere, a driving ambition to become a nurse (a profession hitherto populated mostly by disreputable characters of whom Charles Dickens's Mrs Gamp is an extreme parody). Against parental opposition she had herself trained and at 33 reformed, almost single-handed, the military hospitals serving the Crimean War, where she gained cult status as the 'Lady with the Lamp'. These efforts were, however, insignificant compared with the prodigious energy she then devoted to the development of a nursing profession back in Britain, the design of hospitals, the collection of medical statistics and the promotion of public health. She died, more or less a recluse, in 1910.

Leaving the museum, turn right down Lambeth Palace Road. On the other side is **Archbishop's Park**, created out of the grounds of Lambeth Palace and opened in 1901. Stay on the west (left) side of the road until the end of the hospital buildings, then cross to the river bank to see the view of the Houses of Parliament; because this is London's greatest building (see Chapter 13), the view is arguably London's finest, too. Lambeth Bridge (1929–32) is on your left.

Behind you is the former church of St Mary-at-Lambeth and Lambeth Palace. Cross over to explore them. The church is of ancient foundation, dating back at least to the 11C, but was much rebuilt to match the 14C tower by Philip Hardwick (1851–52). The Archbishop of Canterbury acquired this land in 1197 and many archbishops are buried in the church. Its function now, however, is to house the **Museum of Garden History**. This is a very pleasant place, where nice teas are served by cheerful people. It is less good as a museum, having poor labelling, no story boards and only a limited number of exhibits. The display continues in the churchyard, now a garden, also deficient in labels or other guidance. The venture was set up in the name of the Tradescants, two of whom were gardeners to both Charles I and II and are buried here, as is Captain Bligh of the *Bounty*. Open 10.30–17.00 daily (closed Jan). Admission by voluntary donation. Shop. Café. ☎ 020 7401 8865. www.museumgardenhistory.org.uk

Lambeth Palace, the Archbishop of Canterbury's London home since the 12C, is next door. Famous in name, the Palace is nevertheless a greatly underestimated and unappreciated building. It is not often open but some of its buildings can be viewed from the exterior. Next to the church is Archbishop Morton's gatehouse (1495), an entrance between two solid red-brick towers with black diapering. To its left, just visible from the gatehouse (or it can be peeped at from across the road over the brick wall), is Archbishop Juxon's hall, rebuilt at the Restoration (1660–63), its medieval predecessor having been destroyed during the Commonwealth. Even from the outside you can see it is a unique mixture of motifs from both Classical and Gothic styles, as if no one had ever made the distinction. Beyond the hall, the so-called Lollards' Tower (1435), a water tower where followers of John Wycliffe were allegedly held, is visible.

If there is any means of entry, do not miss the chapel and the 13C undercroft, the interior of the hall with portraits of archbishops by, among others, Hans Holbein and Antony van Dyck, and above all the library, with such treasures as the Lambeth Bible, a masterpiece of Romanesque Art (*c* 1140–50). To enquire about possible visits, ☎ 020 7898 1200.

A possible detour could now be made along the river via the **Albert Embankment**, counterpart of the Victoria Embankment and part of the same programme by Sir Joseph Bazelgette (1866–70). It is a mile long and repeats the dolphin lampposts seen on the opposite bank, but its only real function is as a road (no sewer or Tube line runs here). It is lined with the worst kind of 1960s offices but once, before the embankment existed, at the southern end lay the magical Vauxhall Gardens, now no more than a shabby public space.

At the church of St Peter on Tyers Street, by J.L. Pearson (1863–64), the **Vauxhall Heritage Centre** has information on the gardens. Open 10.30–16.00 Tues–Thur. ☎ 020 7793 0263.

Returning from Vauxhall, from St Mary-at-Lambeth, make your way down Lambeth Road to the east, away from the river. First, on the left, is the churchyard, then an infants' school of 1880, now known as the Ark. Opposite, in a modern block with a crest on the tower, the **Royal Pharmaceutical Society** has an interesting museum that can be visited only by prior appointment, as part of a group. Admission free. For opening times, ☎ 020 7735 9141, ext. 354 www.rpsgb.org.uk

There are one or two good 18C houses on the left of Lambeth Road and through an entrance back into Archbishop's Park, the **Marine Institute**, a fine

Vauxhall Gardens

No trace remains—not even a blue plaque—but for nearly 200 years 'Vauxhall' was a famous London institution. The area was first fenced off and opened as a public garden before 1660, and Samuel Pepys enjoyed visiting it. From historical accounts it is clear that its particular mixture of public music, food and drink, and perambulating and flirting in the gardens among the shrubberies and their surrounding paths and avenues, was already established. The gardens' heyday was in the 18C, largely under the management and later ownership of Jonathan Tyers (commemorated in nearby Tyers Street), when steadily rising admission charges enabled the introduction of better facilities, eating places, statuary and paintings. The gardens became more popular than ever. As late as 1813 a party was held there to celebrate Wellington's victory at Vittoria and Westminster Bridge was blocked by traffic for three hours. But the gardens fell on bad times, and their risqué reputation made them incompatible with the Victorian character. They closed in 1859.

red-brick 19C building. It was founded in 1756 to help recruit boys to the Navy. After going under the railway bridge, look out on the right for the famous Lambeth Walk, though it is not worth exploring. Beyond it are a good 1950s block and then the 1960s Lambeth Towers, on your right, the usual slabs attractively broken up into a range of shapes and sizes.

Imperial War Museum

The main reason for your journey into this very ordinary area is now visible opposite, to the right: the Imperial War Museum (**Map 15,8**), housed in the imposing remains of **Bethlehem Hospital** for the insane, known as Bedlam, which had served that purpose in its original locations in the City since 1246 but was rebuilt here in open marshland in 1812.

• Open 10.00–18.00 daily. Admission free. Archives and library open 10.00–17.00 Mon–Fri. Café. Shop. ☎ 020 7416 5000. www.iwm.org.uk

The Imperial War Museum opened at the Crystal Palace in 1920, moved to South Kensington in 1924 and came to Lambeth in 1936. Its collection had been initiated in 1917, before the First World War was over, and from the start it was decided to include the Commonwealth—hence the now contentious, even wildly inappropriate, name 'Imperial'. But contention is inescapable in the themes of this remarkable place, the appalling conflicts of the 20C, from the First World War to Kosovo. Any sense that some of the displays glorify war—and they used to, more than now—is absolutely offset by a visit to the Holocaust exhibition on the third floor.

The exterior of the 1812 hospital building, by James Lewis, with later enlargements including the copper dome of 1844, retains a certain aura of discomfort, helped by the two 15-inch guns menacingly pointing at you. This is perhaps fitting in a museum commemorating British and Commonwealth involvement in two world wars. Having said that, the interior was converted in the 1960s with great imagination, filling in the open central courtyard and constructing new galleries at all levels. The surrounding **Geraldine Mary Harmsworth Park** is a rather bald open space, named after his mother by Lord Rothermere, who bought the grounds of the old hospital and gave them up to public use in 1926.

Note. You should decide at the outset whether to include the Holocaust exhibition in this visit. The Museum recommends you not to take children under 14 to the Holocaust section, although much of the rest of the museum is very suitable for children. This route reaches the Holocaust exhibit last: if you decide to cover the entire museum, then this must be the right order. It will be a sobering and profound experience.

Courtyard This is an exciting and vividly filled space. Ole Bill, a London Transport bus of 1911 which was used for troop movements in France is eye-catching, but more inspiring are the suspended **aircraft** of both world wars, including a Spitfire and a Mustang. Much more disturbing is a V2 Rocket of 1944 with startlingly complex innards. A separate display shows aspects of Commonwealth involvement in both world conflicts. To the left is a good café and to the right an excellent shop.

Floor 1 Excellent displays on the origins of the First and Second World Wars show the growth of opposing alliances, although they are insufficient to complete our understanding. The reconstruction of a front-line trench at the **Somme** in 1916, which you walk through, is dark, smelly, full of sudden noise, a premonition of hell, and at the same time a reminder of courage, cheerfulness and resilience, qualities perhaps now missing from our more mundane lives. The 10-minute re-creation of the London **Blitz** holds similar ambiguities.

Plenty of space is given to conflicts since 1945. J.F. Kennedy said in 1961 'Mankind must put an end to war—or a war will put an end to mankind.' No one seems to have listened, and the collapse of Communism in Europe, which for over 40 years looked like the biggest obstacle to peace, now seems irrelevant in the light of the ethnic and religious struggles which have replaced it.

Floor 2 Up the stairs (or lift) there are good displays on the Secret War, the workings of the special services, and on the history of the **Victoria Cross and George Cross**. Glorification is avoided but the heroism of individuals inspires. There are also some heavyweight artefacts, including the cockpit of a Halifax bomber. There is an interesting review of the museum's range of collections and a discussion of its collecting policies.

One of the collections is of **art**. This is very professionally displayed, with occasional special exhibitions. From the First World War you should locate John Singer Sargent's *Gassed* (1917), works by Stanley Spencer, William Orpen (*Signing of the Peace at Versailles 1919*—little serious men at the foot of huge mirrors), Paul and John Nash, Wyndham Lewis and C.R.W. Nevinson. From the Second World War the collection includes works by Henry Moore, Graham Sutherland and John Piper. Important paintings are sometimes on loan elsewhere, so if visiting to see a specific work, telephone in advance to check it is there.

Floor 3 The **Holocaust Exhibition**, located in a newly built space, is sometimes crowded. There are two parts. The first traces background developments from the origins of European **anti-Semitism** (including in England, more or less contemporary with the building of Westminster Abbey) to its intensity in Nazi Germany where, again, Jews became blamed for a variety of ills. The readiness of a few people to bully, and of most people to turn a blind eye, could not be more shocking, nor could the perfunctory dismissals of the rest of Europe that this was not their problem. With Jews were lumped the usual targets of Western **social prejudice**—gypsies, radicals, conscientious objectors, homosexuals, racial

1inorities such as Poles, and the disabled. The objective was the creation of a race
f perfect human specimens in an ideal society, a distorting mirror-image of most
ocial policy. We should listen carefully to ourselves when we talk of genetic modi-
cation.

Part Two begins with the onset of war. No more talk: the **final solution**. There
re videos of survivors of the death camps and of the ghettos at Lodz, Riga and
Warsaw. Their testimonies, and their faces, are unbearably moving; the images,
1 still photographs and video, shattering and unforgettable. You learn how the
echnology of a gas chamber was developed to maximum efficiency. There is a
uge model of Auschwitz. Finally, in separate videos, the **survivors** discuss how
Never Again' might be guaranteed: each has an answer. Time will tell, but exhi-
itions like this should themselves be a solemn and forceful deterrent.

eave the museum at the main entrance and walk to the right, past the guns, and
o into a small area of park appropriately devoted to peace, with a Tibetan gar-
en laid out in 1999 and opened by the Dalai Lama. You can walk through this
o exit the park at the northwest corner on to St George's Road. To the left, over
1e crossroads, is **St George's Roman Catholic Cathedral**, an imposing
;othic church by A.W.N. Pugin himself (1839–48). It serves the Roman
'atholic diocese of Southwark and ironically stands near the site of St George's
ields, where anti-Catholic Gordon Rioters assembled in 1780. Sadly there is not
1uch work by Pugin left visible, thanks to bomb damage and an odd but power-
1l 'Gothick' rebuilding of the 1950s. Even so its large scale makes it worth seeing,
10ugh it smells of polish more than incense. The cathedral would have been
1rger still had Pugin's proposals for a massive west tower and spire been accepted.

A short detour down Lambeth Road to the east brings you to **St George's
'ircus**, an important terminus for the street plans of the 1770s, which were
esigned to develop the area south of the new Blackfriars Bridge. In the centre is
n obelisk commemorating the fact.

Turn left into Westminster Bridge Road and immediately take the first right,
Vaterloo Road. On your right is a large example of a **Peabody estate**.

George Peabody

Peabody (1795–1869) was an American, born poor but who proved a highly
successful businessman. In 1837, now extremely rich, he settled in London
and opened a bank; in 1851 he paid privately for the American section of
the Great Exhibition. Concerned about the effects of poverty, in 1862 he
established a Trust for the building of blocks of working-class flats. Similar
initiatives were taken by other philanthropists. Peabody blocks exist to this day,
all over inner London, and are still managed on the principles of a housing
association. Many are easily recognisable from their standardised architecture
of the 1870s, in Italianate yellow brick.

Further on, on the left, are the 1970s headquarters of the London Ambulance
rigade and opposite, on the right, of the Society for the Propagation of Christian
nowledge (SPCK), both good modern buildings. Next on the right is the **Old Vic
heatre**, dating to 1816 when it was built as the Royal Coburg Theatre using
:one and other materials from the Savoy Palace, demolished to make way for
Vaterloo Bridge, over which the rubbish was daily transported.

In 1833 it was renamed the Royal Victoria Theatre in honour of the princess soon to be queen, a title rapidly abbreviated, Cockney-style, to its present name. The interior has been rebuilt many times. Once it had rowdy music hall shows, but later in the 1880s was cleaned up to a higher moral tone by Emma Cons. The Old Vic's heyday was under the direction of Emma's niece Lilian Baylis from 1912 until the Second World War, when it was a Shakespeare theatre before either the Royal Shakespeare Company or the Royal National Theatre had been thought of.

The Old Vic Theatre at Waterloo

Beyond, down The Cut to the right, is the Young Vic, an offshoot founded in 1970. The Cut once had a huge and thriving street market, but all that survives is in **Lower Marsh**, across the road to the left beyond a brand new vaguely Japanese garden, opened for the Millennium and indicative of 21st public garden design. Lower Marsh market is still good for fruit and vegetables later in the week.

Keep straight on up Waterloo Road. On the left the *Fire Station*, in the original building for that purpose (1910), is a recommended pub. Beyond, up on high tracks, is **Waterloo Station**, built by J.W. Jacomb-Hood (1901–22), climaxing at its northern end in the Victory Arch for the First World War—with good carving on the exterior—and Nicholas Grimshaw's snaky train shed for Eurostar services (1993). The line itself dates back to the 1840s. Tubes and buses go everywhere from here.

'Villages': west and northwest

If the term 'village' now seems scarcely applicable to most of the places covered in this section of the Blue Guide, it must be remembered that many of them still retain traces—a church, a pub, some old houses, even sometimes a village green—of the lost world in which they began.

That world was a quiet one of small farms and market gardens generating produce to keep Londoners alive, with its own village centres and independent lives. As our wider analysis explains (p 69), in the age of travel by horse, the encroachment of the city's housing into that peaceful farmland was slight. In Georgian times ribbon development began to creep down the main highways, and some new estates were launched as far out as Kensington but—as the Thameside villas, the 18C communities in Hampstead and Dulwich, and the new capitalist investments at Kenwood and Wanstead demonstrated—essentially these areas were perceived as retreats from London, not as part of it.

The railways changed all this for ever, and the 'Great Wen' festered out to infect and smother village after village. Even before this, in the east, earlier features of the industrial revolution such as the docks had buried any semblance of country life. Now the former villages are a largely indistinguishable part of the whole city and the only traditional English villages you will find within the M25 are in the southeast, such as Downe or Cudham.

But this simply adds to the interest of seeking out the remaining evidence of a significant past, which is still considerable, and exciting to uncover. Every community is different, with its own character and atmosphere—far more so than a group of villages in a typical English county. If you are unconvinced, try a handful of these walks (perhaps Chapters 34, 44, 50 and 66) to find out.

In this section, we circle London clockwise, starting in the west, and completing a ring round London Transport Zone 2 (Chapters 34 to 55). Then we explore a group of riverside villages and towns (Chapters 56 to 64) before resuming the clockwise mode round a selection of more distant places in Zones 3–6 (Chapters 65 to 71). Independent of these explorations are two indispensable visits for those spending some days in London, one to Hampton Court in Zone 6 and one to Windsor, outside the zones altogether (Chapters 72 and 73).

34 • Chelsea

Once simply a riverside village, though quite a grand one, Chelsea has for centuries now been a more complex mixture, often combining opposites—artists and the army, or urban fashion and horticulture. Such contrasts are embodied in this walk, along with a rich collection of domestic housing from a range of periods and some good museums and churches. Chelsea remains a most desirable and expensive residential area. Take care over timing; the Royal Hospital closes for lunch and Chelsea Physic Garden and Carlyle's House are open only on certain days.

Distance: 4 miles. Time: 2 hours + time for museums. Tube: Sloane Square. Map 16 and 17.

We shall begin and end at Sloane Square (**Map 17,1**). As you alight from th train look up: across the tracks, through a large iron pipe, runs the rive Westbourne *en route* from the Serpentine in Hyde Park down to the Thames.

As you emerge from the station **Sloane Square** itself opens up before you. I was first laid out in the 1770s by Henry Holland and named after the note Chelsea resident and Lord of the Manor, Sir Hans Sloane (Chapter 16). To you right is the *Royal Court Theatre*, where many of George Bernard Shaw's play received their first performance, as did later similarly key works such as Joh Osborne's 1956 *Look Back in Anger*. Sloane Street stretches up to Knightsbridg to the north and on the west side the major department store of *Peter Jones* (par of the John Lewis group) flourishes its elegant modern curving façad (1935–37), one of the first curtain walls in Britain.

We set off to the west down **King's Road**. The king in question was Charles I for whom it was laid out as a private highway for his journeys from St James Palace to Hampton Court. Now it stretches in a nearly straight line from Eato Square to Putney Bridge, forming a far from private main artery throug Chelsea. It acquired a special reputation in the 1960s as a place for fashionabl gear (as the word was). It is still a fine street in which to browse, with shops ope late and plenty of attractive housing in the roads either side. We go first past th **Duke of York's Headquarters** on the left, currently under reorganisation bu essentially a plain stock-brick block with a portico (1803), built originally as school for soldiers' orphans and thus related to the Royal Hospital nearby; it now used by the Territorial Army.

After looking at the shops each side, including King's Walk Mall (1987–89), good example of the new genre, turn left down **Royal Avenue**, conceived i 1692 but now with early 19C houses (**Map 17,3**). The back of the Royal Hospit comes into view between the trees. Its formal and grand layout, very unusual fc London, dates back to William III's scheme to create a royal route from his ne Kensington Palace to the Hospital, crossing the royal route to Hampton Cou (the King's Road) at right-angles.

At the foot of Royal Avenue is a large parade field, formerly a parterre, calle Burton's Court. Turn left down St Leonard's Terrace, with a pleasant mixture housing, and right down Franklin's Row to reach the Royal Hospital.

Chelsea Hospital

Cross Royal Hospital Road, which was cut through the grounds in 1860, to reac on the left a small **museum** and **shop**. These are the work of Sir John Soan around 1810, when the Hospital expanded to cope with the Napoleonic War and are worth seeing. After this, cross back across Light Horse Court, throug the hallway of the Governor's House and into the main courtyard, on the nort side of which are the Great Hall and chapel. To the south lie the gardens, inclu ing the former Ranelagh Gardens.

• Open 10.00–12.00 and 14.00–16.00 Mon–Sat, 14.00–16.00 Sun. Admission free. ☎ 020 7730 5282.

It appears that it was Charles II's own idea to emulate Louis XIV's Invalides i Paris (1670), and to repeat in London what had already been achieved for th Irish Army at Kilmainham in Dublin, which formed the stylistic preceden The requirement was a pleasant retirement home for veterans whose welfar in old age was now recognised as the responsibility of the state following the establishment by Oliver Cromwell of a standing army. Chelsea Hospital continues this function to this day, providing accommodation for up to 400 pensioners, whose distinctive scarlet coats make them instantly identifiable.

These buildings (1682–91) formed Sir Christopher Wren's first major public commission: he was working at the time on the City churches and St Paul's Cathedral but Chelsea Hospital predates his work both at Greenwich and Hampton Court. It is near-perfect architecture, not magnificent but restrained (unlike Greenwich), not imaginative but disciplined (unlike Hampton Court), symmetrical, functional but full of individual touches.

Wren's work can be appreciated as you cross through to the **main courtyard**, with its central bronze of *Charles II* in Roman dress by Ginling Gibbons (1676). The central Doric portico is echoed by lesser pilastered porticoes in the two wings which scarcely interrupt the line of windows. In these wings are wards with rows of 9ft by 9ft cubicles for each pensioner. The long inscription along the colonnade of the north block commemorates the Hospital's foundation and establishment by Charles II and James II and its completion by William and Mary.

Go in by the octagonal domed entrance at the centre. The **chapel** on the right is barrel-vaulted, with good plasterwork and an unusually handsome reredos carved by William Emmett, Grinling Gibbons's predecessor as royal carver. The painting of the *Resurrection* in the apse is by the Venetian artists Sebastiano Ricci and his nephew Marco, who were in London together in 1712–16: it is interesting to compare it with the work of Antonio Verrio at Hampton Court, in the Great Hall next door, or of James Thornhill at Greenwich. To pursue the issue, cross the hall to enter the **Great Hall**, a comparatively modest space used mainly for dining, with a plain ceiling and portraits of monarchs on the walls. In particular, at the far end note *Charles II*, shown on horseback in front of the Hospital buildings, begun by Verrio and finished by Henry Cooke.

If you are exploring the **gardens** to the south, remember they were severely truncated by the construction of the Chelsea Embankment in 1874. Until then they were one of the Hospital's proudest features, laid out in the 1690s by George London and Henry Wise, the royal gardeners, with canals and avenues to provide a glorious setting for the Wren buildings from the river. The gardens to the east were formerly those of Ranelagh House (Lord Ranelagh was the first Hospital Treasurer and built himself a house on the site), and were second only to those at Vauxhall (Chapter 33) as a fashionable resort in the 18C. In the centre was a huge rotunda, long since disappeared. The area comes to colourful and fragrant life in the third week of May each year, as the venue for the **Chelsea Flower Show**, which has been held here since 1913. For details of dates and tickets, ☎ 020 7649 1885. www.rhs.org.uk

Leave the Hospital by the west wing into College Court and out into West Road, hence back to Royal Hospital Road. Note Soane's much-admired utilitarian stock-brick stables on the left. Turn left and almost immediately you reach the **National Army Museum** (1968–70). Open 10.00–17.30 daily. Admission free. Café. Shop, with an excellent stock of military books. ☎ 020 7730 0717, ext. 2228. Army life is here presented heroically, rather than analytically. It thus differs ideologically from the Imperial War Museum, but there are some very good displays and plenty of interactive opportunities, videos and convincing models, and

the building has ramps from floor to floor, not an afterthought but well inte
grated into the design. It is best to start in the basement with 'Redcoats. Th
British Soldier 1415–1792', in fact dealing mainly with the 18C, and go up th
ramps, looking at the paintings as you go. The best displays are on Floor 1, 'Th
Road to Waterloo (1793–1815)' and 'The Victorian Soldier (1861–1914)'. O
Floor 2 the 20C exhibit 'From World War to Cold War' is also good, with inte
esting films on video, though not comparable to the Imperial War Museum. 'Th
Modern Army' on Floor 3 is frankly an advertisement.

Outside the museum turn right. A short detour takes you right again, up Tit
Street, then left down Christchurch Street (past a reasonable pub, *A Surprise i
Chelsea*) to see **Christchurch** by the underestimated Edward Blore (1838), wit
a school opposite. ☎ 020 7351 7365.

Go on down Christchurch Street back to Royal Hospital Road, to the **Chelse
Physic Garden**. The entrance is likely to be through a gate in Swan Walk—tur
left, then first right (**Map 17,5**). Open April–Oct 12.00–17.00 Wed; 14.00
18.00 Sun. Admission charge. Café. Shop. ☎ 020 7352 5646.

> This botanical garden, only the second in the country when it was founded i
> 1676 by the Apothecaries Company, became a distinguished location for th
> development chiefly of medicinal plants, and also for the internation
> exchange of seeds and plants. It was in financial difficulties until rescued b
> Sir Hans Sloane in 1722.

Get in if you can: it is an oasis of calm and interesting planting, spoiled only b
the traffic roaring by on the **Chelsea Embankment** outside. Like it or not, w
have to face this traffic next. Continue down Swan Walk, first turning left to loc
up Tite Street, named after the architect of the Royal Exchange who had been
prominent member of the Metropolitan Board of Works, sponsors of this Thamesi
route. Its purpose—like that of the more famous Victoria Embankment, to pr
vide a traffic bypass over a mains sewer (see Chapter 9)—was no doubt a wortl
cause, but it was irretrievably damaging to the river view. Even so, some fine ne
late 19C 'Queen Anne'-style housing was arranged along it, and in **Tite Stre
a colony of artists and writers grew up in the 1890s. These included John Sing
Sargent (at no. 31), and Oscar Wilde (at no. 16, now no. 34), but the guidin
spirit was perhaps J.A.M. Whistler, whose famous Art Nouveau style White Hou
(formerly no. 35) by E.W. Godwin was scandalously demolished in the 1960s.

J.A.M. Whistler

James Abbott McNeill Whistler (1834–1903) was an American expatriate
who lived in London and Paris. His particular feeling for London is shown in
his Thameside *Nocturnes*, painted in Chelsea in the 1870s, where, as elsewhere in his work, the use of musical nomenclature refers to the indistinct
fusion of line, form and colour to convey a mood. Self-confident and witty,
Whistler was a natural leader for the Aesthetic movement of the 1880s:
when an admirer praised a natural landscape view as reminding her of his
work, he replied, 'Yes ma'am, nature is creeping up.'

Returning along the Embankment, note nos 8–11 (especially no. 8, Clo
House), all by Norman Shaw—but the whole run are collectors' items. This
equally true of the block after the Physic Garden, in particular no. 17, Sw

House, again by Shaw (1875–77), which is based on a Tudor house in Ipswich and was one of the trendsetters for a whole movement. Gardens then appear on the Embankment and you can withdraw behind them to walk along the famous **Cheyne Walk**, pronounced 'Chainy' (**Map 16,6**).

This stretch of what was riverside now dates back to the early 18C, and even before that was the site of a house built by Henry VIII for himself. The literary and artistic associations here could hardly be richer: George Eliot, William Dyce and Daniel Maclise lived in different houses along this riverside façade.

In a single house, no. 16, Tudor House (a misleading name—it was built in 1717—but referring to an older use of the site) lived, successively and incredibly, D.G. Rossetti, Algernon Swinburne and then George Meredith. Rossetti is commemorated by a fountain in the gardens. Cross over Oakley Street, with its uniform 1860s terraces and the painfully delicate Albert Bridge (Chapter 55) on your left. Cheyne Walk then continues with no loss of interest. Nos 38 and 39 (1893–94) represent one of the developments arising from Norman Shaw's Swan House, in a Queen Anne turned Arts and Crafts style. The architect was C.R. Ashbee, designer of many Chelsea houses, few of which survive: he went on to establish an artistic community at Chipping Camden in Gloucestershire. In the gardens here, note the statue of *Thomas Carlyle* by Sir Joseph Boehm (1882)—we shall be returning to him soon.

The road bends round to reach **Chelsea Old Church**, or All Saints, red-brick, comfortable and reassuring. Much of the brickwork consists of quite recent repairs of bomb-damage, but it was brick before, the nave built in the late 17C to attach to a surviving medieval chancel, which was then brick-faced. Open 14.00–17.00: do go in if you can, to see the rich collection of monuments. Left to right, if you stand at the back of the church, they include memorials to Charles Cheyne, Viscount Newhaven and his wife Jane by Piero Bernini, son of the great Gian Lorenzo (1672); Richard Jervoise (1563), in a great free-standing arch all to himself; beyond this, Sir Robert Stanley (1632), his portrait-bust looking at you fixedly. To the right of the arch, Sara Colvile (also 1632), rising in her shroud like John Donne at St Paul's. Then comes the altar, and in the corner the badly damaged tomb of Jane Guilford, Duchess of Northumberland (1555); and finally, in the south chapel, restored for his private devotion by Thomas More, his own monument (1532) constructed after the death of his first wife—although he himself was never buried here, being interred at Canterbury after his execution three years later. Nearby is an ambitious monument to Lord and Lady Dacre (1595).

Sir Thomas More

More (1478–1535) was a cultivated and erudite lawyer and a fervent Roman Catholic, and was vividly celebrated in Robert Bolt's play *A Man for All Seasons*. His fame has depended on both his intellectual reputation and his unsuccessful attempt to find a compromise in Henry VIII's desire to split from Rome. A Londoner by birth and temperament, he succeeded Thomas Wolsey as Chancellor in 1532. He advised Henry against divorce, a policy which led first to his imprisonment and then, despite his argument that the evidence against him was perjured, execution. He was canonised in 1939. More can sometimes border on the sanctimonious—see the wording he devised for his epitaph in Chelsea Old Church. (You may well disagree.)

Before leaving the church, note the capitals of the columns in the More chape like Pietro Torrigiano's tomb for Henry VII in Westminster Abbey, these are ver early examples (1528) of Renaissance motifs in Britain. Nearby is a plaque t Henry James, a parishioner who, it defensively records, 'renounced a cherishe citizenship to give his allegiance to England in the 1st year of the Great War ☎ 020 7795 1019.

A rather static black-and-gold statue of this most famous of Chelsea residen by L. Cubitt Bevis (1969) stands in the gardens just outside the church; hi house, long since demolished, was nearby.

Now, a possible detour is to continue along the Embankment past Batterse Bridge. On the right is **Crosby Hall**, originally built in Bishopsgate in the City i the 1460s, and later bought, coincidentally, by Thomas More. It was moved her in 1908–10, arranged quite unhistorically to overlook the river, and has sinc been embroidered with imitation additions. It would be uniquely interesting to b able to see the interior but it is privately owned, and is invariably bolted an barred. Beyond Beaufort Street in the western part of Cheyne Walk, at no 95–100, is **Lindsey House** (1674), perhaps the grandest surviving large hous in Chelsea, even if now divided, having been the headquarters of the Moravia Church in the 18C (**Map 16,5**). It is largely invisible behind the high front fence The Brunels, father and son (see Chapter 37), lived at no. 98.

Now go back to Chelsea Old Church and up Old Church Street. Everything is a pleasing scale, except for the Gothic working-class flats (1878). Peep u Paulton's Street on the left to see Paulton's Square—back to the stucco terrac of the 1830s. From Old Church Street turn right into Justice Walk. At the end ar nos 23–24 Laurence Street (called Duke's House and Monmouth House), with lovely early 18C pedimented doorway. It is a shock to see, as you turn to the righ a standard Peabody block in the usual yellow stock-brick trim. Turn right past and left into Lordship Place to reach Cheyne Row, where at no. 24, part another early 18C terrace, stands **Carlyle's House**. Open late March–O 11.00–17.00 Wed–Sun and Bank Holidays. Admission charge (National Trust ☎ 020 7352 7087. www.nationaltrust.org.uk/regions/thameschilterns

Thomas Carlyle (1795–1881) and Jane Carlyle (1801–66) were born an educated in Scotland and lived there after their marriage in 1826. They move to Chelsea in 1834 and, as a couple, dominated the mid-19C London literar scene. Carlyle was hugely admired for his scholarship (in the field of Germa literature) and historical writings, but in the 20C his reputation declined proportion as his prose became increasingly impenetrable. Jane Carlyle al: had a brilliant mind but, as was the custom of the day, devoted it to domest chores and coping with her temperamental husband. Their letters, includir those to each other when apart, especially Jane's, have perennial appeal.

The Carlyles lived here from their arrival in London in 1834 until his death, as widower, in 1881. It is possible to see several rooms, including the servant miserable basement, Jane's bedroom and sitting room, and Carlyle's special converted attic in which to write. It is fascinating, steeped in Victorian atmo phere, dark, full of books and moods.

Then turn up Cheyne Row into Glebe Place, another artists' haunt, and brin ful of interesting houses. You first cross **Upper Cheyne Row**, where the small houses were cheaper than those near the river. James Leigh Hunt lived at no. 2

1716). An ugly red-brick Board School is on the left, and **Glebe Place** then xtends round two corners. No. 35 is important as a work by Philip Webb (1868), Villiam Morris's architect. No. 4 is by Charles Rennie Mackintosh (1920), his nly work in London, but late, by which time the Glasgow magic had died.

And so we return to the King's Road (**Map 16,4**). On the left at no. 211 is Argyle House by Giacomo Leoni (1723), publisher of the key translation of 'alladio, and thus a seminal influence on Palladianism. Chelsea College of Art is p Manresa Road opposite. Turn right and cross over at the lights to **Dovehouse ;reen**, a former burial ground given by Sir Hans Sloane in 1733: you can cut hrough it—via Chelsea Farmers' Market—to Sydney Street. Here you must see he church of **St Luke**, an early Gothic Revival building by J. Savage (1820–24), nspiring, tall and proud, far from 18C jokiness. It is not quite to the standard of A.W.N. Pugin but easier to live with: even if you cannot get in you can sometimes eer through the glass door.

Go back down Sydney Street to see the attractive **Old Chelsea Town Hall** by M. Brydon (1885–87), with later work by Leonard Stokes (1904–8), in neo-aroque style. Cafés and restaurants are all around here, and more pleasant 'helsea streets to the north. Explore them, or to the west, if you have energy left. 'ou can catch a bus back to Central London from anywhere along here—take os 11, 19 or 22—or wander slowly back along the constantly interesting and njoyable King's Road to Sloane Square, where you started.

35 • South Kensington and its museums

)f all the walks in this Blue Guide, this is the marathon, not because of distance ut content. It contains a walk of modest length but considerable interest and hree of the biggest and richest museums in London. To do all this in a day is carcely possible, but the walk and any one of the museums, or just two of the nuseums, spending a half-day in each, would be perfectly reasonable. Or you night combine the walk in the morning with lunch and afternoon at the Victoria nd Albert Museum: South Kensington and the V&A (as it is invariably known) re all of the same mind-set.

Distance: 2 miles. Time: 1 hour + the rest of the day for museums. Tube: South Kensington. Map 12 and 16.

tart at South Kensington station (District, Circle and Piccadilly Lines). If it is aining you can take a shortcut to any of the museums via the subway thought-ully placed under Exhibition Road. Otherwise, briefly take in the shops and mbience of the short stucco terraces and confusing conjunction of roads round the station (**Map 16,1**). This is uncharacteristic of Kensington as a vhole, which is crammed with more coherent, if varied, 19C housing, a little of vhich we shall see on this tour. If you are interested in seeing more, look at 'ourtfield Road, Harrington Gardens and The Boltons to the west or Pelham treet and Crescent to the east: these are not covered in other walks in this guide. ut our main focus in this chapter is the large, planned (at least in outline) ectangular area to the north, bounded by Queen's Gate and Exhibition Road.

South Kensington Museums

Why so many museums in South Kensington? The impetus for their foundation was the Great Exhibition of 1851 (see Chapter 20) and Prince Albert's
determination to capitalise on its success. In this he was greatly assisted by Sir
Henry Cole, a committee member for the 1851 Exhibition and then secretary
of the co-ordinating body for museum developments.

The idea of a museum is essentially 19C, reflecting Victorian values of
education, scientific collecting and the overlap between them. It seemed to
Albert and his colleagues that the expression of these values required geographical closeness, hence the notion of grouping museums and educational bodies on this large vacant site close to Hyde Park, before speculative
housing spread over it unstoppably. The land was purchased with the profits
of the Great Exhibition and the main institutions arrived over the next 20
years. A long shadow was cast by Albert's death in 1861, resulting in the
commemorative structures of the Albert Memorial and Hall. The layout of a
major International Exhibition held in the centre of the area in 1862 is still
reflected in the curved streets south of the Albert Hall.

Since the 1860s all the institutions have expanded to fill every inch of the
site—and the V&A for one plans further extensions. There is a feast of architecture to enjoy as well as the contents of the museums themselves.

Natural History Museum

We shall begin with the Natural History Museum, on the north side of Cromwell
Road, its long yellow terracotta façade with twin towers behind formal steps
(which have workshops underneath) and gardens giving it a monumental
appearance.

- Open 10.00–17.50 Mon–Sat; 11.00–17.50 Sun. Admission free. Café.
  Restaurant. Shops. ☎ 020 7942 5000. www.nhm.ac.uk

> The building was intended from the start to be filled with the natural history
> collection of the British Museum which in turn had been built up from the
> bequest of Sir Hans Sloane (Chapter 16). The architect was Alfred
> Waterhouse, whose designs were submitted in 1868, and the building, in
> Romanesque style, was opened in 1881. But the guiding hand, who insisted
> on the array of ornament over almost every surface to illustrate the contents,
> was the first superintendent, a Darwinian, Sir Richard Owen.

It is an exciting building, especially the main hall, and as you ascend the steps,
enter, and look around the arched top-lit space, you will definitely feel that frisson
(by now familiar, it is hoped) which Ada Huxtable calls 'the joy of architecture'.
There are two distinct parts to the display: the Life Galleries on four floors
(10–50, 101–8, 201–2 and the Basement), essentially all Waterhouse's building
except for research areas; and the Earth Galleries (60–66) on the three floors of
the former Geological Museum facing Exhibition Road, which you can access
from within. The Life Galleries will take more time, but the Earth Galleries are of
equal originality and importance. The following tour emphasises the highlights.

Life Galleries

In the entrance hall is the cast skeleton of an 85ft-long **Diplodocus** and some
other remarkable phenomena tucked away in the arched bays, including

Coelocanth, a 'fossil fish' thought to have been extinct for 70 million years until rediscovered in the 20C. Climb the stairs to see more of the architecture and take in the section of a **giant sequoia** tree on the second floor.

The 'spine' of the museum is called Waterhouse Way, and on the ground floor galleries lead off it in both directions. Go left first. Gallery 21, on **dinosaurs**, is extremely popular: on crowded days you may be directed to a rapidly moving queue up the stairs and along a walkway from which you can get an impression of the display cases below, with robot Deinonychus on top noisily eating their prey. At the far end you meet a life-size Tyrannosaurus Rex, champing his/her jaws, with heavy, and smelly, breathing. There is much more to see on the same lines as you return through the gallery and a special shop (the Dinostore).

Our own rather unsatisfactory **human species** is considered in Gallery 22: but we have evolved this far, so make the best use of the interactive facilities to understand how our bodies operate. Galleries 23 and 24 (the latter an addition of 1929–32 with a predictable, and oddly likeable, Art Deco feel) are both devoted to a vast display of **mammals**, none vaster than the awesome blue whale suspended from the ceiling. There are plenty of interactive diversions here, too.

Walk along the back of these galleries to see the **fish and marine invertebrates** in Galleries 12 and 13: there is much of interest but in this case live presentation in an aquarium would add value (that it can be done with some species is demonstrated at the Horniman Museum, Chapter 52). There is a café next.

In the other direction Waterhouse Way will take you through Gallery 33, **'creepy-crawlies'**—especially diverting is No. 1 Crawley House, the home where any of us might be sharing our accommodation with large numbers of such creatures. In Gallery 31 opposite a particularly brilliant set of reminders of our **ecological responsibilities** makes one realise what damage we have done to our world. Everyone should see this. Next come a shop and the restaurant. Gallery 38 deals with **birds**, and is less successful.

From here you can go direct to the Earth Sciences section but it is best to complete the tour of the Life Galleries by returning to the first floor above the entrance gallery. Here the Museum deals with **primates** (Gallery 101) and **plants** (Gallery 108). The highlight here is Gallery 105, dealing with **Darwinian theory** and the origin of species: it is dark and largely unvisited but fascinating, given our current disposition to meddle with genetics. Rather inconsistently, **minerals** (Gallery 102) and **meteorites** (Gallery 103) seem to be within the Life Sciences section, and are dreary old-fashioned displays. You can pass quickly through here, admiring Waterhouse's architecture, to reach the middle floor of the Earth Sciences section.

Earth Galleries

The **Earth Lab** in Gallery 66, a space to explore British geology, is of great interest and Gallery 63, which explores the **history of our planet**, even more so. The Museum recommends you spend 30–40 minutes to review these 20,000 million years. Life will certainly be over in another 5000 million years, you will be pleased to know, and the Earth will be extinct in roughly 2000 million years after that. There is not long to go.

Walk down to the comprehensive and spectacular display of the riches of the Earth, **geology**, on the ground floor. From here take the ingenious escalator through 'the centre of the Earth' to the top floor. In Gallery 61 you can explore the process underlying **earthquakes** and in Gallery 62 discover how mountains and deserts will keep shaping themselves. This is all absorbing and adult, but also easily accessible to interested children.

If children lose interest at any point, take them to the basement of the Life Sciences area where **Investigate** is located. This is a hands-on exhibition with plenty of educational content, but you should check opening times—it can be closed in school term time, though never at weekends.

This tour assumes that you will exit from the Natural History Museum's Earth Galleries—there is another good shop by the door—into Exhibition Road (**Map 12,7**). Turn left: the next stop, on the left, is the Science Museum.

Science Museum

The exterior architecture of the Science Museum may be dealt with in a sentence: it is a tedious piece of inter-war Classicism disguising a reinforced concrete structure. Inside there is something much more exciting—the Wellcome Wing—but there is no trace of this from Exhibition Road.

- Open 10.00–18.00 daily. Admission free but charge for IMAX cinema. Café. Restaurant. Shops. ☎ 020 7942 4454/4455/4000. www.sciencemuseum.org.uk. Guided tours on the hour 11.00 to 17.00 (except 13.00) daily.

The Wellcome Wing is devoted to contemporary and future science, with vivid hands-on displays, changing exhibitions and an IMAX cinema (if you want seats in the cinema at a specific time, check at the information desk). On the ground and third floors, and the basement, you can wander from the older historical displays straight in to the Wellcome Wing's futuristic ones, which you may want to avoid. The following tour of highlights takes you through the historical sections first and then the Wellcome Wing separately. Equip yourself with a floorplan at the entrance.

Historical displays

On the ground floor is a riveting display of **early engines**, including Boulton and Watt's rotative steam engine (1788). The much later Harle Syke red mill engine (1903) is often in steam, and awe-inspiring. In the next section, on **space**, is a replica of Apollo 11's lunar lander: such objects are hard to reconcile with the older machines around them, but have now become equally historic.

The best section on this floor comes next, 'Making the Modern World'. It contains George Stephenson's *Rocket*, a Lockheed 10A Electra plane zooming down from the ceiling, the first sewing machine, a copy of Crick and Watson's DNA model as well as the Apollo 10 command module.

If you have children with you, now may be the moment to take in the basement, where there are **hands-on activities** for all ages, well supervised and highly educational as well as being universally popular. Try 'The Secret Life of the Home', 'The Garden' and especially 'Launch Pad'.

On the first floor, the highlight is a general display on **materials**, crossed by a glass bridge which itself illustrates materials' mostly untapped potential. A sculptural structure of 213 different materials endorses this idea. Other displays on this floor deal with **telecommunications**, gas surveying, **time** (mostly through a collection of clocks), and the **weather**. Somehow of particular relevance is a very interesting presentation on the **technology of food**.

The second floor is a rich mixture, strong on **chemistry** and **energy**. The

Chemistry of Everyday Life' display is impressive. Others deal with lighting, showing Edison's earliest lamps, nuclear power, and **computing**, explaining Charles Babbage's pioneering work done in London in the 1860s. There is a large section on ships and marine engineering which needs some re-arrangement to breathe fresh life into it.

On the third floor things improve again, especially in the excellent section on **health**, where multimedia displays trace the history of medicine up to the latest state-of-the-art techniques. For historians there is an interesting, though relatively small, section on science in the 18C, and there are galleries dealing with optics, photography and oceanography. Strongly recommended is the display on **flight** with rides available on a motion simulator and an enlightening history of ballooning, aircraft and similar successful attempts to improve on Icarus.

On the fourth and fifth floors are further displays on medical history, but the third floor is the best place to go through to the Wellcome Wing.

Wellcome Wing

From here you descend by the staircase at the sides of galleries to the lower floors to look at the architecture by Richard MacCormac (2000). As you see by looking down from the third floor, this and the second and first floors are inserted into the huge space like trays of increasing size. It is hugely effective: a cold blue light gives everything a suitably scientific feel. On this floor, 'In Future' is a series of **interactive games** inviting you to participate in a kind of perpetual survey addressing technical and moral issues of the day. You can compare your answers with those of previous participants. It is thought-provoking and important.

Go downstairs—the absence of an escalator has been criticised, and certainly the excitement of the escalator journey in the Natural History Museum's Earth Galleries is notably missing—to the second floor. 'Digitopolis' considers the future of **digital technology**, with appropriate scope for interaction on a massive scale. It could be excellent but inevitably it can be overcrowded and you may have to wait to have a go, or worse (but typical), discover the computer is down.

The display on the first floor, 'Who am I?', is better. It explores how our species is continuing to evolve through its responses to **bio-medical developments**. Again, the material is challenging and thought-provoking.

Back on the ground floor you can find the **IMAX cinema** (entrance up the only escalator) and a vast, regularly changing exhibition on the latest subjects in science. There will always be plenty and varied interactive displays, including items for young children (such as the Pattern Pod). You can not cover it all, so choose first what appeals, perhaps consulting at the information desk. There is a trendy food outlet called the *Deep Blue Café* but no shop in this area: the Museum has excellent shops at the front entrance, where you came in, and which you pass as you leave.

Back out in Exhibition Road turn left, noting opposite a glaringly white Mormon Church (1961)—usually open with a quiet carpeted interior—and then turn left again. You are now walking through **Imperial College** (founded 1910), the main scientific institution within London University: as such it is usually very near the top of Britain's university league table, immediately after Cambridge and Oxford, but is without the architecture to match its importance. Through the trees you will distinguish only 1960s blocks until you come to a huge tower on the right, visible for miles around. This is all that was retained from a rather gross 19C building called the Imperial Institute, constructed after a colonial exhibition on the site in 1886: the architect was T.E. Collcutt. The tower is a distinguished object, but seems out of place in its new context.

Soon you reach **Queen's Gate**, the intended western boundary of the exhibition site. It is worth making a short digression to look at the housing here. First note on your right, on the corner, a fine Norman Shaw house (1888–89) showing the architect in his growing 'Queen Anne' mode (see Chapter 57). On the western side of the road are the stucco ranges we associate with the worst of Victorian Classicism: these can be seen even more comprehensively in Queen's Gate Terrace, off to the left: cross to have a look, to understand what Shaw and others were rebelling against in the 1880s.

Proceed up Queen's Gate to the north, towards Kensington Gardens. Take the right turn into Prince Consort Road, where everything is very tall and impressive (**Map 12,5**). It may be possible to enter **Holy Trinity Church** on the left-hand side. This is one of the last works of George Bodley (1901–3), pupil of Sir George Gilbert Scott and an important late Gothic Revivalist who kept the flag flying into the 20C. Next door is the Imperial College Union Building by Sir Aston Webb (1910–12) in his neo-Tudor mode, and opposite, on the south side of the road, the **Royal College of Music** (1888–94) by Sir Arthur Blomfield, on an axis with the Royal Albert Hall to the north. There is a collection of musical instruments to be seen. Open 14.00–16.30 Weds only, ☎ 0202 7589 3643.

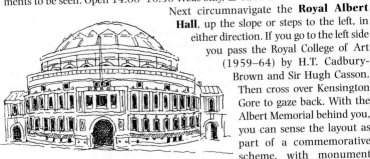

Next circumnavigate the **Royal Albert Hall**, up the slope or steps to the left, in either direction. If you go to the left side you pass the Royal College of Art (1959–64) by H.T. Cadbury-Brown and Sir Hugh Casson. Then cross over Kensington Gore to gaze back. With the Albert Memorial behind you, you can sense the layout as part of a commemorative scheme, with monument pointing down to great hall,

The Royal Albert Hall

below which steps extend and streets curve away to embrace, as we have seen, a series of scientific and cultural institutions. This commemorative aspect was not part of the original scheme but became crucial to it after Albert's tragic death from typhoid at the age of 42.

The idea of the Albert Hall was promoted chiefly by Sir Henry Cole who appointed his own architect from the Royal Engineers, Captain Francis Fowke, and his successor Major-General H.Y.D. Scott. The resultant building, opened in 1871, is unlike other Victorian architecture, plain overall, noble and dignified, with restrained Classical decoration in the form chiefly of a terracotta mosaic frieze; it is thought to have been influenced by the ideas of Gottfried Semper, a Dresden architect and friend of Prince Albert who was in London in the 1850s. The interior is equally interesting in its bald way. Musical events catering to a wide range of tastes, including the Proms from July to September take place inside. For details, ☎ 020 7589 8212. www.royalalberthall.com

Prince Albert

As a foreigner, Albert (1819–61) was never popular, despite his Herculean efforts on behalf of his adopted nation, of which the South Kensington complex is the tangible memorial. A minor German prince, he was the child of parents who divorced when he was seven, perhaps thus emphasising his serious and intellectual nature. He and Queen Victoria fell in love in 1839 and enjoyed a tempestuous but passionate marriage resulting in nine children. She was overwhelmed by his death. It is difficult to see where his career would have taken him from the 1860s, as he was prevented, partly by Victoria herself, from developing a political role and even the staggering success of the Great Exhibition might have left him unmourned. But the Queen's grief guaranteed a clutch of memorials.

The **Albert Memorial** (1863–72), up the steps behind you, is a much more typical, indeed archetypal, piece of High Victoriana, perfectly summed up by Pevsner as the exemplar of its age: 'rich, solid, a little pompous, a little vulgar, but full of faith and self-confidence'. Sir George Gilbert Scott engaged the services of all the leading sculptors of the day to design its 175 life-size figures, free-standing or in relief. The central seated bronze of the Prince, over four metres high, is by J.H. Foley. The groups in the four corners of the monument represent Agriculture, Manufacture, Commerce and Engineering, and at the four corners of the steps, anti-clockwise from the southeast, are Asia, Africa, America and Europe. The columns round Albert are of granite, with Portland stone above, ornamented with Salviati glass mosaic. It was restored in the 1990s: the controversy over the considerable cost was petty, for this is a masterpiece.

Back across the road, move on to the left, or east. You will not be able to miss Norman Shaw's **Albert Hall Mansions** (1879), an early example of the red-brick blocks which sprang up all over west London in the 1880s and 1890s. This one shows no consideration at all for the same architect's **Royal Geographical Society** (founded 1830) just beyond, built as Lowther Lodge in the 1870s in his earlier domestic style.

Turn right, back into Exhibition Road. A detour can be taken here if you are interested in housing. First note the long and assertively handsome façade of **Prince's Gate** continuing east along the main road (**Map 12,6**). It was a speculation which well indicates the sheer scale of the wealth in mid-19C Kensington, and was based on drawings by Harvey Lonsdale Elmes (d. 1847), a young genius whose work is rare in London but whose masterpiece was the great St George's Hall in Liverpool. Down Exhibition Road turn left through Prince's Gardens to Ennismore Gardens, to find on the east side more by the same hand (late 1840s, but finished in the 1860s). Just to the north is the **Church of the Assumption and All Saints**, built for the Church of England (1848–49) but now Russian Orthodox and therefore with an interior of marked interest. Go through to **Rutland Gate**, a slightly earlier development of the 1830s, and at the south end, through a strange gateway that marks a boundary between the original estates, into Brompton Square: the northern crescent is again of the 1830s and the west side built even earlier (1821).

This detour ends with a visit to the **Brompton Oratory**, a significant Roman Catholic church, with an uncompromisingly Italian design by Herbert Gribble

(1878), based on the Gesù in Rome (**Map 12,8**). The interior bristles with sculptures of saints throughout the many side-chapels. Unlike the Anglican churches you enter in London, this one will be full of the faithful at their devotions. ☎ 020 7808 0900.

Victoria and Albert Museum

If you chose not to follow the detour, to get to the Victoria and Albert Museum (V&A) all you need do is continue straight down Exhibition Road to the Henry Cole Wing and enter there. Otherwise, you will now have reached the main entrance in Cromwell Road. Our tour starts from that point.

- Open 10.00–17.45 daily (till 22.00 Wed and last Fri of the month). Admission free. Café. Restaurant. Shops. ☎ 020 7942 2000. Recorded information ☎ 020 7942 2528. www.vam.ac.uk. Guided tours on the half-hour from 10.30; British Galleries 12.30.

The architecture of the V&A is a hotch-potch. The original structure of 1853 by Sir William Cubitt, to house art collections and known rudely as the Brompton Boilers, was removed in 1867 to become what is now the Museum of Childhood in Bethnal Green (Chapter 46). Then Henry Cole's team took over the northern half of the present site, building variations on the Albert Hall form of Classicism, much of which you will see as you tour the interior. The exterior in Exhibition Road, formerly the School of Naval Architecture, has not done very well, looking rather black and gloomy. There have been controversial plans to insert an assertively futuristic block by Daniel Libeskind to incorporate this entrance to the museum. The Cromwell Road façade and galleries (1899–1909) are the work of Sir Aston Webb, though not at his best here, with contributions all over the façade from the cream of Edwardian sculptors as well as contemporary students from the Royal College of Art. It is not very lovable, and entirely lacking the coherence of the Natural History Museum. But at the V&A it is the contents that matter, and these we shall now describe.

Pick up a floorplan at the **information desk**, under the central dome beyond the entrance, and decide on your priorities. It is a challenge to cover the whole museum in one visit. The British Galleries covering the period 1500–1900 were entirely rearranged and opened at the end of 2001 and are certainly a highlight, but to see them alone would be to bypass many other treasures. Sir Roy Strong, a former director of the museum, described it as 'an extremely capacious handbag'. You will see what he meant.

First get your bearings. If you stand under the central dome behind the main entrance, with the excellent **main shop** on your left and the sculpture galleries on your right, the central part of the museum stretches ahead of you (Level A) down a few steps. Galleries extend both left and right and beyond, on a smaller scale, in a square around the central Pirelli Garden Court. Beyond that, far to the left, lie the restaurant and the Henry Cole Wing. Most of this layout is repeated on the floor above (Level B). The British Galleries are entered to the left of the main door just behind you and stretch round the outer edge of the building, with the second half immediately above on Level B. We will start with them.

British Galleries

These galleries chart British design's journey from obscurity to the 'workshop of the world', using four thematic approaches: 'style'; 'who led taste'; 'fashionable living'; and 'what was new?' Within these many aspects of life are examined, from the court to the people, from birth to death, craft to factory and, of course, from Classical style to Gothic Revival to modernity. There are plenty of interactive exhibits: you can try on a ruff, weave a tapestry, feel the weight of a gauntlet. All this works extremely well, being intellectually challenging and satisfying at the same time, a textbook for effective museum display.

Level A We begin in Gallery 58 where, in half of a panelled room from a London house of 1606, there are treasures from the **English Renaissance** from the courts of Henry VIII (a decorated writing box) and Elizabeth I (a jewelled miniature). In Gallery 57 stands the **Great Bed of Ware** (1590), made for a Hertfordshire inn where it was a tourist attraction available for occupation by many guests at once; it was probably the work of German craftsmen living in London.

Gallery 56 explores the 17C, before and after the Civil War, which in terms of art and design was more of an interruption than a turning point. The nobility dressed magnificently before the Interregnum and soon adopted similar practices after the Restoration. The **State bed** (1700) from Melville House in Scotland is more modest in scale but not in grandeur. Britain's increasing colonial interests in the Americas, India and East Asia can be seen in **imported porcelain and silk**, which in turn spawned home industries. By Gallery 43 we reach the 18C with a complete room from a house in Henrietta Street, designed by James Gibbs, in high Palladian style but surprisingly comfortable.

In Galleries 52 and 53 beyond you can explore a range of similar 18C comforts, ceramics, furniture, tea-drinking utensils and an increasing range of **luxury goods**, including clothes, to be enjoyed through a new activity, shopping, the novelty of which has so far failed to wear off. Spending was not the only pleasure: note the family portraits ('conversation pieces'), L.F. Roubiliac's statue of *G.F. Handel* (1738) and the complete **Music Room** from Norfolk House in London, a symphony of white and gold, showing how rich life was, for some.

Level B A change of mood is detectable as you go upstairs, or take the lift, to return through the British Galleries for the years 1760 to 1900. The restraint of **Neo-Classicism** can be felt at once. In Gallery 118, Robert Adam's panelling from Northumberland House in London (1773) and his Kimbolton Cabinet (1776) are in their different ways equally cold and gracious. Furniture by Thomas Chippendale, pottery by Josiah Wedgwood and tasteful Chinoiserie prepare us for Antonio Canova and Bertel Thorwaldsen's chilly statuary. The *Three Graces* 1814–17) and Thomas Hope's furniture and vases in Galleries 119 and 120 introduce us to the austere correctness of Regency Classicism, with its Greek and Napoleonic Empire overtones.

You begin to see where the **Gothic Revival** came from, a longing for the warm fires and candles of medieval England. There are hints in Gallery 120, where a room from **Lee Priory** (1783–94) is cosy in the manner of Strawberry Hill (see Chapter 63). By Gallery 122 we are in the full flow of Gothic romance, with furniture by A.W.N. Pugin and William Burges (a lovely cabinet of 1858), revived religiosity (a cope designed by Pugin in 1848–50) and perhaps most especially the technological triumphalism of the **Great Exhibition**. But the Victorians were nothing if not eclectic: alongside Gothic are furnishings in the style of Louis XV and innovations from Japan.

A reaction was inevitable. The artefacts of Christopher Dresser (1880s) in Gallery 125 have a purging effect, and by the **Arts and Crafts** phase of the late 19C we can glimpse Britain's tentative overtures towards an original or vernacular design vocabulary. William Morris led the way from his Oxford Street shop—see his Bullerswood carpet (1889). The sweet yet revolutionary simplicity of C.R. Ashbee and Charles Rennie Mackintosh's designs are even more inspiring.

International collections
Level A Return to the main entrance to explore the international rooms. Gallery 43, the **Medieval Treasury**, is straight ahead in the centre: search for the ivory Veroli Casket (early 11C) and Gloucester Candlestick (early 12C). Beyond, down a few steps and in the rooms circling the Pirelli Garden Court, is work from **Italy and Northern Europe**, sculpture, woodcarving, majolica, bronzes and glass. In Gallery 21A Giambologna's dominating *Samson Slaying a Philistine* (1562) is worth seeking out, but there are countless smaller masterpieces.

To the left of the Giambologna you can ascend four steps into Gallery 40, the **Dress Gallery**, a large space given over to regularly changing displays from the V&A's huge costume collection. Leaving on the far side you find yourself in a long corridor with galleries for the arts of the Asia leading off it.

Before exploring those you should look into the echoing **Raphael Gallery** (Gallery 48a), which contains nothing but Raphael's cartoons (i.e. huge painted paper templates for tapestry production) of the *Lives of St Peter and St Paul*. Charles I acquired these masterpieces for his collection in 1623, but they have been lent to the V&A since 1865.

Back in the corridor and to the immediate left, in Gallery 41, are cultural objects from **India**. Second left is Gallery 42, for **Islamic art**: on the back wall is the Ardabil Carpet (1539), one of the largest Persian carpets in the world. Continuing back past the Medieval Treasury, Gallery 44 displays **Chinese art**, which also overflows into the corridor. Beyond it you will find **Japanese art** in Gallery 45, and the art of **Korea** in Gallery 47.

Off this gallery to the right is Gallery 50, with some beautiful **English and European sculpture**, including Gian Lorenzo Bernini's *Neptune and Triton* (1630) as well as enormous, almost architectural structures from Italy. In addition, most visitors like to include Gallery 46, the **Cast Courts**, off the Korea gallery to the left. These amazing spaces contain only plaster casts of such objects as Trajan's Column, reproductions collected primarily for the use of students who could not afford to travel abroad—a surviving example of the Victorian educational objectives behind the museum, but still spectacular.

Beyond the Cast Courts, to the north, are Gallery 38, the **Canon Photography Gallery**, and the North and South Courts, which house temporary exhibitions. Making your way via Italian sculpture in Galleries 11–16, detour into the **Gamble Room** and the **Morris and Poynter Rooms** either side of it. These beautifully decorated spaces (sometimes closed for private functions), the work of the three designers after whom they are named, were the Museum's original refreshment rooms: in the Poynter Room you will see an iron and brass grill for chops and steaks. The Morris Room, an early commission for William Morris' new firm (see Chapter 67), is particularly magical.

Down a ramp you reach a small shop and the **main restaurant**, serving good food all day. Above are the galleries of the **Henry Cole Wing**. Don't miss Gallery

202, where Frank Lloyd Wright's original office for Edgar J. Kauffmann in Pittsburgh has been re-erected. It is the only example of Wright's work this side of the Atlantic. The remaining galleries of this wing, which contain mostly prints, drawings, paintings and photographs of the 19C, including a rich fund of works by John Constable (1776–1837), are not described in detail here but are well worth exploring if you have time. The collection of British miniatures is exceptional. Also in the Henry Cole Wing is the Department of Prints and Drawings, which you can visit without an appointment.

Level B The main museum on this level is reached by ascending the stairs covered in glazed terracotta tiles in blue and green. Turn right first to look at Galleries 70–74, a disappointing display on the 20C, though there is better to come in a moment. Return to the top of the stairs to follow a circuit of this level. First come Galleries 65–69, full of **silver**, an amazing, well-presented display with a 'discovery area' and some staggering artefacts. This leads, right, into Galleries 83–84 with **church plate**. In Gallery 85 at the end the **National Art Library** lies to your right. This can be consulted when open (10.00–17.00 Tues–Sat)—access to some items requires a reader's ticket. Otherwise turn left and left again to reach the **jewellery** in Galleries 93–90, exiting through a grilled turnstile. Keep going through galleries of **arms and armour**, usually deserted, and turn right into Gallery 94, to see **tapestry**. This little-visited space is one of the highlights of the V&A but only the more determined visitor reaches it: it contains a group of magnificent and very rare Flemish tapestries of the mid-15C, depicting hunting scenes, formerly in use in Chatsworth House, Derbyshire. They contain fascinating details of costume and facial expression. Don't miss them.

Nor should you miss the **20C design** in Galleries 103–6, creating a smaller circuit alongside. Although somewhat drearily displayed—the V&A are not 20C minded, one feels—this is a great place to marvel at the sheer quality of design throughout the last century.

Galleries 95–101 for **textiles** run down the east side of Level B, which brings you into corridors (Galleries 109 and 102) decorated with frescoes by Frederic, Lord Leighton (see Chapter 36). These were commissioned from Britain's then leading artist in 1868, with a programme typical of the period, the *Arts of Industry Applied to Peace and War*.

From Gallery 109 you can explore **stained glass** in Gallery 111, which leads to a long corridor (Galleries 113–14) of **ironwork** and, far away in Gallery 40a, **musical instruments**. There are other, smaller galleries on Level B as well as a rich collection of **ceramics**, porcelain and pottery at Levels C and D, above, along the Cromwell Road frontage.

From the V&A, you can return in two minutes to South Kensington station. For a few more architectural delights, cross Cromwell Road to reach **Thurloe Square** (from 1840), designed by George Basevi, pupil of Sir John Soane. It is worth going down to the southern end to have a laugh at no. 5, reconstructed in an impossible wedge-shape after the Circle Line was taken past below it. Basevi created some beautiful terraces in this area, amongst which are crescents, a special pleasure and a comparative rarity in London: nearby are Egerton Crescent, to the east, and Pelham Crescent, to the south, both by the same man.

36 • High Street Kensington

This is a mundane name for a prestigious district, but the 'High Street' is the spine of this walk. Kensington Palace is tucked away with astonishing modesty (compared with Buckingham Palace) and is all the more enjoyable as a result. There are fine residential streets, two fascinating small museums of the 19C, a particularly leafy and underestimated park and some good shops. These ingredients add up to one of the richest (in two senses) walks in this guide. Note that Leighton House is closed on Tuesdays.

• Distance: 2¾ miles. Time: 1½ hours + 2 hours for museums. Tube: High Street Kensington. Map 10 and 11.

Travel on the Circle and District Lines can be frustrating but is necessary to reach High Street Kensington station (**Map 11,3**), the start and finish of this walk. You emerge from the station, through a modern shopping mall, to blink in the High Street, with shops stretching away left and right. Opposite, the Bank Melli Iran occupies a compact, very domestic-looking 19C building: it was the **Old Vestry Hall** (1851), a reminder that this was once the village centre, with the church towering behind (see below). Turn right. The first main block of shops you reach is the former *Derry and Toms*, now divided into the usual chainstores, but once second only to Barker's as one of the great department stores of High Street Kensington. It still has a **roof garden**, originally a popular feature and still worth visiting for its planting, views and protected birds. It is open occasionally via a separate entrance at 99 High Street Kensington, ☎ 020 7937 7994.

Cross Derry Street and behold an even bigger emporium, *John Barker & Co.* now divided up but still to be read as a single building in Parisian Art Deco style by Bernard George (1933). The two thin towers with vertical glazing seem both confident and vulnerable, still conveying a past glamour. Opposite is a nasty heavy Classical store, also built for Barker's but ten years earlier and certainly devoid of any glamour whatsoever: this is equally true of Richard Seifert's *Royal Garden Hotel* next door (1965), a 'slab and podium' which manages to make Modernism seem vulgar. There are some interesting blocks on the south side.

Kensington Palace

Cross over into **Kensington Gardens** (see Chapter 20) to visit Kensington Palace. There are two reasons to see the palace. First, it is important historically and architecturally, with work by Sir Christopher Wren and William Kent, and the state apartments provide a fine tour. Second, it is enjoying a growing reputation as a museum of royal dress, with both permanent and changing exhibitions.

Go diagonally towards the Round Pond, up the slope, along the Broad Walk and left past the **sunken garden**, which was created as recently as 1909. As you go, look through the railings at the architecture. The east front—to be seen beyond the statue of *Queen Victoria* at the time of her accession, by her daughter Princess Louise (1893)—shows the beginnings of Palladianism, with the central three bays projecting forward under a pediment.

• Open March–Oct 09.30–17.00 daily; Nov–March 09.30–16.00. Admission charge. Refreshments in the Orangery. Shop. ☎ 020 7937 9561. www.hrp.org.uk. Tube: High Street Kensington or Queensway.

The palace was the preferred London home of William III and Queen Mary (see Chapter 72), who disliked the damp atmosphere of Whitehall. They saw it simply as a private retreat, not a palace, and its modest aspect is the main source of its appeal today. It was also popular with George II and Queen Caroline, in whose time the gardens were developed. The architecture is restrained, and although Wren was involved he seems to have resisted opportunities for exuberance. The south front has been argued to resemble more closely the work of a Dutch architect, Jacob Roman, who had worked for William in Holland.

The **Dress Collection** is met first on the tour, displayed in a series of rooms on the ground floor. Court dress is an extraordinary notion, consciously behind fashion, deeply hierarchical and arcane, and of staggering expense. On occasions it has been reformed—such as when George IV simplified procedures on his accession in 1820, and in the 1920s—but for coronations and similar big events, even today the designers and tailors have a field day. And everyone apparently enjoys either wearing or watching it. The most recent powerful display of the phenomenon was given by Princess Diana, whose clothes we know were part of some wider statement. Dresses from her collection, and the Queen's, are often part of the changing exhibitions.

Diana, Princess of Wales

No one had heard of Lady Diana Spencer (1961–97) when she married Prince Charles in 1981, but she soon became inescapably prominent. This occurred inevitably because of her natural good looks and her role as mother of the next heirs to the throne (William was born in 1982 and Harry in 1984). But it was reinforced by her own inconsistent response to the public gaze, partly delight, as her interest in being seen as a leader of fashion confirms, but also partly fear at intrusions into privacy. Diana's full iconic status developed only in the 1990s, first, after her separation from Charles—part of some kind of inner revolution within the royal family whereby several celebrated marriages were dissolved—and second, after her tragic death in a road accident in Paris in 1997. This was followed by a short-lived but intense outpouring of national grief, during which flowers spread endlessly around the gates of Kensington Palace, where Diana had lived after her divorce.

After the dress displays, you mount the **King's Grand Staircase**, originally constructed by Wren in 1689 but redeveloped during George I's occasional occupation in the 1720s. The most noticeable feature is the *tour de force* of illusionist painting in the Italian style by William Kent, whom we think of as an architect (see Chapter 12), showing members of George I's court as it were 'watching' him ascend the stairs.

At the head of the stairs you enter the **Presence Chamber**, overlooking the small White Court which gives light to the State Apartments: there are three much more substantial courts in the private parts of the palace to the west. The Presence Chamber is again by Kent in a 'grotesque' style, an early example of the fashion that was to be so comprehensively developed by Robert Adam later in the 18C. The overmantel carving is by Grinling Gibbons (1689).

As at Hampton Court, the **Privy Chamber**, which you reach next, was for more intimate guests. It is sparsely furnished today, with busts of important 18C figures and three fine tapestries made in the 17C in workshops at Mortlake, beside the Thames towards Kew. The ceiling, again by Kent, illustrates his particular brand of humour: it shows Minerva and Mars, who wears the Garter Star, giving him membership of Britain's oldest and highest order (see Chapter 73).

Next comes the **Cupola Room**, facing north and, as the original principal state room, the most ornate. It actually feels rather claustrophobic: Kent was less successful here in reproducing an interior of serious Roman grandeur, with Ionic pilasters, arms and a coffered dome. Perhaps the problem is that the *trompe l'oeil* is just not convincing enough. The clock in the centre of the room is later (1743), done for Princess Augusta, mother of George III.

Now go east to the **King's Drawing Room**, the focal point of the east façade. Through the windows you can get an impression of how the gardens were originally laid out, with the Round Pond, then called the Bason, on an axis with this central room and the Long Water, or Serpentine, beyond. There used to be ornate parterres to the north and south. The ceiling and chimneypiece of the room are all that remain of Kent's work, but the great oval of *Jupiter and Semele* sets the tone. *Venus and Cupid*, by Giorgio Vasari (1511–74) after Michelangelo, which George II insisted on keeping as 'my fat Venus', still hangs on the south wall.

The Council Chamber (not always open) lies to the north, but your route goes south into three rooms that, although part of the original conception, have become associated with Queen Victoria's occupation of Kensington Palace as a princess. She lived there with her mother, the Duchess of Kent, from her birth until her accession in 1837. She was asleep in the **Bedchamber** when she was awakened by the news that William IV had died and the job was hers. Thirty years later, these rooms were occupied by the Duke and Duchess of Teck: their daughter Mary, later to marry George V, was born in the Bedchamber. The room is furnished with Victoria's own bed and a painting by George Hayter of the wedding of Victoria and Albert in 1840.

The Ante-Room next leads to the **Dressing Room** of the Duchess of Kent, Victoria's mother, a William III room but wholly Victorianised for our viewing of it. Here there are paintings of the Duke of Kent and his eccentric brother, the Duke of Sussex, who also lived in Kensington Palace for many years but was buried at Kensal Green, among the commoners, in 1843.

Along the south façade is the **King's Gallery**, built by Wren for William III in 1695 as an extension of the original house, but now decorated and furnished as for George I's occupation in 1725. Over the fireplace is a wind-dial (1694) linked to a weathervane on the roof above, in an overmantel by Kent, who painted the story of *Ulysses* on the ceiling.

You return past the staircase to Queen Mary II's side of the palace, developed to her requirements until her death in 1694 as a series of small, intimate rooms leading to a gallery. Her sister Queen Anne also spent time in these rooms and was influential in some of the work on the gardens. Her profile portrait by Sir Godfrey Kneller and a portrait of her husband Prince George of Denmark, who died here, are in **Queen Mary's Closet**. The fine collection of portraits continues in the Queen's Gallery.

Finally, descend the Queen's Staircase and leave via the Garden Room, or probably through the shop. This is a good opportunity to visit the **Orangery**, lying just to the north (**Map 11,1**). This noble building, a cut above the palace in some ways, seems to have been the work of Nicholas Hawksmoor, modified by Sir John anbrugh (1704–5), and somehow you feel the heavy presence of these two personalities. It has a pediment at each end, brick arches with giant windows facing south to keep the orange trees alive in winter, and brick piers with an entablature above for the entrance. Inside are pine and pearwood carvings by Grinling Gibbons and some welcome refreshments.

Queen Victoria (1819–1901, r. 1837–1901)

Victoria's birth resulted from a rush to the altar following the death of George IV's daughter and only child: one of his brothers, the Duke of Kent, married Princess Victoria of Saxe-Coburg and their daughter Victoria was the only offspring of George III's numerous children who survived to carry on the Hanoverian line. She was brought up in Kensington Palace, in a largely female, largely German household.

Victoria was shrewd in politics, quite cultivated in the arts, and retained some of the playfulness of her uncles. Her accession in 1837 occurred during a decade of radical change in Britain which saw political reform, the growth of the railways, Catholic emancipation, and a revival of Gothic architecture. Marriage to Albert (Chapter 35) in 1839 gave full rein to her passionate nature, but brought with it a new seriousness confirmed by his early death in 1861 (to her inconsolable grief), the birth of nine children and sobering responsibilities. All this coincided first with a period of tremendous prosperity and technical innovation followed by economic slowdown. Victoria's 40 years of widowhood became associated with a decline in royal popularity and a parallel loss of direction in English political and economic progress.

Hers was a long reign of staggering change, which the single adjective 'Victorian' oversimplifies, yet the word remains uniquely powerful: 'Elizabethan' is essentially part of the Tudor age, 'Georgian' applies to several kings, but 'Victorian' has come to mean a set of values, a lifestyle, an era. Even Americans talk about their Victorian period.

Return past the south front of the palace. Note the gardens through the railings and the silly, overdressed statue of *William III* by Heinrich Baucke (1907). You exit by pathways across Palace Avenue—look back at the west façade of the palace, private and not otherwise visible, and on a pleasing scale—to reach Palace Green, leading north to **Kensington Palace Gardens**. This is an amazingly opulent street and worth a look, although the presence of guards at the various embassies inhibits staring. The mansions were a Victorian speculation in the 1840s by a builder who went bust, but the whole project had official approval and James Pennethorne laid out the plan on the Kensington Palace kitchen gardens. It is all beautifully looked after.

Take the footpath west back to the real world of Kensington Church Street. Go up a little way to cross and enter the **Carmelite Church** by Sir Giles Gilbert Scott (1954–59), insipid, very late Gothic but with a red ceiling and red altar which are rather effective. Then go down the hill back to High Street Kensington, with a great view of Barker's and nice houses to the right in Holland Street, laid out in the 1720s as a direct link between Kensington Palace and Holland House. There is a Gothic Revival style pub on the left—you can do Gothic in all sorts of ways, as Pugin kept telling us.

Turn right and enter Kensington's primary church, **St Mary Abbots**, via the lychgate. This church, by Sir George Gilbert Scott (1868–72), grandfather of Giles mentioned above, is a magnificent Gothic Revival effort inside and out. The cloistered approach to the south door was by J. Oldrid Scott, younger son of Sir George, in 1889. There are lots of marvellous monuments, some from the previous church—note that of the Earl of Holland (1721) in the south transept—a pulpit given by William III (1697), and a window to Sir Isaac Newton, who was a parishioner.

Leave the church at the west door. There are pleasant gardens all around: one of the seats was dedicated to Sir Alec Clifton-Taylor, doyen of building historians, in 1991. Go back into High Street Kensington but immediately turn right up Hornton Street (**Map 10,4**) to see first the solidly Classical library in red brick by E. Vincent Harris (1955–60) and then behind it, also in brick, the modern **Civic Centre** (1972–76). This 'great red whale of a building', as Pevsner calls it unfairly, is from a design of 1965 by Sir Basil Spence (architect of Coventry Cathedral). Granted it does not conform to its surroundings, but what Modernist building ever did? It seems invigorating in these oh-so-respectable streets.

The streets stretch up to Campden Hill beyond and can be explored with some pleasure even if you are not visiting **Linley Sambourne House**. Continue past the front of the library down Phillimore Walk, across Campden Hill Road and Argyll Road, then turn right and left into Stafford Terrace, to no. 18 on the left (**Map 10,4**). This museum, the home of Victorian cartoonist Sambourne, is currently closed for refurbishment but scheduled to reopen in 2002. For information, ☎ 020 7602 3316. www.rbkc.gov.uk/linleysambournehouse. All these streets were part of a development of 1858–60, by which time, as you see, a straightforward Italianate style was giving way to elaboration.

From Stafford Terrace go up Phillimore Gardens to Duchess of Bedford's Walk and turn left into Holland Park. This has always been a lively spot and remains so to this day, although **Holland House** itself is a poor old thing: a vivid mural recaptures its heyday—or one of them.

The original mansion was Jacobean, called Cope Castle and built by Sir Walter Cope, James I's Chancellor, in 1605–14. It was in the ornate, pre-Inigo Jones style with much decorative carving, which can still be seen in the one-storey stone loggias which have survived. Sir Walter's daughter married the Earl of Holland—hence the name—who was executed as a royalist and Cromwell's men occupied the house. Joseph Addison also occupied it in the early 18C having married the 3rd Earl's widow, and composed his *Spectator* article here. But the house's great days were from the 1760s when it became a meeting place for Whig politicians, including Charles James Fox, one of the family, and literary men including Richard Brinsley Sheridan and later Lord Byron, Sir Walter Scott and Thomas Babington Macaulay, under the management of the outstanding hostess Lady Holland. There was another great flowering in the 1890s and 1900s, when Lady Ilchester, married to another Fox descendant, held garden parties and masked balls. In the Second World War the house was bombed and never restored, and in 1952 the London County Council took it over, converting the east wing into a youth hostel. The aristocratic gardens were turned into a public park.

No specific route through **Holland Park** is recommended but it is worth trying to see what you can of the surviving bits of the house, including, to the south, an original gateway by Inigo Jones, executed by Nicholas Stone (1629). Many events take place here and make use of the remains, including open-air theatre in the summer. The gardens are beautiful, not least the Kyoto Garden on the western side, set up by Japanese companies in 1991. There are places for refreshment.

Leave the park by the Ilchester gate and go down to Melbury Road (**Map 10,6**). This is one of the notable streets of 'arty' Kensington, a rejection of respectable terraces by prosperous artists. On the immediate right is no. 29, Tower House, a Gothic fantasy built for his own use by the architect William Burges (1876–78). Next door, no. 21, and no. 8 along the street are by Norman Shaw, for the artists Sir Luke Fildes and Marcus Stone. Several others are of interest.

Now return down Melbury Road towards High Street Kensington but turn right into Holland Park Road to see, on the right at no. 12, **Leighton House**. Open 11.00–17.30 Wed–Mon; closed Tues. Admission free. Tours (charge) at 12.00 Wed, Thur. ☎ 020 7602 3316. www.rbkc.gov.uk/leightonhousemuseum

This was the house of Frederic, Lord Leighton, (1830–96), another artist and the only one to have been made a member of the House of Lords, so far. He was President of the Royal Academy. The house was designed for him by his friend George Aitchison in 1866, before the later arrivals in Melbury Road. Leighton himself was a practitioner in the later 19C genre of anodyne Classical subjects which have had little following ever since. There are plenty of them inside.

The main reason to go in is the extraordinary Middle Eastern decorative scheme, including an Arab Hall added by Leighton in 1877, with a tinkling pool. Everywhere there are exotic tiles, some from Cairo and some by William de Morgan. It is hard to decide if it is jokey, or spooky, or beautiful—it certainly generates a neurotic feeling.

Fresh air will be needed after this heady interior—even a dash of clear refreshing Modernism would not go amiss. Return up Holland Park Road and down to High Street Kensington, turning left to see the **Commonwealth Institute** by Robert Matthew and others (1960–62), in a manner which follows and develops that of the Royal Festival Hall (Chapter 32). It has a dramatic roof canopy of curving paraboloid shape, best seen from the inside. There are regular changing exhibitions on Commonwealth subjects. Open 10.00–17.00 Mon–Sat, 14.00–17.00 Sun. Admission free but donation appreciated. ☎ 020 7603 4535. There is also a useful reference library. Open 10.00–16.00 Mon–Sat ☎ 020 7603 4535 ext. 210, www.commonwealth.org.uk

Across the road is an Art Deco Odeon, by the regular cinema-design team of Leathart and Granger (1926). Cross over and turn to the right for a little way to find **Earls Terrace** on the left, an ambitious run of houses *à la* Bloomsbury, but early (1811) for this part of the world. Just behind—turn left into it—is **Edwardes Square**, part of the same development but a great deal more modest, with delicious two-storey terraces around a large communal garden, all on a totally different scale from those closer to town, where a square this size would have required much more substantial houses to be profitable to the developer.

On the eastern side there is a good pub, the *Scarsdale Arms*. Beyond that turn left into Pembroke Square, also pleasant but more orthodox (1824). This leads to Scarsdale Villas, which has pleasant but quite grand houses of the 1860s and is leafier and less pretentious than Stafford Terrace above. A Coptic—originally Presbyterian—church (1863) stands on the corner, where you turn left and then right along Abingdon Villas to go left into Iverna Gardens. Here there is another unusual, Armenian church, **St Sarkis**, built by the famous firm of Mewès and Davis (1922) and financed by Calouste Gulbenkian. It is an exact copy of the 13C bell tower at Haghpat, Armenia. As a climax to a London walk, beat that.

Continue into Wright's Lane and turn right. You are back at High Street Kensington station.

37 • Bayswater and Paddington

Bayswater is a rich resource for enthusiasts of 19C housing, more varied than in Notting Hill, if without that area's contemporary buzz. As an area today it is quiet and anonymous, a mixture of housing and small hotels. Paddington, which offers acceptable opportunities for refreshment (and might attract station enthusiasts addicted after Chapter 28), comes about half-way round.

• Distance: 3½ miles. Time: 1½ hours. Tube: Marble Arch. Map 4, 5, 12 and 13

Start from Marble Arch station (Central Line): come up into Oxford Street and turn right, or else locate Exit 12, which brings you to the southwest corner of Edgware Road (**Map 13,1**). Look at Marble Arch itself (details in Chapter 21) then head northwards past a nasty Modernist Odeon cinema block on the right. Take the first left, Connaught Place, into civilisation.

First we are going to explore the area once called **Tyburnia**, from the ancient tributary of the Thames which flowed down past here through Marylebone to Westminster, and the notorious gallows which once stood on the site of Marble Arch.

But Tyburnia, like Fitzrovia and Belgravia, was also a comfortable middle-class housing estate developed on the Bishop of London's Land by S.P. Cockerell, beginning as early as 1805. The land lay between the newly opened Paddington Basin of the canal (Chapter 39) and Hyde Park: its main artery was to be Sussex Gardens, with service streets off both sides, Westbourne Terrace at right angles, and churches to close the vistas. All went well until the 1850s, when Paddington Station thrust its nose in, and again until after the Second World War, when a policy of aggressive Modernism was embarked upon up to the revisionist 1970s, when the word 'conservation' was invented. It all makes for vivid contrasts, and there is plenty of the early building still to be seen.

Connaught Place is an example. These houses, on the left, were part of a new form developed on this estate, 'back-to-front' design, which we shall see much of. The backs looking over Hyde Park and to be seen from the Bayswater Road had the finer façades, stucco-covered as in Regent's Park, but the fronts also needed a grand and dignified entrance: hence the handsome columned and stuccoed porches and otherwise plain brick upper floors.

Turn right into Stanhope Place and up into **Connaught Square**, where the houses are comparatively restrained with brick upper floors somewhat disfigured in particular cases by the later mad (because it can not be eradicated) custom of painting the bricks. Turn left into Connaught Street and then right, up Porchester

Place, to see how the phase of Modernist renewal worked (**Map 12,2**). In Norfolk Crescent and Oxford Square the original street patterns were retained but monstrous rectangular blocks were inserted, with three towers to the west overlooking Edgware Road.

Turn left down Oxford Square and right into Titchborne Row and Hyde Park Crescent to find the church of **St John** by Charles Fowler (1829–30), of Covent Garden Market, meant to close a vista but missing the opportunity. It is a pleasant and welcoming church and is usually open.

To explore more squares, go first into Hyde Park Square, along the north side, into Gloucester Square, a big one that leads down to Sussex Place. If you look to the right you can see an arch of Paddington Station in the distance, but turn left to reach small, pretty **Hyde Park Gardens Mews**, stretching along to an arched entrance at Clarendon Place. Go through the arch, turn right and go nearly as far as the main road to find on the left Sir Giles Gilbert Scott's own house (1925); it is solid, fat, comfortable, vaguely Classical and not at all modern, built in brick and somewhat reminiscent of his power stations.

Sir Giles Gilbert Scott

The grandson of Sir George (Chapter 28), Giles Gilbert Scott (1880–1960) came to prominence when very young with his winning Gothic design for Liverpool Cathedral (1904). He was fairly versatile, but never truly modern. Scott has always been admired for Waterloo Bridge and, more recently, for his red phone boxes; his reputation has been boosted by appreciation of his power stations at Battersea, yet to be rescued, and Bankside, now seen as heroic in its role as the home of Tate Modern. But in maturity he often seems pedestrian, as in the enfeebled post-war Gothic of the House of Commons.

Go on to Bayswater Road to look back up the street, and then return a little and turn left down **Hyde Park Gardens**, one of the grandest of all the 'back-to-fronts' of which you have now seen both back and front. At the end you reach Sussex Square (mostly 1930s) and thence, down Bathurst Street with its attractive 1840s shop fronts, reach traffic-ridden Westbourne Street, with bow windows pushing out so that occupants might catch a glimpse of the park (**Map 12,1**).

Opposite is the truly awful *Royal Lancaster Hotel* by Richard Seifert and Partners (1968). Try not to look and turn right, crossing the dangerous roads to reach the church of **St James**, a late work of G.E. Street (1881–82), building on an earlier, smaller church from the original 1840s estate, which he reorientated to place the altar at the west end. Here again a vista was devised, with a triangular garden in front and Sussex Gardens beyond, splitting into separate crescents behind the church, and the equally prestigious Westbourne Terrace stretching northwest. The traffic is a shame because the street planning is most attractive.

Go up grand Westbourne Terrace and turn right down Praed Street (**Map 4,7**), or go down Sussex Gardens, turning left in London Street and noting dignified Norfolk Square. Either way you reach **Paddington Station**, terminus of the old Great Western Railway, opened in 1854. It was the grandest line in England and until 1892 used the 7ft broad gauge favoured by its engineer, the great Isambard Kingdom Brunel, who was also the designer of the station.

> ### *Isambard Kingdom Brunel*
> Brunel (1806–59) was the son of Sir Marc Isambard Brunel (1769–1849), who had constructed the first Thames Tunnel (Chapter 47), on which as a young engineer Isambard cut his teeth. The son's Great Western line contains much daring engineering, including the Maidenhead Bridge and the Box Tunnel. He also built the Clifton Suspension Bridge (1829), the *Great Western*, which took 13 days to sail to New York in the 1880s, and in the 1850s the giant, ill-fated *Great Eastern*.

The front of the station forms the **Great Western Hotel** by P.C. Hardwic (1851–54), which was grander than anything before it but is hardly in the S Pancras class. Go down one of the ramps either side to the station concourse. Yo can see four parallel sheds (one was built later, in 1913) with long curved roo with wrought-iron ribs. The Crystal Palace, which had been built immediatel beforehand, influenced the structure, but the station is less strictly functiona with plenty of decorative detail, most noticeably the swirling, slightly weir bands of iron against the vertical glazing. There are many modern facilities, as a other stations, but they are especially well handled here (compared with Victori or Waterloo).

Work on a massive scale is taking place to the northwest of the station in th former goods yard and adjacent to the Paddington Basin. This will extend east wards under Bishops Bridge Road and may entail further reconstruction of bot the fourth, later station shed and St Mary's Hospital. It is unclear how rapidl this project will proceed so you must decide how far to explore in that directior In St Mary's, meanwhile, there is an interesting small museum, the **Alexande Fleming Laboratory Museum**. Open 10.00–13.00 Mon–Thurs. Guide tour on the hour. Admission charge. Shop. ☎ 020 7725 6528. it was in this labora tory that Fleming discovered penicillin, by accident, in 1928.

From the station, take a western exit into Eastbourne Terrace, with depressin modern buildings opposite the station, and make your way down Clevelan Terrace. First cross Westbourne Terrace again, then Gloucester Terrace with i memorable double bow windows. Keep going and you will find Clevelan Gardens, a little square all of a piece on three sides (**Map 12,1**). On the fourth, i a totally different idiom, is the assertively modernist **Hallfield Estate**, a postwa showpiece of the 1950s designed by the Tecton partnership and implemented b Drake and Lasdun. Although it is from an era before tower blocks, Hallfield delib erately makes statements opposed to those of the surrounding stuccoed streets— in colour, scale, shape, angle and purpose. There is no dimension in which it con forms, an attitude so far from current planning philosophy that it is hard t believe it could all have been done in one lifetime. As 1950s architecture, how ever, Hallfield looks superb, spacious, abstract, exciting, classless and optimistic The ten- and six-storey blocks, with trees and grass in between, have chequere façades and balconies like opened drawers, in the style of the Festival Hall. At th western side is Lasdun's Hallfield School, also a landmark of its time.

Go down Leinster Gardens, with stucco once more everywhere. Halfway dow is an oddity, sham fronts to cover the District and Circle Lines burrowing under neath. Then Craven Hill Gardens lead down to Craven Hill, with good, big villa leading back to the original estate. Turn right into the last part of Craven Hi Gardens into **Porchester Terrace**, where it is worth walking left down to no

–5 on the left, in the shadow of the giant Hyde Park Towers (**Map 11,2**). This remarkable pair of semis is the 'double villa' which John Claudius Loudon, the gardening writer and architect, built for himself and his mother in 1823. Its glazed porch disguises the fact that it is a pair. The date is very significant: it was before Nash created the Park Villages at Regent's Park, and these houses must therefore have been real trend-setters.

Return up to Queensborough Passage on the left, go through it and out into tall and depressing Queensborough Terrace; turn right and trudge up to Porchester Gardens. Go left and across Queensway to **Whiteley's**. This was a premier department store which William Whiteley founded in 1863, expanding to 17 departments and 6000 staff by 1900; he embarked on this massive building by Belcher and Joass in 1908. The store survived until 1981 but then found itself too far from the West End or Knightsbridge, and so was converted into a shopping mall for chainstores. It is still worth going in to see the original top-lit atrium spaces—one circular and one octagonal—but there is nothing else of interest.

Go along to Princes Square where the street widens. It is rather less salubrious here. Beyond, in Leinster Square and Princes Square, the 'back-to-front' idea was taken to extremes, so that the white 'back' is fine, overlooking a nice garden, while the 'front' has a smart porch but anomalous nasty drainpipes. Down Ilchester Gardens and St Petersburgh Place are three interesting, contrasting but contemporary places of worship built in the 1870s, vividly demonstrating the multi-faith aspect of this community, then as now. First, on the corner of Moscow Road, is the Greek Orthodox Cathedral of **St Sophia** built here for the Greek merchants of Bayswater by John Oldrid Scott (1877), another of Sir George's sons. It is all suitably Byzantine. Next is **St Matthew**, built for the Church of England by J. Johnson (1881) in Gothic Revival style. On the left, and much the most impressive, is the **New West End Synagogue** by George Audsley (1877–79), a red giant in a 'Gothick' mix of styles, with two towers. All three will almost certainly have locked doors,

To avoid stucco-sickness you need go just a step further along Moscow Road and turn left into **Palace Court** (Map 4,1). This is where the Paddington aesthetes of the 1890s congregated. It is in a revival of the Queen Anne style and, after such quantities of peeling, once ultra-respectable terraces, you will deeply sympathise with this minor rebellion. Here is red brick, variety, asymmetry, freshness, light. Look at no. 47 on the right, built for Alice Meynell, the poet, by Leonard Stokes (1889). All the houses are pleasant but at the southern end nos 10–12 are really delightful: they are by J.M. Maclaren (1890).

Unless you want to go on to nearby Notting Hill turn left into Bayswater Road. Note the Yellow House—now the Westmoreland Hotel—in Arts and Crafts/Queen Anne style, by George and Peto (1892). Then peep at **Orme Square**, which is of the Regency period (1818), older than anything else around here. After that, in no time at all you reach Queensway station (Central Line).

38 • Notting Hill

There are three dimensions to Notting Hill. First the area of shops and streets around Notting Hill Gate, with a fair amount of buzz and interest, and some quaint artisan housing all madly fashionable today; second, Portobello Road market, to be seen any day, but in full flood only on Saturdays; and third, for the housing enthusiast, the extravagances of the Ladbroke Grove Estate. This route covers all three aspects consecutively, but it makes quite a long walk. Be aware that the Notting Hill Carnival takes place in the last weekend of August (see below).

- Distance: 3½ miles. Time: 2 hours + extra time for browsing. Tube: Notting Hill Gate. Map 10 and off map.

Start at **Notting Hill Gate** station (Central and Circle Lines). First briefly explore the now attractive streets on the south side of the main road (**Map 10,2**), Hillgate Street or Farmer Street, for example. Hillgate Place running east–west provides a frame. These densely packed terraces date from 1851 and were designed to house artisans providing services for the wealthy all around. It was a hopeless cause and they soon had multiple occupants and turned into serious slums. There is little evidence of that now in the painted façades, window boxes and fast cars in the street. 20C gentrification has had some benefits.

Note the **Coronet Cinema** (1898), converted for cinema use in 1916. Cross back at the station to go up Pembridge Road, forking right: shops have been added to the fronts of the houses. Then go left to begin the long journey up Portobello Road.

Portobello Road

Porto Bello, in the Gulf of Mexico, was captured from Spain by Admiral Vernon in 1739, and a farm in the countryside north of here was patriotically named after it. This road once led to that farm.

Nothing much happens to start with, but after crossing Chepstow Villas—with big Victorian detached houses, as you would expect from the name—you reach very respectable **antique shops** and rather less respectable antique stalls, where there is plenty to explore. Keep going, over Westbourne Grove. At the crossing of Elgin Crescent and Colville Terrace, the street market becomes more conventional, selling fruit and vegetables, but just as vivid.

> There has been a market here since the 1870s, starting with gypsies buying and selling horses for the Hippodrome (see below). It brought down the standard of the neighbourhood, as at Covent Garden, but the overspill of antiques from the closed Caledonian market, after the Second World War, restored the tone somewhat.

After Blenheim Crescent you are in the historic part of Portobello Road. On the left is the **Electric Cinema**, purpose-built and one of the earliest, opened in 1911. ☎ 020 7727 9958. There are also some excellent bookshops, including the *Travel Bookshop* and *Books for Cooks*. To the right down Talbot Road there is an unusual church, **All Saints**, by William White, built in the 1850s to be the centre of a new religious community here, which never materalised.

This is the southernmost point, more or less, in the route of the Notting Hill Carnival, which is relevant if you are walking here at any time near the end of August.

> ### *Notting Hill Carnival*
> The Carnival is the biggest public festival in London, Caribbean in origin and inspiration but increasingly international and multi-racial in spirit and fact. It originated in 1966 as an unofficial response to race riots in Notting Hill in the later 1950s, as a simple street parade with music. In one sense that is still its basis, but now the Carnival is a huge show on the August Bank Holiday weekend, with children's costume parades on the Sunday and adults on the Monday, from morning till night. It is very crowded, noisy, joyful and just occasionally violent. The area affected is only the northern part of the district, north and south of Ladbroke Grove station (which is closed for the day). The location and route may be changed in 2002, which would destroy the essence of a truly 'local' event.

Press on past Westbourne Park Road to Lancaster Road: if you are still interested, go under Westway, where the stalls stretch around into Golbourne Road on the right, getting cheaper all the time.

Ladbroke Grove

Sooner or later you need to return, choosing a suitable point at which to cut through to Ladbroke Grove: Blenheim Crescent is suggested. Turn left to explore the Ladbroke Grove Estate.

As you now see, Notting Hill is indeed a hill, a comfortable mound. From the 1730s it was owned by the Ladbroke family, one of whom decided to open a race course called the Hippodrome here in 1837, erecting a circuit round the brow of the hill. It was not a success, heavy going and unpopular with such local residents as there were, and closed in 1841. That cleared the way for housing development which was placed in the hands of Thomas Allom and W.J. Reynolds. Between them, these two covered the hill with crescents in concentric circles, with St John's church slightly off-centre on the brow. It is a spectacular estate, extravagant in style, ambitious in scale and very green, with the innovation of large communal gardens between the blocks. At the same time it is fatiguing, mentally and physically.

Turn right at any of the crescents, maybe going as far as Lansdowne Crescent, to get an impression of the houses (**Map 10,1**). This is Reynolds's side, with coarse Italianate decorations and the inevitable stucco, but quite a lot of variety. You may spot no. 29½, a tiny modern infill (1973). Villas lie on the upper side.

Go round to **St John the Evangelist** by Stevens and Alexander (1844), an early Gothic Revival church, that is to say of the Victorian variety advocated by A.W.N. Pugin, sited picturesquely on the ground once occupied by the Hippodrome's grandstand. You need to see the other side of the hill to understand just how far Victorian stucco extravagance could go, in the hands of someone like Thomas Allom. Stanley Crescent is the best example, with bow windows galore, balconies, pediments and big cornices. It is overpowering.

Take Stanley Gardens eastwards to where the church of **St Peter** by Allom (1852) closes the vista: a Classical design, it was a long way out of date by then but conforms to the housing pattern. Turn right down Kensington Park Road, then down Ladbroke Square, where you can turn right past pleasant gardens with more modest houses. Then turn left down Ladbroke Grove to Holland Park Avenue.

While you are here, cross over to make a small circuit round **Campden Hi‖ Square**, an earlier development than we have seen so far, by Joshua Hanse‖ (1820s), who was a major developer in Regency Brighton (**Map 10,2**). The‖ have been some later alterations, but it is still a fairly complete entity. It is al‖ worth looking at Aubrey Walk to the south.

Finally, do not miss **Holland Park**—the road, not the park itself, which ‖ covered in Chapter 36. In the northern part of the Holland Park estate, it w‖ developed in the 1860s with 90 identical detached villas, Italian from baseme‖ to roof-tiles, by Francis Radford. Holland Park Mews was built in between at t‖ same time, for humbler persons to keep the main residents in the manner ‖ which they wanted to become accustomed (**Map 10,3**).

To the north return to Holland Park station, back on the Central Line.

39 • Little Venice

This is a delightful, quite self-contained area, with good pubs, spectacul‖ Italianate houses and canal views. It bears no resemblance whatever to Veni‖ and the silly name is of recent origin: it has associations with both Robe‖ Browning and Lord Byron, who would have known better. The walk shows y‖ the exteriors at least of important churches by Street and Pearson and takes y‖ to the lesser known district of Maida Vale.

- Distance: 2 miles (1½-mile optional detour). Time: 1 hour + extra for deto‖ Tube: Warwick Avenue. Map 4 and off map.

Travel to Warwick Avenue station (Bakerloo Line, in Zone 2) and exit throu‖ ironwork vaguely reminiscent of a Paris Metro (**Map 4,5**). Warwick Avenue its‖ runs between the two station exits with a cabman's shelter between. There ‖ Victorian brick and stucco all around. Cross Clifton Gardens to look at the chur‖ of **St Saviour**: it is a rarity, a 1970s replacement of a Victorian church with ‖ eye-catching but painfully thin spire of fibreglass. The interior is unlikely to ‖ accessible.

Walk north up Castellain Road as far as Formosa Street. Little shops cur‖ away to the right and the grand *Prince Alfred* pub stands on the corner. Turn l‖ along Formosa Street and follow it up to the footbridge over the Paddingt‖ Canal. A modern canal-side pub, the *Paddington Stop*, is on the right.

It is worth going over this bridge and turning right to see **St Mary Magadalen‖** a small masterpiece by G.E. Street (1865–72). It, too, is rarely open but you c‖ at least admire the exterior of red brick and stone, with its varied planes, and t‖ way the church was slotted into its narrow site (then a small gap between po‖ houses): it is a High Church trumpet call to downtrodden Paddington.

Along the canals

Both the Paddington and Regent's Canals are ideal for walking, and have so‖ good new canal-side architecture. Villas of the 1820s are much rarer: there is ‖ better selection than here at Little Venice.

Return over the bridge and turn right along Blomfield Road. The high wall ‖ the right protects the villas from the canal moorings, but through the wall y‖ can get onboard *Jason's Trip*, which is both a restaurant and a boat providi‖

anal trips to Camden via the Zoo. Other canal boats also ply the route to Camden from here. In winter most of the trips take place only at weekends, but from April to October run daily at regular intervals, approximately 10.30–16.30. Tickets can be obtained in advance (recommended especially for weekends) or on the boats.

Jason's Trip, restaurant ☎ 020 7286 3428; trips ☎ 020 7286 6752. www.jasons.co.uk.

Jenny Wren, ☎ 020 7485 4433.

London Waterbus Company, ☎ 020 7482 2660.

Paddington and Regent's Canals

The Paddington Canal was built first during the 'canal mania', that period when visionaries saw Britain criss-crossed by canals as it now is by railways and motorways. It was opened in 1801 to connect with the River Brent, which in turn connected the Thames to the Grand Junction Canal going all the way to Birmingham. It was therefore historic, linking the great national canal system to London itself, and vital, bringing cargoes of goods to the London markets from the new areas of manufacturing. Its terminus is Paddington Basin (Chapter 37).

The Regent's canal was a later venture of the 1820s, first planned to go through Regent's Park but in the event going round its northern rim through the Zoo, and via tunnels to Camden Town, Islington and Hackney to join the Thames at Limehouse. The triangular basin at Little Venice is the junction between the two canals.

Another attraction here, well worth visiting if the timing suits, is the **Puppet Theatre Barge**, with afternoon shows for children in the school holidays and for adults in the evening. The barge is at Little Venice from October to June, but in high summer it plies the Thames. For details and bookings, ☎ 020 7249 6876 or ☎ 07836 202745.

Turn left down Clifton Villas to see *Clifton Nurseries* on the right, a well-stocked garden centre with a shop and greenhouse in the Postmodern idiom. In the next turning on the left, in effect at the back of the nursery, is a pleasant pub, the *Warwick Castle*.

From the next bridge, which crosses at the point of the old lock, take a proper look at the triangular basin and canal, and then walk round the edge of the basin to the **Rembrandt Garden**. The choice of Rembrandt is presumably an allusion to Amsterdam, somewhat inconsistent with Venice, and equally irrelevant: as already noted, this distinctive area owes nothing to either. The garden is a disappointment but what gives charm and character to the whole area is the way the villa façades are related to the canal stream, with a modest carriageway inbetween. The stucco-fronted villas themselves (1840s onwards) are often highly ambitious, for example, nos 36–37 Blomfield Road. Warwick Crescent, where Browning lived (see box, p 354), is on the south side of the basin.

Go down Howley Place, averting your gaze from horrible flats on the right to see the only somewhat less dominating 1840s semi-detached houses on the left, with their overpowering cornices. Turn left—there are fine villas either side in Park Place—and reach the Regent's Canal with its attendant terraces, Maida Avenue on this side and Blomfield Road continuing opposite. There will be many boats moored here. The Maida Hill tunnel is to the right, as is the **Catholic**

Robert Browning

Browning's life (1812–89) was divided between Italy and London and over a third of it was spent at 19 Warwick Crescent, overlooking the canal basin, sometimes known as Browning's Pool. He bought the house (which was demolished in 1960) after the death of his beloved wife Elizabeth Barrett (see Chapter 24) and lived here with his father, sister and son, publishing *The Ring and the Book* (1868) and other later works during this time. He had been born in Camberwell. His love affairs with Italy (from his first visit in 1838) and Elizabeth were the starting points for the work of his finest period.

Apostolic Church by the major Victorian architect J.L. Pearson (1891–93) again, you are unlikely to get inside, but the west façade is a powerful composition

If you are interested in cricket, take the following detour (if not, go to the next paragraph). Keep going across Maida Vale, then turn left and first right into St John's Wood Road (Map 4,3), to reach **Lord's Cricket Ground** an eclectic mixture of architecture including some distinguished modern work. The building of the Regent's Canal meant that Thomas Lord had to move his cricket ground again—it had originally been in Dorset Square (see Chapter 24)—slightly to the north. But there it stayed. Lord's is more than a club, the ground of its original and continuing patron, the Marylebone Cricket Club; it is an institution and for cricket fans a sacred place, still resonating with triumphs and disasters, and where Test matches are still played. The ground and museum are open for guided tours (except on match days) at 12.00 and 14.00. Admission charge but no need to book. ☎ 020 7432 1033. Tube: St John's Wood.

Back on the original tour, turn left down Maida Avenue, over the bridge and back to the right along Blomfield Road, roads which Pevsner says 'form one of the most attractive tree-and-stucco landscapes of London'. Turn left again down Randolph Road where the mood changes to something less congenial: there are odd quoins on the stucco and a general heaviness. Cross Clifton Gardens and continue up Randolph Crescent, where the heaviness increases to the point of depression, given the top-heavy attics.

In due course you reach a substantial road junction, with the *Warrington Hotel* on the left, a very grand name for what is only a pub, although a good one. David Ben-Gurion, first prime minister of Israel, lived in a house in nearby Warrington Crescent, and further down, tucked in amongst the red-brick terraces, is a little outcrop of Arts and Crafts building, at nos 63–67.

Cross Sutherland Avenue, which is wide and tree-lined—the mood has changed again, for the better—and in Lauderdale Road note the domed **Spanish and Portuguese Synagogue** (1896). Return to go left up Randolph Avenue which starts on a pleasant scale but then becomes overpowering on the right, in gaunt brick with built-in terracotta heads, obviously portraits, but of whom?

You are now in Maida Vale, named after the Battle of Maida in southern Italy in 1806, where Sir John Stuart won an important, but not decisive, victory over the French army of occupation. Sir John had nothing to do with the area—he is buried in Bristol Cathedral—but several pubs called the *Hero of Maida* were opened and one such by the canal bridge gave its name to the area of new houses along that stretch of the Edgware Road.

Cricket

Although these days definitely second to football, cricket is still an English national sporting obsession. The first recorded games occurred in the 17C, and most of the rules observed today, except overarm bowling, were in place by the mid-18C. Thomas Lord opened his first ground in 1787.

Many developments occurred in the 19C, including Test matches and the competition for the Ashes trophy (the phrase originates from Australia having won the first two series, leading the *Sporting Life* to declare in 1882 that the ashes of English cricket would be buried there). In the 20C many Commonwealth countries joined the international competition and the need for sponsorship introduced a commercial system and shorter games, although the time needed for a match still seems long in the modern world.

Just before you reach Maida Vale station, note **Elgin Mews South**, with its polychrome Gothic entrance. Lord Elgin, who brought back the marbles from the Parthenon in Greece (Chapter 27), gives his name to the pub on the corner. The Tube station with its vintage Edwardian tiles is itself is to be enjoyed as you descend into the depths.

Before ending the walk, you might want to glance up **Abbey Road** where the Beatles made their 1960s recordings. To find the studios, turn right at the station, cross Maida Vale and take the first left off Abercorn Place, namely Hamilton Terrace. At Carlton Hill turn right and left for Abbey Road. The studios and the zebra crossing which featured on the eponymous album cover, are just down on the right.

Villages': north and northeast

0 • Camden

At the centre of this walk, Camden Lock is a cheerful and now enormous are of small shops and stalls, crowded and not at all smart, but full of character and interest. There is a great deal more of interest in the wider area, in terms of open spaces, housing and canals, creating a rich mix. The walk is best attempted when the sun shines. But beware: Camden Lock is very crowded at weekends.

Distance: 4¼ miles (including Primrose Hill). Time: 2 hours + time to see Camden Lock. Tube: King's Cross. Map 7 and off map.

This route begins at King's Cross Station (**Map 7,1**), as there are important things to see on the way to Camden. Set off up Pancras Road between St Pancras and King's Cross stations, noting if interested the working-class flats, gasworks and nature reserve off Goods Way to the right (see Chapter 28). Go under the railway bridges. Our first stop is the green space on the right.

This is the churchyard of **Old St Pancras**, a very ancient church indeed: we know this from the discovery here of a 7C altar stone and from the rare dedication by St Augustine himself to Pancras, a boy martyred in Rome *c* AD 304 who is otherwise commemorated only at Canterbury. There is Norman work in the little church but it has been messed about by many later hands and you are unlikely to gain entry. The churchyard is full of interest, however, and as now restored is beautiful despite its truncation when the railway was built. Do not miss the mausoleum Sir John Soane put up for his wife in 1816, which also contains the remains of his eldest son and the great architect himself. Also commemorated here are the artist John Flaxman (d. 1826) and his wife, and William Godwin and Mary Wollstonecraft (d. 1797), radical thinkers and the parents of Mary Shelley, author of *Frankenstein*.

Beyond the churchyard is grim St Pancras Hospital, with a clock tower (1880s), and next to it Goldington Buildings (1902), early public housing. Next, to the left in Royal College Street is the **Royal Veterinary College**, a truly depressing horror in 1930s red brick. The college was founded on this site in 1791, the first such establishment in Britain; there is a small museum. ☎ 020 7468 5162. Opposite, across Pancras Road, are some early postwar flats, some would say representative of the heyday of confident local authority housing; behind them, and to be contrasted, is more local authority housing, this time low-rise, of the 1970s when doubt had crept in. If you are in a mood to explore, go behind these blocks to see the pretty early 19C terraces in Medburn Street, put up by the Brewers Company who owned the land.

Our route takes you left, along Crowndale Road. At no. 26 is Old St Pancras Church House, with a figure of the saint (1896). On the right is the **Working Men's College** built 1904–6, although the institution dates back to 1854 and was strongly supported by John Ruskin: it still functions as an adult education centre.

When you reach the main road, Camden High Street, note on your right *Camden Palace* (1900), an old music hall with a green copper dome. The statue of the radical MP *Richard Cobden* is by W. and T. Wills (1868), and on the left is Mornington Crescent station in the familiar plum tiles. Across the main road to the left, what was the Carreras Cigarette Factory (1926), in Egyptian style with cats, is a monument to Art Deco. Go behind the factory into **Mornington Crescent**, a pretty curve of 1821–23 spoiled when the factory was built in its garden. Walter Sickert used to live at no. 6. The area around here is also the subject of many works by Frank Auerbach, an important living artist and local resident.

Walter Sickert

Although an artist associated with London, most memorably through his claustrophobic interiors and his interest in music-hall subjects, Sickert (1860–1942) was international in temperament and painted extensively in Dieppe and Venice. He lived in Camden Town and later in Highbury and was an exciting and original writer and critic, as well as a key influence on the artists of the Camden Town Group and the Euston Road School. The former, which he established in 1911, was a society formed for the purpose of exhibiting together. Its artistic philosophy supported Post-Impressionism, as opposed to the New English Art Club, and early members included Spencer Gore, Harold Gilman and Lucien Pissarro (son of Camille).

Take the small turning second on the left along Mornington Crescent and go up Albert Street to the **Jewish Museum** at the top. This is one of the Museum's two sites in London (the other is in Finchley, see p 465). The display here effectively covers the general history of Jewish culture in Britain since medieval times, with a special emphasis on ceremonial art. There are some wonderful objects to admire, including arks, Hanukkah lamps, textiles and illuminated marriage contracts. For more personal recollections and family warmth, you should make the journey to Finchley. Open 10.00–16.00 Mon–Thur, 10.00–17.00 Sun. Admission charge. Shop. ☎ 020 7284 1997. www.jewmusm.ort.org

Return south and turn right to Mornington Street and cross the Euston railway tracks into **Park Village East**, the counterpart of Park Village West (Chapter 25) with which it shared its ideals. Though less compact, it was equally influential. The surviving villas (1824) used to back onto a branch of the Regent's Canal, the bridge over which you can see at the top of the street, carrying Parkway over the dried-up dip. Proceed along Prince Albert Road to a church on the right, **St Mark**: it is High Victorian (1851–52), altered by A.W. Blomfield in 1890 but still fine.

Now decide whether to go onwards the short distance to climb up the 206ft **Primrose Hill**, once famous as a site for duels and still offering a fine prospect of London. The detour is recommended, certainly if the weather is good. Then return to this spot by the church in order to get down to the **Regent's Canal towpath**. We now venture along this evocative and quiet path, away from the cars, to reach Camden Lock. (For the Regent's Canal itself, see Chapter 39.)

On the right bank are the delightful back gardens of houses in St Mark's Crescent. Go under Gloucester Avenue and the railway, but then go up to street level at the next bridge, Oval Road, where it says 'Pirate's Castle': this is a children's playcentre in the form of a toy fort by, amazingly, Richard Seifert and Partners, the tower-block team (1977). Peep down the street to see, on the left, Jamestown Road, with a factory by Serge Chermayeff (1937) and after that on the left Gloucester Crescent, with massive Italianate villas (*c* 1850) and in front the grand Victoriana of Regent's Park Terrace (1845). Then go back to the canal.

In a short time you will reach the area known as **Camden Lock**. Open 10.00–18.00 daily. ☎ 020 7284 2084. The lock itself—the first of a series to lower the canal down to the Thames at Limehouse—is of 1820, still intact, with twin chambers. To the left, off the towpath, are groups of shops and stalls around a square called

Camden Lock

Westyard, with mooring for canal boats. Canal boat services ply from here to the Zoo and Little Venice (see Chapter 39 for details and telephone numbers). Explore this first, then cross over the canal bridge, technically a cast-iron roving bridge

(1854), and walk along as far as Chalk Farm Road. Turn left over the road bridge to visit Eastyard, with more of Camden Lock market. Beyond, up Chalk Farm Road, the location changes to Camden Market, where masses of stalls mostly for clothes but including some antiques, stretch for acres under the arches of the railway. Open 09.30–17.00 daily. ☎ 020 7485 5473. The market reaches almost as far as the **Round House**, built as an engine house for the London North Western Railway Company (1841). The Round House became a theatre in 1965, but failed in the tough, unhelpful 1980s: now it is being revived. The market covers the former railway stables of 1855, where vast numbers of horses were kept to distribute the goods brought from the northwest all over London.

Return to the canal and continue along the towpath to complete the last leg, following the twisting water line under all the road bridges as far as Pancras Way. Then go up to road level, where the enthusiast may like to trek a little way north-east to see the **Agar Estate** at Camden Square and Rochester Square (1840s). Also worth looking at are architects' houses of the 1960s in Camden Mews and Murray Mews. Then return to see the rest of Camden's shops. Make sure you find Lyme Terrace between Camden Road and College Street, beautifully overlooking the canal below.

At Camden Street, pick up Hawley Crescent to return to Camden Lock, but do not miss the former **TV-AM studios** by Terry Farrell (1981–82) brashly advertising in its design the breakfast television idea. When you reach the bridge again, turn left this time. There are more shops on both sides, in the same idiom. You soon reach Camden Town station and its busy crossroads: again there are countless pubs and shops, which continue down Camden High Street as far as Mornington Crescent. Your choice of station will depend on your remaining energy, taste for shopping and the day of the week (because it is important to note, Camden Town tube is exit-only between 13.00 and 17.30 on Sundays, so you must go to Mornington Crescent or Chalk Farm at those times to the Northern Line).

41 • Hampstead

If you have time, you should give up a day to Hampstead. It is a picturesque and historic place full of character and charm: its small streets and corners repay time and trouble and the Heath (an 825 acre green space) is exhilarating even in bad weather.

It is difficult to advise on how long exploring Hampstead will take. There are five separate museums, all good but catering for different interests, as well as Kenwood. Two suggestions are made. The first (a) includes a visit to Kenwood which could be self-contained or followed by a walk across the Heath and an afternoon in Hampstead village. The second (b) allows for a half-day in Hampstead village, touring both streets and museums; Kenwood is omitted or could be seen as part of the Highgate tour (Chapter 42).

- (a) Distance: 4 miles. Time: all day. Tube: Golders Green or Finsbury Park, then bus 210, or Hampstead.
  (b) Distance: 1 mile. Time: 2–3 hours with stops. Tube: Hampstead.
  See map on p 360–361.

Kenwood

If it were easier to reach, Kenwood would certainly be on the list of unmissable London attractions. The best route by public transport is to go to Golders Green (Northern Line) and then take bus 210, which can also be caught from Finsbury Park (Victoria and Piccadilly Lines). Either way, alight in Hampstead Lane at Kenwood. The stop is recognisable at the end of a long, tall brick wall on the left: if you miss it, get off at the next request stop, and enter at West Lodge.

- Open April–Sept 10.00–18.00 daily; Oct–March 10.00–16.00. Admission free. Café/restaurant. ☎ 020 8348 1286. www.english-heritage.org.uk

History

There was a villa on this fine site overlooking London from 1616. It changed hands many times, but the defining moment came in the period 1754–96. First, the place was bought by William Murray, an up-and-coming lawyer who became Lord Chief Justice and Earl of Mansfield. Second, in the 1760s Murray brought in the Adam brothers to remodel the house, giving, as Robert Adam put it, 'full scope to my ideas'. The third strand in Kenwood's history came when Lord Mansfield's nephew engaged George Saunders to extend the house in the 1790s (the wings either side of the portico are his work), and in 1793 called on Humphry Repton to advise on the grounds. The whole landscape was nearly lost to developers in 1924 but Lord Iveagh, of the Guinness family, came to the rescue, acquiring the house which he then gave to the public along with his collection of paintings. Such generosity is too much taken for granted.

Entering through East Lodge, wander through a leafy hollowed drive bordered by rhododendrons (signposted 'House': the sign to 'restaurant' leads also to toilets). It was intended by Repton to give a sense of woodland mystery and is still very picturesque. You emerge into the open to be greeted by the civilised Ionic portico of the Adams's north front. The effect is magical, and the best place in or near London to understand the aims of late 18C landscaping.

Enter the house through the portico into what was originally an entrance hall, refurbished by Adam as a dining-room, but soon reverted to a **hall**. The evidence for the dining-room is to be seen in the plasterwork and the ceiling panels by Antonio Zucchi (1773). There is a portrait of **Lord Mansfield** by J.B. Van Loo on the left and over the fireplace another of **Lord Iveagh**.

The route conceived by the Adams takes you left into the top-lit stair hall, with its iron and cast-brass balusters: it is tempting to go up, but not yet. Continue through to the **Ante-Chamber** with its stunning view of the park, lake and sham bridge. Before the trees grew you could see London, a vista that must have sold Kenwood to Lord Mansfield in the first place. There are two paintings here by Angelica Kauffmann. Then turn left for the *pièce de resistance*, the **Library**, an Adam masterpiece and, as the guidebook justifiably states, 'among the most impressive and memorable of late 18C British interiors'. It was built as a 'Great Room' for the purpose of grand receptions, then the fashion. The ceiling paintings representing *Hercules' Choice between Glory and Pleasure* are by Zucchi (1769). Every detail reveals exquisite sensibility. *Lord Mansfield with his bust of Homer* by David Martin is over the fireplace. The bust itself, by Joseph Wilton (*c* 1760), a gift from Alexander Pope, stands to the left. The bust to the right shows Mansfield without a wig and has a fine profile.

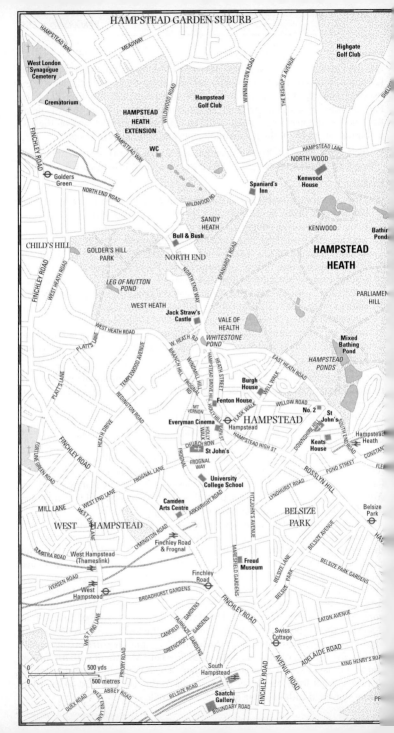

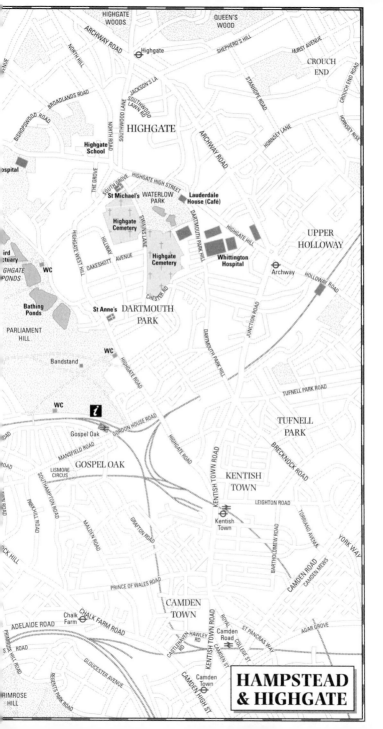

HAMPSTEAD
& HIGHGATE

Return to the northeast wing, added by George Saunders in 1793, through the dining-room lobby with its coffered ceiling and balcony above—a taste which post-dates Adam. You then reach the **Dining Room**, now a picture gallery: take a free pamphlet for more details. The works which are of special note include Sir Joshua Reynolds's *Girl leaning on a Pedestal* (1775) immediately on the left; his portrait of *Lady Chambers* (1752), wife of Sir William, the architect of Somerset House; Frans Hals' famous portrait of *Pieter van den Broecke* (c 1633), merry and bright; and Jan Vermeer's *Guitar Player* (c 1672), a world-class masterpiece. Over the fireplace and on the right-hand wall are portraits by Antony van Dyck; and there are two paintings of Venice by Francesco Guardi. Most unforgettable of all, behind the door on the right, is a Rembrandt *Self-portrait* (c 1665), which seems to speak of humanity triumphant amid adversity.

Now return via the lobby and the Ante-Chamber to view the rooms along the south front. In **Lord Mansfield's Dressing Room** the most significant paintings are Van Dyck's *Unknown Man* (1620s), a *Landscape* by Jacob van Ruisdael, and Claude de Jongh's *Old London Bridge* (1628). In the **Breakfast Room** are two paintings by Thomas Gainsborough, a portrait of *J.J. Marlin* and *Hounds coursing a Fox* (1785), and *Lady Hamilton at her Spinning Wheel* (1782–86) by George Romney. In **Lady Mansfield's Dressing Room** are some medieval paintings (on long loan) and a *Virgin and Child* by Sandro Botticelli.

The **Orangery**, a space to match the Library and give symmetry to the whole, lies at the end: it is often used for recitals.

Finally you reach the northwest wing, first the Green Room and then the Music Room. These rooms are the counterparts in Saunders's 1790s extensions of the dining-room and its lobby, and like them are now dedicated to the Iveagh bequest of paintings. In the **Green Room** are two delightful English portraits of children, Sir Thomas Lawrence's *Miss Murray* (1825–27), skipping along with her pretty flowers; and Henry Raeburn's *Sir George Sinclair as a Boy* (1796)—the sitter was known as the Harrow Prodigy on the strength of producing some early Latin verse, but this proved an exaggeration.

In the **Music Room** are some brilliant Gainsboroughs: *Miss Brummell* (1782), another child portrait; *Lady Brisco* (1776); and, absolutely stunning in pink, *Countess Howe* (1763–64), dazzling from the far end of the room. There are also some Reynolds portraits: it is interesting to compare them with Gainsborough's—less dashing, with perhaps more insight. On the right, Romney's *Lady Hamilton at Prayer* (1782–86) is a far-fetched idea, but presumably she was modelling. It is interesting to see a portrait of another actress later William IV's mistress, in *Mrs Jordan as Viola in Twelfth Night* (1790s) by Sir John Hoppner. You exit via the shop. Upstairs lie a hall and the former family bedrooms, a space now usually used for temporary exhibitions.

Take time to survey the **grounds**. To the west of the house (on the left as you leave) are extensive gardens created out of the former kitchen garden and picturesquely hidden from the entrance drive from West Lodge. Turn left again to experience a typically Reptonian feature, a dark trellis tunnel from which you emerge to experience the same delight as in the Ante-Chamber, a sudden view down to the lake. From the terrace you can descend the lawns to walk by the lake confirming at first hand that the bridge is a sham. Return up the east side for refreshments in the Coach House, part of the service wing added by Saunders in 1793. This approach gives the best, and very photogenic, view of Adam's trans formation of the south front, with its stuccoed pilasters, displaying a catalogue of the Adams's Neo-Classical design repertoire. In summer there are evening **concerts** from an orchestral platform on the far side of the lake and the lawns are covered with picnicking listeners. For dates and details, ☎ 020 8233 7435. www.picnicconcerts.com

If you did not approach Kenwood by this route, you may now decide to walk back over **Hampstead Heath** to Hampstead Village. There are many activities to be enjoyed besides simply taking the air: riding, fishing, swimming. ☎ 020 7485 4491 for details.

The character of the Heath is much wilder than the intentionally 'polite' grounds of Kenwood, but its rural atmosphere has often been threatened by developers, most notably Sir Thomas Maryon Wilson, the lord of the manor in the 19C, who saw an opportunity for speculative housing but was prevented after prolonged legal battles won by local inhabitants. The Heath has always been popular with poets (John Keats and Percy Bysshe Shelley) and painters (John Constable), as it was with Cockney merrymakers on bank holidays.

Hampstead Village

Our walk around Hampstead Village and its museums is circular. If you are omitting Kenwood, it is best to start from Hampstead station (Northern Line), the deepest station on the system, with a 181ft lift-shaft, because the station is high up on the hill. The following description starts from the Tube station. If you come by foot from Kenwood across the Heath you should reach the car park north of Hampstead Heath station: go up Willow Road to Burgh House and then along Flask Walk to the station to join this route.

It is difficult to devise a walk in Hampstead, or even to draw a map of the streets. As you leave the station, look around. Across the road, Heath Street, to the right is the Gothic clock tower (1873) of the former fire station. To the left, down the hill towards Chalk Farm, is Hampstead High Street with pleasant shops and cafés; across the traffic lights Heath Street also runs downhill towards Swiss Cottage, and you can glimpse the *Everyman* (☎ 0845 606 2345, www.everyman cinema.com) repertory cinema.

Turn left. On the right you will see Perrins Court and Perrins Lane, with a minimalist restaurant by Rick Mather (1986) in between. Cut up Perrins Court, where there are some small shops to explore, to join Heath Street, which you cross to go down Church Row.

Church Row is perhaps the finest street in Hampstead. On the south side there is an excellent example of a type of domestic building which began to appear in London's better villages in the late 17C and early 18C—others are to be seen in Highgate and Clapham—calm, dignified, generously proportioned and conforming with the new building regulations for the city. On the north side the style is more rustic, in particular no. 5, which is weather-boarded.

Down the hill you reach the church of **St John** by John Sanderson (1745–47), which has its own interesting history.

The first choice of architect was Henry Flitcroft, Lord Burlington's protégé, but he was too expensive, so the parishioners chose the lesser figure of Sanderson. From the outside the church is quite plain and modest, brick with a tower breaking up through the central pediment. This is the church's east end and there was much argument about the orientation of the altar, only resolved finally in the 1870s when F.P. Cockerell was called in to repair and improve matters. The inside is therefore an odd mix of minimalist 18C and comparatively rich 19C, but is very comfortable with its grey-painted pews and an intimate family feeling.

In the churchyard signs allow you to locate the grave of John Constable. Also buried here are Norman Shaw, the architect, and, in the extension across Church Row, political leader Hugh Gaitskell, author George du Maurier, and film stars Kay Kendall and Anton Walbrook. (Inside the church 'Tomb Trails' also help you to track them down.) Leaving the main churchyard, turn immediately right down the slope into Frognal Way, a private road (meaning it is not maintained by the local council) containing some icons of Modernism including the **Sun House** by Maxwell Fry (1934–35). At the end is **no. 66 Frognal** by Connell Ward and Lucas (1937), according to Pevsner 'in the extreme idiom of the day, now something of a classic', though looking rather shabby.

A short detour can be made a little way down Frognal to the left if you are interested in seeing **University College School**, a fairly spectacular Edwardian collection (1905–7) designed in an exuberant early 18C mode. Opposite the school, at no. 39, is the house Norman Shaw built for the illustrator Kate Greenaway (1884). A similar detour is possible down Frognal Lane to see no. 40, on the left down a path, a nice villa of 1813, and next to it no. 42, a scrumptious 1880s red-brick beauty, built by the architect Basil Champneys for himself. Not far away, down the hill via Arkwright Road, is **Camden Arts Centre**, where there is a lively changing programme of exhibitions and events. ☎ 020 7435 2643.

But our main route is northwards up Frognal, past no. 94, called The Old Mansion (*c* 1700), on the right. Turn right at Mount Vernon where Robert Louis Stevenson used to live at Abernethy House. Turn right briefly at the top of Holly Walk. This leads down to the church you have seen, but do not miss the little area here at the top: two pretty, small alleyways called **Hollyberry Lane** (where the composer Sir William Walton lived) and **Prospect Place**. In between is **St Mary**, one of the earliest Roman Catholic churches in London (1816), in the centre of a further group of cottages. All is sweetly picturesque. Much of Hampstead is rather like this: beautifully looked after, with perfectly tended gardens, a paradise. Just occasionally you long for some grit, but there is plenty of that elsewhere in London, so enjoy Hampstead's honey today.

Walking back to Mount Vernon, you emerge into **Holly Bush Hill**, a small triangular green. The weatherboarded house on the right is called Romney's House, after the artist George Romney, who had it built for himself in 1797. Beyond is Holly Mount, where the *Holly Bush Tavern* awaits your custom, having been created from Romney's stables. Across the green to the north is a fine early 18C terrace behind long front gardens. The building nobody mentions but everybody notices, on the east side, brutally wrecking all sense of scale, is a Consumption Hospital, built high up for fresh air in 1880, but now flats—an early example of the considerations of health and safety squashing all others.

Walk up Hampstead Grove. A very fine five-bay brick house comes into view on your left: this is **Fenton House** (1693), its original architect unknown, now run by the National Trust. The Fenton family owned it between 1793 and 1834, but there have been many other interesting occupants, the last being Lady Binning, whose collection of furniture and porcelain remains on display. Equally impor tant is the Fletcher collection of musical instruments held here. There is also a fine garden. Open 14.00–17.00 Wed–Fri; 11.00–17.00 Sat, Sun and Bank Holidays. Admission charge (free to National Trust members). Tours. Concerts in summer. ☎ 020 7435 3471. www.nationaltrust.org.uk/regions/thameschilterns

A little further on turn left into Admiral's Walk. Another fine house on the right, **Admiral's House** (1700), has a quarter-deck at roof level which is to be seen in the film *Mary Poppins*, and was once occupied by Sir George Gilbert Scott (see Chapter 28). The novelist John Galsworthy later lived at Grove Lodge next door and died there in 1933. Then bear right, across Lower Terrace, to reach Judge's Walk: the impressive views to the north towards Harrow and Hendon were painted by John Constable, who at one stage lived in Lower Terrace.

John Constable

Constable (1776–1837) was born on the Suffolk/Essex border and 'Constable country' refers to that area of England, centred on Dedham. But he lived for many years in Hampstead and painted extensively there as well as in his home area and in Dorset and Wiltshire. Unlike his contemporary Turner he was slow to gain recognition and he left few successors in England, where the Pre-Raphaelites took landscape in a different direction. But he was much admired in France, including by Eugène Delacroix, and his apparently spontaneous style in rendering a sky or a landscape can be linked with Impressionism, although in fact it was mostly constructed carefully, from sketches, in a studio.

Go past a reservoir (1865) to reach, on the left, Whitestone Pond, with more spectacular views: on the far side is the pub called *Jack Straw's Castle*: the original Jack Straw was a leader of the Peasants' Revolt of 1381 (see Chapter 29) and afterwards took refuge in this coaching inn.

Turn right and make your way down Heath Street taking the second left, Stanford Close (easy to miss) to get into Hampstead Square. Here, alongside some attractive early 18C houses, similar to those in Church Row, **Christ Church** (1851) dominates: Pevsner calls it 'correct but dull', but the site and atmosphere are impressive. Go downhill to New End: Elm Row, with a good terrace on the north side, is on your right.

You may notice a perceptible change of tone in the architecture. **New End** was never so smart as the rest of Hampstead and this is where the working classes were corralled. You can see straight away the former **workhouse** (1853), later a hospital and now smart apartments. The morgue, opposite, is now New End Theatre. Turn left then right and briefly right again along Streatley Place, a narrow passage between the workhouse and the ultra-powerful former **Board School** (1905) (see box, p 366), for 600 children, with brilliant if forbidding architecture on a tiny site. At the end wander right up Mansfield Place, a group of tiny cottages either side of their long front gardens.

Now return to New End Square and go down the hill to **Burgh House** (1703), in grander surroundings again. This fine mansion was built for Dr Gibbons, spa physician, but now belongs to the Borough of Hampstead who use it for temporary exhibitions and a display on local history. What is left of the garden was designed by Gertrude Jekyll. Open 12.00–17.00 Wed–Sun. Admission free. Café. ☎ 020 7431 0144.

Board Schools

The earliest board schools in London, apart from endowed establishments like Westminster and Harrow, were tiny and were run by parishes. In the 19C, the Church of England and subsequently the government began to form National Schools, which were often a gloomy Gothic in style. The Elementary Education Act of 1870 introduced primary education for all and established a School Board for London. Over the period to the early 20C, when the London County Council took over, this important body sponsored hundreds of new schools throughout the capital, all in a distinctive architectural style, easily recognized to this day, whether they survive as schools or not. Their tall windows, to introduce light and fresh air, prominent gables with a bell, a date and the logo SBL, proclaim their admirable purpose.

At the corner, decide if you have had enough. Hampstead station is not far away to the right, down **Flask Walk**, with the *Flask* itself, a recommended pub, and some very attractive shops on the way. Otherwise, stay a little longer and turn left along **Well Walk**, past a pub on the right, to locate the well on the left, trickling gently by the road. This was an 18C discovery, a chalybeate spring which became very fashionable (drinking it apparently provides an excellent purge) and brought to Hampstead trippers for whom a Pump Room was erected, now long gone. In its time Well Walk has provided homes for the writers John Keats, D.H. Lawrence, John Masefield and J.B. Priestley.

Opposite the well, peep into **Gainsborough Gardens**, an exclusive and snobbish 1884 development of very handsome houses by various architects. Go back to the *Wells Tavern*, turn left down Christchurch Hill and into Willow Road. There is nothing much here until you reach nos 1–3 at the bottom: these have become another Modernist icon, being a key work by Ernö Goldfinger (1937–39), who himself lived in **no. 2 Willow Road**, which was acquired by the National Trust as its first Modernist property. Open for guided tours only, every 45 minutes 12.15–16.00 Thur, Fri and Sat March–early Nov. ☎ 020 7435 6166. Information ☎ 01494 755570. www.nationaltrust.org.uk/regions/thameschilterns

Now the Heath is before you again. Turn right up Downshire Hill, with lovely houses; at the road junction is a sadly crumbling chapel (1818) with, by all accounts, a delightful interior, but it seems always to be closed. Go round it and down Keats' Grove to **Keats' House**. Open 12.00–17.00 Tues–Sun. Admission charge. ☎ 020 7332 3820. www.cityoflondon.gov.uk/leisure_heritage. **Note**. Building work is in progress: ☎ 020 7435 2062 to check the house is open before visiting. The museum contains many mementoes of his life and work: an atmospheric place.

Return up Downshire Hill, past the chapel and on up to Rosslyn Hill, where you turn right to climb back to the Tube station.

Hampstead contains a further interesting museum which could be combined with parts of the walks detailed above. The **Freud Museum**, in Maresfield Gardens, is the house where the pyschoanalyst Sigmund Freud lived for the last years of his life, dying in 1939. From Rosslyn Hill, follow Thurlow Road (opposite Downshire Hill) to Lyndhurst Terrace, turning left and right into Fitzjohn's Avenue. Turn right, cross the road and find Maresfield Gardens on the left. The

John Keats

Keats (1795–1821) was very much a Londoner, the son of a livery-stable manager in Moorfields who died when Keats was nine years old, and a London resident until his departure for Rome in 1830, where he died of tuberculosis the following year. In his own short lifetime he became prominent in the Cockney School of poets, satirically so-called by the Edinburgh *Blackwoods Magazine* because they were not high-born. Keats trained as an apothecary but turned to poetry, and poverty, as early as 1815, coming to live in the house of his friend Charles Brown in Hampstead, later known as Keats' House, in 1818. Much of his most famous work was published in that 'Great Year' (1818–19), including the *Ode on a Grecian Urn* and *Ode to Autumn*. His letters to Fanny Brawne, to whom he became engaged, and to his friends are almost as noteworthy and as moving as his poetry. He was the epitome of the Romantic poet.

Museum is at no. 20. It contains Freud's consulting room and study, as preserved by his daughter, Anna, and a gallery for exhibitions related to his work. Open 12.00–17.00 Wed–Sun. Admission charge. ☎ 020 7435 2002.

42 • Highgate

This is still one of the most village-like areas of London and most of our walk will confirm this impression. Highgate Cemetery, about two-thirds of the way round, is the spookiest of all the series of cemeteries developed from the 1830s. You may want to adjust your timetable to accommodate the main West Cemetery which can only be entered on a guided tour (see below).

- Distance: 3¾ miles. Time: 2 hours + time for the cemetery tour.
  Tube: Highgate. See map on pp 360–361.

Catch a High Barnet train (Northern Line) to Highgate station. Ascend the leafy path to Archway Road, which you cross at the traffic lights to go up Jackson's Lane. On the corner is the Community Centre, constructed within a former Methodist church (1905) in rich red brick. There are impressive 19C houses in Jackson's Lane. At the top, on the right, is a very narrow roadway with a bulging brick retaining wall looking as if it might collapse at any moment, although it has supported the garden of the house on the corner for over 200 years. Just beyond, off Southwood Lawn Road, is a piece of 1960s Brutalism at its most vivid and exciting, **Southwood Park** flats—worth glancing at as a fine example of a now much-criticised style.

Turn right and immediately left into Southwood Lane, on the left from Kingsley Place. Look out for a stunning view to the left—there are plenty on this walk. Kingsley Place was named after Mary Kingsley the explorer, who lived at Avalon, a little further ahead on your left. Opposite are the many buildings of **Highgate School**, to see more of which turn right into Castle Yard, at the left-hand end of which, it spreads itself along North Road. Highgate School was founded as a grammar school by Sir Roger Cholmeley (pronounced Chumley) in 1565, but most of the buildings you see are by F.P. Cockerell (1860s)—the main hall parallel to the road, classrooms on the left and the domineering chapel on the right. Having digested this, look at the very pleasant mix of mainly 18C houses stretching along North Road opposite. Cross the road and turn north to see them better: the only minus is the garage offensively inserted into the front garden of no. 30. Soon you reach a National School in Gothic style by the important Victorian architect Anthony Salvin (1852).

Soon after this, on the left, you will encounter what are now seen as modern masterpieces, **Highpoint One and Two**, by Berthold Lubetkin and his firm Tecton (1933–35). Highpoint One was the first modern block of flats in London, sited for effect with views to the west, and old trees retained at the front. Although earlier, you reach it second. It seems desperately 1930s, with glass tiles, curves and a concrete canopy under which to alight from a limousine. Highpoint Two is more rectangular and seems less dated (and less interesting, therefore). It contained larger flats which were more expensive, and exhibits jokey, and therefore almost Postmodern, concrete caryatids with their backs to each other.

Keep going north, downhill now; before turning left into Broadlands Road, go just a little further to see **Verandah Cottages**, charitable housing for local workpeople (1863) with a stockade of iron galleries on two sides. Broadlands Road is an Edwardian development, but an exciting Gothic monster lurks at no. 16. Turn left into Bishopswood Road, which surrounds Highgate School's playing fields, full of respectable grey Victorian mansions. When you reach the busier road, Hampstead Lane, turn left and ascend the hill. **Kenwood** lies only 10 minutes' walk to the right. You could include it here, and if not doing the Hampstead walk in Chapter 41, certainly should.

Cross Hampstead Lane and turn right into The Grove to explore the centre of Highgate Village. The Grove, the top of West Hill, and South Grove mark an enclave full of delights. In The Grove, on the right, is the entrance to **Fitzroy Park**, a former Palladian villa, long since demolished but now a secluded leafy lane with some interesting modern houses, including no. 6 (1958) designed Ove Arup, the distinguished engineer, for himself. Keep going along The Grove to see nos 1–6, semi-detached houses of 1688. Samuel Taylor Coleridge died at no. 3 and J.B. Priestley, novelist and dramatist, lived there in the 1940s.

Samuel Taylor Coleridge

Coleridge (1772–1834) was a leading figure in English Romanticism, a poet, philosopher and critic, and friend of William Wordsworth, Robert Southey, Charles Lamb and William Hazlitt. He led a dramatic and chaotic early life, writing, walking, becoming involved in revolutionary politics and, most damagingly, addicted to opium: his famous *Kubla Khan* was written under its influence. In 1816 he found permanent 'care' in the home of a young surgeon in Highgate and lived there until his death. He became a powerful apologist for Christianity: Lamb called him 'an archangel slightly damaged'.

At the end, Highgate West Hill stretches down to the right and on the corner is an Edwardian giant, **Witanhurst**, visible from miles around, but you will have to peer through the padlocked gates as the place is at the time of writing derelict and forlorn. It was once a millionaire's paradise, the millionaire in question being Sir Arthur Crosfield, the soap magnate.

Opposite is **St Michael**, a church in minimalist Gothic style, designed by Lewis Vulliamy and built by the Cubitts (1831). It is open in the afternoons and con ains the grave of Coleridge. At least equally appealing is the *Flask*, a pub on the corner between South Grove and West Hill, with a Georgian interior. Also in South Grove is Old Hall, a tall late 17C house of five bays, and there are some interesting 1950s houses in Bacons Lane. Do not miss a spanking new glass-fronted, prize-winning state-of-the-art house by the architects Eldridge Souverin (2001), behind the wall of The Lawns. Further east is the Highgate Literary and Scientific Institution established in 1840, which contains a collection of Coleridge material. Open 10.00–17.00 Tues–Fri and 10.00–16.00 Sat. ☎ 020 8340 3343.

At the end of South Grove you reach **Highgate High Street**, full of pleasant shops and pubs, apparently a real village centre worth exploring. Then go to the right, downhill. Note on the left some large, handsome 18C houses crowded together (nos 106–110) and beyond them the earlier **Cromwell House** (1637), now the Ghana High Commission. It is a handsome if slightly crudely built pile, with primitive but extremely ambitious brickwork—you realise that you are not in the centre of Charles I's sophisticated London, but out in a country village.

Opposite is **Waterlow Park**, set up as a 'garden for the gardenless' by the philanthropic industrialist Sir Sidney Waterlow in 1889. Waterlow lived at Fairseat, next door up the hill, but acquired these estates, including the 16C Lauderdale House just inside the entrance, and decided to give them to the London County Council. It was generous of him, because this is a lovely park, on a steep slope with fine views and planting. Refreshments and art exhibitions are sometimes to be found in Lauderdale House. Open 11.00–16.00 Tues–Fri ☎ 020 8348 8716.

Cross the park and go out into Swain's Lane. Just downhill are the entrances to **Highgate Cemetery**. East cemetery open 10.00–17.00 daily; in winter 10.00–16.00. West cemetery open by guided tours only at 12.00, 14.00 and 16.00 Mon–Fri, March–Nov; 11.00, 12.00, 13.00, 14.00, 15.00 Sat and Sun all year.

The West side is the older and more spectacular, opened in 1839 as part of the new chain of cemeteries built round the then outer rim of London, and an immediate runaway success with the Victorians. The policy now is to maintain it in a state of 'managed neglect' which, even if rather consciously theatrical, is certainly atmospheric. The mean Gothic gatehouse sets the tone, but inside there are many rich surprises, especially the Egyptian Avenue and the Beer Mausoleum, and innumerable solemn monuments among the dripping trees. Michael Faraday (d. 1867) and Christina Rossetti (d. 1894) are buried here. The East cemetery is less evocative, more Classical and still in use. But it has its distinctions, including the graves of Karl Marx (1883) and George Eliot (1880).

Turn right out of the West Cemetery, or left from the East, to descend Swain's Lane. Turn right into Oakeshott Avenue, the northernmost road of the **Holly Lodge Estate**, built in the 1920s over the grounds of an early 19C house that belonged to Baroness Angela Burdett-Coutts. On both sides are strange forbidding flats for 'Lady workers', and then, after Hillway (the main drive to the former house, with spectacular views south over London, including the ubiquitous London Eye), trim villas of the 1920s behind perfect grass verges. At the end you are back in Highgate West Hill and almost opposite is no. 31, where John Betjeman was brought up and which he immortalised in verse ('NW5 & 6'):

> *I see black oak-twigs outlined in the sky,*
> *Red squirrels in the Burdett-Coutts estate.*
> *I ask my nurse the question 'Will I die?'*
> *As bells from sad St Anne's ring out so late,*
> *'And if I do die, will I go to Heaven?'*
> *Highgate eventide. Nineteen-eleven.*

And indeed, down the hill, to your left, you will find St Anne's, with a fine spire tower (1852).

John Betjeman

Betjeman (1906–84), born in Highgate, became one of Britain's most famous poets, publishing several volumes of verse with sales much higher than average and being appointed poet laureate in 1972. This success made him unpopular with more high-minded critics. He also had a considerable influence on the appreciation of architecture, writing accessibly and with insight on the subject in books and articles, as well as, later in life, popularising it on television. He was resolutely and wittily middle-class. The fact that the British now appreciate their Victorian churches, steam railways and decaying suburbs is more thanks to Betjeman than anyone else.

Beyond St Anne's turn left again back into Swain's Lane to locate, on the right **Holly Village** (1865), a Gothic extravaganza designed to be seen from th Burdett-Coutts estate above (then, and in Betjeman's time, a garden). The architect was Henry Darbishire, who worked mainly on Peabody housing. A notice i severe Gothic lettering says 'Private Keep Out', but take a peep. It is a gem.

Turn right at Chester Road. You now walk through an area called **Highgat New Town**, that is 'new' in 1865–68, when a series of modest terraces wa erected. In the 1960s many of these were demolished by Camden Council an replaced by some remarkable modern flats (1972), serious and formidable, som

Highgate door

of which you can see stretching along i front of you on the left-hand side of Raydo Street. Opposite them, in the different idio of only 10 years later (1981), are som shops, coloured and curved, fun havin returned to architecture.

At the top of Raydon Street, cros Dartmouth Park Hill and go down Magdal Avenue back to Highgate Hill, then tur right. The spectacular building on the left part of the **Whittington Hospital**, but historic part, being the former Holborn an Finsbury Union Workhouse Infirmar (1877), a towering pile of Gothic gloon How nice to be alive and well, or eve unwell, in the 21C.

Archway station (Northern Line) no comes into view on your right.

3 • Islington

he finest aspect of Islington is its rich residue of Georgian streets and squares,
nd this walk takes you through all the best. But it also has more than its share
f local entertainment, a fascinating collection of antique shops and a market,
s well as a range of restaurants, pubs and cafés. Islington was poor until it was
ediscovered from the 1960s, and some parts still are, but rich and poor seem to
o-habit here in reasonable harmony.

Islington was always seen as a convenient point for access to town, in the 18C
s a place to ride out for Sunday afternoon tea, and later as a pleasant suburban
esidential area. It possessed gardens and fine views of London, as well as the pic-
uresque New River and the beneficial waters of Sadlers Wells. Only in the 19C,
fter the railways, did it become slummy.

Distance: 4 miles. Time: 2 hours + time for the Estorick Collection.
Tube: Angel. Off map.

tart at Angel station, where you emerge into the noise and bustle of **Upper
treet**. Opposite, across the traffic-ridden carriageways, you immediately see an
lington characteristic, a raised causeway forming the pavement or sidewalk, an
menity created when the streets were badly churned up by live cattle being dri-
en to London.

Turn right. You soon reach the beginning of the fashionable antique market
onfusingly called **Camden Passage**. It makes its way north along what was the
ld High Street, in a mixture of permanent shops—with a particularly rich col-
ction in the Mall, a former tramway transformer station—and street market
alls, especially on Wednesdays and Saturdays. Briefly turn off to the right at
uncan Street, down to **Duncan Terrace** and **Colebrooke Row**. These attrac-
ve, balanced 18C streets were developed to run either side of the New River, the
queduct brought from Hertfordshire in the early 17C (see Chapter 29). There is
o sign of the river here now, its course culverted under a pleasing garden.
eyond, you see the Regent's Canal emerging from its tunnel. To its left runs Noel
oad, where playwright Joe Orton lived at no. 25 in the 1960s. Of more historic
erary fame was Charles Lamb, who in 1823 moved into 64 Duncan Terrace
ith his sister Mary, 'feeling like a great lord, never having had a house before'.

Charles Lamb

Lamb (1775–1834) was an essayist, letter writer and critic, and above all a
Londoner. Born in the Inner Temple, he lived with his sister at various
addresses in the centre of town and later at Islington, Enfield and Edmonton,
where he died. He was a friend of Samuel Taylor Coleridge, William Hazlitt,
Leigh Hunt and others, and literature was his metier, but he also endured a
full working life as a clerk with the East India Company, taking, with delight,
a pension in 1825. His writings can still be enjoyed in the *Essays of Elia*
which in places, with his letters, can convey more powerfully even than
Charles Dickens the essence of the city.

The next on the right off Upper Street after Duncan Street is Charlton Place,
ith a pleasing crescent down its right-hand side. The heavyweight building to
e seen across Upper Street is the Business Design Centre—we will reach it at

the end of this walk. At the end of the antiques area is an authentically Victoria pub, the *Camden Head* (1899). To the left, Upper Street and Essex Road fork a Islington Green, headed by a crumbling 19C statue of the chief promoter of th New River, *Sir Hugh Myddelton* by John Thomas (1862), with a shady garde behind.

Take the right fork up **Essex Road**: there are still a few antique shops here bu they are downmarket by comparison with Camden Passage. Turn left at Cros Street. Here ascend the characteristic raised pavement, passing cool and refine 18C houses on both sides. At Upper Street turn right—we shall be back here late to see the opposite side of the road—past the Town Hall (1922) in which yo may be able to visit the Islington Museum Gallery. Open 11.00–17.00 Wed–Sa 14.00–16.00 Sun, with some local history exhibits. ☎ 020 7527 2837. The continue to Canonbury Lane on the right. Turning down it, take a look to the le down Compton Terrace (early 19C), long and dignified, looking over garder which separate it from Upper Street. In the middle of the terrace is the startling dominant **Union Chapel**, built for the Congregationalists by James Cubi (1876–77), showing Victorian religious self-confidence at its most extreme. It now a music venue. ☎ 020 7226 3750 for information.

Going along Canonbury Lane you come almost immediately to **Canonbur Square**, an extremely handsome development of 1805–30 though with a too formal garden. It was severed by Canonbury Road, which was laid out at th same time. On the southwest side the houses are on a raised terrace with a palac front, *à la* Bedford Square.

Walk along the north side and cross Canonbury Road to locate at no. 39 Northampton Lodge, a detached villa now housing the **Estorick Collection** **Modern Italian Art**. It is essential to stop here for a coffee, at least, in the exce lent café, but more important to see the fine collection of Italian 20C art collecte by the American Eric Estorick and his wife Salome. It is particularly strong on th fascinating and now somewhat frightening Futurist movement launched by Filip Marinetti in 1909. Works by Umberto Boccioni, Giacomo Balla and Gino Severi are permanently displayed, as well as temporary exhibitions. Open 11.00–18.0 Wed–Sat; 12.00–17.00 Sun. Admission charge. Café. Shop. ☎ 020 7704 952 www.estorickcollection.com

On the east side of the square, looming up inescapably, is **Canonbury Towe** the oldest building in the area, which formed the northwest corner of Canonbu House, a manor house built on an ecclesiastical site reallocated at the Dissolutic of the Monasteries. The tower is perhaps mid-16C. There is still plenty of interi decoration of the period to be seen. Open only by a pre-booked weekd appointment. ☎ 020 7226 6256. www.canonbury.ac.uk. Also the Tow Theatre performs here. ☎ 020 7226 3633 for details.

Down to the right you can see Canonbury Place (1771), with slightly sick green stucco, and Alwyne Villas stretching down over the former gardens Canonbury House. You could detour to the bottom to see **Alwyne Road**, with b later Italianate villas overlooking the New River, now rearranged in a spec riverside walk with Canonbury Grove (1820s) on the other side.

Our main route takes us north up Compton Road, with pompous stucco mid-19C houses, leading up to St Paul's Road, where you turn right, cross ar then turn left into **Highbury Grove**. Highbury is an entity distinct from bo Canonbury and Islington, and developed separately from the later 18C. As

evelopment it was never so co-ordinated or complete, but some individual ter-
aces are as beautiful as any in Islington.

Ascend Highbury Grove. A big 1960s school is on your right and Italianate
illas on the left. Many more such villas can be seen in a detour down Highbury
ew Park, to the right, a complete development of the 1850s. As you walk up
ighbury Grove, Highbury Fields comes into view on your left. Another detour
to the right, round **Aberdeen Park**, gives a text-book lesson on housing with
xamples from all periods from Italianate Victorian to what have become known
s 'Bypass variegated' homes of the 1930s. In the middle of it all is the church of
t **Saviour**, once a large polychrome brick Gothic Revival building by William
White (1865–66), always evoked by John Betjeman's poem ('St Saviour's,
berdeen Park'):

Great red church of my parents, cruciform crossing they knew—
Over the same encaustics they and their parents trod
Bound through a red-brick transept for a once familiar pew
Where the organ set them singing and the sermon let them nod,
And up in this coloured brickwork, the same long shadows grew
As those in the stencilled chancel where I kneel in the presence of God

ou would be hard-pressed to do this today, as the interior is now an exhibition
pace for contemporary artists: but at least this means you have access.

Walk back round to Highbury Grove and turn right to the top of the hill, then
ross over to **Christchurch** by Thomas Allom (1847–48), creator of Ladbroke
rove, spreading around the corner. Outside is an 1897 clock tower and a pleas-
nt street, Highbury Hill, stretching west. But we turn south down Church Path,
hrough a delightful avenue of trees, to **Highbury Fields**, an ancient open space
aved from developers in the 1880s by the Metropolitan Board of Works. They
erhaps felt guilty having located the borough's only proper park, Finsbury,
bout four miles from the area it was meant to serve. At any rate Highbury Fields,
ith its 18C terraces all around, is lovely. Joseph Chamberlain lived at Highbury
lace, on the left.

Cut across the grass diagonally to reach Fieldway Crescent, down which you
roceed to reach Holloway Road. The incredibly grand **public library** (1905–7),
ith statues of *Edmund Spenser* and *Francis Bacon*, is on the left. Cross over to
dmire its Edwardian splendour and then keep going through the churchyard of
t **Mary Magdalene** by William Wickings (1812–14), a large stock-brick
hurch built to meet the needs of the burgeoning community. You soon reach
iverpool Road, which you cross, going down Crossley Street. To the right, in
heringham Road, is **Freightliners**, a city farm. Open 10.00–13.00 and 14.00–
6.00 Tues–Sun.

A giant Board School towers above Lough Road, where you turn left, then right
nd walk down to the end of Bride Street. The high wall opposite is reminiscent
f a prison, not surprisingly, because this is **Pentonville**, built by Thomas Jebb
1840–42), the first appointed surveyor of prisons. It has a formal entrance, less
orbidding then those of many later prisons, in Caledonian Road, but you do best
o turn left here down Roman Way, going over the railway bridge and back from
olloway into Islington; this part is the community called Barnsbury. Beyond a
ower-covered pub, turn right down Huntingdon Street and left into Thornhill
rescent.

The exciting thing here, on the **Thornhill Estate**, is the window pattern Everything is of the 1820s to 1840s but points forward to the more ornat Victorian ideology of decorating every surface. The co-ordinating architect wa Joseph Kay. Thornhill Crescent and Square, apart from the Gothic church of : Andrew (1852–54) in the middle, set the tone. Do not miss Beresford Pite's **Wes Islington Library** (1905–7) on the west side, with odd patterns in th stonework and a stone alphabet round the façades, indicating a very early chi dren's library. Go south through the square to reach Richmond Avenue and tur left. There is infinite variety in the stucco decoration: pilasters, rosettes, bracket even sphinxes and obelisks. Prime Minister Tony Blair used to live here an helped to give, or received from, Islington a trendy reputation: there is no blu plaque to record this fact, yet.

Turn left into Thornhill Road, which has some early shop fronts on the righ hand corner. There is a little garden on the left and then Malvern Terrace, a rura seeming cul de sac. Opposite is a very pleasing pub, the *Albion*, and on the left a unusually attractive street of 1830s' villas with a quaintly rural nam Ripplevale Grove. Turn right into Barnsbury Street and again into **Lonsdal Square**, built for the Drapers' Company, who owned the land, by R.C. Carpent (1838–45), in a very unusual Tudor Revival style.

Beyond, to the south down Stonefield Street, you reach **Cloudesley Square i** the middle of which stands an early Gothic Revival church, **Holy Trinity**, b Charles Barry (1826–29), architect of the Houses of Parliament: it is based o King's College Chapel, Cambridge, but is hardly a competitor. Turn left, back int Liverpool Road, on a raised pavement. To the right, opposite, you can see the o entrance to the Royal Agricultural Hall (1861), known as the 'Aggie', which wa built for cattle shows but is now part of the **Business Design Centre**, enter from Upper Street: both the Royal Tournament and Cruft's Dog Show began her

Cross the road into Theberton Street to see two more squares. First, go left int dignified **Gibson Square** (1830s), with a Classical pavilion in its garden mar ing a ventilation shaft to the Victoria Line. Then go on into **Milner Squar** famous for John Summerson's remark that despite visiting it many times yc 'still could not be absolutely certain that you have seen it anywhere but in a unhappy dream'. It is by Roumieu and Gough (1838–44). Despite being cleane up since Summerson's day it does look awful, with strange vertical bric pilasters. It is best to make a beeline for no. 20, which turns out to be not a fro door but a passageway through to Almeida Street.

Here, on the right, is the **Almeida Theatre**. It was built by Roumieu ar Gough as Milner Square's Literary and Scientific Institute. The theatre is no being renovated and its productions are taking place elsewhere. For detail ☎ 020 7359 4404. www.almeida.co.uk

Now turn right, back into Upper Street: Cross Street, which you saw earlier, just opposite. On your left is Islington's parish church, **St Mary**, with a fine 18 tower displaying many twiddly bits, by Launcelot Dowbiggin (1751–54). Th rest of the church was bomb-damaged but rebuilt by Sealy and Paget (1954–5 and is light and refreshing, if you can get in. To the rear of the church in Dagma Passage is the **Little Angel Puppet Theatre**, London's only permanent pupp show. For details of performances, ☎ 020 7226 1787. Next door is anoth equally important theatrical venue, the **King's Head**, king of pub theatres, wi performances at 20.00 Mon–Sun; matinées Sat and Sun; ☎ 020 7226 1916. C he same side of the road, on the corner of Gaskin Street, is a lovely red-brick Arts and Crafts building, formerly **Islington Chapel** (1887). If the Congregationalists could manage beauties like this, how could they also sponsor a monster like the Union Chapel further north?

Soon you are back at **Islington Green**. There are scores of cafés, pubs and restaurants everywhere you look, and here, on the raised pavement, spilling out onto the footpath. This noisy, busy part of Islington is not really typical as you have seen from the quiet squares, but is an essential element in its character. The front of the Business Design Centre is on the right. It hosts regular specialist exhibitions. ☎ 020 7359 35350 for details. If the subject interests you, you will get a chance to see the Aggie's original 1860s iron hall inside.

Soon Angel station, and buses for the City and West End (the 19 and 38 are particularly frequent and convenient), come into view across the road. Before you leave the area, if not undertaking Chapter 29, you may like to seek out the Crafts Council Gallery in Pentonville Road.

44 • Hackney

The centre of Hackney offers one of the most vivid evocations of past and present to be found anywhere in London. There are plenty of Georgian survivals, mixed with shabby public housing of the 20C. The area is not gentrified to the extent of Islington, indeed it is kept perpetually in motion by the richly mixed ethnic community. There is noise, dirt, colour, sharp images everywhere. Our walk starts in the midst of this bustle, but includes the old Sutton House and ends in the comparative peace of Victoria Park and the Regent's Canal. Choose a Wednesday or Sunday if you want to see Sutton House, or consider ending the walk at the Bethnal Green Museum (Chapter 46)

Distance: 4–5 miles. Time: 2 hours. Off map.

Travel There is currently no Hackney Tube or railway station on a direct line out of London (although Hackney Downs, on the line from Liverpool Street, is close), but this may be corrected when the new Eurotunnel link is completed. Hackney Central station is on the historic but inconvenient **North London Line**, which runs in a loop from Richmond to Woolwich: it stops at a range of mysterious, generally unvisited inner London suburbs (what tourist ever reaches Brondesbury, Gospel Oak, or Dalston?). Change onto it at Highbury and Islington station (Victoria Line) and then ride the three stops east to Hackney Central. There are two good bus routes from the West End, numbers 30 and 38.

Leave Hackney Central station straight into the hubbub. Amhurst Road stretches northwest: it contains the furniture store *E. Gibbons*, the oldest cash-only shop in London, which has been here since 1898. Under the bridge, **Mare Street** rises north and south up a gentle hill, and to the right a bus garage vanishes into infinity. Our route is initially north, up the upper part of Mare Street, now understandably called The Narroway, apparently pedestrianised but buses career down it fast and unexpectedly. Proceed with caution.

On the right is a branch of the HSBC, in extreme Palladian style though the frontage was added only in 1900. This building is the **Old Town Hall** (1803), dating from the period of Hackney's prosperity.

In the 17C and 18C the village became an extremely popular and prosper ous leafy retreat, remaining rural after Islington had been built up. It was a favourite place to found private schools and Samuel Pepys would enjoy trip out here to admire the 'very pretty' schoolgirls. In its earliest days, with churches, chapels and villas, Hackney must have been a delightful and fashionable spot, even if, as quoted by Daniel Defoe (who was born here), it contained more carriages than Christians.

Behind the Town Hall is the oldest object for miles around, the late medieval tower of the old church, **St Augustine**. The rest was demolished when the new church of St John went up just to the east—we shall pass it—in 1794, but the tower was retained temporarily to house the bells. By the time the bells were installed in the new building, a growing antiquarian taste (to which we have today returned) ensured the tower's preservation. Around it are the messy, pleas ant, crowded gardens of the former churchyard.

Continue up the Narroway: there are glimpses of an older façade behind a big shoe shop on the left and of a fine curved corner as you turn right into Lower Clapton Road. The big church then comes into view on your right but we will first explore round its circumference, starting with **Clapton Square** on the left. It is worth going round the left-hand and top sides of this middle-class suburban development of 1811–18. Then make your way down the small Clapton Passage at the northeast corner, with little Victorian Gothic houses of 1880, a design continued in Powerscroft Road opposite, across the busy Lower Clapton Road to which you have now returned. These transitions illustrate the downward path of Hackney's growth—18C rural villas, early 19C genteel semis and terraces descending into wholly suburban lower-middle-class streets, and then into 20C council flats and general shabbiness.

Daniel Defoe

One of London's most significant writers, versatile, prolific, and full of zest for life, Defoe (1660–1731) was the son of a local butcher, and attended a school for Dissenters in Newington Green, north of Hackney. He married in 1683 and established a hosiery business in Cornhill. Even so he travelled in Europe extensively as a young man and throughout Britain all his life, the fruit of which was chiefly *A Tour through the whole Island of Great Britain* (1724), a model for guidebook writers to this day. His capacity to capture the exotic never deserted him and in *Robinson Crusoe* (1719) he created one of the most powerful of all Western romantic myths. But the essence of his work was in radical causes and in London itself. A Dissenter and anti-Jacobite throughout his life, he was several times pilloried or imprisoned. He died at his lodgings in Ropemaker's Alley, Moorfields and was buried in Bunhill Fields.

Across the road is the magnificent **Round Chapel** by Henry Fuller (1869–71), built as a Congregational church and in Pevsner's view one of the finest non-conformist buildings in London: it is still very much in use by the Assemblies of God. Go back round the corner of Lower Clapton Road, to the right: the former electricity showroom opposite in Fascist Classical style (1930s interrupts a grand pilastered early 19C terrace reminiscent of the work of Thomas Cubitt in Bloomsbury.

Then, on the left, is the great church **St John at Hackney** by James Spiller 791–94) and its tower (1810–14). It is a very fine building, a huge stock-brick x, shaped as a Greek cross, with a theme of semicircular porticoes arranged und the north and south arms. The north tower above the chief pedimented trance incorporates a clock-storey with bows (like St Mary-le-Bow) and yet other shape on top with a weather-vane. It is very eye-catching and easy to ew from the generous churchyard. Get inside if you can—the church is usually cked but is sometimes open for organ recitals as well as for services. There is a ant interior square under a canopied roof. From the spacious gallery the organ ojects vertiginously.

Leave the churchyard in an easterly direction into Sutton Place (1820) with a mplete terrace on the south side and paired houses on the north. Turn right d you are in front of the East End's oldest house, **Sutton House**, managed by e National Trust. Open Feb–Nov 13.00–17.00 Fri and Sat, 11.30–17.00 Sun d Bank Holidays. Admission charge. Café. Shop. Art gallery. ☎ 020 8986 ?64. www.nationaltrust.org.uk/thameschilterns

Sutton House, mistakenly named after the founder of Charterhouse School, Thomas Sutton (who lived nearby but not in it), has had an extraordinarily chequered history. It was originally built in 1535 by the courtier Sir Ralph Sadleir, who rose in Henry VIII's service as Thomas Cromwell's assistant: Sir Ralph later built himself a larger house in Hertfordshire and Sutton House became a school. In the 18C it was divided into two houses. In the late 19C it became St John's Institute and was later expanded into a residential college. After nearly perishing entirely through dilapidation, in 1936 it was taken over by the National Trust and sub-let inadequately, becoming by the 1980s squatted and derelict. But then the Trust restored it beautifully as an amenity for community use, a purpose it serves perfectly, for schools, exhibitions, social events, and public visiting. See it if you possibly can.

tour of the house will take you to the Tudor kitchen, the Georgian parlour and en a fine Tudor oak-panelled room, the Linenfold Parlour, the original panel- g recently restored after a range of vicissitudes. The staircase reveals traces of dor decoration. Upstairs there are three fine rooms at the front of the house cluding the Great Chamber with portraits of later members of the Sadleir mily. The cellars can also be seen and coffee or lunch can be had in the Barn at e back, an addition of 1904.

From Sutton House go immediately right down Isabella Road and then right to Isabella Street and right again into Mehetabel Road, another good example Victorian Hackney's speculative housing, this time of the 1860s. Then go left der the railway to Morning Lane. Notice that the ground slopes down and then es. The railway runs along the path of Hackney Brook, flowing to the River Lea, d 18C visitors travelling up Mare Street from London had to cross a ford here reach old Hackney. Turn right along Morning Lane back to Mare Street.

You emerge opposite the **Hackney Empire**, a genuine and complete Frank atcham theatre of 1901, now restored to its former glory. ☎ 020 8985 2424. xt to it to the south is the Hackney Town Hall (1934) behind formal but much ndalised gardens, slightly Art Deco in style and built of Portland stone. Behind, ere is some good Postmodernism in Christopher Addison House, and opposite e Town Hall there is what was the Methodist Central Hall (1926), Classical in yellow stone and converted with the older library next door into an arts centre. On the south side of the Town Hall, at 1 Reading Lane, is the **Hackney Museum**, covering the history of Hackney's rich culture. Open 09.30–17.30 Mon, Tues, Fri, 09.30–20.30 Thurs, 10.00–17.00 Sat. Free. Café. Shop. ☎ 020 8356 3500. And just south again, at 199 Richmond Road, is a contemporary art gallery, *Flowers East*.

You have now seen the best of the public buildings in contemporary Hackney: they are a mixed bag, but full of atmosphere. There is more Georgian and Victorian housing to be seen. Go down **Paragon Road** to the east: soon on the left you reach nos 71–83, built in 1809 and named to replicate the Paragon in Blackheath (Chapter 50). Then turn right down Mead Place and left into Cresset Road, where you encounter **Lennox House**, an unusual example of innovative housing of the 1930s designed by J.E.M. McGregor. This leads you into Well Street on the right and a little street market among the small shops.

Go down Terrace Road to Cassland Road, and turn left for one of the fine Georgian terraces in Hackney, on the right. **Hackney Terrace** was built by William Fellowes (1792–1801), with a palace front and pediment (copying Bedford Square, then recently completed). It was financed by tenant subscribers, an early example of the building society principle. Opposite is an attractive crescent of Victorian villas.

Off Cassland Road you will find Meynell Road and Meynell Crescent (1890s) opposite **Well Street Common**, a survivor of ancient common land. Turn left at Meynell Gardens, a rare 1930s interloper in this sort of area, and go down Church Crescent, where you pass **St John of Jerusalem**, a big Gothic Revival church of the 1840s, and the **Monger Almshouses**, originally 16C but rebuilt in the 19C.

Go down to Southborough Road and cross Victoria Park Road—pleasantly arranged traffic interchanges in the Victorian estate—to reach the entrance of **Victoria Park**.

> Victoria Park, a surprisingly large space, was laid out from 1840 by James Pennethorne, son-in-law of John Nash. Even at that early date, there was pressure to protect some open spaces from the march of speculative housing and thereby establish a public amenity for the escalating local population. Victoria Park was the first such creation, the result of a public petition. Pennethorne tried to recreate the notion of smart terraces and a canal round the edge of the Park, and picturesque planting within, similar to Regent's Park.

A sense of this ideal was achieved and there are some particularly fine trees, but little of the grandeur is left. The completeness of the Park is spoiled by Grove Road cutting through the centre. On the left is a large original hotel, the *Royal Inn on the Park*, now not much more than a pub. Gore Road curves away to the right with pleasant 1870s villas. Explore the Park, as you prefer. To the left, in the eastern half are two lakes and an English garden, a little neglected, many fine trees and much flat space. On the south side runs the Hertford Union Canal connecting the Regent's Canal (Chapter 39) with the River Lea. There is an enormous, ridiculous, drinking-fountain given in 1861 by Baroness Burdett Coutts and designed by Henry Darbishire, her protégé. To the east stand another curiosity, two shelters retrieved from those installed on old London Bridge in the 1760s, after the demolition of its houses.

The lake on the western side of the Park is more scenically ambitious, with a waterfall and islands, and the levels more attractively varied. Leaving on the southwest side you will find the **Regent's Canal** and its towpath, a pleasant way to complete this walk, along to the next bridge. There, ascending to the road, you find yourself in the southern part of Mare Street, where a 26 or 55 bus will take you back into town. If you were to turn left down Cambridge Heath Road, you would soon reach the Bethnal Green Museum of Childhood (Chapter 46) and Bethnal Green station (Central Line).

For separate independent exploration, **North Hackney** and **Stoke Newington** are also recommended. These areas contains some good Georgian houses, the attractive Clissold Park, and the extremely atmospheric Abney Park Cemetery.

Villages': east and southeast

45 • Spitalfields, Shoreditch and Hoxton

This is a walk through three historic areas, from south to north. You are never far from the City (Chapter 3). The past, or different pasts, are startlingly juxtaposed with a lively present, most notably in what is now called Banglatown in and around Brick Lane, analogous to Chinatown in Soho. At the beginning is a vivid modern art gallery and at the end a peaceful little museum with an appealing café. Consider going on a Sunday, to include Columbia Road or Petticoat Lane markets.

Spitalfields' name originates from the area behind the former St Mary's Hospital, a medieval establishment built over a Roman cemetery. It was always a popular district for immigrants, from the Huguenots fleeing oppression in the 17C, and Jews from Europe in the 1880s to Bangladesh in the later 20C. It had periods of prosperity—silk weaving in the 18C—but from the 19C until recently like Shoreditch and Hoxton, it became one of the poorest areas of London.

Distance: 2¼ miles. Time: 1 hour + more for markets and museums.
Tube: Aldgate East. Map 9, then off map.

Begin at Aldgate East station (District or Hammersmith and City Lines), or walk along from Aldgate (Circle Line). This is Whitechapel High Street (**Map 9,4**): it is grim, with traffic and litter blowing about, and is still 'no small blemish to so famous a city', as John Stow said in 1590. But just by Aldgate East is the **Whitechapel Art Gallery** by C. Harrison Townsend (1897–99), a distinguished Art Nouveau façade with a high-tech modern gallery behind. It was part of a late Victorian initiative to bring art to the East End, a mission still in progress, and shows changing exhibitions. Open 11.00–17.00 Tues–Sun (sometimes

Whitechapel Art Gallery

later Wed, Sat and Sun). Admission free. Café. Shop. ☎ 020 7522 7888. www. whitechapel. org

On the library next door there is a plaque to Isaac Rosenberg, a forgotten Jewish poet of the First World War.

Turn back towards the City and then turn right into Middlesex Street. There is nothing interesting to start with but before long (if it is a Sunday) you will be in the thick of **Petticoat Lane** market selling clothes and a whole range of artefacts: this was the former name of Middlesex Street until officially changed by puritanical administrators in 1830 but it has stuck. Although Sunday is the main day, there are signs of life throughout the week, and a fully functioning clothes market in Wentworth Street, to the right.

Proceed north. Look out for Sandys Row and Frying Pan Alley on the right, a good modern block to the south. In Brune Street, on the left, the façade of the **Jewish soup kitchen** survives (refurbished inside), a reminder that the area was once a crowded Jewish community; a century ago, the Jewish Free School nearby, with 4300 pupils, was the largest school in the entire country. Now very few Jews live in this particular area, which is being pulled two ways by the Broadgate ambience to the west (Chapter 3) and the Bangladeshi markets to the east. At the east end of Artillery Lane, at no. 56, is a near-perfect 18C shop front from Huguenot days, which seems, like Artillery Passage to its left, to be deliberating which way to go, city prosperity or eastern variety.

The same struggle is affecting **Spitalfields Market** just to the north—reach it up Gun Street (**Map 9,2**). It was for a century an important fruit and vegetable market but now functions as a kind of Covent Garden (in a sense that is what it always was), with stalls for organic food, crafts, clothes and jewellery, at its liveliest on Sunday.

To the right, down Brushfield Street, a most uplifting sight meets the eye: Nicholas Hawksmoor's great **Christchurch Spitalfields** (1714–29), the finest of his six London churches, soon to re-open after prolonged and expensive restoration. It should be worth the wait: this is one of London's outstanding buildings.

Even from the outside Christchurch is something of a heartstopper, with a huge 225ft tower and spire, wider than it is deep, with the persistent Hawksmoor motif of an arch breaking into an entablature occurring all the way up. Take a look down either side, where the massive north or south façades continue the impression. This was one of the churches built under the Fifty New Churches Act of 1711 (Chapter 47). Here in Spitalfields the objective was to deter the growing number of Huguenot refugees from joining the non-Conformist chapels.

The interior is just as astonishing—square, massive, and noble in the extreme. The plan is to remove the double gallery placed at the back by Ewe

Nicholas Hawksmoor

To those who enjoy architecture, Hawksmoor's London churches are a kind of addiction. Their forbidding, massive appearance is hard to link with the comforts of Sir Christopher Wren, whose assistant Hawksmoor was, and was disliked by the Palladian generation and by the Victorians. But now they are greatly admired and can with initiative be visited as a set. Try it— St George's Bloomsbury, St Mary Woolnoth, Christchurch Spitalfields, St George in the East, St Anne Limehouse, and St Alphege Greenwich: it is a challenging day's tour, both for the mind and the use of London transport. Hawksmoor (1661–1736) also worked with Sir John Vanbrugh at Castle Howard in Yorkshire and at Blenheim Palace in Oxfordshire. Born in Northamptonshire, he lived most of his later life in Westminster, and contributed ideas for the first Westminster Bridge. His personality remains unprobed but has been the focus for imaginative speculation by modern London authors, especially Peter Ackroyd, in his novel *Hawksmoor*.

Christian in the mid-19C, a pity in a way because this used to add yet more grandeur and theatricality. Open 12.30–14.30 Mon–Fri, 10.30–16.00 Sun; ☎ 020 7247 0165. There is an important music festival here in June, ☎ 020 7377 0287.

Now we walk zig-zag fashion northwards, trying to take in both Georgian Spitalfields and 21C Banglatown at the same time: this is no easy task, but they are in some ways set to merge before long. The Georgian streets are Fournier Street, Princelet Street and, to the west, Folgate Street. They have many handsome early 18C terrace houses, sometimes with a side entrance through to the back yard. The attic floors often have long windows to give maximum light to the weavers who occupied them when the houses gradually ceased to be domestic and became commercial premises. One such house, **18 Folgate Street**, was restored and arranged by an American, Dennis Severs (d. 1999), to tell the domestic story of a silk-weaver's family from 1724 to 1914. Now run by the Spitalfields Historic Buildings Trust, it is open for tours: candlelit evening tours Mon, times vary, booking essential; also 14.00–17.00 first Sun of the month and 12.00–14.00 the following Mon, no booking required. Admission charge. ☎ 020 7247 4013. www.dennissevershouse.co.uk

If it is Bangladeshi culture you prefer, go to the eastern ends of these streets to explore **Brick Lane**. The mosque on the corner of Fournier Street perfectly summarises the ethnic transformations of this area: it was built as a Huguenot church in 1740, became a Wesleyan chapel in 1809, a synagogue in 1897 and since 1976 has had its present role. All around are vividly colourful cafés, restaurants and clothes shops. Do not go too far up, but it is worth passing under the bridge of a modern office to reach the former brewery buildings of **Truman, Hanbury, Buxton** (founded in 1666), with a great brick chimney: by the end of the 19C it was the largest brewery in the world, but closed in 1989.

Walk back along Quaker Street, then right into Wheler Street under the long railway arch under the Bishopsgate Goodsyard, an extensive railway storage area whose future is at present uncertain. Across Bethnal Green Road you reach another area once famous, or infamous, for its extreme poverty, the **Old Nichol**—a notorious slum forming the central location for an important but now seldom-read novel, *A Child of the Jago* by Arthur Morrison. The whole network of courts and alleys was cleared away in the 1890s to create something just

Columbia Road Flower Market

as interesting today, th London County Council first ever housing, th **Boundary Street Estat** (1900). The towering red brick blocks now seem a intimidating as the slum which preceded them. G up Camlet Street or Clu Row to reach the centre Arnold Circus, raised hig up in the middle with now enormous plane trees an bushes. In summer it i dark from the shady tree and in winter from th housing blocks all around. It is an odd place, once seen, never forgotten.

If it is a Sunday, leave via Hocker Street to the north to see **Columbia Roa** street market, a mass of flowering plants and interesting small shops—wel worth the detour. On other days go down Calvert Avenue west to Shoreditch Hig Street. On the right, currently under extensive restoration, is **St Leonar Shoreditch**, the bells of which are said to respond 'When I grow rich' in th famous 'Oranges and Lemons' nursery rhyme. It is a fine work of the 1730s b George Dance the Elder, the same architect and date as the Mansion House. H tried to copy the spire of St Mary-le-Bow. Buried here were Richard Burbage Shakespeare's friend and builder of the original theatre nearby, later re established as the Globe, and Gabriel Spencer, the actor killed by Ben Jonson in dual in 1598.

Opposite the church is the spectacular run of Wells and Company's ironwork a chaotic, text-book illustration of the late Victorian period's stylistic confusion Cross over to it and turn briefly left down Old Street—busy with traffic—and not the former Town Hall on the left: there is no confusion here, but highly confiden Italian style. Cross over again with care and look at the former police station, b J.D. Butler (1906), who designed scores of them, all individual and appropriatel magisterial. Turn right into Hoxton Street and then turn left into **Hoxto Square**, which is very old in foundation (1683), contemporary with Soho. It i now much modernised, although something of its original character can be fel Dr James Parkinson, who first diagnosed Parkinson's disease in 1817, lived an practiced at no. 1, and the Gothic ensemble on the north side is by A.W.N Pugin's son (1864–66).

Go west down Coronet Street into **Hoxton Market**, again much renewed bu still 19C in character, with a good Greek restaurant on the east side. Walk ou and right into Pitfield Street. Note the delicious former library on the right by H. Hare (1895–97), who must have been a Norman Shaw enthusiast. Just opposit is a former college, originally Haberdashers' Almshouses (1825–27), very forma and Classical and not reminiscent of almshouses at all. Go north up Pitfiel Street and you soon reach a fine church, **St John the Baptist** by Franci Edwards (1824–26), standing large and dignified in a big churchyard. It woul be grand to get inside, but very unlikely.

Turn right down Crondall Street and Falkirk Street, making your way briskly through this dreary estate back to Kingsland Road, where the more traditional almshouses opposite will immediately catch your eye. They are lovely and moreover form the **Geffrye Museum**. Open 10.00–17.00 Tues–Sat; 12.00–17.00 Sun and Bank Holidays. Admission free. Restaurant. Shop. Garden (open April–Oct). ☎ 020 7739 9893. www.geffrye-museum.org.uk

The almshouses were built in 1715 for the Ironmongers' Company, under the will of Sir Robert Geffrye, a former Mayor of London whose statue appears over the central doors. They were converted to a museum as long ago as 1914 and, because the area had a tradition of furniture-making, it was determined that the subject matter should be a history of domestic furnishing from Elizabethan times to the present. The route of the displays progresses chronologically, starting in 1580. It is beautifully done, with paintings, maps and books left around for you to read as background. At the southern end, a large extension was built in the 1990s to accommodate a restaurant, a good bookshop and an excellent space for temporary exhibitions: modernity here harmonises perfectly with the early 18C, partly because we only experience it from the interior. There is also a beautifully maintained historic garden.

A further fine Victorian church, **St Chad**, by James Brooks (1868–69) is in Dunloe Street behind the museum. From the request bus stop in Kingsland Road a 242 bus will take you back to Tottenham Court Road.

6 • Stepney

This is a good walk on which to gain an impression of the old East End. The character of much of it has been altered but not transformed: there is still plenty of grit around, and not too many signs of gentrification or business. The route goes from Whitechapel through unreconstructed Stepney and ends at Limehouse which, being by the river, has been utterly changed. Bethnal Green, with its important museum, is incorporated as a detour, or could be added to the walk through Hackney in Chapter 44.

Distance: 3½ miles. Time: 1½ hours + time for the Bethnal Green Museum. Tube: Whitechapel. Off map.

Take the Tube to Whitechapel station (District Line) and turn left. You are immediately in a dense street market, largely Bengali and Somali, located on the north side of one of the widest roads in London. A short distance to the right, past the crossroads with Vallance Road on the corner of Fieldgate Street, is the **Whitechapel Bell Foundry** and its small museum. On this site since 1733, many famous bells have been cast here, including Big Ben, and the USA's original Liberty Bell. Open 9.00–17.00 Mon–Fri. Pre-booked tours at 10.00 Sat. Shop. ☎ 020 7247 2599. www.whitechapelbellfoundry.co.uk

Opposite Whitechapel station is the **London Hospital** (Royal, but only since 1990), founded in 1740 and on this site since 1757. The original fine 18C buildings by Boulton Mainwaring have been altered and added to, unavoidably, but the long northern façade remains a noble sight. It is worth going in to see the garden square with a statue of *Queen Alexandra* by George Edward Wade (1908) located to the south and beyond that, in Newark Street, in the former church of

St Augustine, a small museum with some references to John Merrick, th 'Elephant Man', who was treated here until his death in 1890. Ope 10.00–16.30 Mon–Fri. ☎ 020 7377 7608.

Go east to the major crossroads with Cambridge Heath Road. On the corner is th former Mann's Brewery, in very grand yellow stock brick, with a clock tower an pediment. For a detour, turn left here and walk for ten minutes, under the rai way bridge, or take a 106 or 253 bus to Bethnal Green station. The church of **John** on the right is important, having been designed by Sir John Soane (182⁵ but is crumbling away. Just beyond is the **Bethnal Green Museum of Chil hood**. Open 10.00–17.50 Sat–Thur; closed Fri. Admission free. Café. Shop. 020 8983 5200. www.museumofchildhood.org.uk. Tube: Bethnal Green.

> This is a substantial museum, the contents of which do not entirely fill i extensive space, which is perhaps understandable as the structure was origi nally built in Kensington to house the first Victoria and Albert Museu (Chapter 35). It was moved here in 1872 and filled with changing exhibi tions, including, from 1924, a children's section of growing local impo tance. It was redesignated the Museum of Childhood in 1974. If everythin seems a little tired, it still has plenty to offer children.

The ground floor contains dolls' houses, the shop and café, with raised displa of model trains, boats and cars, teddy bears, puppets, games and a huge colle tion of dolls. At the upper level there are rather more 'adult' displays on hi torical approaches to birth and childhood, including clothes and pioneerin methods of education. There is a soft play zone (charge) where under-fives ca safely let off steam while their minders read a complimentary newspaper.

Resume the main route in Whitechapel Road, which at Mann's Brewery becom Mile End Road, and keep going east. The road to the south from Cambridge Hea Road is **Sidney Street**, where in 1911 two anarchists were famously besieged no. 100 and their dwelling burned out, under directions on the spot fro Winston Churchill, then Home Secretary. On the left, in Mile End Road, are som fine almshouses, founded by Trinity House in 1695 (see Chapter 2), for '2 decayed masters and commanders of ships or the widows of such'. In the roa are a grand avenue of plane trees planted in 1910 and a copy of a statue **William Booth**, founder of the Salvation Army, whose first headquarters w opened here in 1867.

A little way further, on the left, are the remains of the East End's only depar ment store, **Wickham's**, with its Selfridges-type façade ridiculously interrupt by a small shop at no. 81, once representing **Spiegelhalter's Jewellers**, wh refused to sell up. Next comes a fine early 18C terrace, nos 107–113, and soc a broad commercial space with stock-brick buildings at the eastern end, deno ing another former brewery, this time Charrington's.

Cross Mile End Road here and go down Hayfield Passage into **Stepney Gree** This lovely wide street can be read, and traversed, as a series of squares, stretchin southeast. Numerous attractive 18C houses survive, especially on the left-han side, and also some interesting galleried late 19C flats on the right, a surviv from Canon Barnett's East End Dwellings Company. In style, they conform wi an excellent late 17C house opposite, no. 37, the oldest house in Stepney. In d course the interesting street pattern widens to an open space on the right wi an eye-catching memorial clock tower (1913) to Stanley Atkinson, a local worthy, whose qualifications are recorded as JP, MA, LLM, MB, BSc, MRCS, LRCP, Barrister and Guardian of the Poor, all achieved before his death at the age of 37.

Turn right at Garden Street, where the old granite cobblestones that once covered most London streets remain in place. Rebels of the Peasants' Revolt assembled here in 1381 and were met by Richard II (see Chapter 29). On the corner, reminding us of those times but actually Victorian, is a ruined Gothic arch, all that remains of College Chapel, part of a training college for Baptist ministers.

> Much bomb-damage was incurred in this area and the sense of openness is misleading in terms of the recent past—but preceding the terraced houses which perished in the Second World War, the land south of Stepney Way was occupied by a moated manor house called the Great Place, leased in the 1530s by Thomas Cromwell. The Rector of Stepney was one of Cromwell's main allies in implementing the Dissolution. Such is the palimpsest of Stepney's history.

Turn left into Stepney Way. On the left, created on the bomb-damaged space, is **Stepping Stones Farm**, one of a number of city farms opened in London in recent years, with the worthy aim of informing urban children of some of the values and problems of rural life. Open 09.30–18.00 Tues–Sun. Admission charge. ☎ 020 7790 8204.

From here, to the east, the pleasing sight of **St Dunstan and All Saints** comes into view. It is one of the most delightful and ancient of all London's parish churches (15C, refaced in the 19C), small scale and comforting, having largely escaped the bombs. Only the tower was damaged, including the bells ('"When will that be?" say the bells of Step-nee'), but still flies the Red Ensign to commemorate the parish's riverside connections to the sea. It is hard to gain entry, but maybe you will be lucky to coincide with a wedding or a service; if so, look out for the Saxon stone rood and 14C panel of the Annunciation.

The large churchyard extends behind. Cross through to the southeast to locate Mercers' Cottages, founded in 1681 but rebuilt in 1856 and strictly Classical in style. Beyond, briefly explore the little streets of Matlock Street, Barnes Street, and Salmon Lane before turning up **Aston Street**. Here are a whole series of unbombed 1850s' terraces, once low quality but today looking dignified, clean and of charming proportions. If they were in Kensington these houses would command £1m each, but in London east is east and west is west.

At the top of Aston Street the dominating 19C gasholders of the former Stepney Gas Works fill the sky. At Ben Jonson Road to the left, you can see mid-20C flats and shops in 'Festival of Britain' style. On the right, on the corner, is a former pub now selling Halal burgers and chips. Turn right and go past the gasworks wall, turning over the canal bridge. The Regent's Canal stretches north and south (Chapter 39). Over the bridge turn left into Copperfield Road, where the absorbing **Ragged School Museum** is established at nos 46–48. Open 10.00–17.00 Wed and Thur; 14.00–17.00 first Sun in the month. Admission free. Café. Shop. ☎ 020 8980 6405. Tube: Mile End.

As you will see from the street, this building has a pedimented centre at roof level, obviously added to give it an imposing appearance. But its history could hardly be guessed.

The presence of the canal behind would imply, correctly, that the origin of the terrace was as commercial warehouses accessible from the towpath. As such they date from 1872, and are the only canal warehouses surviving in the area. Only five years later, Dr Barnardo rented two of them for his Ragged School for children aged five to ten years, who received there a free education along with breakfast and dinner. It was to be some time before the 1870 Act (see p 366) would extend to poor areas of this type and the solution was left to charity. The school was closed in 1908 and the building went through a series of other uses including a Jewish clothing factory. In 1983, through local efforts, it became a museum of the disappearing East End: as such it is a special place, egalitarian, authentic and informative.

Dr Barnardo

Thomas John Barnardo (1845–1905) was an evangelical Protestant from Dublin, who came to work at the London Hospital in 1866. Shocked by the number of homeless and neglected children in the area, he founded for them first a Christian mission and second a series of houses in the East End for boys, which became known as Dr Barnardo's Homes. He also set up schools to fill the gap still unfilled by the state system. Later he established the Girls' Village Home at Barkingside and began sending children to Canada for training and resettlement. It is estimated that he rescued 60,000 children.

To the north, the bomb-damaged area has been turned into a pleasant park with a footpath to Mile End station (Central Line). For the sake of its integrity—unspoiled East End—you should perhaps end the walk here. But it is hoped you will continue a little further to complete the canal theme. Turn onto the towpath to proceed south. The chimney on the left is a sewer vent shaft, serving the Northern Low Level Pipe passing under the canal here on its journey to Abbey Mills and beyond. You then pass under various road bridges to reach, before long, **Limehouse Basin**. This was created in 1812 as the Thames entrance to the Regent's Canal, leading round to Paddington and thence via the Grand Junction up to the Midlands, thus creating the London gateway to the whole of Britain's canal system. Now surrounded by new speculative housing, some quite luxurious, and with a new life as a marina, it is somewhat reminiscent of St Katharine's Dock (Chapter 3).

Having looked at the basin, you need to come up to the busy street, heavy with traffic, Commercial Road, and walk east. There are some good 18C terraces on both sides, and soon, on the right, Mill Place which leads to the accumulator tower remaining from the hydraulic pumping system installed throughout the docks in 1868–69.

Next on the right is a library of 1900, with a bronze of **Clement Attlee** by Frank Forster (1988) in front. Attlee was prime minister 1945–51 and the MP for this constituency from 1922. Then the road crosses a bridge over the **Limehouse Cut**, a very early canal (1767–70) predating the Regent's and the docks, devised to make a link between the Thames and the Lea bypassing the Isle of Dogs. You can see it stretching away northeast, straight as an arrow—there are no considerations of property or the picturesque here. Next on Commercial Road is the very fancy former Town Hall (1879–81). Across the road is the wholly depressing Mission, or Empire Memorial Sailors' Hostel (1923–24).

The best is yet to come. Turn right down Newell Street, where encouraging 18C houses survive. Suddenly, on the left, a little courtyard opens up to reveal the west end of **St Anne Limehouse**. The heart leaps. The huge entrance steps and tower by Nicholas Hawksmoor rise, white and inspiring, pointing to the heavens. The church was begun in 1714, with Christchurch Spitalfields and St George in the East (Chapter 47). St Anne's had the same builder as St George's, Edward Strong, who lived up to his name, but it is slightly more conventional. The interior was refitted in the 1850s by the Hardwicks, father and son, though there is an inconsistency.

Go through the churchyard on the south side, across Three Colt Street, down Renade Street to reach Westferry station (Docklands Light Railway), or return to Commercial Road to catch a 15 bus going west. If you have time before returning, it is worth going south down Three Colt Street to see the Thames Path at Dundee Wharf, with new flats by CZWG, an acquired taste. There is room on the right to survey the entrances to Limehouse Basin and the Limehouse Cut in Narrow Street or left to see the entrance to **Limekiln Dock**, which served the original Lime House. You could do worse than end your walk at the *Grapes*, in Narrow Street, which featured as the Six Jolly Fellowship Porters in Dickens's *Our Mutual Friend*.

47 • Wapping

Wapping is compact, self-contained, dense and complex, perfect for a short but historically challenging walk, with great views and some famous riverside pubs *en route*. What was once a boat-building riverside hamlet became in 1805 the London Docks, which in turn in the 1980s became a mixed community of office space, new middle-class inhabitants renting a river view, old-time Londoners in council flats with no such view, with a dash of Bangladeshi here and there, each in their own little sector. Not many tourists reach Wapping, although plenty find St Katharine's Dock (Chapter 3), which was the most westerly part of it.

Distance: 2 miles. Time: 1 hour. Tube: Shadwell. Off map.

Start at Shadwell station (East London Line). It is also on the Docklands Light Railway (described more fully in Chapter 48). Descend and turn right into **Cable Street**, named from its original function as a straight section in which to manufacture rope or cable. It has usually been associated with East End poverty but the blackened 18C houses on the left, beyond the Library (1860), show that it was once respectable. Cable Street was the scene of a famous 'battle' in October 1936 when Sir Oswald Mosley's fascists found themselves barricaded by local inhabitants. The main route turns left at Cannon Street Road but a small detour to the west can take in Well Close Square, with **St Paul's Church for Seamen** and its pretty school (1869), built on the site of London's first Danish church. Down Grace's Alley, curving away northwest, is **Wilton's Music Hall**, 'the most important surviving early music hall anywhere', with varied programmes ranging from traditional music hall to modern opera. For details, ☎ 020 7702 9555.

Return to Cannon Street Road, and go south. Soon, on the left, the Baroque bulk of Nicholas Hawksmoor's **St George in the East** towers above you. Go up to examine it and then mount the steps. This is one of Hawksmoor's six surviving

London churches, built 1714–26 under the 1711 Act. St George's is one of tl
more extraordinary and although the interior was bombed in 1941, the dr
matic, slightly insane exterior—with huge keystones, castellated towers ar
startlingly plain windows—is a sufficient indication of the workings of tl
architect's mind.

Fifty New Churches Act

In 1711 Queen Anne's new Tory government persuaded themselves that the
time was right to build a series of fifty new churches in London, in order to
bring, or restore, Anglican doctrines to newly expanding areas of London
such as Spitalfields that were perceived to be developing into centres for dis-
sent, religious and political. A commission was set up and designs began to
be approved. The Tories were, however, soon replaced by the Whigs and in
the event only twelve new churches were constructed under the Act. These
include several on what was then the suburban edge, mostly to the east of
London, including three of Hawksmoor's masterpieces.

You can usually enter to find a utilitarian postwar church (1964) tuck
inside the outer walls, nothing special but exhibiting some good photographs
Hawksmoor's interior. Then go outside again round by the churchyard, and tl
red-brick vicarage by Edward Strong, the builder of the church, to see the ea
end and the churchyard. The monument to the Raine family was once fine, b
the figure is now smashed and covered with graffiti.

Exit south onto the Highway, a traffic cut-through from the Tower to the ea
always noisy and full of fumes. Cross over and escape. Cut over the car park
Tobacco Dock, part of the original London Docks. You can get in to explore,
partially explore, because everything is currently in a rather sad state. Tl
evocative interior was the warehouse of Tobacco Dock (1811–14), by Dan
Alexander, constructed to store wine and spirits at the lower level and tobac
above. Its engineering was advanced for its day and generously respected
Terry Farrell in its conversion to a shopping centre in the 1980s. But this was o
Docklands initiative that did not catch on (see Chapter 48). As a shopping cent
it was too far from civilisation and lacked either buses or a Tube stop—fe
showed your persistence by coming to Shadwell on the DLR. So here it is,
ghostly shell, awaiting a fairy godmother.

At the southern end you emerge between two moored vessels, just here f
entertainment, into all that remains of Tobacco Dock itself, now a pleasant b
artificial canal stretching both ways, and creating a friendly and leafy wa
Everything has been prettily softened up but you can still see the dominatir
brickwork of John Rennie's dock walls (1811).

Turn left and cross the canal to reach **Wapping Lane**, an old highway th
ran between London Docks' northern and eastern sections. Turn right. Note
the left, in Raine Street, a fine Baroque former school, with statues of childr
either side of a plaque which commandingly exhorts 'Come in and learn yo
Duty to God and man, 1719'. A little way further on the left through a courtya
is a church, **St Peter**, an inspiring piece of Gothic Revival design by F.H. Pown
(begun 1865–66), denoting the missionary aims of 19C Anglo-Catholicis
to the poor of this area: the large clergy house is an indication of high st.
numbers. In fact the church was not finished until the 1930s, and was th

immediately bombed, and repaired, so it is not all as old as it looks, or feels.

Next down Wapping Lane turn right, towards a pub called *Turner's Old Star*, and continue down to the end of Tench Street. The great wall ahead of you marked the edge of Wapping Basin behind, now filled in as a football pitch. Continue past the sports centre into Scandrett Street. The tower on your left, with its churchyard opposite, belonged to the church of St John (1756): the rest of the church was bombed in the Second World War. Both features determined the shape of the dock entrance, just as the dock walls have sometimes been left to determine the shape of today's street pattern. The church tower is now flats, but some nice 18C houses remain either side as well as another school (1760), with more pretty children over the door.

Then cross Wapping High Street to look down **Pier Head**: here are lovely yellow stock-brick houses (1810) for senior dock officials, lining either side of the original dock entrance, with curved ends to give views of the river. The entrance is grassed over, which is absurd historically but admirable aesthetically, neatly transforming it into a residential square. The original architect, Daniel Alexander, would be surprised but probably, after tactful explanation, pleased. Across the river is a rarity, a large but as yet unconverted warehouse, Chambers Wharf.

Now walk east down Wapping High Street. You immediately reach the *Town of Ramsgate*, one of the surviving riverside pubs, and alongside it Old Stairs leading down to the river, with irresistible beachcombing opportunities if the tide is out. *Oliver's Wharf*, an early riverside apartment conversion (1972) comes next, with overhead gangways across the street. It originally stored tea: to the river it presents a Gothic Revival façade (1870). Time was when Wapping High Street consisted entirely of warehouses with such gangways, dark and wet, with a range of smells from tobacco and spices to the river itself.

Such nostalgic reflections are usually easy in Wapping, but here they are soon severely jarred by an ultra-brash 1970s building for the river police boat maintenance. It is made of blue and white plastic panels: a horrible intrusion. The other police building nearby (1907–10) is much more harmonious, and important, because this is a historic police location: '200 years of surveillance' have taken place from here. The river police were formed in 1798 to prevent piracy, 30 years before the Metropolitan Police proper.

Execution Dock is so-called from the practice of hanging pirates there and allowing the bodies to remain until three tides had covered and exposed them, invariably described with relish in riverboat commentaries. Perhaps appropriately, after Wapping New Stairs, we reach the *Captain Kidd*, another pub named for one of the most notorious of such pirates, hanged in 1701. This pub is not historic but a warehouse conversion. Again there are opportunities to explore the river foreshore, tide permitting.

Continue along Wapping High Street. Wapping station appears, carrying the East London Line through Marc Brunel's **Thames Tunnel**, begun as long ago as the 1820s and planned even earlier, in 1802. If you have a travel card, why not go down to platform level to look at the noble, horseshoe-shaped tunnel entrances.

The tunnel was initially for pedestrians and in due course vehicles, but no one came up with the funding for horse and carriage ramps, and it was converted to a railway in 1869. Many workmen were killed during the construction but it was nevertheless an engineering wonder. Marc Brunel's tunnelling shield has been the model for the construction of all subsequent underground transport systems.

Soon after this is a section of the **Thames Path**, a riverside walkway, beyond new flats: go through the iron gate, which is open even if it looks locked. Here there are places to sit and admire the view of the church of St Mary and historic Rotherhithe opposite (Chapter 51). You are brought back in due course to the High Street at New Crane Wharf, where you turn right along **Wapping Wall**. There is no riverside path here, properly, because the wharves are conversions, not new flats. You can enjoy the landward sides of them, which still survive, as does another famous and characterful pub, the *Prospect of Whitby*. Its customers included Pepys, Dickens and Turner. It was named after a ship, the *Prospect*, from Whitby in Yorkshire, which moored here regularly in the 18C.

In due course you reach the eastern entry to the old London Docks, **Shadwell Basin**. The swingbridge (1930s) has been fixed in place. On the left, first, is the Hydraulic Pumping Station (1889–93), now part restaurant and part art gallery and next the Basin itself, surrounded by decorous 1980s housing by MacCormac, Jamieson, Pritchard and Wright, very effective and pleasing. We shall return in a moment but first cross over to look one more time on the river. Go down into **King Edward VII Memorial Park** on the left-hand side of the dock entrance, where there is a great view downstream past the Isle of Dogs and across to Rotherhithe. In the foreground is a shaft from the Rotherhithe Tunnel (1908), and a touching little memorial of 1922 to 16C explorers such as Martin Frobisher who embarked from here 'to explore the northern seas'. The very green and pleasant park was opened by King George V in 1922 in memory of his father, 'dedicated to the use and enjoyment of the people of East London for ever'.

Returning to Shadwell Basin, walk round the north side to climb the steps to the church of **St Paul**, a clear landmark. The architect was John Walters (1820) who was associated with Daniel Alexander, the main architect of the London Docks. The exterior is in elegant Georgian style, conveying civilised values, and the attractive interior has associations with Frobisher, Captain James Cook and Thomas Jefferson (his mother lived here, and their first plantation in Virginia was named Shadwell), but is usually locked tight. Next to the church are the former church schools and the rectory, all of the same general date, but the schools look more Victorian.

Now you are back in the Highway, not a pleasant experience. Cross over when you can and go up Dellow Street, back to Cable Street and Shadwell station.

48 • Docklands

Nearly everything is new on this walk, built over a largely invisible past. It is a Postmodern walk—more so than any in London—and what Postmodernism does to history is play about with it, and it will be necessary to sort the real past from the pseudo-past. But Docklands is also exciting, futuristic, full of zest and life—a place to feel optimistic, if slightly nervous, about the future.

• Distance: 1¼ miles. Time: 1½ hours. See map on p 393.

Travel This route leads from the entrance to the old West India Dock down the southern tip of the Isle of Dogs, taking the Docklands Light Railway (DL art of the way: you will need a travel card for Zones 1 and 2. To get to the starting point from central London, take the DLR from Bank or Tower Gateway, to Westferry.

escending to road level, cross and go through the modern flats to reach Garford reet. If you miss it, or can not find it, turn left and immediately right down the ide dual carriageway of West India Dock Road and take the right-hand turn ack under the railway. In Garford Street note on the right the **Dock onstables' Cottages**, a rare piece of domestic architecture by the engineer hn Rennie (1802), still nestling dark and cosy in their pretty front gardens nongst the glowing apartments all around. The scene is a fitting introduction what is to come.

istory

In the 18C Britain's overseas trade increased so dramatically that by the end of the century congestion of shipping on the Thames in London was creating impossible problems. Few ships could get past the traffic-jams up to the Custom House or to reach the Legal Quays in front where customs' duty had to be paid. Unloaded cargoes were subject to pillage before they began to rot away, a difficulty that led to the setting up of the first river police force (Chapter 47).

The long-term solution was to construct deep-water docks in the little-populated marshy areas east of the City. Over the 30 years from 1798 different-ent consortia, in competition with each other, dug out docks for themselves in the Isle of Dogs, Wapping, Rotherhithe, Blackwall and at St Katharine's, and enclosed them within high walls. Each dock specialised in a particular section of trade. West India Dock, the first to be completed in 1802, handled sugar, rum and molasses from the Caribbean Islands and other Atlantic trade, including the Canaries (hence Canary Wharf). The London Docks in Wapping took trade from other warm climates, such as coffee, wine and tobacco (hence Tobacco Dock). And in Rotherhithe, the Surrey Docks (hence Surrey Quays) developed trade in timber from Scandinavia and North America (hence Canada Water). Great tea clippers like the *Cutty Sark* raced to bring their car-goes to East India Dock at Blackwall. And so the problem was solved, for a century and a half until the 1960s, when the growth of container shipping required deeper water than London could provide. Almost overnight the trade moved downstream to Tilbury. As happened at the same time in other great ports, the docks in London, dirty, smelly, bristling with masts and cranes, with their own cultures, populations and secrets, disappeared for ever.

But a renaissance has happened, allowing a separate transformation to each dockland area. A special body, the London Docklands Development Corporation, was set up to coordinate the redevelopments. Those at St Katharine's, Wapping and Rotherhithe are described in Chapters 3, 47 and 51. The most spectacular has been here at West India Dock, where after one or two false starts in the 1980s the gods of commerce now reign supreme: glittering towers, fast-moving offices, bars, shops and people have entirely dis-placed the former community. Before we get too sentimental, however, remember that it was to honour the gods of commerce that the docks were needed in the first place.

The Docklands Light Railway, which is now such a delight to tourists, was one of those false starts. It was far too small to cope with the influx of workers which the new towers would demand. Much of this problem was solved by extending the Jubilee Line—and that would never have reached here without the irresistible deadline of the Millennium and the ill-fated Dome.

Turning into Hertsmere Road, you pass on the right the *Dockmaster's House* (1807), now a pub but a building which had been through many previous transformations. Then go past the original **dock gate piers** (1809) and turn right. You are now inside what was the secure area of the West India Dock and can see straight ahead of you the giant sugar warehouses of North Quay, built by George Gwilt (1802–3).

Go to the right along Hertsmere Road. On the right, originally outside the secure area, are two buildings which were Seamen's Temperance Homes and, on the roadside, in red brick with a Doric portico, the former Port of London Authority Police Station (1914). Stay on this side of the road and go past the Guard House and right, into **Cannon Workshops**. These were originally workshops for the dock services designed by John Rennie (1825), but are now a relic of the early 1980s approach to Docklands development, small businesses establishing themselves in run-down areas—a kind of basic Thatcherism, soon overtaken by the economics of the multi-nationals. The little round building is a former guardhouse, denoting that this was the main entry through the inner wall.

Cross Hertsmere Road to enter North Quay. On the left read the wonderful stone plaque of 1800, two huge proud sentences commemorating the dock's opening. Then, also on the left, comes the Ledger building or Dock office by Rennie (1827), with a small but perfectly formed Doric portico, now the inevitable pub. In the first of the warehouses the new **Museum of Docklands** is opening in summer 2002. The museum will focus on the development of the Dockland area within the port of London as a whole, including its contemporary regeneration. Plenty of interactive displays are planned, and a shop and restaurant. ☎ 020 7001 9800.

The sugar warehouses stretch away to the east, still with their original barred windows but now all converted into restaurants and bars. On fine days everybody sits outside looking over the water which still lies in the **North Dock**, the one import dock, with the office tower beyond. Two cranes are preserved, a mockery, on the dock side. The contrasts with the past are the same as at Covent Garden, but even more telling. Here for 150 years, men lost the skin on their fingers from a lifetime of grasping and dragging the rough, leaking sacks of molasses from ships' holds into dark warehouses. Now we sip cappuccino in the sun.

Cross over the footbridge to the right. As you go get your bearings. On your left the DLR is passing through West India Quay station into Canary Wharf station, in the centre of the

One Canada Square, Canary Wharf

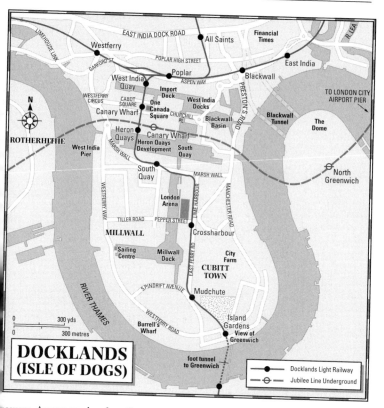

**DOCKLANDS
(ISLE OF DOGS)**

towers. As you go ahead up the steps, you are on what was once the central quay between the import and export docks, but you would never know. No more warehouses survive: the past is over.

The steps are unaccountably called Wren's Landing: at the top you cross a road and enter **Cabot Square**. There are fountains, trees defining the square shape, plenty of seats and almost always a strong wind. Look around. They call it little Manhattan, but little Chicago might be better. The co-ordinating architects for the project were SOM of Chicago, and most of the buildings you can see from here are by American architects. The northwest corner, nos 1–5 Cabot Square, built for Credit Suisse, is by I.M. Pei's firm (Pei built the pyramid at the Louvre), and the blocks in both the southwest and northeast corners are by SOM themselves. The last mentioned, no. 25, built for Morgan Stanley, is in a style based on Chicago buildings of *c* 1900, while no. 10, the most eye-catching, is supposed to be a reference to London buildings of roughly the same period, in yellow stock brick with lots of stone dressings, pediments up at penthouse level and an arcade inspired, it is said, by the Ritz in Piccadilly (which in turn was inspired by Paris). This is all very enjoyable and Postmodern, but what does it mean?

To the east, Canary Wharf's first tower, officially called **One Canada Square**, dominates the pseudo-Art Deco entrance to the shopping mall. The tower is by

Cesar Pelli, architect of the World Financial Centre in New York, to which this bears an uncanny resemblance. It was Britain's first skyscraper, and when finished in 1991 surpassed all other British towers and all but one in Europe (at Frankfurt). It has 51 storeys and is 800ft high; encased in grey stainless steel it is intended to be compatible with the English climate. As a landmark, Londoners generally have taken to it well, seeing it on the horizon as a sign of home as they drive down the M11 or up from Gatwick on the M23. Here at its foot, and as in New York, or in a Gothic cathedral, you can not help being reminded of your extreme littleness.

You can easily take a short detour west from here down West India Avenue, and it may be worth it to see the river, a reminder of origins. First you reach **Westferry Circus**, a much pleasanter green space than Cabot Square, and beyond that a viewing point over the Thames to Rotherhithe. Just to the right were Limehouse Stairs, in other words a former access point to passenger boats on the river, and an original dock entrance, although the main one was on the eastern side. Beyond, to the right, you can see the warehouse conversions of Wapping. Across the river the most prominent buildings are Columbia and Canada Wharf (1864) with its Gothic Revival windows, both former 19C granaries and now apartments. Rotherhithe was the first site in England to be used for the bulk storage of grain, by the 19C cheaper to import from Canada then to grow at home. To the left the stream bends round towards Greenwich.

Return to Cabot Square and go through into the shopping mall. You can look around at this level, or at floors below or above. Canary Wharf DLR station is up some escalators at the half-way point. There are innumerable places for coffee or other refreshment here. Keep going through the building to reach the main entrance to One Canada Square, where security will prevent you getting any further. But you can admire or deplore the opulence of the gleaming marble surfaces. Go down to basement level to emerge on the other (east) side.

Here you find yourself in **Canada Square** itself, a grassy enclave with the two newest towers before you, that on the left, rounded and cool, built for HSBC by Foster and Partners and modelled on the same firm's HSBC building in Hong Kong, and that on the right, more blocky and edgy, a further work of Cesar Pelli for Citibank. Both seem to defer in spirit to One Canada Square.

Norman Foster

Foster (b. 1935) is one of Britain's most noted contemporary architects, whose work achieved an international reputation with the Hong Kong and Shanghai Bank (HSBC) Headquarters in Hong Kong. In London, he has built Canary Wharf station, the finest of all the fine new designs for the Jubilee Line extension, and designed a giant, gherkin-shaped tower for the City, planned for the Baltic Exchange site as well as City Hall and Stansted Airport. His firm was also the architectural consultant for the Millennium Bridge. Foster's large practice has been outstanding in the amalgamation of engineering technology with aesthetic appeal.

Beyond here you could walk to Blackwall Basin and thence to an unchanged area of the old Isle of Dogs called Coldharbour. It may not be unchanged for long. This is a considerable detour and most will prefer to turn right from Pelli's tower and then down steps to the right of Citibank towards the old export dock, now alled **South Dock**. Curious clocks on posts will catch the eye and then on the left, Norman Foster's beautiful **Canary Wharf station** (Jubilee Line). If you have not travelled to it before, explore it now—there is no need to pass a ticket barrier—going down the escalators into a cavernous grey rectangle, lit from above. It shows a brave new world, brilliant but at the same time discomfiting.

Coming out again, you have a good view of the building filling the last corner of Cabot Square, no. 20, which as you now see makes an integrated composition along South Dock. It is by the American firm of Kohn Pedersen Fox (KPF). Another clearly American concoction, it proclaims its Postmodernist credentials by the extended open girders over the DLR tracks, jokingly implying that they would like to have built a continuous façade to make a tunnel for the railway.

If building works are not too intrusive, explore a little way east, under the DLR line at Heron Quays. Beyond, **Heron Quays** itself is further modest architecture of the Docklands workshop phase, coloured plum-red and very much low-rise, by Nicholas Lacey (1980s). It is made to look astonishingly dated by its surroundings. You can see, at the eastern end, a traffic-light tree (1997) and beyond, to the left, you can not miss the very much more assertive Cascades by CZWG 1985–89), unquestionably high-rise, with many nautical references such as the crow's-nest balconies. Pevsner praises Cascades' 'sense of fun' and 'delightful details', but in style terms time is not treating it kindly.

In the South Dock further great works are being undertaken. It is hoped that the fine **footbridge** to South Quay will be reinstated, and not designated too 1980s'. It is usually possible to mount the stairs to Heron Quays station to travel south of the river, towards Lewisham: Heron Quays is closed until autumn 2002 so until then you will need to return to Canary Wharf station to make this connection.

As you travel you will see, on the right of the train, **Millwall Dock**, a later creation of the 1860s, surviving as a marina. More prominent from the railway is the London Arena (1985–89) at Crossharbour, a conversion of a former shipping shed belonging to the Olsen Line. It presents regular ice shows, pop concerts and ice hockey. For details, ☎ 020 7538 1212. Then the track drops down to **Mudchute**, where you could alight to see the city farm opened in 1977. Open 09.00–16.00 daily. Admission free. ☎ 020 7515 5901. The Mudchute area is a curiosity, a landscaped park formed from the dredgings created by Millwall Dock. Just south of the station, at 197 East Ferry Road, is the **Island History Trust**, an archive of 5000 photographs of the Isle of Dogs in the 20C. Open 13.30–16.30 Tues, Wed and first Sun in each month. Admission free. ☎ 020 7987 6041.

The climax of this walk is the best river view in London after the Houses of Parliament, for which you must walk south or rejoin the DLR to alight at Island Gardens and make your way up, across Manchester Road, to the riverside. **Island Gardens** is a small park laid out by the London County Council in 1895 for the purpose it still serves: to survey Greenwich Royal Hospital across the stream. This is the only place to obtain the ideal view (to interpret it all, consult Chapter 49). Canaletto painted it from here in the 1740s, when the Isle of Dogs was no more than a marsh: his painting is sometimes on display at the Queen's House, Greenwich. As you have seen, a lot has happened since those days, but his view is unchanged.

To the right is the entrance to the **foot tunnel** to Greenwich (1900–02). You

can resume your DLR journey to Cutty Sark station there, or to go back to town
Why not satisfy the child in you and endeavour to get a front seat?

49 • Greenwich

There should be no question of missing Greenwich. If it is less 'royal' than
Hampton Court or Windsor, it has finer architecture; if it is less central than
Westminster, it is nobler; and the view of the assembly of buildings from across
the river, or from the hill in the park, stays with you for life.

As usual, this chapter is presented in the form of a walk, arriving by train, but
the circuit can be joined or abandoned at various points, depending on transport
preferences.

- Distance: 2 miles. Time: 1 hour + perhaps the rest of the day for all the sights
See map on p 397.

Travel The most scenic way to arrive is by boat (see p 497): you will find
return ticket much better value but may be frustrated by the last boat returning
as early as 17.00. If coming by train you need a travel card for Zones 1 and 2
Travel from Charing Cross (you may need to change at London Bridge) c
Cannon Street and alight at Greenwich, which is also on the Docklands Light
Railway. The walk starts at Greenwich station, but if you are coming by boat o
leave the DLR at Cutty Sark station, connect with the walk at Cutty Sark below.

Greenwich, just like Hampton or even Windsor, is essentially no more than
small riverside town for boat building and local trade, without distinction
These places were never planned as centres for royalty, as Versailles was fo
example. The palace of Placentia at Greenwich was popular with Tudor mon
archs and Henry VIII and Elizabeth I were both born there, but royalty
departed Greenwich as long ago as the 1680s. Since the decision of William
III and Mary to move their palace to Kensington, its *raison d'être* has been
naval charity, then naval education, and now, it is to be feared, only
tourism—although there are hopes that the ambience of a university town
may spread (see below). Also, the Greenwich and Docklands Festival in June
introduces a cultural theme.

The façade of **Greenwich station** (1878) is very handsome and the location is
historic as the original terminus of London's first railway line, from London
Bridge to Greenwich. Turn left along Greenwich High Road.

It is not a prepossessing start to the walk. On the right are the brick tower and
offices of the former Town Hall (1939), Scandinavian Modernism now oddly dated
Then, as you come round the bend, the giant east end of Nicholas Hawksmoor's
St Alfege (1712–48) looms into view. Alfege was an archbishop martyred by the
Danes in 1012. This is one of Hawksmoor's six great London churches, erected
under the Act of 1711 (see Chapter 45); it was justified by the fact that the for
mer building was in ruins and Greenwich had by that time a high profile, while
the Naval Hospital was being built. You can appreciate the special massiveness
and central bias of Hawksmoor's work, though less so here than elsewhere. The
tower is more delicate, a clear enough indication that it is from other hands: it
was added by John James (1730), designer of St George's Hanover Square. The
church is often open. ☎ 020 858 6828.

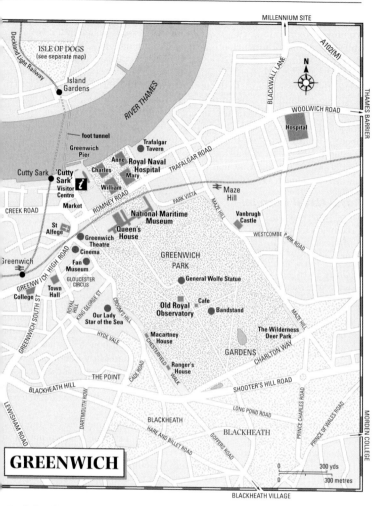

MILLENNIUM SITE

ISLE OF DOGS
(see separate map)

Island
Gardens

RIVER THAMES

Dockland Light Railway

A102(M)

BLACKWALL LANE

THAMES BARRIER

WOOLWICH ROAD

Hospital

foot tunnel

Greenwich
Pier

Trafalgar
Tavern

Anne
Charles

Royal Naval
Hospital

TRAFALGAR ROAD

Cutty Sark

'Cutty
Sark'
Visitor
Centre

Mary

William

Maze
Hill

Market

ROMNEY ROAD

PARK VISTA

MAZE HILL

CREEK ROAD

St
Alfege

National Maritime
Museum

Vanbrugh
Castle

Greenwich

Greenwich
Theatre

Cinema

Queen's
House

WESTCOMBE PARK ROAD

GREENWICH HIGH ROAD

Fan
Museum

GLOUCESTER
CIRCUS

GREENWICH

PARK

General Wolfe Statue

Town
Hall

College

GREENWICH SOUTH ST

ROYAL HILL

KING GEORGE ST

CROOM'S HILL

Our Lady
Star of the Sea

Old Royal
Observatory

Cafe

Bandstand

MAZE HILL

The Wilderness
Deer Park

HYDE VALE

Macartney
House

GARDENS

CHARLTON WAY

THE POINT

CADE ROAD

CHESTERFIELD WALK

Ranger's
House

SHOOTER'S HILL ROAD

BLACKHEATH HILL

LEWISHAM ROAD

DARTMOUTH ROW

LONG POND ROAD

PRINCE CHARLES ROAD

PRINCE OF WALES ROAD

MORDEN COLLEGE

BLACKHEATH

HARE AND BILLET ROAD

BLACKHEATH

GOFFERS ROAD

GREENWICH

0   300 yds
0   300 metres

BLACKHEATH VILLAGE

Look briefly at the churchyard—the composer Thomas Tallis (d. 1585) and General Wolfe (d. 1759) are buried here—then continue round the bend towards the river. Little shops and façades on the opposite side of the road form a square, put together in the 1830s by Joseph Kay, by that time architect to the Greenwich Hospital, with suitable street names, Nelson Road and King William Walk. In the centre of the square is a pleasant **covered market** selling 'antiques' on Thursdays and crafts and organic food at the weekend. Open 09.30–17.00 Wed–Sun and Bank Holidays. ☎ 020 7515 7153 or 020 8293 3110. There are similar goods in an open-air market off Stockwell Street at weekends.

The market used once to extend down to the river, past the DLR station, but now that space is taken up by the dry dock of the **Cutty Sark** (launched in 1869), one of the last and finest of the 19C tea clippers, laid to rest here in 1957 and a fitting memorial in many ways. An object of great beauty, the ship is very exciting to tour round, with a well-presented display, including a collection o ships' figureheads, and helpful, seadog-like attendants. Open 10.00–17.00 Admission charge. Shop. ☎ 020 8858 3445. www.cuttysark.org.uk

Very visible at the river's edge is a brick cylindrical building with a glazed dome: this is the entrance to the **foot tunnel** (1900–02) under the river to the area called Island Gardens on the Isle of Dogs (Chapter 48). Canaletto's great view of Greenwich Hospital was taken at Island Gardens: if you want to experi ence it, a walk through the tunnel (there are lifts at each end) and back take about 30 minutes, or take the DLR one stop. Alternatively, you can experience a version of this view by walking east along the riverside, from the pier or foot tunnel entrance, to halfway along the main hospital frontage, and looking south towards the Queen's House.

Royal Naval Hospital

Make your way up the east side of the *Cutty Sark* to enter what is called the Greenwich Experience, a populist term for a good display on the area as a whole with useful literature. It sells tickets for the Hospital, but the Greenwich Experience itself is free.

• Open 10.00–17.00 daily (last admission 16.15). Café. ☎ 020 8269 4744 www.greenwichfoundation.org.uk

Hospital? College? University? or Palace? This guide has adopted the term hos pital for the key group of buildings at the heart of Greenwich—meaning accommodation for pensioners, not necessarily the sick. This is how its chie architect Sir Christopher Wren thought of it, and how his buildings func tioned from the 1690s until 1869. William III and Mary intended to create here a naval hospital on the lines of the Chelsea Hospital for soldiers and Louis XIV's Invalides in Paris. As it happened, the result was grander than either because of the precedent set by the King Charles Block, which had been created as part of a new palace for Charles II.

After the Hospital closed in 1869, the buildings functioned as the Royal Naval College until the 1980s, when the Ministry of Defence moved in Meanwhile, the Queen's House and related buildings in the south became and remain, the National Maritime Museum. Now some of the former Hospital buildings have become premises for Greenwich University (including the Queen Anne block) and Trinity School of Music (the King Charles block) and others tourist attractions managed by the Greenwich Foundation.

Make your way through the exhibition space and out into the grounds of the former Hospital. The first area has been recently named Pepys House, for no obvious reason except that Samuel Pepys came here from time to time on naval business, though the new Hospital was not his department. Cross an internal road: the **Dreadnought Library** is opposite. It was the infirmary of the Hospital, built by James 'Athenian' Stuart who was surveyor here in the 1770s and is now part of Greenwich University.

Walk left until you reach the open quadrangle at the centre. As you go look a the western elevation of the building to the right, called the King William Block the massive forms indicate the work of Hawksmoor, it is thought, but could be that of Sir John Vanbrugh, who was surveyor here at the time.

In the quadrangle pause and look around. As you face the river, on your left is the **King Charles Block**, the first to go up as part of that monarch's intended new palace, by the architect John Webb (1661–69). On the right, designed to match it but within the conception of a hospital, is the **Queen Anne Block**, begun in 1699. A statue of *George II* (1735) by J.M. Rysbrack stands, irrelevantly, in the centre. Turn round and look south: up the hill in the park, to the right, is the Royal Observatory and in the foreground are two domed and colonnaded buildings, the **Queen Mary Block** to the left and **King William Block** to the right, both by Wren. In the centre, diminutive but important as we shall explain, the little Queen's House bravely makes its own un-naval statement. Dr Johnson later said this architectural ensemble was all too magnificent for charity: you can see what he meant, but it has no equal in London.

On the right in the King William Block is the **Painted Hall**. Designed by Wren it is a genuinely Baroque creation, with space at three levels separated by stairs, and overpowering art: 'the most effective piece of Baroque painting by any English artist, grand, abundant, and of a perfectly easy flow' (Pevsner). The artist was Sir James Thornhill, William Hogarth's father-in-law. At the bottom right-hand of the furthest wall he recorded himself, with hand proffered as if for payment: certainly the Hospital took a long time to settle up. The themes of the painting are royal celebrations: William and Mary appear in the main ceiling handing peace and liberty to Europe; Anne and her husband Prince George of Denmark are depicted in the ceiling of the Upper Hall, while the walls below show the arrival of George I and his family in 1714. The body of Nelson lay in state here in 1805.

The Hall was judged too grand for the naval pensioners, who normally had to eat in the vault below. To this you will now descend and pass through a linking underground passage, the Chalk Walk, to a similar vault under the Queen Mary Block. Here a display of replica crown jewels from around the world is set out. Proceed up the stairs to see the **Chapel**, where a tape of religious music is likely to be playing—tacky but not entirely incongruous. You will immediately be struck by the contrast in style: compared with the bombast of the Hall it is refined, delicate, flat, we might even say 'feminine', indicating a later date. Indeed it was rebuilt in the 1770s, after a fire. This was during James Stuart's surveyorship but the design is attributed to William Newton, his Clerk of Works. A large painting of *St Paul and the Viper* by Benjamin West is above the altar. The pulpit is exceptionally exquisite.

When you leave, see if you can gain entry to either of the inner quadrangles of the Queen Mary or King William Blocks; these are worth seeing, especially that in the King William Block, by Hawksmoor again, but they are usually roped off.

If you need refreshment go east to visit the recommended *Trafalgar Tavern* facing the river, by architect Joseph Kay (1837), associated with Dickens and once famous for its whitebait dinners: these little fish are now reputed to be venturing up the Thames again. If not immediately heading south, across Romney Road, see Trinity Hospital just to the east, an establishment of 'Gothick' almshouses rebuilt in 1812.

The original line of Romney Road, which goes east to Woolwich (see below), marked the division of the palace from the park, and the Queen's House, most peculiarly, was originally built as a bridge over it. In 1693 the road was rerouted to where you see it, marking a new division between the Hospital and the other spaces. They were re-integrated in 1807–12, visually at least, when the colonnades either side of the Queen's House were added by Daniel Alexander, leading to new wings to accommodate schools for the children of pensioners and serving naval men—now the National Maritime Museum.

National Maritime Museum, Queen's House

Cross the road to visit the National Maritime Museum and the Queen's House, which is now used to present part of the Museum's fine collection of paintings.

- Open 10.00–17.00. Admission free. Café/restaurant. Shops. Library.
  ☎ 020 8858 6565. www.nmm.ac.uk

The **Queen's House** is a surviving palace building dating back to the period of royal usage. It was a late addition to the palace of Placentia.

Architecturally, it is a seminal building. Inigo Jones (Chapter 12) returned from Italy in 1614 having fully absorbed not only the architectural principles of Palladio but also the ideology of the country villa, to which a gentleman could escape from the stresses of town. It was these twin themes which he imported for James I's queen, Anne of Denmark, in 1616, bringing Classical architecture to London. Its main public demonstration had to await the completion of the Banqueting House in the centre of London and it took a generation longer to catch on. But the Queen's House was the first product of 300 years of Classical building in England.

The Queen's House, Greenwich

It has been changed quite a lot. John Webb added the wings either side in the 1660s, broadening the bridge across the road. Stucco was used to cover the upper floors, which were originally limewashed brick. But the Palladian ideas are easy to see: rustication, the central bays projecting forwards, a curved staircase from the modest basement entrance, carefully proportioned windows (although the originals were casements) and a balustrade round the roof level. Go round to see the loggia at first-floor level on the south side, with Ionic columns. The building was finished for another queen, Henrietta Maria, wife of Charles I, in 1637 and some of the most 'Palladian' features may have been introduced at the second stage of the building, and are therefore later than the Banqueting House.

Although the interior cannot now be viewed as a furnished space, the proportions of Jones's design can be admired: there is a cubic hall on the north side of the 'road' and to the east a spiral staircase, with a 'tulip' motif, cantilevered and therefore free of supports. There are state rooms on the first floor, formerly a drawing room to the east and a bedroom to the west. Henrietta Maria occupied this accommodation when she returned to England on the restoration of her son as monarch in 1660: you can see her monogram in the ceiling of the drawing room.

The rest of the **National Maritime Museum** is entered usually from the

orth, to the west of the Queen's House. The museum was refurbished and imaginatively re-presented in 1999, with a glass roof over the central Neptune Court
y Rick Mather. It offers a rich series of exhibits on Britain's maritime history.

Take a free ground plan to find your way around. The organisation of space in
ne museum consists of a central structure, surrounded by 'streets', East, South
nd West around three sides. The outer sides of the streets contain galleries at
three levels and a centre of two levels, of which the higher is called Upper Court.
Above South Street, overlooking all, is the reconstructed stern of the last ship-of-
ne-line, *Implacable*, captured from the French at Trafalgar (1805) and in the
ritish service until scuttled in 1949.

At level 1 both sides of East Street (Galleries 3 and 8) commemorate **Explorers**,
ext to them (9) is a display of naval uniforms and (10), of particular interest here,
n audio-visual display on **Maritime London**. A connected exhibit, in South
treet, is the Rococo barge designed by William Kent for Frederick Prince of Wales
1732). Off West Street are galleries on trade (**Cargoes**) and the submarine.

At level 2, the Upper Court looks to the future of the sea, assessing such worry-
ng subjects as pollution and global warming. The sea already covers 71 per cent
f the planet. How much more will it take? The **Global Garden** (11) tells the
tory of the globalisation of plants, thanks initially to people like Captain Cook
nd Sir Joseph Banks. A bridge leads across to 19, **Art and the Sea**, part of the
useum's rich holdings of the visual arts, including film, and round the corner
o 16, **Trade and Empire**, which doesn't hesitate to tackle slavery. Stairs lead
o 14, a search station where you have computer access to details of the collec-
on increasingly visitors' first port of call when seeing specific information at
arge museums.

Now you go up to level 3, where there are special exhibits in 22, inter-active
isplays, for children primarily, in 21 (sail a Viking long boat) and 25 'All
ands': fire a gun, etc, and a more serious consideration of War at Sea in 24. Do
ot miss 23, through separate stairs, the gallery devoted to **Nelson**, including
ne uniform he was wearing when killed at Trafalgar. Finally, it is downstairs in
nis block to see **Seapower** and so into the pleasant café which in turn leads
nto the Park.

Old Royal Observatory

eave by the south exit and make your way into **Greenwich Park** (see also
hapter 50). Straight ahead of you is a steep slope that rises to the **Old Royal
Observatory**. If you climb up the path in front of the shrubs, with railings either
de, you cross the prime meridian, but you can see it more precisely if you
xplore inside.

Open 10.00–17.00. Admission free. Shop. ☎ 020 8312 4422. www.rog.nmm.ac.uk

Wren was the architect of the original dual-purpose building in 1675–76:
the two requirements were an observatory for the measurement of the stars
and living accommodation for the 'observator', with 'a little for pompe', as
the architect put it. But only a little: it was very economically done, and the
apparently stone quoins, for example, are made of wood. Charles II sponsored
the venture due to the pressing need to learn how to measure longitude, a
problem not fully solved for another 100 years. The first Astronomer Royal,
John Flamsteed, occupied the observatory from 1676 until 1719, hence its

name, Flamsteed House. He never discovered longitude but his achievement did lead, as recently as 1884, to the choice of Greenwich for the prime meridian, longitude 0°, the division between the eastern and western hemispheres—a division you can straddle, and be photographed on, just inside.

The observatory was added to in the 1870s and 1890s—in the separate 1893 building a planetarium is shown—but in the 1950s the actual task of observing the stars was transferred to Herstmonceux in Sussex.

Even so, this is an evocative and important place. The tour begins with a display on Flamsteed's occupation of the domestic rooms, all appropriately modest. You then mount the stairs to the **Octagon Room**, a more prestigious space probably intended for important visitors as well as day to day observation of the stars. There are portraits of Charles II and James II, and Thomas Tompion's clocks of 1676, each with a 13ft pendulum; they require winding only once a year.

A related function at Greenwich, associated with defining longitude and the meridian, has been the accurate measurement of time, which began with the installation of Tompion's clocks. The first visible symbol of 'Greenwich Time' was the ball on one of the exterior towers of Flamsteed House, installed in 1833 and programmed to drop from the top to the bottom of its shaft at 13.00 hours daily for the benefit of ships in the Thames to set their chronometers. Greenwich Time is commemorated every day with the 'six-pip' time signal on the BBC, launched in 1924. Downstairs again to an absorbing display of John Harrison's first four chronometers and other evidence of the longitude saga.

> ### John Harrison
> An unsung hero until the publication of Dava Sobel's book *Longitude* (1998), clockmaker Harrison (1693–1776) struggled to satisfy the requirements of a specially established committee to encourage research into the measurement of longitude. The challenge was to devise a clock that, despite the motion of the sea, still told the time accurately. With such a clock, a seaman could check his local position, by the sun and stars, against a known time on a fixed meridian such as Greenwich, and thus measure how far east or west he was. Until this was achieved, there were many wrecks, and their numbers increased as vessels became faster. Finally, in 1763, Harrison convinced the committee with a clock with an error of only five seconds between London and Jamaica. But they did not pay him the prize money for another ten years.

Beyond, across the grass outside Flamsteed House are further buildings constructed later as the official definition of the meridian moved marginally eastward. Successive Astronomers Royal were intent on setting up more accurate instruments to measure the stars. You are able to observe these and admire their engineering, finally reaching a useful shop and the exit. To the south (right) lie the separate observatory buildings referred to above. To the left—you will have already noticed it—in front of the statue of General Wolfe by Tait Mackenzie (1930; see Chapter 50), is a spectacular view of the Thames with the City to the left, Docklands straight ahead, and the Millennium Dome, designed by Richard Rogers (1999) to the right. At the time of writing the fate of the Dome is unclear. Whatever the retrospective view of the Millennium experience itself, the structure more than simply eye-catching: it is powerful and imaginative. But it was never intended to be permanent, so if it cannot find a role, London will shed no tears.

You may like to explore the park further: it is attractively laid out, and well planted and maintained. The last phase of the walk takes you to the foot of **Croom's Hill** on the western side. The upper parts of Croom's Hill are covered in chapter 50 and are worth exploring, especially the Ranger's House, but down here at the foot, note the **Greenwich Theatre** (1871). For details and bookings, ☎ 020 8858 7755.

Opposite at no. 12 is the small, and unique, **Fan Museum**, devoted to a collection of 3000 fans. These are worth seeing, but a bonus is the opportunity to explore the excellently restored interior of an 18C town house. Open 11.00–17.00 Tues–Sat; 12.00–17.00 Sun. Admission charge. ☎ 020 8858 7879. www.fan-museum.org

A few yards up the hill from the Fan Museum, turn right into **Gloucester Circus**. The south side is an indication of the quality of housing Greenwich aimed for in its 18C naval heyday: this development was by Michael Searles (1791). Go through it to cross **Royal Hill**, a very pretty street with a couple of nice pubs and small houses, more the sort of domestic housing Greenwich finished up with, but no less appealing. Just up Royal Hill, turn right into Circus Street, which has similar housing, as do the streets off to the south.

Turn right into Greenwich South Street, then left and you are back at the station. If you are returning to a boat, the DLR or a bus, turn right down the High Road to reach the town centre again.

East of Greenwich down the straight route formed by Romney, Trafalgar and Woolwich roads lies **Woolwich**, important historically because of its former naval and military associations, and now because of a new defensive measure, the **Thames Barrier**. You can take a boat or a 177 or 180 bus there from Greenwich. Erected in 1974–82 to protect London from increasingly high surge tides, the barrier is extremely advanced engineering: the visible supports operate huge rotating gates out of sight under the water. A visitors' centre explains it all. Open 10.30–16.30 in summer; 11.00–15.30 in winter. Admission charge. Shop. ☎ 020 8305 4188. www.environment-agency.gov.uk

Nearby, and also worth visiting, is a lively new-ish museum in the historic Royal Arsenal, called **Firepower** and recounting the history of artillery from Roman times to the present day. It is interesting, although inclined to make war sound like jolly good fun. Open 10.00–17.00 daily. Admission charge. Café. Shop. ☎ 020 8855 7755. www.firepower.org.uk

Finally, to the west of Greenwich (take a 188 or 199 bus) lies the historic shipbuilding centre of **Deptford**, where Henry VIII founded the British navy and the Royal Naval Dockyard. There is still some evidence of the 18C victualling yards. But the greater reason to visit Deptford is Thomas Archer's Baroque masterpiece, **St Paul's** (1713), towering above its now decrepit surroundings. Albury Street, to the north, gives an idea of Deptford's long-lost respectability. The 188 bus will return you to town.

50 • Blackheath

Blackheath itself is a windswept open space criss-crossed by roads and feels we[l]
named on a cold, cloudy day. But in summer, when the sun shines, kites are alo[ft]
and cricket is peacefully played, the views over London make it lovely. The mos[t]
important feature of the village is the exceptional domestic architecture of i[ts]
houses, terraces and streets which established themselves round the edges of th[e]
heath from the 1790s. In reasonable weather this will be a delightful walk. [It]
could be combined with adjacent Greenwich (Chapter 49) but this is not recom[-]
mended, as Greenwich is a major site.

• Distance: 4 miles. Time: 2½ hours + more time for Ranger's House. Off map

Travel Take a train from Charing Cross or London Bridge to Blackheath, ever[y]
30 minutes; you will be returning from Lewisham, on the same line but wit[h]
more frequent trains. For train times, ☎ 08457 48 49 50.

As you emerge from the station you get the feeling of being in a village, a dens[e]
and crowded village certainly, but very much of non-urban dimensions. Th[e]
station itself is of 1848, in yellow stock brick, typical of the early railways. Th[e]
busy street runs in front and rising to left and right. First explore to the left, roun[d]
the triangle of Tranquil Vale, Royal Parade and Montpelier Vale. There are man[y]
small shops and restaurants to enjoy here if not many signs of early 19C buil[d-]
ings, although these can be re-imagined from the scale of the whole area an[d]
evidence behind the shop fronts.

Go up **Tranquil Vale** to where the shops end and the heath begins. On the le[ft]
is Grotes Place and other small-scale developments of the late 18C, attractive[ly]
sited to face the heath. To the right are more shops and, across the road, dom[i-]
nating the grassland beyond, **All Saints**, built by A.W.N. Pugin's pupil Benjami[n]
Ferrey (1857–67) and therefore in standard Gothic Revival style. It was aligne[d]
with the Wolfe statue in Greenwich Park and the Queen's House beyond.

Turn right again down the hill and back past the station to explore the su[r-]
roundings of Blackheath Village. First, ascending the hill on the south side of th[e]
station, turn briefly left into Cresswell Park, where there are some tall Georgia[n]
houses and further down, the **Presbytery**. This was the first major house in th[e]
then new Blackheath Park, a substantial estate developed from the 1780s, some[-]
times called the Cator estate after the owner at the time.

Go on up the hill, then fork left into Village Road. On the bend are some heav[y]
late 19C red-brick buildings, in non-delicate Arts and Crafts style, still housin[g]
local cultural institutions—all very worthy and characteristic of the period–
including an art school, the music conservatoire and a large concert hall. Fo[r]
information about events at **Blackheath Halls**, ☎ 020 8463 010[0]
www.blackheathhalls.com

Next on the left is **Blackheath Park**. Turn down it to see a model of how t[o]
merge mid-20C with early 19C housing. The original lay-out of the Cator esta[te]
left many large gardens and other tempting gaps of unbuilt land, irresistible t[o]
20C developers, and there was considerable bomb damage in the area durin[g]
the Second World War. The combination of Georgian terraces or villas wit[h]
later work, especially the distinctive white weather-boarded Span developmen[ts]
of the 1950s and 1960s, is remarkable successful. There is a Span block on th[e]

right-hand corner of Blackheath Park, to give you an idea what to look for.

Go as far as Pond Road. The estate continues, just as attractively, down Foxes Dale to the right, to explore if you wish, but our route is to the left. Do not miss the painfully thin, Gothic church of **St Michael** on the corner, built by George Smith (1826–29), before the Gothic Revival. Pugin would not have liked it but you will, with its needle sharp, historically inaccurate, brilliantly delicate spire.

Pond Road crosses the railway—peep over the wall to the right to see the tracks in their deep cutting curving in two directions like a toy lay-out. There is an open green space on your right and some rather institutional looking mid-20C blocks, certainly not a success. Go up the hill to reach South Row, with the heath beyond: there is a pond to the left and opposite it, on your side, **Colonnade House** by Michael Searles (1804), a notable South London architect of the period. Searles also built Paragon House on the corner to your right: if you find yourself admiring the doorcase in Pond Road, you will not be surprised to learn it was brought here from the Adam brothers' demolished Adelphi (Chapter 10).

Turn right and right again into the **Paragon** itself, the finest terrace in Blackheath, again by Searles (1794–1807), masking the northern boundary of the Cator estate. It has a distinct and unusual rhythm: tall semi-detached blocks are interspersed with ground-level colonnaded pairings, containing the front doors, accessed by steps over the areas. It has all now been converted into flats but still looks achingly beautiful and original.

Go to the end, down a little slope, to face the entrance to **Morden College**. The boards say 'No public admission' but you can get a closer view of this most interesting place by going down a footpath just to the left, which winds through the grounds. It was built as, and still is, an almshouse, once for 'decayed Turkey merchants', elderly importers of Middle Eastern products. The sponsor in 1695 was Sir John Morden and the builder Edward Strong, one of Sir Christopher Wren's favourite practitioners. The architect is not known but could have been the great man himself; the building's quality makes the attribution reasonable enough. The statues in the pediment are of the founder and his wife. The gardens are always beautifully tended.

Return to St German's Place and go north. There are some nice early 19C houses here: many are semis sharing a pediment, rather a pleasing idea of which there are numerous examples in this area, but few elsewhere. The heath stretches away on your left. It is easy to imagine it as a place for assembling troops, or groups, and so it often was. Wat Tyler's peasant rebels assembled here in 1381 (see Chapter 29), as did Jack Cade's 40,000 followers in 1450. Today it is the starting point of the London Marathon each April (see Calendar).

Cross over Prince of Wales Road and the busy Shooter's Hill. Then take Maze Hill and cross Charlton Road. (**Charlton House**, about one mile to the east from here, is an important Jacobean survival, extremely rare this near London: it has a west front of remarkable extravagance.) We are going to take the entry into Greenwich Park on the left, but if you are energetic enough for a short detour an interesting building lies a little further down Maze Hill on the right. **Vanbrugh Castle** was built by Sir John Vanbrugh for his own use: he lived in it from 1719 until his death seven years later. He was surveyor to Greenwich Hospital at the time. It is a strange, not very appealing, Gothic pastiche in yellow brick, but presumably he liked it: compared with his great buildings it seems crude. There is another park entry opposite.

Sir John Vanbrugh

Son of a Flemish refugee, Vanbrugh (1664–1726) was born in London and brought up as a gentleman. A man of many parts, he was first an army officer: arrested as a spy, he was imprisoned in the Bastille. Then he became a dramatist, writing *The Relapse* in 1696 and *The Provok'd Wife* in 1697. Finally he was an architect, working on Castle Howard in Yorkshire from 1699 and on Blenheim Palace in Oxfordshire from 1705. He had no training in architecture and perceived buildings in a wholly theatrical or scenic way—unlike Inigo Jones, who also worked on theatre designs—and relied heavily, it is thought, on Nicholas Hawksmoor for technical advice. His Greenwich excursions into Gothic can be seen as crucial in the way this national style 'hung on' during the 18C and came to incorporate the romantic overtones seen in the Houses of Parliament, for example.

Now go into **Greenwich Park**. The northern half, which contains the Ol Royal Observatory and abuts the Queen's House, is explored in Chapter 49. Th is the southern part, on higher ground.

Like other royal parks, Greenwich was formerly a hunting ground, attache to the palace of Placentia. It was the first to be enclosed and designated park, in 1433, when the land belonged to Henry V's brother Humphrey, Duk of Gloucester. The present wall dates from James I's time. Twice a year, a spec tacular fair used to be held in the park, but it became too riotous and wa closed in 1857.

There are still deer here but they are now confined to The Wilderness. There ar also the (invisible) remains of a Roman temple, Anglo-Saxon barrows, Victorian bandstand and, of course, the Royal Observatory. Cross the park fro either of the gates mentioned, walking westwards. Note a plan at the entranc The Wilderness and Flower Garden will be to your left and the Observatory your right: you may want to locate the statue of *General James Wolfe* at th northern end of Blackheath Avenue, to enjoy the view, or visit the Observator There is a place for refreshments by the new observatory building (1897), whic houses a planetarium. Then continue along the avenue of trees towards Croon Hill Gate.

Leaving the park, turn left up Chesterfield Walk. First you pass **Macartne House**, a jumble of buildings, some of them late 17C: it was the home of Gener Wolfe's father and the place where his body rested on its return from Quebe Soon you reach a bowling green on your right and on the left, the **Ranger House** (1700), grandly facing west, with Venetian windows and a cupola. It wa occupied in the 18C by the Earl of Chesterfield, celebrated for his letters to h son, who added the galleries. The house was so-named from 1815, as the res dence of the Ranger of the Park, an ancient but largely honorary appointmen The collection of portraits which used to be housed here has now been broke up, but the interior is to be filled with the Wernher Collection of furnitur tapestries, silver and other artefacts. It is now managed by English Heritag Open 10.00–18.00 Wed–Sun. Shop. Study centre for building material an techniques, open by appointment only. ☎ 020 8853 0035. www.englisl heritage. org.uk

General James Wolfe

Wolfe (1727–59) was a colourful professional soldier promoted to major-general very young by William Pitt the Elder. His great assault on Quebec in 1759 turned the course of the war with France, the climax of an *annus mirabilis* of English victories. His military tactics were questionable but undeniably successful and his heroic death at the age of 32 assured his lasting fame. He said he would rather have been the author of Gray's *Elegy* than the victor at Quebec. He is buried in St Alfege's church in Greenwich.

After this, explore the terraces on the west side of the heath before descending to go back to town. Turn right out of Ranger's House down Crooms Hill, going past some spectacular houses including the **Manor House** (1695), facing the heath. Going downhill, note no. 68, five bays wide (1692), and beyond the church, the remarkable no. 66 with the ornate rubbed brickwork of its period (1630s), known as Artisan Mannerist. Between these two is a high-powered Gothic Revival Roman Catholic church, **Our Lady Star of the Sea**, by William Wardell (1851), an acolyte of Pugin, its chancel and a chapel decorated by Pugin himself.

Keep going past a gazebo outside the **Grange** (no. 52, various dates), supposedly by Robert Hooke, Wren's deputy in the rebuilding of the City after the Great Fire. Turn left into King George Street, which is much more modest, with little terraced houses either side to serve the grand folk round about. This leads to the grander terraces in Hyde Vale (third left), which you ascend. Detour round Diamond Terrace to the right. Gradually you climb back to the Heath. Turn right at Westgrove Lane to reach The Point, an open space, with **West Grove**, an 18C house. Underneath this, in the 18C, gravel famous for its quality was removed—and even, it is said, sold to Louis XIV for use at Versailles.

Cross over Shooter's Hill Road again and walk south down **Dartmouth Row**. There are more fine houses here, some dating from the late 17C (nos 20–22). Nos 24–26 are early 20C Arts and Crafts, perhaps coming as a relief after so much Georgian correctness and reminding you, for the first time today, that English architecture can sometimes be warm, cosy and comforting. On the left, nos 21–23 (1688) are quite spectacular, with keystone heads: they are followed by the more intimate Church of the Ascension (originally late 17C) on the left, then Dartmouth House (1750).

Go past a tongue of the heath on the left, your last sight of it, and depressing Victorian villas on the right, down Lewisham Hill into Lewisham Road. You are undoubtedly back in the modern world, if not civilisation, with Citibank's offices stretching up beyond the railway bridge, Tesco's brimming with customers to the right, and a massive, confusing roundabout packed with buses. You are in **Lewisham**.

Turn right, and right again and you will find the station. Your ticket takes you back to Charing Cross, but if you have a Zone 2 travel card you could enjoy going on the DLR to Bank or Tower Gateway (get a front seat).

51 • Rotherhithe

Like the rest of the former dock areas, Rotherhithe was transformed in the 1980s (Chapter 48). The creation of the docks had itself been a transformation, though less dramatic here because of the existence of Tudor shipyards in Deptford, adjacent to the south. Before that, Rotherhithe had been a maritime riverside village with very distinct and distinguished historical associations. Evidence of these three existences, each with its own charms, can be seen on this walk.

• Distance: 4 miles. Time: 2 hours. Tube: Canada Water. Off map.

Begin in the immediate present by disembarking at Canada Water, one of the new Jubilee Line's best stations: its architect is Ron Herron. Take the exit to Lower Road, and look across Canada Water itself—wildfowl and islands, surviving capstans and anchors—to the Surrey Quays shopping centre. Our circuit will end on the other side of these disappointing monuments to late 20C commerce.

> Rotherhithe was known as Redriff, a combination of two Saxon words for mariner and haven. The *Mayflower* sailed from here in 1620, to create the first English permanent settlement in North America. Jonathan Swift's Gulliver was born here and Samuel Pepys was a regular visitor in his capacity as a naval administrator. The first wet dock in London was opened in 1697 by John Howland, with funds obtained by the marriage of his daughter to the Marquess of Tavistock, one of the Russell family. It became the Greenland Dock, used by whalers, and still exists. From 1801 the whole area was developed as the Surrey Commercial Docks, comprising at its peak nine docks, six timber ponds and a canal. Scandinavia, the Baltic and North America were the main destinations for ships leaving Rotherhithe, and the Surrey dockers were a distinct breed, with their own slang and special hats for carrying planks of wood. The docks were closed in 1970 and were filled in and rebuilt over the next 15 years.

Walk away from the water and shops towards the clock tower of the former **Dock Manager's Office** (1887). Opposite is a small park: go through into Moodkee Street, with 1920s council flats, and right into Neptune Street, round to Albion Street. A pretty copper spire topped by a Viking ship weathervane will immediately catch your eye: this is the **Norwegian Seamen's Church** by J.L Seaton Dahl (1925). Open 12.00–22.00 for the use of Norwegians in port. It is a friendly place, with good 19C stained glass from an earlier church. The small complex is called St Olav's Square.

Keep going down Albion Street. Next is the **Finnish Seamen's Church**, assertively Modernist in style, by Cyril Sjöström (1954). Open 15.00–21.30 for the use of Finns in port. The same architect designed the brick civic buildings opposite, with a statue of a musician by Tommy Steele himself (a local), in the centre

Next on the left, you could take vertiginous steps down to see the **Rotherhithe Tunnel** opened in 1908: it is for road traffic, do not venture in. Proceed at the higher level by crossing Brunel Road and, keeping Rotherhithe station on your left, go along to the chimney of a much more exciting tunnel, still in use and commemorated here by its engine house. Open as a museum 13.00–17.00 Sat and Sun April–Oct, Sun only in winter. ☎ 020 7231 3840. Marc Brunel

Thames Tunnel, begun in 1825, was, as the plaque proclaims, 'the first thoroughfare under a navigable river in the world'. (For more detail, see Chapter 47.)

Now you have reached the western end of Rotherhithe Street, one of London's longest streets and once one of its most memorable, with warehouses and water either side. The site ahead of you is filled by new Postmodern apartments by CZWG. Make a detour to the left—past the *Mayflower* pub, first built in 1553: the present building is only a copy—to explore the old riverside village. Its close connections with the USA—in 1618 the Pilgrim Fathers set out from here in the *Mayflower*, under the command of local mariner Christopher Jones, who is buried in the church on the left—mean that the pub is licensed to sell American stamps (and beer, too). The church is reached later.

> ### Pilgrim Fathers
> The Pilgrim Fathers were the leaders of the Plymouth settlement on Cape Cod, Virginia. As religious dissidents they had first left Nottinghamshire to settle at Leiden, Holland, but in 1620 decided to sail to America, many embarking from Rotherhithe in the *Mayflower*. A self-governing covenant was signed on board on 21 November 1620, forming the basis for the new state constitution. The first Thanksgiving for the Pilgrims' survival was held a year later.

A short distance beyond the pub you encounter the first of many views of the river. Opposite are the wharves of Wapping, mostly converted into apartments. Tower Bridge is far to the left. Take in the view, and the smell, and reflect on the deathly hush and emptiness after centuries of hubbub and congested toil. Keep going west past **Prince's Stairs** and **King's Stairs Gardens**: most of the stairs on the river no longer exist but were places, between the wharves, where the public could embark on ferries or other craft. When the river was London's main highway, from Roman times to the 19C, river stairs were the equivalent of bus stops. Prince's Tower is now simply Riverside Apartments, fine late Modernism by Troughton McAslan (1986–90).

Just beyond the *Angel* pub, another riverside inn that is not as old as it looks, on the left is an unusual survival, the remains of a medieval moated **manor house** rediscovered in 1902. It has been identified as belonging to Edward III from 1353, and originally had a hall, kitchen, chamber, gatehouse and garden. Storyboards round the site, reasonably free of graffiti, tell the tale. Following the circuit, make your way back along Paradise Street through King's Stairs Gardens, past a children's playground and St Peter, a Roman Catholic church (1902). The path through the flats is called Cottle Way and emerges beside the *Ship*, a pub (1920s) more typical than the imitations by the river. Go back up to the parish church of St Mary and its surrounding buildings, including the **Charity School** (rebuilt 1746), with figures of school children, and the **Watch House** (1821).

The church of **St Mary** is the rebuilding of a medieval structure by John Jones (1714–15): compare his St George's Hanover Square (Chapter 19). The fine tower is later (1746), with the spire above. The interior—the church may be open—was restored by William Butterfield in the 1870s but has largely recovered. The reredos is by Joseph Wade, King's Carver at the Deptford shipyard, and the table in the Epiphany Chapel is formed from the timber of the *Téméraire*,

finally broken up at Rotherhithe and the subject of J.M.W. Turner's masterpiec
in the National Gallery.

Just south of the church is the interesting **Rotherhithe Picture Research
Library**, established by a local filming company but for general public use. Ope
10.30–16.00 Mon–Fri. ☎ 020 7231 2209. It contains a vast range of historica
images useful for publication or just browing.

Then return, past the Mayflower, and past no. 135 Rotherhithe Street, a sur
viving barge-repair workshop, to the **Thames Path**, which now takes you eas
for a stretch of river views. The housing on the right is all new, typical of the post
wharf, post-commercial Thames world, not unattractive to look at and certainl
pleasant to live in, but enfeebled in spirit. Soon you reach a Rotherhithe Tunne
airshaft and beyond that **Surrey Lock**, an 1860 entrance to the former dock
partly filled in in the 1980s, but incorporating the original lock gates and a lift
ing bridge. Beyond is the *Spice Island* bar and restaurant and beyond that a
architecturally notable youth hostel (1989–92).

Opposite, across the river, the architecture is more dynamic, but is it a
improvement? The red Lego bricks randomly arranged certainly relieve th
tedium, but are too dominating: they represent the apartments of Free Trad
Wharf, Wapping, by Holder Mathias Alcock (1985–87). The riverside path o
the south side continues, intermittently, with the tamer kind of development.
you decide to go that way you will reach the **Lavender Pumphouse** (1928
housing a local history museum. Open 10.00–15.00, but irregularly. ☎ 02
7231 2976. The Lavender Pond was a timber store for Surrey Docks and ha
been converted into a pretty garden. The river path ends and you will need to us
Rotherhithe Street, past Nelson Dock and **Nelson House**, a shipbuilder's man
sion (1730), both part of a Holiday Inn hotel. After that comes the city farn
described below.

A more vivid impression of the change in Rotherhithe is achieved by turnin
inland at Surrey Lock, under Salters Road, to see, first, **Surrey Water**, converte
from the old Surrey Dock. Keep left and reach Gunwhale Close, then right an
immediately left up Dock Hill Avenue. These new streets are all part of the 198C
infilling and public re-housing programme—less grand than the private riversid
apartments, somewhat scruffier but more homely. Dock Hill Avenue leads into
small park and up the newly created **Stave Hill**. Ascend to the top and loo
around. In the centre of the small summit is an iron model of the old pattern c
docks: compare each perspective with the present. From here the present has it
virtues too, in the form of an exhilarating panorama. Straight to the north is th
top of Nicholas Hawksmoor's St Anne's Limehouse (Chapter 46). To the east ar
Docklands and Canada Square and in the foreground, Cascades (Chapter 48). T
the south you can see the Crystal Palace radio mast and to the west the Londo
Eye and Tower Bridge, St Paul's Cathedral and the Telecom Tower.

Look out, to the east, for a straight-edged path, clearly visible from the sum
mit, and then descend to follow it southwest. The path is straight because it fol
lows the original granite edge of the former Russia Dock. All around is th
newly constructed Ecological Park: it could be pleasant and attractive, bu
seems down-at-heel already. Go out of the park to the east, under or across th
new Salters Road to reconnect with the east end of Rotherhithe Street if you wis
to see the **Surrey Docks City Farm**, a good collection of domestic animals an
attractively laid out gardens (1986–90). Open 10.00–17.00 Tues–Sun; close

Fri in school holidays, sometimes closed for lunch, 13.00–14.00. Admission charge. Café. Shop. ☎ 020 7237 6525.

After the farm, leave Salters Road by Norway Gate to see **Norway Dock**, a really beautiful new waterside housing development by Shepherd Epstein (1988–96), created from one of the earliest docks in the Surreys (1813). Walk round it, either way, to reach Finland Street and Quay. You are now looking on to **Greenland Dock**, formerly Howland (see above) where scores of whalers were once moored. It is very pleasant, with facilities for water sports. Walk east to traverse the dock entrance over South Sea Street. The original swing bridges and their mechanisms have been left in place. There are many storyboards around to tell the history but most are covered with graffiti.

Go towards the river and look across to the Isle of Dogs. An original lock-keeper's cabin and tide-gauge house survive. From **Greenland Pier** you can take a boat trip to central London, but only at times to suit commuters (see p 35). Turn right into **South Dock**, originally built 1855–60, late in the overall complex, and now a marina. Go along Rope Street, its dead straight line surviving from the rope-making trades, with new and not very interesting housing all around. Then walk past the sports centre, back along Greenland Quay, the line of the Surrey Canal, turning right at the end and under the main road up to **Surrey Quays** shopping centre. Tesco's looms on the right. The shopping centre is part of the whole scheme but is 'a sad disappointment...it has a nasty temporary air and contributes little to a potentially fine urban landscape' (Pevsner). So much in Rotherhithe's history has been exciting that the ordinariness of some of the latest transformation is hard to accept.

Surrey Quays station (East London Line) is close by; or you can walk through the shopping centre back to Canada Water; or catch a 1 or 188 bus back to town.

'Villages': south and southwest

52 • Dulwich

'One of the most delightful intellectual trips which the neighbourhood of the metropolis affords', says a guidebook of 1832 about Dulwich. It is still true. The combination of fine houses, an excellent art gallery, a pleasant 1890s' park—to which, with a short walk, an unusual and recently renovated museum can be added—make this a very worthwhile excursion, enjoyable on a number of levels.

- Distance: 4 miles. Time: 2½ hours + extra time for the Gallery and Museum. Train: North Dulwich. Off map.

Travel You must brave the railway system of South London to get to Dulwich, but it is easy enough: the best route is from London Bridge to North Dulwich (Zone 2). You can also go from Victoria to West Dulwich (Zone 3), trains every

30mins. Either route takes less than 15mins. Our walk begins from North Dulwich, but West Dulwich is slightly closer to the Picture Gallery.

North Dulwich station is in a lovely leafy cutting. It is an original station, built with some pretension to grandeur by Charles Barry Jr (1866), son of the architect of the Houses of Parliament, who was the architect of Dulwich College. Its coat of arms appears on the façade. As we shall see the College has been the major influence on the development of the area, like Eton College at Eton (Chapter 73).

Turn left down Red Post Hill. If you wish to start with a detour there are areas of interest to the north, to the right. Not far away is the **Sunray Estate**, one of the most ambitious housing developments of the 'Homes fit for Heroes' campaign after the First World War, patriotically cottagey with steeply pitched roofs. Beyond that is **Denmark Hill** where John Ruskin lived from his birth until 1872: both his houses have gone but a park has been named after him. Felix Mendelssohn stayed at a house in Denmark Hill and wrote 'Spring Song' there.

John Ruskin

Born in South London, Ruskin (1819–1900) was a writer of great influence on Victorian taste in art and architecture, and to some extent social policy, too. His tastes were specific and ideal—for Venetian Gothic, for work to be done by the hands of craftsmen not machines, and for nature as the sole source of beauty. (This was the origin of his support for both J.M.W. Turner and the Pre-Raphaelites, including John Everett Millais, whom Ruskin's wife married after seven years of their own failed relationship.) His writings, even if little read today, were prodigious and influential, notably on William Morris. He was an early protagonist for education of the adult working class, among whom he acquired many admirers (see the Working Men's College—Chapter 40).

On our main route south, across the traffic lights, these presences can be felt as you walk through Victorian Dulwich: the place was already prospering in the 18C, as will be shown in our walk through the village, as it is still euphemistically known. First there are big red 19C houses on the right, with Victorian cottages visible in Gilkes Crescent to the left. Also on the left, where the road divides into Court Lane, there is an 18C burial ground with wrought-iron gates. Soon, major 18C houses (nos 57 and 59, for example) set the tone. There are also many small shops and pleasant restaurants of which you may like to take advantage, and the *Crown and Greyhound* (1895), a vulgar Victorian pub, recommended.

Soon the road forks. Go left down College Road; Dulwich Park is on your left. On the right is the **Old College** building which formed the original Dulwich College, founded by Edward Alleyn (1619), an actor who performed in Christopher Marlowe's plays and helped found the Rose Theatre (Chapter 31). The Old College is no longer part of the school, which lies further south, and the buildings have been much altered over time, although they still form a picturesque group.

Dulwich Picture Gallery

Immediately on the right is Dulwich Picture Gallery, where you should spend the next hour or two. The excellent café will provide sustenance. Open 10.00–17.0

Tues–Fri; 11.00–17.00 Sat, Sun and Bank Holidays. Admission charge (free Fri). Café. Shop. ☎ 020 8693 5254. www.dulwichpicturegallery.org.uk

The Picture Gallery is one of Sir John Soane's most cerebral works, to be enjoyed as architecture almost as much as the paintings it contains are to be enjoyed as art. It needs to be seen in the context of the Old College buildings, which was its original rationale, and how Soane conceived it in 1811. The bequest of paintings was chiefly that of Sir Francis Bourgeois, Soane's client, who had inherited them from his friend Noel Desenfans, a dealer, who had in turn collected them for the King of Poland. The commission was to create a building to house them, as part of the school, with some almshouses for elderly women and a mausoleum for Sir Francis's and Desenfans' remains. Most architects would have demurred faced with such a complex project, but Soane rose to the challenge, and the mix of mausoleum, almshouses and gallery succeeds triumphantly. The café and buildings next to it were designed recently by Rick Mather (2000).

As you go through the entrance hall and shop you are entering, as Soane intended, the central square gallery, Room III. Rectangular galleries extend left and right and beyond each is a further square gallery. These five rooms (I–V) were Soane's original hanging space: Rooms VI–IX were created out of the almshouses and Rooms X–XIII are later additions at the front. Straight ahead of you is the **mausoleum**, self-contained and decently roped off, but easily visible between Rooms III and VIII. Suitably solemn and dignified, it shows Soane's minimalist form of Classicism, once to be seen on a grand scale at the Bank of England (Chapter 1).

Room III contains 18C English portraits, notably by Sir Joshua Reynolds, including *Mrs Siddons as the Tragic Muse*, and a *Self-portrait* (1788), showing him wearing tiny glasses. **Room I** is given over to French 17C works, with Nicolas Poussin's famous *Triumph of David* (1630–33), Goliath's head gawping on David's spear, and the remote magic of Claude Lorrain's *Jacob and Laban's Daughters* (1676). **Rooms V, VI and XIII** beyond contain works by Tiepolo, Rembrandt and Bartolomé Murrillo among others. **Room XII** contains 18C European painting and a delightful early work by Thomas Gainsborough showing an unidentified couple enjoying a rest in the country (1755), and more importantly two paintings by Jean-Antoine Watteau. A special favourite is Soldi's portrait of the sculptor L.F. Roubilliac.

In the other direction, **Room II** is devoted to Peter Paul Rubens and Sir Anthony van Dyck, including the latter's *Samson and Delilah* (1619), with Delilah craftily calculating when to snip the scissors. In **Room XI** to the left is Rembrandt's *Girl at a Window*, allegedly once hung in a window and mistaken by passers-by for reality—and certainly the girl is an archetype.

Room I has some wonderfully humane Gainsborough portraits, including several of the multi-talented Lindley family. **Room IX** has Dutch landscapes, for those who like Aelbert Cuyp's cows, and **Room X** an eclectic mix of 17C English work including Sir Peter Lely's early, and surprisingly sexy, *Nymphs by a Fountain*.

Leave the Gallery gardens by the west exit, into Gallery Road, and turn left. All is pleasantly green. On the right, in a small park, is a handsome villa called *Belair*, by Richard Shaw (1785), now a restaurant. Soon you reach Thurlow Park Road and West Dulwich station.

Turn left: there are some pleasant 18C villas here and there on the left and on the right the present **Dulwich College**, spreading itself comfortably over its grounds. This ambitious rebuilding (1860s) for the Old College north of the Gallery was achieved as a result of a deal made with the railway companies, in compensation for their lines being allowed to cross the College's estates. The architect was Charles Barry Jr but there have been many later additions.

Turn right at College Road to get the full view. Do not miss, on the left, **Pond Cottages**, picturesquely grouped by the millpond. Return to the corner and walk east along Dulwich Common.

Soon, on the left, appears Queen Mary's Gate into **Dulwich Park**: the formal entrance was opposite the Picture Gallery in College Road. No route is given, so explore to the extent you are interested. There are some fine trees and azaleas and rhododendrons flowering May/June; there is also a sculpture by Barbara Hepworth, *Two Forms (Divided Circle)* (1970). The park was developed in 1890 after the College transferred the land to the new London County Council (LCC) in the late 19C flurry of enthusiasm to create new public spaces (see Chapter 53).

Leave the park by the Rosebery Gate at the southeast corner: Lord Rosebery, an ineffectual prime minister in 1894–95, was the first chairman of the LCC in 1889. Keep going along Dulwich Common: it is rather full of traffic, with soul-destroying flats on your left, but fairly soon you will spot the *Grove* public house on the left. Turn right into Lordship Lane and walk to the brow of the hill. An alternative pleasant detour, if the weather permits, is to turn right before the main road, up a private wooded footpath called Cox's Walk. This takes you into the public woodland of **Sydenham Hill Wood Nature Reserve**, a pleasant stroll (well signposted), from which you will emerge onto Sydenham Hill. Turn left and go to the roundabout, where fine views are to be seen towards Surrey or north towards London: Tower 42 (Chapter 4) can be identified, as can the all-seeing Eye.

If you were to walk south down Sydenham Hill, you would reach **Crystal Palace Park** after approximately one mile. This is certainly of interest if you enjoy 19C parks, but is not worth the tramp otherwise. It was here that Joseph Paxton's giant (1600ft long and 282ft high) modernistic wonder from the 1851 Great Exhibition in Hyde Park (Chapter 20) was rebuilt on an even larger scale in 1854, and dominated the south London skyline until 1936 when it was burned to the ground. The radio mast remains a landmark. A fine sports stadium was opened in the park in 1964, and there is a natural amphitheatre. The 19C curiosities are the archaeological remains of the Crystal Palace terraces and the 29 prehistoric monsters, made of brick and iron but stucco-covered (1854), which prowl near the lake.

From the Sydenham Hill roundabout, locate Eliot Bank and descend through LCC housing (1950s) to London Road. The **Horniman Gardens and Museum** will come into view on the opposite side. The shorter Lordship Lane route will have brought you to the same point. The museum is being widely extended to accommodate its collection of musical instruments and more interactive exhibits: this work should be completed by summer 2002. Open 10.30–17.30

Mon–Sat; 14.00–17.30 Sun. Admission free. Café. Shop. ☎ 020 8699 1872. www.horniman.demon.co.uk

The **building** by C. Harrison Townsend (1897) is an eye-catcher in itself (compare his Whitechapel Art Gallery in Chapter 45), with typical massiveness and curvy distinction, a huge mosaic by Anning Bell, and a clock tower: 'No doubt one of the boldest public buildings of its date in Britain' (Pevsner). Over the door is the brave and inspiring inscription 'Dedicated to the public for ever as a free museum for their recreation, instruction and enjoyment'.

The benefactor behind all this was Frederick Horniman, a tea merchant, who assembled the core of the collection on his travels abroad, giving it the theme of anthropology and natural history.

The Africa Gallery is challenging and thought provoking, and contains many beautiful objects. The Natural History Gallery has an aquarium. The museum of musical instruments will reopen later in 2002. The **gardens** next door, also part of Horniman's generous gift, are to be integrated into the museum. They contain more powerful views of London, a bandstand (1912), and the conservatory (1894) moved from Horniman's house in Croydon. They are also lovely to walk round.

Opposite the museum you can catch a 176 bus back to Waterloo, Charing Cross or Oxford Circus. Eight minutes' walk away downhill to the left is Forest Hill station (Zone 3), from which trains take 13 minutes to reach London Bridge.

53 • Brixton

Transformations in cities take place sometimes through planning decisions, as at Covent Garden, sometimes through disasters, like the Great Fire, and sometimes through the people themselves. Brixton is in the third category. It was once a stuffy Victorian suburb, became between the wars a slightly seedy area on the route south, and has now been transformed by its Afro-Caribbean residents into a new cultural entity within its original streets and buildings. Few architects have been employed here. It is vivid, gritty and cheerful—except when you penetrate to the still seedy parts. On this walk you experience both aspects.

• Distance: 3½ miles. Time: 1½ hours. Tube: Brixton. Off map.

Start at Brixton station (Victoria Line): the buzz reaches you as you ascend the escalators, and out in the street you are part of it. Turn left out of the station and immediately left again into the appropriately named **Electric Avenue**, so-called because it was one of the first streets to be lit by electricity in 1888. It is a busy Caribbean market with a startling range of foods and other products.

Go only a little way at this stage—you will come back to it—and turn right into Electric Lane. The tall curving terraced houses (1885) and the inescapable railway tracks above to the left make it dark yet colourful. Turn right into Coldharbour Lane, back to the traffic lights, to a sense of openness combined with traffic.

Dominating the view is **Lambeth Town Hall** (1906–8). It is on a steeply angular site, thin but very Edwardian in its energy, with a rich sculpture collection of allegorical figures. Who are the figures? Cynically Pevsner says 'hardly one passer-by in a hundred thousand will have the wish to work out for himself but Blue Guide readers can push that miserable proportion up. (The answers are on p 418 at ★.)

Ahead you are looking at the church of St Matthew, described below, and on the left the lively **Tate Free Library**: many such opened in the 1890s. There is a bust of Sir Henry Tate (of sugar and Gallery fame) in front. Alongside is a memorial to the victims of the Sharpeville massacre of 1960. Such juxtapositions are characteristic of Brixton. To illustrate the point you now cross Windrush Square, named after the vessel which brought the first Caribbean immigrants to Britain in the 1950s, to reach an ornate memorial to the Budd family, distinguished residents of the 19C.

St Matthew is one of the four very handsome 'Waterloo' churches built in Lambeth in the 1820s. The name comes from the location of the first, St John, Waterloo Road, which in turn came from the bridge, opened two years after the great victory. The four Lambeth churches are also named after the four evangelists and, although built by different architects, were a self-contained set within the huge programme of church-building, most of it on a tight budget, which was undertaken following the Napoleonic wars. St Matthew's, characterised by big strong Doric all over, even up to the second stage of the tower, is by C.F. Porden (1822). Since the 1970s it has been a community centre, with a bar in the crypt.

Make you way up Brixton Hill, either side of the road. The residual Rush Common survives on the left—otherwise there is not much to see. A huge incomplete Roman Catholic Gothic church, by J.F. Bentley (1880s), who was later to produce Westminster Cathedral, is on the right at Horsford Road. Turn right down Blenheim Gardens to locate an astonishing survival, a **windmill** (1816), well preserved in the midst of Lambeth Council's low-rise 1970s housing: it is a reminder that until the coming of the railways there was working countryside all around here. Other uses could be detected even then: only three years after the windmill, Thomas Chawner built the Surrey House of Correction just to the south of it in Jebb Avenue, now much enlarged as **Brixton Prison**, although the Governor's House is part of the original.

Make your way from Brixton Hill across intervening 1880s suburbia to the other old arterial road from central Brixton, **Tulse Hill**. Arodene Road and Leander Road will give you an idea of how incredibly unimaginative Victorian suburban housing could be. Individually the little houses are of a pleasing design, with a pretty porch, generous windows, grey brick and a variable skyline. In bulk, they are boring. It is almost a relief to get into the more open and widely spaced brick blocks of the Tulse Hill Estate—but not quite, because the Victorian terraces, however tedious, at least have warmth and comfort, whereas 20C public housing is windswept and bleak.

Cross Tulse Hill and go down the steps into **Brockwell Park**. A pleasant circuit to the right will take you up the slope past the water gardens to a walled area known as the Shakespeare Garden, laid out in the 1890s to display the plants and flowers mentioned in Shakespeare's plays. This is the former kitchen garden of an earlier house on the site, worth exploring *en route* to the house, which is on the crest of the hill. This is the former **Brockwell Hall** by D.R. Roper (1811–13), a fine villa built for John Blades, a glass merchant in the city who had bought the estate. Some of the interior can be seen by visiting the café inside. There are good

Public parks in London

The idea of a public park is Victorian, and was intended to create or conserve open space in crowded urban areas for recreation of many sorts, with grass, flower beds and amenities such as fountains, greenhouses, children's playgrounds, and, increasingly, sports facilities. The first major parks were in northern industrial cities such as Liverpool, Preston and Glasgow. London had been privileged over earlier centuries to have its royal parks, but in the 1840s Victoria Park, Hackney, was opened, reflecting the new values, followed by Battersea Park in 1853.

After the establishment in 1855 of the Metropolitan Board of Works, later the London County Council, and later still the Greater London Council, the focus shifted to the acquisition of former manor houses and villas such as Brockwell Hall with their surrounding estates. Brockwell was purchased in 1891. Most of the parks now creating green 'lungs' in London's suburbia originated in this way.

In the 20C, the chief pressure on the parks was provision for sport, especially football and cricket. Meeting this need has limited the creation of space for public walks and horticulture. Brockwell is no exception.

views all round, especially to the centre of London in the north. To the west is the park's still-popular Lido.

Descend the hill from the villa past the various pitches, cycle tracks, bowling greens and pavilions to reach the gate at Brixton Water Lane. Turn right. There are some attractive 1830s' houses here, contrasting in their modest scale with the massive semis to be seen stretching down Dulwich Road, backing on to the park.

Cross over to go down **Effra Parade**. The name refers to a river that starts in Norwood to the south and flows through Brixton to reach the Thames at Vauxhall. Although downstream it is now mostly enclosed as a sewer, its water is still visible higher up. 'Effra' derives from the Celtic word for torrent. This street is a mixture of the brave new world of 1950s' flats and the safe old world of mid-Victorian speculative housing. At the end is something which came between public or chartitable housing for those of the poor who were perceived as 'deserving', in this case, as often, a galleried block of flats, with 'St George's Residences' proudly inscribed on the eastern end.

Turn left into **Railton Road**, now peaceful enough but the place at the heart of demonstrations in 1981 and 1985, when the people of Brixton became tired of discrimination. By crossing Coldharbour Lane you soon return to the market area around Brixton station. At the crossroads is the **Archive and Museum of Black Heritage** in Coldharbour Lane. Open 10.00–16.00 Mon–Fri. The museum is in the course of expansion, but visitors welcome by appointment. ☎ 020 7738 4591.

Entering Atlantic Road you are back amongst the railway arches. Turn right down Pope's Road to Canterbury Crescent with its Victorian almshouses and huge red-brick, rather forbidding flats, Dover Mansions. The police station on the right is again of the 1950s.

Across the main road is the façade of the former *Bon Marché*, a department store from Brixton's middle-class era, now long gone. To the right is the **Brixton Academy**, a mecca for live music. ☎ 020 7771 2000. Walk back to the left to return to Brixton station.

★ (The figures on Lambeth Town Hall represent Justice, Science, Art and Literature.)

54 • Clapham

The fortunes of Clapham, an early suburb, have varied. Its most attractive architecture and the essence of its character are datable to the early 19C, when a group of evangelical Christians formed there, becoming known as the Clapham Sect. The Common, still a notable open space, was drained in the early 18C and by the mid-19C its green acres were surrounded by Victorian terraces, which in turn became shabby by the mid-20C. There has been a renaissance in recent years, with new money giving the place a face-lift. Our walk covers all the best parts.

• Distance: 4½ miles, including a detour to Lavender Hill. Time: 2½ hours. Tube: Clapham Common. Off map.

Go south to Clapham Common station (Northern Line) in Zone 2. If the train's destination indicator says Kennington, change there to continue your journey south. Note the single-platform stations at Clapham North and Clapham Common unique to the Northern Line and dangerous when crowded (but nearly a century old, remember).

From Clapham Common station you emerge into the middle of the road. Cross busy Clapham High Street and go down the south side of Clapham Common a short way to **Crescent Grove**. Enter between two identical houses to find yourself in a D-shaped area of garden surrounded by exceptionally elegant 1820s stuccoed houses, all beautifully maintained: this is one of the most attractive residential developments in London. Explore down to the end and return.

Much of Clapham was like this once, before its decline and renaissance. There are a few other nice houses back in South Side but nothing to compare with Crescent Grove. Cross back over the main road and venture on to **Clapham Common**. To your left will be a small enclave around the *Windmill*, a picturesque old pub. Keeping Long Pond on your right make your way west towards the band stand (1862), transferred from the International Exhibition at South Kensington. The greensward stretches away on all sides (220 acres)—if it is a weekend there will be many people around, especially dog-walkers. It is not beautiful but it is certainly atmospheric, and suitably reminiscent of Graham Greene's *The End of the Affair* (1951), which is set on and around Clapham Common.

As you walk, look to the right to digest North Side, always the most fashionable parameter, which we shall explore later. Note how two enormous white blocks wreck the proportions: they will be explained. Continuing past the bandstand

---

Graham Greene

Greene (1904–91) was one of the 20C's outstanding novelists. Most of his work was located in exotic and dangerous places but several of his lighter novels, or 'entertainments', including notably the *Ministry of Fear*, have London settings. *Brighton Rock* reeks of the seedier part of that resort. Above all *The End of the Affair* (1951) is inextricably linked with wartime Clapham. Greene's serious novels wrestle with the moral dilemmas inherent in a Roman Catholic life-view: 'the appalling strangeness of the mercy of God'.

there is a more wooded area, and then you reach The Avenue, close to the west side (the 'wrong side', as Greene's narrator would put it). Turn right to reach North Side, cross and make your way up **Sugden Road**. This is a detour which demonstrates just how tedious Victorian speculative building could be, although no worse than that of the early 20C: countless streets like Sugden Road surround London, and make the Ruskinian snootiness about the repetitiveness of Georgian domestic architecture appear outrageous. Present-day attempts to introduce colour are only too understandable.

At the top, we reach **Lavender Hill**. We are now in Battersea (but not close to the walk described in Chapter 55). Opposite is the spectacular church of the **Ascension** by James Brooks, completed in the 1880s. It is worth getting inside if you can to admire the 'noble design of great simplicity' (Pevsner). If you are fairly energetic, walk a little way west down Lavender Hill; off Altenburg Gardens on the left is a delicious Arts and Crafts public library, and in the main road nearly opposite, on the same side as the church, the **Battersea Arts Centre**, once the Town Hall, by E.W. Mountford (1892), architect of the Old Bailey (Chapter 6). It specialises in new and experimental theatre. ☎ 020 7223 2223.

These are all worthwhile buildings but what you have been led up here to see primarily is the **Shaftesbury Park Estate**, down the hill on lower ground to the north of the Ascension church. As you descend Acanthus Road to the left of the church you will see the little towers marking the formal entrance into Grayshott Road, which you can explore, or turn right down Elsley Road. This was a trend-setting place, in terms of design and ambience, a self-contained estate of cottages erected in 1876 (as the dates over the porches show), in straight roads on a grid but with a distinctly rural air. The aims of the designer, William Austin, who created his own company, the Artisans, Labourers and General Dwellings Company, were charitable, like Peabody's large blocks, and the consequences equally far reaching but in a different way. Shaftesbury Park can almost be read as an embryo garden suburb, with varied but integrated designs, a few shops (they can be seen at the end of Tyreham Road), an institute, but no pubs. It is fun to pick out the variety of architectural motifs, Classical and Gothic.

Once back on Lavender Hill, go east via Ashley Crescent and into Queenstown Road. To the left is the Gothic and showy **Park Town Estate** by James Knowles Jr (1860s). This was built not for charity but as part of the area's attempt to become a middle-class enclave, a goal attempted even more positively in Clapham by the same architect.

Turn right down Queenstown Road to the traffic lights, cross, go left into Wandsworth Road and then right into Victoria Rise. There are dominating Victorian houses either side, but they are on a slightly more comfortable scale as Clapham Common comes again into view. When you reach it, turn left into North Side, but do not miss to the left the **Cedars**, by Knowles again, one of a pair either side of the adjacent Cedars Road. These were the dominating blocks you spotted when crossing the Common and marked the entrance to Knowles's Clapham estate: that led to his Battersea estate above, and thence in theory via Queenstown Road over the new Chelsea Bridge (1858) to Thomas Cubitt's Pimlico (Chapter 15), a processional route, if you like, for the middle-class. The Cedars are simply vulgar, with twiddly bits all over the place, too big, too forceful, with no taste whatsoever. Think back to the demure Shaftesbury Park estate and contemplate how money corrupts.

Our route now runs east, along North Side, which shortly diverts you to the left. A beautiful group of three mid-18C houses now functions as **Trinity Hospice**. The third, no. 29, was called the Elms (1754) and was at one time occupied by the architect Charles Barry. Next, after the Chase, comes an early 18C terrace, cool, well proportioned and dignified: it is followed by others in similar style, such as nos 5–9 (1830s). After that there is a library (1888) and opposite, the plain brick church of **Holy Trinity** by Kenton Couse (1774) architect of Richmond Bridge. Here the Clapham Sect mostly worshipped.

> ### Clapham Sect
> This was the term given, at the end of their period of influence, to a network of humanitarian evangelical Anglicans, many of them MPs, who lived at Clapham and worshipped at the parish church. The most famous were William Wilberforce, Henry Thornton, the banker, and Zachary Macaulay, father of the historian. As a group they could claim decisive influence in the abolition of the slave trade (1807), and of slavery itself in the British Empire (1833).

Keep going to reach **Old Town**, the original centre of Clapham, where more pleasant 18C houses are to be seen. There is a 'village' feeling attributable to the street pattern. With the triangular Polygon area to your right, across the road is a good row of three houses, nos 39–43 by J.F. Bentley (1907), architect of Westminster Cathedral (Chapter 15): he used to live at no. 43.

Turn left and then fork right into Rectory Grove, another old street curving away picturesquely. Rectory Gardens, now a slum, were originally cottages for artisans to serve the middle-class householders. Rectory Grove leads gradually up to the parish church of **St Paul**, an absolutely plain Georgian box (1815) replacing a medieval building: every expense was spared. Inside is a remarkable 17C monument to the Lord of the Manor, Sir Richard Atkins, and there are nice later monuments in the churchyard.

Returning from the church, turn left into Larkhall Rise and right into **Clapham Manor Street**, with some very pleasing terraces put up in the 1830 by local builders for the developer Thomas Cubitt (also active in Pimlico Bloomsbury and elsewhere). Cubitt himself provided the design for the pub, now called the *Bread and Roses* (1846). James Knowles came along in 1860 and inserted at no. 42 what was once a dispensary, and is now a taxi school, again totally incompatible in style.

At the 1970s health centre, on the right, turn right through pedestrian walkways to reach Belmont Road and then **Grafton Square**, an ambitious development of the 1850s. There are grand terraces on three sides, stuccoed and with ornate window surrounds. The style illustrates the way things were going, from the dignified restrained work of Cubitt to over-the-top Knowles. Through Grafton Square you return to Old Town, and now turn left down The Pavement, back the Common.

There are some pleasant shops here, or rather were, for example, no. (1824). Opposite, on the Common, is an ornate **drinking fountain** by German sculptor F. Muller (1884), in sentimental mode. Now you are back at Clapham Common station. There are plenty of local pubs and restaurants to sample before you descend to the Northern Line. If you feel like a more scenic return route catch an 88 bus to Oxford Circus via Westminster and Trafalgar Square.

55 • Battersea

Battersea was once a riverside village—the suffix 'ea' or 'ey' derives from the Saxon for island, as in Chelsea and Bermondsey. There are some traces of this still to be seen, including a delicious riverside church, as well as a fine Victorian park and surrounding houses. The best part is not well served for transport.

• Distance: 3 miles. Time: 1 hour. Train: Clapham Junction. Map 16, 17 and off map.

The suggested starting point is **Clapham Junction Station**, which is extremely simple to get to from Victoria or Waterloo. Hardly a beauty spot, it is interesting in that it was once the busiest station in the world, with 2500 trains a day passing through. Before the station's arrival in 1863 the busy crossroads outside was known as the Falcon after a wayside inn that stood there. After the railway, the area became a popular 19C commuter suburb, with its own department store, *Arding and Hobbs*, at the foot of Lavender Hill (Chapter 54). It is suggested you leave the station at the Grant Road exit. Opposite you will see the eye-catching little modern **Church of the Nazarene** (1968–70), but otherwise a desolate landscape of bus stands and parked lorries.

Make your way to the right and then left up Falcon Road. There is nothing much here but council flats to either side, but press on to cross York Road/Battersea Park Road into the largely pedestrianised **Battersea High Street**, which curves attractively round a bend: there are signs of the pre-railway world here, as in Simpson Street on the right. Continue under the railway bridge, with a 19C school on the right, now turned into flats, and a social centre on the left, the Cedars Club, 'rebuilt 1905, the foundation stone laid by Miss Lloyd'. On the right, in Trott Street, is the Roman Catholic church of the **Sacred Heart** (1892, by F.A. Walters), in red brick with a green copper spire. There are several pubs and a 1970s development made to co-ordinate with its older neighbours, such as pubs like the *Woodman* (and the clearly much newer *Original Woodman*!)

Beyond the Original Woodman pub is a fine school, **Sir Walter St John School**, a Victorian Gothic building replacing an older one, part of it by William Butterfield (1858–59). Then a really pleasant little urban space opens up, somewhat inaccurately called **Battersea Square**, with food shops, bars and restaurants spilling out under the trees, spoilt only by traffic along Westbridge Road.

After enjoying this, turn left down Vicarage Crescent, where you come alongside the river. On the left-hand side, behind a wall, is the remarkably fine **Old Battersea House** (late 17C), which faced the river before wall, road, and bankside were constructed. The house is now owned by *Forbes Magazine*, and can sometimes be visited by organised groups. Within it, the ground floor houses the De Morgan Foundation Collection (mostly paintings by Evelyn de Morgan, a female Pre-Raphaelite). Open by appointment Wed (afternoon). Reservations in advance, ☎ 020 8871 7037.

Get up on to the riverside path and walk east. The views are quite good: **Chelsea Harbour** (1980s) opposite, with it pagoda-type tower, is one of the better examples of Thames-side renewal (Map 16,7). **Lots Road Power Station** (1902) is to the right, fat and red: widely hated when it first appeared, ruining the Chelsea riverscape, it was built to empower the District Line. It is hard to imagine that once upon a time this stretch of river was quiet countryside, with no wharves, let alone embankments, and the marshy fields full of lavender and watercress.

Soon you reach a remarkable gem from those days, the church of **St Mary** by Joseph Dixon (1775–76), in old London stock brick with two tiers of windows, a west porch with Tuscan columns and a square tower and spire. The church was originally 12C, and still has 17C glass in its east window. The west end faces the river, a fact of which the architect took advantage, making it a real eye-catcher from the water or either bank. William Blake was married here in 1792. Inside there are some fine monuments. The church may be open 11.00–15.00 June–Sept.

Carry on along the river path to **Battersea Bridge (Map 16,6)**. On the opposite bank is Cheyne Walk (Chapter 34). The bridge is not that in J.M. Whistler's painting, which was of timber and designed by Henry Holland (1771), but a cast-iron replacement by Sir Joseph Bazalgette (1886). The gilded fascia of the arches disguises narrower curves and indeed, for its date, the bridge is quite steeply arched.

At the bridge cross the roadway and go on along the river path to Albert Bridge. On the right, half-way along, is **Ransome's Dock**, which you cross by a swing-bridge; the dock leads to a little enclave with a good, eponymous restaurant. **Albert Bridge** (1871–73), most refined and delicate of the Thames bridges, was by the engineer R.M. Ordish, built on the principle of rigid wrought iron suspension. It has never been strong enough and a notice on it famously asks troops to break step—a useful reminder that the Millennium Bridge problems were not unique.

Turn right at Albert Bridge Road and shortly you will enter **Battersea Park** on the left **(Map 17)**. This is a lively, interesting 200-acre park with attractive gardens and leisure facilities, a children's zoo, a delightful boating lake, and regular special events such as antiques fairs and art shows. Park open 07.30–22.00 daily. Café. ☎ 020 8871 7530. Pump House Gallery open 11.00–16.00 Wed–Sun. ☎ 020 7350 0523. Children's Zoo open Easter–Sept 10.00–17.00 daily, Oct–Easter 11.00–15.00 Sat, Sun only. ☎ 020 8871 7540.

Battersea Park was a characteristic Victorian initiative, proposed as early as 1844, aimed at improving public health and areas of unpleasant reputation. Battersea Fields had that sort of reputation, boggy in winter and attracting undesirable types in summer. Developer Thomas Cubitt suggested that the marshy ground could be built up by the transfer of earth upstream from the docks, and James Pennethorne designed the layout. The river was embanked from 1861. The precedent for this kind of amenity was Victoria Park, Hackney (Chapter 44), but the lake at Battersea is the most romantic and picturesque feature of all the new 19C parks. In the 1890s the Park became the centre of the new craze for bicycling, and in 1951 part of it was laid out as the Festival of Britain Gardens, by Osbert Lancaster and John Piper.

Maps at the entrances show the amenities available and the walker can select any preferred route. Recommended are the English Garden, the formal garden, the lake with its 1930s café and the neglected but evocative Festival Fountain. By the river is the Peace Pagoda (1985), one of a series built world-wide by a Buddhist order: it is 100ft high with wind-bells on each corner and four gilded statues representing scenes from the life of Buddha. How the idea promotes peace is unclear, but it looks vivid enough. Sculpture elsewhere in the Park

:ludes a Henry Moore, *Three Standing Figures* (1948) and a Barbara
pworth, *Single Form* (1961–62).

Leave the Park at the southeast corner, to find Queen's Circus (**Map 17,8**),
 pleasantly dominated by the railway from Victoria on one side but leading off,
the south and west, along very grand, tall, late-Victorian terraces, designed to
ιulate those at Kensington, though Battersea has never reached those heights.

Battersea Dogs' Home

Perhaps the one thing everyone knows about Battersea is the Dogs' Home. It
:onstitutes a temporary refuge for stray dogs, and cats, 500 or so at any one
:ime, rescued from the street and returned to their owners or re-housed with
new owners, who are carefully vetted for suitability. Over 20,000 animals
are taken in each year. The home was not always in Battersea. It was
founded in 1860 in Holloway by Mary Tealby, who was obliged to move in
1871 in response to neighbours' complaints, and successfully relocated to
the present site, a no-man's land surrounded by railways.

Along Prince of Wales Drive to the left, under the bridge, you will reach
ιttersea Dogs' Home—perhaps you will hear the inmates barking—and beyond
at, from the railway bridge, you have a good view of the sad and neglected
ιttersea Power Station by Sir Giles Gilbert Scott and others (begun 1929), a
ɜwar version of his Tate Modern building (**Map 17,6**). There are plenty of ideas
 what should happen to it—from a theme park to a giant club—but insuffi-
nt cash to carry them out. Demolition and an extension of the riverside park
ɜms an option worth considering, but many would dismiss this as philistine;
storically the power station is a rare example of early British industrial
)dernism.

The best way back to town from here is a 137 bus from Queen's Circus to
ford Circus; or you could take a 44 or 344 bus along Battersea Park Road to
uxhall station (Victoria Line). For the really energetic, it is not that far over
ɩelsea Bridge to Sloane Square station.

Villages': upstream

5 • Fulham and Putney

ɩese two former riverside villages on either bank of the Thames are linked by a
e bridge. In character they make an interesting contrast and both have dis-
ɩctive features, including Fulham's Bishop's Palace staring across at Putney's
at clubs.

Distance: 4¼ miles in total. Time: 2½ hours + extra time to see Fulham Palace.
Tube: West Brompton. Off map.

The full walk starts from West Brompton station (District Line) in Zone 2; ta▌ Wimbledon train. A much shorter version of the walk could start from Put▌ Bridge station on the same line (see p 425).

Fulham

The first pleasure is seeing **Brompton Cemetery**, by turning right from ▌ station and in through the forbidding brick gates. Inside it is quite formal, des▌ being of the same date (1840) as the more mysterious and extensive cemeter▌ Kensal Green, and is usually populated by local people enjoying it as a quiet pa▌ like retreat, exactly as the founders intended. Explore as you wish, moving n▌ to south. On the left in the central avenue is the grave of Emmeline Pankh▌ (d. 1928), the most famous of the Suffragettes. At the southern end of the ce▌ tery, long colonnades begin either side, with catacombs below, leading ▌ central circle crammed with monuments, and on the south side an octag▌ chapel. The designer was Benjamin Baud.

Leave at the southern end and turn right into Fulham Road. A barely not▌ able bridge takes you over Chelsea Creek. Soon afterwards you become awar▌ a major presence on your right, hard to define at first but dominating. ▌ **Stamford Bridge** (the name of the miniature crossing just mentioned), now fam▌ only as the ground of Chelsea Football Club. The stands were built 1972–74▌ with football stadia for clubs such as Arsenal and Tottenham Hotspur, Chels▌ has become multi-purpose, with cafés, restaurants and shopping, much ▌ designed to market the club. If it is a Saturday you will be wholly caught up i▌ on weekdays it is no doubt quieter than the proprietors would wish.

Football

Like cricket, rugby and tennis, modern football was a British invention, b▌ unlike them had its origins among the working class, in particular in th▌ industrial cities of the North. Forms of football were played in China and th▌ ancient world, but the regulations of the contemporary game—with 1▌ players in two teams, only one from each able to handle the ball, playing o▌ a standard-sized pitch and scoring goals—were devised in Britain in 1863▌

The Football Association was formed soon afterwards and its Cup was fir▌ played for at the Oval in Kennington in 1872. The Football League wa▌ formed from northern teams in 1888, but extended south to include Chelse▌ and other London clubs in 1914. The Premier League is a recent inventior▌

From the start, football created heroes, as it still does. After a dip in th▌ 1980s, the game is now restored as the chief sporting preoccupation for mi▌ lions throughout the world, spawning multi-million-pound businesses.

Past the ground is Fulham Broadway, ironically the station for Chelsea s▌ porters, but not really worth a detour to see even for the Neo-Renaissance T▌ Hall (1881). It is more interesting to take a left turn down one of the mid-▌ stucco-fronted streets such as Britannia Road or Waterford Road to the Ki▌ Road. Many antique shops spill over from Chelsea. In the distance to the so▌ Chelsea Harbour's Belvedere stretches up beyond the railway but is inacces▌ from here. More immediate are the remains of the former gas works at Sa▌ End. There is much new housing here, but a grand Victorian pub, the *Impe*▌ *Arms*, survives on the corner of Cambria Street and in Rewell Street, to the e▌

Sandford Manor, now occupied by a construction company but originally a 7C manor house, in brick later covered with roughcast. Return down Michael reet and Harwood Terrace, turning left at Imperial Road to find **Imperial quare**, a perfect enclave of little 19C houses built for the Polish immigrants ho staffed the Imperial Gas Company's works behind. Gasholder no. 2 is sup->sed to be the oldest in the world (1830). The rest of Sands End is a confusing ixture of Victorian terraces and new development.

Return via Bagley's Lane to **Walham Green**. This was the Victorian centre of ilham. Wandsworth Bridge Road, stretching south, makes a pleasant stroll, full little cafés, a few better restaurants, and innumerable shops selling pine furni- re. The streetscape is distinguished by lions on the gables of the little red-brick >uses (1890s), a modest forerunner of the Edwardian shopping streets of the :xt decade. Although modest originally, the whole of this area is very fashion- le today. Turn right anywhere after Clancarty Road to cross South Park. In :terborough Road there is a piece of pure 1950s style, always worth looking out r, **Hurlingham and Chelsea School** by Sheppard Robson and Partners 956). Make your way through to Broomhouse Lane.

Turn left for a short detour and a river view. Just downstream to the left is /andsworth Bridge (1936–40), with only two piers supporting steel-plate rders, but quite steep for a modern bridge. Opposite is the mouth of the River /andle and to its left the Solid Waste Transfer Station from which containers of >mpressed rubbish are to be seen regularly commuting down the river—you ill notice them on any river trip (Chapters 74 and 75): all come from here.

The main route is up Broomhouse Lane, past the Castle Club, built as a school 1854, a pretty symmetrical Tudor revival. On the left is the firmly excluding all of Hurlingham House (1760), once famous for polo and now for croquet: ill a private club, it can be glimpsed only from the river whose bank it hogs. >on, on the left you can cross **Hurlingham Park**, formerly the club's no. 1 polo -ound but now public, with a stand which must be the most extensively graffi- :d object in London. Cross westwards to make your way down Napier Avenue > Ranelagh Gardens, and the huge solemn blocks of flats comprising Riverside >urt. After **Putney Bridge station**, follow the railway down to the river. The iilway bridge (1887–89), huge and black, was constructed for the London and >uth Western Railway, now the District Line. Turn right along the riverside path > the very fine **Putney Bridge**, elegant, curving and grey, by Sir Joseph azalgette (1882–86).

Now we are at the riverside part of Fulham. Go up on to the road, and across your eye is caught by All Saints' church, tucked in behind the trees. Before you :plore it, go a little way past the church gate to find the **Powell Almshouses** by ?. Seddon (1869), a delicious mixture of favourite Victorian ideas.

Go back to **All Saints**. It has a sturdy tower with diagonal buttresses, built in 1e 1440s from Kentish stone. The rest of the church was rebuilt in 1880, in othic style, Perpendicular as was the original, but it is uninspiring nevertheless. here is a fine collection of monuments inside from the earlier church and in the 1urchyard the tombs of no less than ten Bishops of London. The reason why ill shortly be made clear.

Go along the riverside gardens, quite attractively designed but poorly main- ined. There is a central fountain (1953) with figures representing *Adoration*, *rotection*, *Affection* and *Grief*, a curious mixture, but each with her own charms. There is then a magnificent run of plane trees alongside the river for ing a grand avenue. Turn right at the end to enter what remains of **Fulha Palace**, which Pevsner calls 'one of the best medieval domestic sites London...of far greater interest than might be expected from its undemonstrat exterior'. Even if this seems a little excessive, it is a place worth exploring ca fully. Palace open March–Oct 14.00–17.00 Wed–Sun; Nov–Feb and Ba Holidays 13.00–16.00 Thur–Sun. Group tours possible. Admission char Shop. ☎ 020 7736 3233. Grounds open all year. Admission free.

> There is no doubt about the site's long history. There was a settlement h even before the Bishop of London first acquired the manor in 704, includi a mile-long moat indicating pre-Saxon origins, filled in 1921. The palace l been built and rebuilt several times, but remained the Bishop of Londo chief residence until 1973. The gardens are, or were, of special interest. A a period of shameful neglect, the place is now undergoing some refurbis ment, but remains sadly and surprisingly down-at-heel.

You enter at a late 19C lodge with roads forking in two directions. Go to the ri to look into the late 15C **courtyard**, an oddly domesticated space, with a cen fountain, original diapered brickwork all around and straight ahead, a la castellated porch with a cupola above. Behind this porch is the original Gr Hall, which can be seen only on group tours.

Return to the other fork, which leads round to the east wing, added in the m 18C and completed in the early 19C. In here is a small **museum** partly hous the Porteous Library, established in 1780. Sometimes you can see Bish Sherlock's Dining Room (1750) with Rococo decoration.

After this explore the **grounds**, which also enable you to see the rather d Georgian exterior of the east wing, and the exterior of a Gothic chapel by Willi Butterfield (1866–67). The gardens, inside their ancient walls, were once unique botanical interest: they were planted by Bishop Compton in the late 1 with many new species imported for the first time, including the magnolia, w nut, maple and cork oak. There is not much sign of any of this now, but crumbling 19C vinery reminds you how beautiful it must once have been.

Leaving the palace you can explore a little further up the river path. The pl centre for children with disabilities (1976) was a pioneer of its type. Before lo you reach a dead end at another football ground, this one belonging to Fulha Football Club and known as The Cottage after **Craven Cottage**, formerly on t site. Fulham is the oldest of all the main London clubs. Turn back to Putney Brid

Putney

Note the attractive lamps on the bridge. For the only time in this guide, a walk taken you across the Thames. Now you are in Putney, a middle-class area of t later 19C, against Fulham's more humble mid-19C terraces. The church on t left is **St Mary**, looking across to All Saints Fulham. Do not forget that wh these medieval churches were conceived, there was no bridge here: the fi bridge, an amazing timber structure, was erected in 1729, beating that Westminster by 20 years. The church tower is 15C, but the rest, with its beau ful 16C chantry chapel, was rebuilt in 19C, and again, after a fire, very succe fully in 1980.

Putney has a tolerably pleasant and busy shopping street stretching south. T

ost picturesque area to explore is the **Embankment** alongside the river to the
ght, which has a mixture of Victorian boathouses. The tide sometimes washes
er the road. There are some pleasant gardens at the end.

This is the starting point for the Oxford and Cambridge boat race held here
every year in March since 1845, over the 4½ mile, bending course to
Mortlake. It used to command a great following, with thousands who had
never been near either university expressing, for no traceable reason, an
unshakeable allegiance to the light (Cambridge) or dark (Oxford) blues. But
today we prefer football.

short way further on by the river path you can cut across to Barnes and its
etland Centre (Chapter 58). Unless pursuing that option today, it is best to
turn down the Embankment, and perhaps have a drink at the *Duke's Head* or
e *Star and Garter* (look for the Universities' Stone), or something more at the
utney Bridge* restaurant and bar. Proceed up Putney High Street to Putney
ainline station (still in Zone 2) to catch the frequent trains to Waterloo, or
turn over the river to Putney Bridge station.

7 • Chiswick

ιe three attractions of this walk are a little spread out, but you could call a halt
ter the first (Chiswick House and Hogarth's House), or the first and second
hiswick village). The third (Bedford Park) is also interesting, and important if
u enjoy London's housing history: it is not much further, or can be approached
parately.

Distance: 3 miles in total. Time: 1½ hours + extra time for Chiswick House.
Train: Chiswick. Off map.

ains run on the Hounslow line from Waterloo every half-hour, for current
nes ☎ 089457 48 49 50. Alight at Chiswick. Cross over the footbridge and
rn right. An uneventful short walk along Burlington Lane leads you to the
belisk entrance to the grounds of Chiswick House.

hiswick House

ιe grounds of the House, the country villa of Richard Boyle, 3rd Earl of
urlington, are a public park managed by the Borough of Hounslow, but remain
mecca for garden historians because of the retention, or restoration, of most of
e garden features devised by Burlington in conjunction with William Kent. You
ill see some as you walk towards the villa, and more later.

House open April–Sept 10.00–18.00 daily; Oct 10.00–17.00 daily;
Nov–March 10.00–16.00 Wed–Sun. Admission charge. ☎ 020 8995 0508.
www.english-heritage.org.uk

rst note that three straight **paths** lead from the obelisk, the left-hand one to a
idge, the central one to a temple and the right-hand one to the villa. The layout
called a *patte d'oie* ('goose foot'). It was done in the 1730s after Burlington had
quired this piece of land as an additional part of his estate and laid it out as a
/ilderness', which in an 18C context means a formal wooded area with straight

Richard Boyle, 3rd Earl of Burlington

Burlington (1694–1753) has become known as the chief spokesman in England for Palladianism, the cultivation of an architectural style based on the work of the late Renaissance Italian architect Andrea Palladio and its interpretations in England by Inigo Jones.

As a young man Burlington inherited both an estate in London, north of Piccadilly, which included Burlington House (now home of the Royal Academy, Chapter 18), and the Chiswick estate. He was already an architectural enthusiast and a supporter of the growing view that Sir Christopher Wren, Nicholas Hawksmoor and company had interpreted Classicism too freely, and that the time had come for a return to the principles of Palladio and Jones (statues of whom you may be able to see on either side of the south front of the villa). He developed the London estate with houses including some of his own design, and employed Colen Campbell, publisher of *Vitruvius Britannicus*, to alter Burlington House. Already disillusioned with public life, in 1727 he decided that at Chiswick he would design a small villa to attach to the earlier house (later demolished) and use it for receptions of guests travelling out the short distance from London. It was thus a showpiece to illustrate how a chaste and correct revival of the antique could be applied to a new and comfortable Whig lifestyle. The design was loosely based on Palladio's Villa Rotonda near Vicenza, with interiors by William Kent, who had returned with Burlington from Italy.

paths. Take the more winding path immediately to the right of the entrance.

On your right as you walk the earth has been raised up. This is the terrac along which Lord Burlington's guests would wander to look out over the fl unbuilt land towards the river—all now suburbia. Soon you reach a **lake** and cascade. The lake has been formed from a natural brook. Under Burlington's fir design it was laid out as a canal, but later, perhaps under the influence of Ken the shape was made less formal and some minor bends were introduced, the fir hints of the ideology of the picturesque. On the right, the cascade, which may l splashing away noisily, was another item for which Kent provided designs.

Up the slope and to the left is the villa: to the right is the main entrance fro the road. Look at the **south façade**. Its perfect symmetry and crisp Corinthia detail embody Palladian features, such as a more important first floor with a po tico and a rusticated ground floor, but also refer to other Roman ideas, as in th Diocletian windows and stepped dome. Other features are more Baroque, such the twin staircases and, on the other sides of the house, Venetian windows, this is not simply a Palladian pastiche, but a collection of Italianate forms.

You enter through the modest door straight ahead. In Burlington's time di tinguished guests would have ascended the staircase to the *piano nobile*, but yo first view will be of the more mundane **ground floor**. There is a worthwhi introductory video in the first room on the left; then you can wander round th quite small spaces. Note that the outer rooms surround a central octagon. At th lower level it may be possible to see the wine cellar. It may also be possible to s the ground floor of the link building of 1732, which was designed to connect th villa with the older house but is now a corridor to nowhere. From the window the link building you can see an important original axis for the garden.

Climb the spiral staircase to the **first floor**. Here you see the ground-floor lay-out repeated, but in a grand manner appropriate for Burlington's guests. You begin in a suite of three rooms along the north façade, known collectively as the **Gallery**, the central one with coffered apses: they were for the display of Burlington's antique artefacts acquired on his Grand Tour. You will see that the two outer spaces are not symmetrical: one is circular and the other, which leads

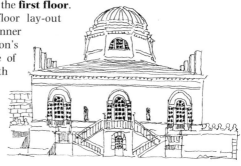

Chiswick House

again to the link building, octagonal. The decoration in the circular room tells the story of the Corinthian capital. The chimneypiece designs are based on Inigo Jones, whose drawings Burlington also collected.

In the centre is the main upper octagon, under the dome, known as the **Saloon**, lit by the Diocletian windows and decorated with antique busts and portraits from Burlington's art collection. This is the grave, formal space guests would have entered first of all from the portico by a rather dark passage. Rooms lead off either side, and in both further paintings were to be hung, hence the limited wall space given over to windows.

On one side is the **Red Velvet Room**, with a ceiling by Kent showing *Mercury promoting the Triumph of the Arts* (Burlington's own objective) with a self-portrait and a bust of Jones. Leading off to the south is the **Blue Velvet Room**, originally Burlington's study, an inner sanctum with an extraordinarily elaborate ceiling, in the centre of which Architecture herself is celebrated. Lord and Lady Burlington's monograms may be seen on the walls.

On the opposite side of the octagonal saloon, the **Green Velvet Room** contains some most interesting contemporary paintings of the grounds before Burlington's second series of changes, when they were still in their formal, early 18C stage. Beyond is another small room which Lady Burlington used as a bedroom after her husband's death and in which she herself died.

Once outside again look at the rest of the grounds. Leaving by the door you came in, turn right, round to the west façade, with a lawn sloping down to the lake, and then round again to the north façade. At the far end of the terrace is a **gateway**, worth going down to see because it is an original by Inigo Jones, brought here from a demolished house in Chelsea and re-erected by Burlington, Jones's disciple.

You can see stretching away the axis path from the link building, leading down to another *patte d'oie*. Next to it is a lawn with portrait busts and a semicircular end, known as an exedra, a form copied from the antique for the display of sculpture. Behind it, make your way down one of the *patte d'oie* paths to the left. On the left are an amphitheatre, the **temple** which you first spotted from the obelisk entrance, and a further obelisk. Beyond that the path reaches the Classical bridge, built after Burlington's time, in the 1770s.

In the early 19C Chiswick came into the hands of the 6th Duke of Devonshire.

He made some changes to the grounds, only some of which have been allowed to survive (Burlington's ideas having been in the main restored), and now we must retrace our steps to see the most notable of them: the **Italian gardens**, a 19C taste, and the **conservatory** (1813). The latter is of some interest, with a large central dome on cast-iron columns, earlier than those at Kew or Syon, and earlier than the Duke's important glasshouses at Chatsworth, Derbyshire, for which Joseph Paxton, who was to build the Crystal Palace, was responsible. Paxton in fact worked here at Chiswick as a young man, and was promoted to Head Gardener at Chatworth.

Locate Duke's Avenue beyond a leafy path and forsake the Chiswick grounds for the traffic nightmare of the A4 (Great West Road). Turn right to reach, after a mercifully short distance, your next destination on the right in Hogarth Lane.

Hogarth's House is a very modest country cottage—single pile, which means it has just one row of rooms with a windowless wall at the back—acquired by the painter and his wife for the same reasons as might be the case today: to escape from town. He certainly did not intend to entertain his friends here. Indeed, it is hard to imagine that the Hogarths could ever have been regarded as Lord Burlington's neighbours. The house has been restored to display engravings o most of Hogarth's best-known painting series, as well as an interesting outline o his life. It does not take long to see, but should certainly be included in your Chiswick tour. Open 13.00–17.00 Tues–Fri (closes 16.00 in winter); 13.00–18.00 Sat, Sun and Bank Holidays (closes 17.00 in winter). Closed Mon and Jan Admission free. ☎ 020 8994 6757.

> ### William Hogarth
> William Hogarth (1697–1764) has been called the father of English painting, indicating his key role as the first painter of English nationality to achieve an international reputation. His influences were substantial, through his efforts to establish a national academy, to develop a theory of painting via his *Analysis of Beauty*, and his readiness to exploit the commercial market for printed engravings. His 'moral subjects' were a new form (such as the *Rake's Progress* at Sir John Soane's Museum, Chapter 23), promoted by him but consistent with the literary trends of the day as seen in the novels of Samuel Richardson and Henry Fielding. His wonderfully painted portraits are free of the fashionable postures of Sir Joshua Reynolds and Thomas Gainsborough, and bring 18C personalities sharply into our contemporary focus. His own personality shifted between an optimistic and ambitious energy and crusty conservatism, and in his later years depression got the better of him.

If you are leaving the walk at this point, the pleasantest route is to retur through Chiswick House grounds to Chiswick station or from Burlington Lar take a 190 bus to Hammersmith. Otherwise, turn right out of Hogarth's Hou to the roundabout and take a subway underneath, over to Fuller's brewery whi you will see later. For now, keep it on your left and go down **Church Street** beautiful but short street winding down to the river. You pass several fine 18 houses and the *Old Burlington*, a former inn with exposed timber framing.

On the right, **St Nicholas** is a church with a surviving medieval tower, oth wise rebuilt by J.L. Pearson (1882–84). It is usually closed, but there are ma teresting graves to study in the large churchyard, including Hogarth's own, with railings and an urn on top, just to the south of the church. From here it is only a step to the river.

First look upstream from a private footpath to the right, open during daylight hours. You can see Barnes Bridge in the distance. Then stroll in the other direction along **Chiswick Mall**, a dignified riverside street with 18C houses. These vary in style but each repays a careful look, so take your time. Particularly impressive is **Walpole House**, once the home of Barbara, Duchess of Cleveland, one of Charles II's favourite mistresses, and later a school, which W.M. Thackeray attended. Many houses have gardens on the river frontage, which is otherwise unembanked. Chiswick Eyot can be seen dividing the stream. The Mall can be followed all the way along to Upper Mall, Hammersmith, which contains similar though less extensive houses and terminates with that of William Morris, **Kelmscott House** (1780), which he occupied from 1878 until his death in 1896 (Chapter 67).

Turn left up Chiswick Lane (near the Chiswick end of the Mall if you have wandered further). On the left is the eastern end of **Fuller's Brewery**, or the Griffin Brewery. Some buildings within go back to the late 18C but most have been rebuilt. Tours at 11.00, 12.00, 13.00 and 14.00 Mon, Wed–Fri. Admission charge. It is best to book in advance, ☎ 020 8996 2063. www.fullers.co.uk

Fuller's beer is one of the more highly prized among true beer drinkers—they have been making London Pride for a century or more. Several of the recommended pubs in this guide are part of this group.

Chiswick Lane continues after a subway under the A4. Keep going to the top of it—it is rather less interesting here—to reach Chiswick High Road. Suddenly here is lots of buzz, with cafés spilling onto the street, trees, traffic and hubbub. Cross the road, turn left and wander along until you reach Turnham Green Terrace, then go right and up under the railway bridge to the Tube station. Acton Green is on your left. You are now in the trend-setting garden suburb of **Bedford Park**. It stretches a little way east, west and north from here, with the church and the inn (around the corner from where you are standing) at its centre.

Bedford Park was the first genuine example of a garden suburb, that strand of the English approach to housing that embodies the continual preoccupation of the English with the idea of the countryside—its looks, its colours, its lifestyle—even in the centres of cities (see also Chapter 66). It was begun in 1875 by Jonathan Carr and is closely associated with its main architect, R. Norman Shaw, but others, E.W. Godwin and E.J. May, were involved, too.

The church of **St Michael** is by Shaw (1879) although it was completed by Maurice Adams (1887), and is generously kept open. It is in the Anglo-Catholic tradition, and so has high steps to the altar, candles, and so on, but what catches the eye is the openness, not darkness and mystery. The green pews were Shaw's own design.

Opposite is the *Tabard Inn*, which was part of the suburb's original plan, with the former stores and art school (bombed) next door. The inn, functioning as a perfectly normal pub, has William de Morgan tiles inside. Walk west, turning left into Priory Gardens, past the vicarage, to wander round the estate. Note The Priory (1880) by May. Turn left into Priory Avenue and Woodstock Road, where there are many Shaw designs. Go along Bedford Road and across The Avenue,

> ## R. Norman Shaw
> Shaw (1831–1912) was one of the most productive and versatile architects
> of the 19C, and one of the least easily categorised, unlike A.W.N. Pugin
> (Gothic) or Decimus Burton (Classical). He developed early an 'Olde English'
> mode, with much fake timber-framing, to be seen at Grimsdyke, near
> Harrow, but gradually moved towards the particularly pleasing vernacular
> or Neo-Dutch which we see at Bedford Park. He did not remain there: by the
> 1890s he was practising the more full-blooded Queen Anne style to be seen
> at New Scotland Yard now flatteringly called Shaw Buildings (Chapter 12)
> and finally the forceful Edwardian Classicism of the Meridian Hotel
> Piccadilly (Chapter 21).

which is the rather less interesting central roadway. To the left, the former Ch
has been altered and, on the left in Bedford Road, Carr's own original Tower
House, a showpiece, was replaced by depressing flats in the 1930s (the idea
'conservation' had not been invented then). Go left down either Newton Grove
The Orchard. You then reach **South Parade** with Acton Green opposite.
right a little way to see no. 14, an early work by C.F.A. Voysey (1891), now se
as an early Modernist. White, clean and horizontal, it certainly seems delib
ately to oppose Shaw's red-brick idiom all around. If forced to live in either t
Voysey house or one of equivalent size by Shaw, which would you choose? T
answer may be the key to your architectural temperament.

Walk back along South Parade or across the Green, perhaps stopping fo
drink at the Tabard to consider the question in depth. Catch the Tube at Turnh
Green (District Line).

58 • Barnes

There are two things to see at Barnes: an attractive village centre, related to t
Thames, and the new Wetland Centre, essential visiting for anyone with a co
cern about the planet we are busy destroying. The walking here is less happy, b
buses can be used as an alternative. Take binoculars.

• Distance: 4¼ miles in total. Time: 1½ hours + 1½ hours for the Wetla
Centre. Off map.

Travel Go to Barnes station (Zone 3) from Waterloo, or to Hammersmith stati
(District or Piccadilly Line) and locate a 283 bus. The walk from Barnes stati
can take you across Barnes Common, which is pleasant but not direct, and in t
end you will have to walk along Rocks Lane: it may be better to catch a 33 or
bus from outside the station, alighting at Queen Elizabeth Walk. Turn right to t
Wetland Centre's main entrance, where the 283 bus terminates.

London Wetland Centre
The Centre is an extremely worthwhile and visually attractive venture which c
be viewed as analogous to Kew Gardens in terms of conservation and ecologi
significance. Open 09.30–18.00 daily (closes 17.00 in winter). Admissi
charge. Café. Shop. Art gallery. ☎ 020 8409 4400. www.wwt.org.uk

Opened in 2000, it was created from four Victorian reservoirs at Barn Elms, adjacent to the Thames, made redundant in the 1980s by the creation of the Thames Water Ring Main. (The Ring Main takes supplies from the upper Thames via underground pipes to reservoirs in the Lea Valley.) The drained land could have been developed for housing or commerce, but greater enlightenment prevailed. The credit is due to Thames Water, Berkeley Homes and the guiding hand of the Wildfowl and Wetlands Trust, founded in 1946 by Sir Peter Scott (d. 1989), son of the Antarctic explorer R.F. Scott. The Trust runs nine Wetlands centres in the UK.

The re-landscaping of the four reservoirs has resulted in the construction of 30 different wetland habitats, where 130 species of wild birds, 24 of butterflies, 260 of moths, and 18 of dragonflies and damselflies have been recorded in the first year. The arrangement for viewing is effectively a division into two separate explorations, one called World Wetlands and the Wildside, and the other, less dramatically, Waterlife: they are quite different in tone. In between, at the entrance point, are a shop, art gallery (where you can buy but not hire binoculars), discovery centre, observatory and tower, and the *Waters' Edge Café*. The observatory is certainly worth visiting first; it gives a good idea of the site, and it is good architecture as well, providing some fine views back towards London.

World Wetlands is a series of 14 environments created to replicate habitats from Siberia to South America, via Iceland and Asian paddyfields (rice, depended on by half the world's population, grows only in wetlands). There are two hides, the further (Wildside) giving views over the northern lagoon which still functions as a deep-water reservoir for the rest of the site: it has fish reefs to attract diving ducks, herons and cormorants.

The other walk, **Waterlife**, is larger and quieter, and in some ways more thought-provoking. It contains interesting permanent displays on pond life, living in wetlands and the creation of sustainable gardens. There are several hides, including Peacock Tower on three storeys (with a lift). It is as good as, or better, than a safari holiday!

Leave the Wetland Centre the way you came in. Turn right, back to the crossroads or, to give yourself a longer and very pleasant riverside walk, turn left to reach the Thames Path, then go left along it, round the bend in the stream to Barnes Bridge. You can enter Barnes village from there.

Castelnau to the right is a straight avenue to **Hammersmith Bridge**, and was laid down in 1827 for this purpose. The present Hammersmith Bridge was built by Sir Joseph Bazalgette (1887), but replaced an earlier suspension bridge. 'Castelnau' derives from the ancestral home near Nîmes of the former landowners, the Boileau family. The *Red Lion* pub at the crossroads leads you into **Church Road**, the nicest street in Barnes. There are several pleasant houses and buildings from different periods here, all small scale, opening up into a green. The church on the right, **St Mary**, has a 17C brick tower and a medieval appearance outside. Inside you discover a completely new, steep-pitched structure making much use of steel and wood, traditional in tone but refreshing. This was done by Edward Cullinan after a fire in 1978. Before the church Homestead House, and after it, Strawberry House, the former rectory, look most handsome.

After that come small and attractive shops, a Gothic-style school on the right and a pompous Classical bank, and then the scenic pond on the left. Turn right into the High Street, which is disappointing in comparison, with uncongenial 1930s' flats on the right. But soon the river is reached, and The Terrace leads left and right.

Cross over onto the rather crude concrete embankment. Opposite is the green space of Duke's Meadows, near the end of the University Boat Race course. To the right Lonsdale Road leads round to **St Paul's Boys School**, which moved here after the Second World War. On the left is Barnes Railway Bridge, built in two parts (1846 and 1890). The Thames looks empty and peaceful here, a fine view for the 18C houses to the left, some of which are particularly handsome, though not improved by the traffic outside. No.10 was occupied by Gustav Holst, the composer, who taught at St Paul's Girl's School in Hammersmith.

You can go on down The Terrace to explore the next riverside village, **Mortlake**, which has a moderately interesting church and churchyard. In the 17C until the Civil Wars England's most famous tapestry workshop flourished here: there is no trace of it today. At the end of Mortlake High Street is Young's Brewery, industrial compared with Fuller's at Chiswick. In the centre of the brewery buildings is Ship Lane, which leads to a lovely riverside pub, the *Ship*, and Thames Bank, an attractive and unspoiled mall overlooking the Thames. This leads to Chiswick Bridge (1973) where you can get a 190 bus to Hammersmith. None of this, unlike the Wetland Centre, is unforgettable and you might prefer to return to Waterloo from Barnes Bridge station.

59 • Brentford and Isleworth

Brentford and Isleworth are old Thameside villages with long histories—Brentford was the county town of Middlesex—and potentially much charm although in both cases the charm takes some seeking out. Even without the major prize of Syon Park which lies between, a walk is justified by the surviving treasures and a couple of interesting museums. Syon House itself is open only in the summer but there are many other attractions to be enjoyed on the site all the year round.

The really committed may want to add a visit to Osterley Park, described here as an appendix. To achieve this you need energy, and to get to Kew Bridge by 10.30, and would have to omit the Musical Museum: but it could just be done.

• Distance: 6½ miles in total. Time: 2½ hours + 6 hours for all the museums, Syon and Osterley. Train: Kew Bridge. Off map.

Set out from Waterloo station to Kew Bridge (Zone 3). The line goes to Hounslow with trains every 30 minutes; the journey takes around 25 minutes. If you have plenty of time, from the station cross the busy Chiswick High Road to look at **Strand on the Green**, originally a fishing settlement but surviving as a very pretty collection of riverside houses, mostly of the late 18C. Zoffany House was the home of the painter John Zoffany between 1790 and 1810. The riverside is good place from which to admire the three broad grey arches of **Kew Bridge**. The third bridge on this site, it is by Sir J. Wolfe Barry (1903) of Tower Bridge fame.

The main route is west down the unpleasant Kew Bridge Road. Inescapable in front of you is the enormous 19C brick tower which marks the site of the **Kew Bridge Steam Museum**, formerly the historic premises of the Grand Junction

Water Company. Open 11.00–17.00 daily. Engines 'in steam' weekends and Bank Holidays. Admission charge. Shop. ☎ 020 8568 4757.

The museum entrance is in Green Dragon Lane. The whole place is a celebration of steam, with a wonderful collection of pumping engines from various periods, including two rare Cornish beam engines in the Eastern Engine House (1845). Two steam railway engines puff up and down on a small track. It is very exciting, even awe-inspiring, especially for enthusiasts, but of equal interest is the exhibition on the supply of water to London from Roman times to the Thames Ring Main of the 1980s, a piece of which you can walk through. The great tower itself is not a chimney or a water tower but a collection of standpipes.

Continue along Brentford High Street, but take a look at the Thames to your left. There is first a pleasant but narrow riverside stretch known as the Hollows, which returns you to the road, and then a second, more extensive river path, Waterman's Park. Across the water is **Brentford Ait**: the word is an Old English version of 'islet', a small island, sometimes spelled 'eyot', from which the place names Chelsea, Battersea and Bermondsey also derive.

Between the two Thameside stretches, on the road, you will see the tower of the former church of St George (1887) which now houses the somewhat inaccessible **Musical Museum**. It contains a collection of automatic musical instruments, the ingenuity of which is demonstrated by volunteers. The star turn is a giant Wurlitzer cinema organ but there are many other remarkable sights and sounds to be encountered. Open April–Oct 14.00–17.00 Sat, Sun; July, Aug also 14.00–16.00 Wed. Admission charge. ☎ 020 8560 8108.

The **Waterman Arts Centre** (1982), on the left-hand side of the road, was a theatre, cinema and gallery space, and may also provide coffee or a drink. ☎ 020 8232 1020. Keep going until you reach Dock Road, on the left. Turn down it, noting the fan-shaped cobbles, and you will find yourself in a strange mixed area of 1980s flats and ancient riverside trades.

This is the mouth of the River Brent, which from 1794, from here to Hanwell, became the Grand Junction Canal (renamed from 1929 the Grand Union Canal). The canal was a waterway of key importance, designed by William Jessop (d. 1814) to create a junction between routes from the Thames and from Braunston in Warwickshire, in the industrial Midlands. From Hamwell, the river continues on a meandering route up to its source near Barnet.

There are still plenty of decaying boats and mud around **Brentford Lock** to give a flavour of the past, and there is also the opportunity to embark on a walk along the canal towpath.

This walk, however, returns to the main road and continues left to the traffic lights, where you turn right up Half Acre to **The Butts**, on the left. Here are 'some of the most appealing groups of houses in west London' (Pevsner), even if the intervening space, on which parliamentary elections for Middlesex were once held, has now descended to the role of a car park. Walk round the square, and perhaps explore Upper Butts and Somerset Road. The development began in the late 17C and continued until the early 18C, with some particularly elegant houses, such as nos 24–26 on the north side. The style is rural rather than urban, with original front gardens: it is suburban in the best sense.

Return down Brent Road to the magistrates' court in the High Street. Turn right and before long cross the bridge over the canal, noting the development of canalside industry. The poor redundant church on the left is **St Lawrence** (1764), the nave designed by Thomas Hardwick, the first of the distinguished family of architects. Cross the road to follow a sign on the left for the pedestrian entrance to Syon. The path takes you down a curving passageway between old brick walls into an unprepossessing area where signposts point to different attractions.

Syon Park

You are now in the centre of Syon Park, the only major estate in London still in private hands—the owner is the 12th Duke of Northumberland. The signs of independent capitalist enterprise, as opposed to English Heritage/National Trust correctness, are all around: children's playgrounds, garden centres, shops, fisheries and places of refreshment. The main, overwhelming, reason to be at Syon is to see Robert Adam's 1760s decorations of the interior of the house, or, if it is winter (when the house is closed), simply the gardens.

- House open mid-March–late Oct 11.00–17.00 Wed, Thur, Sun and Bank Holidays. Admission charge. Gardens open daily 10.00–17.30 or dusk. Admission charge. Many shops. Restaurant/café. ☎ 020 8560 0881. Butterfly House open 10.00–15.30 (dusk in summer). Admission charge. ☎ 020 8560 0378. www.butterflies.org.uk

> ### Syon and the Dukes of Northumberland
> The Percy family date back to the Norman conquest and, before their enno-blement, included Harry Hotspur, who fought with Henry V. The 9th Earl acquired Syon in 1597. Named after Mount Zion in the Holy Land, it had been founded as an abbey for Brigettine nuns, from whom it was brutally snatched during Henry VIII's Dissolution of the Monasteries. His coffin rested at Syon in 1547, *en route* for Windsor, and must have been most unwelcome. The estate was then taken over by the Earl of Somerset, Edward VI's protector, who built the present house. The Percys successful cultivation of their estates in Northumberland and Syon has enabled them to maintain a position as one of the nation's senior families. The most important dukes from Syon's point of view have been the 1st, who employed Robert Adam from 1761, the 2nd, who built the stables and developed the river through the estates, and the 3rd, who laid out the gardens in the early 19C.

Entry is through the west door into the **Great Hall**, where Adam created a frigid, precise space with almost no colour, crisp plasterwork (by Joseph Rose, one of his favourite craftsmen) and a black-and-white marble floor. There are busts and statuary from the antique, including copies of the **Apollo Belvedere** and a bronze of the *Dying Gaul*, cast in Rome by Valadier. Leaving by the stairs at the southern end, nothing in the Great Hall prepares the visitor for the multi-coloured **Ante Room**, with its marble columns and Ionic capitals in gold with golden statuary above.

Adam's intention was that you should progress through these rooms, which had been 'finished in a style to afford variety and amusement'—the understate-ment of the year. From the Ante Room, you move into the **Dining Room**, cooler again but not like the Great Hall. Statuary in niches adorns the walls, with a relief of the *Three Graces* over the fireplace. At each end is a regular Adam feature, a short colonnade which both divides and extends the space (as in the Library at Kenwood).

Next comes the **Red Drawing Room**, so named for its wall-hangings of red Spitalfields silk: it is another ante-room intended for the ladies withdrawing from the dining room *en route* to the Long Gallery. The Red Drawing Room's coffered ceiling is to be contrasted with the 'Adamesque' ceilings in the rooms either side, but the carpet, also designed by Adam, deliberately reflects these ceilings. Note Sir Peter Lely's masterpiece *Charles I and his son James, later James II*, two of a kind one suspects, commissioned by the 10th Earl. The next space is the amazingly long **Gallery**, running 136ft along the length of the house but only 14ft wide. Far from being awkward, it contains much colour contrast and interest deriving from the books, decorated pilasters and medallion portraits of the family. The domed turret rooms at the northeast corner have a clock-cum-birdcage. You leave the house by way of the **Oak Passage**, an addition by the 3rd Duke in the 1820s, with oak panelling saved from the original Jacobean house, before Adam got to work on it.

The history of the **gardens** (which are open all the year) is even richer than that of the house: its changes have been dramatic but few, whereas many earls and dukes imposed their preferences on the gardens. Even before the Percys, the Earl of Somerset sponsored his physician, William Turner, to write at Syon in 1548 one of the first systematically devised herbals. The most significant changes came from the appointment of Capability Brown to lay out the gardens and park in the newly fashionable landscape style—in contrast to the formality of previous generations—from the 1750s to the 1770s; and later, in the 1820s, the 3rd Duke's rebuilding of the conservatories and development of the plant collection. Charles Fowler built the Great Conservatory (1826/7), which influenced Joseph Paxton at Chatsworth and his Crystal Palace (and thus, many argue, all modern architecture), and here the great waterlily Victoria Regia was first cultivated in England. Also in the gardens today are an **aviary** and **butterfly collection**. At Syon, Britain's first **garden centre**, a phenomenon which has become the destination of many a Sunday afternoon drive throughout the land, was opened in 1964.

The main exit from Syon (not recommended) is London Road to the northwest, down an avenue of limes and across Brown's serpentine lake via a bridge by James Wyatt. Marking the road entrance is an extravagantly decorated Adam **gateway** with the Percy lion in Coade stone on the top. From here you can walk north to Syon Lane station.

For completeness you should continue your walk to see Isleworth, and it is therefore recommended that you follow the cars along the road to the southwest, and out into Park Road and Church Street. On the left is **Ferry House**, in the grounds of which, alongside the river and shortly visible from the riverbank, is a meltingly beautiful pavilion, built alongside a now-demolished boathouse, erected in 1802 for the second Duke by Robert Mylne, his last work of architecure.

Across the road, facing the river and very picturesque, is the 15C tower of **All Saints** church. The rest of the building was burned in 1943, not by a German bomb but by two local boys playing with matches (they did the same to Hounslow Church nearby). The new building, in modern style (1963, by Michael Blee), is usually locked tight, as modern churches almost invariably are. Alongside is the *London Apprentice*, an old pub, much extended.

The riverside is very pretty. In summer a manual ferry can take you across to the opposite bank: you may have to call it over. After this the rest of old **Isleworth village** is frankly disappointing, being full of 1980s Docklands-type housing for new capitalists, all brick, wood and terracotta, with delicatessens nearby. The most interesting route to take is that posted 'Riverside Walk to Whitton' (although it does not go there). The river in question is the Duke of Northumberland's—cut through in the 16C from the River Crane to provide extra power for his mills: after rain it still has a rapid current. The mills are gone but along Mill Plat, on the left, you cannot miss the **Ingram Almshouses** for former mill-workers (1664), with flood boards across the doors. Through a little park you reach Twickenham Road. Turn left and then right into St John's Road, noting on the corner **Sermons Almshouses** (1849) in the new fashion of polychrome brick and, opposite, the fine Gumley House (1700), now a convent school.

Continue along St John's Road to find the church of **St John**, by James Deason (1855), built on the Duke of Northumberland's land by his 'river' and partially at his expense. It is worth walking around the church to find **Farnell's Almshouses**, School and St John's Cottage, an appealing Gothic stone ensemble (1857) paid for by the local brewer, John Farnell. This is followed, on the left, by the typical mid-19C suburb of Woodlands, generated by the railway and seedy now but still with Victorian dignity. Go down Woodlands Road and Woodlands Grove to sample how early train commuters lived in their perfect respectability. It is sad and nostalgic.

To return to central London, go through the shops, under the bridge, and turn right for Isleworth station, from which trains leave every 30 minutes.

If you want to see Osterley, at Isleworth station turn left down London Road and take the first right, into The Grove. You now enter a rather grander Victorian suburb than Woodlands, poetically called **Spring Grove**, after the house of Sir Joseph Banks, the botanist and explorer, in the centre of the estate (now a college). Go up The Grove and turn right into Osterley Road: in each you will find a few remaining gloomy 19C villas, glaring out from their surrounding trees.

When you get to the church of **St Mary** by J. Taylor Jr (1856), who faced it with his own patent stone, turn left down Church Road and right into Thornbury Road. Then cross the murderous Great West Road and continue up to the gate of Osterley Park in Jersey Road. It is not far and there is a pleasant walk down the estate drive.

Osterley Park

Osterley is much less commercial than Syon, with more trees, and is run by the National Trust. Soon you reach the lake and the house comes serenely into view.

• House open April–Oct 13.00–17.30 Wed–Sun. Admission charge. Restaurant, Shop. Park open 09.00–19.30 or dusk. ☎ 020 8560 3918.
www.nationaltrust.org.uk

Osterley was originally the home of Sir Thomas Gresham (from c 1575), the City polymath who founded both Gresham College and the first Royal Exchange. In the 18C, the badly dilapidated house was acquired by the Child family of prosperous bankers, of whom Robert (d. 1782) seems to have been the initiator of Robert Adam's involvement from 1763.

As at Syon, the Adam brothers created within a Jacobean, or earlier, house a series of exquisitely decorated rooms as an *enfilade* running anticlockwise from the open portico. Although the rooms are smaller and quieter than those at Syon, they are more detailed and delicate, and are approached more spectacularly. The entrance entails a flight of steps, via the transparent portico, raising the level to the first floor and filling in what must once have been a ground-level courtyard.

Mounting the steps and crossing the raised courtyard you enter the **Hall**, preciously decorated in Adam mode, in Wedgwood green: the oval on the marble floor reflects the plaster ceiling. Turn right to reach the North Vestibule which leads down, first to the **Breakfast Room**, with pier glasses and side tables, and then the **Library**, with wall paintings by Zucchi, and where even the bookshelves are constructed like a Classical exterior.

Next comes the **Great Stair**, set off by Corinthian columns and refined iron balusters. The stairs were designed to hold a painting of the *Glorification of the Duke of Buckingham*, perhaps by Peter Paul Rubens (1627), which had been purchased by Robert Child's grandfather. Four rooms, Mr Child's bedroom and dressing room, Mrs Child's dressing room and the Yellow Taffeta Room are open upstairs.

Return down to the **Eating Room**, which is exquisite in a different way, as Adam intended. He wrote, '[eating rooms should not be] hung with damask, tapestry etc. But always finished with stucco, and adorned with statues and paintings, that they may not retain the smell of the victuals.' This one reflects such a policy in extravagant detail, with plaster vines all over the ceiling.

After this, the **Gallery**, which runs the length of the garden front, as at Syon, is filled with paintings and has two fine fireplaces, but unlike Syon has a plain ceiling. All the sharper is the contrast with the more comfortable **Drawing Room**, with an exceptionally ornate ceiling a design taken from the Temple of the Sun at Palmyra, but used by Sir Francis Dashwood at West Wycombe, Buckinghamshire. Dashwood is thought to have been the source of Adam's introduction to Robert Child. Continuing down the south wing of the house, you reach the **Tapestry Room**, with a ceiling of contrasting delicacy to offset the Boucher medallion Gobelin tapestries.

Finally, in the **State Bedchamber**, the furniture is more intentionally important then the decoration: Adam designed it all, including the State Bed. Last is the wholly different **Etruscan Dressing Room**, intended as a total contrast to everything before it, and reflecting the new interest in the antique sparked by recently unearthed Etruscan vases: Adam at his most innovatory.

The **grounds** of Osterley are well worth exploring if time allows. The lake, a circuit round the exterior of the house (Adam added a fine staircase entrance at the back) and a visit to the 16C stables for tea should happily complete the day.

If you have seen both Syon and Osterley, no one should ever second guess you on Adam again. But, to make absolutely sure, you ought not to miss Kenwood (Chapter 41). The best way back is to return down the drive and Thornbury Road, and turn right along the Great West Road to reach Osterley station (Piccadilly Line).

60 • Ealing

'Queen of the suburbs' was Ealing's advertising slogan in its late 19C phase of suburban development. It was a contentious claim, but can be justified. In Ealing the usual developments—taking over an ancient village, with the help of a railway, and the imposition of streets of housing—were achieved with a rich mixture of styles and intended for a range of income levels, and at the same time retained a centre with necessary amenities including green space and, in places, a surviving sense of the past. This walk is quite short but could be extended in several directions by anyone interested in 20C suburban housing. There is a rich gem, Pitshanger Manor, towards the end.

• Distance: 8¼ miles in total (essentials only 2½ miles). Time: 3–4 hours.
  Tube: Ealing Broadway. Off map.

This route makes a circle from Ealing Broadway station (District Line and Central Line, and national rail from Paddington). Turn left. Immediately you reach the Broadway, and turn left into **The Mall**. Opposite is a fine run of turn-of-the-19C shops. Windsor Road, on the right, is an indication of the kind of superior stucco-trimmed 1870s houses that filled inner Ealing after the railway arrived. A little further along The Mall, nos 42–43 are villas with giant pilasters showing that a couple of decades earlier an even higher standard was the aim.

If you turn left at Hamilton Road and left again up the busy Hanger Lane (part of the designated North Circular Road, but not purpose-built), you will reach Queen's Drive, second right. It leads to North Ealing station and beyond that the **Hanger Hill Garden Estate**, a group of half-timbered houses (1928–36), full of English nostalgia, both its own for the Elizabethan age, and now ours, for the 1930s. Ian Nairn called it 'a marvellous nonsense'. Further still up Hanger Lane, again on the right, take Corringway and turn left into **The Ridings**. This is an even smarter estate (1930s), laid out as a series of concentric crescents on Hanger Hill, with several rather daring pieces of Modernism amongst the traditional vernacular pastiche.

Back at The Mall, take the turning on the right called The Common: **Ealing Common** then stretches to the left. This is a pleasant area of open space and good trees, spoiled only by the North Circular Road roaring by on the far side. The Common has some more handsome 19C houses. Such houses needed servicing and, off to the right, St Mark's Road and St Matthew's Road were built in the 1880s as terraces for artisans. At the corner of Warwick Road is a huge pub, the *Grange*, and a small restaurant, *Charlotte's Place*.

Turn right down Warwick Road, then left at Ascott Road and right into Ranelagh Road, a 10-minute walk through streets of pleasant 1860s housing. If you were to continue south down Ascott Avenue, you would reach Elderberry Road, taking you across Popes Lane to an entrance to **Gunnersbury Park**. This large and pleasant public park contains many sports facilities, walks, trees and two lakes. More significantly, perhaps, it has two fairly substantial houses known as the **Large** and **Small Mansions**, the former mainly the work of Sydney Smirke (1835), brother of Sir Robert and famous as the designer of the British Museum Reading Room. It is a handsome affair, done for Nathan Mayer Rothschild, and now functions as a museum of local history. Open 13.00–17.00 Mon–Fri, 13.00–18.00 Sat, Sun (closes 16.00 in winter). Admission free. ☎ 020

8992 1612. Nearby are the remains of interesting gardens created by the Rothschild family and their predecessors who included, in the earlier house, Princess Amelia, George III's aunt. This house, the Small Mansion, is sometimes open as an arts centre.

If you decide against this detour and continue along Ranelagh Road, you come out into St Mary's Road. Turn left to see an unmissable Victorian church, **St Mary**, by S.S. Teulon (1860s). In fact it was an 18C church that Teulon took over and Gothicised in his own overpowering way. There is a huge tower, to which Teulon wished to add a spire, but cash ran out. Inside all is wilder still, with iron columns like stovepipes supporting a wooden gallery and a forest of wooden tracery up to roof level. At the east end there are horseshoe arches, and all the arches are punctuated by notched bricks. Once it was all richly coloured, but in the more sober 1950s it was painted pale blue and cream. The pulpit is also by Teulon. ☎ 020 8579 7134.

Outside, the scale of the surrounding small Georgian terraces of St Mary's Square and Church Lanes is that of the 18C chapel, which makes Teulon's church seem even more crushing. It is worth poking around these little streets and the others to get a feeling for their cosy domesticity. Then turn north up St Mary's Road, which divides into two with a row of trees in the centre, recalling Ealing's village days.

Soon, on the right, comes a taste of the 1950s, now **Thames Valley University**, with Festival of Britain ironwork. Soon after that, on the left, is a different taste of the same period, **Ealing Studios**, where the great film comedies and other British classics were made.

In fact the studios were set up here as long ago as 1904, in the gardens of a house owned by early cinematographer William George Barker: by 1912 Barker had developed his five acres into the largest film-making location in Britain. The heyday of Ealing Studios, under Basil Dean and Michael Balcon, lasted from 1931 to 1955, but they are still operative and planning a revival.

Next come more pleasant houses and an appealing former school of 1860, now the Kingdom Hall, Gothic in polychrome brick. Now the roadway widens to accommodate **Ealing Green**, with some equally pleasant mid-19C houses in the roads opposite such as The Grove. On the left we have reached something special.

Pitshanger Manor

Pitshanger Manor was the architect Sir John Soane's country house.

• Open 10.00–17.00 Tues–Sat. Admission free. Occasional exhibitions. ☎ 020 8567 1227.

There was a 17C house on the site, acquired in due course by the Gurnell family, who in 1768 commissioned George Dance the Younger to add to it a wing with two reception rooms on two floors. This wing is still there, on your left as you face the building. In 1800, Soane, who had trained in Dance's office at exactly the time the extension was being built, and was now a prosperous architect seeking a country house for himself, bought Pitshanger. He demolished all the old house except Dance's wing and put up the central block which you now see, the façade an imitation of the Lothbury Court of the old Bank of England, which he had recently completed. Earlier precedents for the idea, which certainly influenced Soane, were Adam's Kedlestone Hall, Derbyshire, but first of all the Arch of Constantine in Rome. It is an erudite, antiquarian scheme, columns with prominent entablatures supporting figures, and intermediate reliefs. In fact Soane did not stay long. He intended the house to be used by his sons, who were to become architects, but they had other ideas, and the estate was sold in 1810.

Soane's spirit prevails here and, the interior now having been restored after use for many years as a public library, a tour will invoke similar architectural sensations as does his museum at 13 Lincoln's Inn Fields (Chapter 23).

The **entrance hall** is cramped and peculiar, with stairs all about and light coming from unexpected sources. There is a little dressing room on the left, akin to a downstairs cloakroom, which you pass to descend first into Dance's wing, which Soane used as a dining-room. In 1901 it was doubled in size to push out into the garden. The geometric ceiling owes more to Dance than Soane.

Returning, descend into Soane's basement. The room on the left was called the **Monk's Dining-Room**, a Soane joke, which he later repeated at Lincoln's Inn Fields. (There was once an even worse joke in the garden at Pitshanger, an overgrown ruined temple, intended to fool the more gullible of Soane's guests into thinking it had been there since Roman times.) The corridor leads on through the basement into a room for temporary exhibitions, erected as part of the library in the 1940s. Soane's kitchens were in a separate building (now demolished), accessed via this corridor.

Return back upstairs to see the three main rooms in Soane's own building. First comes a small drawing room, quite plain, through which there was originally access to a conservatory. Next, on the left, is the slightly larger **library**, with a starfish ceiling, another Soane trademark. Lastly, the **breakfast room** is still more idiosyncratic, with caryatid pilasters and a shallow domed ceiling with Greek decoration and sky and clouds painted in the centre. You may love it or hate it. The redecoration of these rooms replicates Soane's colour scheme.

The upper part of the Dance wing, used as a drawing room, is very handsome but not Soanian in character. One bedroom is furnished as in Soane's day. But Mr and Mrs Soane apparently very seldom slept here, preferring to return at night to London after using Pitshanger during the day and evening. This very odd 'reverse commute' is entirely in character. In a room at the northern end of the house is a collection of pottery by the Martin Bros of Southall (from the 1870s): odd work, birds, jugs, grotesque faces, etc.

It is worth looking round the back of the house to explore the grounds, now called **Walpole Park**. The cedars are from the 18C and the ornamental gardens were landscaped in 1800 by a gardener from Kew, presumably with Soane's approval. Many changes have been made since but it is still a congenial place, enhanced by the gateway at the northeast corner.

It is in this direction that you should now go, up Bond Street to the Broadway. The surroundings here are the familiar terraces of an Edwardian shopping street. Broadway is full of bustle, noise and traffic, but the shopping centre on the right is not the usual late 20C mall, or not entirely. **Ealing Broadway Centre** (1979–85) has the usual ingredients but in the centre is an open piazza with seats and a library, grandly called Town Square. The designers were Building Design Partnership, a group whose work is worth exploring.

Back in Broadway, you will see, to the west, a grandiloquent Town Hall (1888) bullied by a Civic Centre (1980–83) in Longfield Avenue to the right. Opposite the Broadway Centre is a noble church, **Christ the Saviour** by Sir George Gilbert Scott (1852), boring on one level—if compared with Teulon—but inspiring at another. It has a fine interior, with interesting furnishings by G.F. Bodley (1906).

Next to the church is Spring Bridge Road. Go up it, over the railway and into **Haven Green**, a small but popular space, heavily yet respectfully used by the locals (that is, the flower beds remain unvandalised). Ealing Broadway station is now back in view on the east side of Haven Green and our circular route ends.

A further interesting exploration into suburbia is possible from here. Go up Mount Park Road. The roads left and right, Mount Park Crescent, King Avenue and Park Hill, all illustrating the later Victorian and Edwardian tone of Ealing, with a climax at the top of the hill in the virtuoso Gothic church of **St Peter** (1889) by J.D. Sedding (see his Holy Trinity, Chapter 16), which is always open.

Finally, beyond St Peter's, across a little park, is a garden suburb, **Brentham Park**, hardly comparable with that in Hampstead (Chapter 66) but embodying the same principles. Architects Parker and Unwin were involved here (1905–08) and it shows in the twisting street patterns, richly varied but integrated house designs, with much use of red and white, and freedom from rigid building lines. The roads to explore are Brentham Way, Fowler's Walk, Brunner Road, Neville Road and Meadvale Road, where (again as in Hampstead) there is a community centre now functioning as a sports club. Beyond lies a delightful park with the River Brent meandering through—but it is a long way back to Ealing Broadway station. Look out for an E2 bus or go via Brunswick Road east to Hangar Lane station, slightly closer (Central Line).

61 • Kew

Kew Gardens are special all the year round, lovely to walk in and study plants, admiring their beauty or reflecting on the natural world. Kew is also the site of a small royal palace, a village green and a pleasant suburb on a bend in the river. The walk looks at these lesser aspects as well as the key elements in the gardens.

Distance: 3 miles. Time: all day. Train: Kew Bridge. Tube: Kew Gardens, District Line, where this walk will end. Off map.

The better impression of Kew apart from the gardens is achieved by beginning at Kew Bridge railway station (Zone 3), which is reached from Waterloo. Cross the hideous road outside the station and take the right-hand side of the bridge. If you like the left-hand side, and are interested in the Thames, you can detour to the left for 10 minutes to see **Strand on the Green** (see Chapter 59). Opposite, a little downstream, is the new Public Record Office (1973–77), the national archive of England, Wales and the United Kingdom, www.pro.gov.uk. ☎ 020 8876 3444. Then return to Kew Bridge and cross to the right-hand side.

Kew Bridge itself is quite handsome, the work of Sir John Wolfe Barry (1903). There are good river views in both directions. The main road on the south side crosses Kew Green, the best part of which is on the right-hand side. The entrance to Kew Gardens is at the far end to the right; as you go, do not miss the handsome 18C houses. A little way to the south but easily visible is the parish

church, **St Anne**, originally a small early 18C chapel for the newly arriving vil
lagers (Kew Gardens was just beginning its career as a show place), steadily
extended and revamped over the years, but looking good nevertheless. Th
painters Thomas Gainsborough (d. 1788) and Johann Zoffany (d. 1810) ar
buried here. Sometimes cricket is played on the green.

Kew Gardens

Soon you see very substantial gates of stone and iron, denoting the gran
entrance to Kew Gardens. They were put up by Decimus Burton (1845–46),
key figure in Kew architecture, who also worked at Regent's Park and Hyde Par
Corner. He was a resolute Classicist but, as we shall see, he and his partner a
Kew, Richard Turner, could produce something akin to Modernism.

- Open 09.30–16.00 daily in winter (closes later according to season, 19.30 o
  summer weekends). Admission charge. Cafés. Restaurants. Shops. ☎ 02(
  8940 1171. www.kew.org.uk

  If you have seasonal flexibility for your visit, the following may be helpful:

January: camellias	June: roses
February: crocus, rock garden	July/August: giant water-lily, summer beddin
April: magnolias, tulips	September/October:autumn colour
May: bluebells, rhododendrons	November/December: berry and bark colour

Walk straight ahead down the most prominent avenue. On your right is a green
house known as the **Nash Conservatory**, one of a pair John Nash designed fo
Buckingham Palace gardens. This one was moved here as early as 1836. Behin
it, mainly out of sight, are some scientific buildings named after Sir Josepl
Banks, the distinguished 18C botanist, traveller and Royal Society president wh
brought back numerous specimens from around the world and bequeathed ther
to Kew. On the left is the back of the Orangery (with toilets) to which we sha
return, but straight ahead, on the right is the diminutive red-brick **Kew Palace**
not looking remotely like a palace but the best place from which to grasp the his
tory of the gardens.

History

Officially the Royal Botanic Gardens, Kew was developed and put togethe
from different royal initiatives in the 18C. When George II and Quee
Caroline occupied a house in the grounds of Richmond Palace (Chapter 62
they began to develop a garden under the guidance of Charles Bridgeman an
William Kent, as they were doing at Kensington. This area now forms th
south part of the gardens at Kew. They were on bad terms with their son
Frederick, Prince of Wales and his wife Princess Augusta (the parents o
George III) and from 1730 Frederick established a rival palace at Kew, built b
Kent, called the White House, now demolished, but then right next to the rec
brick 1630s merchant's house to which you are currently adjacent. August
particularly liked gardens and over the years commissioned buildings fror
her favourite architect, Sir William Chambers, many of which still adorn th
landscape. It was Augusta who in 1759 laid out the first botanic garden.

Having in 1765 employed Capability Brown to replan further the souther
part of the gardens, George III and Queen Charlotte, who also loved the place
began to build their own new palace nearby (also now demolished) an

meanwhile took up temporary residence in the red-brick house. From 1802 to 1806 they lived here full time and so, modest though it is, Kew Palace was a real palace for a while.

The palace is an interesting house in its own right. It was built by a merchant of Dutch descent, Samuel Fortrey, in 1631 and is representative of a distinct architectural mode of that period—not following Inigo Jones into formal Classicism, but breaking away from Jacobean and Tudor extravagances. The style is essentially Dutch but the showpieces are virtuoso performances in decorative brickwork. The interior was naturally altered for royal occupation and is to be re-opened for public tours in due course.

Behind the house, on the river side, is a perfectly re-created **physick garden**, with many specimens that are contemporary with the early 17C house. Explore this at leisure. Then return past the front of the Palace to the **Orangery**, where you may feel like some refreshment. This is one of Chambers's buildings (1761) and was adjacent to the White House when that existed. It is still covered with the stucco Chambers prepared according to a secret recipe.

Across the lawns in front of the Orangery you will see the **Princess of Wales Conservatory** (1986) (that is Diana, the recent Princess of Wales, not Augusta mentioned above), when opened a state-of-the-art design for energy efficiency, without side walls and mostly below ground-level: the principle has been taken further at the National Botanical Garden of Wales which opened in 2000. The plants inside, arranged in five different environmental zones, are able to live in computer-controlled conditions replicating their natural habitats. Behind the conservatory is an older creation, the very beautiful **Rock Garden** (1930s), which creates a quaintly contrasting non-computerised world. Beyond that, in a walled area, is a large extent of preparatory beds (order beds, comprising a kind of living plant classification) and to the left, the **Alpine House** (1979). The **Kew Gardens Gallery**, with temporary exhibitions, is nearby.

Your main route should be south, towards the lake, to see the architectural masterpiece of Kew. All around you are contemporary plantings, labelled for botanical study. If this guide focuses on architecture at the expense of botany, the reader must not see an implied prejudice: Kew is a garden above all and chiefly to be enjoyed as such. But we can not help reminding you to look out on the left for the **Temple of Aeolus** on a little hill, one of Chambers's confections (1760–63), rebuilt by Burton. The lake is a Victorian conception and here you come across the next phase of Kew's development

After a period of neglect following the deaths of both King George III and Sir Joseph Banks in 1820, Kew was given to the state by Queen Victoria in 1841. It soon became the serious scientific establishment of today, while attempting to retain, as it successfully still does, some of the pleasure-garden atmosphere. The chief promoters of the new discipline were Sir William Hooker, the first Director, and his son Joseph, friend of Charles Darwin. The great glasshouses were commissioned and opened under their management.

Beyond the lake is the **Palm House**, the remarkable creation of Burton and Richard Turner (1844–48), placed here so that its outline can be reflected in the water. Pevsner calls it 'one of the boldest pieces of 19C functionalism in existence—much bolder, and hence aesthetically more satisfying, than the Crystal Palace ever was'. It was earlier than the Crystal Palace, too, and bearing in mind the significance the latter had in the development of modern architecture, this makes the Palm House very special. It was Turner, the engineer, who came up with the idea of wrought-iron ribs as used in shipbuilding to cover the maximum space without internal supports. Wrought-iron, as opposed to the cast-iron of the Crystal Palace, enabled the roof to curve and with the enhanced Victorian technology for glass production the whole structure is plastic in a wholly late-20C way. It houses the awesome plants of the tropical rainforest.

To the north of the Palm House is the smaller **Waterlily House** by Turner (1852), designed to accommodate Victoria Regina, first grown at Syon. To the east are toilets, a café and an excellent shop and, for Burton enthusiasts, the **Campanile** (1847) disguising the furnace chimney of the Palm House, showing that Burton was not totally modern.

Nearby, as you walk south past Victoria Gate, you will encounter several of Chambers's structures built for Princess Augusta, including the Temple of Bellona (1700) and the Ruined Arch. Just before the Ruined Arch is the **Mariannne North Gallery**, built by the important 19C theorist James Fergusson (1872–85) to house, in a top-lit space, a huge collection of her flower paintings.

Through the arch turn right towards the *Pavilion Restaurant* and, looming up beyond it, the **Temperate House** by Burton (1859–62), much more conserva-tive than the Palm House, with straight windows that could be opened on hot days, a perfectly reasonable functional requirement. The interior should be explored, as should a very interesting separate house to the north, which shows the evolution of plants over the last 600 million years.

Then go south, where your eye will be caught, first, by a Japanese gateway, the Chokushi-Mon, designed for the Japan-British Exhibition of 1910, surrounded by a fascinating Japanese garden. In view from there is another spectacle Chambers's **Pagoda** (1761), ten-storeys and 163ft high, not particularly authentic but quite extraordinary both for the period and in the context of the buttoned-up Palladianism of Chambers's Somerset House (Chapter 9). It was much more ornate when first constructed.

George III (1738–1820, r. 1750–1820)

When he became king, George III said he 'gloried in the title of Englishman'. It sounds contrived, but he intended to distance himself from his grand-father (George II) and great grandfather (George I) whose preferences had been German. It was a timely pronouncement, because the concept of nationality was then a growing element in public self-consciousness. It was also true: George III does appear more 'English' than most British monarchs (except those of the 20C): a family man, respectable, traditional, firm, not very imaginative, stuffy.

His long reign was full of crises: the loss of the American colonies; the risk of revolution as in France; his own illness (porphyria), which was incor-rectly treated; and his largely uncontrollable children. But he worked hard, involving himself in politics, including complex relationships over the years with Bute, North, Fox and Pitt, and led with Queen Charlotte an exemplary family life. His apprehensions about his eldest son's suitability to follow him—exactly what George I and II felt about theirs—were in his case justified.

He and his queen loved Kew and its gardens, and seem to have preferred a quiet domesticated existence to pomp and ceremony.

The lake lies nearby to the west of this, filling a dell, and should be seen especially in the rhododendron season (May). One more little architectural gem should be searched out, in the southeast corner: **Queen Charlotte's Cottage** (1772) was designed for her, even maybe by her, in which to enjoy picnics and has decorations on the first floor by her daughter, Princess Elizabeth. The domestic tastes of George III and his queen remain remarkably appealing.

After exploring at leisure, and gaining a sense of the Thames behind the trees to the west, you need either to retrace your steps to Kew Bridge station, or leave by the Victoria Gate for Kew Gardens station (District Line and North London Line). To do this, cross Kew Road and go up Broomfield Road or Lichfield Road to Station Approach. In the parade of shops is a recommended restaurant, the *Glasshouse*, where a late lunch or early dinner might round off the day to perfection. Alternatively, you might lunch there and then do the walk in reverse. Happiness is guaranteed either way.

2 • Richmond

Although now suburban to an extent, Richmond remains distinctive, refreshingly unpretentious and enormously likeable. A riverside town with a rich history, it has good architecture, including the remains of a royal palace, a theatre, shops, the Thames for views and boat trips, and a wonderful extensive park for walks in all weathers. This chapter also describes Ham House, to be seen in addition or as an alternative to Richmond Park.

Distance: 3 miles, further to see Ham House. Time: 6 hours in total. Off map.

Travel Richmond is an easy journey by mainline train from Waterloo or Victoria (change at Clapham Junction), or on the North London Line, or by Tube (District Line). It can also be reached by boat from Westminster in summer—journey time 2 hours. ☎ 020 7930 2062/4721 and see Chapter 75.

Richmond station itself is a genuine Art Deco creation by Southern Railway architects (1936–38), not masterly like those of Charles Holden on the Piccadilly line but in the same idiom. Turn left towards the town. Distances are short and the streets compact and crowded. You come first along a shopping street called the Quadrant, which leads left into The Square, which is hardly more than a junction. There is a brick clock tower and former fire station on the left and a narrow terrace of cottages, Waterloo Place. Go right, across The Quadrant, down Duke Street.

Immediately, you experience the shock and pleasure of **Richmond Green**. You are suddenly away from noise and traffic in a large, peaceful space across which you can roam, surrounded by old trees and dignified houses. It is unlike anywhere else in London—too informal to be read as a square, too small to be a park, but too urban to be a village green.

Its origin was common land for grazing for anyone who chose to use it, and it was later used as a space for jousting, attached to Richmond Palace, the stables and outbuildings of which spread onto it. It is therefore smaller than it once was, but the miracle is its survival at all in a London suburb.

Explore first Little Green to the right, where three relatively unsuitable late 19
buildings extend, the most eye catching being the **Richmond Theatre** by Fran
Matcham (1899), architect of the Coliseum and Hackney Empire. For details o
events, ☎ 020 8940 0088.

Then return to go down the left-hand side of the Green, where everything
Georgian in feel. Many houses merit individual attention: the Richmon
Society's excellent series of walks, available from the Information Office in th
Old Town Hall, give detailed information. Look out for the fine carved doorcase
and porches. **Brewer's Lane**, on the left, deserves separate exploration. Vis
Britannia or the *Cricketers* for a drink.

At the southern end of the Green do not miss the almost separate little squar
with **Old Palace Terrace** on one side. This is an early suburban terrace o
1692, at the beginning of a trend, similar examples of which are to be seen as fa
afield as Highgate and Clapham. Continuing along the southwestern side are fin
houses such as Old Palace Place (1700) and Old Friars (1687), and the long ru
of **Maids of Honour Row** (1724), built for the staff of Queen Caroline whe
she was Princess of Wales and living in Richmond Lodge (not the Palace) nearb

Richmond Palace was originally medieval, associated with Edward III wh
died there. Demolished and rebuilt, it was burned down in 1497 and rebui
again by Henry VII who made it very much his own. It was partly demolishe
during the Commonwealth, but James II would like to have rebuilt it ye
again, asking Wren to make plans. The fragments we see today are surviva
from the Tudor building.

The mood changes, to darker brick and smaller dimensions: Old Palace Hou
and Palace Gatehouse were built into the surviving wall of Henry VII's palac
Next to them you turn left through a surviving arch of the Outer Gateway in
Old Palace Yard. On the left is a block called The Wardrobe, renovated in th
1680s but retaining Tudor brickwork. At the bottom of the Yard stan
Trumpeter's House (1702–4), built on the former Middle Gate and now co
verted into flats, a modification continued to the right as Trumpeter's Inn, whi
looks 18C but is actually of the 1950s, indicating the dangers of historicism.
William IV bollard has been installed to confuse you further. Admire it if you lik
but do not be fooled.

You now reach **Old Palace Lane**, an attractive little street with 19C cottag
and a tempting pub, the *White Swan*. Turn left and you soon reach the river. '
your right are a steel railway bridge (1908) and the vaguely Art De
Twickenham road bridge, of reinforced concrete (1928–33). More important
round to the left is **Asgill House** by Sir Robert Taylor (1757–58), a riverside vil
built for the banker Charles Asgill. It is lovely, perfectly restored and beautiful
cared for, but it is privately owned so all you can do is peer through the railing
The same is true of the handsome portico at the back of Trumpeter's Hous
beyond its fine garden. Keep going along the delightful riverside path.

After Friars Lane, you reach boathouses that lie under St Helena Terra
(1835), and next to them the *White Cross Hotel* of similar vintage: this is 1
Richmond. Water Lane stretches up into the town but first we must look
Richmond Riverside, an ensemble put together by Quinlan Terry (198
Again, the difficulty is to sort out the genuinely old from the good imitatio
Heron House, in red brick, is *bona fide* later 17C; the central façade of the origin

oyal Hotel is of the 1820s and the tower of the building near the bridge the 850s. The rest is pastiche, including Whittaker House to the left, new offices sed on a design by Sir William Chambers done when George III toyed with the ea of restoring Richmond Palace. It all looks attractive and, with the genuinely d bridge, makes a delightful river view, even if the grass slopes are looking a bit orn. But is it honest? It is done so well that most people will never sort out the enuine from the fake. If it pleases, does it matter?

Make your way up the grassy banks into Heron Square, part of the Quinlan erry development, and go through to the **Old Town Hall** (1893): it ceased to e a town hall in 1965. It houses the useful information office, a local studies brary, an art gallery and an interesting local museum. Open 11.00–17.00 ues–Sat; 13.00–16.00 Sun. ☎ 020 8332 1141.

Return down the steps by the side of **Richmond Bridge**—there is a pleasant afé, *Tide Tables*, at the foot next to the old boathouses, where rowing boats may e hired. The bridge still bears constant heavy traffic. Despite widening and rengthening in 1937 this must be a strain for a structure erected in 1777, esigned by Kenton Couse and James Paine: it is a rare example of Paine's work London. Except for Waterloo, it is the handsomest bridge on London's Thames. ontinue under the bridge by the river. Boat trips are available from here to eddington and, on summer afternoons, to Westminster. For details, ☎ 020 948 3303 or 020 7930 2062.

Ignore the Postmodern apartments on the opposite bank and concentrate on e rich mixture of riverside development to be enjoyed on this side, some a bit ilapidated but enlivened by the odd new item here and there. Keep going until e path moves away from the bank into Buccleuch Gardens, at the top of which a little tunnel (a former grotto, it appears) under the road and up steps into **errace Gardens**. These were laid out in the 1880s over the grounds of two for-er large houses. Up the slope you will spot a Coade-stone figure of the *River hames* by John Bacon Sr (1784) only recently raised to magnificence here—nere is a twin god at Ham House. Keeping the river on your right, go through nd enjoy the rest of the gardens, leaving through a small gate.

If you are visiting Ham House (see below), cross Petersham Road and continue long the riverside for about 30 minutes. If staying with the town walk, possibly ncluding the park, turn left up Nightingale Lane. You soon pass the *Petersham lotel*, a Victorian eyesore by John Giles (1865), the extravagant architect esponsible for the outrageous Langham Hotel north of Oxford Circus. At the top ou join **Richmond Hill**. Look back at the view, admired for centuries. Built to njoy it are two fine houses (both 1770s) on your immediate right: first is The Vick, by Robert Mylne, and then Wick House, built by William Chambers for Sir oshua Reynolds. Opposite are an attractive mixed group of 18C terraces, now perating as hotels.

This route now continues up the hill to Richmond Park, but if you do not wish o go as far, turn left down Richmond Hill, past more interesting houses, to rejoin he centre of the town. You can reconnect with this walk at Ormond Road.

Jp the hill you soon reach the somewhat gross **Star and Garter Home** by Sir dwin Cooper (1921–24), a dominant landmark from both the road and down n the riverbank. It was built for, and still houses, invalid servicemen. At the end f the terrace on the opposite side of the road is Ancaster House (1772). Two fountains come next, and then the gates to **Richmond Park**. The gates them selves are attributed to Capability Brown (1798).

Richmond was used by successive monarchs for hunting up to the 19C: it still a royal park, enclosed by the brick wall built under Charles I (1637 Much the biggest of the royal parks—2470 acres and 2½-miles across— contains herds of red and fallow deer, and large numbers of historic oak tree Apart from the Isabella Plantation, a rhododendron garden in the southwes Richmond Park has never been landscaped, unlike the London parks: i rolling slopes, bracken, ponds and trees comprise natural countryside unchange since medieval times. The other example near London is Epping Forest.

You can walk for miles in the park, and it is an exhilarating experience, but th short incursion described here will take you to the right inside the gates, to th entry to Pembroke Lodge Gardens. Follow the path and on your left you will soc find the so-called **Henry VIII Mount** from which, allegedly, the king wou watch the progress of the hunt. From the top on a clear day you can see St Paul Cathedral in one direction and Windsor Castle in the other. Continue t **Pembroke Lodge**—formerly the home of Lord John Russell, the Victorian prim minister, and boyhood home of Bertrand Russell—where the café may provid welcome refreshment. So will the spectacular views to the west. The other impor tant house in the Park is **White Lodge**, built in 1727–29 for George I, now use by the Royal Ballet School; it lies well to the east of the area we have explored.

Either retrace your steps to Richmond Gate, or more enterprisingly cross ove the grass and roads northwards to the pedestrians-only Cambrian Gate. Go dow Cambrian Road and across Queen's Road, with many 19C villas, and dow Marlborough Road to Friars Stile Road, where you turn right. The *Marlboroug* pub is to the left, but dominating the view now is the church of **St Mathias** b Sir George Gilbert Scott (1861–62), the finest church in Richmond, in inspirin Gothic Revival style.

At the church turn left down Mount Ararat Road as far as The Vineyard, the turn left again. Note the austere former British Schools on the right, opened b Lord John Russell in 1867, now apartments. Past Halford Road on the right, wit Halford House (18C), are different groups of pretty almshouses of various date Clarence House (1696) and early Roman Catholic (1824) and Congregation (1831) churches. At the main road, Hill Rise, turn right and you are back nea the shops.

Ormond Road then appears on the right, with Ormond Terrace, a lovel Georgian group, and a Unitarian church where the first Labour prime ministe Ramsay Macdonald, was a lay preacher. On the left is an unusual feature, house built back-to-back, The Rosary and The Hollies (1699).

Turn left down Church Terrace and across Red Lion Street to reach the paris church, **St Mary Magdalene**. It is a mixed bag, with a tower of 1500, a nave c 1750 and an east end by G.F. Bodley of 1903, but it is very pleasing and stand in a pretty churchyard. Of many interesting monuments within, particularl appealing is the grief-stricken widow on the memorial to Major Bean (1815 killed by a cannon ball at Waterloo: 'He fell, it is true, in the field of glory.' Nearb is the grave of the actor Edmund Kean (d. 1839). Not far away, in Paradise Roa is Hogarth House, an 18C house in which Virginia and Leonard Woolf initiate the Hogarth Press in 1915. To the north of the church you can get back int

eorge Street. Turn right, through The Square, and along The Quadrant back to
e station.

am House

) see Ham House, an atmospheric place with handsome interiors, catch a 65
.s from Richmond station to Ham Polo Ground; the 15-minute walk from there
the historically correct approach to the house. Or, as indicated above, reach it
a the riverside walk from Richmond. It can also be approached by ferry from
wickenham.

House open April–Oct 13.00–17.00 Sat–Wed. Admission charge. Restaurant.
Shop. ☎ 020 8940 1950. Gardens open 11.00–18.00 Sat–Wed.
www.nationaltrust.org.uk/regions/southern

Although begun in 1610, Ham House essentially reflects two periods, the
1630s and 1670s. The first set of alterations were by William Murray, first
Earl of Dysart, progressively adopting the new fashions of Inigo Jones; and
the second by his daughter the Countess of Dysart and her husband the Duke
of Lauderdale. This unpleasant-sounding couple, who were at the heart of
Restoration intrigues, spent lavishly on the house, extending it and filling it
with the finest furniture of the day, much of which remains there.

rom the south, the garden side, the exterior shows a smooth brick elevation
ade more or less flat by the addition of extra rooms in the 1670s. The original
nd more complex shape of the house may be seen from the main entrance on
e north side, facing the river: here the projecting bays at each end mark the feet
the original H-shape, focusing attention on the central entrance set back in
e five-bay inner façade. Enter here, through gate piers added in 1671 and pass-
g another cast of John Bacon's *River Thames* (see above).

The immediate space, stretching to the left, is the **Great Hall** with, above it, the
all gallery, originally a separate dining-room before the later 17C alterations. The
eiling (1630s), by Joseph Kinsman, was very progressive for its time, divided into
ompartments in the manner Inigo Jones had brought back from Italy only a few
ears before and applied at the Queen's House in Greenwich and the Banqueting
ouse in Whitehall. There are numerous family portraits and a fireplace with fig-
res of Mars and Minerva. From here go into the **Staircase Hall** and up the fine
ak flight (1630s), with innovative panels instead of balusters, and newel-posts
ith fruit. The carving, including the doorcases, is incredible, from the genera-
on before Grinling Gibbons.

here are more family por-
aits in the **Hall Gallery**,
nd a chance to look at the
eiling plasterwork close up.

You then reach the **North
rawing Room**, with
nother fine ceiling of the
630s, and remarkable
urly pilasters. Next lies the
ong Gallery: its dimen-
ions derive from the fact
at it is one of the legs of

Ham House

the H of the original plan, but it was redecorated in the 1670s. It is interesting to compare the two types of carving. In the 1670s greater restraint was shown in, for example, the fluted Ionic pilasters and more delicate cornice. Is this moderation from the sobering effect of the Interregnum, even if we normally associate the Restoration with a Baroque exuberance? There are many more portraits, including one by Anthony van Dyck of *Charles I*, given by the King to William Murray and still in its original frame. There are also a generous number of paintings by Sir Peter Lely, chief portraitist of Charles II's age.

> ### Sir Peter Lely
>
> Lely (1618–80), a Dutchman who settled in England in the early 1640s, became the leading portraitist of the royal and aristocratic families in the period after Van Dyck. He worked for Charles I and kept working during the Commonwealth, but was even so re-appointed under Charles II. His portraits of distinguished women, such as the 'Windsor Beauties' series, all convey rather similar sleepy and provocatively dressed figures, but their male equivalents are more diverse and sharply characterised. Pepys did not like Lely, describing him as a 'mighty proud man and full of state'.

In the **Green Closet**, off the Long Gallery, is a remarkable coved ceiling of William Murray's time by Franz Cleyn, much ornate carving, and a fine ebony table with caryatid legs. At the other end of the Long Gallery is the **Library** (1670s) and, along the south front, the **Queen's Ante-Chamber, Bedchamber** and **Closet**. The queen in question was Catherine of Braganza, who paid a visit here in 1673, as indicated by crowns over the chimneypiece.

From this point return to the ground floor via the **Volury Room** to see the Duke and Duchess of Lauderdale's apartments. The strange name of the first room is a reference to flying: in the 1680s it housed birdcages, but its original purpose was a bedroom for the Duke, with a closet on one side and a dressing room on the other. The furniture dates from the 1740s when the 4th Earl of Dysart turned the space into a drawing room. The White Closet next door has a ceiling by Antonio Verrio (who worked at Hampton Court) with the Duchess's Private Closet beyond.

Beyond the Volury Room is a withdrawing room, designed for use after eating in the **Marble Dining-Room**, which is reached next. This room, with its fine parquet floor, was at the centre of the garden axis, like the Queen's Bedchamber above, but was for more intimate meals than the original dining-room above the Great Hall. It leads to the **Duke's Dressing Room**, beyond which, perversely, the **Duchess's Bedchamber**—although in fact it was originally used by the Duke; from it the Duke's Closet is reached. A few other rooms may be seen in the northwest corner, and the service rooms in the basement.

Do not miss the **gardens**, which are gradually being reconstructed in a layout of the 1670s. This is controversial, because unlike the house their design has been substantially changed since the 17C. The 18C **dairy** has also recently been restored. There is a most attractive restaurant in the **Orangery**, offering 'historic menus', which must be worth trying.

Return the way you came to catch the 65 bus to Richmond. Alternatively, if you have time, the river path back to Richmond is beautiful.

3 • Twickenham

we have seen, successive monarchs liked to establish their palaces by the
ames, to live by the river among idyllic scenery and appropriate neighbours.
ny lesser mortals have chosen to emulate them, for comparable reasons, and
the 18C a succession of Thames-side villas became established along the west
nk at Twickenham. You can understand the attraction: even today the water-
le route is delightful. If you expect to go as far as Strawberry Hill, check the
ening times (see below).

Distance: 2¾ miles. Time: 1½ hours + extra time for visits.
Train: St Margaret's. Off map.

art this walk from St Margaret's mainline station (reached from Waterloo) or
e an H37 bus there from Richmond (Chapter 62). From the station turn right
d pass Crown Road on the right. Go down the third turning to the right after
at, Sandycombe Road. On the left is a curiosity, **Sandycombe Lodge**, designed
d largely built by the painter J.M.W. Turner for his own use in 1812, when he
s 37 years old. Its odd looks are probably the result of Turner's legendary
htfistedness, which made him refuse to employ either architect or contractor
apter 10).
At the end of the road cross Richmond Road and go into Marble Hill Park, with
e white, Palladian north façade of the villa of **Marble Hill** gleaming across the
vn. Open 10.00–18.00 daily April–Sept, 10.00–17.00 daily Oct, 10.00–16.00
ed–Sun Nov–March. Admission free. Café nearby. Shop. ☎ 020 8892 5115.
ww.english-heritage.org.uk

This little gem was built (1724–29) for love, or love-making at least. It was
commissioned by the mistress of George II when Prince of Wales, Henrietta
Howard, Countess of Suffolk, with financial help from the Prince. She was an
eminently respectable and intelligent person (as her portrait inside the house
shows). The Countess was friendly with Alexander Pope and later Horace
Walpole, both neighbours. Pope gave advice and Charles Bridgeman designed
the gardens stretching down to the river.

e architect of Marble Hill was Roger Morris, taking advice from Lord Herbert,
er the Earl of Pembroke, an architectural enthusiast who sponsored the first
estminster Bridge. Palladian ideals were scrupulously applied: the villa has a
odest ground-level entry with some features of rustication, a pedimented
;ade at front and back—the latter, facing the river, is the more delicate—a single
and room on the first floor and a restrained symmetry.
Enter at a side door on the north front, from which the staircase hall is
ached. A fine carved staircase—there is also a servants' staircase—takes you in
e grand manner up to the **Great Room**, a perfect cube. It is decorated in gilt
d white, with an elaborate architrave but a plain ceiling. The precedent may be
rd Pembroke's cube room at Wilton House, near Salisbury, then thought to
ve been designed by Inigo Jones.
The doors at either end lead, to the left, to Lady Suffolk's bedchamber and to
e right, her dressing room (this is the kind of absurdity that Palladian symme-
′ necessitates). The bed alcove lies between Ionic columns. On the north side of
e house are the Damask Room and servant's bedchamber. Among the rooms

on the attic floor above, most notable is the gallery along the east side of th
house. Back on the ground floor are a breakfast room and dining parlour.

Leave by the door you entered, turn left and follow the path round to the ear
19C coach house, where there is a café. Take the path alongside this to rea
Orleans Road, with small cottages and stables stretching down to the river. B
before going in that direction you may like to turn right and right again in
Chapel Road to see **Montpelier Row** (1720) at the end, 'one of the best exar
ples near London of well-mannered, well-proportioned early Georgian terra
development' (Pevsner).

The route runs beside the river as much as possible. Back down Orleans Ro
on the right is an entrance to **Orleans House**, of which all that survives is th
Octagon, itself important because it is the work of James Gibbs (see Chapter
You reach it through the trees. With the recent additions behind it is now used
a local art gallery, with frequently changing and always interesting exhibitior
Open April–Sept 13.00–17.30 Tues–Sat, 14.00–17.30 Sun; Oct–Marc
13.00–16.30 Tues–Sat, 14.00–16.30 Sun and Bank Holidays. Admission fre
☎ 020 8892 0221. www.richmond.gov.uk/depts/opps/leisure/arts/orleanshous

The Octagon (1720) was a garden room, commissioned by the owner
Orleans House, James Johnston, Queen Anne's Secretary of State. Gibbs w
working on St Martin-in-the-Fields at that time, using the Italian plastere
Artari and Bagutti for the nave. He gave them a field day here at Twickenha
Two of the medallion portraits are of George II and Queen Caroline (f
whose visit this luxurious extension was created in 1729—how did she fe
about her husband's mistress comfortably installed next door?). The thir
done later, is of Louis Philippe, Duc d'Orléans, after whom the house w
named. He lived here in the years 1800–14 and 1815–17 and as King
France in 1844 paid a sentimental return visit. Scandalously, the house w
demolished in 1926.

Walk towards the river, going through a small gate into the road, called Riversid
the rest of Orleans House garden lies opposite and was always divided by th
road. Just to the left, in Marble Hill Park, you can catch the **ferry** across th
Thames to Ham House (Chapter 62). To see more of Twickenham, turn rig
along the road, past good houses, although the river is frustratingly out of sig
most of the time, with high garden walls each side. Soon you reach the **Whi
Swan**, a lovely 18C pub with riverside seats. Turn right up Sion Road, with
pretty 18C terrace, go under a bridge—which you will soon go over—and up
the right to see the church.

St Mary is a beauty, with a 14C tower and a noble and generous 18C bod
built, after the old church collapsed, by John James (1714–15), architect of
George Hanover Square. The chief façades are clearly meant to be those to th
north and south, a scenic consideration as the pedimented and projecting sid
face the village and the river respectively. There is a monument on the exterior
Alexander Pope's nurse for 38 years and to the 18C actress Kitty Clive, wh
undertook many acts of local charity, a feature which her glowing epitaph cle
erly links with her stage career:

Such deeds on life's short scenes true glory shed
As heavenly plaudits hail the virtuous dead.

Alexander Pope

Born in Windsor as the only child of Roman Catholic parents, Pope (1688–1744) suffered at the age of 12 a disabling disease that left him with curvature of the spine. As a young man he came to live in London, joining the circles of Joseph Addison and Jonathan Swift. He settled in Twickenham with his mother in 1718, gradually developing his riverside villa in Palladian style and creating a remarkable garden and grotto. Of this only the grotto survives. Pope's poetry is distinguished by its rhyming couplets and unforgettable epigrams. A true Augustan, as a person he was combative and waspish, yet in a certain way passionate.

There are many fine monuments inside including one by Francis Bird to Pope nd his parents. Open 14.00–16.00.

To get into the gardens and locate the bridge you came under a while ago, ake your way from the church round to the north side of **York House**. This is w council offices but remains a very handsome building, much altered from its 7C origins, when the owner was the Earl of Clarendon. You may be able to peep and see one or two rooms and perhaps the 17C staircase, but the best effect is hieved by going past the front entrance to the east side of the house, to view e gardens. They are beautifully laid out and planted with a fine sunken lawn at e back of the house. At the south end of this you find the bridge. Go over to see e riverside gardens with the messy boatyards of Eel Pie Island across the water. alk westwards and enjoy a laugh at the amazing sculptured fountain installed an owner in 1910: large numbers of life-size nude nymphs splash about, procted from vandals by an ornate, and much more recent, structure of painfuloking iron spikes. Beyond, in a separate space, is some interesting modern ulpture, unlabelled for some reason.

Rugby football

The much-disputed story is that W.W. Ellis, playing football at Rugby School, Warwickshire, in 1823, picked up the ball and ran with it. The Football Association's regulations of 1863 (see Chapter 56) separated rugby as a distinct game in which handling was widely permitted and an oval ball used for the purpose. It was widely adopted at independent, fee-paying schools, thus becoming socially distinct as well. The Rugby Football Union, of London clubs, was formed at a Pall Mall restaurant in 1871 and tried for over a century to maintain its amateur status despite the existence of a separate professional game, Rugby League, in the north.

Now you find yourself at the riverside **Embankment**. So far there has been no nbankment, the river inaccessible beyond private gardens. It is all very public re. Swans welcome crumbs. There will be ice-cream vans and a major pub lled the *Barmy Arms*. Twickenham's shops lie in York Street and London Road st to the north, where Twickenham station is also to be found. Ten minutes' alk north from the station is what is for some Twickenham's most famous ilding, '**Twickers**', the mecca of Rugby Union in England and headquarters the Rugby Football Union. It has a museum which opens 10.00–17.00 Tues– t, 11.00–17.00 Sun. Admission charge. Guided tours. ☎ 020 8892 8877.

You may be curious to cross the footbridge to **Eel Pie Island**, where the tavern

was famous in the 19C as a resort for boat-trippers from London who came to e
eel pies. In the 1960s it developed a reputation for risqué parties. Today there m
still be parties, but for the visitor there is no tavern, no entertainment, and no ca
but a great many bungalows with 'Private' firmly inscribed on their gates.

Only a little more riverside is accessible, past a fine but derelict Art Deco buil
ing; then you have to cut up to the main road. Turn left along Cross Deep, whic
is busy and dusty, past a fine house (1700) of the same name, and past St Jame
and St Catherine's schools. This is where Pope had his villa, with an unde
ground passage under the road—the **Grotto**—to his riverside garden. So
afterwards, on the left, come Radnor Gardens, a delightful green oasis by the riv
on the site of Radnor House, destroyed in the Second World War, with a surviv
ing octagonal summer house and a disconcertingly triumphalist war memoria

Go back to the road and, unless you are going to visit Strawberry Hill, take
33 or R68 bus back to Crown Road for St Margaret's station or into Richmond.
it is Sunday and the time is right, cross the road and fork right down Waldegra
Road to **Strawberry Hill**, on the left. Open April–Oct 14.00–15.30 Sun. Guide
tours only. Admission charge. ☎ 020 8240 4224.

> Horace Walpole, writer, critic, connoisseur and son of Prime Minister Robe
> Walpole, acquired Strawberry Hill in 1747. Almost immediately, as a kind
> joke, he began to Gothicise it. Over the next 18 years he finished the job, b
> by the end it was less of a joke and more of a serious piece of archaeologic
> reproduction. As such it is often referred to as the beginning of the Goth
> Revival, although to true revivalists of the 19C such as A.W.N. Pugin it wou
> have remained trivial. Yet Strawberry Hill was very influential and has hu
> appeal: today's Postmodernist ethic approves strongly of this kind of imit
> tion. You are advised to see it if you can.

In addition to Walpole's building there is a large 19C wing constructed by a lat
owner, the political hostess Lady Waldegrave, and the extensive 20C buildings
St Mary's College, who now own it. There is much to see of Walpole's work, bo
on the exterior and during the 90-minute guided tour of the interior.

To return to town, take the 33 bus, which stops in Waldegrave Road.

64 • Kingston

Kingston-upon-Thames, more than anywhere else so near to London, still fee
like a country town, with a central market place and medieval streets and alle
ways: you could be anywhere in England. There are some excellent shops, and
course Father Thames. This route does not involve much walking but makes
very pleasant day, or half-day, which could (just) be combined with Hampt
Court or Wimbledon, or a walk in Richmond Park.

- Distance: 2 miles. Time: 1½ hours. Off map.

Travel Trains go to Kingston from Waterloo (on the line to Shepperton) at 1
minute intervals. A Zone 6 travel card would allow you to combine your journ
with a visit to Hampton Court, a bus ride or walk away, or change at Wimbledo

Kingston is a historic place, going back to Saxon times. Seven Saxon kings were crowned here, including the admirable Athelstan and the unfortunate Aethelred II (see below). The town received its first charter in 1200 making it the oldest of only three royal Boroughs in England, and King John lived here. The key was its location, on the Thames and on direct routes from London to Portsmouth or across the river to the west. A bridge was built here in 1193 and was the first one upstream from London.

You will not feel much of this as you walk from the station. Turn right along the higher pedestrian path by the railway and when it descends to road level cross the main road to Bentalls. The walk begins by going through this mega-store and one other; if shops do not appeal, keep going by road to Kingston Bridge.

Bentalls was founded in 1867 and grew to be Britain's largest privately owned department store. It is huge, taking up a whole block, with a bridge across the street you were in to its own car park. The 'Wrenaissance' façade by the 1930s Kingston architect Maurice Webb was retained in redevelopment. Re-cross Wood Street to the branch of **John Lewis**, nearly as big, in progressive architecture of 1990. John Lewis extends across its own bridge and finally provides an exit, via its own car park, to the bridgefoot by the river. In the construction process, a **medieval undercroft** was discovered and conserved. These two excellent and enormous retail outlets contribute to Kingston's claim to be the seventh largest retail centre in Britain.

But there is more to Kingston than shops. You are out on **Kingston Bridge** now, with the Thames flowing by beneath you. This handsome bridge was built by Edward Lapidge in 1828 of brick faced with Portland stone, but widened on the upstream side in the 1914: you can see evidence of this under the arches. A pleasant riverside path stretches under the bridge—follow it past a riverside pub and then turn left past a car-park entrance into Bishops Hall and then Thames Street. Opposite, through another gap, is a churchyard and the west end of the parish church.

The exterior of **All Saints** is of flint, late medieval, with a fine tower to which a brick top with pineapple finials was added in 1708. It was quite heavily restored in the 19C but the walls partly incorporate a much older building. To the south, in the churchyard, there are markers to denote a pre-1066 chapel where the Saxon coronations may have taken place. Inside, you are aware of a very sizeable space, with transepts: this was a church for a large, prosperous town, and the centrally placed altar denotes a recent adaptation to what are no doubt smaller congregations. There are some particularly fine monuments: look out for Sir Anthony Benn (d. 1618) lying in his red robe, and the seated Countess of Liverpool by Sir Francis Chantrey (1825), shown elegantly meditating.

Leave the church to the south to enter the bustling Market Place. The atmosphere is that of a country town. Straight ahead is the Italianate **Market House**, once the Town Hall (1838–40): inside you will find an information office, and on the front a gilded statue of **Queen Anne** by Francis Bird (1705), the important sculptor whose work can be found extensively in St Paul's Cathedral.

Facing Queen Anne, take in the buildings of the Market Place. Immediately behind is the **Shrubsole monument** (1882)—to a local worthy. Further behind on the left are the façade of the **Griffin Hotel** and the **Druid's Head**, still a pub. On your immediate left, in the passageway, the weatherboarded side denotes an old building; next to it is the proud façade of **Nuthall's** (1901), once the smartest restaurant in town. Ahead to your left, on the corner of Thames Street, no. 14 (now a branch of Next) is a genuine 16C timber-framed house, leaning quaintly. Adjacent to it, nos 15 and 16 are also covered in timber-framing, but this is entirely fake (1909). Behind the Market Hall to the right, stretching round the corner, is a façade which looks more genuinely old but is also fake, in that it is a restored copy done after a fire (1976). On your immediate right is a former inn, marked 1422, which seems unlikely: next to it is a passageway typical of a medieval town. The centre of Kingston has many such and the criss-cross street pattern denotes the original lay-out.

Go through this passageway and turn right into a smaller space, known as **Apple Market**, also ancient, and then turn right, into the curving High Street. On your left is the Guildhall, 1930s-looking, by Maurice Webb, though not daring like some town halls of the period, in brick with a curved façade and a central tower filled with Classical references. Sometimes temporary exhibitions are held inside. On the right of the entrance is something remarkable: encircled by Victorian railings modelled on Saxon spears is a **sandstone slab** on which seven different kings were crowned between AD 900 and 979. This was the period when the West Saxon kingdom was asserting its domination not only over the Danes, who occupied the north and made frequent invasions, but also over the Mercian (Midland) section of the Saxon community. The choice of Kingston for the coronations (as opposed to Winchester) is probably an indication of its geographical position on the Thames—critical in this defensive context.

Anglo-Saxon England

This least studied, and least understood, period of English history started with invasions from North Germany from the 4C and 7C and lasted until the Norman Conquest. The Anglo-Saxons gave England its name, its Christian religion, its towns and shires, a literature and culture (see the Sutton Hoo Burial in the British Museum, Chapter 27) and a distinct, though now largely lost, architecture. Themselves invaders, their enemies were the invading Danes, or Vikings, who populated much of the north and east. Only through the skill and courage of Alfred in the later 9C was a precarious single English kingdom established. The rulers crowned at Kingston over the next century were his descendants, but the last of them, Aethelred II, mismanaged matters to allow a successful Danish invasion, including London, in 1016 by Cnut (Canute). Cnut's stepson was Edward the Confessor.

From both the coronation stone and from back across the High Street examin the small bridge over the River Hogsmill, which flows down into Surrey. You wi see that the stone has been erected almost precariously above the stream. Th **Clattern Bridge**, as it is called, is by far the oldest on any London waterway an one of the oldest in Britain. Its piers date from the 12C. A little path on the wes ern side enables you to see them.

Proceed down the High Street. On the right, no. 52 is **Amari House** (1730s with a weatherboarded back similar to the one you saw in the Market Place: i the 1790s it was the home of Caesar Picton, a wealthy black businessma brought as a slave from Senegal at the age of six by a local gentleman, wh gained prosperity from a coal business set up with a bequest from his owner wife. Across the road (and now a Pizza Express) is a much older survival, datin from about 1550, an open **hall house**, that is, a house without chimneys; the smoke from fires inside was directed through a hole in the roof, as in medieval halls such as that at Hampton Court.

Return up the High Street, or the parallel path by the Thames, to the Clattern Bridge and turn right along the pathway prettily constructed by the Hogsmill, with the Guildhall on your left and other office buildings. You come out in St James's Road. Turn right, across Kingston Hall Road and down Penrhyn Road as far as the **Surrey County Hall**, a handsome building (1892–93) with additions by E. Vincent Harris (1930–38). You will be able to distinguish Victorian work from that of the 1930s: the former is much more exuberant, less respectable. The building is still used by Surrey Council, confirming Kingston's important status, although the county town is Guildford.

Go back again up St James's Road and turn right into Eden Street. A grand United Reformed Church stands on the opposite corner. On the left is another shopping centre, Edenwalk, and opposite that, on the right, is a Gothic former post office (1875). Go past this down Lady Booth Road and cross Wheatfield Way. On the other side is a delightful, warm, beautifully proportioned Arts and Crafts style **library and museum** (1904): the architect was Alfred Cox, the benefactor Andrew Carnegie. Open 10.00–17.00 Mon, Tues, Thur–Sat. Admission free. Shop. ☎ 020 8546 5386. www.king.mus@rbk.kingston.gov.uk

The museum has a good display of local history on the ground floor, with a vivid model showing the town in 1813, and changing exhibitions on the first floor. A particularly interesting theme is the work of Eadweard Muybridge (born 'Edward', but he changed his name to match that of one of the Saxon kings), a local man who found fame and moderate fortune in the USA in the 1870s as one of the inventors of the movies. He returned to Kingston to die, in 1904, and left his zoopraxiscope to the museum, where it is on display.

From the museum turn right, past the bus station and across Fairfield North, turning right into London Road. You will not be able to miss *Out of Order*, a joke sculpture by David Mach (1989) consisting of a series of telephone boxes collapsed domino-style. Opposite is a police station (1864). No. 30, on the right, is supposed to be the oldest surviving brick house in the town (1660). Soon after this, on the left, are **Cleave's Almshouses**, dateable only a little later; intended to house 'six poor men and six poor women of honest life and reputation', they still do.

A little way further along London Road is Kingston Grammar School, founded by Elizabeth I in 1561. On the opposite side, across Cromwell Road, **Lovekyn Chapel** is a chantry founded in 1309 that survived demolition at the Reformation by being re-incorporated as the original school. It is thought to be the only remaining freestanding chantry chapel in England. Beyond it is another school, Tiffins, in a super yellow-brick 18C mansion.

All good things must come to an end, and there is nothing more to see in London Road, so return to Clarence Street. Some more shops in this pedestrianised road may engage your attention. Turn right up Dolphin Street to return to the station. Alternatively, a 65 bus will take you to Ham House (Chapter 62). Plenty of buses run to Hampton Court (111, 216, 411) from Wood Street.

65 • Harrow

Harrow is the name of both a school and a town, the old part of which stands on top of a hill 200ft high, its church a landmark to the surrounding suburbs. The 19C houses climbing up the hill and the fine school buildings make a place of some character. It is worth spending a half-day here, especially if that is extended briefly by adding the excursion suggested at the end.

• Distance: 2 miles. Time: 1½ hours, or spend the day. Tube: Harrow-on-the-Hill. Off map.

Start at Harrow-on-the-Hill station (Metropolitan Line) in Zone 5. After the ticket barriers, turn left and go down the steps. Toilets are available at this station—a rarity on the Tube. Go forward to Lowlands Road, cross it and set off up Lansdowne Road. The open space to your left is called the Grove, and high above and through the trees the spire of St Mary's church points heavenwards.

Go down the footpath between the fences to reach Roxborough Park, which you cross to continue the footpath. A sign says 'St Anselm's School' as if the path were exclusively theirs: it is not. On the left stands the Roman Catholic church of **Our Lady and St Thomas of Canterbury** (1894), and beyond, St Anselm's School (clearly of the 1950s). Then the scene opens out beautifully with common land on all sides: St Mary's again appears on high on the left. Your path stretches away slightly to the left; once over the ridge, descend towards 19C houses in stock brick mixed with recent Arts and Crafts Postmodernism. Soon you find yourself in West Street. Turn left and then right into Crown Street. These little streets grew up on the hillside to house those providing services to the great 19C school on the summit, 'above' them in both senses.

Crown Street leads to Middle Road where **John Lyon School** lies on both sides, in 19C houses. It was founded in the 19C when Harrow School lost sight of its original purpose—and that of John Lyon, Harrow's original founder—to serve the local community. The buildings include part of the Red House (1883–85) by E.S. Prior, an interesting Arts and Crafts architect, who lived in the area.

Turn left up Byron Hill Road: this is the first reference to the Romantic poet who went to school at Harrow and whose presence here is still felt more strongly even than Winston Churchill's. As you ascend you will see a spectacular 1880s house (no. 10) on the left, with fine views. The summit is an open area called The Square—oddly, because it is triangular—with the rambling **King's Head** pub on the left (closed) and a few restaurants and former banks: a little community that is no more. Join the High Street and go left, taking a route that passes along the ridge of the hill. It has an eclectic mix of houses from a range of periods. Some are boarding houses of Harrow School.

Harrow School

After passing on the left the ironically named **Old Etonian**, a French restaurant, you will see the main buildings of Harrow School. It is best to mount the steps through the gardens on the left-hand side of the road, face the iron gate and turn clockwise to look at each. Several distinguished architectural names are represented.

Lord Byron

Byron (1788–1824), the great Romantic poet, 'mad, bad and dangerous to know', has left us a reputation rather than a love of his works. Yet his influence was enormous, especially in Europe, and not just on poetry but also on music, the novel, opera and painting. Born with a clubfoot, to unstable parents, his succession to a title was unexpected, and did nothing to temper his wild nature. At school in Harrow, he loved the place and wrote affectionately about it afterwards:

> *As I trace again thy winding hill*
> *Mine eyes admire, my heart adores thee still.*

He was ostracised for supposed incest with his half-sister Augusta, and from 1816 Byron left England never to return: he died from a fever while becoming involved with the cause of Greek nationalism. His five-year-old daughter Allegra by Claire Claremont, a friend of the Shelleys, is buried in an unmarked grave in St Mary's churchyard.

The school was founded in 1572 by a local farmer, John Lyon, who obtained a charter from Queen Elizabeth I for the purpose. A very early if not original building of 1608 survives (the Old Schools). Besides Lord Bryon and Sir Winston Churchill, former pupils over time have included Robert Peel, Richard Brinsley Sheridan and Anthony Trollope (who hated it).

Behind the gates and almost on the brow of the hill (the church is behind) is **Old Schools**. The 17C schoolroom is still inside, with benches and the headmaster's throne at one end. But the attractive red-brick building consists mostly of later extensions, primarily those by the Classicist C.R. Cockerell (1819–21), here performing very effectively in Tudor style.

Next, across a small road up to the church with more, oddly constructed steps in front, is the **War Memorial Building**, begun in 1921 by Sir Herbert Baker, of Bank of England fame (a plaque pretentiously says: Architectus Herbertus Baker). His is a recognisable style, a kind of smoothed-out late Classicism, sub-Lutyens but in some ways more grandiose. It is a very well-behaved building, making the **Chapel** by Sir George Gilbert Scott (1854–57), next across the main road, look quite original. This is in uncompromising Gothic Revival style, flint-faced, with many spirelets and gables, lovely against the spectacular view behind.

Next door to the Chapel is Scott's **Vaughan Library** (1863), built to commemorate the famous head of the school who in 15 years expanded it from under 100 pupils to nearly 500: it too is Gothic but this time in multi-coloured brick and approached by a tiled path. Then comes a much more sober but substantial red-brick building: this is the **Headmaster's House** by Decimus Burton (1840–46), another Classicist here working in brick. There is a little Gothic peculiarity beyond it. Out of sight from here, down past a pleasant garden and cascade, is the Shepherd Churchill dining hall (1976), by Dennis Lennon, in traditional mood.

Finally, completing the circle back across the road, is **Druries**, a boarding house by C.K. Hayward (1864): he was the brother of a housemaster and architect of several buildings on the site. It is Gothic in multi-coloured brick again, but whereas Scott's buildings are under control, this one is wild. With the views on all sides this group of buildings makes a lovely place; although close to London its charm is rustic against Eton's more distant urbanity.

Make a short detour to look down Football Lane, a right-hand turn beyond the Chapel and the neo-Tudor New Schools (1855), to see the **Museum Schools**, delicious Arts and Crafts building by Basil Champneys (1884–86), an object lesson in how the later Victorians escaped from Gothic. Return to the main road, across which you are now faced by the **Speech Room** by William Burges (1874–77), Victorian extremist. His idea here was Sicilian Gothic. The statue of *Queen Elizabeth* by Sir Richard Westmacott (1815) was added incongruously in 192. The asymmetrical towers are also later, but as you return up Sir Herbert Baker steps and turn right you can see at the back the semicircular shape comparable Sir Christopher Wren's Sheldonian Theatre at Oxford. A small public art galle here is open in term-time, 14.30–17.00 daily (except Wed).

Now climb the last stretch of hill to the church, going through a lych-gate an past the graves: there are many interesting headstones. The church of **St Ma** is an ancient foundation (12C) and was a 'peculiar' of the Archbishop Canterbury, which is to say, the Archbishop was responsible for it directly, not th local diocese. The roughcast tower with the eye-catching spire has Norman win dows, but most of the church was heavily restored or rebuilt by Sir George Gilbe Scott (1846–49). It still looks good and has fine brasses and monuments inside including John Flaxman's moving relief to John Lyon (1815).

Go beyond the church to the west end to see the view and, inscribed on a sto by the grave of John Peachey, where Byron often sat, his ode recalling his days Harrow, ending in full Romantic vein 'Take, while thou cans't, a lingering la farewell.'

Return to the east end of the church and go left down Grove Hill. **The Grov** an 18C house, appears on the left—once the vicarage, it is now another boar ing house—as do other good houses as you descend. Take Davidson Lane to t right to see a Gothic monstrosity by Hayward, called **Garlands**, acro Peterborough Road. Go on down either of these parallel roads to Lowlands Roa

You may want to look at Harrow town, for shopping or refreshment. It is not ing special, but then it never was: unlike Eton, town and school are unconnecte There are two large, perfectly ordinary shopping malls, St Anne's and George's. Or you can return direct to Harrow-on-the-Hill station.

While in the area, it may be worth going two stops on towards Watford a alighting at **Pinner**, with a medieval church at the top of the old High Stre several timber-framed houses and pubs, and pleasant parks and gardens. It h an old village at the centre and, all around, suburbia at its leafy best. Metrola has its merits.

Another pleasant excursion might be to take a 350 bus to Headstone Lane a there, in a local park, locate **Headstone Manor** (1344), the only moated man house left in Middlesex, built for the Archbishop of Canterbury (the same o was connected with St Mary at Harrow). It is slowly being restored. Nearby in tithe barn is a modest local museum with changing exhibitions. Op 12.30–17.00 Thurs–Sat, 10.30–17.00 Sun. Free. Shop. ☎ 020 8861 2626.

·6 • Muswell Hill and Hampstead Garden Suburb

ardly a place on every visitor's itinerary, Muswell Hill is included here as an lmost perfectly preserved example of an Edwardian suburb, free of shopping ialls, supermarkets and stations. To get there you are taken via another curios- y relatively unknown to tourists, the Alexandra Palace. The walk may be com- lemented with a visit to the contemporary, but very different and architec- irally superior, Hampstead Garden Suburb, only a short bus ride away.

Distance: 2 miles + 1¼ miles for Hampstead Garden Suburb. Time: 1¼ hours + 1 hour. Station: Alexandra Palace. Off map.

ıart from the station called Alexandra Palace, reached on the frequent national ıil services northbound from Finsbury Park (Victoria and Piccadilly Lines). This the great main track from King's Cross to Scotland, opened in 1844, careering ırough the little tunnels of north London. When the Palace was built in 1875 special branch line was laid to it, but has long since gone.

Walk up the steps over the tracks, turn left, then left again into Alexandra Park 'ay. Ignoring the asphalt turning, fork left again along a sandy footpath. This ikes you across **Alexandra Park**, laid out in readiness when the Palace was ıly a plan, conceived in the 1860s as part of the contemporary mania for huge :hibitions but remaining unbuilt due to lack of finance. The slope to the left is ırprisingly rural—you could be in Hertfordshire—with fine trees and central ɔndon visible not far away to the south. At the end of the golf course, push up ıe grass slope to the right towards the Palace. The planting, paths and terraces ɛre are all Victorian. Climb up to the main terrace, across the road, to take in ɔth the view of London and the south façade of the building.

The **view** is stunning. The separation, and rivalry, between Docklands to the ft and the City (look out for Tower 42) is vividly clear, with the West End inte- ːated yet distinct with its more interesting Centre Point and Telecom Tower. The ɛarby ridge of hill to the right is Highgate.

Alexandra Palace itself, vulgarly but affectionately known as 'Ally Pally', is ɔ beauty, but an ambitious effort nevertheless. The precedent was the Crystal ılace, rebuilt at Sydenham and already the finest possible landmark for south ɔndon. But the design of the Alexandra Palace had different predecessors, not ›seph Paxton's modernising glass and iron, but the gabled brick halls of South ɛnsington, still to be seen at the Bethnal Green Museum (Chapter 46). This one ıas to have a long central nave, crossed by three transepts—you are in front of ıe central one—with a tower at each corner.

The Palace, named in honour of the Princess of Wales, opened in early May 1873. Sixteen days later it was burned down as a result of a coal falling from a workman's brazier. The 124,000 visitors who had come in the first two weeks encouraged the promoters to rebuild, and the new version was opened in 1875, with a Great Hall to seat 12,000 and the largest organ in the country. Commercially, however, the building was never a success. By the First World War it had ceased to function, becoming successively a barracks, a home for Belgian refugees and a prison camp for 17,000 captured Germans. It had a new lease of life in 1936 when, on 26 August, the world's first live television transmission took place from here. The Palace was used by the BBC for several decades, but in 1980 another fire necessitated much rebuilding.

Alexandra Palace now accommodates a lively programme of exhibitions all th
year round: you may be lucky enough to coincide with one. For advance detail
☎ 020 8365 2121.

Queen Alexandra (1844–1925)

The eldest daughter of the Danish King Christian IX, Alexandra was married in 1863 to the Prince of Wales, who became Edward VII (see Chapter 9),
purposely perhaps to calm him down after a tempestuous young manhood.
Alexandra as Princess of Wales was popular as well as beautiful and elegant.
She suffered her husband's infidelities and when Edward VII was dying, she
insisted that Mrs Keppel, his mistress of the time, should be summoned to his
bedside. Her life was devoted to family, domesticity and good causes, and she
pioneered Alexandra Rose Day, raising funds to care for sick children.

Walk west along the terrace, past the *Phoenix* pub insensitively inserted in
the corner. If there is an exhibition, enter at the west end: even if not, try to catc
a glimpse of the Palm Court. Then go down the slope and away from the roadwa
to the right into the pleasant parkland of The Grove, once a fine 18C house occu
pied by Dr Johnson's friend Topham Beauclerk but now demolished. There a
some remains of 18C planting and several old trees. Cross over the grass to th
left to locate a covered footbridge out of the park leading into Muswell Hill, an
turn right.

At first sight, **Muswell Hill** proper is no more than a busman's shelter in th
middle of a roundabout and several rather large buses, but look around: the cen
tre does not in the least detract from the dignified shopping façades elegantl
arranged round the circumference, covering the brow of the hill, with matchin
avenues descending in different directions. John Betjeman should have writte
about this place. To the immediate right Duke's Avenue dips downhill, with
Baptist church on the right. Next, anticlockwise, comes the Broadway wit
shops; then a residential street, Queen's Avenue; and finally to the left the con
tinuation of the Broadway in your direction. The whole ensemble was created b
a firm of local builders, Edmondsons, between 1897 and 1914, repeating wit
even greater success a formula they had used at Crouch End, not far away. Toda
you will find plenty of coffee bars and cafés here to refresh yourself.

As you go left along the Broadway, look out on the left-hand side, dow
Summerland Gardens and Hillfield Park, for sweeping views southeast. Opposit
is a pretty Presbyterian church (1903), now an Irish pub, a bizarre outcome ce
tain to distress the original elders. The Church of England is still alive and well
the church of **St James** straight ahead, with a proud spire (1909).

Turn right into Fortis Green Road. Opposite is a fine cinema (1930s) in crea
and black with a linked Art Deco shopping parade curving round the corner. O
the right-hand side of the road are more, but different, Edwardian shops wit
large arched windows, a familiar design. The Edmondsons' curving terrac
stretch away down Prince's Avenue. Then, by contrast, comes the rustic bric
work of **Birchwood Mansions** (1907), in Arts and Crafts style, an entirely di
ferent idiom from Edwardian suburbia—it is a foretaste of what you will see
you go on to the Hampstead Garden Suburb. At the end of the road is anothe
Gothic church, the **United Reformed** (1897), built as Congregational and st
in business.

Now wander round the Edmondsons' streets, such as Queen's Avenue and King's Avenue, to return to Muswell Hill Broadway and the Alexandra Palace. There are plenty of buses to Highgate where you can catch the Tube (Northern Line) or to the City or West End (43 or 134). Or walk along Fortis Green, which has several pretty 19C cottages, early villas and an old pub, to reach East Finchley station (Northern Line): turn left at the *Bald Faced Stag* pub.

It is only one stop from East Finchley to Finchley Central where, nearby, in East End Road (look at the map in the station) is the second branch of the **Jewish Museum** (see also Chapter 40), on East End Road. It is based in the former Finchley Manor House built by Thomas Allen (1723). This branch contains an archive of tapes, photographs and documents recording Jewish experience in Britain and reconstructions of workshops and homes. It also runs an educational programme on the Holocaust. Open 10.30–17.00 Mon–Thur, 10.30–16.30 Sun (closed Sun in August). ☎ 020 8349 1143. www.jewmusm.ort.org. Tube: Finchley Central.

Hampstead Garden Suburb

Alternatively, in Muswell Hill or at East Finchley, get on a 102 bus for Hampstead Garden Suburb. It is always called this locally; and residents will say they live 'on', not 'in', the Suburb. Alight at Temple Fortune, a shopping parade not far from Golders Green station—sit downstairs and ask the driver to call out the stop. Start up Hampstead Way into the Suburb.

Garden suburbs

Suburbs are always by definition within a conurbation. Garden cities were a separate development, self-contained towns on green-field sites. The English fascination with rural living can be seen in London squares, in the establishment of communal gardens in Notting Hill (Chapter 38), and in the first garden suburb, Bedford Park (Chapter 57). This had red-brick Arts and Crafts architecture and winding streets, in which old trees survived unfelled, and not least an art school, church and tavern, epitomes of middle-class culture. It was not radical in trying to combine town with country, but it was radical in adopting for its design, not Classical or Gothic, but a rural English vernacular which owed something to Arts and Crafts and which was to develop into 'Queen Anne' style.

In 1907, thirty years after Bedford Park, Dame Henrietta Barnett, wife of Canon Barnett, a tireless worker for improvement in the East End, conceived the idea of a large area of mixed housing, to bring working-class residents in contact with 'the contagion of refinement' from middle-class neighbours. The area she chose lay north of the Barnetts' own country place near Hampstead, which the Northern Line now conveniently reached.

As social policy this was original enough, but employing Barry Parker and Raymond Unwin to design the street plans and architecture generated a genuinely radical ideology: artisans and managers lived on a single estate in houses varying in size (according to class, it must be admitted) but in a co-ordinated vernacular style. Hampstead Garden Suburb has been an example ever since, and its style has worn well. If the middle class now rules here, you could say that was exactly Dame Henrietta's intention.

Temple Fortune was to be the Suburb's only shopping centre, the idea of shops in Central Square, which we shall see, having been foolishly rejected. Go up Asmun's Hill or via The Orchard, or explore independently this earliest part of the development, aimed at working-class or artisan occupants. Try to locate examples of 'twittens', footpaths between the houses, sometimes with arched entrances. It is villagey and quaint, decidedly 'English' in its use of traditional forms, a logical development of the Arts and Crafts style without reverting, via the 'Wrenaissance', to Classicism.

But Classicism does creep in, as you see when you make your way to Central Square, formal, rectangular, with processional entrances north and south. The main, Anglican church is **St Jude** (1909–11), by Sir Edwin Lutyens, highly eclectic in style, though at first sight Gothic, as manifested in the spire. The other Free church, also by Lutyens (1911), with a dome, balances both spire and square. The Institute and School on the east side complete the formality and, in theory, the community. But there are no shops, and certainly no pub. On the south side are houses for the middle classes.

Again you may want to explore independently, but do not miss Meadway where it crosses Hampstead Way: nos 6–10 Meadway and no. 22 Hampstead Way are by the increasingly-admired M.H. Baillie-Scott (1909), middle class yet still strongly vernacular. Who would not want to live here?

If you go down Hoop Lane and turn left, you soon reach Golders Green station (Northern Line) or a bus stop: take the 13 or 113 bus back to town.

67 • Walthamstow

Walthamstow has a huge street market four days a week, a delightful secret area round its old church with a good local museum, an unbelievably forceful town hall, and the William Morris Gallery. Unfashionable it may be but Walthamstow undoubtedly merits a half-day from anyone with more than a few days to spend in London. This walk can easily be combined with that in Barking (Chapter 68) with Barking preferably coming first.

- Distance: 2¼ miles. Time: 1½ hours + 1 hour for the William Morris Gallery. Tube: Walthamstow Central. Off map.

Start from Walthamstow Central station (Victoria Line or national rail from Liverpool St). If you have come from, or are going on to, Barking, you must use Walthamstow Queen's Road station (on the North London Silverlink line) approached via Shrubland Road.

Almost opposite is Selbourne Walk shopping centre. Go through that to discover the **market**, which is mentioned here first because markets are better earlier in the day. Open Tues, Thur, Fri and Sat. This is supposed to be the longest street market in England, although Portobello Road must beat it. As at Notting Hill there is plenty of variety, but no antiques, and lower prices. The grand former public library has a bust of *Passmore Edwards*, the 19C philanthropist, who endowed it and so many others.

From the market cross Hoe Street to ascend Church Hill. On the corners are some crazy flats with a clock tower (1950s), and several other interesting buildings as you go along—not least Walthamstow Girls' School on the right. Soon afterwards, turn right towards the church, **St Mary**, not very prepossessing with its plaster rendering but historical: it is originally 12C, but much messed about in the early 19C. A guide is on sale inside if the church is unlocked. Do not miss the fine collection of monuments and monumental brasses.

Peaceful, too, is the ancient group of buildings around the church. To the north lie the **Monoux Almshouses**, restored after bomb damage, but dating back to the 16C when Sir George Monoux, City Alderman and Master of the Drapers' Company, endowed them. As you come from the churchyard, to the south on your right are **Squires' Almshouses** (1795), 'erected and endowed for ever by Mrs Mary Squires for the use of six decayed tradesmen's widows of this parish and no other.'

Opposite is a former National School of 1819 and beyond that the **Vestry House** (1730), now a museum. It was intended for meetings of the Vestry (i.e. the elders of the parish) and used as a workhouse for 20–30 of the parish poor. It later served as a police station—one of the prime exhibits is a police cell of 1861. Another lock-up for difficult citizens was attached to the exterior wall and can still be seen. Open 10.00–13.00 and 14.00–17.30 Mon–Fri, 10.00–13.00 and 14.00–17.00 Sat. Admission free. Shop. ☎ 020 8509 1917.

Return along Church Lane: note on the right the **Ancient House**, a 15C timber-framed hall house, and nearby the *Nag's Head*, a relatively venerable pub. Then walk north along Church Lane to Shernhall Street, where you turn left. There are various schools on either side, one of which occupies a fine house at the top of the street on the right. This is **Walthamstow House**, built in the 1750s and obviously sited on high ground to take advantage of the views. It was for two generations the home of the Wigram family, having been bought by Sir Robert Wigram (1744–1830), an Irish surgeon who became an East India merchant, acquired considerable wealth and fathered 23 children.

Going over the brow of the hill you descend to busy Forest Road, running east–west. On the right is another substantial Georgian villa, **Thorpe Combe** (1760), now a hospital. But what catches the eye, on the north side of the road, is **Waltham Forest College**, demonstrating semi-Fascist, 1930s Classicism, with reliefs of people undertaking a range of healthy activities. Stay on the north side of the road and walk westwards. An even more remarkable 1930s ensemble soon comes in to view: the **Town Hall and Assembly Hall** (by P.O. Hepworth) are set out beyond much well-tended grass and flowerbeds around a circular fountain. Over the door of the Assembly Hall is the categoric statement 'Fellowship is life and lack of fellowship is death'—a questionable if not altogether odd pronouncement, but since it is a quotation from William Morris, its selection is probably understandable. Local government in London has often allowed itself the luxury of ambitious public buildings but few dared go this far, even in the 1930s. It is an unforgettable ensemble, the effect only slightly modified by the magistrates court on the western side (1960s) showing more restraint.

On the south side of the road is a powerful piece of orthodox Modernism, the YMCA, and further along yet another Georgian villa, Brookscroft (1760s), now also owned by the YMCA. Continue west, across Hoe Street and Chingford Road, to reach the final 18C villa for the day, built as Water House and so-named because of the moated area behind it, now part of Lloyd Park. Since the 1950s Water House has been known as the **William Morris Gallery**, although his own connection with it was not especially close: it was occupied by his mother (1848–56) when Morris was at boarding school and university. Open 10.00–13.00 and 14.00–17.00 Mon–Sat and first Sun of each month. Admission free. Shop. ☎ 020 8527 3782. www.lbwf.gov.uk/wmg

---

William Morris

Morris (1834–96) was a man of extraordinary, diverse talent. After Oxford he studied architecture with G.E. Street and then sought to become a painter under the influence of his friend D.G. Rossetti. His true vocation, however, was as a designer, and with friends he established the firm of Morris Marshall, Faulkner and Co. in Oxford Street. His ideas were original, but always tempered by admiration of medieval forms and practices. His first house, Red House at Bexleyheath (1858–60), was designed for him by Philip Webb. In later life he became a socialist, making many speeches and writing pamphlets, poems and novels in support of his ideas. He established his own printing press, the Kelmscott Press. His later years were spent in Kelmscott House in Hammersmith Mall (Chapter 57), Kelmscott being his country house in Oxfordshire. He has been massively influential but he never resolved the paradox that hand-made products cost more than those made in a factory, and would therefore be bought only by the prosperous middle class of whose values he disapproved, sickened, as he put it, of 'ministering to the swinish luxury of the rich'.

This is a museum more than a gallery, but no less interesting for that. Four rooms are set out with a well-displayed and explained collection of Morris's designs and objects he owned, illustrating his dictum 'have nothing in your houses you do not know to be useful or believe to be beautiful' (the opposition between 'know' and 'believe' is neat).

Across the corridor is a gallery of Pre-Raphaelite and other paintings (see Chapter 27), including some by Sir Edward Burne-Jones (Morris's closest associate) and, most interesting, John Ruskin's *West Porch at Rouen*, clearly stuck together from various separate attempts. Rossetti's favourite model was always Morris's wife Jane and he painted her whenever he could get near: the portrait here is of another model, *Alexa Wilding* (1872), but she has been made to look like Mrs Morris anyway. There is also a work by Ford Madox Ford, *Jacopo Foscari in Prison* (1870).

Upstairs, besides a gallery for temporary exhibitions, are several items relating to the Century Guild, an early Arts and Crafts movement with which Morris was involved. Its enduring image is the title page of a book on *Wren's City Churches* (1883) by A.H. Mackmurdo, which is said to foreshadow the entire Art Nouveau ideology, with its swirling natural forms. In another room there is a substantial show of vivid paintings by Sir Frank Brangwyn (d. 1956), a generous donor to the museum and himself a reasonably important 20C British artist.

Behind the William Morris Gallery is **Lloyd Park**. Edward Lloyd brought the house from Mrs Morris and was also important in his way, as founder of the *Illustrated London News* and the father of 25 children. Is there something in the air in Walthamstow? Wander round Lloyd Park, behind the house: both it and the garden were generously offered to the local council by one of Edward Lloyd's sons in 1899. At the back of Lloyd Park is a small gallery called **The Changing**

Room, showing temporary exhibitions. Open 10.00–18.00 Sat, Sun. Admission free. Café. www.lbwf.gov.uk/org

The best way back is to re-cross Forest Road and climb Gaywood Road to Hoe Street, turn right and return over the hill down to Walthamstow Central station. If you are going on to Barking, make your way to Walthamstow Queen's Road for a mainline train.

As you go, consider this final quote from Morris (apposite for all readers of guide books and others): 'I love art and I love history; but it is living art and living history that I love. If we have no hope for the future, I do not see how we can look back on the past with pleasure.' *History of Pattern-Making* (1882).

68 • Barking

Barking is only seven miles from the City but, like Croydon or Richmond, keeps a sense of its own identity. It was one of the earliest Saxon settlements in Essex and later owed its growth to two phenomena now altogether vanished, an abbey and a fishing industry. For the most part today it is a relatively dreary place and you may have to use your imagination to get a sense of its interesting past.

A short walk covers the main items. It could be followed or preceded by a short train journey to Walthamstow, a richer resource. The two together make a worthwhile day in northeast London.

• Distance: 1½ miles. Time: 1 hour. Tube: Barking. Off map.

Barking is in Zone 4 and is easily reached by Tube (District Line), arriving at modern, impersonal Barking station (rebuilt 1956–61).

Turn right, and you soon reach a pedestrianised area, East Street, with a street market. An ordinary sort of 1970s shopping mall, called Vicarage Field, covers the ground to the left; inside is a central atrium with struggling palm trees and a fountain. Turn left down Ripple Road and then, turning right, an open square comes in to view containing the Library (1974) and a rather impressive red-brick **Town Hall** designed in the 1930s but in emphasis and tone unmistakably of the 1950s, when it was built: it is worth comparing with Waltham Forest Town Hall (Chapter 67). The designer was Reginald Edmonds. At the rear of the Town Hall is an **Assembly Hall**, even more of the 1950s, with wriggly iron balconies, by Herbert Jackson.

To the west of this, across North Street/Broadway, a green space pleasingly stretches out. The whole town plan was determined by this area, which represents four commons and the grounds of Barking Abbey next to the River Roding, which lies beyond. In the foreground is all that remains, the **Curfew Tower** built as late as the 15C, which functions now as a gateway to the church.

St Margaret is an excellent example of a medieval town church. There are plenty to be found in England, but few others as close to London (compare Kingston). It is long, low, wide and comfortable with a fine original timber roof. The west tower, with its higher stair-turret, is 15C but parts of the church are older. Open 10.00–15.30 Mon–Sat.

Enter via Church Centre, where coffee and tea are served. Inside the church are large, comfortable 19C pews. There are some moving monuments, especially those to Sir Orlando Humfreys (1737) and, in alabaster, Sir Charles Montague

(1625), shown in a military camp dozing (or dying?) in his tent. Another, to Robert W. Hall and erected by his son (early 19C), is referred to touchingly as the younger man's 'sincere though feeble testimony of gratitude and love'. Captain James Cook, the explorer, was married here in 1762.

The churchyard has many well-kept graves and extends into the grounds of **Barking Abbey**. Its walls are composed of Abbey stones. Recent excavations have shown the layout of the Abbey, but it is all shamefully neglected, with no storyboards or guidance of any sort. You can, however, walk around freely to gain impressions of this important place.

It was founded around AD 666 as a Benedictine nunnery by St Erkenwald, Bishop of London, with his sister St Ethelburga as first abbess. Later abbesses included another saint, three queens—including Maud, wife of Henry I and Matilda, wife of Stephen—and two princesses. William I stayed here. The Abbey is connected with the church of All Hallows Barking (Chapter 2). After the Dissolution of the Monasteries in 1539, it was the most important Benedictine foundation in the country, but the buildings were demolished and the stone taken by river to improve Henry VIII's palace at Greenwich.

Leaving the Abbey area to the west, cross Abbey Road and go down to **Town Quay**. All will be deserted. Three stones have been placed and inscribed to commemorate 'an island of grass beside the Roding'. And 'gulls soar over the icy water, smell the sea, feel the silky air'. From this place for 500 years, the town's main industry derived from its fishing fleet, which sailed down to the Thames at Barking Creek and out to the sea. In the 19C there were 220 smacks crewed by over 1400 men and boys. There is not a trace of a boat today, but you can see the river flowing placidly by.

Return across the common to East Street and the market, with a suitably forbidding magistrates court (1893), and reach the station. To go to Walthamstow catch a Gospel Oak train from Platform 1.

If it should be the first Saturday in the month between March and December (but not Aug) you may like to go one station further on the District Line to Upney, to see **Eastbury Manor House**, owned by the National Trust but managed by the local authority. It is an important example of Elizabethan architecture, a brick built H-shaped manor house, with recently revealed wall-paintings and alleged connections with the Gunpowder Plot. Open 10.00–16.00 first Sat in month Mar–Dec (except Aug). Admission charge. ☎ 020 8507 0119. www.national-trust.org.uk

69 • Eltham

The chief and essential reason for going to Eltham is to see Eltham Palace, but there are other sights of interest if you do not mind walking a little further—these are included as options.

• Distance: 2¾ miles. Time: 2 hours + 2 hours for Eltham Palace. Off map.

Travel Take a train from London Bridge, Charing Cross or Waterloo East t Eltham, on the line to Dartford via Bexleyheath. Almost as close is Mottinghar (same termini, different line), from which you will return. For train times out and back, ☎ 08457 48 49 50.

From Eltham station you have the option of a detour: skip this and the next paragraph to go straight to the Palace. Turn right out of the station. Take the third right, Prince Rupert Road, and cross Rochester Way to explore briefly the **Well Hall** (or Progress) **Estate**. It is picturesque and villagey, reminiscent of the Hampstead Garden Suburb of ten years earlier. Its origin (1915) was as a show estate, built at speed in 12 months, for supervisors and skilled workers in the armaments factory at Woolwich to the north, and was designed by Frank Baines, who had trained with C.R. Ashbee, a noted Arts and Crafts architect. It could have been a model for post-First World War public housing estates, but Well Hall was regarded as a little too fancy for the average public-housing tenant, for whom something more modest was judged sufficient, and more affordable, by the authorities.

Return down Well Hall Road towards the station and cross to take a look at what remains of **Well Hall** itself, a former moated manor house once occupied by Sir Thomas More's daughter, Margaret Roper. There is still good evidence of the inner and outer moats. The remains of the hall were later incorporated into a farmhouse.

Eltham Palace

Now proceed past the station down Well Hall Road to the crossroads with Eltham High Street, a pleasant suburban shopping centre with a few older buildings. Go south down Court Road and fork right into Court Yard to reach Eltham Palace, a unique site run by English Heritage.

• Open April–Sept 10.00–18.00 Wed–Fri, Sun and Bank Holidays (closes 16.00 in winter). Admission charge. Audio guide. Café. Shop. ☎ 020 8294 2548. www.english-heritage.org.uk

Eltham Palace is in part a surviving medieval royal palace and at the same time an important Art Deco house designed for Stephen and Virginia Courtauld. The following tour takes these two elements in reverse order, and indeed follows the route which visitors in the 1930s might have taken.

The original house was built by Anthony Bek, Bishop of Durham, who presented it to the Prince of Wales, soon to be Edward II, in 1305. Extension and rebuilding took place under Edward II, Richard II (Geoffrey Chaucer supervised the work), Henry IV and Edward IV, who had the Great Hall built. Henry VIII spent much of his boyhood here and built a new chapel, but at the end of his life favoured nearby Greenwich. Eltham fell into disrepair and was largely wrecked during the 17C Commonwealth. The Great Hall survived but was subsequently used as a farm and later as an indoor tennis court, until the arrival of the Courtaulds, who took the lease in 1931. Their new house was completed in 1937.

You enter over a stone **bridge**, dating from the time of Edward IV's occupation of the Palace in the 1470s, which crosses the moat that defended the original house. After obtaining your ticket, make your way to a turning circle for cars, with a fine tree in the centre, the Courtauld's house on your left, the Great Hall straight ahead, and views of London stretching away on your right, to the west.

Look at the curved **arcade** through which you will enter. It is based on Sir Christopher Wren's work at Hampton Court and Trinity College, Cambridge, with the upper part of the arches blocked—a Postmodern conceit, because here, unlike in Wren's buildings, there is no need for the arches to be blocked at all. Above the balustrade to the right you may be able to see three 15C gables from the old Palace, apparently cleverly conserved and integrated—in fact they were taken down and rebuilt here as surrounds for bedroom windows.

The Courtaulds' architects in the 1930s were the interesting firm of John Seely (later Lord Mottistone) and Paul Paget. We have encountered some of their post-Second World War church restorations, for example, All Hallows by the Tower (Chapter 2). At Eltham they were being employed early in their career on an ambitious project with a big budget—every architect's dream. The result, when taken with the furnishing policy of the interior, is Postmodernist before its time. As we have seen elsewhere, Postmodernism can be very enjoyable and that is the mood created here. Puritanical 1930s Modernists, only too ready to cause outrage themselves, must have found it shocking.

On either side of the entrance are substantial toilets, part of the Courtaulds' original requirements and an indicator of the scale of their entertainment. Then you enter the pure Art Deco space of the **entrance hall**, a top-lit triangle with curved corners, marquetry-panelled walls and curving staircases. In the centre are chairs and occasional tables by the Swedish designer Rolf Engströmer, islanded on a very typical circular abstract carpet by Marion Dorn. These leading designers of the period were no doubt delighted to receive the Courtaulds' patronage. The role of Swedish design as a trendsetter is confirmed by the inclusion of an image of Stockholm Town Hall in the marquetry panelling. The back of the entrance hall leads to a loggia and a flower room (not open) which contains a bamboo ladder down which Virginia Courtauld's pet ring-tailed lemur, Mah Jongg, would descend from his upstairs quarters to join the company below. (The whole Eltham world is reminiscent of early Evelyn Waugh novels.)

From the entrance hall you enter the **drawing room**, a relatively quiet space designed by Peter Malacrida, an Italian aristocrat friend of the Courtaulds, whose work was the pinnacle of fashion. The panels by the windows are the work of Gilbert Ledward. The original paintings hung by Stephen Courtauld in the room are now mostly in Zimbabwe. The ceiling beams are plaster with built-in lighting but are painted to look like timber with Italo-Hungarian motifs, a reference to Virginia's parentage.

Via the corridor you reach Virginia's **boudoir**, also by Malacrida, with Art Deco lighting. The sofa is an early example of built-in furniture. Next to it is the **library**, a male space for Stephen, with a giant coved ceiling, wood panelling all around on which watercolours from his collection were arranged behind the Soane Museum-type shutters, a hanging map and a walnut desk. You can almost smell the pipe smoke. There is a haunting bronze called *The Sentry*, by Charles Sergeant Jagger, a reminder of Stephen's war service in the Artists' Rifles, at the end of which in 1918 he was awarded the Military Cross.

Go back to the corridor, and with a further but different sense of shock, you find yourself in the screens passage of the **Great Hall**. Such a passage was the convention at the service end of a medieval hall, connecting with the kitchen

The Courtaulds

The Courtauld family were Huguenot refugees who established in the 18C a textile business which developed into the multi-national manufacturer. Samuel Courtauld (1876–1947), at one time chairman of the company, was a passionate and early collector of Impressionist and Post-Impressionist paintings. It was he, with Lord Lee of Fareham, who founded the Courtauld Institute, as part of London University, to which he later left his private collection, now on show at Somerset House (see Chapter 9). Samuel's younger brother Stephen (1883–1967) was also an art connoisseur but no businessman. In 1923 he married Virginia Peirano, recently divorced from an Italian aristocrat. At Eltham they lived what now appears a charmed life, terminated by the Second World War. In 1944 they moved first to Scotland and later to Zimbabwe, where Stephen died after leaving many of the Eltham paintings to the National Gallery in Harare.

and pantry; at the opposite end would be a dais for the king or owner. The Great Hall (101ft by 36ft, height 55ft) was built for Edward IV around 1470, and thus lies in date and scale somewhere between Westminster Hall (roof of 1390s, but the rest older; see Chapter 12) and Hampton Court (built by Henry VIII in the 1520s; see Chapter 72). The hammerbeam system here is 'false' in the sense that the beams are braced into the posts, but they are of original construction—more than can be said of the minstrel's gallery and the timber screen at the dais end, which are the creations of Stephen Courtauld and his architects. The stained glass of 1936 depicts some of the royal owners of Eltham.

The Courtaulds used the Great Hall for musical performances. Under this great medieval hammerbeam roof, Art Deco novelties seem no more than trivia. It has been argued that the source of some of Stephen's ideas for re-medievalising the Hall came from his connections with the film industry. Alexander Korda's *Private Life of Henry VIII* was produced in the same year that the Courtaulds discovered Eltham, and Stephen himself later became the chief sponsor of Ealing Studios. But before we are too scathing about this cardboard-cutout medievalism, it must be remembered that before the Courtaulds came along and 'restored' it the grounds of Eltham Palace were eroding into suburbia.

Return to the entrance hall and go upstairs to the principal landing, back to the Evelyn Waugh world. Here is a copy of an evocative portrait of Stephen and Virginia (1934), by L. Campbell Taylor, with lemur, and next Stephen's **bedroom**. It is restrained, as befits his personality, with Kew Gardens on the wallpaper and a bathroom in swimming-pool colours. In total contrast is Virginia's suite next door, created by Malacrida, and like the film set of a Joan Crawford movie, with a bathroom of extreme luxury.

Back on the landing, and behind bars, are Mah Jongg's sleeping quarters, comfortably in proportion. Also on the first floor you should be able to see some of the guest suites, on a corridor which led down to servants' rooms: in the later 1930s the full staff numbered 15.

Downstairs again, the **dining room** forms a suitable climax: it is Art Deco at its most sophisticated. The ceiling is of aluminium leaf, the walls maple flexwood and the black Belgian marble fireplace contains the original fake-coal electric fire. The remarkable original cupboard doors show applied lacquer animals and birds, but the pink dining chairs are reproductions.

Before reaching the garden you can refresh yourself in the tea room and shop. In the **garden**, survivals of the medieval Palace were shaped to form a mixed 1930s layout. Walk along the north side of the Great Hall to the squash court with a statue of *St George* (1930), by A. Hardiman, at the end, and then around to the south side. Over the lawned moat there is a pretty timber bridge, a quasi-balustrade by Seely and Paget resting on medieval brick piers, a strange mixture in itself. You can look back at the south façade of both Hall and house, a remarkably harmonious mixture of real late Gothic and Neo-Neoclassical.

From here you descend into the moat space to wander through a sunken garden and series of garden 'rooms', past a fountain and round to the north stone bridge again. On the right, in the former enclosing wall, are bay windows inserted in the early 17C, in the last stages of Eltham's use as a royal palace. Beyond the stone bridge is a loggia and wisteria-covered pergola.

Leave the Palace via signs to the car park. This will bring you back to Court Road, which slopes downhill to the right. Before you go this way, look out for a turning on the opposite side pointing to Royal Blackheath Golf Club. This is private, but you may feel able to go up a little way to look at the clubhouse, formerly **Eltham Lodge**, a ravishing mid-17C house by Hugh May (1664), earlier than Wren. It is of red brick, with seven bays and a central pilastered pediment, generous windows and a strong, dignified cornice. It was built for Sir John Shaw, a banker and friend of Charles II, who leased Eltham Palace to him, though Sir John preferred to build his own lodge nearby.

Go back to Court Road, now turning left, downhill. This route will take you shortly to Mottingham station for trains to London Bridge and Charing Cross. Intervals between trains can be as long as 30 minutes; for details, ☎ 0845 748 4950. Allow 10 minutes to reach the station from Palace or Lodge.

70 • Croydon

There was a time in the 1960s when it looked as though Croydon would compete with London itself—as Docklands does now, against the City. Office towers and shopping centres sprang up, big firms moved in and commuting from north London to Croydon was not remarkable. That heyday is over, but Croydon is still a bustling, energetic place with its own independent attractions—some far preceding the 1960s—of which this short walk shows you the best.

• Distance: nearly 2 miles. Time: 1 hour. Off map.

Travel Trains to East Croydon (Zone 5) are very frequent from Victoria Thameslink or London Bridge; some trains go to West Croydon (Zone 5) from Charing Cross. Besides innumerable buses the area has the additional benefit of a new tramway system, running partly on the road, partly on old railway, which enables you easily to combine this walk with Wimbledon (Chapter 71): an All Zones travel card would be necessary.

Croydon's origins date from its location where the Roman road from the south coast cut through the North Downs, an aspect of geography which gave the place renewed importance in the canal and railway eras. It was always favoured by the Archbishops of Canterbury, who built themselves palace here, now a school; six archbishops are buried in the parish church, including John Whitgift who founded Whitgift School in the 16C. London's first airport was opened here during the First World War (1915), and was the starting point for Amy Johnson's flight to Australia in 1930.

Start the walk at East Croydon station, which has been rebuilt and is light and airy. First look left from the station. The building which immediately strikes you, an octagonal tower with a richly textured, pale-brown surface, on its own round-about, is **NLA House** by Richard Seifert and Partners (1968), creators of Centre Point and many less impressive tower-block offices. It looks as if alternate floors have been twisted out of alignment with those above and below. The other big blocks are of the same period, also for insurance companies—General Accident and Commercial Union—who were riding high in the 1960s.

You soon become conscious that there is not much of a town plan about 1960s Croydon, although high priority was clearly given to traffic. Turn right from the station and left at the road junction. The rather grim 1950s and 1960s buildings all around including the **Fairfield Halls**, a cultural centre with a gallery, and the Ashcroft Theatre. For details of events, ☎ 020 8688 9291.

Make your way across the busy road into Katharine Street. Here on the left you will find the grand **Town Hall and Library** by Charles Henman (1892–96) and 1960s' municipal offices. There is a tourist information office in the clock tower, ☎ 020 8253 1009, and a well-stocked local museum with interactive displays. Open 11.00–17.00 Mon–Sat; 12.00–17.00 Sun and Bank Holidays. Café. Shop. ☎ 020 8253 1030.

Go to the end of Katharine Street and reach the old High Street. To the left a huge flyover brings traffic down to the 1960s area. Just beyond it is one of the finest buildings in Croydon, an early 18C house called **Wrencote**, in red brick with a carved frieze, entirely dominated by the flyover and other intrusions.

Go back up the High Street. The west side contains a series of buildings of the same period of development as the Town Hall, from late Victorian Croydon, proud of its prosperity and links with the capital. One of the most eye-catching is nos 32–34 with an archway leading to an arcade which stretches down to Surrey Street, making imaginative use of the slope.

Go down here, or turn left down Crown Hill. There has been a large market area in Surrey Street for 700 years, and there is still a daily street market here. As you reach Church Street the character changes again because you have moved further back in time, to the oldest part of the town. To prove it, there are some half-timbered buildings here, in Church Street and Church Road. Turn left down Old Palace Road to locate the former **Archbishop of Canterbury's palace**, which archbishops occupied from medieval times until 1780. Medieval senior clergy took care of themselves very nicely, and had a series of palaces from Canterbury to Lambeth. This one now functions as a girls' school. There are extensive survivals from the medieval building around two enclosed courtyards, including a Great Hall, Guardroom and Chapel. Open for guided tours only at 14.00 and 14.30 in school holidays. ☎ 020 8668 2414.

Close by, at the west end of Church Street, is the parish church of **St John the Baptist**, a substantial building by Sir George Gilbert Scott (1870), replacing a perpendicular church destroyed by fire. Some traces of the older church remain inside, in deference to which Scott's design is more Perpendicular than usual.

There are also several interesting monuments from the former church.

Make your way back up Crown Hill to the High Street, turning left into North End. On the corner opposite are the **Whitgift Almshouses**, dating back to 1599, established for 16 men and 16 women and still used for their original purpose. John Whitgift, Archbishop of Canterbury, endowed these almshouses as well as his school, and lived here himself in a suite of rooms on the south side. Some of the original furniture remains inside.

There are still plenty of attractive 1890s buildings to be seen all around. You are walking towards West Croydon station but turn right before you reach it into Poplar Walk, where there is an exceptional 19C church, **St Michael**, by J.L. Pearson (1820–23). This important architect was a firm follower of the Gothic principles laid down by A.W.N. Pugin, John Ruskin and company. His masterpiece is Truro Cathedral in Cornwall but plenty of his work can be seen in London. Here at St Michael's the interior is dark, in undisguised stock brick but fully rib-vaulted, with prominent stone shafts and string-courses: it is peaceful and cool, with none of the draining emotionalism of All Saints Margaret Street.

To the south you can walk through the **Whitgift Centre** (1965–70), a huge pedestrianised shopping centre stretching north–south, with separate open squares in the centre. Having explored, exit east at first-floor level into Wellesley Road, the main through route that you crossed earlier. If you locate Lansdowne Road opposite, go down it and turn right into Dingwall Road to see more of 1960s Croydon. This will confirm the impression of three worlds—one medieval, though with minimal remains, another of the 1890s, and a third of the 1960s—each of which has left architectural calling cards to remind us of its values.

At George Street turn left and you are at East Croydon station. Do not forget the possibility of exploring the tramlink, including going to Wimbledon (Chapter 71).

71 • Wimbledon

In most minds, Wimbledon means one thing, the tennis championships held in June/July, but there are other attractions open all the year: a pleasant shopping centre; a smart, old-fashioned High Street; a tennis museum; Wimbledon Common and some of its surrounding houses. It is too spread out to treat as a single walk and for what follows you are recommended to hop on and off a 93 bus. In this way the chapter can be combined with part of the tour of Putney and Fulham (Chapter 56); or with that of Croydon (Chapter 70), reached by tram.

• Distance: 4 miles, shorter by bus. Time: 3½ hours. Tube: Wimbledon. Off map

There are frequent trains to Wimbledon (District Line) in Zone 4, also from Waterloo or Clapham Junction. In the Broadway, look around at the shops appearing somewhat unplanned but all quite pleasing. Note **Bank Buildings** on the right, at the bottom of Wimbledon Hill Road, a later 19C building with the usual red terracotta.

Turn left from the station and walk east for a while. On the right is Wimbledon Theatre, a rare survival (1910) with a dome and mock 18C interior. The **Polka Theatre**, further along on the left, is strongly recommended for children, with an excellent programme of age-related shows all the year round. For details ☎ 020 8543 4888.

Now return, taking a 93 bus towards Putney Bridge station if you wish, and travel up Wimbledon Hill. Ridgway, only two or three stops away on the left, marks the beginning of the High Street. Detour down Ridgway where, on the right in Linfield Road, is a small **museum** of local history. Open 14.30–17.00 Sat, Sun. Admission free. ☎ 020 8296 9914.

Return to the High Street. Note, on the north side, set back from the road, Eagle House (1613), and the handsome Natwest Bank on the corner (1895). Locate on the same side Church Road. At the top, to the right, is the church of **St Mary**, medieval in origin, and still so in the chancel. Much later rebuilding has taken place to give the church its present handsome appearance, mainly by Sir George Gilbert Scott, twice over (1843 and 1860). Inside you may be able to see the Cecil Chapel (1626–36): the Cecil family, descending from William Cecil, Queen Elizabeth's Chancellor, were local landlords. Of significance for any Londoner is the grave of Sir Joseph Bazalgette, who came to live here.

Sir Joseph Bazalgette

This engineer had more influence on London's health, hygiene and appearance than almost anyone else. Of French descent, Bazalgette (1819–91) was trained as an engineer from the age of 17. He was involved in the railway mania of the 1840s, but not prominently; his first major appointment was as surveyor to the Commissions for Sewers in the 1850s. These Commissions, and their concerns about the pollution of the Thames, led to the setting up of the Metropolitan Board of Works, with Bazalgette as Chief Engineer. In this capacity he organised the system of intercepting sewers which still serves London, carrying sewage far downstream where, these days, it is processed and recycled. (In Bazalgette's time it was taken out to sea.) For this purpose he built the Victoria and Chelsea Embankments and the Albert Embankment. He also designed bridges and many major new roads, including Charing Cross Road, Queen Victoria Street and Southwark Street.

Return to the High Street, off which you soon turn left down Southside Common. **Wimbedon Common** starts to open out on your right. The fact that 1000 acres are still open land is thanks to the operations of the Commons Preservation Society in the 19C, who campaigned as at Hampstead Heath to stop the local lord of the manor developing it. On the left is **Southside House**, with a fine late 17C façade, extended and altered in 1776, with statues of *Plenty* and *Spring* in niches either side of the front door. These are portraits of the wife and daughter of the original owner, Robert Pennington. There are several interesting paintings and artefacts inside. Open Jan–June for guided tours only at 14.00, 15.00, 16.00 Wed, Sat, Sun and Bank Holidays. ☎ 020 8944 7643.

A detour can be made down West Side Common past many Georgian houses and cottages to Cannizaro House (now a hotel in a separate park) on the left. Even more fine houses lead to the ancient *Fox and Grapes* pub beyond and Camp Road stretching west. 'Camp' is a reference to **Caesar's Camp**, an Iron Age hillfort at the end past a clubhouse. Return down the Causeway to the High Street war memorial where you can catch a 93 bus again, up Parkside to Somerset Road on the right.

To the west of Parkside lies a large stretch of the Common, the wildest area of public common land in London (not counting Richmond Park, as a royal park)

and more extensive than Hampstead Heath, though flatter and less picturesqu
To the northwest, a short tramp along bridleways, is the **windmill**, one of th
largest of its type (1817–18, altered 1893). Open 14.00–17.00 Sat, 11.00–17.0
Sun and Bank Holidays. ☎ 020 8947 2825.

Alternatively, go east of Parkside, down Somerset Road, turning left and fo
lowing the road round past Burghley House, site of the Cecils' mansion, to th
All England Lawn Tennis Club. Within this internationally renowned site
the **Wimbledon Lawn Tennis Museum**, located in the Centre Court structu
with views of that famous grass. It has tennis memorabilia, equipment, pain
ings and videos of the great players in action. There are also separate guide
tours of the grounds. Open 10.30–17.00 daily, but check for special arrang
ments during the Championships. Guided tours of the grounds must be pr
booked. Admission charge. Café. Shop. ☎ 020 8946 6131. www.wimbledo
org. Tube: Southfields (15min walk).

> ### Tennis
> Lawn tennis evolved from real, or royal, tennis in the 19C. Standard rules
> were drawn up in 1875 and the Wimbledon Championships first held in
> 1877, at the grounds of the All England Lawn Tennis and Croquet Club.
> (Croquet is still one of Wimbledon's official responsibilities.) The strange
> scoring system for tennis is supposed to be based on the quarter-hours of the
> clock. The game's huge popularity in the 20C originates from women's
> participation, a so-far unresolved limitation to cricket and football.

It seems appropriate to end with tennis in Wimbledon. A fairly easy walk nor
along Church Road and Wimbledon Park Road will take you to Southfiel
station (District Line). Or you can return down Somerset Road to Parkside a
catch the 93 bus, either back to Wimbledon station or, in the opposite directic
north to Putney (mainline trains to Waterloo) or Putney Bridge stations (Distr
Line).

2 • Hampton Court

you have more than three or four days in London, a visit to Hampton Court—
ual to Greenwich in architectural interest (almost), more important histori-
lly than Windsor (just)—is indispensable. It is not difficult to reach and it is
autifully presented. There is a great deal to see, and a good place for lunch, so
ve it a whole day if you can.

Distance: negligible, unless taking a walk in the park. Time: 3 hours at least,
whole day recommended. See plan on p 481.

avel Hampton Court station is in Zone 6: mainline trains run every half-hour
om Waterloo (takes 30 minutes). Hampton Court is at the end of the line.
lternatively, take a boat trip down the Thames from central London (for details,
e Chapter 75).

om the station go over the **bridge**, reflecting that in Hampton Court's golden
e visitors always arrived by boat. Before 1750 there was no bridge: the one you
e crossing is the fourth and was designed by Sir Edwin Lutyens (1930–33). As
u reach the north bank, you will see some very fine houses on the far side of
ampton Court Green, to the left, several built in Sir Christopher Wren's time for
nior Palace officials, including the Royal Gardener and the Master Carpenter.
But your eye will not rest on these, with the Palace clearly in view on the right.
u should enter via **Trophy Gates**, built for William III. The ticket office and
cellent shop are in the Cavalry Barracks on the left, with toilets beyond. This
ur will take you through the two main areas of the Palace, and then list the
maining attractions from which to choose.

Open March–mid-Oct 09.30–18.00 Tues–Sun, 10.15–18.00 Mon; mid-
Oct–March closes 16.30. Admission charge. The Privy Garden and the Maze
can each be entered separately, for a lower admission charge. Entry to the Park
is free. Restaurant. Café. Shops. Audio tours and costumed guides (for some
areas). ☎ 020 8781 9500. www.hrp.org.uk

story

Although always thought of as a royal palace, Hampton Court was essentially the creation of Cardinal Thomas Wolsey (see below), who acquired the
manor from the Knights Hospitaller (see Chapter 29). He was the inspiration
behind the main plan and developed it as an establishment of considerable
luxury for himself. Henry VIII was piqued by this and in 1525 Wolsey
thought it diplomatic to present Hampton Court to the King. It was not
enough to prevent his downfall.

Henry then built himself a new Great Hall (1532–35) and other apartments, and completed the Chapel. He also lived here quite extensively, as did
his queens. Edward VI was born here in 1537. Thereafter little was changed,
except for Charles II's work on the grounds, until William and Mary. Disliking
Whitehall, they decided in the 1680s to develop their palace here, employing
Sir Christopher Wren. Some of Henry VIII's work was demolished and much

new work done, most notably the Fountain Court and the King's Apartment in two phases, with the Privy Garden completed *c* 1700.

The last period of royal involvement and building was during the reign George II and Queen Caroline, when the Queen's Apartments were complete (1732). There has been no royal occupation since 1737. In 1838 Que Victoria decided to open Hampton Court to the public, retaining some accommodation for grace-and-favour residents. In 1986 a serious fire broke o above the King's apartment, causing considerable damage.

The Great Gatehouse at Hampton Court Palace

Go up to Wolsey's **west façad** with the Great Gatehouse at th centre, and gaze at it for a whi Little by little a 16C feeling com over you: the warmth of the bric the fiddliness of the detail, t castellation where none is neede and the ornate chimneys. Th terracotta medallions of Roma emperors, attributed to Giovan da Maiano, are early evidence the Renaissance in England and tribute to Wolsey's innovato taste. The heraldic animals ha been regularly renewed. Th unnecessary moat was later fill in. Normally you will then ent

from here to the **Base Court**, unchanged from Wolsey's time and reminiscent an Oxbridge college, predictably, as its purpose was accommodation for gues These courts form the ground plan of Hampton Court—next comes the Clo Court, with Wren's Fountain Court beyond (see below).

Cardinal Wolsey

Thomas Wolsey (*c* 1472–1530), son of a butcher in Ipswich, became a uniquely powerful Lord Chancellor, second only to King Henry VIII, being given special authority by the pope which placed him in a far more influen tial position than the Archbishop of Canterbury. He lived with great pomp and ceremony at both Hampton Court and Whitehall Palace, both later taken over by the King, whose jealousy of his lifestyle was increased further by Wolsey's failure to organise a clean divorce from Catherine of Aragon. As Simon Schama puts it, Henry 'had no use for a Mr Fix-it who couldn't fix it'. Wolsey's unpopularity and inevitable path towards execution ended in his death, at Leicester, on his way to London to conduct his defence.

Henry VIII's apartments

But before exploring the courts, turn left up the worn stairs to see Henry VII apartments. Here more than anywhere in England you can get a feeling for t personality of this difficult and unappealing character, whose influence has be greater than that of any other monarch.

Immediately you enter the **Great Hall** (106ft long by 40ft wide), looking mu

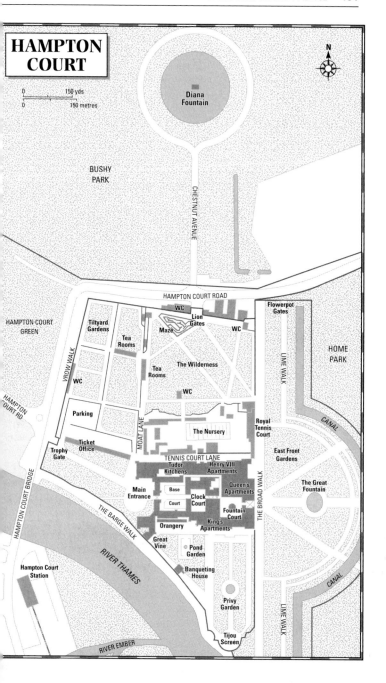

HAMPTON COURT

0   150 yds
0   150 metres

N

Diana Fountain

BUSHY PARK

CHESTNUT AVENUE

HAMPTON COURT ROAD

HAMPTON COURT GREEN

Tiltyard Gardens

Tea Rooms

WC

Lion Gates

Maze

WC

Flowerpot Gates

HOME PARK

VROW WALK

WC

The Wilderness

Tea Rooms

WC

LIME WALK

HAMPTON COURT RD

Parking

MOAT LANE

The Nursery

Royal Tennis Court

East Front Gardens

CANAL

Trophy Gate

Ticket Office

TENNIS COURT LANE

Tudor Kitchens

Henry VIII Apartments

THE BROAD WALK

The Great Fountain

HAMPTON COURT BRIDGE

Main Entrance

Base Court

Clock Court

Queen's Apartments

Fountain Court

Orangery

King's Apartments

THE BARGE WALK

Great Vine

Pond Garden

RIVER THAMES

Hampton Court Station

Banqueting House

Privy Garden

CANAL

LIME WALK

Tijou Screen

RIVER EMBER

as it did during its founder's time. Henry built it to emphasise his own presenc
here after the demise of Wolsey, to function as a grand entrance, and more pra
tically as a dining-hall for the 600 or so Palace staff who ate here twice daily.
is interesting to sort out what is Tudor and what is 19C pastiche. In the first ca
egory are the hammerbeam roof, spanning the wide space, the tapestrie
ordered by Henry for this very Hall, and the screens passage, behind which th
servants would come and go. The carved and painted cornices and stained gla
are Victorian, as are the stags' heads and the fact that the roof is mostly bare tin
ber, no longer painted all over. There are no fireplaces: an open fire burned in th
centre of the hall.

Next, through the Horn Room (recently so arranged and not historical a
such, but note on the left the original ancient timber staircase to the kitchens
you reach the **Great Watching Chamber**, where guests would wait among
the permanent detachment of the Yeomen of the Guard before presentation t
the King. The tapestries and ceiling are part of the original decorative schem
The apartments for Henry to receive his guests, which lay beyond this chambe
were demolished in Wren's time, but your route enables you to reach the Chap
via two original corridors, now called the **Haunted Gallery** (from the unlike
story that Catherine Howard, under house arrest here for adultery, tried t
escape towards the Chapel where Henry was at prayer, but was detected an
dragged back screaming to her rooms). In the second part of the Gallery is a
interesting painting showing Henry and Jane Seymour (who had in fact died
with their son Edward and the princesses Mary and Elizabeth, in Whiteha
Palace (1545).

Henry VIII (1491–1547, r. 1509–1547)

Perhaps the most famous of all English kings, Henry has been admired too
much. He squandered the advantages, financial and political, left to him by
his father Henry VII and, a poor judge of people, allowed courtiers to gain
too much power which had then, by their removal or execution, to be
restored to the throne. The first such example was Wolsey.

Henry is most famous for his six marriages. The first, to Catherine of
Aragon, the widow of his brother Arthur, lasted over 20 years, but failed to
meet Henry's near-neurotic wish for a male heir. The consequent pursuit of
a legitimate divorce, against the wishes of the pope, led to the separation of
the English Church and the establishment of the monarch's position as its
head (which is still retained today). The next queen, Anne Boleyn, mother of
Elizabeth I, was beheaded for adultery. The third, Jane Seymour, died soon
after the birth of Henry's only son, who became Edward VI. The next marriage, to Anne of Cleves, was in effect arranged for political purposes by
Wolsey's successor Thomas Cromwell, and resulted in Henry's rapid divorce
and Cromwell's execution. Catherine Howard was also executed, for adultery. His last wife, Catherine Parr, was already a widow when Henry married
her and lived on to become his.

Although Henry's influence on events in the England of his time was
enormous—the establishment of the Church of England, the Dissolution of
the Monasteries and the redistribution of their wealth into royal and aristocratic hands—his motivation for introducing such radical change was
largely personal selfishness.

To the left is the **Chapel** with the royal pew in which the monarch sat, at this upper level; from here you descend into the space below. This too was part of Wolsey's original Palace, but has a ceiling made for Henry (1535–36), and further changes, including the enormous reredos by Grinling Gibbons, which Wren inserted at the same time as the royal pew and gallery structure made for Queen Anne. The current arrangement is Victorian, to provide seating for the grace-and-favour residents of the Palace.

Leave the Chapel by the corridor that leads to the **Tudor kitchens**, which are enormous, naturally enough for a household of 600. Their role diminished at the end of that period, but they are most interestingly presented and do not take long to wander through.

The next important area to tour is designated the **King's Apartments**—the king in question being William III. Return to **Clock Court** and cross it. But look around first at the jumble of styles. Behind you is Henry's Great Hall, with windows high up and a blank wall for the kitchens below, thrust up against Wolsey's west range, and the **Astronomical Clock** above more roundels. The clock was Henry's introduction (1540), giving endless information including the times of high tide at London Bridge. Next comes a colonnade, built by Wren, to lead to William III's apartments, blatantly Classical and slightly ridiculous in these Tudor surroundings. No such mistake was made by William Kent, the architect commissioned by George II to add rooms for his family, including his son the Duke of Cumberland: Kent's range (see '1732' above the gateway) is in convincing Tudor style.

William III's apartments

The entry to William III's apartments (1689–1702) is up a grand Baroque flight of stairs with long treads and low risers making it a comfortable ascent. The ceiling was decorated by Antonio Verrio who, although Italian, always seems less effective at these Baroque extravagances than Britain's own Sir James Thornhill. The subject is the mythical idea of *Alexander the Great triumphing over the Caesars*, to be read here as William triumphing over the Stuarts, an insensitive notion which could only have been sustainable after the death of Queen Mary in 1694 and before the succession of Anne in 1702.

William III (1650–1702) and Mary II (1662–94)

Britain's only joint monarchs, this Protestant couple reigned together for only six years but were of considerable international significance. William, Prince of Orange, represented the Dutch Protestant tradition, making him the enemy of Louis XIV and an uneasy ally of Charles II. In 1677, he neatly married Mary, Protestant daughter of Charles's brother James, who was to become a Catholic in 1680 and King in 1685. Concerns about James II's Catholic policies led British patriots to welcome William and Mary as joint monarchs in the 'glorious', and also bloodless, revolution of 1688. The marriage was childless and Mary's death in 1694 left William prostrate. Afterwards his policies seemed to harden but he ensured the subsequent unbroken Protestant succession after Anne. William and Mary's influence on royal architecture was very substantial, not only at Hampton Court but also at Greenwich and Kensington.

At the head of the stairs, a formal series of rooms stretches in a standardise order along the south façade. The progress along these rooms is the same kind of *enfilade* created at Versailles to approach Louis XIV, though it is restrained and 'English' in comparison. The first is a **Guard Chamber**, as for Henry, but here made distinctive by the display of 3000 arms. The Privy Garden can be seen from the windows—we reach it later. Next is the **King's Presence Chamber**, for general audiences, with a giant portrait of *William III on Horseback* by Sir Godfrey Kneller (1701), painted to hang in this very place. The tapestries are Henry's but were selected for hanging here by William.

Then follows the **King's Eating Room**, where William would sometimes dine ceremonially, watched by his courtiers. After it comes the most high-powered room, the **Privy Chamber**, centred on the axis of the garden, where ambassadors and guests of similar status were received. It was above this room that the 1986 fire broke out: at the top of the fireplace panel you can see traces of the scorched woodwork above Grinling Gibbons's surround, which was removed and saved. The chandelier was not removed and crashed to the floor amid a pile of waterlogged debris.

After this the ideology of the route becomes more personal, although still formal. The next room is the **King's Withdrawing Room**, access to which was confined to known people, senior courtiers and officers of state: the King sat in an ordinary chair, not a throne. Even more intimate is the **King's Great Bedchamber**, in which a privileged few courtiers could be present when the King was dressed. Here there is a painted ceiling by Verrio and more limewood carvings by Gibbons.

Now the ceremony has almost entirely died away and we reach the **King's Little Bedchamber**, where he actually slept, beyond which is the King's Closet lavatory and the back stairs leading down to similarly intimate rooms running back along the ground floor. These still have Grinling Gibbons overmantels but also much more personal, even slightly erotic, pictures apparently listed here in an inventory taken at the King's death, and implying a more relaxed monarch than history has encouraged us to think. These rooms lead through to the **Orangery** in which the tender plants from the garden outside would be assembled in winter.

Finally the **King's Private Drawing Room** and **Dining-Room** complete this section. In the Dining-Room the table is laid for the dessert stage in a contemporary dinner party, with the plate not in use, but displayed to underline the King's wealth and power. Round the walls are the so-called 'Hampton Court Beauties', paintings of ladies attending Queen Mary, whose images she commissioned from Kneller. William hung these portraits here after Mary's death.

You now emerge into **Fountain Court**, where there is indeed a fountain playing. This is the inner court of the block where the King's Apartments look over the garden. It certainly does not show Wren at his best: the windows are too close together and in an inconsistent programme, and the height of the ground floor arcade is awkwardly truncated. These infelicities are probably accounted for by a serious hiccup in the building project, brought about by Mary's death and William's resultant loss of interest, and separately, a crisis of cost escalation.

This may be a good moment to leave the interior to examine the **East Front** (Your ticket enables you to return inside at any stage, or visit any of the gardens except the Maze.) Here we see the outer side of Wren's conception, and to much greater effect. The central pedimented block in stone is brought forward, with two further stone bays either side, succeeded left and right by brick with stone dressings, stretching symmetrically and generously north and south. This fine façade looks out on the formal gardens punctuated by avenues of enormous yews, leading to and crossing a semi-circular canal dug in Queen Anne's time. Beyond this is the **Long Water**, a great canal on the lines of that at Versailles, created for Charles II in the 1660s, surrounded by the Home Park with its deer.

The *Tiltyard Restaurant* may appeal at this point: turn left and left again at the end of the wall.

Further attractions

There are other gardens to see, and many more interesting interiors. The following gives brief descriptions of these in no particular order.

Queen's State Apartments This suite, which overlooks the gardens we have just seen, was originally for Queen Mary, then taken over by William and Mary's successor, Queen Anne, but furnished in the main for Queen Caroline, wife of George II. If the style is restrained compared with William's rooms, the scale is no different, as its origin under a joint monarchy would imply.

Enter from the Queen's staircase (decorated by Kent) in Fountain Court, through another Guard Chamber with an insane Yeoman of the Guard fireplace, apparently by Gibbons although it seems very out of character, and decoration in the heavy style of Sir John Vanbrugh. Then comes a Presence Chamber, which includes a painting of *Satyrs and Sleeping Nymphs*, done by Peter Paul Rubens with Frans Snyders, and the Dining-Room. Go round the corner to an *enfilade* series, from Audience Chamber, via Drawing Room (with a Verrio ceiling), and Bedchamber (with a Thornhill ceiling—note the difference) to the Queen's Gallery, an impressively long chamber intended for Andrea Mantegna's *Triumphs of Caesar* (see below), but now with 18C Brussels tapestries. You leave after the Queen's Closet.

Georgian Rooms This suite is entered from Clock Court. The rooms were used by George II's queen, Caroline, during the last visit of the full court in 1737, during which occurred a fateful quarrel with their son Frederick, Prince of Wales. Included are the Cumberland Suite furnished by William Kent (1732) for the couple's second son, the Duke of Cumberland, and a small closet with a Tudor ceiling surviving from the Wolsey era. This leads into the **Communications Gallery**, which sounds very up-to-date, but means simply a gallery communicating between the King's and Queen's separate apartments, where a series of paintings known as the *Windsor* (sic) *Beauties* are displayed. These are portraits by Sir Peter Lely of the most beautiful women in Charles II's court. Next you reach the **Cartoon Gallery**, purposely designed by Wren to display Raphael's drawings of the *Acts of the Apostles* (1516) which Charles I had purchased in 1623. The original drawings are now in the Victoria & Albert Museum, but these copies were done in 1697. Finally in this section of the tour you reach Queen's Caroline's private apartments, with her bath and other curiosities.

Wolsey Rooms and Renaissance Picture Gallery These rooms are also entered from Clock Court. As implied, they are part of the earlier Tudor palace. The collection of paintings is particularly fine, and includes many important

16C and 17C works by Flemish, German and Italian masters such as a Bronzino portrait, **The Massacre of the Innocents** by Pieter Bruegel the Elder (1565) and a fascinating view of Hampton Court by Leonard Knyff (1703): there has been little change in the architecture, if some change in the gardens.

Privy Garden This area, to the south of the Palace, appears not to have changed since Knyff's view was taken but was actually completely restored from scratch in the 1990s, with great attention to accuracy in planting and arrangement. What you see is the garden more or less exactly as William III would have walked in it, down to the restored gates of Jean Tijou, with the river beyond. It is a perfect complement for Wren's south façade, which is nearly as effective as that on the east.

South Gardens Through the Privy Garden you reach the South Gardens, which include Henry VIII's pond gardens, not authentically restored. After this the **Lower Orangery** is reached. This now houses the **Triumphs of Caesar** (c 1484–1505), painted by Mantegna for his patrons the Gonzagas of Mantua but later acquired by Charles I. Close by is the **Great Vine**, planted in 1768 by Lancelot 'Capability' Brown, the Royal Gardener of the day, and still producing fruit: it is the oldest known vine in the world.

East Gardens. You saw Queen Anne's canal and the Long Water from the East Front. You may want to wander further. Do not miss the 'real' tennis court by the wall, and the great herbaceous border.

North Gardens. This area was planted as a so-called Wilderness, which means an area of evergreen shrubs, in William III's time. Most of this has gone but within it, still famously surviving, is the **Maze**, actually created in 1702, and surprisingly tricky. There is also a beautiful Rose Garden.

If you leave Hampton Court via the Wilderness, through the Lion Gate, you can cross the road to enter **Bushy Park**. Wren laid out the central avenue, leading to the Diana Fountain (by Francesco Fanelli and originally conceived for the Privy Garden) in the 1690s, with a view to a grand processional route to a new north entrance to the Palace, *à la* Versailles again. Only the park was completed. Beyond it is much wilder although flat, and has deer, as it has for centuries. To the west is the Waterhouse Woodland Garden with beautiful rhododendrons in May.

If you have strayed to the east Kingston station will be nearer (Chapter 64). Otherwise, walk back to the station at Hampton Court.

73 • Windsor

Windsor is not, by any definition, in London, but is readily accessible from the capital and is recommended for its history, art and architecture. England's foremost, and largest, castle is home to one of the occupied royal palaces: if your visit coincides with an official event such as the Garter ceremony, you are more likely to achieve a royal sighting at Windsor than elsewhere. After touring the Castle you may want to see a little of the town, visit **Eton** or take children to **Legoland**. This chapter covers each of these possibilities.

• Distance: 5 miles in total. Time: 4½ hours, or up to a whole day at Legoland. See plan on p 489.

Travel Windsor is well outside London Transport zones. There are two mainline rail stations at Windsor, Central, reached from Paddington (change at Slough), and Riverside, reached direct from Waterloo; the journey takes *c* 45 minutes.

Windsor Castle

Central station is directly opposite the Castle. Riverside is a 5-minute walk from the town centre along Thames Street. The ticket office is in St Alban's Street, off Castle Hill to the right.

● Open 09.45–17.15 daily. Last admission to State Apartments and St George's Chapel March–Oct 16.00; Nov–Feb 15.00. Admission charge. Shops.
☎ 01753 869 898. www.royalresidences.com
St George's Chapel is open only for worship on Sundays. It may be wise to telephone before setting off from London in case the State Apartments are closed for an official function.

History

More popular with monarchs than any other palace, Windsor was founded for defence purposes by William the Conqueror, on a cliff overlooking the Thames. Stone-built from Henry II's time (1165) it became a royal mausoleum following Edward IV's construction of St George's Chapel (1475) and a long-term residence from the reign of Charles II (1660s). Major refurbishments were made for George III by James Wyatt (1796) and for George IV by Sir Jeffrey Wyatville (1820–30) but these suffered badly in a fire of 1992, after which they were restored or, more controversially, reconstructed. Queen Victoria designated the Henry III Chapel (13C) a memorial chapel for Prince Albert, who died at Windsor, and commissioned other buildings for the Home Park, which had once been a hunting ground.

Climb up Castle Hill and circle Middle Ward. In the centre is the **Round Tower**, an artificial mound, or motte, dating back to William the Conqueror's first development of the site. The tower itself was built in Henry II's time and made higher by Wyatville in the early 19C, for deliberate pictorial effect. You can not enter: today it houses the royal archives. The moat surrounding it never contained water.

You are then taken through the curtain wall onto the **North Terrace**, which was developed in the reign of Henry VIII and extended for Charles II. It may be sunless but offers fine views to the north, especially in winter when the trees are bare: you can see Eton College Chapel, the M4 motorway, Slough beyond and the wooded Chiltern hills in the distance. The State Apartments lie ahead to the right.

State Apartments

When you enter, and for most of your tour, you are in the architecture of Wyatville or Wyatt—they left behind little of Hugh May's work for Charles II. On the left is a room containing **Queen Mary's Doll's House**, given to her in 1924 when she was 57). It was designed by Sir Edwin Lutyens on a scale of 1:12 (it measures 8ft by 5ft) and intended as an accurate record of contemporary design. It is fully plumbed and has two lifts. The wine in the cellar is genuine. Even the books in the library were specially hand-written by prominent authors of the day, including J.M. Barrie and Sir Arthur Conan Doyle.

There is an exhibition of china in the undercroft which precedes the **Grand Staircase**. The staircase itself, top-lit and uncompromisingly Gothic, as altered by Anthony Salvin for Queen Victoria, serves as the showpiece entrance to the State Apartments. An enormous figure of *George IV* (1828–32) by Sir Francis Chantrey, part of Wyatville's scheme, towers above the half-landing. At the top of the staircase you enter the **Grand Vestibule**, the work of James Wyatt, in the phoney Gothic of the 18C. On display is a serious quantity of arms and most interestingly the bullet which killed Admiral Nelson.

Turn right through the Waterloo Chamber, to be seen more fully later in the tour, to the Ante-Throne Room, once, when larger, Charles II's audience chamber. This leads to the **King's Drawing Room** (the King in question being again Charles II), redecorated in both the 18C and 19C, and an ensuing sequence of rooms for first the King and then the Queen. There are fine views north from the windows and besides the decorations and furniture, many masterpieces from the Royal Collection. In the Drawing Room, there are three works by Peter Paul Rubens, most prominently the *Holy Family with St Francis* (1626–28) over the fireplace, a well-nourished, worldly group compared with the ascetic Renaissance treatments of similar subjects. Also by Rubens, and almost more interesting, are *Winter* and *Summer*, from a series (1620–30).

The **King's Bedchamber** was used by visiting monarchs on state visits. The paintings include several views of Venice by Canaletto, collected by George III, and two portraits by Thomas Gainsborough. The chimneypiece is to a design by Sir William Chambers and the decoration is by Wyatville, although he retained the cornice from Charles II's day, carved by Grinling Gibbons.

Next are two smaller rooms, the **King's Dressing Room** and **Closet**, hung with suitably small but outstanding paintings. In the former is Antony van Dyck's *Charles I from Three Positions* by (1635–36), from which Gian Lorenzo Bernini was to produce a bust. There are several other fine portraits including a Van Dyck of *Queen Henrietta Maria* (1632), a Rubens *Self-portrait* (1622) and a portrait of an *Old Woman* (c 1629) by Rembrandt. The arms are those of William IV, who was once in the navy. In the Closet next door are the arms of his queen, Adelaide. A large Canaletto and a portrait by Sir Joshua Reynolds dominate, but one of the most attractive is a double portrait by William Hogarth of *David Garrick and his Wife* (1737), a happy couple, having fun.

Next comes one of the Queen's apartments, the most private, a **drawing room** remodelled by Wyatville to conform with the rooms you have just viewed, retaining the cornice but adding new ceilings in Charles II's style. There are some very important portraits here, including a masterpiece by Hans Holbein, *Sir Henry Guildford* (1527) and several others by the same artist. The subjects are as interesting as the artist: see the slightly embarrassed look of *James I* (1620), *Elizabeth I* (1546), a princess with a tense expression, and the much-lamented *Henry, Prince of Wales* (1605), eldest son of James I, clearly pleased with his work at the hunt. The windows in this room retain their original plate glass of the 1830s, the earliest date for it in England.

You now double back to see the **King's Dining-Room**, which lies behind his suite of apartments on the north side; originally it had windows to the south before Wyatville's extensions, and is now therefore rather dark. The ceiling is by Antonio Verrio (1680s) and the carvings, which Wyatville left alone, are by Gibbons. There are some odd portraits: a cross-looking *Catherine of Braganza* (1664) over the chimney piece, the *Chinese Convert* (1687) by Sir Godfrey Kneller and *Bridget Holmes* (1686), a portrait of a royal servant, by John Riley-

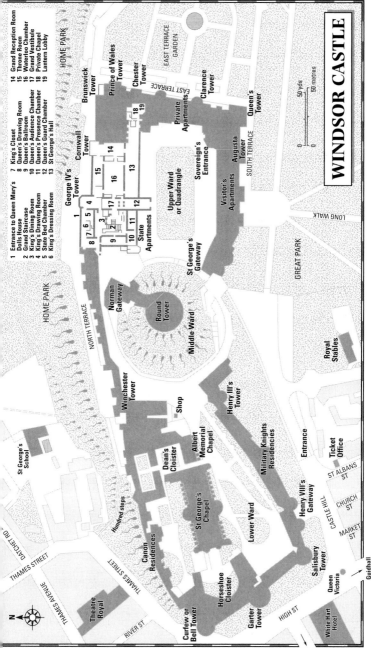

WINDSOR CASTLE

1 Entrance to Queen Mary's Dolls House
2 Grand Staircase
3 King's Dining Room
4 King's Drawing Room
5 State Bed Chamber
6 King's Dressing Room
7 King's Closet
8 Queen's Drawing Room
9 Queen's Ballroom
10 Queen's Audience Chamber
11 Queen's Presence Chamber
12 Queen's Guard Chamber
13 St George's Hall
14 Grand Reception Room
15 Throne Room
16 Waterloo Chamber
17 Grand Vestibule
18 Private Chapel
19 Lantern Lobby

HOME PARK

Brunswick Tower
Prince of Wales Tower
Chester Tower
EAST TERRACE GARDEN
Clarence Tower
Queen's Tower
Private Apartments
EAST TERRACE
Cornwall Tower
George IV's Tower
Sovereign's Entrance
Augusta Tower
SOUTH TERRACE
Upper Ward or Quadrangle
Visitor's Apartments
State Apartments
St George's Gateway
0   50 yds
0   50 metres
LONG WALK
GREAT PARK

HOME PARK
NORTH TERRACE
Norman Gateway
Round Tower
Middle Ward
Winchester Tower
Shop
Henry III's Tower
Royal Stables

St George's School
Dean's Cloister
Albert Memorial Chapel
Hundred steps
Military Knights Residencies
Entrance
Ticket Office
ST ALBANS ST
CHURCH ST
MARKET ST
Henry VIII's Gateway
CASTLE HILL

DATCHET RD
THAMES STREET
Canon Residences
St George's Chapel
Lower Ward
Horseshoe Cloister
Garter Tower
Salisbury Tower
Queen Victoria
White Hart Hotel
HIGH ST
→ Guildhall

Theatre Royal
THAMES AVENUE
Curfew or Bell Tower
RIVER ST

N

WINDSOR & ETON CENTRAL STATION

the last two are especially interesting but inevitably patronising. There is some fine French and English furniture and some grim tapestries placed here apparently by George V's queen, Mary.

Go back to the Queen's rooms and to the left into the **Ballroom**, or Gallery, with wonderful George III glass chandeliers, delicate blue walls, and a whole collection of Van Dyck portraits: particularly likeable are the *Five Eldest Children of Charles I* (1637), plus an extremely large dog—the expressions are worth studying—and the *Villiers Brothers* (1635). Along the window side of the room is rare silver furniture from the late 17C: the fashion came from Louis XIV but all his was melted down to fund war campaigns.

Next, go into the **Queen's Audience Chamber**, lighter due to the windows on the south side. Here the Charles II scheme has survived best of all: the ceiling is higher than Wyatville's interventions, and on it Verrio depicted Queen Catherine in a chariot drawn by swans. It is an English version of Versailles in its scale, the use of wood rather than marble (by Gibbons and his workshop), the absence of mirrors and comparative sobriety. The French tapestries are later, acquired by George IV.

The **Queen's Presence Chamber** is a little less important than the Audience Chamber—remember you are touring these rooms in reverse order—but has the best of all the Verrio ceilings, with Queen Catherine seated at the centre. Gibbons's carvings surround the overmantel portrait, above a too-ornate late 18C fireplace. George IV acquired these tapestries, too, from the firm of Gobelins; they fit the spaces perfectly.

The Queen's apartments end with a **Guard Chamber**, where we return to Wyatville's version of Gothic and a more military world, with arms all over the walls and a portrait of *Frederick, Prince of Wales* (1727), by Joachim Kayser over the fireplace. The ivory throne was a gift to Queen Victoria from the Maharajah of Travancore, shown at the Great Exhibition of 1851. Look through the window behind, over the quadrangle to the George IV gateway, beyond which, on the same axis, the Long Walk stretches for three miles straight as an arrow across the Home Park. You may think it merely picturesque but it, too, was part of the ideology of Versailles (also seen in the Long Water at Hampton Court) of long straight lines to signify royal splendour, authority and extent. Wyatville, working in the heyday of the picturesque, was perhaps not immune to such ideas. In this context it is fascinating to note how he adapted 17C Classicism for the Apartments but chose Neo-Gothic for the processional rooms. One begins to understand how the Houses of Parliament came about.

The point is illustrated in the next spectacular space, **St George's Hall** (185ft long). This is the ancient site of the Castle's medieval hall, redone for Charles II and redone again by Wyatville in his version of Gothic, with a timber roof. But this is not what you see now. The undeniably magnificent oak hammerbeam roof is a creation of the 1990s, designed by Giles Downes. St George's Hall was the chief casualty of the 1992 fire, when the ceiling and east wall were entirely destroyed. The decision was taken to recreate the hall in the George IV style but not to replicate it, although that could have been done. The stylistic term for this doubtful compromise must be Neo-neo-Gothic. The coats of arms of the present knights of the Order of the Garter (see below) adorn the ceiling. The source for the romantic interpretation of Gothic here conveyed was George IV's admiration for the novels of Sir Walter Scott. The knight on horseback at the east end

The Wyatts

The Wyatts were an architectural dynasty—two separate ones to be exact—whose members have featured prominently in London building. The most famous was James (1746–1813), whose main work, the Pantheon in Oxford Street, is now remembered only by name in a branch of Marks and Spencer but was also responsible for Ashridge in Hertfordshire (a National Trust garden easily accessible by train). His brother Samuel (1737–1807) worked on many of the dock schemes and his son Benjamin (1775–1855), a favourite of the Prince Regent, created Drury Lane Theatre, the interior of Lancaster House, Apsley House and the Duke of York's Column. Thomas Henry (1807–80), resident of Bloomsbury Square, and Sir Matthew Digby Wyatt (1820–77), who worked with Sir George Gilbert Scott on the interior of the Foreign Office, were brothers in a separate branch. The Windsor Wyatt, Sir Jeffrey (1776–1840), was a nephew of James. For added distinction he changed his name to Wyatville when he gained the commission for the work at the Castle. His improvements for George IV and William IV showed equal facility in both classical and 'gothick'. Windsor Castle is his masterpiece.

nother recent piece of antiquarianism, re-created in the 1990s to revive a long-defunct figure ritualised in coronation ceremonies and last used at George IV's wn. Take time to study the marvellous series of portrait busts by Roubiliac, ysbrack, Bacon, Chantrey and numerous distinguished sculptors of successive onarchs and their relatives, as well as paintings by Lely, Kneller and others.

The next space is the newly built chapel (not open), followed by the **Lantern obby**, completed in 1997 as a memorial of the fire which began in this space, e Victoria Chapel. The Lobby is said to be inspired by the octagon in Ely athedral. It displays fine workmanship but a feeble artistic philosophy. There are lso fine displays of silver gilt.

There now come yet more State Apartments—the Green Drawing Room, the rimson Drawing Room, the State Dining-Room—but they are open only in winter: e present Queen uses the rooms in summer for private and official entertain-ent. They are Wyatville's work, damaged by fire but restored more closely to his ork than St George's Hall.

The next room on the main tour is the **Grand Reception Room**, a French reation attributable to George IV's own preferences, with 18C panelling nported from Paris. Wyatville was doubtful about it, and his Gothicky windows ead as a reproach. But it is a dazzling space, perfectly restored after the fire, and ith the Gobelins tapestries the most beautiful in the Castle. It is used by the ueen to greet her guests before a State banquet.

Next is the **Garter Throne Room**, where the Garter Knights and Ladies are vested (see box, p 492). It is part of Wyatville's work for William IV, whose ortrait, by Sir Martin Archer Shee (1833) hangs on the left-hand wall. The arter insignia are shown in the ceiling.

The last interior is now reached by returning to the **Waterloo Chamber**, the rgest room in the Castle. The space is properly dominated by Thomas awrence's portrait of the *Duke of Wellington* (1814–15). There are numerous ther fine Lawrence portraits of contributors to Napoleon's defeat, including *eorge III* (1820) at the end of his life and *Frederick, Duke of York* (1816). The nnual Garter lunch is held here.

> ### *Order of the Garter*
> This is the oldest and highest royal decoration, founded by Edward III in 1348, and still awarded each year by the sovereign at Windsor to a chosen few, usually already members of the aristocracy. There are 24 knights and ladies at any one time. The ceremony in June is a great show and the procession to St George's Chapel attracts large crowds. The insignia are a star, a garter worn below the left knee, and a blue sash. The story goes that Edward III saw the Countess of Salisbury's garter slip off and, as any gentleman would, returned it to her with the comment *'Honi soit qui mal y pense'* (meaning 'Shame on those who think evil thoughts' or 'Let's hope no one gets the wrong idea.') The phrase, comically, remains the royal motto.

As you leave, look over the railings across the Upper Ward or Quadrang When the Queen is in residence, in the private apartments on the south and ea sides, the Changing of the Guard takes place here at 11.00 Mon–Sat April–Jun on alternate days July–March (not Sundays). (When the Queen is not in res dence, the Changing of the Guard takes place in the Lower Ward, near the Cast entrance.) The Quadrangle is also a good place to see the way in whic Wyatville's idiosyncratic Gothic has determined the aesthetic of the entire stru ture. He deserves a reputation not far short of those of Charles Barry and A.W. Pugin.

St George's Chapel

None of these names could match the sheer spatial beauty achieved by the arch tects of St George's Chapel, which you will visit as you descend back past t Round Tower into the Lower Ward. They are recorded as Henry Janyns a William Vertue. The exterior of St George's is initially confused by the Albe Memorial Chapel (formerly Henry III's Chapel) which you pass first and will s from inside.

> The first chapel was Henry III's (13C) and the first St George's Chapel w begun by Edward III in the 14C. The present St George's is later (begun 147 and was an initiative by the Yorkist King Edward IV to accommodate t growing number of Garter Knights he had created to prop up his claims to t throne. The present building is analogous to King's College Chape Cambridge, and the chapel of Eton College, both sponsored slightly earlier Henry VI, Edward IV's Lancastrian rival. St George's goes one better including transepts but placing them half-way down the structure so that t chancel equals the nave in length, and thus becomes symmetrical Renaissance novelty).

You will enter the nave by the south transept. It is best to tour the nave clockwi followed by the chancel north aisle, choir and chancel east aisle. The ove whelming feature is the **vaulting** with its decorative bosses: this, with the hu but delicate windows, is a triumph of the late Gothic style peculiar to Englan known as Perpendicular. Much of the vaulting here was not complete until t early 1500s, which makes it contemporary with the Henry VII chapel Westminster. The centre of the nave is a good place to stand to let the effect of t design, with its stars and quatrefoils, enter the spirit.

There is much else to see as you tour. Of particular note is the **font** in t outhwest corner, designed by J.L. Pearson (1887), depicting the baptism of Edward II. In the northwest corner, the early 16C **Urswick Chantry** contains an unexpected masterpiece, the tomb of Princess Charlotte, only child of George V who died in childbirth in 1817. She lies under an all-covering shroud from which only four fingers protrude, but also rises to heaven, accompanied by angels, one of whom carries the stillborn baby. The sculptor was Matthew Cotes Wyatt, another of the tribe (see above). Nearby is the tomb (1939) of George V (d. 1936) and Queen Mary (d. 1953). There are many more interesting monuments for you to examine as you proceed, including the **Roos tomb** (1513–26), with vivid recent embroideries by Beryl Dean (1970–74).

Beyond the Hartings Chantry in the north chancel aisle is the lengthy tomb of Edward IV (1483), who was 6ft 4in tall, with a monument designed when the tomb was rediscovered in the late 18C. Go into the **choir** and note the glass of the east window and the carved reredos below, designed by Sir George Gilbert Scott (1863) as yet another memorial to Prince Albert. On the left are late 15C iron gates made for Edward IV's tomb. Now look at the choir itself. The stalls are original, carved by William Berkeley (1478–85). Some changes were made in the late 18C, with some new fronts and misericords added with very great skill: it is enjoyable trying to distinguish between 15C and 18C carving. The top level is for the Knights of the Garter, each of whom has a unique memorial enamelled plate, of which some 670 are displayed at the back of the stalls (although there have been over 900 knights in the 600 years of the Order's existence). The sovereign's stall is by the chancel exit.

Leave the chancel to return to the nave. Look at the screen supporting the organ—it is made of Coade stone and was installed in 1790. Turning round, the west window's glass is mostly *c* 1500 but the window itself was enlarged, and some new glass added. There is a **shop** in the Bray Chapel, after which you proceed up the south chancel aisle, where there is plenty of interest still, including the tomb of Henry VI (d. 1471), tactfully placed well away from that of Edward IV.

Exit into the Dean's Cloister, built in 1240, well before St George's but contemporary with Henry III's chapel, which you now enter. This has been much altered over time, including major rebuilding by Henry VII as a burial place for Henry VI. In the 1860s it became the **Albert Memorial Chapel**. As such it contains the strangest monument in this entire guide, the tomb of the Duke of Clarence, Edward VII's eldest son, by Sir Alfred Gilbert (the sculptor of 'Eros' in Piccadilly). He started it in 1892, went bankrupt and moved to Belgium, returning in 1926 to finish the job. Nothing closer to Art Nouveau exists in England. To the east is the cenotaph to Prince Albert, plain and dignified by Baron di Trinqueti.

You may want to wander a little more around the Castle interior before embarking on the town walk.

own walk

Start at the statue of *Queen Victoria* (1887), by Sir Edgar Boehm, at the foot of Castle Hill. Stand alongside her, with your back to the Castle. To your right, Thames Street descends round the Castle perimeter to Riverside station. Central station is just off Thames Street on the left, with a grand entrance. Opposite is an information office.

First take a look at the little streets behind you, Market Street and Church Street. Turn left from the statue and left again up **Queen Charlotte Street**, the shortest street in England, it is claimed. This tight street pattern dates back to the medieval days of the Castle. On the right is Market Cross House (1680). In Church Street, note the very ancient *Old King's Head* and next door Nell Gwyn's house (1640)—Charles II liked Windsor, remember. To the left is Henry VIII's gateway to the Castle. To the right, down Church Lane on the corner of the High Street, is the **Guildhall**, designed by Sir Thomas Fitch (1687–89) but the construction supervised by Sir Christopher Wren. Inside on the ground floor (usually open) you may be able to see four Tuscan columns which stop short of the ceiling: the story goes that Wren was asked by the council to insert these for the security of the construction but, knowing they were unnecessary, left them free-standing.

Take a look at the church of **St John the Baptist** (1820–22) just alongside, amazingly mean and basic compared with the Castle: it makes a powerful statement about the role of the people in a royal town. But, as if to balance that point, the railings in the South Chapel are by Grinling Gibbons himself (1680–82) even if originally intended for the chapel in the Castle. Then go down Peascod Street (pronounced 'Pesscot'). There are various shops here and on the right, King Edward Court shopping centre, a typical 1980s affair. Then go right, up to Windsor Central station, built early in 1849 to facilitate Queen Victoria's arrival by train from London. Its viaduct over the water meadows to Slough is the longest run of brick arches in the world.

Returning to Thames Street, turn left down the hill. On the left, in **no. 1 Curfew Yard**, Oliver Cromwell, refusing to enter the Castle, allegedly signed Charles I's death warrant. Next on the left, next to Boots, is a passageway with a view of Windsor by Wenceslaus Hollar inscribed on the tiles.

Just past River Street is the Theatre Royal (1910, but with a theatre on this site since 1815), but we turn down River Street to the **Thames**, a miniature here compared with the London views you have seen. Turn right for a good view of the bridge, now too weak for traffic, despite being the work of the great Thomas Telford (1823). There should be many swans; all of those on the Thames are owned by either the Queen, the Dyers' Company or the Vintners' Company. Each year, in a ceremony called Swan Upping, they are rebranded, the Vintners' bird receiving a nick either side of the beak, the Dyers' on the right side only. The Queen's are mercifully left alone.

Walk to the bridge and climb the steps. On the right is *Sir Christopher Wren House*, now a hotel, allegedly built as his own home: this is a possibility, as he was MP for Old Windsor and his father was Dean here. Go past it, turning left to reach the delicious small-scale Gothic Windsor Riverside station (1850), with many references to Victoria and Albert; or go back over the bridge to explore Eton.

Eton

Eton, north of the Thames, is in Buckinghamshire. Its chapel bears comparison with that of St George at Windsor, and the relationship between college and town makes a striking contrast with Harrow (Chapter 65). At Harrow the school and the suburban town remain unconnected, but Eton is a school and nothing else, having swallowed its town whole.

The walk along the High Street from the bridge passes some pleasant shops and galleries, with little villagey alleys between. No suburban development has ever been allowed. Even the Victorian Gothic **parish church** (1852–54) to the eft has been largely taken over by the College as a sanatorium and staff flats, although you can still worship in the chancel.

Over a small bridge (Barnes Pool), Eton College starts to open up all around you, as if you were in Cambridge. The school quadrangles are usually open to the public from spring to autumn.

> The atmosphere is collegiate as its founder in 1440, Henry VI, intended. He based it on the recent precedent of Winchester School, created by William of Wykeham as the counterpart of New College, Oxford. The counterpart to Eton, also founded by Henry VI, is King's College, Cambridge with its famous Chapel. Eton was to be a mixed charity, with a Provost, ten fellows, four clerks, six choristers, a schoolmaster, 24 scholars and 24 elderly or infirm men. The composition soon began to change, with the number of scholars steadily increasing—there are now over 1300 pupils, comprising one of the world's great schools—and the number of old men declined rapidly to nil. There is still a Provost and separately a Headmaster, and still two types of pupil, scholars who live in the College itself and oppidans who live with housemasters.

Turn right through the arch to see the main quadrangle, **School Yard**. Above the arch is Upper School, modestly located in this range of the late 17C: you may be able to get inside during school holidays. In School Yard, Lower School (c 1630) stretches along on your left. In the centre of the square is an 18C statue of *Henry VI* and on the right the Chapel, also sometimes open. This consists of a choir (1460s) and transepts (1470s) only—no nave was ever built—and is comparable with the other great Perpendicular masterpieces of the period except that the fan-vault is considerably less venerable, having been built in 1957–58. There are modern windows by Evie Hone (1942–52) and John Piper (1958–61).

On the far side of School Yard is Lupton's Range, buildings associated with an important Provost of Henry VIII's time. The gatehouse is typical of the period and may remind you of Hampton Court. Go through it into **Cloister Court**. This is all work of the 1440s or of 80 years later, but with later additions. It too is very like an Oxbridge college, with cloister walks. On the right is College Hall, the dining-room, with the College library in front of it.

You may also get into **Brewhouse Yard** from the corner of School Yard, a picturesque space which leads you back to the town, and down to Windsor. The rest of Eton is nearly all College buildings of different periods.

Legoland

Legoland is an entirely separate adventure, and it does not make sense to combine it with anything else at Windsor except possibly the walk around the town. Shuttle buses for Legoland stop in Thames Street.

- Open mid-Mar–end Oct 10.00–17.00/19.00. Admission charge. Cafés. Restaurants. Shops. ☎ 08705 040 404. www.legoland.co.uk

The fairground (for that is what it is) was opened in the 1980s by the Danish toy manufacturer, and nearly everything is built, or appears to be built, from Lego bricks. It makes an excellent, though quite expensive, day out with children of all ages.

If you have more time for exploration in Windsor, you might like to look at the **Home Park**, on the north side of the Castle, stretching over to the river, and scene of the annual Horse Show in May. Also to be seen is the **Great Park** to the south, where you glimpsed the Long Walk in your tour of the Castle. This fine avenue, laid out in Charles II's time, stretches for 3 miles to terminate at a huge equestrian statue of *George III* (1824–30), known as the Copper Horse, by Sir Richard Westmacott.

To the east of the Long Walk is **Frogmore**, a late 17C house, revamped by James Wyatt for Queen Charlotte (1792). Frogmore's grounds were designed by Sir Uvedale Price, the amateur exponent of the picturesque. They contain the Royal Mausoleum of Prince Albert and Queen Victoria (1862–71) by A.J. Humbert, with a grand High Renaissance interior and a rather more appealing domed rotunda mausoleum to the Duchess of Kent (1861). Open a few days each year, ☎ 01753 868286, ext. 2347.

Finally, 5 miles south of the town within the boundaries of the Great Park is the **Savill Garden**, 35 acres of woodland with a range of trees and other features, daffodils and magnolias in spring and ferns in autumn. The innovative temperate house (1995) can raise completely one of its walls on fine days to extend, so to speak, the garden inside. Open 10.00–18.00, Mar–Oct; 10.00–16.00 Nov–Feb. Admission charge. Café. Shop. ☎ 01753 847518.

River trips

The following two chapters describe not walks but boat trips on the Thames, the first going from the centre of the city downstream, and the second upstream. Both give a unique view of London. Several separate short cruises round the Pool of London are also available.

For departure and arrival times and durations of journeys, see London Transport's *River Thames Boat service guide*, which is often to be found at stations. There is direct competition on the main routes. From Westminster you have a choice of two passenger operators: *Westminster Cruises* and *City Cruises*. At Embankment there is only one: *Catamaran Cruisers*. Whichever operator you choose, you will hear a commentary with useful information and many tired old jokes, for which donations are invited. If you have a travel card it may entitle you to a discount on the boat fare (and see p 35).

Westminster Cruises ☎ 020 7930 4097. www.wp.cr.co.uk

City Cruises ☎ 020 7930 9033. www.citycruises.com

Catamaran Cruises ☎ 020 7987 1185.

The following tours point to the main landmarks, as will the boat commentary, but here we shall try to link them with the walks in earlier chapters—chapter numbers are shown in brackets—where more detail about specific buildings can be found.

4 • Downstream: Westminster to Woolwich

This journey to Greenwich takes about an hour, and a further 25 minutes, usually in a separate boat, to the Thames Barrier. This description starts from Westminster: if you are boarding at Embankment, pick it up from there (see below).

Behind you is **Westminster Bridge** (13), but as you pull away all eyes are likely to be drawn to the **London Eye** (32), balefully surveying you as it slowly turns. On its right is the noble but now humiliated **County Hall**, and climbing up behind the Shell building. The green space is Jubilee Gardens, at present under threat as a site for more concert halls and a new National Film Theatre (all 32).

On your left, on the west bank, you will see first Michael Hopkins's **Portcullis House** (1999), then R. Norman Shaw's former **New Scotland Yard**, now government buildings, overlooking the stream; on the Embankment the RAF War Memorial stands appropriately in front of the Ministry of Defence, with its green roof. Next is the delightful **Whitehall Court**, and the National Liberal Club (all 2). The vessels moored here are the *Tattershall Castle*, a Clyde paddle-steamer, and the *Hispaniola*; both are now pubs.

The first bridge you go under is **Hungerford Bridge** (10), built as a footbridge by I.K. Brunel in the 1840s but taken over by the railway soon afterwards: new footbridges are being added to it at a painfully slow pace. Under it, Embankment pier is on the left with **Embankment Gardens** behind. Towering above Charing Cross station is Terry Farrell's **Embankment Place** (11). **Cleopatra's Needle** comes into view with the 'new' Adelphi, Shell Mex House and the **Savoy Hotel** (10) behind.

It is more inspiring by far to view the South Bank, where you see the **Roya Festival Hall** at its finest. Next to it are the much-disliked Queen Elizabeth Hal Purcell Room and Hayward Gallery (all 32): they may have disappeared by you next visit. The bridge ahead is the beautiful **Waterloo Bridge**, for which Sir Gile Gilbert Scott was the architectural consultant. The commentary will almost ce tainly say it is known as the 'Ladies bridge' because female labour was used in i wartime construction, but no-one is conscious of the point, except on the boat On the left, the restaurant boat is the *Queen Mary*. As you go under the bridg look through the piers at the sweep of the arches.

Now the river has turned directly east. **Somerset House** (9), obscured b both Sir Joseph Bazalgette's Embankment and plane trees, stands on the lef long and magnificent: it is one of London's masterpieces. On the South Ban Denys Lasdun's **National Theatre** makes a blocky and uncompromisin Modernist response, echoed by his IBM building next door. Then comes a mo mixed collection of buildings on both sides, from which, on the south sid beyond LWT's boring tower block, the **Oxo Tower**, a former warehouse, may l picked out (all 32).

As you go past the north bank remember that it once displayed numerous fir edifices of the quality of Somerset House, noble houses of the aristocracy, all th way from Westminster. A reminder of such a past soon comes into view: **Templ Gardens** (8), with the buildings of Inner and Middle Temple behind, are the on riverside gardens to survive to the present. In front of them is a memorial George V after whom this stretch of the river was named King's Reach. You ma be able to see the emblematic dragons marking the border of the City. HC *Wellington*, which acts as the livery hall for the Master Mariners' Company, an HMS *President* are moored here. The attractive buildings by the bridge on th north bank are the Gothic, red-and-white Sion College and the former City London Boys' School, which looks like a French château (8).

Then come a series of bridges: **Blackfriars Bridge** (8) is first, the road brid; built by Joseph Cubitt in 1869, resplendent in vividly painted cast iron. Next a the redundant piers of the former railway to Holborn Viaduct—will they find new purpose? The winner of the railway competition next to them is the St Paul railway bridge of 1884 by Sir J. Wolfe Barry and H.M. Brunel, now carryir Thameslink trains.

Once you are out the other side of this forest of piers, to the left **St Paul Cathedral** (7) stands supreme, and **Tate Modern** (31) in the former Banksi power station dominates the south side. It is not within the range of many of to see the Tate as an object of beauty, but that was never intended: let us call 'honest' or 'brave'. The **Millennium Bridge** (6), however, is certainly beautift although it has lost some its millennium shine. Before it, on the north side, is th present City of London School for Boys.

On the left, just before Southwark Bridge (6), is the **Vintners' Hall**, a pastich portico of the 1980s, giving an impression of antiquity only partly appropria to what lies behind but creating an architectural absurdity: a portico with i entrance. Opposite, the **Globe** (31) is a straightforward replica of the early 1 theatre, with some suitable imitatory service buildings. There are glamorou new apartments alongside.

After Southwark Bridge is the railway bridge to Cannon Street built in 1886 b Sir John Hawkshaw, with squat Doric piers, minus their capitals, which a ather appealing. On the north side is a good 1970s block for BT, Mondial House, and then the very handsome **Fishmongers' Hall** (all 6), where the portico means an entrance, and grandeur besides. On the south side, **Southwark Cathedral** looks clean and crisp after renovation, and is largely on view despite an insensitive 1970s office block pushing in, next to which is the **Golden Hinde** (replica) in its small dock (both 31) .

Before you now is **London Bridge** (2), so famous but really not very distinguished: this one was built in 1962 to replace John Rennie's nobler version of 1832, which was sold to an enterprise in Arizona, USA, where it was re-erected. The boat commentary will say the Americans thought they were buying Tower Bridge: it seems an inexplicable deal otherwise.

Tower Bridge is ahead. First, on the north side, is Adelaide House (1924), with Sir Christopher Wren's **St Magnus the Martyr** (2) tucked in next to it and the **Monument** behind. Then come two 1980s' offices, both quite pleasing, the blue one likely to generate one of the boat commentary's better jokes. After that is the former **Billingsgate Fish Market** (2) of 1874 by Sir Horace Jones, refurbished as a dealing room a century later but now redundant again, such is the speed of change. On the south bank there is first a pointy 1980s' monster, then **Hay's Wharf**, a rare piece of 1930s' Modernism in London, not wonderful but with interesting Art Deco letters. Not far away is the prominent arch of **Hay's Galleria**, a new shopping centre made by filling in and covering the former dock of Hay's Company, which had been on this site since the 17C (30).

Turning back to the north you will see a superb riverside building, Sir Robert Smirke's **Custom House** (2)—with trees absurdly (this was built as a vital quay) obscuring the architecture—completed in 1827 after subsidence, and behind it Minster Court, Neo-Neo-Gothic offices. The north bank has some pretty good buildings, all of quality. You can not say the same of the south, with Southwark Crown Court looking like the kind of prison it may be sending its defendants to. But **HMS Belfast** (30), a 1938 cruiser fascinatingly exhibited as a warship, obscures it to some extent. To its east is the new **City Hall** (2002), by Norman Foster Associates, functional in shape and forward-looking in concept.

On the north side the **Tower of London** (3) fills the bank with its familiar mixture of history and sinister deeds. The White Tower was built to humble Londoners into submission but the outer wharves, apart from Traitor's Gate, were for more comfortable landings. **Tower Bridge** (3), advanced engineering enclosed inside Disneyland Gothic, now reached: it will not raise its bascules for our cruise, but they still go up for major vessels. It opened in 1895; the architects were Sir J. Wolfe Barry and Horace Jones. Most people love it, and only a few cranks wish it were in Arizona.

This is more than can be said for the **Tower Thistle Hotel** next downstream, a great brown 1970s' slab, about as sensitive to its surroundings as a giant tank. **St Katharine's Dock** (3), prettified into a marina, peeps out behind it. Things look a lot better to the south. First comes the former **Anchor Brewery** (30), now new apartments but with '1895' proudly proclaimed on the chimney. Next is the long and impressively integrated block of **Butler's Wharf**, a great warehouse now handsomely converted by Terence Conran into apartments and restaurants. Past a gap is the **Design Museum** (30), a piece of minor 1950s' Modernism given a fine new lease of life under the same guiding hand.

At this point the boat commentary will start to dry up, but there is still a great deal to note. On the right is **St Saviour's Dock**, a pioneer in warehouse conversions, and to its left **China Wharf** (both 30), not a conversion but a Postmodern creation by CZWG. On the north bank **Wapping** (47) begins, first with eye catching new housing and the offices and printworks of News International behind, followed soon by Wapping Pier Head, the old entrance to London Dock now exclusive housing round a gentrified square. **Wapping Old Stairs** can still be seen next door, and then Gothic Oliver's Wharf, now apartments.

The blue-and-silver building on the left is a **police boat maintenance depot** an oddly strong statement: the river police started life here. The more subdued and dignified late 19C police station, in stock brick with a prominent gable, is close by. On the south bank much has been opened up, but there are still historic survivals, such as the *Angel* pub and the isolated 'leaning house'. The Surrey Docks may have gone but there is still **Rotherhithe**'s ancient village (51), with the *Mayflower Inn* (rebuilt authentically) and St Mary's parish church.

We are now able to see that the course of the river ahead is weaving south round the Isle of Dogs towards Greenwich. On the north bank, look out for the famous pub, the *Prospect of Whitby* (47), followed by a splash of green, which is the King Edward Memorial Park with the red-brick cylindrical air-vent to the Rotherhithe Tunnel, opened in 1908. Its counterpart on the south side is alongside the main entrance to the Surreys, as these docks were called.

At the bend, Free Trade Wharf, a Lego-brick development of the 1980s reduces the riverside to a Mediterranean seaside resort, but on its right, notice the dignified former late 18C **warehouses**, the only survivals all along this stretch. On the south bank is seemingly endless but not unattractive new housing, all vaguely imitating warehouses. Round the bend, the *Holiday Inn*, with its own pier, includes Nelson House and the former **Nelson Dock** (52).

On the left all eyes are likely to be on the skyscrapers of **Canary Wharf** (48) recreating Manhattan or Chicago—the lead architects are a Chicago firm. More and more towers are sprouting up, a deafening gesture of faith in the contemporary world. The new work makes the efforts of the 1980s—Heron Quays squatting miserably against the water, and the sail-shaped Cascades with its jokey crows-nest references—look passé: Postmodernism on the wane.

On the Surrey side you may see the old entrance to **Greenland Dock**, still available for water sports, and **South Dock**, a marina (both 51). Some way after this is the dignified façade of the old **Navy Victualling Yards** where rum and provisions were stored. In the shameless 1960s they were incorporated into the GLC's showpiece Pepys Estate: so, astonishingly, those East European slab-blocks are part of the same social environment as the 18C stock brick—but, at least they left the 18C alone. This area, **Deptford**, is in fact historic, the birthplace of Henry VIII's navy. There is little of interest on the Isle of Dogs side, although the Italianate **Plate House** (1854), now flats, marked the centrepiece of Burrell's Wharf, from which Brunel's great steamship the *Great Eastern* was launched.

After the mouth of the River Ravensbourne, on the south side, the little domed structure denoting the stair to the Greenwich Foot Tunnel, the *Cutty Sark* and the later, c 1800 buildings of the Royal Naval Hospital at **Greenwich** will have come into view (49). The c 1700 layout co-ordinated by Wren is just to the left, but you will not see it properly until you have disembarked, or by continuing to the Thames Barrier. The best view of all—the one painted by Canaletto—is to be found on the north bank, at the lowest tip of the Isle of Dogs called **Island**

Gardens (48), distinguishable by the Foot Tunnel's domed counterpart. Behind the Hospital you may be able to spot the **Royal Observatory** at the brow of Greenwich Park (49 and 50), the division between the east and west hemispheres.

If continuing to the Barrier, you will see, on the right, after the *Trafalgar Tavern*, the attractive domestic Gothic of **Trinity Hospital** (1613–14, restored 1812), dwarfed by the ugly Greenwich Power Station. Opposite is the unregenerated area of the Isle of Dogs on the left, Cubitt Town (after William Cubitt, one of the early developers). Blackwall Tunnel is under the water beneath you and on the right, on the promontory, seeming confident even if humiliatingly redundant, the **Dome**. On the north side, after massive new development going on in Blackwall Basin, the old entrance to East India Dock, and then full of muck and mess, the mouth of the River Lea, the largest of the Thames's London tributaries, wending its way up into Hertfordshire.

Most river trips then end at the **Thames Barrier** (49), erected in the 1980s to protect London from flooding. This also necessitated raising the banks on both sides for several miles downstream. The barrier is being brought into operation with increasing frequency. There is a visitors' centre to explore if you are leaving the boat. **Woolwich** nearby contains much of interest—see end of Chapter 49.

Just before the Barrier, on the north bank, are some new developments by Barrett Homes, looking impressive and spacious, with a tower by the river and fingers' extending east or west. Between them is a brand new open space, **Barrier Park**, the first in London for 50 years, French-designed, very distinct and angular, with disciplined, military-style planting. Is this the shape of parks to come?

75 • Upstream: Westminster to Hampton Court

This second boat trip also begins from Westminster Pier and can go as far as Kew (1½ hours) or Hampton Court (3 hours). It is not recommended that you undertake Hampton Court as a return trip: the journey back by train takes 30 minutes and a travel card (which you will have to obtain at a station first) earns a discount on the boat fare. Again, figures in brackets refer to earlier chapter numbers.

The boat heads upstream, under the **Westminster Bridge** of 1854–62, which replaced old Westminster Bridge, only the second bridge in London, built in 1750. On the right are unforgettable river views of the **Houses of Parliament** (13) with the terraces for the Commons (with green awnings) and then for the Lords (red awnings). Victoria Tower Gardens is next. Opposite, on the east bank—the river flows south–north just here—is **St Thomas's Hospital**, known locally as Tommy's, part in a 1970s block and part in Florence Nightingale-inspired pavilions of 1860. Visible before Lambeth Bridge is the Archbishop of Canterbury's London establishment, **Lambeth Palace**, with its 17C hall sandwiched between older towers. The river used to run alongside it until Sir Joseph Bazalgette constructed the Albert Embankment in the 1870s. Next to the Palace, a church now functions as the **Museum of Garden History** (all 33).

Lambeth Bridge, red and brown with obelisks, dates from 1929–32. On the east side is tedious, inexcusably second-rate architecture of the 1960s. Avert your gaze to the west bank, where things are only marginally better, with solid government buildings of the 1920s and then Millbank Tower. Some relief come with **Tate Britain** (15), an example of flowery Edwardian Classicism with Jame Stirling's Clore extension alongside.

Vauxhall Bridge (15) built in 1906 is the second on its site, and on its east ern flank is the eye-catching **MI6 building**, otherwise known as the Gree Goddess, by Terry Farrell and built in the 1980s. Rather too prominent on th further side of the bridge is St George's Wharf, a new housing development, wit curvy penthouses. Opposite, in Westminster, is a 1960s' showpiece for sma flats, Crown Point and beyond that its 1930s equivalent, Dolphin Square, heav and lumpy. Beyond is the **Grosvenor Bridge** approaching Victoria Statio (when built in 1860 it was the first railway bridge to cross the Thames i London's centre): it is no beauty. Nor is the giant on your left, **Battersea Powe Station** (55) by Sir Giles Gilbert Scott, although many people are keen to see conserved, and if finance is forthcoming it will be turned into an entertainmer centre of some sort. Immediately after the railway bridge is **Chelsea Bridge**, suspension bridge built in 1934 on modern engineering principles.

Now comes a lovely stretch of the river, Chelsea Reach. Sir Christopher Wren **Royal Hospital** for army pensioners is on the right, beautifully laid out to fac you, if somewhat obscured by the Embankment (34). On the left is **Batterse Park** (55), with the Peace Pagoda donated by a Buddhist community in 198 Back on the right, fine later 19C riverside houses by R. Norman Shaw and othe precede the **Chelsea Physic Garden**, and more fascinating houses in th famous **Cheyne Walk** (both 34).

Albert Bridge of 1871–73, delicate in appearance and rather too fragile fe proper use, makes a fine picture. Beyond it are more Chelsea houses, Chelsea o church (34) and opposite, Ransome's Dock in Battersea. The red-brick Tudc building on the right is **Crosby Hall** (34). Beyond the cast-iron **Batterse Bridge** built by Bazalgette in 1886, the mood again changes.

First, on the right bank, the embankment soon ends, exposing Lots Roa Power Station, another old hulk overdue for demolition but still supplying powe to the Underground. Then you will see the new housing development of **Chelse Harbour**, consciously swish, with its belvedere tower. Opposite stands a ros between thorns, **St Mary Battersea** (55) sandwiched by bullyboy blocks. Ne is a little railway bridge of 1863 carrying Silverlink trains, followed by muc mixed development on both banks, as old-time riverside industry gives place modern flats and shopping complexes. The curiously steep **Wandswort Bridge** of 1938 is now reached: after this, bridges become less frequent.

On the left are the mouth of the River Wandle and the Solid Waste Transfe Station, packing its containers to float downstream. Taking a river trip is the on way to catch a glimpse of the **Hurlingham Club** (56) on the north bank, famous sports club resolutely holding on to its prime riverside land.

After another railway bridge comes the very handsome **Putney Bridge**, als built by Bazalgette, with a church on either bank, in Putney (left) and Fulha (right), with what is left of **Fulham Palace** beyond (all 56). This is where th Oxford and Cambridge Boat Race starts. Look out for the boathouses on th Putney shore, and Fulham Football Club's ground opposite. Soon afterwards yo will see the extremely worthwhile **London Wetlands Centre** (58) on th Surrey side, opposite architecture by Richard Rogers, including the famous *Riv Café*, run by Rose Grey and Ruth Rogers, wife of the architect.

Hammersmith Bridge, another built by the versatile Bazalgette in 1887, now appears: it is sweetly proportioned but unable to cope with today's heavy traffic. On the right comes the dignified Upper Mall with 18C houses and excellent pubs. William Morris lived here in the last years of his life. Opposite is **St Paul's School**; one of the foremost in Britain, founded in 1509, it moved here from the City in the 1960s. On the north bank is **Chiswick Mall** (57) with more 18C dignity, hiding behind Chiswick Eyot. Fuller's Brewery soon follows, and **St Nicholas** (57), a medieval church partially rebuilt by J.L. Pearson.

There is not a lot of interest for a while after this. Barnes railway bridge (58) was built in 1849, which makes it the oldest bridge reached so far on this cruise. **Barnes** village riverside precedes it on the left. Round the bend, at **Mortlake** (58), is the finishing post for the Boat Race and Chiswick Bridge of 1938. In due course, a large building which is the new Public Record Office and Kew railway bridge appear. Kew Pier, where you may be disembarking, is close by. **Strand on the Green**, a row of fishing cottages, is on the right, and then Kew Bridge (all 61).

Kew Gardens (61) now stretches blissfully along on the south side of the river, opposite **Brentford**, somewhat hidden behind Brentford Ait, but with the chimney of the Steam Museum towering up (59). The mouth of the River Brent, connecting to the great canal system which covers the whole of industrial England, can be spotted among new flats and a marina. This is followed by **Syon Park**, still the Duke of Northumberland's London home (59), and a long stretch of peaceful river with not a building in sight on either bank.

The riverside village of **Isleworth** comes into view on the right, with its church, pub and its own Ait, while the Old Deer Park of the former **Richmond Palace** (62) continues the greenery on the left. Note Richmond Lock, the first you have reached, on the left with a footbridge, and soon the vaguely Art Deco road bridge of Twickenham, opened in 1933, and a railway bridge.

Now comes one of the finest stretches, through **Richmond** riverside (61 takes you along the towpath), under Richmond Bridge—the first historic bridge on the river so far, a meltingly beautiful curve, built in 1774 by Kenton Couse and still carrying a full load of traffic—and on. This is perfect riverside scenery, with people, boats, waterfowl, and the land stretching up on the left-hand side to the houses on Richmond Hill. As the river bends past Petersham Meadows on the left, you will begin to see, on the Middlesex bank, the survivors of the age of 18C riverside villas (63), first **Marble Hill**, commissioned by the mistress of George II; then, harder to spot from the boat, Orleans House by James Gibbs; and after that York House. Opposite stands the earlier and grander **Ham House** (62). A ferry runs between these places in summer.

Twickenham riverside is less scenic than Richmond but full of character, with Eel Pie Island a mysterious enclave. On the right, beyond it, Alexander Pope had his villa—the grotto still exists, at the top of Radnor Gardens (63) on the right. On the left all is water meadows. Next on the right, barely visible, is Horace Walpole's Gothic confection at **Strawberry Hill**.

Soon **Teddington Lock** is reached, where the tidal part of the Thames ends. There has been a lock here since 1811. From here on the Port of London Authority's control gives place to that of the National Rivers Authority. Thames Television's studios are on the right. Round a long, slow bend, you pass Canbury Gardens, on the Surrey side, a railway bridge, and then **Kingston Bridge**, a fine Regency structure comes elegantly into view (64). The branch of John Lewis, one of Kingston's excellent shops, protrudes on Kingston's pleasant riverside. Watch out for the Hogsmill River, on the left, moving under its medieval bridge; and later on the same side St Raphael's church, 19C eclecticism gone mad.

Past Raven's Ait on the left, there are filter beds and in due course Thames Ditton Island. Stretching away on the Middlesex side is the Home Park of **Hampton Court**. The River Ember branches away to the left but look to the right for a sight of Jean Tijou's great gates with the Privy Garden beyond. The Palace's riverside gardens and buildings are spread in a leisurely manner along the bank. You will disembark on the opposite side just before Hampton Court Bridge, designed by Sir Edwin Lutyens, a fine name on which to end, ready to tour the great palace (72).

Glossary

This list mainly covers architectural terms. See also the list of monarchs on p 81.

Aisle in a church, the longitudinal corridor either side, or one side, of a nave, separated from it by piers or an arcade.

Ambulatory a semicircular aisle round a chancel.

Apse a semicircular space, with a half-domed ceiling.

Arcade a series of arches.

Architrave the lowest section in an entablature, or the framework round a window or door.

Art Deco a minor but now popular sub-division of Modernism, arising from the 1925 Arts Décoratifs Exhibition in Paris, characterized by streamlined and 'Cubist' effects.

Art Nouveau a wave of 'new art', spreading across Europe in the 1890s, fading fast and dying completely with the First World War, characterised by flowing naturalistic forms.

Arts and Crafts a movement to promote the aesthetic and values of hand-made products, named after the Arts and Crafts Exhibition Society of 1882 (see also Chapter 16).

Baldacchino a canopy supported by columns.

Balustrade a row of small columns or shafts along a roofline, or supporting the handrail of a staircase.

Banqueting house usually an upper floor in a large house, or a separate building, offering views over the estate or gardens, for guests to relax after eating in the dining hall. Inigo Jones's building in Whitehall is not typical.

Baroque a rich, exuberant architectural style emanating from 17C Rome, but watered down in England. In London, can be seen in late Wren (St Paul's, City church towers, Greenwich), and Hawksmoor's and Archer's churches.

Basilica the shape of early Christian churches, stemming from a standard form for Roman public buildings: a rectangle entered at one end, often with a nave, leading to an apse at the other.

Bastion a projecting tower in a fortification or wall.

Bay a vertical section of a façade; a bay window projects from the façade.

Boss a decorative feature covering the intersection of ribs on a ceiling.

Brutalism a movement of late Modernism in England characterised by chunky concrete blocks of concrete.

Campanile a bell tower.

Capital the top part of a column.

Chamfering cutting the edge of a block at 45 degrees to the two surfaces.

Chancel the part of a church where the main alter is located, sometimes reserved for clergy, containing the choir and sanctuary, often separated by a screen.

Chantry a small chapel established to celebrate masses for the soul of its founder or someone of his or her choosing.

Choir similar to a chancel, but specifically to accommodate singers.

Classical referring back to the architecture and styles of Greek and Roman antiquity, sometimes as recycled through the Renaissance.

Clerestory the upper level of a church, often with windows, created by the projection of the nave roof above the aisle roofs.

Coade stone an artificial, cheaper alternative to Portland stone or other quarried masonry, manufactured in Mrs Coade's Lambeth factory, flourishing in the late 18C/early 19C.

Coffering a pattern of sunken squares or diamonds on a ceiling.

Column a single support, usually for a beam or entablature.

Colonnade a series of columns with an entablature.

Composite a combination of Ionic and Corinthian orders.

Corinthian an order characterised by capitals with acanthus-leaf decoration.

Cornice the projecting upper part of an entablature; or a separate, decorative longitudinal section within a wall, or at the top of it, to keep the rain off. Also, in interiors, the moulding between wall and ceiling.

Crossing the central point in a cruci-form church.

Cupola a small dome crowning a roof.

Cusping the pointed edge created by leaf-shaped foils (in Gothic architecture).

Decorated a period of Gothic architec-ture (*c* 1250–1350) characterised by detailed tracery and elaborate carved decoration.

Diapering surface decoration in squares or diamond shapes.

Diocletian window a semicircular window with two prominent uprights (or mullions), based on the Baths of Diocletian in Rome.

Doric an order characterised by a plain undecorated capital, and a frieze of metopes and triglyphs.

Early English the first stage of Gothic architecture (mid-12C to early 14C) with simple tracery and vaults.

Edwardian relating to the reign of Edward VII (1901–10).

Elizabethan relating to the reign of Elizabeth I (1558–1603).

Engaged column a column attached or sunk into a wall.

English Heritage a public body set up in 1983 to care for and maintain historic buildings and ancient monu-ments. Membership gives free admission to properties in their care.

Entablature a beam forming the upper part of a structure, supported by columns and itself sometimes supporting a pediment. It has three parts, architrave, frieze (often decorated) and cornice.

Façadeism retaining a conserved frontage and building a completely new structure behind it.

Fanlight a lunette over a door.

Fluting vertical grooves up a column.

Flying buttress an additional support for a wall extended outwards by a freestanding semi-arch.

Foil in Gothic architecture, the leaf-shape created by dividing a circular form or window, e.g. into three (trefoil) or four (quatrefoil).

Fresco a wall painting, usually done when the plaster is still wet.

Frieze middle section of an entabla-ture, usually decorated with carvings; or decorated band along the top of an internal wall, below the cornice.

Gallery in Gothic architecture, an upper storey above an aisle.

Georgian in architecture, relating to the reigns of George I, II, III and IV and William IV (1714–1837).

Gothic medieval architecture charac-terised by the pointed arch. It was out of fashion during the main Classical period of the 17C and 18C, but never entirely abandoned and revived with a new sense of purpose from the 1830s.

Greek cross a cross with arms of equal length.

Grotesque a range of small decorative forms of ornament, deriving from Roman antiquity.

Ha ha a ditch supported on one side by a wall, and invisible from the walled side, thus providing a barrier without impairing the view.

Hammerbeam an additional beam projecting from a wall, from which a central beam can be raised, thus allow-ing a wider span.

Hanoverian relating to the branch of the monarchy from Hanover, Germany, from George I onwards.

High tech a British contribution to Postmodernism, emphasising engineer-ing or technological elements as visual features.

Ionic an order characterised by capitals with volutes or spiral scrolls.

Jacobean relating to the reign of James I (1603–25).

Jacobite a supporter of the senior

ranch of the Stuart dynasty, following the displacement of James II as king in 1688.

Keystone the central stone or voussoir in an arch, often larger or more prominent than the rest.

Lancet window a narrow window with a pointed arch.

Lantern a small tower with windows or openings in a roof or dome.

Latin cross a cross with one member longer than the other three; the usual shape for medieval Gothic churches.

Lectern a stand for holding a book, from which lessons are read.

Listed having a grade given by English Heritage, either I, II* or II. Grade I applies to the most important, and untouchable, buildings. In 'Conservation Areas', determined by local authorities, development is extremely restricted: these often contain listed buildings.

Lunette a semicircular space or window.

Metope a space, often carved, between triglyphs in a Doric frieze.

Mews a row of stables with accommodation for grooms above.

Modern (sometimes **International Modern**) an architectural style developed separately both in the USA and Europe in the early 20C, characterised by cubic metal and glass frameworks, and/or reinforced concrete; minimal decoration and emphasis on function. In London, Modernism was slow to arrive and prompt to depart in the 1970s.

National Trust a membership body founded in 1895 to hold and conserve significant buildings and areas of the countryside. It is the custodian of over 200 such properties and places.

Nave the main body of a church.

Neo-Classical reviving the Classical from antiquity; more specifically, the period (c 1760–1830) when the Classical style was influenced by new archaeological discoveries.

Neo-Georgian a revival of the Georgian style, esp. brickwork with

some stone dressings, partly associated with George V (1910–35), but seen earlier (e.g. in the work of Lutyens).

Non-Conformist not conforming to the forms and practices of the Church of England.

Norman see Romanesque.

Ogee a double curve, bending first one way, then the other.

Order in Classical architecture, a term denoting the style of the column from base to capital, and the entablature above. There are conventionally five orders: Tuscan, Doric, Ionic, Corinthian and Composite.

Palladian in Classical architecture, a style (or an architect adopting the style) based on the work of Andrea Palladio, a 16C Italian architect.

Parterre a level area of lawn or patterned flower-beds with intersecting paths.

Patte d'Oie radiating avenues from a central point.

Pediment a triangular structure at the top of a portico, supported by piers/columns and an entablature.

Pendentive a concave spandrel.

Perpendicular the last phase of English Gothic (c 1350–1600), characterised by wide, flatter arches and large windows giving increased light.

Picturesque essentially, like a picture, specifically the paintings of Claude Lorrain and Salvator Rosa; an aesthetic concept of the later 18C and early 19C, based on a scenic view, perhaps with mountains and ruggedness, and 'quaint' or asymmetrical architecture.

Pier a solid support for a beam or within an arcade.

Pilaster a flattened, or rectangular, column or pier attached to a wall.

Plinth base of a wall, column, or statue.

Portico a collective term for an entrance comprising steps (possibly), columns, entablature and pediment.

Postmodern after, or even opposed to, Modernism; in favour of a partial return to historicism and/or eclectic shapes and styles, richer surface decoration and texture, playful and inventive.

Pre-Raphaelite a group of mid-19C artists who formed a Bortherhood committed to the styles and technique of painting applicable before Raphael, b. 1483.

Pulpitum a stone screen between the nave and crossing/choir.

Putto/putti a little boy or boys, used as a decorative motif in Classical architecture.

Queen Anne in architecture normally refers to the late 19C revival of early 18C red-brick domestic styles

Quire see choir.

Quoin a chamfered stone on the corner angle of a building.

Regency the period 1811–20 when George IV, as Prince of Wales, acted as Regent.

Reredos a screen behind an altar.

Restoration refers to the reinstatement of Charles II in 1660.

Retrochoir a rectangular space behind the choir, like a square ambulatory.

Rib a projecting ridge (usually of stone) on a ceiling or a vault.

Romanesque a style of architecture from Normandy, France, based on Roman motifs, in particular the rounded arch, imported to Britain from the mid-11C until the mid-12C.

Rustication a means of drawing attention to the stone blocks forming a wall by chamfering the edges and possibly roughening the surface.

Sanctuary an area round the main altar in a church.

Shuttering temporary retaining form for wet concrete, made of timber or metal, leaving its shape imprinted when removed.

Spandrel triangular surface between the upper parts of adjoining arches.

String course a horizontal band of stone or moulding in a wall.

Stuart relating to the Stuart branch c the monarchy, from James I (whose mother was Mary Stuart, Queen of Scots) and including Charles I and II, James II, Mary II (of William and Mary and Anne (1603–1714).

Swordrest a stand against which to lean an unwanted sword when indoors

Tester a sounding-board over a pulpit

Tracery intersecting arcs formed by ribs in the upper part of a Gothic lancet or panel.

Triforium the middle storey of a church, either blind (i.e. filled in) or treated as an arcaded wall-passage.

Triglyph a block with vertical groove separating metopes in a Doric frieze.

Tudor relating to the reigns of Henry VII, VIII, Edward VI, Mary I and Elizabeth (1485–1603).

Tuscan the plainest of the orders, wit unfluted columns and undecorated capitals.

Vault an arched ceiling, usually of stone, but can be of brick, constructed in various shapes (e.g. tunnel, groin, ri or fan).

Venetian window an archway or window with three openings, the outside two rectangular and the central or taller and arched; a Palladian motif, als called a serliana.

Vermiculation stone blocks carved with wriggly patterms like worm casts.

Victorian relating to the reign of Victoria (1837–1901).

Voussoir a wedge-shaped stone forming an arch.

Weepers small mourning figures on the sides of medieval tombs.

ndex

This index includes sub-indexes for the following subjects: bridges; churches; museums and galleries; parks and gardens; streets (including squares, roads, terraces, etc); stations; theatres, cinemas and concert halls. Page numbers highlighted in bold refer to items covered in 'boxed text'.

M

Seventeenth edition, May 2002
Published by A & C Black Publishers Limited
37 Soho Square, London W1D 3QZ

www.acblack.com

Maps drawn by RJS Associates and H.B.C. Consultants Ltd. Maps based upon the Ordnance
Survey mapping with the permission of The Controller of Her Majesty's Stationery Office
© Crown copyright 398454.
Map of London Underground reproduced by permission of Transport for London.

ISBN 0–7136–4889–9

Published in the United States of America by
W W Norton & Company, Incorporated
500 Fifth Avenue, New York, NY 10110

Published simultaneously in Canada by
Penguin Books Canada Limited
10 Alcorn Avenue, Toronto
Ontario M4V 3BE

ISBN 0–393–3247–1 USA

The author and the publishers have done their best to ensure the accuracy of all the information in Blue Guide London; however, they can accept no responsibility for any loss, injury
or inconvenience sustained by any traveller as a result of information or advice contained
in the Guide.

Cover photographs: central image of St Paul's Cathedral, and details of *Newton as the
Ancient of Days* by Sir Eduardo Paolozzi, and the London Eye, courtesy of www.robert
harding.com; detail of the Great Court, British Museum, courtesy of the British Museum.

Dr Roger Woodley is both an architectural historian and a Londoner, who, after a career
in the City, took a degree in art history at University College London and a PhD at the
Courtauld Institute of Art. Besides teaching and lecturing, he is currently at work on a
biography of Robert Mylne, architect and engineer of the first Blackfriars Bridge, and a
new edition of *Blue Guide Museums and Galleries of London*.

A&C Black uses paper produced with elemental chlorine-free pulp, harvested from managed
sustainable forests.

Printed and bound in Great Britain by Butler & Tanner Ltd, Frome and London.

Acknowledgements

The author's taste in architecture was formed over a long period, originating with his father, in boyhood treks round cathedrals and any parish church where the door could be pushed open. This was followed by intensive reading of Ian Nairn and Nikolaus Pevsner and continuous debates over the years, in front of, aside and about London buildings, with his partner Jane and their family who have been similarly conditioned, and with the author's good friend Clive Weeks. Here interest was honed into knowledge and, it is to be hoped, judgement, through Elizabeth Carey's classes with the London University Extra Mural Diploma, followed by studies with Tom Gretton at UCL and John Newman at the Courtauld Institute. His gratitude to these and other tutors is immense.

For the production of this Blue Guide itself, he is grateful to Charles Ford for thinking of him; to Gemma Davies, editor at A&C Black, for her wise counsel and unfailing encouragement, and to her colleagues Judy Tither and Kim Teo; to Alison Effeny, whose hawk-eyed and tireless checking of the text greatly enriched the final result; to Peter and Sheila Dorey for rehearsing some of the walks; to Quentin, Justine, Owen, and their partners, and to Molly, for their warm and continuous support; to all the author's friends for their unflagging interest; and to Jane for every one of these things and much more besides.

The publishers would like to thank John Murray (Publishers) Ltd for permission to reproduce extracts from *N.W.5 & 6* and *St Saviour's, Aberdeen Park, Highbury, London N,* by John Betjeman from his *Collected Poems.*

For permission to reproduce the colour photographs at the front of the book, grateful thanks are due to the following:

Title page: statue of **Queen Boudicca**, with Big Ben, courtesy of www.robertharding.com

Henry VII Chapel, Houses of Parliament, Albert Memorial, Cornwall Terrace, St Paul's Cathedral, St Anne Limehouse, Whitehall Court, Royal Festival Hall, Tower Bridge, London Eye, River Thames upstream, © Roger Woodley.

City Hall, Somerset House: exterior, north block, © Courtauld Institute Gallery 2002.

Horniman Museum: the Clock Tower, © Horniman Museum, photographer M. Harding.

National Theatre: view from the stone circle, courtesy of the National Theatre.

Palm House, Kew, courtesy of Royal Botanic Gardens, Kew.

The Blue Guides

ty Guide
athens

- **unrivalled coverage of Athens, past and present. The city explored in 15 walks, featuring the ancient city, Pláka (old Athens), the National Archaeological Museum and, of course, the Acropolis. An enthusiast of all things Greek, author Robin Barber is an archaeologist with 40 years' experience of travelling Greece.**

- Robin Barber
  5th edition, 2002
  320 pp
  ISBN 0–7136–6129–1
  £14.99

City Guide
New York

- **According to the *New York Daily News*, 'Possibly the most comprehensive guide there is to New York...' Detailed walking tours through Manhatten, Queens, Brooklyn, the Bronx and Staten Island, Blue Guide New York offers an accessible approach to exploring the city.**

- Carol von Pressentin Wright, Stuart Miller and Sharon Seitz
  3rd edition, 2002
  816pp
  ISBN 0–7136–6316–2
  £17.99

City Guide
Paris and Versailles

- **the most comprehensive cultural guide to Paris; no other guidebook provides such detailed coverage of the city's fabulous museums and galleries. Packed with information about Paris's many writers and rulers, artists and architects. Day trips to the châteaux of Versailles, St-Germain-en-Laye, Malmasion, Ecouen and Fontainebleau**

- Delia Gray-Durant
  10th edition, 2001
  432pp
  ISBN 0–7136–5294–2
  £14.99

BLUE GUIDE • CITY GUIDES • BLUE GUIDE

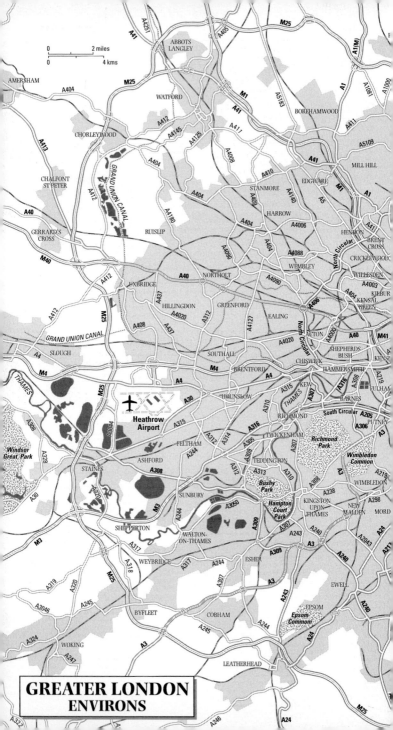

GREATER LONDON
ENVIRONS

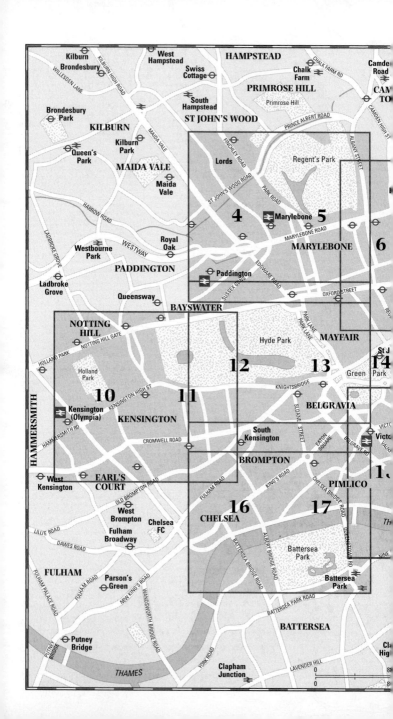

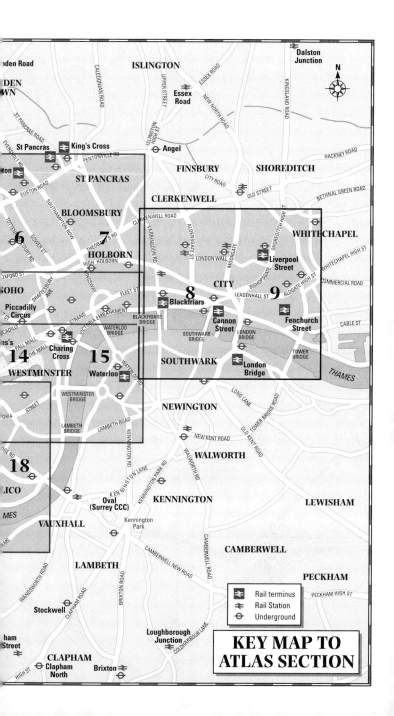

den Road

ISLINGTON

**DEN
WN**

St Pancras ⇄ King's Cross

Angel

FINSBURY   **SHOREDITCH**

ST PANCRAS

CLERKENWELL

BLOOMSBURY

6   **7**

HOLBORN

HIGH HOLBORN

WHITECHAPEL

London Wall

SOHO

Piccadilly
Circus

CITY

8
⇄ Blackfriars

9

Cannon
Street

Fenchurch
Street

⇄ Charing
Cross

14   **15**

Waterloo

WESTMINSTER

SOUTHWARK

London
Bridge

NEWINGTON

18

LICO

Oval
(Surrey CCC)

KENNINGTON

LEWISHAM

VAUXHALL

Kennington
Park

CAMBERWELL

LAMBETH

PECKHAM

Stockwell

Loughborough
Junction

CLAPHAM   Clapham
North   Brixton ⇄

⇄	Rail terminus
⇄	Rail Station
⊖	Underground

**KEY MAP TO
ATLAS SECTION**

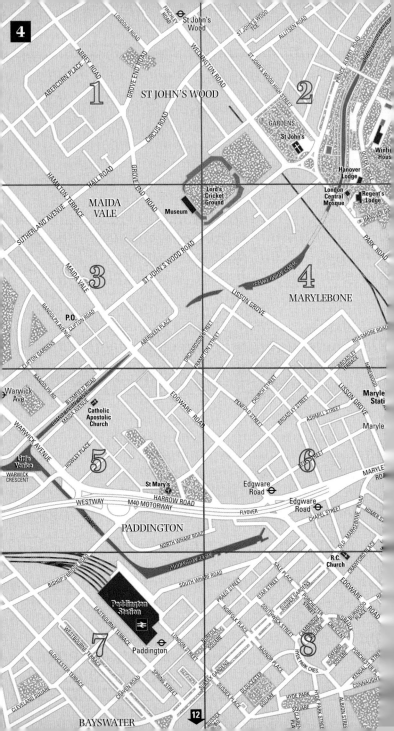

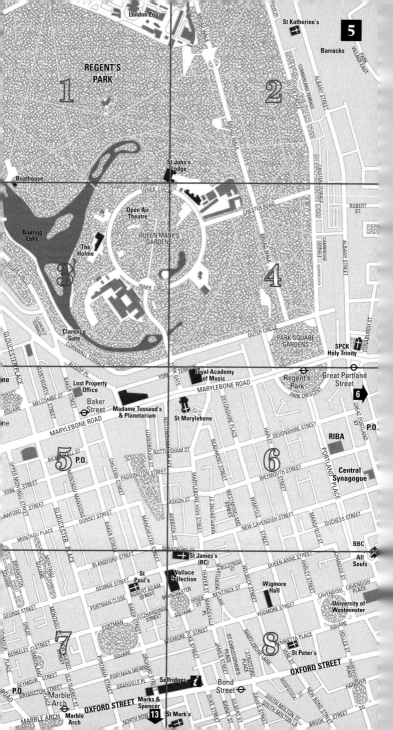

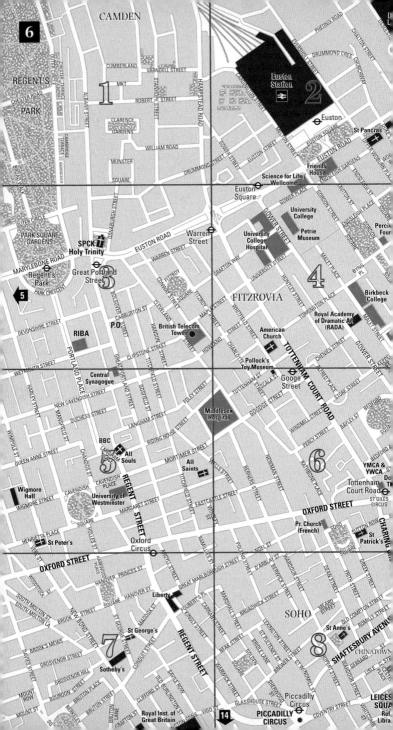

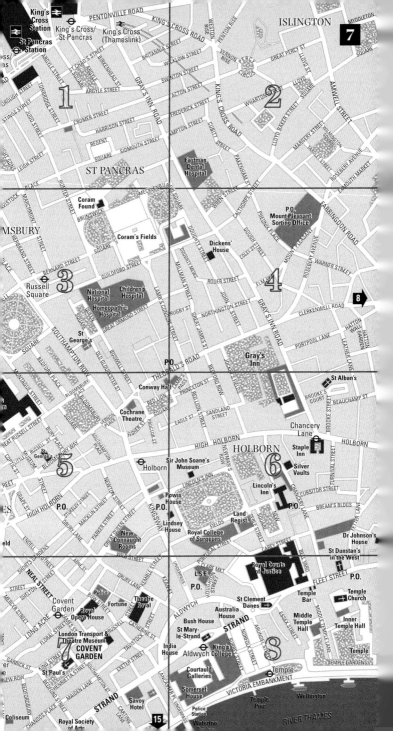

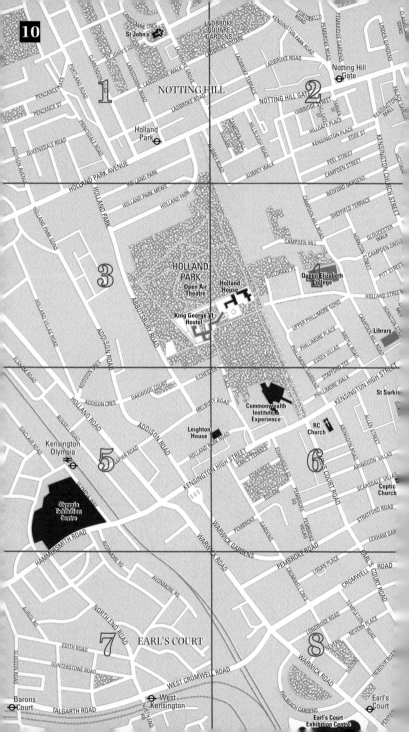

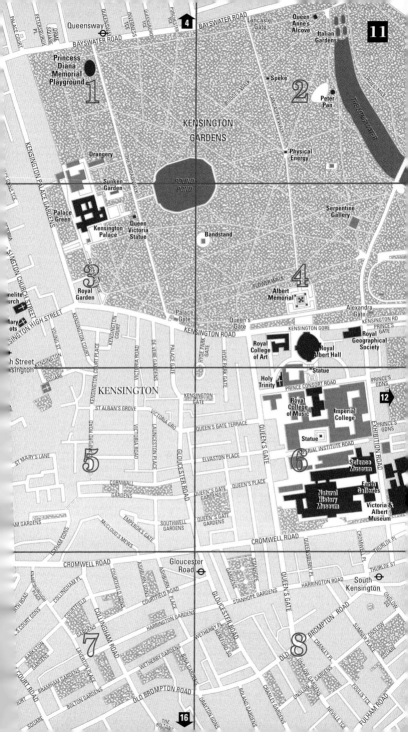

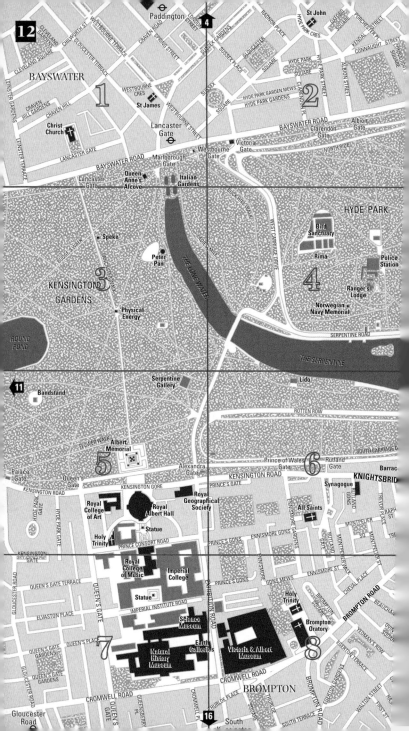

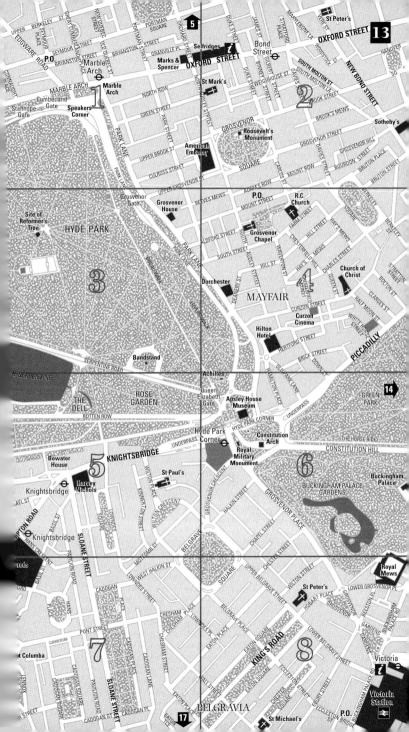

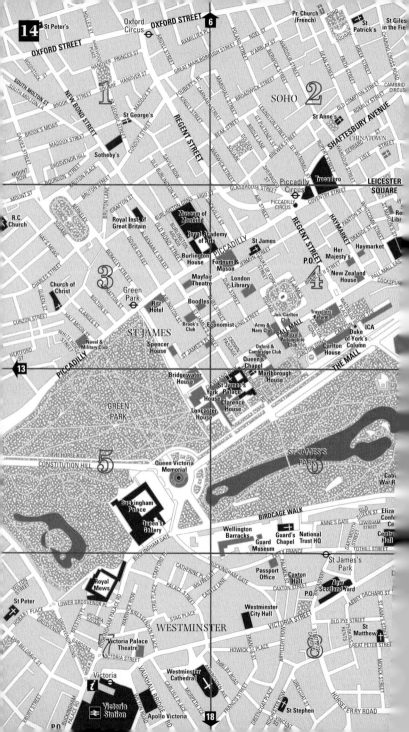

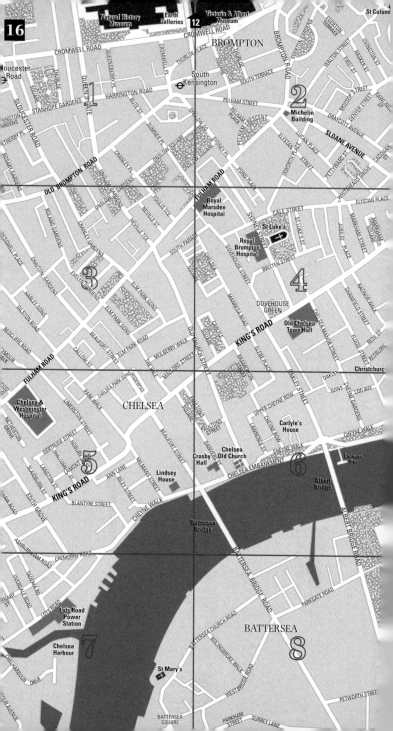

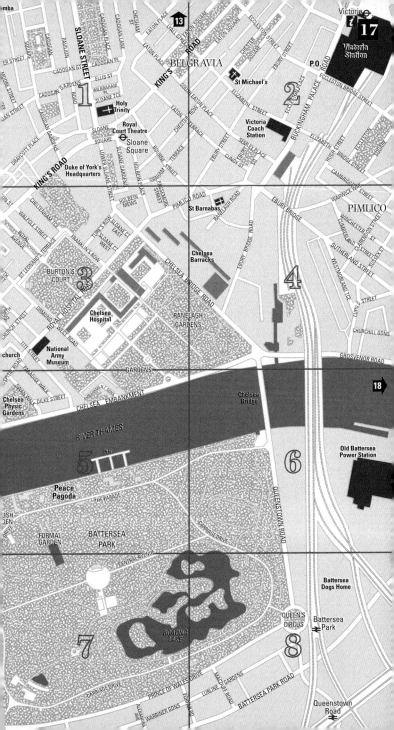

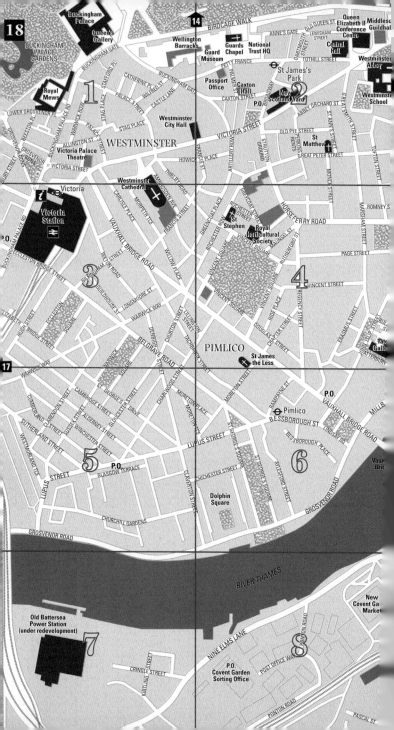